# Discovering
## Arguments

# Discovering Arguments

## An Introduction to Critical Thinking and Writing with Readings

### THIRD EDITION

**WILLIAM PALMER**

*Charles A. Dana Professor of English*
*Alma College*

PEARSON

Prentice
Hall

Upper Saddle River, New Jersey 07458

**Library of Congress Cataloging-in-Publication Data**

Palmer, William

  Discovering arguments : an introduction to critical thinking and writing with readings / William Palmer.--3rd ed.

    p. cm.

  Rev. ed. of: Discovering arguments / by Dean Memering and William Palmer. 2nd ed. 2006.

  Includes bibliographical references and indexes.

  ISBN-13: 978-0-13-602646-4

  ISBN-10: 0-13-602646-X

1. English language—Rhetoric.   2. Persuasion (Rhetoric)   3. Critical thinking.   4. College readers.
5. Report writing.  I. Memering, Dean, 1936–2006 Discovering arguments. II. Title.

  PE1431.M49 2008

  808′.0427—dc22                                      2008017270

**Editorial Director:** Leah Jewell
**Senior Acquisitions Editor:** Brad Potthoff
**Editorial Assistant:** Tracy Clough
**Production Liaison:** Joanne Hakim
**Director of Marketing:** Tim Stookesberry
**Senior Marketing Manager:** Sandra McGuire
**Marketing Assistant:** Adam Merten
**Permissions Specialist:** Lisa Black
**Senior Operations Supervisor:** Sherry Lewis
**Cover Art Director:** Jayne Conte
**Cover Design:** Studio Indigo
**Cover Photo/Illustration:** Digital Vision/Getty
  Images Inc.
**Director, Image Resource Center:** Melinda Patelli

**Manager, Rights and Permissions:** Zina Arabia
**Manager, Visual Research:** Beth Brenzel
**Manager, Cover Visual Research & Permissions:**
  Karen Sanatar
**Image Permission Coordinator:** JanMarc
  Quisumbing
**Photo Researcher:** Rachel Lucas
**Full-Service Project Management:**
  Dennis Free/Aptara®, Inc.
**Interior Design:** Rose Design
**Composition:** Aptara®, Inc.
**Printer/Binder:** Edwards Brothers
**Cover Printer:** Phoenix Color Corporation

Credits and acknowledgments borrowed from other sources and reproduced, with permission, in this textbook appear on page 604.

Pearson Education LTD., London
Pearson Education Singapore, Pte. Ltd
Pearson Education, Canada, Inc.
Pearson Education–Japan
Pearson Education Australia PTY, Limited

Pearson Education North Asia Ltd., Hong Kong
Pearson Educación de Mexico, S.A. de C.V.
Pearson Education Malaysia, Pte. Ltd.
Pearson Education, Upper Saddle River, New Jersey

10  9  8  7  6  5  4  3  2  1
ISBN 13: 978-0-13-602646-4
ISBN 10: 0-13-602646-X

# Dedicated to
# Dean Memering
# (7 Jan. 1936–25 Aug. 2006)

---

Dean Memering was my professor, my mentor, and my friend. He showed me the way.

Dean's presence as a teacher always inspired me. I watched him each day struggle to walk into the classroom, first with a cane and then crutches—yet always with a smile, with an expression of *Yes* on his face. He would prop himself up on a table and teach.

In front of a class Dean possessed a glow I loved to see. He was smart. I was in awe of his sharp intellect and his ability to communicate clearly. I remember when he demonstrated how to give a lecture; he spoke on existentialism. I was stunned. He had an ability to resonate with me and countless other students. Surely his existence was important: he helped us grow as writers, readers, and thinkers. He helped us care about language and thought.

Dean inspired me with his character. I trusted him and knew he was honest and fair-minded. He had a life-giving spirit, so I naturally wanted to be around him. Others did too—especially his wife Joan. I took as many classes as I could with Dean.

I kept the papers I wrote for Dean. He always wrote something positive first and then in his own way addressed what needed work. Here are a few of his comments. They carry his voice.

> Pretty cute, Palmer. The satire on potato chip ads is pretty sharp. It's a good thing you kept it short—I don't think the reader could stand much more. Very subtle. You have a terrific concept here—sharing a fragile moment with your old aunt. Very good ideas. The colors are great. Maybe it is just a bit over-done—a little too lush—you must work hard to control your imagery.
>
> Beautiful work, Bill. You have 100% got it. There are some clinkers here and there (I marked one—rather enthusiastically). [He had written in the margin "Phooey, blah, poop"]. But this is pretty mature and controlled writing. What you need, I dare say, is a year or two of serious writing with an absolute friend of an editor to help you get rid of the clinkers.

Dean's comments gave me hope that I could, perhaps, become a writer and a teacher of writing like him.

Dean became my absolute friend of an editor. He helped me get rid of the clinkers. After I graduated from Central Michigan University, I wrote an article about teaching the concept of *quality*, drawing from the popular book at the time, <u>Zen and the Art of Motorcycle Maintenance</u>. Dean kindly read it and wrote three and half pages of detailed notes. After I revised the paper, the <u>English Journal</u> accepted it, my first major publication.

Fast forward 25 years and Dean asked me to co-write his next textbook for Prentice Hall. He had recently suffered a brain hemorrhage. As a hemophiliac, he didn't know if he could write anymore. Surprised and grateful to be asked, I accepted his offer.

It took us four years to write the first edition of <u>Discovering Arguments</u>. Dean had not lost his touch as a writer. His mind was as sharp and clear as ever. As a co-writer he was kind, patient, and generous. He was my wise elder.

Dean Memering was my professor, my mentor, and my friend. He showed me the way: the way to write, the way to teach, the way to be. I celebrate Dean with deep gratitude and dedicate this edition of <u>Discovering Arguments</u> to him.

*William Palmer*

# Contents

**INTERCHAPTER 2**
## VOICE AND EMPHASIS     161

**CHAPTER 3**
## STRATEGIES OF ARGUMENTATION     176

**CHAPTER 7**
**RESEARCH STRATEGIES**

**CHAPTER 8**
# EVALUATING EVIDENCE 449

**CHAPTER 9**
# DOCUMENTATION 486

**CHAPTER 10**

# WRITING YOUR RESEARCH PAPER 526

## CONCISE HANDBOOK OF GRAMMAR, MECHANICS, AND USAGE    557

# Preface

<u>Discovering Arguments: An Introduction to Critical Thinking and Writing, with Readings</u>, 3rd edition, helps students communicate clearly, argue persuasively, and read carefully.

Students discover the impact of persuasive appeals—logos (reason), pathos (emotion), and ethos (ethics)—when they write and read. They learn that ethos—a writer's credibility of character—is the most essential appeal. They learn the importance of being trustworthy and fair-minded when arguing. They learn the value of presenting opposing arguments before presenting and defending their own arguments. They learn that a writer's use of logic and emotion can contribute to ethos or weaken it. These appeals give students powerful tools that form the center of thinking, writing, and reading activities in the book.

<u>Discovering Arguments</u> helps students write better. The book presents a holistic view of content and style. Through the chapters, students learn to excel at what they say; through the **interchapters on style,** students learn to excel at how they say it. No other textbook contains style interchapters or presents elements of style in such accessible and useful ways as this book does. The interchapters promote learning by doing. Students can do activities in class or out of class and immediately apply what they learn to their own writing.

The book's stylistic tools enable students to use language in positive ways. With a minimum of grammatical jargon, the interchapters help students develop stylistic maturity. A style interchapter follows each of the first five chapters so that instruction and practice can begin early in the semester, as students revise their writing. The interchapters help instructors present tools of style one at a time, letting students discover for themselves patterns of diction, punctuation, and sentences and then applying them to their own writing. The interchapters also help students solve common problems such as avoiding needless words, run-on sentences, and comma splices.

<u>Discovering Arguments</u> is a multifunctional textbook. **As a rhetoric,** it shows students a variety of strategies for communicating clearly and persuasively, including a chapter on the Toulmin method of argument and problems in reasoning. **As a reader,** it contains selections that appeal to students logically, emotionally, and ethically. **As a guide to research writing,** it features concise yet comprehensive sections on library strategies, evaluation of evidence, plagiarism, techniques of documentation, and detailed guidelines for writing reports and argument papers using either the latest MLA

or APA style. The book also includes **a concise handbook of grammar, mechanics, and usage.** Accessible and engaging, the book prepares students for critical thinking, writing, and reading at the college level.

## KEY FEATURES OF THE THIRD EDITION

- Discovering Arguments includes a major revision on research writing. The research chapters are more clear, concise, and useful. The complex topic of stem cell research is gone, replaced by a model report, "Saturated by Color," which examines the effects colors have on human behavior. The model argument paper is "Grain or Grass: What's the Beef?" This paper draws on the extensive research done by Michael Pollan in his book The Omnivore's Dilemma. Students will find these model research papers clear, engaging, and thought-provoking. In addition, the research chapters contain "Ryan's Process Notes" in which a student discusses his journey of finding a topic, doing research, and writing his argument paper.

- Chapter 8, "Evaluating Evidence," includes a new section called "The Wikipedia Dilemma," which presents different viewpoints on whether or not students should use Wikipedia as a source in their research papers. Scott Jaschik, an editor for Inside Higher Ed, writes "A Stand Against Wikipedia" about Middlebury College banning the use of Wikipedia in student papers. T. Mills Kelly, a professor in the Department of History and Art History at George Mason University, writes "Why I Won't Get Hired at Middlebury," explaining how and why he assigns his history students "to create or substantially edit one historical entry in Wikipedia." This dilemma provides a relevant case study for students as they learn about evaluating evidence.

- Chapter 8, "Evaluating Evidence," also contains a new research assignment, "Going Beyond the Information Given." This name draws on the title of a book by the renowned psychologist of learning, Jerome Bruner. He argues that students learn best by actively constructing their own knowledge. In the new assignment students are asked to take one article from a newspaper or magazine and then to do research on the information presented within that article. Chapter 8 provides a model showing a student reading Nicholas D. Kristof's essay "Save the Darfur Puppy" (from the New York Times) and going beyond this information to do research. The student first writes a reaction to Kristof's essay and then researches authorities and facts mentioned in the essay. The student writes a report on what he finds, using quotes, citing sources, and compiling a Works Cited list. This activity enables students to evaluate evidence by focusing on one article yet going beyond it. This new assignment models what students should do when they work on a report or argument paper. It shows students that doing research is a process of discovering and opening doors, which lead to other doors. Going through these doors, reading information and evaluating it, helps students see whether information is credible, accurate, and trustworthy.

- <u>Discovering Arguments</u> contains new information on humor. Chapter 1 includes a section on humor as a form of pathos that stirs emotions in readers. Chapter 3 includes a full treatment of humor as a strategy of argument, involving humorous tone and satire. Examples of humor are presented by Dave Barry, Stephen Colbert, Anne Lamott, and Rick Reilly. Some examples from the satirical Web site <u>The Onion</u> are also included. Humor as a strategy of argument not only can cause laughter and delight but can also expose serious problems and suggest surprising ways to solve those problems.

- The Toulmin method of argument now begins Chapter 4. The presentation of this method has been revised and improved with new activities and reading selections. The section includes a close analysis of an essay, "The Tense Middle," by Nobel Prize–winning chemist and teacher Roald Hoffmann. After the presentation of the Toulmin method, Chapter 4 offers a comprehensive treatment of logical fallacies in the section "Problems in Reasoning."

- Chapter 2, "Arguments and Controversies," includes new essays for students to analyze and evaluate: Mike Gallagher's "Preventing Another Massacre" and Hillary Hylton's "The Gun Lobby's Counterattack" about the Virginia Tech mass shooting; Kathleen Parker's "Children Last" about young children in military families; Rebecca Hagelin's "Video Game Violence and Our Sons"; Ellen Goodman's "No Change in Political Climate" about global warming; Bob Herbert's "The Divide in Caring for Our Kids" about national health care for children; and Leonard Pitts Jr.'s "Expedience No Reason to Kill a Man" about capital punishment. The chapter also contains a new case study on drinking age.

- <u>Discovering Arguments</u> draws many new examples from positive psychology, which students will find thought-provoking and personally relevant. What is happiness, and can people learn to be more happy? What is the science behind positive psychology? Students will read examples from recent books such as <u>The Happiness Hypothesis</u> by Jonathan Haidt.

- Chapter 6 contains new poems, stories, and literary nonfiction. This chapter on literature is more comprehensive and engaging than similar chapters in other argument textbooks. It features a new student essay on Robert Hayden's classic poem "Those Winter Sundays," serving as a model for analyzing and evaluating a literary text.

- Interchapter 5 includes a new section on students presenting themselves through e-mail. In an e-mail exchange between a student and an instructor, the instructor raises the issue of the student using careless grammar and spelling in her e-mails.

- <u>Discovering Arguments</u> contains new biographical notes for writers whose selections are featured throughout the book.

## UNIQUE COMPONENTS OF THIS BOOK

- <u>Active-Discovery Learning</u>.   The book emphasizes an inductive approach in which students discover for themselves key strategies of argumentation and tools of style. With less lecture, students are invited to do more, encouraging them to make discoveries on their own. For example, Chapter 1 asks students to write an opinion essay while (not after) they read the chapter and learn to appeal to logos, pathos, and ethos. In the style interchapters students are asked to perform a task—such as writing a sentence with a colon to introduce an explanation—before they read about how to do it. After students make an attempt in their notebook, they read three examples of sentences containing colons used in this way. From these examples, students can infer the pattern on their own. Then students are directed to apply the new tool of style to their writing.

- The Foundation Chapter. In Chapter 1, students learn about writing an opinion essay using their own experience and knowledge for supporting evidence. They examine three model essays written by college students and published in the "My Turn" column of Newsweek. Students see that they too can write about issues that matter to them and to others. Chapter 1 introduces students to the process of thinking: of examining problems and discovering eureka moments of possible solution. The chapter introduces students to the persuasive appeals of logos, pathos, and ethos, guiding students to use them intentionally in their opinion essay. The chapter also includes the clearest, most comprehensive advice on writing engaging titles, introductions, and conclusions of any textbook on the market. Chapter 1 provides a strong foundation for students as they progress through the book.

- The Power of Opposites. Chapter 3 begins with an expanded section on using opposites to help students generate ideas as well as analyze and evaluate ideas. Students examine contradictions and paradoxes to find topics for their own writing. They learn to develop a higher tolerance for ambiguity and a lower tolerance for either/or thinking. No other textbook encourages students to examine dialectical opposites as fully as this book does. New to this strategy is information called "Flip It" from the book Why Not? How to Use Everyday Ingenuity to Solve Problems Big and Small by Barry Nalebuff and Ian Ayres. Flipping it is when people turn an idea upside down to see an opposite point of view. Students also discover ways to use creative thinking skills—such as writing analogies—to complement critical thinking skills. Students are invited to write an essay using an analogy to explain how they think.

- Discovering Arguments labels many activities in the style interchapters "Revision," prompting students to apply tools of style immediately to drafts of their writing.

## SUPPLEMENTS FOR INSTRUCTORS AND STUDENTS

### Instructor's Manual

A comprehensive instructor's manual is available online that includes sample syllabi, teaching tips, and other information. Please contact your Pearson representative for access.

## *MyCompLab*

MyCompLab is a Web application that offers comprehensive and integrated resources for every writer. With MyCompLab, students can learn from interactive tutorials and instruction; practice and develop their skills with grammar, writing, and research exercises; share their writing and collaborate with peers; and receive comments on their writing from instructors and tutors. Go to <http://www.mycomplab.com/> to register for these premiere resources and much more.

## ACKNOWLEDGMENTS

My deepest thanks goes to my family for their support and love: Bonnie, Brenden, Ean, and Ryan.

Thanks to the Prentice Hall staff, ever professional and helpful: Brad Potthoff, Senior Editor, English; Tracy Clough, Editorial Assistant; and Maureen Benicasa, Project Manager.

Special recognition to Jennifer Starkey, reference librarian at Alma College, who helped fine-tune Chapter 7, "Research Strategies."

Thanks to members of the profession who provided constructive criticism and suggestions:

Anthony Annunziata
*(LeMoyne College)*

Harryette Brown
*(Eastfield College)*

Rebecca Finlayson
*(Rhodes College)*

Gloria Hochstein
*(University of Wisconsin)*

Heidi Huse
*(University of Tennessee at Martin)*

Debra Knutson
*(Shawnee State University)*

Brett Millan
*(South Texas Community College)*

Beth Nardella
*(West Virginia University)*

Amanda Petrona Hoover
*(Louisiana State University)*

Ruth Porter Pajka
*(Luzerne County Community College)*

Mary Vandiver
*(Henderson State University)*

# Discovering Arguments

## CHAPTER 1

# Communication and Persuasion: Logos, Pathos, Ethos

## **N**OTICING AND THINKING

*When you give more attention to the doing than to the future result . . . your doing then becomes not only a great deal more effective, but infinitely more fulfilling and joyful.*
(Eckhart Tolle, <u>Stillness Speaks</u>)

Have you noticed this? If you engage in an activity—such as writing a paper, let's say—and you pay more attention to the process of writing it than to finishing it, you will do a far better job, and you will enjoy the experience much more. Paying such attention is not always easy. But it is essential.

Consider an example of paying attention to something positive. Here is a parable that Buddha told:

A traveler, fleeing a tiger who was chasing him, ran till he came to the edge of a cliff. There he caught hold of a thick vine and swung himself over the edge.

Above him the tiger snarled. Below him he heard another snarl, and behold, there was another tiger, peering up at him. The vine suspended him midway between two tigers.

Two mice, a white mouse and a black mouse, began to gnaw at the vine. He could see they were quickly eating it through. Then in front of him on the cliff-side he saw a luscious bunch of grapes. Holding onto the vine with one hand, he reached and picked a grape with the other.

How delicious! ( *from* <u>Zen Buddhism</u>)

How can this parable possibly shed light on critical thinking, writing, and reading? Although this situation is utterly extreme, it shows that the traveler was somehow able to notice an unexpected gift of grapes and to focus on them—on a moment of possible sweetness—instead of his impending doom. Not blinded by despair, he paid attention to eating one grape and exclaimed "How delicious!"

Writing an essay, of course, is not perilous, though at times it may feel that way. When you write, you too are a traveler, but there is no tiger above or below you— unless perhaps these tigers are symbols of your fear ("I can't do this paper") and your doubt ("I'll never do a good job on this"). Along the way, if your eyes are open to it, you will discover surprising gifts that can nourish you.

This book concerns critical thinking and its relationship to writing and reading. You may encounter surprises. Some readings might make you laugh. Tears might come. You may feel angry. You may be provoked to think in new ways that will not only help you in this course but in your life.

## The Process of Thinking

**FIGURE 1.1** Sally Forth cartoon.
Source: SALLY FORTH ©King Features Syndicate.

When you read this cartoon, did you experience a surprise? Cartoonist Greg Howard presents a contrast: although you have heard the phrase "Founding Fathers" many times, have you considered the idea of "Founding Mothers"? This opposite produces a sudden awareness, helping you realize that American history classes and textbooks often leave out women, as if women did not take part in founding our country. Hilary's point makes her father realize something he did not know. This is a hallmark of critical thinking: realizing viewpoints and ideas you did not consider before.

You were born with the ability to think. But skilled thinkers have learned a procedure for thinking that the unskilled lack. Generally the process works this way:

## THE PROCESS OF THINKING

1. You notice a problem: you feel something is wrong and you identify it.
2. You explore the problem consciously by asking questions and subconsciously by incubating it (putting it on a back burner).
3. You discover a possible solution for the problem, and you experience a *eureka*: the moment of *aha!*, as if a small light turns on in your mind.
4. You test the solution to verify that it works. If your solution does not solve the problem, you must explore the problem again and find other possible solutions.

You use this thinking process naturally but usually without awareness. Suppose you are in a shopping mall and in the distance see a young man you think you know—but you realize you've forgotten his name. You want to say hi. For a few minutes while you shop, you try to remember his name and ask yourself questions: "Did I go to junior high with him? Wasn't he on my soccer team? Is his name unusual?" While browsing CDs in a music store, you experience a eureka—a sudden moment of illumination: "His name is Seymour! How could I forget?"

When the man in the Zen parable suddenly notices "a luscious bunch of grapes," he has a eureka. It helps save him, albeit for a moment.

Eurekas come in all sizes. You may experience eurekas by noticing something surprising within a word. The name *Seymour* fits an extremely perceptive person who can *see more* than most people. Perhaps you once had trouble spelling *separate*, putting an *e* after the *p*, until a teacher pointed out that the word contains *a rat*. Perhaps you had a eureka while deciding what college to attend. Albert Einstein valued eurekas. In 1907 when he struggled to make sense of Newton's theory of gravitation, he experienced "the happiest thought of my life." He "concluded that a person falling from the roof of a house was both in motion and at rest *at the same time*."[1] Although Einstein's idea seemed illogical, it made paradoxical sense and generated his theory of relativity.

## ACTIVITY 1

In your notebook, make a list of eureka moments you have experienced in your life—large ones and small ones. Choose one and write about how it made a difference for you. ▪

## The Paradigm Shift

A name for a major eureka is *paradigm shift*. In Stephen Covey's book <u>The Seven Habits of Highly Effective People</u>, he discusses the importance of paradigm shifts in our thinking. He defines *paradigm* as "a theory, an explanation, or model of something else." Although his definition is general and not very clear, Covey uses a personal illustration to show what he means:

> I remember a paradigm shift I experienced one Sunday morning on a subway in New York. People were sitting quietly—some reading newspapers, some lost in thought, some resting with their eyes closed. It was a calm, peaceful scene.
>
> Then suddenly, a man and his children entered the subway car. The children were so loud and rambunctious that instantly the whole climate changed.
>
> The man sat down next to me and closed his eyes, apparently oblivious to the situation. The children were yelling back and forth, throwing things, even grabbing people's papers. It was very disturbing. And yet, the man sitting next to me did nothing.

---

[1] Albert Rothenberg, "Creative Contradictions," <u>Psychology Today</u>, June 1979: 55–62.

It was difficult not to feel irritated. I could not believe that he could be so insensitive as to let his children run wild like that and do nothing about it, taking no responsibility at all. It was easy to see that everyone else on the subway felt irritated, too. So finally, with what I felt was unusual patience and restraint, I turned to him and said, "Sir, your children are really disturbing a lot of people. I wonder if you couldn't control them a little more?"

The man lifted his gaze as if to come to a consciousness of the situation for the first time and said softly, "Oh, you're right. I guess I should do something about it. We just came from the hospital where their mother died about an hour ago. I don't know what to think, and I guess they don't know how to handle it either."

Can you imagine how I felt at that moment? My paradigm shifted. Suddenly I *saw* things differently, and because I *saw* differently, I *thought* differently, I *felt* differently, I *behaved* differently. My irritation vanished. I didn't have to worry about controlling my attitude or my behavior; my heart was filled with the man's pain. Feelings of sympathy and compassion flowed freely. "Your wife just died? Oh, I'm so sorry! Can you tell me about it? What can I do to help?" Everything changed in an instant.

The essence of Covey's paradigm shift—and of all paradigm shifts—is his sentence "Suddenly I *saw* things differently, and because I *saw* differently, I *thought* differently, I *felt* differently, I *behaved* differently." His dramatic experience helped him become more aware of what changed his thinking.

When you write, you experience the process of thinking continually. You encounter problems involving your choice of topic, supporting evidence, organization, and style. You may not experience many paradigm shifts when you write, but you will experience countless eurekas. If you notice them, they will help you "give more attention to the doing." They will motivate you to keep writing. As you work through this book, the more eurekas and paradigm shifts you notice, the more you will enjoy thinking, writing, and reading.

What follows is a student paper about a paradigm shift she experienced. Do you think it works well? Why?

## Ruby's Cane

### *Renée Bancroft*

"Hi, Ruby? . . . My name is Renée, and I'm the college student that'll be coming to spend time with you. Would that be okay?" The woman paused over the phone. After a moment, she reluctantly agreed, claiming she didn't remember having signed up for this "thing." I took a deep breath. What had I gotten myself into?

She asked what we were going to be doing. I told her we could go for walks, play cards, or whatever she'd like to do. She replied curtly, "Well, I don't think I'll play cards with you." Okay, then, I thought. I took another deep breath and I told her I would come see her.

That Tuesday, I followed directions up to Ruby's room. The door was slightly ajar; I could see a wrinkled woman reclining in a chair, watching a blaring television. I knocked softly, waiting for her to acknowledge me: nothing. I knocked again and looked around the hallway. I knocked once more—this time loudly—and called her name through the crack in the door.

A shrill voice cut through the strange-smelling home. "COME IN, I said!" I entered, breathing deeply, apologizing that I had not heard her. She did not budge from her chair, nor did she look at me. I walked over to her side and extended my hand. She didn't even bother to take her eyes off the television. I carefully took her hand resting on the arm of the chair and then she tentatively shook it. Gosh, what a crabby, rude woman, I thought. She told me to sit on her bed so we could talk. As I did so, I glanced at this white and red cane propped up on the other side of her chair. I looked carefully, quickly, and holding my breath sat down on the bed feeling like a complete fool.

"I don't know what we're going to do," she said, turning her head towards me. I stared at her empty eyes, searching them, testing them almost suspiciously, like I didn't believe what I interpreted as rudeness was actually blindness. "You know I'm blind, right?" I hadn't. I searched her eyes the entire hour I was there; I searched myself, and I was ashamed at my initial reactions to this woman before I had even met her. Everything made sense. I realized why she didn't want to play cards, I understood why she didn't extend her hand, and I realized she hadn't been watching the television at all. I wanted to slap my own face.

This wasn't some crabby old bag. She was a nervous, timid woman who needed a little attention and understanding, and I hadn't wanted to give that to her at first. I wanted to apologize. She wasn't the only one who was blind. The experience was humbling and made me examine myself: I was surprised at how quickly I judge people.

I visited with Ruby once a week for an entire semester, and I will never forget the lessons she didn't even know she taught me. I got a look at her life as an elderly blind woman in a nursing home. It is too easy to make snap judgments about someone. It isn't until you realize a person's circumstances that you can even begin to understand him or her as a person. I learned to see Ruby as she was: a mother, a grandmother, an Eastern Star. We ceased talking like volunteer and resident; we formed a friendship, some special bond that went beyond class requirements. I'll always remember Ruby and—as a constant reminder of my own premature judgments—that white and red cane.

## ACTIVITY 2

To help you think more about the process of thinking, write about a paradigm shift you have experienced—a shift of understanding that made you more aware of something. First, *describe* what happened to cause the shift; *then explain* the significance of the shift to you. Suggestions: Have you ever prejudged someone—a fellow student or a teacher, for example—and then discovered you were wrong? Have you gotten upset with your parents for a decision they made only to find out there was a significant reason why they made that decision? Bring this writing to your next class.

## COMMUNICATING CLEARLY AND EFFECTIVELY

How do writers create their effects? If you want your readers to do something, what language should you use? Because all writers attempt to create some effect with their words and sentences, you can say that, in general, all writing is to some degree persuasive. You may not want your readers to get up and clean the local river or park, but there are many other effects of language. Writers may seek agreement from their readers. They may seek acceptance.

Thinking, communicating, persuading—they all go together when writers are in control. But how? Read the following essay by Amy Wu, a 20-year-old history major at New York University when <u>Newsweek</u> published her essay for its "My Turn" column. As you read, consider how Wu identifies and explores a problem, how she notices things, and how she communicates and persuades. *to Convince*

### Stop the Clock

*Amy Wu*

My aunt tends to her house as if it were her child. The rooms are spotless, the windows squeak, the kitchen counter is so shiny that I can see my reflection and the floors are so finely waxed that my sister and I sometimes slide across in socks and pretend that we are skating.

Smells of soy sauce, scallions and red bean soup drift from the kitchen whenever I visit. The hum of the washing machine lulls me to sleep. In season, there are roses in the garden, and vases hold flowers arranged like those in a painting. My aunt enjoys keeping house, although she's wealthy enough to hire someone to do it.

I'm a failure at housework. I've chosen to be inept and unlearn what my aunt has spent so much time perfecting. At 13, I avoided domestic chores as my contribution to the women's movement. Up to now, I've thought there were more important things to do.

I am a member of a generation that is very concerned with saving time but often unaware of why we're doing it. Like many, I'm nervous and jittery without a wristwatch and a daily planner. I am one of a growing number of students who are completing college in three years instead of four—cramming credits in the summer. We're living life on fast-forward without a pause button.

In my freshman year, my roommates and I survived on Chinese takeout, express pizzas and taco take-home dinners. We ate lunch while walking to class. Every day seemed an endless picnic as we ate with plastic utensils and paper plates. It was fast and easy—no washing up. My girlfriends and I talked about our mothers and grandmothers, models of domesticity, and pitied them. We didn't see the benefits of staying at home, ironing clothes and making spaghetti sauce when canned sauces were almost as good and cleaning services were so convenient. A nearby store even sold throwaway underwear. "Save time," the package read, "No laundry."

We baked brownies in 10 minutes in the microwave and ate the frosting from the can because we were too impatient to wait for the brownies to cool. For a while we thought about chipping in and buying a funky contraption that makes toast, coffee and eggs. All you had to do was put in the raw ingredients the night before and wake up to the smell of sizzling eggs, crispy toast and rich coffee.

My aunt was silent when I told her about utensils, microwave meals and disposable underwear. "It's a waste of money," she finally said. I was angry as I stared at her perfect garden, freshly ironed laundry and handmade curtains. "Well, you're wasting your time," I said defensively. But I wasn't so sure.

It seems that all the kids I know are time-saving addicts. Everyone on campus prefers e-mail to snail mail. The art of letter writing is long gone. I know classmates who have forgotten how to write in script, and print like 5-year-olds. More of us are listening to books instead of reading them. My roommate last year jogged while plugged in. She told me she'd listened to John Grisham's The Client. "You mean read," I corrected. "I didn't read a word," she said with pride.

My nearsighted friends opt for throw-away contacts and think the usual lenses are tedious. A roommate prefers a sleeping bag so she doesn't have to make her bed. Instead of going to the library to do research, we cruise the Internet and log on to the Library of Congress.

Schoolkids take trips to the White House via Internet and Mosaic. I heard that one school even considered canceling the eighth-grade Washington trip, a traditional rite of passage, because it's so easy to visit the capital on the Information Highway. I remember how excited my eighth grade classmates and I were about being away from home for the first time. We stayed up late, ate Oreos in bed and roamed around the Lincoln Memorial, unsupervised by adults.

It isn't as if we're using the time we save for worthwhile pursuits like volunteering at a soup kitchen. Most of my friends spend the extra minutes watching TV, listening to stereos, shopping, hanging out, chatting on the phone or snoozing.

When I visited my aunt last summer, I saw how happy she was after baking bread or a cake, how proud she seemed whenever she made a salad with her homegrown tomatoes and cucumbers. Why bother when there are ready-made salads, ready-peeled and -cut fruit and five-minute frosting?

Once, when I went shopping with her, she bought ingredients to make a birthday cake for her daughter. I pointed to a lavish-looking cake covered with pink roses. "Why don't you just buy one," I asked. "A cake is more than a cake," she replied. "It's the giving of energy, the thought behind it. You'll grow to understand."

Slowly, I am beginning to appreciate why my aunt takes pleasure in cooking for her family, why the woman down the street made her daughter's wedding gown instead of opting for Vera Wang, why the old man next door spends so much time tending his garden. He offered me a bag of his fresh-grown tomatoes. "They're good," he said. "Not like the ones at the supermarket." He was right.

Not long ago, I spent a day making a meal for my family. As the pasta boiled and the red peppers sizzled, I wrote a letter to my cousin in Canada. At first the pen felt strange, then reassuring. I hand-washed my favorite skirt and made chocolate cake for my younger sister's 13th birthday. It took great self-control not to slather on the icing before the cake cooled.

That night I grinned as my father and sister dug into the pasta, then the cake, licking their lips in appreciation. It had been a long time since I'd felt so proud. A week later my cousin called and thanked me for my letter, the first handwritten correspondence she'd received in two years.

Sure, my generation has all the technological advances at our fingertips. We're computer-savvy, and we have more time. But what are we really saving it for? In the end, we may lose more than we've gained by forgetting the important things in life.

Why did <u>Newsweek</u>'s editors choose to publish Amy Wu's essay? Wu communicates an important truth: obsessed with saving time, she and her generation don't spend their extra time usefully. Consequently, they have forgotten the value of doing simple activities with their own hands like gardening, making meals, and writing letters. Her argument applies to many older people in our culture as well. Thus, her essay appeals to a wide audience.

How exactly does Wu communicate her truth? Is her meaning clear? What effects does she create through her choice of words and sentences? First, try contrasting Wu's essay with this condensed version of it:

I don't understand why some people spend hours cooking and cleaning. I hate doing these things. I'm always in a rush. I eat fast food. I'm squeezing four years of college into three. I mean, my friends are the same—we're always hurrying. But we don't do much of anything useful with the time we save. It's pretty crazy really. But I do have a relative who likes to clean and cook, and she's been rubbing off on me. Recently I cooked a home-made meal for my family. They really liked it. I even wrote a letter instead of using e-mail. I think I'm going to start slowing down and start spending my time in more productive ways.

How is this paragraph different from Amy Wu's essay? Although the basic idea is essentially the same, is it clear and persuasive? Not really. It's general and vague—there aren't any images to help readers see what she means. Its language does little to create effects in readers: to engage them, to make them interested or surprised, to move them to say, "Yes, that's exactly how it is with me too." The condensed version is less convincing because it lacks reason and emotion; it lacks any real sense of the writer's personality or voice.

## Specific Evidence

Having a valid opinion is not enough for clear communication and persuasion. An opinion or idea must be supported with specific evidence: convincing reasons, examples, and details. Amy Wu goes to great lengths to use specific evidence to prove her point. As a reader you can *see* what she means because she uses language that appeals to your senses of sight, smell, sound, touch, and taste. You can see her aunt's house in Wu's first paragraph, feel Wu sliding across the "finely waxed" floors, and smell her aunt's "soy sauce, scallions and red bean soup." You can sense Wu's own handmade meal too—"the pasta boiled and the red peppers sizzled."

Wu notices and shares so many details that she makes it hard for readers to miss her point—her thesis: "I am a member of a generation that is very concerned with saving time but often unaware of why we're doing it." You can appreciate the VCR metaphor that restates her thesis: "We're living life on fast-forward without a pause button." You can see that by the end of her essay Wu has a paradigm shift: she cares more about slowing down and enjoying the pleasure of making things instead of buying them. She moves from an obsession with saving time to an appreciation of savoring time.

When a writer like Amy Wu communicates clearly, she takes the time to defend her ideas with evidence that will persuade readers to identify with her and to consider whether they too are "time-saving addicts." Critical thinkers take time to support their ideas with details. When Wu asked her aunt why she didn't buy a cake instead of making one, her aunt replied, "A cake is more than a cake. . . . It's the giving of energy, the thought behind it." Excellent writing and thinking require such a giving of energy—a commitment to clarity and persuasion.

When you talk, do you usually communicate clearly? Suppose you are walking on campus and see a friend. She asks how you are, and you reply, "Fine, and you?" She smiles and responds, "Great." In this brief exchange, does your friend know what you mean by *fine*? Do you know what she means by *great*? Perhaps you weren't feeling fine at all but said so anyway. When you talk to people, you often use general language. But when you write and want to communicate clearly and persuasively, you need to give specific reasons, examples, and details as Amy Wu does.

## ACTIVITY 3

To practice communicating clearly, write two paragraphs about a quality of a person you know well: perhaps your roommate is caring, a friend of yours is funny, or your mother is wise. In the first paragraph try to communicate poorly—that is, intentionally be general and vague. In the second paragraph, communicate clearly—present specific reasons, examples, and details. Bring these paragraphs to your next class.

Here is another "My Turn" essay written by a college student, Brian A. Courtney from the University of Tennessee, that Newsweek published. As you read it, consider how Courtney identifies and explores a problem, how he notices things, how he communicates and persuades. Also, notice what he does with words and sentences to create certain effects in readers.

### Freedom from Choice

#### *Brian A. Courtney*

As my friend Denise and I trudged across the University of Tennessee campus to our 9:05 a.m. class, we delivered countless head nods, "Heys" and "How ya' doin's" to other African-Americans we passed along the way. We spoke to people we knew as well as people we didn't know because it's an unwritten rule that black people speak to one another when they pass. But when I stopped to greet and hug one of my female friends, who happens to be white, Denise seemed a little bothered. We continued our walk to class, and Denise expressed concern that I might be coming down with a "fever." "I don't feel sick," I told her. As it turns out, she was referring to "jungle fever," the condition where a black man or woman is attracted to someone of the opposite race.

This encounter has not been an uncommon experience for me. That's why the first 21 years of my life have felt like a never-ending tug of war. And quite honestly, I'm not looking forward to being dragged through the mud for the rest of my life. My white friends want me to act one way—white. My African-American friends want me to act another—black. Pleasing them both is nearly impossible and leaves little room to be just me.

The politically correct term for someone with my racial background is "biracial" or "multiracial." My mother is fair-skinned with blond hair and blue eyes. My father is dark-complexioned with prominent African-American features and a head of woolly hair. When you combine the genetic makeup of the two, you get me—golden-brown skin, semi-coarse hair and a whole mess of freckles.

Someone once told me I was lucky to be biracial because I have the best of both worlds. In some ways this is true. I have a huge family that's filled with diversity and is as colorful as a box of Crayolas. My family is more open to whomever I choose to date, whether that person is black, white, biracial, Asian or whatever. But looking at the big picture, American society makes being biracial feel less like a blessing than a curse.

One reason is the American obsession with labeling. We feel the need to label everyone and everything and group them into neatly defined categories. Are you a Republican, a Democrat or an Independent? Are you pro-life or pro-choice? Are you African-American, Caucasian or Native American? Not everyone fits into such classifications. This presents a problem for me and the many biracial people living in the United States. The rest of the population seems more comfortable when we choose to identify with one group. And it pressures us to do so, forcing us to deny half of who we are.

Growing up in the small, predominantly white town of Maryville, Tenn., I attended William Blount High School. I was one of a handful of minority students—a raisin in a box of cornflakes, so to speak. Almost all of my peers, many of whom I've known since grade school, were white. Over the years, they've commented on how different I am from other black people they know. The implication was that I'm better because I'm only *half* black. Acceptance into their world has meant talking as they talk, dressing as they dress and appreciating the same music. To reduce tension and make everyone feel comfortable, I've reacted by ignoring half of my identity and downplaying my ethnicity.

My experience at UT has been very similar. This time it's my African-American peers exerting pressure to choose. Some African-Americans on campus say I "talk too white." I dress like the boys in white fraternities. I have too many white friends. In other words, I'm not black enough. I'm a white "wanna-be." The other day, an African-American acquaintance told me I dress "bourgie." This means I dress very white—a pastel-colored polo, a pair of navy chinos and hiking boots. Before I came to terms with this kind of remark, a comment like this would have angered me, and I must admit that I was a little offended. But instead of showing my frustration, I let it ride, and I simply said, "Thank you." Surprised by this response, she said in disbelief, "You mean you agree?"

On more occasions than I dare to count, black friends have made sweeping derogatory statements about the white race in general. "White people do this, or white people do that." Every time I hear them, I cringe. These comments refer not just to my white friends but to my mother and maternal grandmother as well. Why should I have to shun or hide my white heritage to enhance my ethnicity? Doesn't the fact that I have suffered the same prejudices as every other African-American—and then some—count for something?

I do not blame my African-American or white friends for the problems faced by biracial people in America. I blame society for not acknowledging us as a separate race. I am speaking not only for people who, like myself, are half black and half white, but also for those who are half white and half Asian, half white and half Hispanic, or half white and half whatever. Until American society recognizes us as a distinct group, we will continue to be pressured to choose one side of our heritage over the other.

Job applications, survey forms, college-entrance exams and the like ask individuals to check only *one* box for race. For most of my life, I have marked BLACK because my skin color is the first thing people notice. However, I could just as honestly have marked WHITE. Somehow when I fill out these forms, I think the employers, administrators, researchers, teachers or whoever sees them will have a problem looking at my face and then accepting a big X by the word WHITE. In any case, checking BLACK or WHITE does not truly represent me. Only in recent years have some private universities added the category of BIRACIAL or MULTIRACIAL to their applications. I've heard that a few states now include these categories on government forms.

One of the greatest things parents of biracial children can do is expose them to *both* of their cultures. But what good does this do when in the end society makes us choose? Having a separate category marked BIRACIAL will not magically put an end to the pressure to choose, but it will help people to stop judging us as just black or just white and see us for what we really are—both.

Like Amy Wu, Brian Courtney writes about something that matters to him and to many others. If the problem of being biracial affected only him or a few people, <u>Newsweek</u> would not have published his essay. How does Courtney communicate and persuade clearly and effectively?

He focuses his essay on an important problem—being biracial and having to choose to be black or white.

He states a clear thesis: "American society makes being biracial feel less like a blessing than a curse." He introduces this thesis in his second paragraph in which he refers to his life feeling "like a never-ending tug of war" between being black or white.

He supports his thesis with sound reasons: being biracial is difficult because of our country's "obsession with labeling." To cope with this problem, he has tried to "reduce tension . . . by ignoring half of my identity and downplaying my ethnicity." The problem is severe, he argues, because society does not "acknowledge us as a separate race." Then, he offers a reasonable solution to the problem: our society should recognize biracial people as a separate race by including "Biracial" or "Multiracial" categories on all forms that ask people to mark their race.

He supports his thesis with convincing evidence: specific examples and details. His introduction serves as an interesting example—while he walks on campus his friend Denise is bothered because he greets a white female friend. Later he describes his parents and himself so you can visualize them: "My mother is fair-skinned with blond hair and blue eyes. My father is dark-complexioned with prominent African-American features and a head of woolly hair. When you combine the genetic makeup of the two, you get me—golden-brown skin, semi-coarse hair and a whole mess of freckles."

He uses language well to create certain effects in readers. His comparisons help readers see what he means: "I have a huge family that's filled with diversity and is as colorful as a box of Crayolas," and "I was one of a handful of minority students—a raisin in a box of cornflakes, so to speak." These images and others make Courtney an appealing and friendly person. His voice—the sound of his personality—is believable, credible, honest, friendly, sincere. You sense you can trust him.

He persuades readers that the problem of being biracial is real and important.

## WRITING AN OPINION ESSAY

Writing opinion essays is useful because as a citizen of any community, you may be asked to express your opinions and to defend them with persuasive arguments. How much of your daily life involves expressing your opinions? Much of it. Yet writing an opinion essay enables you to think more deliberately and carefully than you would in normal conversation.

## ACTIVITY 4

### OPINION ESSAY

Write an essay in which you support an opinion about something that matters to you, that concerns you and other people. What problem can you examine? What do you value that you feel other people could benefit from reading and thinking about? What do you care about that you'd like your readers to care about too?

- To get started, in your notebook explore at least three possible ideas for an essay. Talk to yourself on paper about what's been on your mind lately that you'd like to address to a certain audience. Also, ask yourself these questions: Am I going to write about a problem that concerns only me? Is my opinion already obvious to most people? What reasons, examples, and details can I use for supporting evidence?

- Your initial audience for your essay should be your classmates and teacher. However, if your final essay works well, you can submit it to your school newspaper, your local newspaper or a major newspaper in your state, or a magazine like

Newsweek for its "My Turn" column. Your essay should be 700–1200 words (3 to 5 pages), containing an effective title, introduction, body, and conclusion.

- You have read two opinion essays that Newsweek published. Both Amy Wu and Brian Courtney explore a problem that concerns them personally yet also concerns our broader society. I invite you to do the same: write about a problem that you can support with specific evidence from your own experience and knowledge.

  *Note:* For this opinion essay, avoid deeply complex controversies such as abortion, capital punishment, or stem cell research. These topics usually require examining opposing views and doing research (as you will see in Chapter 2).

- Start writing your essay soon—today or tomorrow. After you do your exploratory writing to find possible ideas, begin a draft of your essay. While you write during the next few days, read the rest of this chapter and try to apply the principles of persuasion presented.

  *Note:* It's not uncommon to write a draft and realize it's not working. Keep in mind the process of thinking: to solve the problems of what to write about and how to support it well, you may need to try a different topic. This is natural. ▬

## Finding Your Subject

Noticing things—problems, possible solutions, distinctive details—leads to wondering what they suggest or mean. Amy Wu in "Stop the Clock" noticed contrasts between herself and her aunt, contrasts in how they spent their time and behaved. Brian Courtney in "Freedom from Choice" noticed his own and other people's problems of being biracial. Wu and Courtney both felt a need to write about their situations.

Do you feel a need to write about a particular problem? If so, that problem is your *writing situation*, which motivates you to write. For students, the beginning of a writing situation is often the writing assignment; however, look beyond the assignment for something in the real world, something that concerns you and other people, something that matters.

---

### GUIDELINES FOR FINDING A SUBJECT

There aren't any definite rules about what is or isn't worth writing about, but consider these guidelines.

1. Write about something that you honestly care about, that concerns you and other people, something that others might benefit from reading. If you are genuinely interested, not faking it, you can usually get your reader interested.

2. What do readers want from the writer? They hope you will tell them some *truth*, something new, something different, and if possible something interesting, entertaining, or enlightening. Nobody wants to read about what is already obvious. Nobody wants to read an essay and say "So what? Who cares?" Brian Courtney in

*Continued . . .*

"Freedom from Choice" educates readers who never thought about the problems of being biracial in our society. Readers also want writers to remind them of some important truth or value, as Amy Wu does in "Stop the Clock." Her idea that we should savor time is not new, but her presentation of the idea by using her own specific evidence makes her essay new.

3. How much evidence do you need? How many reasons, examples, and details? The writer's problem is usually not enough evidence rather than too much. The quantity of evidence depends on the writing situation: if your boss asks you to write a one-page memo about a problem in your department, you must condense what you know. In a persuasive essay or a letter to an editor, you can present more specific information. Writers must decide how much is enough information in whatever they write. How many examples and details do Amy Wu and Brian Courtney use in their essays? Many. They both draw from their own personal experience and knowledge for their evidence. Try to do the same: draw on your own experience for evidence.

## WRITING PERSUASIVELY

Persuasive writing attempts to move your reader. The persuasive writer uses evidence—reasons, examples, details—to cause readers to respond in some way. You can't force your readers, but you can appeal to them. You can appeal to your reader's mind, emotions, and character.

A persuasive writer attempts to get readers to respond as the writer wishes. To convince readers you need specific evidence such as facts. You can't get your readers to accept the claim, for example, that fast food is not healthy for you, if you don't know the facts about it. Also, you can tell people the truth about smoking tobacco, and readers may even agree with you. Still, that may not produce the desired change in their behaviors. Speakers and writers have known since ancient times that truth and logic alone are not always sufficient to move people. People sometimes rebel at being told what to do, even when they recognize that the advice is in their best interests. Many people are suspicious of anyone who seems to be trying to manipulate them.

Philosophers and orators of ancient Greece and Rome struggled with this conflict. Some philosophers insisted that argumentation should concern only facts, logic, and absolute statements with which all reasonable people must agree. They admired statements like this: Socrates is a man; all men are mortal—therefore Socrates is mortal. The beauty of such reasoning could be shown with mathematics, the philosophers said: "A is B; B is C—therefore A is C." The philosophers believed that such *truth* would persuade people. On the other hand, the orators said, such statements seem not very useful in real life. For one thing, you can't always know what the truth is: in most cases you can only say what is *probably true*, not what is *absolutely true*. If two people accuse each other of wrongdoing, each denying the other, it's difficult to say what *truly* happened. The ancient orators knew that to persuade people it was often necessary—

in addition to giving reasons and facts—to stir their emotions and to convince them of the morality of both the argument and the speaker.

Even now many people believe only verifiable facts should constitute evidence. Our courts are founded on that presumption. Anything else is considered trickery. However, to get the facts, our courts are founded on the adversarial system. Thus you can find courtroom scenes awash more in emotion than facts and reason, tearful witnesses, and shocked, enraged lawyers. In addition to emotion, modern lawyers and politicians often rely heavily on moral arguments. "The defendant is a moral person," the jury is told, "with a family to support, is a regular churchgoer, a solid member of the community. What a shame for this community that such a fine, upright citizen should be dragged into court," the lawyers argue.

Although ancient orators introduced emotions and morality into arguments, the philosophers insisted that students must be taught to use only logic and reason. Persuading audiences through emotional pleas or ethical presentations, the philosophers thought, was manipulation. However, one of the most important philosophers of the time, Aristotle, said speakers needed all three appeals in order to move audiences. His advice continues to hold true. Persuasion then and now requires all three appeals: logos, pathos, and ethos.

## THE PERSUASIVE APPEALS

Skillful writers appeal to their readers: to their minds with *logos*, their emotions with *pathos*, and their ethics with *ethos*.

### Logos

To appeal to your reader's mind, you give reasons. If your reasons make sense and your examples and details are specific and clear, your logos will be convincing. However, critical thinkers know that people can—and often do—resist logos. Writers can show facts and evidence yet still fail to move people. Suppose you were hired to write a flyer for a campaign aimed at getting more people to keep a fire extinguisher in their home. You might explain all the reasons why every home should have an approved fire extinguisher and why all adults and older children should be trained to use it. You can show pictures of fires destroying homes, fires that could have been stopped with a home extinguisher. All these reasons could make a strong argument for the home fire extinguisher. Nevertheless, many readers might do nothing. Logic alone often fails to move people.

Using all the appeals together, effective writers convince through good reasoning, a careful stirring of emotions, and their own trustworthy character. Logos is most powerful when it deals with absolute or *certain* information. Unfortunately most of the time you have only *probable* evidence. You can't say the house will *certainly* burn down if you have no fire extinguisher, nor can you say your house is absolutely safe from fire if you do have an extinguisher. Logos is an important element of persuasion, but often you need other elements to convince readers.

How reasonable is Deborah Prothrow-Stith, M.D., in this passage from her book <u>Deadly Consequences</u>?

> While much about human aggression is not known, one fact is indisputable: Among all races, all classes, and in every corner of the globe men are more violent than women. This truth had led researchers to look for a particular male substance that explains violent outbursts. Discredited work done in the 1970s attempted, but failed, to establish the presence in violent males of an extra Y chromosome. Researchers today believe it is the male hormone testosterone that causes male violence. Testosterone courses through the bloodstream of all males. Do violent males have more testosterone than peaceful ones? This question has not yet been fully answered, but according to a small study done by the respected Swedish psychologist Dan Olweus, they do. "Testosterone poisoning," is the term Olweus uses to describe displays of male aggression. What is not clear, however, is whether testosterone causes violence or whether aggressive feelings and violent acts cause increased amounts of testosterone to be produced.
>
> I think there is a likelihood that testosterone plays some not yet fully understood role in male sex role differentiation and aggression. However, I feel certain that neither this hormone, nor any hormone, is totally responsible. Presumably males in all nations possess reasonably equal amounts of testosterone, and yet rates of violence are far from equal worldwide. Socialization is the factor that differs from place to place. Some societies, like our own, clearly encourage young males to enact their violent feelings. Other societies convey to their young that non-violent outlets must be found for aggressive feelings.

In this passage Prothrow-Stith asserts an argument that men are more violent than women—she claims this is a "fact" and "indisputable." You and I don't have the scientific data that support her statement—all men everywhere are more violent than women—but neither can we dispute it. She summarizes some research that has attempted to build on this idea. Questioning the role of testosterone, she wonders if it causes violence or whether violence causes it to increase. She concludes that this hormone cannot by itself cause male aggression (else we cannot explain differences in male behavior around the world)—socialization also plays a significant role. We can infer, on the whole, that Prothrow-Stith appears to use effective logos: her appeals to reason make sense, and she seems fair-minded.

You may question her statement that our society "clearly encourage[s] young males to enact their violent feelings." This seems a broad generalization; however, upon further reflection, you may agree that many popular movies, television shows, and video games do glorify violence, and you may have observed peer groups encouraging violent behavior among males. In this passage Prothrow-Stith doesn't attempt to stir emotions in readers; she offers arguments and reasons. Her writing here appeals to logos.

By contrast, later in her book, Prothrow-Stith combines pathos—the appeal of emotion—with logos.

> Why shouldn't the movie hero enjoy using violence? Why not, indeed, when only bad guys, never heroes, get hurt. You won't see Bruce Willis or Arnold Schwarzenegger shot through the spine, a quadriplegic, a paraplegic, a young man without sexual function, a young man

with a permanent breathing tube who can only whisper his words from a hospital bed where he will pass the rest of his life. Who, then, if not the mass media, will tell our young that these are the true consequences of violence?

Again Prothrow-Stith displays her questioning mind. Her long third sentence, however, appeals to your emotions: the image of a young man whispering from a hospital bed is sad and real; it seems odd to consider Bruce Willis or Arnold Schwarzenegger in this situation. Prothrow-Stith moves readers to think about violence and to feel its effects.

Then too, readers can catch a glimpse of her ethos in her effort to be fair-minded in her book. Prothrow-Stith acknowledges that media do not always promote violence.

> It ought to be noted, however, that not all of television's lessons are violent ones. Social learning does not just involve the modeling of negative behaviors. Researchers have shown that positive behaviors can be modeled, too. The people who produce <u>Sesame Street</u> and <u>Mr. Rogers</u> do a great job of providing models of desirable social behavior for young kids to emulate. Concern for others. The willingness to delay gratification. The capacity to compromise. All these behaviors and many more are made available to small children who watch these programs. These lessons will not become patterns of behavior, however, unless home and schools provide reinforcement. When a child sees another child sharing on <u>Sesame Street</u> and then tries sharing at home, parents need to be vigilant. Positive behavior needs reinforcement or it will not reoccur.

In showing different points of view, Prothrow-Stith conveys the impression that she is a careful critical thinker, being fair to both sides.

What might you infer about Prothrow-Stith's ethos—her character? Does she seem trustworthy, believable, credible? That she cares about the complex problem of violence in our culture is a reason to respect her. If you knew more about her background, would her ethos have more persuasive appeal? Prothrow-Stith is a physician and former Massachusetts commissioner of public health who is now a professor at Harvard University. She has worked in emergency rooms and witnessed firsthand the deadly consequences of violence. If she were not a doctor of medicine and a public health expert, you might not accept her appeals to reason and emotion. Even without this biographical information, readers can hear the voice of a concerned individual discussing a serious problem in our society. Further, she seems fair. Prothrow-Stith does not overdo the pathos or exaggerate the reality. Overall she uses the restrained voice of the objective writer, a scientist, yet she persuades readers to care about this problem.

Logos, pathos, and ethos interplay with one another differently in any given act of communication. Critical thinkers pay attention to persuasive appeals. Noticing these appeals will enable you to use them intentionally while you write and to analyze them while you read.

## Recognizing Logos

*Logos* is a Greek word for *word*, by which the Greeks meant "divine words," reason, the word of God. From *logos* comes our word *logic*. An appeal to logos is an appeal to reason: the writer tries to reach the reader's mind with reasons, examples, and facts. For example, consider this thesis: Parents know they should not leave pans with handles protruding over the edge of the stove. Reason [because]: Curious children may reach for the handles and pull hot pans down on themselves.

Analyzing logos usually requires careful reading or listening. You can improve your ability to analyze logos by following these guidelines:

## GUIDELINES FOR ANALYZING LOGOS

- What clues are there that the writer is trying to be logical?
- Where does the writer use reasons that make sense?
- Is the writer's thesis reasonable and worth considering?
- Is the writer's supporting evidence clear, specific, and convincing?
- Does the writer use accurate facts, examples, and details?

As you read the following passage from S. I. Hayakawa's book Language in Thought and Action, consider Hayakawa's use of persuasive appeals—especially logos.

## On Human Survival

### S. I. Hayakawa

People who think of themselves as tough-minded and realistic, among them influential political leaders and businessmen as well as go-getters and small-time hustlers, tend to take it for granted that human nature is selfish and that life is a struggle in which only the fittest may survive. According to this philosophy, the basic law by which man must live, in spite of his surface veneer of civilization, is the law of the jungle. The "fittest" are those who can bring to the struggle superior force, superior cunning, and superior ruthlessness.

The wide currency of this philosophy of the "survival of the fittest" enables people who act ruthlessly and selfishly, whether in personal rivalries, business competition, or international relations, to allay their consciences by telling themselves that they are only obeying a law of nature. But a disinterested observer is entitled to ask whether the ruthlessness of the tiger, the cunning of the fox, and obedience to the law of the jungle are, in their *human* applications, actually evidences of *human* fitness to survive. If human beings are to pick up pointers on behavior from the lower animals, are there not animals other than beasts of prey from which we might learn lessons in survival?

We might, for example, point to the rabbit or the deer and define fitness to survive as superior rapidity in running away from our enemies. We might point to the earthworm or the mole and define it as the ability to keep out of sight and out of the way. We might point to the oyster or the housefly and define it as the ability to propagate our kind faster than our enemies can eat us up. In Aldous Huxley's

> Brave New World, we see a world designed by those who would model human beings after the social ants. The world, under the management of a superbrain trust, might be made as well integrated, smooth, and efficient as an ant colony and, as Huxley shows, just about as meaningless. If we simply look to animals in order to define what we mean by "fitness to survive," there is no limit to the subhuman systems of behavior that can be devised: we may emulate lobsters, dogs, sparrows, parakeets, giraffes, skunks, or the parasitical worms, because they have all obviously survived in one way or another. We are still entitled to ask, however, if *human* survival does not revolve around a different kind of fitness from that of the lower animals.

Hayakawa appeals to reason in this passage. He doesn't give emotional examples; he doesn't stir your feelings. Rather, he helps you consider the familiar idea of "survival of the fittest" in a new way. He questions whether only "beasts of prey" apply to human fitness. He offers readers a different perspective from which to see, describing less predatory kinds of animals and the ways they survive. In using this contrast, he enables you to see a problem in the notion of survival of the fittest. In his book Hayakawa presents this thesis: "Human fitness to survive means the ability to talk and write and listen and read in ways that increase the chances for you *and fellow-members of your species* to survive together." (His italics.) Thus, what distinguishes humans from other animals is our ability to cooperate with each other through our use of language.

Because Hayakawa uses effective logos or reasoning, many readers are also impressed with his ethos or character: he seems intelligent, knowledgeable, and believable. In fact, Hayakawa was a professor of semantics (the study of human interaction through communication), president of San Francisco State College, and then a U.S. senator from California. This information might further impress you about his character, which in turn might help you find his thinking more credible and persuasive.

However, you don't always have biographical information about writers. You must rely on the ethos you infer or sense in the writing. In Hayakawa's work you can sense the ethics of a man who challenges people who use slogans like "survival of the fittest" and "the law of the jungle" to justify their own selfish behavior. He challenges conventional thinking by asking which animal is appropriate if people must make analogies for human survival. Animal analogies omit the important fact that humanity has survived not with claw or fang but with mind, language, and cooperation.

## ACTIVITY 5

### REVISION

Look over the draft of your opinion essay. Examine your use of logos. Put a checkmark wherever you have used reasoning. How might you use reason more effectively? Supply additional reasons, facts, and examples if you can. ▪

## Pathos

Any single appeal by itself may not be enough to move people. If you want people to "think about" a problem, logos is a good appeal. But if you want to move people to do something or stop doing something, pathos is essential.

Suppose a group of city engineers presents this argument:

> The old bridge out of town is weak and may soon collapse. It should be repaired or replaced. We need taxes to pay for this work.

The engineers report the truth. Except for the implication in *collapse* there is no emotion here. However, though the argument may be true, the voters are reluctant to vote themselves a tax increase. You can see the *logic* of the engineers' argument; nevertheless, that may not move the taxpayers. The old bridge has lasted this long: it will probably last a while longer. It's difficult to get the public to respond . . . until you involve their emotions. What is needed is a speech writer who can create some passionate images. With pathos and logos together, writers may be able to reach an otherwise reluctant audience:

> The old bridge is not safe. The school bus must cross it twice daily. Think of it—a busload of our children crossing over the steep ravine under that shaky bridge. The bridge is old and rusting. It creaks and groans—it moves. One day soon it *will* give way. Our kids may crash through and fall screaming to their death. A small increase in taxes can prevent an enormous tragedy. If we don't act now, we will be responsible for what is sure to happen.

*Pathos*, the ancients discovered, could overthrow logic. You have to think about reasons and examples, but your emotions stir you automatically: fear, pity, hope, anger, guilt. Officials try to get people to use seatbelts in their cars, but statistics don't have as much impact on people as fear does.

In short, people can be moved with emotional appeals; pathos is often stronger than logos. However, the early philosophers recognized there were dangers in pathos, too. They knew people might be persuaded to act against their better judgment. If a speech could be delivered with enough pathos, the emotions of a jury might be moved in sympathy with a criminal. Thus, pathos is an appeal easily abused. Critical thinkers must beware of arguments aimed at their emotions. You must not let others use guilt, fear, and pity to manipulate you. Also, you must take care in using pathos yourself. Be sure the pathos is legitimate, appropriate, and used with restraint.

Here is a scene by Richard Selzer, a surgeon who became a writer, from his book <u>Mortal Lessons: Notes on the Art of Surgery</u>. Notice how Selzer uses pathos:

> I stand by the bed where a young woman lies, her face post-operative, her mouth twisted in palsy, clownish. A tiny twig of the facial nerve, the one to the muscles of her mouth, has been severed. She will be thus from now on. The surgeon had followed with religious fervor the curve of her flesh; I promise you that. Nevertheless, to remove the tumor in her cheek, I had cut the little nerve.
>
> Her young husband is in the room. He stands on the opposite side of the bed, and together they seem to dwell in the evening lamplight, isolated from me, private. Who are

they, I ask myself, he and this wry-mouth I have made, who gaze at and touch each other so generously, greedily? The young woman speaks.

"Will my mouth always be like this?" she asks.

"Yes," I say, "it will. It is because the nerve was cut."

She nods, and is silent. But the young man smiles.

"I like it," he says. "It is kind of cute."

All at once I *know* who he is. I understand, and I lower my gaze. One is not bold in an encounter with a god. Unmindful, he bends to kiss her crooked mouth, and I so close I can see how he twists his own lips to accommodate to hers, to show her that their kiss still works. I remember that the gods appeared in ancient Greece as mortals, and I hold my breath and let the wonder in.

Through his description Selzer enables you to imagine and visualize the young woman whose facial nerve like "a tiny twig" has been severed. Although she appears "clownish," her husband shows his love (and his moral character) for her by claiming he likes her new mouth and by forming his lips to kiss hers. The scene is at once sad yet full of love. Selzer's use of emotion can help you think about how you might act if someone you loved suddenly changed physically. Would you be as supportive as the young man in this scene?

Consider Selzer's ethos. What does this scene reveal about his moral character? Is he uncaring, disinterested, cold? Not at all. As a doctor, he witnessed this act of love and was moved both emotionally and intellectually. When it happened, he had a eureka moment: he compares the husband to a god from ancient Greece. Readers respond to Selzer's ethos because he cares about this young couple.

Each piece of writing has a different combination of logos, pathos, and ethos. Some writing, such as objective reports or summaries, appeals entirely to logos. Other writing, such as personal essays, may appeal more to pathos than to logos. Even within the same essay, speech, or book, the combination of appeals may change. Martin Luther King Jr.'s renowned "I Have a Dream" speech contains powerful logos, pathos, and ethos; however, he appeals most strongly to pathos at the end when he repeats "I have a dream." His emotional refrain stirred his audience to action: to demonstrate nonviolently for civil rights.

Pathos is a powerful tool you can use to put your audience into a receptive mood, to help them feel your messages. But if your audience senses that you are manipulating their emotions, your pathos will backfire and cause your audience to question your moral character (ethos). For example, some critics of Vice President Al Gore's speech during the Democratic National Convention in 1996 accused him of being too heavy-handed with pathos. In her essay, "Gore's Tear-Jerking Speech Belies Tobacco Background," columnist Joan Beck writes:

> Those delegates to the Democratic convention who were moved to tears by Vice President Al Gore's poignant story about his sister's death from lung cancer might not have been so misty-eyed if they knew about Gore's long and profitable relationship with tobacco.
>
> With uncharacteristic emotion, Gore told the audience that he was called to the hospital one day in 1984 as his sister, Nancy, lay dying.

"All of us had tried to find whatever new treatment or new approach might help," Gore said, "but all I could do was to say back to her with all the gentleness in my heart, 'I love you.'"

Gore went on: "Tomorrow morning, another 13-year-old girl will start smoking. I love her, too. Three thousand young people in America will start smoking tomorrow. One thousand of them will die a death not unlike my sister's. And that is why, until I draw my last breath, I will pour my heart and soul into the cause of protecting our children from the dangers of smoking."

Gore comes late to the fight against tobacco. He and his family made money by raising tobacco on their Tennessee farm for years–profiting from a product that killed lots of other people's sisters.

Joan Beck also acknowledges in her essay that Gore's family stopped producing tobacco after his sister died, but she raises questions about Gore's ethos because of his manipulation of emotion in his speech.

Lawyers often use pathos to persuade juries; other lawyers warn juries not to be swayed by emotion. In the infamous O. J. Simpson trial, jurors saw many gruesome photographs of Nicole Brown and Ronald Goldman. They heard intensely tearful testimony from Brown's sister and Goldman's father. But the defense persuaded the jury not to convict Simpson by pointing to the emotional and prejudicial nature of the evidence against him.

In the case of Timothy McVeigh, convicted in the Oklahoma City bombing, the prosecutor used pathos when referring to the victims killed in the blast:

Using McVeigh's own words against him, prosecutor Larry Mackey said the 168 people who died in the April 19, 1995 blast were not "tyrants whose blood had to be spilled to preserve liberty."

"And certainly the 19 children that died that day were not storm troopers who had to die because of their association with an evil empire," he said. . . .

Mackey described how McVeigh set the fuse on the truck bomb and could see the toys and cribs in the federal building's day-care center on his way to his getaway car, with only a "wall of windows" to protect the children from the blast.

"America stood in shock. Who could do such a thing?" he said. "It has fallen to you, members of the jury, to answer this question. . . . The answer is clear—Tim McVeigh did it."

. . . By the end, one juror and more than a dozen bombing survivors and relatives were crying.

The defense attorney used logos in the following excerpt to counteract the effect of Mackey's emotional appeals:

But in the defense summation, lead attorney Stephen Jones said the prosecution based much of its case on emotion. He urged jurors not to be swayed by sympathy the way the O. J. Simpson jury was swayed by race. . . . Rather, Jones argued, jurors should focus on the prosecution's evidence, which he said was badly flawed.

When people's lives are at stake, the use of pathos and logos can make a dramatic difference in finding an accused person guilty or innocent. Whoever sends you messages—lawyers, TV reporters, essayists, advertisers—shapes messages with persuasive appeals of logos, pathos, and ethos.

## Recognizing Pathos

*Pathos* comes from the Greek word for *suffering*; we use it to mean appealing to the emotions. From *pathos* comes the word *sympathy*: to have appropriate feelings for another person's emotions, to "feel for" that person. We also have *empathy*, which means to feel the same or similar emotion as another person. The word *pathetic* means pitiable, sad. Without emotions, people seem cold, mechanical, and less than human. But unscrupulous speakers can take advantage of emotions, and many people believe that emotions should be ruled out when you try to determine truth. Did the defendant commit the crime, yes or no? The fact that the defendant sits in court weeping piteously should have no bearing on the question. (The defendant may be faking anyway.)

Certainly critical thinkers must be aware that emotions may or may not have anything to do with "truth." In many cases emotions can be essential. It's possible to tell people all the scientific data about HIV and AIDS and how they are transmitted, but until you move people emotionally, not much will change. Critical writers must recognize not only "logical or factual" truth but "emotional" truth as well.

The breadth and depth of our emotions are part of the human miracle:

---

**Pathos**

Affection, anger, contempt, delight, disgust, despair, embarrassment, envy, excitement, fear, guilt, hope, horror, humiliation, humor, jealousy, joy, love, loyalty, passion, pity, pride, joy, remorse, ridicule, sadness, shame, shock, shyness, sorrow, vengeance

---

Human emotions can be difficult to analyze: crying for joy can look similar to crying for sorrow; silence might indicate anger, fear, or hurt feelings. Experience will help you develop your ability to identify human emotions.

## G UIDELINES FOR ANALYZING PATHOS

- What clues are there that the writer is appealing to the reader's emotions? Does the writer use vivid description, examples, personal stories, or shocking facts to move you?
- What emotions do you think the writer is trying to rouse: sorrow, fear, guilt, hope . . . ?
- Where does the writer use emotional appeals: at the beginning, toward the end, or throughout?

*Continued* . . .

- Is the pathos appropriate and used with restraint—not faked or exaggerated in order to manipulate an audience?
- How does the writer's appeal to emotion reinforce his or her appeal to reason?

Here is a "My Turn" essay that <u>Newsweek</u> published, written by Julia Kraus, a high school student from Wichita, Kansas. As you read it, consider how Kraus identifies and explores a problem, how she notices things, how she communicates and persuades. In particular, consider how she uses pathos as an appeal to help readers feel and think.

## If I Told You, Would You Want to Hear?

*Julia Kraus*

It's a normal conversation, really. It's the first day of 11th grade. I've just met my biology-lab partner. He mentions his brother. Then he asks me The Question.

It isn't earth-shattering. It isn't even unusual. The Question is: how many brothers and sisters do you have?

After 10 seconds of silence I say, "I can't remember." I really can't. Does he mean how many siblings I have at this moment? Or does he mean every sibling I've ever had in my life?

When I left home this morning, I had three siblings. When I come home tonight, I could still have three. Or I could have only two. Or four. And as for all the siblings I've ever had, the tally is nearing 250. Foster care is so hard to explain.

Every time someone asks The Question, it ends up becoming a conversation. I could say "two" and have that be the end of it, because I do have two sons-of-my-parents brothers, but that answer is incomplete. I could say, "More than 200," but that leads to witticisms such as "What do you do, run a sweatshop?" I could just say, "We do foster care," and lead right into the inevitable conversation. Any way I truthfully answer The Question sparks scores more.

How long have we been doing this? Eight years. Yes, sometimes it's hard to give them up. No, I don't usually mind them—I like kids. No, I'm not a foster kid myself. No, I don't know your cousin Rosie who got put in foster care last year. I couldn't tell you even if I did know her. Why? Against the law. No, I can't tell you stories.

That last thing was a lie. I could tell you stories if I wanted to, if I left off the names of the kids. But you wouldn't want to hear.

There's the 3-year-old girl who was stripped, doused with cold water and force-fed. In her front yard. In January.

There's the developmentally delayed teenage mother who doesn't know who her daughter's father is. The young woman's stepfather swears up and down that it can't be him because he's had a vasectomy. Not because he's never had sex with his stepdaughter.

There's the 6-month-old boy, eyes goggling almost sightlessly, hooked up to God-knows-what machine, whimpering. He's been sent to us because he was shaken at a previous foster home, shaken hard, shaken fast, shaken violently until his eyes popped out, whereupon his shaker pushed them back in with his thumbs. His vision will never exceed 20/100.

There's the 3-year-old boy with eyes swollen shut by a huge double shiner. His two bottom left ribs were broken. He had fist-size bruises on his chin and cheeks. He complained only once, when he was eating. He said his mouth hurt. My mom looked. His teeth were rotted through.

There's the baby we had for just a day or two. Not long after she went home, her father flew into a temper and killed her. She was less than a year old, I do remember that.

Are you covering your ears? Are you screaming at me to stop? Good. That'll teach you to ask me to tell you stories.

I remember being 14 and at a sleepover. Everyone was talking animatedly about a TV show. "Fill me in, guys," I said, "I've never heard of this show."

A girl I didn't know well stared at me. "Never?"

I shook my head. "I don't really have time to watch TV . . . "

"You're pretty naive, aren't you?" she interrupted. "Pretty sheltered."

I stared at her. "Naive?"

"I can just tell," she said, "you are."

I wanted to scream at her, tell her stories that made her cringe and cry and beg me to stop. Instead, I said firmly, "You've never seen a newborn addicted to cocaine. I am not naive."

I'm not.

I think about them all. Pictures come, nonsequential pictures that tell no stories and give no names. My mother, sleeping in a rocker with our first foster baby. My father, checking the sprinklers in the yard with a toddler clutching his hand. A pair of sad, too-old eyes. A tiny hand curled around my finger.

Sounds come. Cries mainly, terrified, or resigned, or painful, or hungry, or angry. Laughs, sometimes. The sighs of a sleeping newborn. Computerized toddler toys.

Smells come. Formula. Lysol. Clean hair. Spit-up. Diapers. Lotion. Detergent. Dryer sheets. Lemony air freshener.

And names come. Nique. Typani. Zanna. Devonte. Isaiah. Kevin. Leticia. Rosa. Angel. Sometimes the name brings a picture, usually not. I am not naive.

I stopped being naive the day after I turned 9 years old, the day our first baby arrived. I will never be naive again.

See what one question will do?

## ACTIVITY 6

Does this essay by Julia Kraus have power? Why? In your notebook, write about how she uses pathos. What does she specifically do to stir emotion in readers—in you? Consider these questions too: How does her use of pathos strengthen or weaken her ability to communicate and to persuade? Does she use too much emotion—do you feel she manipulates you? How would you describe her voice—the sound of her personality?

Also, why does she use many incomplete sentences? Is this a problem, or does her style help her achieve her purpose? ▆▆▆

When writers use emotion well, they can touch a reader's heart and open up a door inside that may have been closed for a while. Consider this essay by Rick Reilly, who writes a weekly column for <u>Sports Illustrated</u>. How does he use pathos to help him communicate clearly and to persuade readers to feel what he says?

## Making Up for Lost Time

### *Rick Reilly*

Your blank screen mocks you and the tower of unopened mail pulls at your coat, and you wonder why you didn't go into the insurance business.

And you check in on your snoring 19-year-old son, home from college, and he's rounding noon and heading toward one and you wonder how you missed the typhoon that came through his room.

And so you trudge back to your desk and open a letter. And when you've finished, you go down, kiss your son on the forehead and wonder how you ever got so lucky.

*Dear Mr. Reilly or whomever might take the time to read this:*

*I am not much of a writer, but since about 1996 I have wanted to nominate this kid for FACES IN THE CROWD.*

*I should have started with all the junior golf tournaments he won at ages six to 10. I should have sent in something when he was written up as a golf prodigy in our paper at age 12. I should have sent in something when he got two holes in one in the summer after eighth grade.*

*I should have nominated him for being a three-time state qualifier and holding most all individual scoring records at his high school.*

*I should have sent in many of his wrestling accomplishments . . . but I'm having trouble remembering everything.*

*This young man was my very best friend. We were golfing partners for 16 years. You see, this young man was my son.*

*He was killed in a motorcycle accident.*

*So what I am doing to honor him is to nominate Cory Lemke for FACES IN THE CROWD.*

*Cory's real accomplishments were being the best friend a guy could ask for, the most loving and best son a father could ask for and a truly gentle and loving kid with the greatest smile in these United States.*

*I don't know how I will cope without him. I hurt so much, and I miss him so much, just to talk to or watch sports together. God, I loved that boy so much!!*

*Please accept this nomination!!*

*Mark Lemke—Cory's Father*

You call him. He's a 51-year-old truck driver in Sheldon, Iowa. He's on the road four or five days a week, just him and his rig and his sorrow.

Even on the phone, you can tell he's one of those tough guys who's not used to fighting off tears. And you can hear that he's losing.

He tells you how he and Cory played golf together every day they could—"thousands of rounds" he says—kidded each other endlessly and then, when it got dark or cold, played video golf together or watched the Vikings or just shot the bull. How his son gave him 16 shots the last time they played and still took $20 off the old man.

He remembers telling the kid that night, July 7, as Cory left to go to a car show in Hull, "Get some sleep, buddy. You gotta play tomorrow." And later: the phone ringing and the sickening cry in his wife Maud's voice from the kitchen, moaning, "Is he dead?"

He didn't even wait to see what it was, he just sprinted to his car and floored it to Hull. But he couldn't get there fast enough because Cory was as good as dead the second he hit that van. "No brain activity at all," the doctor said. Great idea. *Let me test drive your motorcycle.* No helmet. Kids.

The next morning they unplugged the respirator. On the way home he picked up his cell and played Cory's last message—"Got us a tee time Sunday over at Spencer," Cory says. "Let's leave at 7:30. Gonna kick your butt."

God, that Sunday morning came down hard on the big truck driver. He just sat in his chair, numb, like somebody'd cut off his arms. And Maud walked in, tears pooling in her eyes, holding out the car keys. "You better go," she whispered. "He'd want you to."

And he did. He pulled his two-ton heart out of that chair and mummy-walked through 18 holes, because buddies don't let each other down. And all the way he ached about all the things he never said or did for his son.

And later on he took out his pen and paper and fixed one of them.

Why did Reilly write this essay? He read a letter from a grieving father whose son had died. His son is the same age as Reilly's son. Mark Lemke's letter wakes up something in Reilly: he goes into his son's bedroom, kisses him on the forehead, and realizes how lucky he is that his son is alive and doing normal 19-year-old things like sleeping in past noon. The letter activates love Reilly takes for granted and deep compassion for the man who asks Reilly to include his son in a regular feature Reilly uses called "Faces in the Crowd," a photo with some description of a person Reilly wants readers to appreciate.

Pathos not only helps readers feel sorrow and compassion here, but it helps readers appreciate the mystery of life and how quickly loved ones can disappear. Remember that Reilly is writing primarily to men who read Sports Illustrated. His essay shows how sports can connect fathers and their children in profoundly loving ways. Notice how Reilly uses the pronoun *you* to help readers put themselves in Reilly's place as he recounts his experience with Mark Lemke. Reilly's essay is a tribute not only to Cory Lemke but also to his father. That Reilly did this and did it so well shows why many readers consider him one of our country's best writers.

## Humor as Pathos

Pathos is not always sad. You can touch readers' hearts through laughter as well, though this is much harder to do. When a writer uses humor, it can help us think about an idea and help us respect that person for causing some delight in us.

Anne Lamott, an essayist and novelist, often writes with humor. She uses humor in her book <u>Traveling Mercies</u> when writing about serious situations, as when she had a fight with her son Sam and "grabbed him by his pipe-cleaner arm and jerked him in the direction of his room." She writes, "It's so awful, attacking your child. It is the worst thing I know, to shout loudly at this fifty-pound being with his huge trusting brown eyes. It's like bitch-slapping E. T."

Her last sentence is funny because it surprises you, yet it makes you think too. She is honest here, writing about what matters: sorry for being rough with her son, she is able to use humor to help her and us understand what happens between parents and children.

Rick Reilly often uses humor to help him communicate and persuade. In his essay "The Way to a Man's Heart," he writes directly to women, arguing that women should try to understand men more—especially when it comes to sports and being men. Here are some excerpts:

> When you say, "Rub aloe on that cut. It'll reduce the scarring," you don't get it. We want it to scar *more*.
>
> Just because we haven't played catcher in years, it's not O.K. to throw out our jock and cup. Do we throw away your pom-poms? . . .
>
> You say it boggles your mind how we can watch a college basketball game that was played in 1969. We say it boggles our mind how you can watch Rachael Ray make a meatloaf. . . .
>
> When you say, "If your team frustrates you so much, why do you still watch them?" That would be like us asking you, "If your kids frustrate you so much, why don't you sell them?" They're our teams, forever.

It's hard not to appreciate Rick Reilly here. When someone makes us smile and wonder at the same time about men, women and sports, we can easily like and respect him.

Dave Barry is one of our country's most popular humorists, able to make readers laugh and think at the same time. Many of his columns involve Mr. Language Person, who discusses problems with diction and grammar. Here is an excerpt from an essay called "Mr. Language Person: Some Words of Wisdomality":

> Welcome to "Ask Mr. Language Person," written by the foremost leading world authority on the proper grammatorical usagality of English, both orally and in the form of words. In this award-winning column, which appears nocturnally, we answer the grammar and vocabulary questions that are on the minds of many Americans just before they pass out. . . .
>
> Q. I have trouble remembering the difference between the words "whose" and "who's." Should I put this in the form of a question?
>
> A. In grammatical terminology, "who's" is an interlocutory contraption that is used to form the culinary indicative tense.
>
> EXAMPLE: "You will never guess who's brassiere they found in the gumbo."
>
> "Whose" is the past paramilitary form of "whomsoever" and is properly used in veterinary interrogations.

What makes this funny, and so what? It's ironic. An expert on language would know what he was talking about, but this person is making up most of what he says. He's a fraud. His name alone, "Mr. Language Person," is funny; he could say Mr. Language Man but strains to be politically correct. Instead of being clear and concise, he makes up words to impress readers: such as "wisdomality," "grammatorical usagality," "interlocutory contraption," and "past paramilitary form of 'whomsoever.'" What is Dave Barry's purpose here? To make readers laugh and smile, and to wonder whether he makes any sense at all—and whether language experts make much sense.

Humor in the hands of experts such as Anne Lamott, Rick Reilly, and Dave Barry looks easy. But it's hard for most writers to pull off well. As a form of pathos that causes surprise and thought, humor is delightful.

But what if a writer's purpose is to ridicule someone or some idea? That kind of humor is far more risky. Consider this excerpt from Doug Giles's essay, "Anna Nicole Smith's Death Blamed on Global Warming":

> Our globe would probably cool off several degrees if Al Gore would just shut up and loose [sic] some weight. First things first, Al.
>
> The unsubstantiated hot air that emits from Gore's pie hole, the friction heat his chunky thighs generate when he waddles, plus the greenhouse gas he bellows out his backside after scarfing down the grande enchilada platter at Casa Ole are enough to make a polar bear bust a sweat.
>
> Speaking of polar bears, I do hope it gets a little warmer up north. I've always wanted to hunt polar bear, but it's just been too cold. Go warmer temps!
>
> Back to Gore. You and I both know that Gore would be warning us about the negative effects of Spider Monkey urine if it would ingratiate him to the voting public. And that's what this global warming, god awful warbling is all about: the unavoidable Presidential aspirations of Albert Gore. Jose Feliciano can see that.

Giles is a conservative columnist appearing on <http://Townhall.com>. He has a book titled <u>10 Habits of Decidedly Defective People: The Successful Loser's Guide to Life</u>. His audience for this essay is fellow conservatives, most of whom don't like Al Gore and are suspicious of the threat of global warming.

Is Giles's humor mean-spirited? Not if you agree with him and tend to laugh when someone makes fun of a person's weight. Yes, if you disagree with him and don't like sarcasm. Humor like this is edgy. Giles is not kind, but he doesn't want to be kind here. He doesn't acknowledge other views on global warming; he ridicules it, even claiming he'd like to hunt polar bears (which many liberals and scientists fear will soon become extinct because of climate change). "Go warmer temps!" He reduces the complex causes of global warming, claiming it's about "the unavoidable Presidential aspirations of Albert Gore." This doesn't show keen logic on his part, but his purpose is not to use keen logic.

Pathos is complex. It's not all about touching hearts and expanding compassion. It can involve humor that delights or that ridicules—and various purposes in between. As a critical thinker, you can judge whether a writer uses too much sadness or too much humor to make readers feel and think. For more on humor, see Chapter 3.

## ACTIVITY 7

### REVISION

Look over the draft of your opinion essay. Examine your use of pathos. Put a check-mark wherever you try to appeal to your reader's emotions. How might you use pathos more effectively? Do you need to tone down your use of emotion?

Remember that your use of pathos depends on your purpose. To help readers feel the deep pain of foster care, Julie Kraus uses intense pathos. But Amy Wu and Brian Courtney use less, and they use different ways to help readers feel and think about their main ideas. There is no recipe for using pathos or any appeal. Your use of appeals depends on what you are trying to do with your readers. ▄▄

## Ethos

The most important attribute of any writer or speaker, Aristotle said, is *ethos*, the writer's character. Nothing is more important than the writer's credibility. You must believe writers for them to persuade you.

If readers don't trust a writer's character, they won't trust the writer's appeals to reason or emotion. Did you find Julia Kraus honest and trustworthy in her essay on foster care? If so, then you likely find her use of emotion and reason persuasive. Richard Selzer expresses concern and awe in his scene about the young couple; however, in other essays his ethos may appear less sensitive. Much depends on the subject matter and Selzer's purpose and tone. (See Selzer's essay "Brute" in Chapter 6.) Thus, you should not assume that the ethos of a writer in one particular essay will be the same ethos of that writer in another essay. Nor should you assume that a writer's ethos is an absolute reflection of the writer.

*Voice* is the sound of a writer's personality you hear in a text. The writer's ethos or character is part of that voice and has much influence on readers. When you write, your voice becomes a dominant element of how well you communicate and persuade. Critical thinkers are aware of this. (For more on voice, see Interchapter 1.)

However, ethos as an appeal can be abused. To create a favorable impression on an audience, irresponsible persons can present themselves as responsible, and immoral persons can present themselves as moral. Critical thinkers know that ethos can be exploited to serve unethical ends. Several television ministers of the past found themselves ruined, even jailed, when the media discovered money collected "for God's work" had really been for the ministers' private use: expensive cars, mansions, high living. While pretending to be moral, honest preachers, they pulled an old-fashioned swindle on the public.

Ethos tells you whether the writer shares your morality—your beliefs of right and good conduct. This was Aristotle's solution to the potential for abuse in persuasion. He said that persuasion could be misused unless the speaker was a good person. The writer has an obligation to be a person of good intentions, someone dedicated to truth and accuracy. That is, as a reader you need to believe the writer is moral, that the ethos you hear is true and honest. Your readers must also believe that you are true and honest, that you know your subject, that you offer sound reasons, that you are fair-minded, and that if you use an emotional appeal it is justified. Losing credibility with your readers is easy. But once lost it is nearly impossible to recover.

## Recognizing Ethos

From the Greek word *ethos*, meaning character, comes the word *ethics*. When you say that speakers or writers have *good* character, you imply that you approve of their morals, their sense of right and wrong: you share their values. What writers say and how they say it can be clues to their character. Most people respect writers who have a strong moral character, even if they don't agree with everything the writers say. The audience perceives whether the speaker is fair, honest, trustworthy, well prepared (showing respect for the audience), and intelligent. It doesn't matter what speakers or writers say if you don't believe them.

As a critical thinker and writer, you must care about your character and how others see it. Here are a few of the attributes of character that most people recognize:

---

**Ethos**

benevolence, courage, credibility, decency, dedication, dignity, enthusiasm, good-will, honesty, honor, idealism, intelligence, morality, nobility, patriotism, resolve, respect, responsibility, seriousness, sincerity, strength, trustworthiness, valor, vigor, wisdom

---

## GUIDELINES FOR ANALYZING ETHOS

- What clues in the writing make you believe the writer is trustworthy, fair-minded, and credible? Is there anything specific that suggests a good person to you?
- What clues, if any, make you believe the writer may be untrustworthy, not fair-minded, and not credible? (Remember that actors can project any ethos needed for the situation.)
- What authority does the writer have on this subject? How can you tell the writer has had experience with the subject?
- What is the writer's tone (attitude) toward the subject? Serious? Sincere? Indifferent? Sarcastic? Playful?
- What is the writer's tone toward the audience? Friendly? Concerned? Indifferent? Arrogant?
- What voice do you hear in the writer—the sound of his or her personality? How does the voice suggest the writer's moral character?
- How does the writer's character reinforce his or her appeals to reason and to emotion?

In August of 1963 at the Civil Rights rally, hundreds of thousands of people gathered at the Lincoln Memorial in Washington, D.C. to hear Martin Luther King Jr.'s "I Have a Dream" speech. King's ethos comes through in many places in the speech. For example:

> There is something that I must say to my people who stand on the warm threshold which leads into the palace of justice. In the process of gaining our rightful place we must not be guilty of wrongful deeds. Let us not seek to satisfy our thirst for freedom by drinking from the cup of bitterness and hatred. We must forever conduct our struggle on the high plane of dignity and discipline. We must not allow our creative protest to degenerate into physical violence. Again and again we must rise to the majestic heights of meeting physical force with soul force. The marvelous new militancy which has engulfed the Negro community must not lead us to a distrust of all white people, for many of our white brothers, as evidenced by their presence here today, have come to realize that their destiny is tied up with our destiny and their freedom is inextricably bound to our freedom. We cannot walk alone.

Calling for unity with "white brothers," King reveals his concern for moral responsibility by asking all who desire justice not to seek their "rightful place" through "wrongful deeds." He believed nonviolence could be a moral power. In his call for blacks and whites to work together, King showed that the civil rights movement affected not only the oppressed but the entire nation: the ethos or character of all America was at stake.

Consider a more recent example of a national figure using the appeal of ethos. On March 1, 2004, the day before Super Tuesday—the Democratic presidential primary—Senator John Edwards from North Carolina, one of the leading candidates, published an opinion editorial in the <u>New York Times</u>. As you read his essay, look for any signs that show his appeals to logos, pathos, and especially ethos.

## A Trust Worth Winning

### John Edwards

"Take it," he typed, his fingers fumbling on the keyboard. "Take it."

Howard E. G. Sawyer was once a towering man with strength and energy. He walked. He played golf. And he was trying to get his life back together when tragedy struck.

His best friend and employer had helped him check into St. Joseph's Hospital in Asheville, N.C., to get sober. E. G. drank a lot, but he was determined to get things right. He was on that path until he was prescribed three times the recommended dose of a medicine called Antabuse, which was used to help patients stay sober.

Instead of helping E. G. get back to his home, his job and his life, that dosage landed him in a coma. And the once broad-shouldered man now spent his days hunched in a wheelchair, surrounded by fast-food containers, overflowing ashtrays and plastic bags filled with his own urine. He was forced to communicate by typing words on a keyboard.

When I said the defense lawyer had offered to settle at $750,000, E. G. once again typed, "Take it." Even though his expression never changed, I knew what that meant to him. I was only 31 years old, this was my first big case, and I wanted E. G. to get everything that he needed to live his life the way he wanted—with dignity.

It was a lot of money for someone who grew up in a working-class world. E. G.'s father drove a bus in Weaverville, just north of Asheville; my own dad had spent much of his life in the textile mills of North and South Carolina. At the time, my wife, Elizabeth, still wore the $11 wedding ring I had bought for her seven years before.

When he typed, "Take it," I understood completely. But when he typed, "I trust you," everything shifted.

We expect our spouses and parents and children and loved ones to put that complete trust in us—not someone met just a few months before. But E. G. did; he trusted me to make a decision that would either guarantee him $750,000 or risk that he not get a penny.

We all have those moments when we see life with stunning clarity. I had had many moments before that night: experiencing the effects of segregation in the South during the 1950's and '60s; watching my dad try to learn statistics from the math show on public television with the hope of a promotion at the mill; my mom refinishing furniture to help me go to college; that first day I entered college, and the day I had to leave Clemson because I couldn't afford the tuition; meeting my wife, Elizabeth; and the birth of my children.

Those were personal. That evening in December 1984 with E. G. in an empty room on the ninth floor of the Buncombe County courthouse, overlooking downtown Asheville, N.C., was the moment the personal and professional collided.

I will always remember what I told E. G. that night: $750,000 was less than he deserved. It was less than he needed—and the jury knew it, too.

E. G. sat there, his otherwise expressionless eyes welling up, and then in a slow and halting manner, he typed, "I trust you."

I was telling this ruined man to turn his back on what must have seemed to him a fortune. I was claiming to know what the jury was thinking. If I was wrong, E. G. would suffer even more for the rest of his life—and I'd go home to my wife and children and on to my next case. I was all he had, and God help him, he trusted me.

That's when I really understood what I was doing. Even though I had written an essay when I was 11 years old titled, "Why I Want to Be a Lawyer," I did not truly understand what I would do as a lawyer until that night. While I had worked my way through law school, clerked for a judge, worked in a law firm, I understood that night how much E. G. and hundreds like him would count on me to make sure that the law protected them—even in difficult cases like E. G.'s, which I also recount in my book Four Trials.

What happened to E. G. was tragic but preventable. To help him maintain his sobriety, his doctor recommended what they called "aversion therapy." After taking Antabuse, a patient who takes a drink becomes nauseated and gets sick. The normal dose was 500 milligrams; E. G.'s doctor prescribed 1,500 because he had heard such aggressive therapy discussed at a convention. The hospital's pharmacists filled the prescriptions, and the hospital's nurses administered them to E. G.

Now, his doctor claimed that the reason E. G. went into a coma and suffered was that he drank while on the drug. The hospital claimed that a nurse supported his statement. When we found the nurse, she testified that E. G. never had a drop. But juries in North Carolina never awarded much. It was entirely possible that even after closing arguments, even after expert testimony that the doctor was at fault, the jury could award him nothing.

That's the responsibility E. G. entrusted in me when I advised him to turn down that $750,000. The figure represented the sum of his lost potential wages, but that hardly meant anything for someone who could no longer walk or talk or keep himself clean.

The jury deliberated for four hours. They handed the judge the verdict sheet and I watched his jaw drop. The verdict was read and they awarded E. G. $3.7 million.

"I trust you" are humbling words, and I have carried them with me always: in the courtroom, in the Senate, along the campaign trail. That's what Americans say when they vote. They cast their ballot, and they're giving you their trust. They are asking you to be their voice every single day. It's something I've been doing since that night in Asheville, and I won't ever stop.

Although John Edwards lost the nomination to Senator John Kerry—and became Kerry's running mate—do you think he presents himself well in his essay? He appeals to pathos. He tries to help readers feel sorry for his client's tragic situation: seeking help to stop drinking, Howard E. G. Sawyer received an overdose of medicine that put him in a coma and caused him to be confined to a wheelchair, to lose bladder control, and to express himself only by typing. Edwards uses pathos with restraint, not overdescribing his client's misfortune. Edwards appeals to logos by helping readers think about whether his client was treated unfairly by his doctor and hospital and whether he deserved a jury award higher than the settlement offer.

But Edwards appeals most strongly to ethos in the essay. As his client trusted him to decide what was best for his well-being, Edwards wants readers to trust him—to trust his judgment and his moral character and to elect him as the Democratic nominee. Throughout the essay he uses details to help readers see him as a humble and honest person: he "grew up in a working-class world"; at the time of E.G.'s trial, Edwards' wife "still wore the $11 wedding ring" he "had bought for her seven years before." He recounts several personal examples of special moments "when we see life with stunning clarity," as when he experienced "the effects of segregation in the South," his mother "refinishing furniture" to help pay for his college education, and his children being born. He expresses his gratitude for these moments—which were paradigm shifts shaping him into the person he is today. But Edwards's illustration of his client's preventable tragedy suggests that he is a person willing and able to fight for others who cannot fight for themselves. The three words "I trust you" represent the essence of ethos. Although it is a cliche for politicians to proclaim they are trustworthy, Edwards offers a clear, persuasive illustration.

A writer's appeals aren't always right or wrong, yes or no choices with which all readers can immediately agree. John Edwards did not win the Democratic presidential nomination. Many readers may have found his essay too self-serving, a final effort to make a difference before Super Tuesday. As a critical reader you should be able to cite evidence and provide reasonable explanations for your interpretation of a writer's persuasive appeals.

Ethos—having good, credible character—is one of the most important ideas any critical thinker can consider. This idea can help you reflect on your character as a person as well as your character on the page. But ethos is complex. In public and private life, a person's character can be contradictory: positive one day and negative the next, and both many times within the same day. Writing and reading can enable you to examine ethos more carefully than you usually would do. Consider this editorial published in the <u>New York Times</u> on August 17, 2005. What does it suggest about ethos?

## A Moment of Grace

*Editorial, The New York Times*

In an age whose crabbed sense of justice finds expression in dismal phrases like "zero tolerance" and "three strikes and you're out," the events in a Long Island courtroom on Monday came as an undeserved gift, something startling and luminous.

It happened when Ryan Cushing, a 19-year-old charged with assault for tossing a turkey through a car windshield last fall, approached the driver he nearly killed, Victoria Ruvolo. Ms. Ruvolo, 44, suffered severe injuries and needed many hours of surgery to rebuild her shattered facial bones.

When Mr. Cushing left the courtroom after pleading guilty, he came face to face with his victim for the first time. He said he was sorry and begged her to forgive him.

She did. She cradled his head as he sobbed. She stroked his face and patted his back. "It's O.K.; it's O.K.," she said. "I just want you to make your life the best it can be."

Mr. Cushing was one of six teenagers out for a night of joyriding and crime, which often happens when childish aggression and stupidity merge with the ability to drive and steal credit cards. The five others have pleaded guilty to various acts like forgery and larceny, but Mr. Cushing, who threw the turkey, could have faced 25 years in prison. At Ms. Ruvolo's insistence, prosecutors granted him a plea bargain instead: six months in jail and five years' probation.

The prosecutor, Thomas Spota, had been ready to seek harsh punishment for a crime he rightly denounced as heedless and brutal. "This is not an act of mere stupidity," Mr. Spota said. "They're not 9- or 7-year-old children."

That is true. But Ms. Ruvolo's resolute compassion, coming seemingly out of nowhere, disarmed Mr. Spota and led to a far more satisfying result.

Many have assumed that Ms. Ruvolo's motivation is religious. But while we can estimate the size of her heart, we can't peer into it. Her impulse may have been entirely secular.

Court testimony by crime victims is often pitched as a sort of retributive therapy, a way for angry, injured people to force criminals to confront their shame. But while some convicts grovel, others smirk. Many are impassive. It's hard to imagine that those hurt by crime reliably find healing in the courtroom. Given the opportunity for retribution, Ms. Ruvolo gave and got something better: the dissipation of anger and the restoration of hope, in a gesture as cleansing as the tears washing down her damaged face, and the face of the foolish, miserable boy whose life she single-handedly restored.

Why is this editorial called "A Moment of Grace"? The word *grace* is defined in the article as "an undeserved gift." Many people would argue that Ryan Cushing did not deserve such a gift. That Victoria Ruvolo forgave him, "cradled his head as he sobbed" and insisted that he receive a plea bargain suggests that she is a person of great character. She shows how much she values character when she told him, "I just want you to make your life the best it can be." Of course, this editorial also appeals to pathos and logos, if you feel moved by it and if it makes you think whether you could also be so forgiving.

You never know what impact your character will have on others. You may be kind and generous to a friend one day; then years later that friend writes to thank you. Several months after Rick Reilly wrote his essay about Mark Lemke wanting to honor his son Cory who died in a motorcycle accident, Reilly wrote another essay concerning Mark and Tony Dungy, the coach of the Indianapolis Colts football team. Reilly begins his essay, "Maybe you could use a happy story after what happened at Virginia Tech, and maybe I've got one." He tells about Tony Dungy calling Mark Lemke to offer his condolences and asking if there is anything he can do. Reilly writes,

> Now, you've got to understand, this was October. The Colts were into the teeth of their schedule, the most critical season in Dungy's life, not to mention Peyton Manning's, not to mention the millions of Colts fans. . . .
>
> But Dungy has his own sorrow to swallow. His 18-year-old son, James, hanged himself three days before Christmas in 2005. And Lemke knows this. So maybe Dungy, who's the same age as Lemke, is a guy who can relate. So they talk, and the coach tells Lemke to keep in touch.

Reilly describes the bond that develops between Lemke and Dungy, how they talk on the phone and e-mail each other. Dungy invites Lemke to be his guest at the Super Bowl. Lemke "watches his new buddy win it all."

In this essay called "Coaching the Grief-stricken," Reilly illustrates the ethos of Tony Dungy. He is kind, compassionate, generous.

> And this is only one stranger whom Tony Dungy has befriended. There's the former high school coach in Wisconsin whose son committed suicide. There's the young kid in Indianapolis who lost his mother and brother in a car wreck. Heartbroken people all over are suddenly getting a hand up from a man who himself should be a puddle but is instead a river of strength.
>
> Yet Dungy refuses to talk to the media about these good deeds, which only makes them better.
>
> "I'm awfully grateful to him," Lemke says. "He helped me keep my faith. He taught me that he and I—we're not alone."
>
> After two weeks of hearing about how low man can sink, isn't it nice to know how high he can rise?
>
> Tony Dungy stands as a reminder to every parent who's grieving right now that there is a way through the pain. And that way is through each other.

This moving essay, however, is not only about the benevolent ethos of Tony Dungy. It indirectly shows the ethos of the writer. Rick Reilly gives grieving parents and a grieving nation a needed story of hope. That Reilly does this shows his own strong, moral character. How can readers not appreciate and respect him for doing this?

## ACTIVITY 8

### REVISION

Look over the draft of your opinion essay. Examine your use of ethos. Put a check-mark wherever you try to appeal to your reader's sense of your character. How might you use ethos more effectively? Should you do anything else to make yourself more trustworthy and credible?

The rest of this chapter will help you revise your opinion essay. It will focus on examining thesis statements and strategies you can use to write engaging titles, introductions, and conclusions.

## THESIS STATEMENTS

A thesis is the statement of a writer's opinion that shapes an argument. In a well-developed essay, a subject is not enough. To reach readers, writers need a point they wish to make. A thesis requires an opinion about a subject. The subject is *what* you write about; your thesis is *so-what* about it. For example:

| The Subject: The What | Point of View: The So-What |
|---|---|
| Our need for immediate gratification | produces time-saving addicts who ironically don't use time well. |
| Being biracial in our society | is a tug-of-war between being white or black . . . or red, brown, or yellow. |
| Foster care | is so hard to explain. |

Critical thinkers know they can't write everything about a subject; they need a way to narrow it. The thesis serves this purpose: it limits and focuses your subject. Then too, with the thesis as a guide, your readers can see how well you have accomplished your purpose—to communicate clearly and to persuade them to agree with you.

### Evaluating Your Thesis Statement

When you try to persuade readers, a thesis statement presents and clarifies your position. It helps readers follow your arguments.

Your thesis is the point of your composition. It is the idea you want your readers to accept. For example, suppose you are concerned about marriage. You have observed several marriages breaking up within your extended family, and it bothered you when pop singer Britney Spears married and divorced within two days in Las Vegas in 2004.

A good thesis might be: "Marriage—the ultimate commitment of two people to each other for the rest of their lives—is not taken seriously enough today by many people." What is the subject of this statement? *Marriage.* What is the point of this subject? *It is not taken seriously enough today by many people.*

If you present a thesis, you must support it with specific evidence. Most readers will want to know your reasons. Some readers may say, "I disagree: if a couple is unhappy they should divorce, even if they have children." Then you should ask, "Why? What are *your* reasons?" In short, reasonable people may discuss with each other what they believe about issues if (and only if) they can give evidence that supports their beliefs.

You can write your thesis statement so that it commits you only to one side: "Lying and cheating are unethical." Or, if you prefer, your thesis can be more complex: "Lying and cheating may not always be unethical." Suppose you are writing on an extremely complex topic that requires research. Your thesis could be "Human cloning is unethical." But you and your paper would be more credible if you examined the issue more fully: "Although human cloning may provide exciting medical and scientific benefits, much research suggests humans should not be cloned until animal cloning has been tested extensively and ethical questions have been examined fully."

In some cases when you write you may have a point to make that is not argumentative: for example, a historical paper, a process paper, or a news report.

| | |
|---|---|
| Capturing Saddam Hussein | (a historical paper) |
| How to Perform Comedy | (a process paper) |
| Tiger Woods: Golfing Wonder | (a news report or biography) |

Some writers describe these as "statements of intent," meaning they identify the paper's main point when there may be no arguable thesis.

However, for persuasive papers, you need a thesis: an opinion you can support with specific evidence—reasons, examples, details.

## GUIDELINES FOR THESIS STATEMENTS IN PERSUASIVE ESSAYS

1. A thesis statement is an arguable opinion that can be supported with specific evidence.
2. A thesis statement should be clearly worded so readers can readily identify and understand it.
3. A thesis should be focused, not so broad that it's pointless, such as "College is an interesting experience."
4. A good thesis statement should not argue the obvious: "Racism is wrong." "Criminals must be punished." A thesis should not argue simple matters of fact such as "Washington, D.C., is the nation's capital."

5. A good thesis statement should be worth thinking or arguing about. In a persuasive essay you should try to get your readers to say, "I never thought about it that way—you may be right."

6. A thesis should not be a statement of your personal preferences. There is no point in claiming you like chocolate ice cream better than vanilla. You must find a way to show that the reader too should prefer one or the other flavor. Better yet would be to find a different thesis.

7. Most readers prefer to find your thesis statement early, followed by your evidence. Although many teachers may ask you to state your thesis as the last sentence in your introduction, you can state your thesis as the first or middle sentence. In less formal writing situations, you can place the thesis later in your paper, even in your conclusion. Occasionally writers may use two sentences to state their thesis: the second sentence clarifies the first. Also, writers may restate their thesis in different words in their conclusions.

## ACTIVITY 9

Where do Amy Wu, Brian Courtney, and Julia Kraus place their thesis statements in their essays? How does the placement of their thesis statement affect their readers? Do they restate their thesis anywhere else?

## ACTIVITY 10

In your notebook, give your opinion about each of these thesis statements for a persuasive essay. Is each thesis statement effective? Try to give reasons why it is or isn't.

1. America is becoming a second-rate country.   *too broad, audience?*
2. Spanking is an act of discipline that parents should be able to do without worry of repercussions.
3. Music is the gift that keeps on giving.
4. Road-rage drivers need to see the consequences of their actions firsthand.
5. You can feel close to someone who is very far away.
6. Smoking tobacco causes cancer.
7. TV and movies must accept some of the blame for the violence in our country.
8. The lessons you learn away from home are things no professor could ever teach you.
9. Obesity is common in our society.
10. People of the same sex should be able to have a union that has the same benefits of a marriage, though I do not think that they should call it a marriage.

11. Cheating in school is not only wrong and risky, but is also an addictive habit that fools people into believing they can't succeed without it.

12. Measuring someone's knowledge has nothing to do with how fast or slow they complete the ACT or SAT. Time limits should be removed in these standardized tests.

13. Affirmative action in schools is not right because it tries to create equality through inequality by giving minorities priority over white males.

14. Smoking should not be allowed in restaurants or other indoor, public places—no exceptions.

15. While being slightly unrealistic at times, Thank You for Smoking is a well-made film with believable characters, good acting, and important insights, all the while being very funny.  ▪

## ACTIVITY 11

### REVISION

Look at your own persuasive essay. How well does your thesis work? Where do you state it? Would it help readers if you restated it? Write an evaluation of your own thesis statement according to the criteria in the "Guidelines for Thesis Statements in Persuasive Essays."  ▪

## ENGAGING YOUR AUDIENCE: TITLES, INTRODUCTIONS, CONCLUSIONS

If you can't get readers to go beyond your title or to finish your introduction, you can't persuade them. You need to motivate them to start reading your essay and to finish it. Paying close attention to titles, introductions, and conclusions is essential.

### Features of Good Titles
- Good titles suggest or state the point of an essay.
- Good titles are concise but informative.
- Good titles catch readers' attention.
- Good titles stir thought, often raising small questions for readers such as "Well, how can that be?"

  "Stop the Clock" . . . "Why stop it?"

  "Freedom from Choice" . . . "From what?"

  "If I Told You, Would You Want to Hear?" . . . "Told me what?"

### Title Strategies

*Use a contrast of some kind* that carries a little surprise. The New York Times ran an editorial on Labor Day called "A Day On." Their argument was, "Instead of a day off, perhaps it should become a day on, a day devoted, across the nation, to helping out—a day, in fact, of national service" (5 Sept. 2005). A <u>Newsweek</u> "My Turn" essay on 22 May 2006 used a title with a contrast of expectation: "Study Hard and You, Too, Can Deliver Pizza." Contrast—doing something different or opposite from what is usual—often works well for titles.

Contrast takes various forms. "A Convenient Truth" by Peter Singer (<u>NYTimes</u>, 26 Jan. 2007) plays off Al Gore's book and film title <u>An Inconvenient Truth</u>. Maureen Dowd's "A Woman Who's Man Enough" combines genders and raises curiosity (<u>NYTimes</u>, 22 July 2007).

*Use three words for a title.* Consider "Stop the Clock," "Freedom from Choice," and "A Day On." Noble Prize–winning chemist Roald Hoffman titles an essay "The Tense Middle"; for him, extremes are too polar, too simple, too black and white (see Chapter 4). "Hooked on Violence" (Bob Herbert, <u>NYTimes</u>, 26 April 2007). "Eating for Credit" (Alice Waters, <u>NYTimes</u>, 24 Feb. 2006)—see Chapter 4. Three words satisfy the mind (see Interchapter 3 on using threes).

*Use your thesis as your title.* William Safire titles an essay "Character Is Destiny" about how character shapes our nation (<u>NYTimes</u>, 12 Jan. 2005).

*Use a question as your title.* "What Is the Value of Algebra?" (Richard Cohen, <u>Washington Post</u>, 16 Feb. 2006.) "Why Aren't We Shocked?" (Bob Herbert, <u>NYTimes</u>, 16 Oct. 2006).

*Use alliteration or word play in your title.* A little alliteration (the repetition of initial consonant sounds) can help readers hear and notice your title. "Stem Cells: The Hope and the Hype" (Nancy Gross, <u>Time</u>, 7 Aug. 2006). "The War of the Words" (Jerry Adler, <u>Time</u>, 16 April 2007). "The Politics of Pot" (Editorial, <u>NYTimes</u>, 22 April 2006). "Dingbats, Dodos and Doozies" (Rick Reilly, <u>Sports Illustrated</u>, 27 Nov. 2006). Be careful, however, not to overuse alliteration, unless you want to create a humorous effect as Reilly does.

## Titles to Avoid

- Avoid general, boring titles such as "An Interesting Problem" or "School and Work."
- Avoid renaming the assignment such as "Essay #1" or "Persuasive Essay."
- Avoid titles that strain for effect like "Suppose You Were a Toe."

Some writers compose the title first; others wait until the paper is finished before deciding on the title. Some titles present themselves like eurekas midway through a draft.

## Features of Good Introductions

- Like titles, good introductions need to catch the attention and interest of readers.
- The first sentence is important: it can engage readers from the start. Consider Amy Wu's opener; she uses a comparison: "My aunt tends to her house as if it were her child." Compare this with the general statement "My aunt cares about her house." Yet a general statement can work well if it sets up what comes next. Julie Kraus begins "If I Told You, Would You Want to Hear" with "It's a normal conversation, really." There are no absolute right and wrong ways to begin an introduction. But a weak first sentence is like a flat tire: readers get a feeling the ride will be bumpy.

- The main purpose of an introduction is to present a writer's thesis statement announcing what the essay will illustrate. Although the strategy of presenting the thesis as the last sentence of an introduction works well for academic essays, less formal essays—like Amy Wu's, Brian Courtney's, and Julie Kraus's—may take a little longer before stating a thesis. An informal essay may spend two or three paragraphs describing a scene or telling a story before stating a thesis.

- Your introduction, like the paper itself, depends on your situation: What are you writing about, whom are you writing to, what is your purpose? If your situation is formal, such as addressing the board of trustees at your school for money to build a new fitness center, your introduction is likely to be serious and direct.

- Your introduction reveals your voice right away—the sound of your personality that you want to project. If you want to sound serious, your introduction should convey a serious tone (or attitude) toward your subject and your audience. If you want to sound humorous, your introduction should convey a humorous tone toward your subject and your audience. Do you want to sound friendly, concerned, serious, passionate . . . ?

## Introductory Strategies

*Start with a dramatic incident,* like Mark Schoofs's description of splicing eye genes into different species.

> It was an experiment that could have come from a horror movie. Geneticist Walter Gehring took a gene that controls the development of eyes in mice and inserted it into fruit fly embryos, among the cells that normally develop into legs. Legs they became—but with eyes all over them.
>
> Researchers at the National Eye Institute recently repeated the experiment, this time splicing in the eye gene from a squid. The flies grew eyes on their wings, legs, and antennae—eyes that could actually respond to light. But because they were not wired to the brain, the flies could not see through them.
>
> Such grotesque flies are more than insect versions of Frankenstein's monster. They are dramatic evidence that many genes are interchangeable among species, that vastly different organisms use similar genetic building blocks. In fact, the gene for eyes—called *Pax-6* in mice and squid—helps form the eyes of humans, too.

*Start with a story relevant to the subject,* such as Brian Courtney's introduction in "Freedom from Choice" or as Clive Thompson does in his essay "The Honesty Virus":

> Everyone tells a little white lie now and then. But a Cornell professor recently claimed to have established the truth of a curious proposition: We fib less frequently when we're online than when we're talking in person. Jeffrey Hancock asked 30 of his undergraduates to record all of their communications—and all of their lies—over the course of a week. When he tallied the results, he found that students had mishandled the truth in about one-quarter of all face-to-face conversations, and in a whopping 37 percent of phone calls. But when they went into cyberspace, they turned into Boy Scouts: only

1 in 5 instant-messaging chats contained a lie, and barely 14 percent of e-mail messages were dishonest.

Dave Barry uses a humorous anecdote to begin his essay "You've Got Trouble":

A few years back, when my son was in college, he had to mail a letter. I don't remember the specific reason, but I do remember having a conversation with him in which he complained bitterly about the amount of work involved—finding a place where he could purchase a stamp, figuring out what kind of stamp he needed, actually writing the letter, locating an envelope, putting the letter into the envelope, having to physically leave his dormitory room to mail the envelope and so on. I grew exhausted just listening to him describe this series of arduous tasks, one coming right after another. I was glad, for my son's sake, that he never had to live in a world—as I once did—where the only way to change channels was to walk all the way to the TV set and manually turn a knob.

Unlike my son, I did not grow up with e-mail and texting, but I have come to agree with him: electronic communication is superior to the old-fashioned paper kind. I do almost all of my communicating by e-mail. I've been known to e-mail people who were literally standing next to me, which I know sounds crazy, because at that distance I could easily call them on my cellphone. But I prefer e-mail, because it's such an effective way of getting information to somebody without running the risk of becoming involved in human conversation.

*Start with a description,* as Amy Wu does in her introduction in "Stop the Clock" or as Pam Houston does in her essay "Above It All in Colorado":

Maybe it's growing up under a bowl of bluebird colored sky, or among groves of quaking aspens, or surrounded by snow that falls and falls and never turns black. Maybe it's learning to ski double black diamond slopes at the age of 3, or the possibility inherent in 53 peaks that rise 14,000 feel above sea level. Maybe it's because the median household income in Colorado is well above the national median, and the people per square mile average is well below it, but Coloradans consistently tend toward the optimistic, rarely confuse cynicism with intelligence and are willing to articulate their hopes for the future without fear.

Thomas L. Friedman uses description in his powerful introduction in "Breaking Death's Grip" in the <u>New York Times</u>:

I learned something new the other night in Tel Aviv. I learned that your neck is actually the weakest part of your body. The Israeli police spokesman taught me that as he explained why the Palestinian suicide bomber's head was blown straight up, like a champagne cork, and was still sitting on a ledge atop the bus stop, like a human gargoyle.

*Start with a contrast,* such as this short introduction by Nicholas D. Kristof in "Gold Stars and Dunce Caps": "In this presidential campaign, we need somebody who wants to address the question President Bush once raised: 'Is our children learning?'"

Consider this example of contrast—seeing the opposite of what you would expect—by Daniel Gilbert in his essay "Compassionate Commercialism":

> In an advertising campaign that began last week, Nissan left 20,000 sets of keys in bars, stadiums, concert halls and other public venues. Each key ring has a tag that says: "If found, please do not return. My next generation Nissan Altima has Intelligent Key with push-button ignition, and I no longer need these."

Many introductions combine strategies. Denise Grady in her article "Struggling Back from War's Once-Deadly Wounds" uses contrast and description:

> It has taken hundreds of hours of therapy, but Jason Poole, a 23-year-old Marine corporal, has learned all over again to speak and to walk. At times, though, words still elude him. He can read barely 16 words a minute. His memory can be fickle, his thinking delayed. Injured by a roadside bomb in Iraq, he is blind in his left eye, deaf in his left ear, weak on his right side and still getting used to his new face, which was rebuilt with skin and bone grafts and 75 to 100 titanium screws and plates.
>
> Even so, those who know Corporal Poole say his personality—gregarious, kind and funny—has remained intact.

*Start with a question*, as Charles Krauthammer does in his essay "When John and Jim Say, 'I Do' ": "Gay marriage is coming. Should it?"

In her essay "Sounding the Global-Warming Alarm without Upsetting the Fans," Alessandra Stanley writes,

> If less is more, then why is biggest better?
>
> Al Gore declared Live Earth "the largest global entertainment event in all of history," but this seven-continent, multimedia eco-extravaganza was colored by the very complacency it vowed to combat: No matter how dire the problem, the solution can be small and painless.

Or you can raise a series of questions, as former senator Bill Bradley does in his essay "A Can Do Nation" in <u>Time</u>:

> Why are we still addicted to oil? Why do 47 million Americans lack health insurance? Why haven't we made Social Security solvent for the long term? Why are too many of our public schools mediocre? Why have we lost respect around the world?
>
> The answers to these questions lie in the story we're being told about America. It's a "can't do" story . . . .

*Start by explaining the thesis*, as Nicholas D. Kristof does in "In India, One Woman's Stand Says 'Enough' ":

> The central moral challenge we will face in this century will be to address gender inequality in the developing world. Here in India, for example, among children ages 1 to 5, girls are 50 percent more likely to die than boys. That means that every four minutes, a little girl here is discriminated against to death.

Robert Wright starts off with his thesis in "E-Mail and Prozac": "I have a theory: the more e-mail there is, the more Prozac there will be, and the more Prozac there is, the more e-mail there will be. Maybe I should explain."

*Start with specific examples that lead to a thesis*, as Steven Pinker does in his essay "The Known World":

> A baby sucks on a pencil and her panicky mother fears the child will get lead poisoning. A politician argues that hydrogen can replace fossil fuels as our nation's energy source. A consumer tells a reporter that she refuses to eat tomatoes that have genes in them. And a newsmagazine condemns the prospects of cloning because it could mass-produce an army of zombies.
>
> These are just a few examples of scientific illiteracy—inane misconceptions that could have been avoided with a smidgen of freshman science. (For those afraid to ask: pencil "lead" is carbon; hydrogen fuel takes more energy to produce than it releases; all living things contain genes; a clone is just a twin.) Though we live in an era of stunning scientific understanding, all too often the average educated person will have none of it.

*Start with a historical review*, like the first sentence from the editorial "Human Cloning Requires a Moratorium" in the science journal <u>Nature</u>: "The history of science suggests that efforts to block its development are misguided and futile."

Consider this example by physicist Brian Greene in his essay "The Universe on a String":

> Seventy-five years ago this month, <u>The New York Times</u> reported that Albert Einstein had completed his unified field theory—a theory that promised to stitch all of nature's forces into a single, tightly woven mathematical tapestry. But as had happened before and would happen again, closer scrutiny revealed flaws that sent Einstein back to the drawing board. Nevertheless, Einstein's belief that he'd one day complete the unified theory rarely faltered. Even on his deathbed he scribbled equations in the desperate but fading hope that the theory would finally materialize. It didn't.

*Start with a surprising statistic*, as Michael Siegel does in "Unsafe at Any Level": "According to a report released last week by the Harvard School of Public Health, cigarette companies have been steadily increasing the nicotine yield of their cigarettes—the report describes an average total increase of 11 percent from 1998 to 2005."

David Broder uses this strategy in his essay "The Dropout Challenge":

> They number in the millions—3.5 million Americans between the ages of 16 and 25 who have dropped out of high school and were not enrolled in school in 2003, the most recent year for which an estimate is available. Of every three young men and women entering high school, only two will emerge with a diploma. For minority students, the odds are worse. And the losers pay a price all their lives.

*Start with a quotation.* In his essay "On Comparing Global Warming Denial to Holocaust Denial," Dennis Prager writes,

In her last column, <u>Boston Globe</u> columnist Ellen Goodman wrote: "Let's just say that global warming deniers are now on a par with Holocaust deniers . . . "
     This is worthy of some analysis.

Suppose you are writing about women and character. You could begin an essay with this: Eleanor Roosevelt said, "A woman is like a tea bag—you never know how strong she is until she gets in hot water."

*Start with a definition:* the definition of the key term or some significant concept in your paper. Here is an example from columnist Ellen Goodman in her essay "Uncomfortable Truth for Japan":

> The name is what first grabbed my attention. *Comfort women?* What a moniker for the sexual slaves who were coerced, confined, and raped in the Japanese military brothels strung across Asia during World War II.

*Start with an idea to be refuted.* Consider this introduction by Mary Beth McCauley in her essay "Students Make Case for Virginity" in <u>The Christian Science Monitor</u>:

> You won't find Cristina Barba's shorts advertising "JUICY" across the backside. Nor will her neckline plunge or her belly button make an appearance. And when she dates, the 22-year-old Penn State grad may part with a simple kiss. But that's it. She's saving herself for marriage and doing whatever it takes to hold true to her intentions.
>      Ms. Barba is an alien, it seems, in a culture draped in ever more aggressive layers of sexuality. By many accounts, the random hookup has become this generation's peck on the cheek.

An Associated Press story uses the strategy of refutation in "Knight: New Rule Hurts College Basketball": "The new rule that says players must be at least one year re-moved from high school before entering the NBA is 'the worst thing that's happened to college basketball since I've been coaching,' says Texas Tech coach Bob Knight."

*Start with a hypothetical example.* Mitch Albom tries to refute the logic of a presidential veto by using a hypothetical example in his essay "Bush's Stem Cell Veto: Whom Does It Save?"

> Consider this scenario: Many years from now, some great-granddaughter of President George W. Bush is crippled in a car accident. There are treatments available that will heal her wounded spinal cord. But the doctor shakes his head and says, "I'm sorry, your great-grandfather didn't support our research, so we're not going to help you."
>      That would be cruel, right? Turning your back on someone in need?
>      No crueler than what Bush did last week.

Consider the power of this introduction that also uses a hypothetical example, from Jeffrey Kluger's essay "Why They Kill" in <u>Time</u>:

> If you want a sense of just how terrible Monday's crimes were, here's something to try: imagine yourself committing them. It's easy enough to contemplate what it would feel like to rob a bank or steal a car; you might even summon a hint of the outlaw frisson

that could make such crimes seem appealing. But picture yourself as Cho Seung-Hui, the 23-year-old student responsible for the Virginia Tech bloodbath, walking the halls of the school, selecting lives to extinguish and then . . . extinguishing them. It is perhaps a measure of our humanity that we could sooner imagine ourselves as the killed than as the killer, and find it easier to conjure up what it would feel like to plead for our lives than to take someone else's.

These introductory strategies are commonly used by writers. They can help you when you write essays or research papers. Notice how many of the strategies appeal to logos, pathos, and ethos right away.

## Introductions to Avoid

- Avoid empty introductions that wander vaguely around the subject without saying anything, such as "Critical thinking is very interesting. There are many people who think critically. The rewards of critical thinking can be tremendous. There is nothing like witnessing a true critical thinker."
- Avoid boring first sentences in introductions, such as "E-mail is common on college campuses." This statement is already obvious to readers.
- The one sentence introduction rarely works well in essays, especially in academic writing where readers expect a full introduction.
- Avoid boring conventional openings such as "In this paper I will . . . "
- Avoid apologizing: "I'm not really an expert on this subject, but I'll try to explain it."

## Features of Good Conclusions

- The conclusion brings the essay to completion and gives readers a sense of closure.
- The conclusion reminds readers of the thesis or restates it in different words. It answers the question "So what?"
- The conclusion provides a brief but well-worded analysis of the point of the paper.
- The conclusion is memorable—the writer saves something interesting for the end.
- The conclusion ends with a distinctive sentence: it may be a short sentence; it may be an especially well-worded or thoughtful sentence; it may be an image that stays with readers.

## Concluding Strategies

*End with a hook:* Refer back to an image or an idea you begin your essay with. This gives your readers a satisfying sense of closure like a circle coming round. Consider Julia Kraus's essay "If I Told You, Would You Want to Hear?"

### First sentences

It's a normal conversation, really. It's the first day of 11th grade. I've just met my biology-lab partner. He mentions his brother. Then he asks me The Question.

## Conclusion

See what one question will do?

The hook is an extremely effective strategy. Many writers rely on it. Notice how <u>New York Times</u> film critic A. O. Scott uses a humorous hook in his review of Mel Gibson's <u>The Passion</u>:

### First sentences

There is a prophetic episode of <u>The Simpsons</u> in which the celebrity guest star Mel Gibson, directing and starring in a remake of <u>Mr. Smith Goes to Washington</u>, enlists the help of Homer Simpson, who represents the public taste (or lack of it). Homer persuades Mr. Gibson to change the picture's ending, replacing James Stewart's populist tirade with an action sequence, a barrage of righteous gunfire that leaves the halls of Congress strewn with corpses. The audience flees the theater in disgust.

### Conclusion

On its own, apart from whatever beliefs a viewer might bring to it, <u>The Passion of the Christ</u> never provides a clear sense of what all of this bloodshed was for, an inconclusiveness that is Mr. Gibson's most serious artistic failure. The Gospels, at least in some interpretations, suggest that the story ends in forgiveness. But such an ending seems beyond Mr. Gibson's imaginative capacities. Perhaps he suspects that his public prefers terror, fury and gore. Maybe Homer Simpson was right after all.

*End by reflecting on the importance or implications of your thesis*, as Amy Wu does in "Stop the Clock":

Sure, my generation has all the technological advances at our fingertips. We're computer-savvy, and we have more time. But what are we really saving it for? In the end, we may lose more than we've gained by forgetting the important things in life.

*End with a call to action.* Nicollette Hahn Niman offers a direct plea to conclude "The Unkindest Cut": "Given the suffering it causes animals and its dubious benefits, tail docking should be stopped." Michael Siegel is also direct in "Unsafe at Any Level":

It's not enough to regulate the varying degrees of nicotine in cigarettes. Ultimately, there's only one way to deal with the addictive effects of nicotine, especially on children: grant the F.D.A. the authority to get nicotine out of cigarettes altogether. Anti-smoking groups shouldn't settle for anything less.

Thomas L. Friedman in the <u>New York Times</u> addresses college students in his essay "The Greenest Generation" and concludes with this call:

You need to become what the writer Dan Pink calls "the Greenest Generation," and build the institutions, alliances and programs that will turn back the black tide of climate change and petro-authoritarianism which, if unchecked, will surely poison your world and your future as much as fascism once threatened to do to your parents' world and future.

This is your challenge. Will you rise to it?

*End with a vivid image or contrast* that reinforces your thesis as Leonard Pitts Jr. does in his essay "Let's See Some Talent There, Janet" on Janet Jackson exposing herself during her

2004 Super Bowl halftime show: "So the headline here is not that a woman exposed a breast. It is, rather, that a breast exposed a woman."

*End with a quotation* that reinforces your thesis in a memorable way as Jacob Sullivan does in his essay "Thinking about Drinking":

> The addiction psychologist Stanton Peele, who has long decried the all-or-nothing attitude reflected in such statistics [on drug use], cites cross-cultural evidence indicating that people who are gradually introduced to alcohol under family supervision are less likely to have drinking problems as adults. The people at Drug Strategies would benefit from a visit to his Web site (<http://www.peele.net>), where he observes, "American public health does not do well at conveying the idea that drinking is a double-edged activity, one with potential benefits as well as real dangers, and that moderation is the distinguishing feature between the two."

In her essay "Outing the Out of Touch" about gays in the military, Maureen Dowd uses a short conclusion with a powerful quote:

> The Republican field seems stale and out of sync. They should have listened to the inimitable Barry Goldwater, who told it true: "You don't have to be straight to shoot straight."

*End with surprising facts* as the editorial "Rescuing the National Parks" does in the <u>New York Times</u>:

> The money we spend on the parks, about $2.4 billion a year, is one-tenth of 1 percent of the total federal budget of $2.4 trillion, not much more than a rounding error. Surely a nation as wealthy as this one can do better. These are our jewels, deserving of far more jealous safekeeping than we are giving them now.

*End with a question* that leaves readers pondering the significance of your essay. In her essay "Television and Free Time," Marie Winn argues that television programs what a child experiences. Her last sentence is, "When, then, is he going to live his *real life*?"

> Bob Herbert in "The Divide in Caring for Our Kids" ends with a question in his conclusion: "There's plenty of give in America's glittering $13 trillion economy. What's the sense of being the richest nation on the planet if you can't even afford to keep your children healthy and alive?"

*End by offering a solution to a problem* your essay concerns, as Brian Courtney does.

> One of the greatest things parents of biracial children can do is expose them to *both* of their cultures. But what good does this do when in the end society makes us choose? Having a separate category marked BIRACIAL will not magically put an end to the pressure to choose, but it will help people to stop judging us as just black or just white and see us for what we really are—both.

*End with a prediction or warning* that logically follows from your thesis and evidence as Linda Chavez does in her essay "Women in Combat Will Take Toll on Our Culture."

> In the name of equal opportunity for women in the military, we've chosen to ignore nature—or worse, we're committed to altering it. We may succeed in training succeeding

generations of young women to become warriors, but we can't begin to know the toll our hubris will take on the individuals involved, their families and our society.

*End by striking a note of reasonable hope* about a problem or an issue as Maggie Gallagher does in her essay "Stem Cells Heal Hearts":

> Let's shut the door on cloning and embryo consumption. Let's open wide the door to alternative solutions. Because adult stem cells work. Because they are consistent with our highest traditions of respect for human life, because it is more fair and sensible for taxpayer dollars to fund treatments that can benefit all taxpayers. Because doing things the right way always pays off in the end.
> Let's get going.

## Conclusions to Avoid

- Avoid the one-sentence or very short conclusion. Like the one-sentence introduction, the one-sentence conclusion suggests there may be something wrong with the structure of your paper. The conclusion has a real purpose: tell your reader what the evidence means—what insight you draw from your paper.
- Avoid merely summarizing your paper or restating your thesis word for word. The summary ending is a cliché.
- Avoid using an overused phrase such as "In conclusion" or "To sum up." Try to be more original.
- Avoid drawing attention to yourself instead of drawing attention to your point: "Now that I have reached the end of this time-consuming paper. . . . "
- Avoid raising any new or irrelevant subjects in the conclusion.

By using effective titles, introductions, and conclusions, you will engage your audience more fully—you will help them pay attention to your thesis and supporting evidence as well as your appeals to logos, pathos, and ethos.

## ACTIVITY 12

### REVISION

Evaluate the title, introduction, and conclusion of your own opinion essay. Do they work well? If not, how can you improve them? Consider using some of the strategies just presented. ▪

While you read this chapter and worked on your opinion essay, did you "give more attention to the doing than to the future result" as the quote beginning the chapter advised? Were you able to notice more details, ideas, and eurekas along the way? If so, terrific. If not, then know that breaking habits takes time.

With thoughtful practice you can strengthen your critical thinking, writing, and reading abilities. Using logos, pathos and ethos, you can learn to communicate persuasively and powerfully.

## ACTIVITY 13

### ACTIVELY READING AN ESSAY

Here are two opinion essays that appeared in <u>Newsweek's</u> "My Turn" column. After you read them, select the one you like most and follow these directions:

1. Make a photocopy of the essay so you can write on it.
2. Notice as much as you can in the essay. To do this, annotate your photocopy: that is, take notes on it—on the margins, between lines, even on the back of the paper. Take notes on what you notice about the following:

   - How does the writer communicate and persuade? What is the thesis? What reasons, examples, and details work especially well as supporting evidence?
   - How does the writer engage the audience—especially you? How do the title, introduction, and conclusion work?
   - How does the writer use logos—clear reasoning and evidence?
   - How does the writer use pathos—appeals to emotions to help readers care about the issue?
   - How does the writer use ethos—appeals to ethics or morality, to what is right and good? How does the writer create appeals to her or his own character? Do you find the writer trustworthy, fair-minded, and credible?
   - How does the writer use words and sentences—what do you notice about the writer's style? What phrases or sentences catch your attention? What does she or he do with words to create certain effects in readers? Do you like the writer's voice—the sound of her or his personality? Why?

3. At the bottom of the page or on the back of it, write a brief paragraph giving your overall opinion of the essay. Do you find it excellent, okay, or weak? Why? Bring your annotated copy to the next class for discussion. ▉

## **H**OW TO ANNOTATE

When you annotate, you're free to create your own style. You can underline important sentences such as the thesis statement. You can write brief or extended comments in the margins on why you agree or disagree with the writer's reasoning or why you like or dislike a particular word, detail, or example. Note any clues you see of logos, pathos, and ethos. Put stars above or beside any words or lines you like. You might use braces {they look like wings} to mark key supporting evidence. Put question marks wherever you have a question or beside any place you're confused. Write out some of your questions. Put exclamation marks where you're surprised by something as you read—anytime you have a little eureka. Also, be aware of your biases: must you enjoy the subject to give the writer's essay a fair reading?

## My Smile Is Worth More Than Face Value

### *Vicki L. Wilson*

"The surgery," the doctor said, "could result in permanent right-sided facial paralysis." "Which means?" I asked. "You could lose feeling on that side of your face. You might not be able to blink your eye. You might not be able to smile."

He was not being impassive about this. I had thought that when doctors delivered bad news, they used a med-school cultivated matter-of-fact delivery. My doctor's voice broke.

I had come to him thinking I had an enlarged lymph node in my neck. I was 31, hadn't been sick, and was a little nervous about a random bump appearing at the corner of my right jawbone. The doctor diagnosed a parotid gland tumor. The only option was surgery to remove it. I shuddered to think my smile would be removed with it.

I have always been a smiler. I was a happy little girl with blond curls and a perpetual smile. Every picture I'm in shows me grinning. Smiling has been my secret weapon for making it through nerve-racking job interviews and successfully eating cabbage served by a friend who didn't know I couldn't stand the stuff. The chances were slim that my parotid tumor would be cancer—it didn't fit the profile. But my doctor couldn't tell me the chances of partial facial paralysis.

"I won't know until I'm in there," he said. These types of tumors often lie on top of or are entangled with the facial nerve. The nerve could get stretched or cut.

A few weeks before surgery, I went to have a CT scan. In the waiting room, I sat next to a woman in her 70s. She smiled at me. I smiled back. "You're very pretty," she said. "You are, too," I answered. But when I turned away, I stopped smiling.

I rebel against the traditional stereotypes of beauty. I see joy in unique-looking people. I deplore fashion magazines and have vowed that no daughter I have will think looks are more important than brains. I will go to my grave saying that beauty is only skin deep. But when there was a chance I could lose the thing I liked most about my own face, I became a narcissist.

I began to see perfect, smiling, winking faces everywhere. I practiced smiling in the mirror, holding the right corner of my lips down to see what I looked like. The effect was bad, physically and mentally. My smile went away long before I was ever under anesthesia.

The night before surgery, I was frantic. I lay awake, talking to my husband. I turned the slim chance of cancer into an inevitability and started thinking about how I could quit my job and order groceries online, avoiding public outings. He let me babble. When I gave him a chance to talk, he said, "I love you. Everything will be OK." How many times have people in this world said that to each other before operations? But I did my best to believe him.

It was an early morning surgery. In the operating room, I looked up at the doctor. I wondered if he was apprehensive. A nurse, with a round face and a grandmotherly air, held my hand, and then I went under. I didn't have any funny dreams, epiphanies or anything I can remember. For me, it felt as quick as a blink, and I woke in the recovery room to the doctor's voice. "Vicki. Vicki. Smile for me, Vicki. Come on."

The room was fuzzy, made blurrier by the fact that everything was white and gray and green. But I saw my doctor, surrounded by nurses. It felt like the scene in "The Wizard of Oz" where Dorothy wakes up in the end and says, "And you and you and you were there!" The thought made me smile. And I could.

I doubt that people often cheer in the recovery room of hospitals. The grandmotherly nurse clapped. My doctor laughed, and left quickly. I found out later that he went right out to tell my husband and family in the waiting room that everything had gone just fine; no cancer, and the tumor had only been near the facial nerve. He was able to work around it.

Because of the surgery, I've lost a little feeling in my right ear, and it feels strange to put in earrings or when I can feel a cold breeze on the top half of my ear and not the bottom. But I have complete use of my eyes and lips, and only a little numbness in my right cheek. My smile works perfectly.

The only visible remnant of the surgery is a four-inch scar near the corner of my right jaw. It's light pink, and curves up from my jaw to my ear. I have to wear sunscreen to protect it; if it gets a little redder, it will look just like a little smile. But I wouldn't mind that. I've learned that smiles shouldn't be taken for granted.

## Bigger, But Not Better

### Ryan Grady Sample

I grew up a fisherman. It was predetermined. My father was a fisherman, my grandfather and his father, too. I could tie flies before I could tie my own shoes. I could catch a feisty cutthroat trout long before a baseball, and for second-grade show and tell, I brought mounted fish instead of teddy bears. I was raised on Saturday-morning fishing shows, not cartoons, and I'm still a sucker for spinning-lure infomercials. I was outfishing my eldest brother by the time I was 9.

Of course, the biggest contributor to my premature fishing prowess wasn't my heredity or the Saturday-morning tutorials. It was that I grew up amid some of the best freshwater fishing in the world. I'm a Montanan, and proud of it, despite the Unabomber, the Capitol gunman and the Freemen.

Today, despite my big beginnings, I'm no Bill Dance or Bud Lilly. I'm not even my dad. I fish for the love of it and I catch-and-release as much as I catch-and-feast. I go home happy with nothing and I tell fish-fibs like every other self-respecting fisherman.

Four years ago, on a fishing foray with my father, he told me about an "invasion" of lake trout (which are approximately three times larger than the cutthroat trout indigenous to the lake) in one of America's most prized fisheries: Yellowstone Lake. At the time, an invasion seemed too strong a word to describe anything a species of fish could do. I remember thinking, "Who cares?" I knew the exotic lake trout were bigger than the cutthroats, and what's a few more big fish for a fisherman?

Several summers later, having hooked my fair share of cutthroats, lake trout and sticks, I asked myself again, "Who cares?" I do. And so should you, if you have any interest—not necessarily in fishing—but in wildlife in general, in environmental preservation or outdoor recreation. If none of that baits you (attention, politicians), does money? Yellowstone Lake isn't just the premier surviving inland trout fishery in North America, it's a big industry. In 1994, it was estimated that the cumulative 30-year value of the fishery, if lake trout were absent, was more than a billion dollars. The estimated value depreciates $640 million if the lake trout remain.

To the novice fisherman, the notion of a big fish's being somehow bad is foreign. The only thinking such a fisherman does while in his element is: "Small fish, good. Big fish, great." It may well have been one of these novice fishermen who introduced the lake trout to Yellowstone Lake. The Park Service is sure that someone transferred the lake trout from a nearby lake. It's not possible that the lake trout's presence is the result of anything except human meddling.

Why will these bigger fish lessen the value of the fishery? The first concern is that the lake trout prey on the smaller cutthroats. The cutthroats, having evolved without any water-dwelling predators, make for easy meals for the lake trout, and because they are so plentiful, the lake trout's population will continue to flourish until the cutthroat population is all but demolished. This isn't scientific speculation; it's been well-documented. Similar introductions of lake trout into large, northwestern cutthroat fisheries have rendered them former cutthroat fisheries.

The lake trout, if allowed to dethrone the cutthroats, will then proceed to rule Yellowstone Lake's ecosystem in a very different manner. Experts have designated the lake trout a keystone predator, likely to drastically alter the energy flow from the aquatic to terrestrial ecosystems of the Yellowstone valley. Because lake trout dwell in significantly deeper waters than do cutthroats, they are almost entirely unavailable to terrestrial predators. Grizzly bears, bald eagles, river otters, osprey—a total of 42 species—will suffer greatly with the loss of cutthroat abundance.

The decline in such a significant food source will force species to feed elsewhere, putting an enormous amount of pressure on an already delicate balance of resources in the park. Eventually, those species less apt to change will die out. It's as if the lake trout, not the grizzly bear or the wolf, is the park's greatest predator. Its presence preys upon the well-being of the park as a whole.

Experts have assigned the Yellowstone fishery a value of "a billion dollars" in an attempt to put a conceptual price tag on the priceless. But if you've ever hiked, fished or even driven in Yellowstone National Park, then a billion dollars doesn't seem to pick up the tip, much less the tab, when you consider the adverse effects the loss of the cutthroat trout will have on the entire park.

I'm not an environmental fanatic. Sometimes I throw aluminum cans in regular garbage containers when the recycling bin imposes a 10-step detour. I'm a fisherman. I've never called myself an "angler" because I manage to disobey the most practical laws of physics while fishing. I've purchased fishing equipment at Kmart, I always misremember either the size or number of fish I've caught in an outing, and I always tell my fishing-mates I "had a bite" when I didn't feel a tug.

But I'm not worried about me. I'm happy fishing in a wading pool under a Montana sky if you tell me there are fish in there. I'm worried about my children and yours.

Yellowstone Lake (and its surrounding ecosystem) is one of an uncountable number of natural areas humans have already altered or destroyed in ignorance, but it is one of the few we can still repair.

After considering many potential solutions, including those as farfetched as introducing seals to prey on the lake trout, the Park Service prescribed a dose of good old-fashioned fishing to fend off the invading species. While fishermen are limiting the lake trout, park experts will be evaluating other means of eradication.

So, I don't know about you, but there's lake trout out there that need to be caught. I just bought a new lure for my rod from a Saturday-morning infomercial, and I'm armed with some experience, limited skill and a lot of desire.

Chances are good that something is invading where you live. It might be zebra mussels, it might be a coal-mining project, and such things may not make for easy fishing. But do what you can. I'll walk back to that recycling bin next time if you will.

## ACTIVITY 14

### REVISION

Evaluate your own opinion essay by annotating it. Then revise your essay once more: see if you should replace any weak supporting evidence with stronger reasons, examples, and details. See if you should reorganize your evidence so you save the best for last. Do you communicate clearly and persuasively? Try to imagine yourself as a reader who does not have your experience: will your essay be clear and convincing to that person? (Be sure to number or date each draft of your essay to avoid confusion.)

Last, proofread and edit your essay. Pay close attention to your diction (word choice) and your sentence patterns. If readers discover many errors in your words and sentences, they will assume you don't care much about communicating clearly. This, in turn, will reflect poorly on your ethos or credibility as a writer.

As you proofread and edit your essay, consider the following questions:

- Are your words carefully chosen—more specific than general?
- Could you omit any needless words?
- Are your sentences easy for readers to follow and understand?
- Do you use variety in punctuation and in sentence patterns?
- Have you found and repaired common problems such as comma splices, run-on sentences and sentence fragments, or incorrect use of apostrophes or quotation marks?

As you revise your essay, work through Interchapter 1. It will help you pay attention to your diction and sentences. It will show you how to use semicolons, for example. To learn how to use colons and dashes, see Interchapter 2. Also, refer to the Handbook toward the end of the book for information on common sentence problems.

## ACTIVITY 15

### REVISION

Sharing your writing with fellow students can be useful and important if you all genuinely agree to help each other. To share writing, bring three copies of your essay to your next class to give to other students. You can read the essays in class or out of class, as your instructor thinks best. If you read the essays out of class, you will have more time to annotate each essay and to provide constructive comments. Either way, try to read and evaluate each essay three times:

1. For clarity of communication—thesis, supporting evidence, and organization
2. For persuasive appeals—use of logos, pathos, and ethos
3. For style and voice—use of word choice and sentences

To evaluate classmates' essays and your own, you can use the Guide for Evaluating Writing at the end of this chapter. When you meet to discuss essays, follow this advice:

- Point out *at least three* features that you like about each essay.
- Point out *no more than three* features that you think could be improved in each essay. Suggest possible solutions to the problems.
- Underline any misspellings or problems in grammar, mechanics, or usage (see the following note). Don't correct these problems for your classmates; point them out for the writers to fix. If you aren't sure if something may be a problem, say so: "I'm not sure if this semicolon works properly here." The group can then discuss it.

You don't need to be hypercritical. It doesn't help to point out every little flaw; too much criticism is usually more harmful than helpful. Look first for what works well. Writers need some applause before taking some criticism.  ▮

## A NOTE ON DEFINING GRAMMAR, MECHANICS, AND USAGE

*Grammar* refers to the way sentences are constructed. Is a certain sentence a complete thought . . . or a fragment? (See Handbook.)

*Mechanics* includes correctness of words and punctuation; for example, do you see errors such as comma splices or run-on sentences? Are there any spelling errors or problems with apostrophes, quotation marks, underlining, or capitalization? (See Handbook.)

*Usage* refers to commonly confused words or phrases well-educated people believe are used either correctly or incorrectly. Should you use "effect" or "affect," "imply" or "infer"? (See Handbook.)

## A CRITICAL THINKER'S GUIDE
## FOR EVALUATING WRITING

| | Weak | Okay | Strong |
|---|---|---|---|
| **Thesis**: clearly stated and focused | | | |
| **Supporting Evidence**: clear reasons, examples, and details | | | |
| **Overall Organization**: clear, easy to follow paragraphs that build toward the strongest evidence | | | |
| **Engaging the Audience** | | | |
| Title | | | |
| Introduction | | | |
| Conclusion | | | |
| **Persuasive Appeals** | | | |
| Logos: use of reasoning | | | |
| Pathos: use of emotion | | | |
| Ethos: sense of writer's character being trustworthy, fair-minded, and credible | | | |
| **Stylistic Tools** | | | |
| Diction: words are more specific than general; apt similes or metaphors; no cliches; needless words omitted | | | |
| Sentence variety: sentences with different beginnings and patterns | | | |
| Punctuation variety: semicolons, colons, dashes | | | |
| **Sentence Skills** | | | |
| Grammar: complete sentences; no comma splices, run-ons, or unintentional fragments | | | |
| Mechanics and Usage: apostrophes, quotation marks, capitalization, proper spelling, no confusion between similar words such as "effect" or "affect" | | | |
| **Comments:** | | | |

# Style and Voice

## Dɪᴄᴛɪᴏɴ

*How you say your message is part of what you say.*

Diction means *word choice*: the words you choose when you write and speak. Your diction depends on your writing situation. If you write about a rock concert you attended and your audience is your peers, your language will be informal; if you write a letter to your college president arguing that tuition should not be raised, your language will be more formal.

Language can be compared to styles of clothing. *Informal language* is like wearing comfortable, everyday clothes; *formal language* is like wearing a suit or a dress. Yet there are various degrees of informal and formal diction: "Hey." "Hi." "Hello." When you use formal language, you try to use correct grammar and avoid slang. In short, you use your best manners with words.

What does all this have to do with critical thinking? It is true that "I ain't got no money" conveys a similar thought to "I'm broke," "I don't have any money," and "I am out of funds." But these language choices also convey information about the writer. Your diction—word choice—enables readers to interpret your meaning as well as get a sense of you (your ethos). *How* you say your message is part of *what* you say.

To write clear and accurate sentences, you must pay attention to diction. Choosing words carefully is an absolute law for writers.

### Monosyllabic Words

Before you read about monosyllabic words, please do the following.

## ACTIVITY **1**

Write a fully developed paragraph of at least half a page:

1. Use words of one syllable only. (You can have up to three exceptions.)

2. Try to express something that has meaning or truth. Don't settle for "See Spot run." Spend at least 10–15 minutes writing a draft of this paragraph in your notebook. Then type the paragraph and bring it to class.[1] ▬

*Note on Doing Activities: You will discover more about writing if you do the activities in the Interchapters. If you read ahead without doing an activity, you will limit your chances to experience eurekas and to learn.*

## ACTIVITY 2

Answer the following questions below your paragraph.

1. What problems did this activity pose for you?
2. What did you discover about diction from writing your paragraph?
3. Agree or disagree with each of the following statements:

    a. Nothing meaningful can be addressed in words of one syllable.
    b. There is no way to make such a paragraph interesting.
    c. No one talks like this. ▬

There are no "right" answers to the above questions. The answers depend on the paragraph you wrote and your experience writing it. Most students who do this activity write paragraphs that are more meaningful and interesting than they had thought possible. Consider the diction and voice in this writing by a student:

### Songs

#### *James Young*

Not a lot of guys or girls like the same songs I do. You see, I like all kinds of songs. I love rap songs, pop songs, funk songs, all songs with a good beat, fresh words, and those small bumps in the road that make me grin. This goes for jazz and big band songs with tons of small quirks, tweaks, and snaps, right down to the <u>Doug</u> theme song. And it seems that when they hear my songs or see them on a song list, they scoff and look at me like I'm some kind of green man from Mars with big ears and a nose the size of a pop can. Yet from time to time I meet a guy or girl who does like a song of mine. Once, a girl in my class heard me start to hum the song "I'm Like a Bird." She was shocked to hear it come from my lips and stunned when I told her I knew all the words. But she did too, so we spent the start of math class singing it. I just like all sorts of songs.

---

[1]Activity adapted from Dona J. Hickey, <u>Developing a Written Voice</u> (Mountain View, CA: Mayfield, 1993) 31–32.

Despite the limitations of using monosyllabic words, James's writing contains a clear *voice*—the sound of his personality. He succeeds with this assignment because he found a way to write about something he cares about—songs—and do so in a lively way. His writing contains some surprises for readers: such as "those small bumps in the road that make me grin," "songs with tons of small quirks, tweaks, and snaps," and "a nose the size of a pop can." The speaker in this paragraph is not bored, and he's not boring readers.

Here is another student example:

## Fear

### *Elaina Joyce Paulson*

I hate fear. It slows me down. It's all that stands in my way from reaching my goals. I had one bad smack and that was it. That's all it takes, and from then on each time I get on the board fear gnaws at me. If I had more strength I would not let fear get to me, but now I am not as brave. I let all the bad thoughts win more than the good ones. I stand there as my legs freeze and my hands shake. I'm so scared. All I can think of is the pain from my last dive. Fear can crush the "I think I can's" and the "I will be fine's." It blocks out all the skills I must think of as I set up for each dive. "Big knee lift." "Stand it up." "Throw." "Hold onto it." "Wait for the call." "Kick out strong." "Reach out and squeeze." All those thoughts are gone. Fear chews them up and spits them out so they don't make sense. At this point I'm too scared to try once more. I don't trust I can do it. In the past I would not let fear win, but now it's all I can think of. Now fear slows me down and stands in my way. I hate it.

Elaina's writing also contains a clear voice. She sounds knowledgeable about diving and the frustrations of it. Her *tone* is clear as well: her attitude toward her audience shows that she wants readers to understand the fear she feels after hurting herself from a bad dive. Her attitude toward her subject shows that she cares deeply about this sport and about fighting fear. Also, her description of fear goes beyond the subject of diving: she expresses the mental and emotional struggle with fear that most people have felt, no matter the cause.

Writing with one-syllable words helps you think more about diction and see that monosyllabic words can often replace multisyllabic words. One-syllable words can sound down to earth, real. You talk like this—at times.

"I possess an aspiration." What famous American speech contains that repeated sentence? None does. Why do you suppose Martin Luther King Jr. choose "I have a dream" instead? King's sentence resonates. With King's sentence of four syllables, less is more. Then too, King was speaking to a vast audience, and the short, simple *dream* was easier to understand than *aspiration*.

Strings of short words can carry power and clarity. Consider what Victoria Ruvolo told Ryan Cushing, whose senseless act of violence almost killed her: "I just want you to make your life the best it can be." (See Chapter 1.) At the end of her essay about Hurricane Katrina, "United States of Shame," Maureen Dowd writes a simple yet powerful sentence: "Who are we if we can't take care of our own?" (3 Sept. 2005). According to surgeon Richard Selzer, this is the most beautiful sentence in the English language: "There but for the grace of God go I." Why would Selzer make such a claim about a string of nine monosyllabic words? He values the elegant simplicity of the message.

On September 11, 2001, Rick Rescorla was working as the security head at Morgan Stanley when the second plane hit the World Trade Center. Using a bull-horn and singing "God Bless America" and other songs, he led more than three thousand employees out of the south tower. At one point, he called his wife and told her, "If something happens to me, I want you to know that you made my life." Then the phone died. The diction of his main thought—"I want you to know that you made my life"—is simple but powerful. These ten words stir pathos, expressing his deep love for his wife. (For more on Rescorla and his rescue, see "Presidential Medal of Freedom: Rick Rescorla" <http://www.medaloffreedom.com/RickRescorla1.htm>.)

Strings of monosyllabic words can clarify and emphasize thoughts and feelings. But it is easy to forget this lesson if you assume good writing must always involve complex words. E. B. White in <u>Elements of Style</u> advises writers, "Do not be tempted by a twenty-dollar word when there is a ten-center handy, ready and able."

## Multisyllabic Words

When you write and speak, you naturally use a combination of multi- and monosyllabic words. But using an abundance of long words does change a writer's voice. Consider this paragraph by a student:

### Precipitation

#### *Dan Scripps*

Linguistically, the English language offers speakers fewer varieties in expressing the concept of precipitation—what is commonly referred to as *snow*—than many Eskimo languages. Perhaps this stems from the reality that snow occupies a greater importance to the people of the Eskimo community than those living closer to the equator. Critics argue that the variety of expressions for this particular concept indicates that Eskimos are unable to process thoughts abstractly and therefore have an inherently inferior language to standard English. Others disagree, arguing that this variety indicates a far greater capacity for differentiation. Still others argue that it indicates nothing more than a difference in reality: the amount of snow in Eskimo regions necessitates a greater number of options for expressing this seemingly uninteresting English word.

Dan's writing here sounds more intellectual than James's and Elaina's more personal paragraphs using single-syllable words. His language reflects the kind of academic style most college teachers will expect you to use in formal papers.

## Pretentious Writing

*Pretentious writing* is a kind of overstatement: through inflated diction and complex sentences, the writer "pretends" that the writing is more important than it really is. Such writing is full of words like *precipitation* rather than *snow*.

Although children enjoy saying super-long words like *antidisestablishmentarianism*, writing and thinking can sound humorous or foolish if diction is inflated too much. Consider the accompanying cartoon.

**FIGURE I1.1**    For Better or Worse cartoon (19 Feb. 2006) showing boss using pretentious language.
Source: ©2006 Lynn Johnston Productions, Inc./Dist. by Universal Press Syndicate.

This cartoon shows an extreme example of pretentious language. One of the effects of the publisher's diction is that it's hard for people to pay attention to him. One employee, Al, has a eureka while playing a game of bingo instead.

You don't need pretentious writing. Write to express—not to impress. Using needless big words is a sure sign of amateur writing and questionable ethos. Choose any word because it is the most accurate word to express your thought. Dona Hickey in her book <u>Developing a Written Voice</u> explains that big words often cause separation between writers and readers:

> Multisyllabic words are often used to create wide distance between speaker and audience, sometimes for the sake of objectivity and high seriousness. But at other times, they are used to create intentional ambiguity, to establish superiority, and to exclude a general audience—those listeners who are not insiders, not members of a profession.

George Will writes his <u>Newsweek</u> column for a wide general audience, but he sometimes uses diction that many readers find hard to understand:

> Postmodernism is the degenerate egalitarianism of the intelligentsia.

Why does Will do this? His diction reflects his voice—the sound of his personality. Highly intellectual, he knows what he means and doesn't always care if many readers don't. His tone toward his audience may seem superior or elitist at times.

Scientific language is often multisyllabic. Students studying anatomy and physiology, for example, must know words concerning hamstring muscles like *semitendinosus* and *semimembranosus*. As a boy Richard Selzer loved to read his father's medical textbooks. They introduced him to long words in a positive way:

> It was then and there that I first became aware of the rich, alliterative language of medicine. I remember that some of the best words began with the letter C. "Cerebellum," I said out loud and let the word drip off the end of my tongue like melted chocolate. "Carcinoma"—it sounded rather like that aria from <u>Rigoletto</u> that Mother used to sing. And then I learned the word that made a surgeon of me—"Choledochojejunostomy." All those syllables marching across the page, ending in that terminal y. It didn't matter what it meant—if that was the way surgeons talked, I was going to be one of them.

To be a writer, you must be a reader—like Richard Selzer. You must learn to care about words. To write with care, you must choose words to express your thoughts and to persuade your audience. Do you own a good dictionary? If not, a good online source is Dictionary.com: see <http://dictionary.reference.com/>. The site also contains a thesaurus you will find useful. It's important to find the accurate, precise words you need, and it's important to replace needlessly difficult words with simpler ones. Thoughtful writers want their voice to be heard, not suffered through.

A comment by a student reveals an important lesson about diction and voice: "Big words make BS-ing instructors easier." But critical thinkers should not use words to con people, because other critical thinkers can usually detect "BS." Using inflated diction to impress others reflects poor ethos. Credibility is easy to lose and difficult to recover.

When you write essays, your voice should sound like you—your natural voice. Careful attention to diction will help you present your ideas the way you want them to be heard.

## ACTIVITY 3

### REVISION

Look at the diction—your word choice—in your recent writing. Do you use any strings of monosyllabic words for emphasis? Do you use any needlessly complex (multisyllabic) words that you could replace with simpler words? Do you present your voice the way you want it to be heard? Revise your writing to improve its diction. ▆

## OTHER FEATURES OF DICTION

In addition to monosyllabic and multisyllabic words, other features of diction you should know are specific or general, concrete or abstract, literal or figurative, and the power of precise words.

## Specific or General

A specific word is one that refers to particular things, persons, or events. Specificity involves precise details: strawberry ice cream, LeBron James, Battle of the Little Bighorn. A general word, on the other hand, is one that refers to a group or class; it "generalizes" where we wish the writer would be specific: dessert, athlete, conflict. Specific details help readers visualize and comprehend information.

### General

Many species will suffer greatly without the smaller fish.

### Specific

*Grizzly bears, bald eagles, river otters, osprey*—a total of *42* species—will suffer greatly with the loss of *cutthroat* abundance.[2] (Ryan Grady Sample)

### General

In one country, an unusual method is used to catch certain animals.

### Specific

In Thailand, hunters have a special trap to catch monkeys. The hunters hollow out the shell of a good sized coconut and put a ripe banana inside. A monkey's hand is small enough to reach inside the opening of the shell, but too big to come out holding the banana. The hungry monkey reaches in, grasps the banana, and discovers he is caught! He screams and cries, trying desperately to escape this trap. And of course he could, quite easily, but in most cases, the monkey doesn't want to let go of the banana. So he is swiftly captured by the hunters. (Diana Winston, Wide Awake: A Buddhist Guide for Teens)

General language often will cause readers to ask, "What do you mean? Can you give an example?"

### General

Earplugs are cheap and come in different styles.

### Specific

For roughly the cost of *bus fare*, anyone can buy a pair of *drugstore earplugs*. Their noise-reduction levels (ranging from about *20 dB* to *30 dB*) and styles (*foam, silicone* and *wax*) aren't all that important. (Claudia Kalb, "Our Embattled Ears")

Too much generalizing robs your writing of clarity and power. Then too, writing in generalities can suggest writers don't respect their readers. Giving specific details makes your writing sound informed; it tells your reader you know what you're talking about. The more specific your language is, the clearer you will communicate. Yet, it is possible to be too specific and bore readers, like a friend who brings 300 photos from his vacation to show you.

---

[2] All italics to indicate emphasis are by the author of this textbook, unless otherwise noted.

## ACTIVITY 4

### REVISION

Look again at the diction in your recent writing. How specific are your words? Try to find some very specific ones. Then see if you should make some other words more specific. ■

## Concrete or Abstract

Concrete refers to things that can be perceived by the senses: words referring to sight, sound, smell, taste, and touch. They bring to mind *images*.

> The frog wasn't *green* at all, but the color of *wet hickory bark*.
> (Annie Dillard, <u>Pilgrim at Tinker Creek</u>)

> As the *pasta boiled* and the *red peppers sizzled*, I wrote a *letter* to my cousin in Canada. At first the *pen* felt strange, then reassuring. I *hand-washed* my favorite *skirt* and made *chocolate cake* for my younger sister's 13th birthday. It took great self-control not to *slather* on the *icing* before the *cake cooled*. (Amy Wu)

> My mother is *fair-skinned* with *blond hair* and *blue eyes*. My father is *dark-complexioned* with prominent African-American features and a *head of woolly hair*. When you combine the genetic makeup of the two, you get me—*golden-brown skin, semi-coarse hair* and a whole *mess of freckles*. (Brian Courtney)

Abstract means ideas and qualities we cannot detect with our physical senses, such as *freedom, democracy, education*. This sentence contains very abstract diction: *The philosophy of existentialism is transformational*. Abstract diction is similar to general diction: both operate at the level of ideas. Concrete diction is similar to specific diction: both operate at the level of supporting evidence. However, the more abstract writing is, the harder it is to read and understand. Without concrete evidence, your readers may feel you haven't thought through your ideas.

There are legitimate uses for abstract language: philosophy, scientific discussions, legal documents, governmental documents, and any language about ideas. Is there a common denominator in these? Yes, educated writers communicating with educated readers:

> Congress is considering proceedings against the president. The report and other evidence submitted by the independent counsel suggest that the president may have committed impeachable offenses.

When educated writers write to educated readers, they may resort to abstract language like this, though not for long. To clarify abstractions, writers must use specific and concrete evidence.

## ACTIVITY 5

### REVISION

Examine the diction in your recent writing. Do you use any concrete words that provide images to show what you mean? Try to find some. Would your writing be stronger if you used more?   ▄▄▄

## Literal or Figurative
### Literal Language

The literal meaning of a word is its plain sense. It is the objective or dictionary meaning. A literal or denotative meaning of *chair* is a seat, furniture for sitting, traditionally supported by four legs and a back piece, though there are a number of variations today such as beanbag chairs.

In addition to denotation, many words have *connotation*: implied or associative meanings. Words can acquire positive or negative connotations—overtones of meaning not listed in a dictionary. *Chair* carries connotations of *electric chair*, *wheel chair*, and *dental chair*. The word *dog* indicates a canine animal, but it can be used to indicate people as well. "You dirty dog" implies a negative use; "you old dog" can imply a positive meaning. The word *home* carries connotations of shelter, security, and love for most people, but it can carry negative associations of abuse as well.

### Figurative Language

Comparisons can show what you mean and give your writing energy. You can make *literal* comparisons: Private colleges are smaller in size than public universities.

You can also make figurative comparisons. Metaphors and similes are the most common figures of speech:

#### Metaphor

A metaphor is an implied comparison:

> We're living life on fast-forward without a pause button. (Amy Wu)

> You are the sunshine of my life. (Stevie Wonder)

> When you write, you lay out a line of words. The line of words is a miner's pick, a woodcarver's gouge, a surgeon's probe. You wield it, and it digs a path you follow. Soon you find yourself in new territory. Is it a dead end, or have you located the real subject? (Annie Dillard, "The Writing Life")

#### Simile

A simile is a direct comparison using the word *like* or *as*:

> ALS is like a lit candle: it melts your nerves and leaves your body a pile of wax. (Mitch Albom, <u>Tuesdays with Morrie</u>)

> The stars were as close as berries on a bush. (Anne Lamott, <u>Grace</u>)

> I tend to go through life like a vacuum cleaner, inhaling all the interesting tidbits in my path. (Ellen Goodman, "On Being a Journalist")

## Avoid Clichés

As a critical thinker you should notice and avoid *clichés*: old familiar expressions considered trite and no longer forceful. They are the opposite of effective figures of speech. Avoid clichés such as the following:

| | | |
|---|---|---|
| anything and everything | end of my rope | ripe old age |
| a chip off the old block | few and far between | rude awakening |
| as busy as a bee | gentle as a lamb | short but sweet |
| as soft as silk | going down the drain | sigh of relief |
| a spoiled brat | hard as a rock | sight for sore eyes |
| at a loss for words | in this day and age | sink or swim |
| at the crack of dawn | last straw | stand in awe |
| clear as day | needless to say | tried and true |
| crying shame | nipped in the bud | white as snow |
| drop in the bucket | pain in the neck | |

Clichés are signs of weak or lazy thinking. They suggest a writer's inexperience with using careful diction. If you cannot think of another way to say something, it's usually better not to say it at all than to use a cliché.

How does the accompanying cartoon play with a cliche?

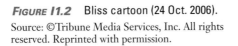

"You eat like a bird."

***Figure 11.2*** Bliss cartoon (24 Oct. 2006).
Source: ©Tribune Media Services, Inc. All rights reserved. Reprinted with permission.

The cartoon produces surprise by the man saying "You eat like a bird" and the woman literally eating like a bird—pulling a noodle as if it were a worm.

Style isn't simply a matter of fixing up words after ideas have been written. Ideas are composed of words, and when the words are not accurate, the ideas will not be accurate.

## ACTIVITY 6

Try writing some metaphors and similes about yourself or someone you know. Write three of each in your notebook. For example, "When I'm depressed, I'm a car without fuel." "When I'm tired, I'm like a library with its lights out." ■

## ACTIVITY 7

### REVISION

In your recent writing, do you use any metaphors or similes that help show what you mean? If you don't use any, would your writing be stronger if you did? Also, do you use any clichés? If you do, try to omit them or revise them. ■

## Precise Words

Well-chosen words are not just ornaments. They bring energy and strength to your sentences. They can help your readers listen and understand. Jennifer Woodruff, a student, wrote this:

> I was taught that it was better to be analytical than personal. So I began to saturate my work with long sentences and big words to make my writing sound more intelligent.

Her precise verb *saturate* works well; it suggests drenching. It's a stronger word than *fill* because of its associations with heavy soaking. Note what happens when Stephen Jay Gould uses an ordinary word in an unexpected context:

> DiMaggio dribbled one down the third-base line, easily beating the throw because the third baseman, expecting the usual, was playing far back.

You don't usually hear or read *dribbled* in reference to baseball, but this word helps readers visualize the ball.

Here are some other examples of precise words:

> Experience, particularly in childhood, *sculpts* the brain.
> (Daniel Goleman, <u>Emotional Intelligence</u>)
>
> I remember the air *carved* by bees. (Richard Selzer, <u>Confessions of a Knife</u>)
>
> Fireflies *throbbed* in the heavy blackness, sending out ardent messages.
> (Louise Erdrich, <u>The Blue Jay's Dance</u>)

Well-used words like *sculpts*, *carved*, and *throbbed* help readers enjoy sentences.

A common problem in student writing is overusing the word *thing* or variations of it such as *things*, *anything*, *everything*, *nothing*, and *something*. *Thing* is the opposite of precise diction: it is extremely general. Notice the effect of the word in the following sentences:

> *Things* were fine when I left. But I have not been able to discuss *things* with him. I wonder how *things* could have changed so dramatically.

One reason why inexperienced writers often use *things* is because they assume readers know what they mean. But readers don't. Readers need specific and precise words to understand what a writer means.

All writing, all reading, all speaking is composed of diction—word choice. Although you usually take words for granted, as a critical thinker try to pay fresh attention to words. They are building blocks of thought: you construct meaning with them; you create your voice on the page with them.

## ACTIVITY 8

### REVISION

Are your words precise enough in your recent writing? In particular, look to see whether you use *thing*, *things*, *anything*, *everything*, *nothing*, and *something*. You may not be able to change these words every time you use them, but you usually can. For example, instead of writing "I learned many *things* this year," you can write "I learned many *lessons* this year."  ▪▪▪

## VOICE

> Writing *with voice* is writing into which someone has breathed.
> (Peter Elbow, <u>Writing with Power</u>)

*Voice* is the sound of a writer's personality on the page. Readers hear this voice talking to them, telling them about the subject matter. Your information—your subject matter—is carried in your writer's voice. You can hear differences in voice when you read the "My Turn" essays in Chapter 1 by Amy Wu, Brian Courtney, Julie Kraus, Vicki Wilson, and Ryan Grady Sample.

## The Writing Situation and Voice

When you write different papers, you will often change your voice. Which voice you use will depend on your *writing situation*:

## FOUR ELEMENTS OF A WRITING SITUATION

**Your motivation** A problem, an assignment, a personal need.

**Your audience** In school your audience is usually your instructor and perhaps some classmates, but your instructor may require you to vary your audience—to write a letter to the editor of your college paper, for example, or a letter to a former employer. You may choose to write a letter to your parents about a problem or an issue you'd like them to consider.

**Your subject** If you write a film review of <u>Juno</u>, your voice will likely be more informal than if you write a research paper on the effects of secondhand smoke.

**Your purpose** What you intend to do in your writing: explain, persuade, evaluate, entertain, explore for self-understanding, or some combination of these.

Each time you write, ask yourself about your writing situation: What is my motivation for writing this particular piece? Who is my audience exactly? What is my subject exactly? What is my purpose in writing this? Answering these questions can help you determine the voice you want to use.

## TONE

What you write and how you write depend on your *tone* of voice: your attitude toward your audience, subject, and self. Writers can't afford the attitude that readers don't matter. You have an obligation to communicate with the reader. You must anticipate the reader's reactions.

### Analyzing Attitude Toward Readers

In the following two letters, one by President Abraham Lincoln and one by Kaiser Wilhelm, what attitudes toward their readers can you infer?

Executive Mansion,
Washington, Nov. 21, 1864.

To Mrs. Lydia Bixby [Boston, Mass.]

Dear Madam,—I have been shown in the files of the War Department a statement of the Adjutant General of Massachusetts that you are the mother of five sons who have died gloriously on the field of battle.

    I feel how weak and fruitless must be any words of mine which should attempt to beguile you from the grief of a loss so overwhelming. But I cannot refrain from tendering to you the consolation that may be found in the thanks of the Republic they died to save.

    I pray that our heavenly Father may assuage the anguish of your bereavement, and leave you only the cherished memory of the loved and lost, and the solemn pride that must be yours, to have laid so costly a sacrifice upon the altar of Freedom. Yours, very sincerely and respectfully, [A. Lincoln]

His Majesty the Kaiser hears that you have sacrificed nine sons in defense of the Fatherland in the present war. His Majesty is immensely gratified at the fact, and in recognition is pleased to send you his photograph with frame and autograph signature.

Try to imagine what might have caused the two men to use such words. Consider the recipients of the letters. You don't know anything about Mrs. Bixby or the German mother of the nine sons who died. But unless these are highly unusual mothers, you can imagine mothers reacting to such news: all their sons have died in the war.

Look again at President Lincoln's letter. Lincoln was a man who had read a great deal and that fact may give his letter a somewhat formal sound, but ask yourself whether Lincoln understands the situation—does his letter seem appropriate? Does it seem that the president understands Mrs. Bixby's loss? Try to imagine yourself in Lincoln's situation. Suppose you were the one who had to write that letter. Suppose it was your mother who received the letter from the War Department.

The president's tone is sad, respectful, and heartfelt; he speaks of Mrs. Bixby's grief. The president's voice is eloquent with words and phrases like "tendering," "solemn pride," and "altar of freedom." It isn't easy to find words of sympathy for someone who has lost a loved one, much less five loved ones. But Lincoln tries, ending his message with a prayer that God may soften her anguish and leave her with "only the cherished memory of the loved and lost."

Historians tell us that President Lincoln was misinformed. As sometimes happens in war, messages are not always accurate. Historians now believe that not all five of Mrs. Bixby's sons died. Nevertheless, you can hear in Lincoln's words his feelings for a mother he believes to have suffered so terribly. He is thinking about *her*.

By contrast, the brief note from Kaiser Wilhelm—apparently not from the Kaiser himself but some member of the war office—during World War I barely acknowledges the tragedy with the use of the single word *sacrifice*. Instead of compassion from one human being to another, the nameless bureaucrat sends the Kaiser's photograph. This message sounds impersonal, like a machine response. The Kaiser's letter ignores or fails to appreciate the situation—sending a meaningful condolence. "His Majesty's" note focuses more on the Kaiser.

## ACTIVITY 9

Write a brief letter to two different people. Write about the same subject for both readers—perhaps your impression of college so far compared to high school. The point of the activity is to show the effect of audience on tone, so don't simply write the same letter twice. Select readers you might actually change your writing for, such as a close friend versus someone more distant such as a school administrator or a teacher. ▨

## Analyzing Attitudes toward Subject and Self

*Tone* in writing not only means a writer's attitude toward audience but also a writer's attitude toward the subject, such as taking the subject seriously or lightly. Lincoln takes his subject seriously in his condolence to Mrs. Bixby. Also, what we hear tells something about the writer's self-image. Who do these writers think they are? Consider again the Kaiser's note to the German mother who lost nine sons. What kind of person writes such a note? Who tells this mother that "His Majesty" is "gratified" that she has lost so many sons?

When you write, your tone tells readers whether you like, dislike, or are indifferent to them and/or the subject, and also what you think about yourself.

How you use words and sentences to create your meaning, your persuasive appeals, and your voice is the central purpose of these Interchapters.

## ACTIVITY 10

### REVISION

What do you notice about your voice in your recent writing? Do you present your voice the way you want it to be heard? If not, try to revise your writing so it sounds like the voice you want. Also, what do you notice about your tone—your attitude toward your audience, subject, and self? Does your tone do what you want it to do? If you seem indifferent to your audience and your subject, these problems need your attention. ▨

## SENTENCE TOOLS

*Sentences embody thoughts.*

All decisions about diction take place within sentences. Just as you need to use a variety of diction, you need to use a variety of sentence structures. The more aware you are of the sentence patterns you use, the more you can control them. In some respects, sentences are like diction: there are simple forms and more complex forms.

## Simple Sentences

Let's start simple and build toward complexity. As we go, you will be asked to practice sentence tools and to apply them directly to your own writing.

## ACTIVITY 11

In your notebook write as many short sentences as you can in one minute. Try to make the sentences complete thoughts, but keep them short. The shorter the better.

> Short sentences help readers stop and think. They work. They can add variety and vitality to your writing. Writers use short sentences to add emphasis and surprise to their thoughts: *I disagree. Trust me. So what? Think critically. Pay attention. I don't know. He was right* (Amy Wu). Short sentences can say a lot—and many long sentences can say little. Thus, short sentences often have persuasive power. They can, of course, occur anywhere in a paragraph. Here psychologist Mary Pipher begins and ends a paragraph with a short sentence:

> Volunteers are happy people. The person who turns off daytime TV and teaches an immigrant to read feels better about his/her life. Sometimes volunteers unite against a common enemy, such as tornadoes, floods or fires. Sometimes they unite around a desire to do good work—to build a trail, paint a house or do health screenings for children. Working with others can rekindle idealism and rebuild a sense of community. Work cures despair. (The Shelter of Each Other)

Pipher concisely states a point, supports it with specific evidence, and repeats her point with a short sentence.

Daniel Goleman begins the conclusion to his essay "The New Thinking on Smarts" with a short sentence that contrasts with his thesis:

> IQ matters. But if we want to give our children the strongest foundation for life, we can't ignore EQ [emotional quotient or intelligence].

Short sentences, as Goleman shows, help writers make points clearly and concisely. By definition, they are *simple sentences: complete thoughts containing a subject and a verb*. Useful tools for style, they often contain monosyllabic words.

Short sentences shift rhythms of thought—at a glance readers can see and comprehend them. Use short sentences occasionally: they will give your writing more variety, emphasis, and power. Experiment. See how they work for you. Keep your eye out for them when you read.

## ACTIVITY 12

### REVISION

Review your most recent writing to see if you can use an occasional short sentence for emphasis.

## Joining Complete Thoughts: Coordination

What comes to your mind when you think of *coordination*? A dancer? An Olympic gymnast? A juggler? These are all forms of coordination. Certain types of sentences are classified under the term *coordination* for similar reasons—they contain a balancing of some kind.

## ACTIVITY 13

In your notebook try to write a compound sentence. If you aren't sure how to do this, don't worry: you will soon learn how. ▬

   You use various sentence patterns every day when you speak, but you probably aren't aware of them. With more awareness you will have more control, and with more control you will be a more effective writer. A pattern that builds on a simple sentence is the compound sentence: *A compound sentence contains two complete thoughts.* Grammatical labels like *coordination* and *compound* often confuse students. The labels, however, are not what's most important; what's important are the patterns.

   Four sentences in the above paragraph are compound—the first three and the last. They all contain two complete thoughts. The sentences are different because the thoughts within them are joined in different ways. In this section you will learn how to write sentences like those.

   The most basic pattern of a compound sentence is combining two complete thoughts with one of these connecting words (called coordinating conjunctions): *and, but, or, for, nor, yet,* and *so.*

   The blue jay is an opportunist, *and* opportunists are survivors in every sense. (Louise Erdrich, The Blue Jay's Dance)

   Try hard to find good arguments for your position, *but* then try even harder to find arguments to refute yours. (Peter Elbow, Embracing Contraries)

   You can write a draft without using an outline, *or* you can use an outline to write a draft.

*Comma rule:* Put the comma *before* the connecting word, never after.

## ACTIVITY 14

### REVISION

In your notebook write three compound sentences, each using a different connecting word. Then check your current writing to see if you use any compound sentences. If not, experiment and see whether you might combine some sentences to make them compound. ▬

## Using Semicolons to Join Complete Thoughts

Many people don't know how to use semicolons because they were never taught how. But using semicolons can add variety and power to your writing.

### ACTIVITY 15

In your notebook write a sentence using a semicolon. If you aren't sure how to do this, you are about to learn a distinctive tool of style. If you already know how, prove it.

How do semicolons function in the following sentences?

Seymour pays attention; he notices details.

Men have better spatial abilities; women have better verbal abilities.
(Ellen Goodman, "In the Male Direction")

This isn't scientific speculation; it's been well documented. (Ryan Grady Sample)

Each sentence above contains two complete thoughts joined by a semicolon instead of a connecting word such as *and, but,* or *or.* A semicolon is a hybrid of a period and a comma: like a period it signals a stop between two complete thoughts, but the stop is not as full or definite. The advantage of using a semicolon is that it shows a close relationship between two thoughts.

Some writers feel that the semicolon is more formal than a comma, suggesting a more sophisticated use of language. It takes a little more thought about language to decide whether a semicolon is appropriate.

*Semicolon Rule:* You need a complete thought on each side of a semicolon, and both thoughts should closely relate to each other in meaning.

### ACTIVITY 16

#### REVISION

In your notebook write three sentences that contain semicolons. Compare these sentences to the one you wrote at the beginning of this section. Did you use a semicolon properly then? Next, look at your recent writing to see if you can connect two closely related sentences into one sentence with a semicolon. When you write fresh drafts of papers or write e-mails, use some semicolons. Practicing this tool is the best way to learn it.

## Using Semicolons with Formal Transition Words

How are the following sentences containing semicolons different from the ones you've seen so far?

The catastrophe is over; however, we still feel afraid.

Seymour understood the idea; therefore, he didn't need any more examples.

Deborah Tannen argues that men prefer independence while women prefer intimacy; consequently, this difference causes countless misunderstandings.

Each of these sentences contains a semicolon followed by a transition word. This structure is useful because it shows cause-and-effect relationships between thoughts. It also gives the impression of formal reasoning. This sentence tool is especially useful in any formal essay, essay exam, or research paper. If you wrote a letter to a prospective employer, this tool could help you look professional. Here is a list of common transition words that can follow a semicolon to join two complete thoughts:

| | | | |
|---|---|---|---|
| also | furthermore | instead | otherwise |
| anyway | hence | likewise | still |
| besides | however | moreover | then |
| consequently | in addition | nevertheless | therefore |
| finally | indeed | next | thus |

The most commonly used transition words are *however*, *therefore*, and *consequently*.

As a writer you have many options on how to connect complete thoughts. For example, you can usually exchange *however* with *but* and keep the same meaning. Consider this example and revision:

> I'm considering a vegetarian diet; *however*, I'm unsure of the health risks.
> I'm considering a vegetarian diet, *but* I'm unsure of the health risks.

The first sentence may sound more formal, but the revision expresses the same thought. The word *but* is monosyllabic and simpler. When you want your voice to sound more formal, you can choose *however*. In addition, using transition words provides variety, helping you not to overuse common connecting words like *and*, *but*, or *or*.

*Comma Rule:*   A comma usually follows a transition word in a sentence containing a semicolon. However, the comma may be omitted for less effect.

## ACTIVITY 17

### REVISION

In your notebook write three sentences that contain semicolons followed by transition words. Then look at your recent writing. See if you can use this sentence tool at least once. ▮

You have used coordination in your sentences since you began to talk. You naturally combine complete thoughts. But with the help of formal connectors such as semicolons and transition words, you can gain more control over the effects of your sentences and your thoughts.

## SOLVING TWO COMMON SENTENCE PROBLEMS

### Comma Splices

Connecting two complete thoughts properly can help you solve two common sentence errors. Consider this sentence:

> Franny saw a shooting star, it felt like a eureka.

What's the problem? This mistake is called a *comma splice*. In formal writing the comma is not considered strong enough to separate complete thoughts. Connecting complete thoughts requires *both* a comma and a connecting word such as *and, but, or, for, nor,* or *yet.*

> Franny saw a shooting star, and it felt like a eureka.

Another way to revise a comma splice is to use a semicolon.

> Franny saw a shooting star; it felt like a eureka.

### Run-On Sentences

Another sentence problem is called the *run-on* or *fused sentence.* This punctuation error has nothing to do with a long sentence rambling on and on with needless words. The error is two complete thoughts fused together without punctuation or a connecting word. For example:

> Critical thinking is important creative thinking is important too.

In this example the first complete thought runs into the second complete thought. There is a collision. A basic way to solve this run-on problem is to use a period to separate the thoughts:

> Critical thinking is important. Creative thinking is important too.

To connect two complete thoughts, you need some punctuation. Here are other options:

> Critical thinking is important, but creative thinking is important too.
> Critical thinking is important; creative thinking is important too.
> Critical thinking is important; however, creative thinking is important too.

Another option, perhaps the best, is to revise for conciseness.

> Both critical and creative thinking are important.
> Although critical thinking is important, so is creative thinking.
> Critical thinkers need to be creative also.

Comma splices occur more frequently than run-on sentences. As a critical thinker you should be able to identify and repair comma splices and run-on sentences. An essay, report, business letter, or research paper containing these errors will not reflect well on your ethos. Readers may infer that you don't proofread carefully—or don't think carefully.

## ACTIVITY 18

### REVISION

Proofread your recent writing to find any comma splices or run-on sentences. If you find some, repair them by using (1) a comma and a connecting word (such as *and, but,* or *or*), (2) a semicolon, (3) a semicolon and a transition word (such as *however, therefore,* or *consequently*), or (4) one complete thought instead of two by omitting needless words. ▨

# Arguments and Controversies

## CRITICAL READING AND WRITING: AGREE, DISAGREE, OR MAYBE BOTH?

**Speed Bump**

*FIGURE 2.1* Speed Bump cartoon (26 June 2002).

Source: Speed Bump ©2005 Dave Coverly. All rights reserved. Used with the permission of Dave Coverly and the Cartoonist Group.

Does the way you argue depend on who you are and what you see? It often does, but you are more complex than an elephant and a zebra. As a critical thinker you can learn to see and argue about various perspectives. You can learn to argue about controversies.

The word *controversy* means "discussion of a question in which opposing opinions clash" (Webster's New World). A controversy involves two or more conflicting views for which there is no easy agreement, as, for example, gun control or same-sex marriage. The more extreme the disagreement, the more controversial the issue. A controversy usually goes beyond the experience of one person—it affects many people. It often has profound implications for society.

Reading an essay about a controversial topic involves considering different views of a debatable issue. Writing an essay about a controversial topic does also. Careful attention to logos, pathos, and ethos is essential for both.

You may *assume*—take for granted—that you know the meaning of words such as *controversy*, *argument*, and *assumption*, but unless I tell you what they mean to me, you might misunderstand. When you think of the word *argument*, what connotations does it have for you? A fight? A way of reasoning? A body of convincing evidence? Is the word positive or negative—or both?

Let us define *argument* as giving reasons for or against an opinion—or for some middle perspective. Middle perspectives are vital for critical thinkers: without them, we have nothing but extremes: yes/no, either/or, for/against. The middle perspectives can provide much truth that is not oversimplified by widely divergent views.

Can you argue without fighting—and without concentrating on what you're going to say next instead of listening closely to another person's view? This chapter will present strategies for you to use whenever you argue about controversial issues.

Critical thinkers analyze what they read. They wonder as they read whether they agree or disagree with an author; they may agree with certain ideas and examples but disagree with others. Before you encounter some essays concerning controversial issues, here is an article by Deborah Tannen, a professor of linguistics at Georgetown University and author of The Argument Culture from which this article is adapted. As you read, notice where you agree and disagree with Tannen.

## How to Turn Debate into Dialogue

### *Deborah Tannen*

Balance. Debate. Listening to both sides. Who could question these noble American traditions? Yet today, these principles have been distorted. Without thinking, we have plunged headfirst into what I call the "argument culture."

The argument culture urges us to approach the world, and the people in it, in an adversarial frame of mind. It rests on the assumption that opposition is the best way to get anything done: the best way to discuss an idea is to set up a debate; the best way to cover news is to find spokespeople who express the most extreme, polarized views and present them as "both sides"; the best way to settle disputes is litigation that pits one party against the other; the best way to begin an essay is to attack someone; and the best way to show you're really thinking is to criticize.

More and more, our public interactions have become like arguing with a spouse. Conflict can't be avoided in our public lives any more than we can avoid conflict with people we love. One of the great strengths of our society is that we can express these conflicts openly. But just as spouses have to learn ways of settling their differences without inflicting real damage, so we, as a society, have to find constructive ways of resolving disputes and differences.

The war on drugs, the war on cancer, the battle of the sexes, politicians' turf battles—in the argument culture, war metaphors pervade our talk and shape our thinking. The cover headlines of both <u>Time</u> and <u>Newsweek</u> one recent week are a case in point: "The Secret Sex Wars," proclaims <u>Newsweek</u>. "Starr at War," declares <u>Time</u>. Nearly everything is framed as a battle or game in which winning or losing is the main concern.

The argument culture pervades every aspect of our lives today. Issues from global warming to abortion are depicted as two-sided arguments, when in fact most Americans' views lie somewhere in the middle. Partisanship makes gridlock in Washington the norm. Even in our personal relationships, a "let it all hang out" philosophy emphasizes people expressing their anger without giving them constructive ways of settling differences.

### Sometimes You Have to Fight

There are times when it is necessary and right to fight—to defend your country or yourself, to argue for your rights or against offensive or dangerous ideas or actions. What's wrong with the argument culture is the ubiquity, the knee-jerk nature, of approaching any issue, problem or public person in an adversarial way.

Our determination to pursue truth by setting up a fight between two sides leads us to assume that every issue has two sides—no more, no less. But if you always assume there must be an "other side," you may end up scouring the margins of science or the fringes of lunacy to find it.

This accounts, in part, for the bizarre phenomenon of Holocaust denial. Deniers, as Emory University professor Deborah Lipstadt shows, have been successful in gaining TV air time and campus newspaper coverage by masquerading as "the other side" in a "debate." Continual reference to "the other side" results in a conviction that everything has another side—and people begin to doubt the existence of any facts at all.

The power of words to shape perception has been proved by researchers in controlled experiments. Psychologists Elizabeth Loftus and John Palmer, for example, found that the terms in which people are asked to recall something affect what they recall. The researchers showed subjects a film of two cars colliding, then asked how fast the cars were going; one week later they asked whether there had been any broken glass. Some subjects were asked, "How fast were the cars going when they bumped into each other?" Others were asked, "How fast were the cars going when they smashed into each other?"

Those who read the question with "smashed" tended to "remember" that the cars were going faster. They were also more likely to "remember" having seen broken glass. (There wasn't any.) This is how language works. It invisibly molds our way of thinking about people, actions and the world around us.

In the argument culture, "critical" thinking is synonymous with criticizing. In many classrooms, students are encouraged to read someone's life work, then rip it to shreds.

When debates and fighting predominate, those who enjoy verbal sparring are likely to take part—by calling in to talk shows or writing letters to the editor. Those who aren't comfortable with oppositional discourse are likely to opt out.

**How High-Tech Communication Pulls Us Apart**

One of the most effective ways to defuse antagonism between two groups is to provide a forum for individuals from those groups to get to know each other personally. What is happening in our lives, however, is just the opposite. More and more of our communication is not face to face, and not with people we know. The proliferation and increasing portability of technology isolates people in a bubble.

Along with the voices of family members and friends, phone lines bring into our homes the annoying voices of solicitors who want to sell something—generally at dinnertime. (My father-in-law startles phone solicitors by saying, "We're eating dinner, but I'll call you back. What's your home phone number?" To the nonplused caller, he explains, "Well, you're calling me at home; I thought I'd call you at home, too.")

It is common for families to have more than one TV, so the adults can watch what they like in one room and the kids can watch their choice in another—or maybe each child has a private TV.

E-mail, and now the Internet, are creating networks of human connection unthinkable even a few years ago. Though e-mail has enhanced communication with family and friends, it also ratchets up the anonymity of both sender and receiver, resulting in stranger-to-stranger "flaming."

"Road rage" shows how dangerous the argument culture—and especially today's technologically enhanced aggression—can be. Two men who engage in a shouting match may not come to blows, but if they express their anger while driving down a public highway, the risk to themselves and others soars.

**The Argument Culture Shapes Who We Are**

The argument culture has a defining impact on our lives and on our culture.

- **It makes us distort facts,** as in the Nancy Kerrigan-Tonya Harding story. After the original attack on Kerrigan's knee, news stories focused on the rivalry between the two skaters instead of portraying Kerrigan as the victim of an attack. Just last month, <u>Time</u> magazine called the event a "contretemps" between Kerrigan and Harding. And a recent joint TV interview of the two skaters reinforced that skewed image by putting the two on equal footing, rather than as victim and accused.

- **It makes us waste valuable time,** as in the case of scientist Robert Gallo, who co-discovered the AIDS virus. Gallo was the object of a groundless four-year investigation into allegations he had stolen the virus from another scientist. He was ultimately exonerated, but the toll was enormous. Never mind that, in his words, "These were the most painful and horrible years of my life." Gallo spent four years fighting accusations instead of fighting AIDS.

- **It limits our thinking.** Headlines are intentionally devised to attract attention, but the language of extremes actually shapes, and misshapes, the way we think about things. Military metaphors train us to think about, and see, everything in terms of fighting, conflict and war. Adversarial rhetoric is a kind of verbal inflation—a rhetorical boy-who-cried-wolf.

- **It encourages us to lie.** If you fight to win, the temptation is great to deny facts that support your opponent's views and say only what supports your side. It encourages people to misrepresent and, in the extreme, to lie.

### End the Argument Culture by Looking At All Sides

How can we overcome our classically American habit of seeing issues in absolutes? We must expand our notion of "debate" to include more dialogue. To do this, we can make special efforts not to think in twos. Mary Catherine Bateson, an anthropologist at Virginia's George Mason University, makes a point of having her class compare three cultures, not two. Then, students are more likely to think about each on its own terms, rather than as opposites.

In the public arena, television and radio producers can try to avoid, whenever possible, structuring public discussions as debates. This means avoiding the format of having two guests discuss an issue. Invite three guests—or one. Perhaps it is time to re-examine the assumption that audiences always prefer a fight.

Instead of asking, "What's the other side?" we might ask, "What are the other sides?" Instead of insisting on hearing "both sides," let's insist on hearing "all sides."

We need to find metaphors other than sports and war. Smashing heads does not open minds. We need to use our imaginations and ingenuity to find different ways to seek truth and gain knowledge through intellectual interchange, and add them to our arsenal—or, should I say, to the ingredients for our stew. It will take creativity for each of us to find ways to change the argument culture to a dialogue culture. It's an effort we have to make, because our public and private lives are at stake.

Do you think Tannen's argument makes sense? Do you agree with her thesis and supporting evidence? Does she persuade you? Yes? No? Sort of? To analyze and evaluate any text, you should read the text again, but this time more actively.

## ACTIVITY 1

Photocopy Tannen's essay and annotate it. In particular, write notes in the margins about what you agree and disagree with. Consider using these notations:

Write "T" beside any statement you find *true* and a "?" beside any statement you *question* or doubt.

Underline any key sentences that surprise you with their *insight* or seem especially well worded. Put a star by these in the margin.

Underline any sentences that contain problems of reasoning such as overgeneralizations.
    Put a question mark by these in the margin.
Write comments in margins if you remember a personal example that *supports* or *challenges*
    what Tannen says.

See if you notice more of Tannen's reasoning.    ▭

Critical thinkers often read a text more than once, especially if it challenges their usual way of thinking. They try out ideas on themselves—wear them around for a while in their minds. They also reflect on their own experience by asking themselves questions: Do I argue the way Tannen claims most people argue? Have I, at times, had to "fight" to defend myself or someone else? When? What happened? Do I know anyone who argues in a mean-spirited or violent way? Who? Do I know anyone who argues the way Tannen recommends, who is able to create a dialogue during an argument?

# READING TOOLS

Suppose your instructor asks you to write an essay in which you analyze and evaluate Tannen's article. In addition to annotating it, what could you do? To analyze (take apart) and to evaluate (judge) any essay, you can ask yourself questions about it and you can notice insights, assumptions, and overgeneralizations in it.

## Asking Questions

Critical thinkers ask questions. It's natural. To think is to notice and to inquire. What questions did you ask yourself as you read Tannen's essay? Here are some questions:

*Is it true that in our culture, "'critical' thinking is synonymous with criticizing"?* This is largely true. However, like Tannen, this book will aim to present other perspectives on critical thinking—more positive ones.

*Is it true that "in many classrooms, students are encouraged to read someone's life work, then rip it to shreds"?* Perhaps. Although the word *many* qualifies the statement somewhat, Tannen provides no example to show what she means here.

*Is it possible not to view controversial issues as heated debates or wars of words? Do most people "always prefer a fight"* as Tannen claims? In television news shows such as <u>Hardball</u> with Chris Matthews, debates are depicted as "fights" or "wars." Seeing controversies in this either/or way is convenient and simplistic. Changing the way most people are conditioned to view arguments is no easy job.

## Noticing Insights

One of the pleasures of reading is noticing insights or statements of truth: statements that surprise you with their wisdom and often concise expression. Tannen's sentence in her conclusion, "Smashing heads does not open minds," is insightful. This restatement of her thesis closes her essay well along with her metaphor of a "stew" of various views rather than an "arsenal."

Not everyone agrees on what is insightful, but that's okay. What's important for you as a reader is to notice insights and to think about them. Consider the best-selling book <u>Tuesdays with Morrie</u> by Mitch Albom, about his professor/mentor Morrie Schwartz dying from ALS. One of the reasons this memoir continues to be popular and important is because many readers find insights in it that help them with their own lives. Here are some insights spoken by Morrie:

> Without love, we are birds with broken wings.

> When you learn how to die, you learn how to live.

> Remember what I said about finding a meaningful life? I wrote it down, but now I can recite it: Devote yourself to loving others, devote yourself to your community around you, and devote yourself to creating something that gives you purpose and meaning.

Some readers may consider one or more of these examples as corny or trite. That's okay. Insights are debatable.

If you notice insights often enough when you read, the process will become a habit: you will experience moments of eureka. The more reading eurekas you experience, the more you will enjoy and value what you read.

## Noticing Assumptions

In using the word *assume* in the following sentences, Tannen notices what people take for granted when they argue:

> Our determination to pursue truth by setting up a fight between two sides leads us to *assume* that every issue has two sides—no more, no less. But if you always *assume* there must be an "other side," you may end up scouring the margins of science or the fringes of lunacy to find it. (emphasis added)

Critical thinkers notice assumptions—unexamined beliefs or values that people take for granted. Our assumptions often limit our thinking: we may assume that gun control is either good or bad. But truth often exists in the complex middle ground of extreme views.

If you are reading <u>Moby Dick</u> at the beach, some people may assume you enjoy serious literature—but you may be reading it for a course you will take in the fall, and you're trying to read ahead. Suppose a friend of yours who attends a private college says, "Students who attend Michigan State University—with more than 40,000 students—are treated like numbers in their classes." This assumption is proven wrong in the case of first-year writing classes and graduate-level seminars, which are small and personal.

Try to notice assumptions when you read. You will find that analyzing and evaluating ideas and supporting evidence will soon follow naturally. Noticing assumptions will enable you to go underneath arguments, to see how they are constructed.

## Noticing Overgeneralizations

> *"TV is the enemy of reading."* True? Do children's shows like <u>Reading Rainbow</u> cause kids not to read?
>
> *"I think interacting with the elderly is always a refreshing experience."* Always? You don't know my great-uncle Frank who. . . .
>
> *"All students in college love to learn."* All? Surely many students find learning difficult and don't "love" to learn, and learn what? Doesn't loving to learn depend on what is being learned?
>
> *"Life is not complete until you've dared to do everything life has to offer."* Everything? Does this include stealing, rape, and murder?
>
> *The overall effect of technology has been to dehumanize people.* Overall effect? How do you know this? What about the use of medical technology to save lives?
>
> *You can't have fun at parties unless you drink alcohol.* This does not hold true for *all* people. Some prefer not to drink at all and don't need to drink to enjoy themselves.

An overgeneralization is an extremely broad statement that covers too many cases; it assumes that exceptions don't exist. Critical thinkers notice overgeneralizations as sweeping statements that contain weak reasoning.

You can spot overgeneralizations easily by noticing certain key words: *all, always, anything, everybody, everyone, everything, no one,* and *nothing. All* kids love ice cream. Wealthy people can get away with *anything.* Old people *always* have a wealth of knowledge to share with young people. *Everyone* enjoys sports. *No one* ever proofreads papers anymore. *Nothing* my parents say makes sense.

To disprove or refute an overgeneralization, you need only a single exception. My nephew Ernie hates ice cream. Ken Lay, founder of Enron and multimillionaire, was convicted of corporate fraud. A grandparent with Alzheimer's no longer has a wealth of knowledge to share. My roommate Karen has no interest in playing or watching sports. My friend Zooey proofreads. Certainly, at least some of what your parents say makes sense.

A popular country-western song by Ray Stevens goes "Everything is beautiful in its own way." *Everything?* What about the Holocaust? Okay, Hitler and others like him may have felt this genocide was beautiful. But now the statement has become absurd.

When you discover overgeneralizations, a red flag should go up in your mind and you should say "What? Really?" Consider the introduction to an essay, "Professor Simon Says," by columnist Mike S. Adams:

> One characteristic of liberal professors is that they actually get dumber as time goes by. Conservative professors just keep getting smarter because we're always under fire from the liberals.

As a columnist for Townhall.com and a criminology professor at the University of North Carolina Wilmington, Mike Adams might be exaggerating to hook readers right away. But readers should question his sweeping overstatements: he doesn't use the word *all* in referring to liberal professors, but his first sentence implies it. That he uses *always* in his second sentence should make critical thinkers wonder if he's kidding or serious. Using overgeneralizations in this way might make many conservative readers chuckle and agree. Whether you overgeneralize or not might depend on your audience. However, usually, making such overstatements reflects poor logos and questionable ethos.

Please don't assume that it is wrong to generalize. People can't help but generalize—that is, state conclusions or opinions. As a critical thinker, however, you must learn to *qualify* your generalizations. Thoughtful writers qualify any generalization that seems too sweeping or is likely to create doubt in a reader's mind. Qualifiers like *many, some, a few* work well, usually. The word *most* is a common qualifier, yet it too might be difficult to justify. "Most men don't like to shop for clothes." This is someone's opinion that is impossible to verify. How many does "most" mean—55%, 75%, 95%? The statement needs more qualification such as "Many men don't like to shop for clothes" or "Most men *I know* don't like to shop for clothes." The ability to qualify generalizations is a hallmark of critical thinking.

Consider this statement by Tannen: "In the argument culture … nearly everything is framed as a battle or game in which winning or losing is the main concern." Her word *nearly* does qualify *everything*, but *everything* is a tremendously broad word that literally means every thing. Is walking down the street a battle or game? Is reading the weather report? Is eating your favorite dessert? *Note:* For more information on overgeneralizations, see Chapter 4.

In sum, when you read an essay or article carefully, you can analyze and evaluate it by asking questions about it and by noticing a writer's insights, assumptions, and overgeneralizations. These same reading tools will also help you analyze and evaluate your own writing as well.

## ACTIVITY 2

Make a list of at least 5 overgeneralizations—ones you've heard before or said yourself. Then rewrite them by adding a qualifying word. Bring your list to class.

## EXPLORING TWO ESSAYS ON A CONTROVERSY

**FIGURE 2.2**  Clay Bennett cartoon (2006).
Source: Christian Science Monitor.

## ACTIVITY 3

Look carefully at Clay Bennett's cartoon. What is the image of the gun suggesting? If Bennett is presenting an argument in this cartoon, what is his argument? Do you agree with it? ▪▪▪

Because controversial issues involve extreme disagreements, they often involve extreme emotions. How writers control their emotions in an essay is one way for readers to evaluate that essay. One of the most emotional issues today is gun control. A strictly logical presentation of facts and figures—how many guns there are and how many people die in gun-related incidents—makes little impact. Writers usually need to appeal to pathos and ethos as well. Here are two essays on this issue, each with a different perspective on gun control. Although they were not recently written, their arguments are still relevant, especially in light of the Virginia Tech massacre.

### Analysis and Evaluation of Mitch Albom's Essay

Author of the bestsellers <u>Tuesdays with Morrie</u>, <u>The Five People You Meet in Heaven</u>, and <u>For One More Day</u>, Mitch Albom has been voted number one sports columnist in America for more than a decade. He writes sports and opinion essays for the <u>Detroit Free Press</u>. As you read the following essay by Albom, consider how well he argues: What is his thesis and how well does he support it? How does he use logos, pathos, ethos? Does he persuade you to consider his arguments and to agree with him? Try to practice the reading tools presented so far in this chapter: asking questions and noticing insights, assumptions, and overgeneralizations.

### Don't Shoot Holes in Gun Control Bills

*Mitch Albom*

Maybe they had an argument. I don't really care. All I know is a man was driving a Ford Bronco on the Lodge Freeway last week and a Cadillac pulled alongside him with several passengers inside and next thing you know, someone in the Cadillac was firing bullets. Three of those bullets hit the driver of the truck. He veered off the highway and began to die.

An hour later, there was one less person in our city.

Tell me again about how gun control is a stupid idea. Tell me again how all it will do is take guns away from innocent people who want to protect themselves. Tell me again how guns don't kill people, people do.

Alan Johnson, the dead man, was killed by a gun. Sure, a person fired it—in a day and age when all we see are guns, everything we watch has guns, every story we hear involves guns. Alan Johnson is not the first man to have an argument with someone. But not so long ago, people settled arguments by yelling louder, or ignoring one another, or, if they were crude, taking a swing.

Nowadays they pull up alongside your car and open fire.

Bang, bang. Take that, jerk.

This is hardly an isolated tale. People in Los Angeles can tell you how their highways have turned into shooting ranges. Cut someone off, they pop you with a bullet. In Detroit, just a few months ago, a guy didn't like his Rally's hamburger, so he threw it back through the pickup window. The female worker threw a drink at him. He drove off, came back with a gun and shot her.

Bang, bang. Take that, jerk.

We live in an age of hair-trigger tempers—and that is no place for hair-trigger weapons. Yet guns, guns, they seem to be everywhere, even places we once considered perfectly safe, like a busy highway during rush hour. What if the bullets meant for Alan Johnson had sprayed into a passing car instead? The gun used, police say, was an AK47 assault rifle, one of the weapons specifically banned in the previous year's crime bill.

This is the same measure opponents said was a waste of time, an unfair burden, the one they are trying to get repealed.

Tell me again.

### Frontier Justice

Am I the only one bothered by this? That you can't honk your horn on the highway anymore without wondering whether the driver is some maniac you just pushed over the edge, and now he's coming after you, rolling down his window and taking aim?

Are we not moving back to the days of frontier justice, the Wild Wild West, where getting upset over a card game was reason enough to kill a man? Think about it. In June, a Detroit firefighter was shot while putting out a blaze. Nobody knew why. Someone just shot him. In January, gunmen rode past a house in southwest Detroit, allegedly angry at a young man who lived there, and sprayed the place with bullets. One of them hit a visiting relative, a 16-year-old boy, and killed him.

He had been sleeping on the couch.

Just a few weeks ago, friends and family were sobbing for a young man who was killed for his Jeep. It wasn't enough that they took the vehicle. They had to shoot him, dump him, let his body rot while they rode around town.

Where does this stop? Because there is no bottom, folks, there is no lowest level at which things don't get any worse. It keeps getting worse as long as we allow it. Who's to say we don't go back to the Old West? We lived that way once. What makes us so different now?

Well. One thing that might is legislation. Stop allowing guns to be as easy to buy as cigarettes. Yes, I know the problem begins at home. And until parents teach their children to respect life, to be shamed by violence and until we stop glorifying TV shows that bring us "real life crime drama" and music that brags about killing cops—until that happens, we will never stomp the killing gene in our society.

But you have to start somewhere.

### Memories Linger

Ten years ago, when I first arrived in this town, I went to a Southfield dry cleaners to pick up a jacket. I saw no one in the store except a customer at the counter. He had his back turned to me. I asked whether anyone was working and he turned around and pointed a gun at my face. He was robbing the place. He told me to get in the closet, or he'd shoot me dead, right there.

I survived that, but for weeks I saw the gun in my sleep. I thought there could be no worse horror, to enter an innocent situation and be looking down the barrel of a gun. Now I realize I was wrong. The worst horror is to look down the barrel just before it fires.

Alan Johnson died that way, and I don't care what might have precipitated it. We cannot live where disputes are solved by bullets. And until we take the guns away, we will make no dent in this. We just keep arguing, until another window rolls down.

Work Cited

Albom, Mitch. "Don't Shoot Holes in Gun Control Bills." <u>Detroit Free Press</u> 19 Nov. 1997: F1.

Many writers have attempted to argue for or against gun control, with little success. There are powerful groups on both sides of this question, and there doesn't seem to be much left for writers to say on either side. Mitch Albom doesn't attempt to deal with the standard arguments concerning the Constitution (does the Second Amendment give individuals the right to have guns?), nor does he cite factual data concerning how many millions of weapons there are in the United States.[1] But he does cite several cases of gun-related crime. He insists that we need to pass laws that restrict gun ownership. Is he right?

### Amendment II

A well-regulated Militia being necessary to the security of a free State, the right of the People to keep and bear Arms shall not be infringed.

## ACTIVITY 4

In your notebook, write a response to Albom's essay. Do you agree or disagree with him—or perhaps both?

### Albom's Writing Situation

Note that the "situation" that prompted this article was the death of a man on the Lodge Freeway (in Detroit), a drive-by shooting by someone in another car. The death of Alan Johnson motivated Albom to address the controversy of gun control, to relate other similar examples, and to share his own frightening experience facing a gun. His thesis is that no matter what provocation may exist between individuals, we must not accept guns and killing as the way to resolve a dispute.

---

[1]"There are an estimated 215 million firearms in civilian hands in the U.S." (ix). Bureau of Alcohol, Tobacco and Firearms. "Crime Gun Trace Reports (1999)." Nov. 2000. 28 June 2007 <http://www.atf.treas.gov/firearms/ycgii/1999/natrpt.pdf>.

## Albom's Introduction

Albom uses the power of first-person narration (storytelling) to pull the reader into the events. He does not distance himself from the topic of gun control by trying to be purely objective. Instead, he pulls the reader into the story. His first sentence, "Maybe they had an argument," causes readers to wonder—an argument about what? But then readers may conclude it doesn't matter what it was about. His second sentence says just that. Albom's first paragraph ends with a powerful sentence: "He veered off the highway and began to die." Alan Johnson's death was not instantaneous. The appeal to pathos builds toward the end of his introductory sequence: "An hour later there was one less person in our city." He sets this sentence off in its own paragraph, for emphasis. He uses one-sentence or one-line paragraphs eight times for emphasis in the article; this is a feature of Albom's style.

## Noticing Albom's Insights, Assumptions, and Overgeneralizations

Mitch Albom insightfully writes, "We live in an age of hair-trigger tempers—and that is no place for hair-trigger weapons." The repetition of *hair-trigger* works well to emphasize his point. The statement provokes thought.

Albom assumes—takes for granted or believes—that guns are everywhere in our culture: "in a day and age when all we see are guns, everything we watch has guns, every story we hear involves guns." This assumption is also an overgeneralization or exaggeration. Surely not every TV show or movie you watch involves guns—many do, but not all. Although his assumption is questionable, it is true that guns are a dominant feature of our culture.

Albom assumes that abolishing guns will help solve the problem of violence: "And until we take the guns away, we will make no dent in this." He may be right; he may not be. Albom assumes that we, the people, have the power to change chronic violence: "It keeps getting worse as long as we allow it." He assumes that if we motivate our legislators to enact tougher gun laws, this "might" help. He assumes there is a "killing gene" in our society. Would you say this killing gene—if it exists—is related solely to guns?

## Responding to Other Arguments

How important is it for a writer to respond to other or opposing arguments? Extremely important, though many writers don't do it. If Albom did not represent the other side, he would not appear fair-minded: his ethos would be less credible. How much does Albom present the other side? Not in depth. Instead, he *acknowledges* opposing arguments with an ironic attitude:

> Tell me again about how gun control is a stupid idea. Tell me again how all it will do is take guns away from innocent people who want to protect themselves. Tell me again how guns don't kill people, people do.

His repetition of "Tell me again" suggests that he has heard these pro-gun arguments countless times from those who fear they will lose their guns and who fear some conspiracy exists against which guns are their only protection. Later he writes,

The gun used, police say, was an AK47 assault rifle, one of the weapons specifically banned in the last year's crime bill.

This is the same measure opponents said was a waste of time, an unfair burden, the one they are trying to get repealed.

Tell me again.

Again he briefly acknowledges the pro-gun view that the crime bill was "a waste of time."

Many people want so much to win their argument that they find it difficult to concede anything to an opposing side. Yet the ability to concede increases your credibility. Your audience (readers) can see that you are fair.

## DIFFERENT WAYS TO PRESENT OTHER ARGUMENTS

As a writer you have various options in presenting other arguments:

- Briefly acknowledge them while conveying your disagreement with them (as Albom does).
- Summarize them objectively in a paragraph; then convey your disagreement with them.
- Fully and fairly present other positions, pointing out their merits and weaknesses before presenting your own position and evidence.
- Present your own position and evidence first and then respond to other arguments.
- Not acknowledge other arguments at all, as if other views don't exist. This is not a wise strategy.
- Misrepresent other positions, exaggerating their weaknesses, making up examples and other kinds of evidence to make the writer appear wrong or foolish. This option is, of course, dishonest—a sign of fatally bad ethos.

### Albom's Use of Logos, Pathos, and Ethos

Using logos, Mitch Albom shows that the gun problem isn't just happening in Detroit. He cites Los Angeles where you can get "popped" with a bullet on the highways for cutting someone off. But it's not only driving that can get you killed. Albom cites a Detroit fast-food place where a worker was shot because the customer didn't like his burger. Again he repeats, "Bang, bang. Take that, jerk," sounding like a child playing guns. This switch from narrator to participant puts you momentarily in the story. As an emotional appeal, it helps you feel and think. You read from the shooter's point of view—but the logic of the shooter seems incomprehensible. What is going on? How are you to understand this epidemic of murders over trivial disagreements?

Albom uses logos and pathos in asking probing questions. "What if the bullets meant for Alan Johnson had sprayed into a passing car instead?" "Are we not moving back to the days of frontier justice, the Wild Wild West, where getting upset over a card game was reason enough to kill a man?" People are getting killed for no apparent reason—like the Detroit firefighter shot while battling a blaze and the 16-year-old boy sleeping on a couch. Albom's use of specific examples and details stirs readers' emotions and makes them think about the problem. "Where does this stop?" he asks.

Although Albom's article combines appeals to logos and pathos, the most important appeal for persuasion is ethos. None of the appeals works unless you believe the writer. The writer's credibility is crucial. Not another unknown victim, Mitch Albom is a well-known, prize-winning author. It doesn't hurt to have external information about the writer, but the ethos in an essay must be built in: you must try to judge from the writing itself whether Albom is a man of good will, a moral person, someone who deserves your respect.

There is no way for you to know absolutely, of course, whether Mitch Albom is being truthful; it's possible that he could have invented much of his evidence. But unless there are obvious clues in the writing that make you suspect the author's truthfulness, you owe the writer a fair reading. Authors have the right to presume you believe them, until you come across something that makes you think otherwise.

Assuming the author to be truthful, you can see that he has taken the trouble to put all this information together carefully, skillfully, so that you can follow it and be open to his point of view. Albom's concern for the individuals killed, his concern for society as a whole, suggest a thoughtful, compassionate person.

You have to ask yourself—is this a reasonable man? Do you believe him? You may not agree with his position, but it's hard not to accept his presentation of the problem.

## What Is the Solution?

Because the gun problem appears to be getting worse, Albom claims we need legislation that will make it harder to buy guns. "Stop allowing guns to be as easy to buy as cigarettes." He argues that we need parents to teach children respect for life, and we need to stop TV shows and music that feature guns and killing. We need a change in attitudes about guns. Albom invokes a metaphor: we must "stomp out the killing gene in our society." Loose in our society is a mad impulse to assert one's dominance with a lethal firearm. He calls for action from readers: more legislation and more respect for life.

## Albom's Conclusion

Albom could have ended his article with the sentence "But you have to start somewhere." Instead, he ends with a personal experience, describing his own encounter when a gunman held up a dry cleaners. He explains the horror he felt facing a gun and seeing the gun in his sleep afterwards. His personal example at the end of his essay stirs pathos, logos, and ethos. Readers feel and think about Albom's personal experience; he and his arguments become even more credible.

Hooking his last paragraph to his first by referring to Alan Johnson again, the drive-by shooting victim, Albom ends his article with this prediction: "We cannot live where disputes are solved by bullets. And until we take the guns away, we will make no dent in this. We just keep arguing until another window rolls down." His last image is a haunting reminder that another drive-by shooting is bound to occur soon.

## Analysis and Evaluation of Thomas Sowell's Essay

Thomas Sowell is a well-known conservative newspaper columnist. He is a senior fellow on public policy at the Hoover Institution, a research center devoted to advanced study of politics, economics, and international affairs. He has written several books on economics, including <u>Affirmative Action Around the World</u> (2004). As you read the following essay, notice whether his arguments are convincing and whether he appeals to your emotions and ethics. Does he persuade you to consider his view, to agree with him? Ask yourself questions as you read; look for any insights, assumptions, overgeneralizations.

### Mass Shootings and Mass Hysteria

#### *Thomas Sowell*

In a world of emotional-outburst TV shows and dumbed-down education, it may not be so surprising that the deaths of 15 people have stampeded Congress toward laws affecting more than a quarter of a billion Americans and their descendants.

That stampede is called "gun control."

The tragic irony is that such laws are much more likely to increase shooting deaths than to reduce them. For those of us old-fashioned enough to think that facts still matter, comprehensive research has shown that allowing law-abiding citizens to carry concealed weapons reduces gun violence, as well as other kinds of violence.

Unfortunately, facts may carry very little weight politically, in the midst of an emotional orgy with rhetorical posturing. Yet the evidence is overwhelming that allowing law-abiding citizens to be armed has reduced violence in general and mass shootings in particular.

For those to whom facts still matter, John Lott's book <u>More Guns, Less Crime</u> presents overwhelming evidence. Another study of his, with Professor William Landes of the University of Chicago as co-author, addresses mass shootings, such as those which have been taking place in schools, post offices and other public places. These shooting rampages have been far more common in places where there are strong gun control laws. No matter what other factors these authors take into account—poverty, race, population density, etc.—the results are still the same. Places with many armed citizens have fewer mass shootings. Their data cover mass shootings in every state and the District of Columbia, going back nearly two decades.

Congress would do well to call Lott and Landes as witnesses who could provide some much-needed education for the public and the media, as well as for the legislators who are being rushed toward ill-considered legislation. Gun control laws have a bad track record, however popular they may be in some quarters.

Think about it: People who are committing illegal acts are not going to be stopped because guns are illegal. What does stop them then? Often it is somebody else with a gun. Indeed, such shootings may not occur at all in places where there is a high probability of encountering armed resistance, either from an intended victim or from someone else on the scene in a public place. If those who are asking emotionally, "How can we stop these school shootings?" were serious, they might discover that some of these shootings have in fact been stopped by an armed adult at the school. None of them would have been stopped by the kinds of gun control laws that Congress is currently being stampeded into passing.

Waiting periods? The young murderers in Colorado waited longer than any waiting period ever suggested before carrying out their well-planned orgy of death. "Assault weapons" ban? Such bans would not have applied to the kinds of guns that were used. Nor would the Columbine High School tragedy have been prevented by programs for "troubled youths." The Columbine killers had already been given a clean bill of health by shrinks running such programs. So had the young killers in another school mass shooting. The track record of psycho-babble is miserable, however popular it may be in the media.

Some people support gun control laws simply because they are opposed to guns. We may all agree that the world would be a better place if guns had never been invented. The same could be said for everything from bows and arrows to nuclear weapons.

But there is no way to unring the bell. The only options available to us today involve choices about what to do now, given that all these deadly things exist and cannot be made to disappear, no matter what kinds of words we put on paper.

In a country where there are millions of guns available illegally to criminals, the real question is whether we should allow potential victims to be armed as well. Even people who never carry a gun are less likely to become victims in a community where concealed weapons are widely permitted to law-abiding citizens, because the criminal has no way of knowing who is armed and who isn't.

Statistics on gun accident deaths need to be weighed against statistics on reduced murders where gun ownership is widespread. The latter far more than balance the former—but only if facts matter.

Work Cited

Sowell, Thomas. "Mass Shootings and Mass Hysteria." <u>Jewish World Review</u> 10 June 1999. 15 Sept. 2007 <http://www.jewishworldreview.com/cols/sowell.html/>.

## Two Methods for Analyzing an Essay: Outlining and Summarizing

To help you understand anyone's thesis and supporting evidence—especially someone whose position you disagree with or oppose—you can make an outline or a summary of the person's essay.

### Outline of Sowell's Essay

I. Anti-gun laws promote killing (paragraphs 1–4)

    A. Fifteen deaths in Littleton, Colorado will affect all Americans if gun control is "stampeded" in Congress.

    B. Facts show that gun laws increase shootings deaths.

    C. Research shows that concealed weapons, lawfully owned, reduce gun violence.

II.  Supporting evidence (paragraphs 5–9)

    A.  John Lott's book <u>More Guns, Less Crime</u> "presents overwhelming evidence."

        1.  Mass shootings happen more often in states with restrictive gun laws.

        2.  Mass shootings happen less often when citizens are armed with guns.

        3.  Lott and co-writer Landes should testify before Congress to educate lawmakers and the media.

    B.  Sowell questions three common arguments that favor strong gun control.

        1.  If guns were illegal, this would not stop criminals; guns stop criminals.

        2.  Waiting periods will not stop murderers.

            a.  The two Littleton students waited and planned their act.

            b.  They had received counseling, which did not stop them.

        3.  Some people oppose all guns and therefore support total gun control, but their view is unrealistic.

III.  Concealed weapons reduce murder (paragraphs 10–12)

    A.  We must choose to act now on how to deal with violence.

    B.  Should potential victims be allowed to arm themselves? This is the essential question in the gun control controversy.

    C.  More concealed weapons owned by lawful citizens will reduce violence because criminals will not know who is armed or not.

---

## FEATURES OF OUTLINING

- Outlines should be objective, without showing your own agreement or disagreement with the author.
- Use your own wording as much as possible; use quotation marks whenever you use direct quotes.
- Outlining gives you a skeletal view of an argument: you and other readers can quickly view it.
- Making an outline helps you think more clearly about your own position on an argument.
- An outline helps you understand an essay so you can write about it.

---

## Summary of Sowell's Essay

Writing a summary, like making an outline, is an aid for understanding. It is useful because it enables you to condense an essay into a paragraph. Also, when you write your own essay on a controversial issue, if you can present summaries of other sources opposing your view, you will appear more fair-minded. Here is a summary of Sowell's essay:

> In his essay "Mass Shootings and Mass Hysteria" (10 June 1999), Thomas Sowell argues that gun control fails to protect lawful citizens from criminals who have guns. He cites John Lott's book <u>More Guns, Less Crime</u> as presenting factual evidence that mass shootings don't happen in states with "armed citizens." States where lawful citizens can own concealed weapons have less mass violence because murderers don't know who is armed or not. After fifteen deaths at the high school in Littleton, Colorado, a "mass hysteria" for more gun control swept the nation. But history shows that gun control laws don't work: criminals get guns; waiting periods don't prevent anyone intent on murder; and people who support gun control because they oppose guns in general don't help solve the problem. What matters is whether lawful citizens should have the right to conceal weapons for their own protection. This question is more important than whether Congress should pass more gun control laws.

## FEATURES OF SUMMARIZING

- Summaries, like outlines, should be objective. Condense without showing your own agreement or disagreement with the author. Make no references to yourself. In a summary your own opinion does not matter—later when you analyze and evaluate an argument you can state your opinion and support it.
- Start your summary by referring to the author's name, the title of the source and its date, and by stating what you think is the author's thesis.
- Use present tense in your summary: Sowell argues, not Sowell argued.
- Use your own wording as much as possible; use quotation marks whenever you use direct quotes.
- Follow the organization of the source you summarize: the main reasons and examples the author uses.
- A summary should be a condensed re-creation of the author's thesis and evidence. The length of a well-developed paragraph will usually suffice.
- A summary should show that you are accurate and careful in presenting an author's thesis and evidence.

Outlining and summarizing are extremely useful tools for critical thinking. Condensing an essay into your own words requires analysis (breaking the essay into component parts) and synthesis (reassembling the parts). Whenever you want to understand any author's argument, you can use these tools.

## ACTIVITY 5

In your notebook, write a response to Sowell's essay. Do you agree or disagree with him—or perhaps both?

### Sowell's Writing Situation

Sowell wrote this essay a few weeks after two students at Columbine High School had killed fourteen students and a teacher. This violence generated a wave of support for greater gun control across the nation. This motivated Sowell to argue his belief that tragedy should not prevent us from examining factual evidence: we should not be swayed by our emotions when such tragedies occur. Like many debaters, Sowell believes only logos can lead to truth.

### Sowell's Introduction

Sowell uses the strategy of contrast to catch his reader's attention: "In a world of emotional-outburst TV shows and dumbed-down education, it may not be so surprising that the deaths of 15 people have stampeded Congress toward laws affecting more than a quarter of a billion Americans and their descendants." His tone is clear in this one long sentence introduction: he dislikes the exhibition of emotions on TV and dislikes the watering-down of education. In such a culture it's natural for masses of people to feel more emotional than logical about gun violence.

The word *stampede* works well to express Sowell's opinion that like a stampede the fervor for gun control is out of control. Sowell's one-word metaphor is loaded with suggestions. *Stampede* refers to "1. a sudden, headlong running away of a group of frightened animals, esp. horses or cattle  2. a confused, headlong rush or flight of a large group of people  3. any sudden, impulsive, spontaneous mass movement" (Webster's New World). His word may offend staunch believers of gun control. But Sowell gets to his point immediately while conveying his tone about gun control and about those people who support it. He may risk alienating readers who strongly oppose his view, but he may also persuade other readers who are uncommitted.

### Noticing Sowell's Insights, Assumptions, and Overgeneralizations

Sowell's statement that "facts may carry very little weight politically" is insightful. Facts should carry weight—for politicians and nonpoliticians alike. However, facts are open to interpretation, which creates much of the tension in the gun control issue. Sowell assumes that the gun-control argument has become irrational as the media focus on the emotions of the events and do not examine the facts. He assumes that facts should carry great weight. Would you disagree? Sowell also assumes that gun control is a "stampede"—not any systematic, orderly quest for solving the complex problem of gun violence. His stampede metaphor may be an overgeneralization, but it effectively questions the character of gun-control enthusiasts. Sowell assumes the gun-control movement is "an emotional orgy with rhetorical posturing." Loaded with negative meanings, this phrase may also be considered an overgeneralization. Surely not all advocates of gun control base their arguments on emotion and inflated language. Sowell also assumes gun control is like trying to "unring the bell." Like many who oppose him, Sowell knows the power of metaphor. The bell image invokes a comparison: once a bell is rung, it can't be unrung; likewise, so many guns exist in the hands of so many criminals that this problem can't be undone. But is this comparison valid?

## Responding to Other Arguments

Sowell questions three common arguments that favor strong gun control. (1) If guns were illegal, this would not stop criminals—guns stop criminals. (2) Waiting periods will not stop murderers. (3) Some people oppose all guns and therefore support total gun control, but their view is unrealistic. Sowell chooses to respond to these opposing arguments *after* he presents his supporting evidence. He doesn't first acknowledge other views and then present his view. It's as if Sowell's message is urgent. He is direct, confident in his beliefs and assumptions. Placing the most important information first is a standard journalistic strategy. This has the effect of diminishing the opposing view, especially since Sowell does not concede anything to the opposition. His organization conveys the idea that his is the truthful, logical view, and the opposing view is only "an emotional orgy" which has no truth. However, this strategy also may damage his ethos, making him seem arrogant.

## Sowell's Use of Logos, Pathos, and Ethos

Sowell appeals to logos much more than Mitch Albom does. He criticizes extreme emotion in our culture. What Sowell does in this essay that Albom doesn't do is present authorities as evidence: John Lott and William Landes, both professors at the University of Chicago. Lott wrote a controversial book called <u>More Guns, Less Crime</u> which Sowell adopts as his thesis in his essay: gun control "laws are much more likely to increase shooting deaths than to reduce them." Sowell doesn't cite statistics from Lott's book; rather, he says the book "presents overwhelming evidence." Sowell also offers reasons why the quest for gun control is dangerous for our society.

Sowell further uses logos when he repeats *stampede* three times and the idea that "facts matter" or should matter four times. This repetition serves as an echo, reinforcing Sowell's conviction that facts should matter, and if facts do matter, then readers should follow Sowell's conclusion that more concealed guns will produce less crime.

Sowell's use of logos is his strongest appeal. He cares about the facts of gun control and about the American public not being unduly swayed by the media's blitz of emotional appeals. His arguments are plausible, and his supporting evidence is verifiable. He persuades readers to consider his thesis. While he may offend staunch advocates of gun control with his negative tone toward them, he acknowledges some of their leading arguments as he tries to refute them.

## What Is the Solution?

Clearly, Sowell argues that more gun control is not the solution. According to Sowell, more guns mean less crime. Most people would assume that more guns would mean more crime. But this is not so, claims John Lott and Sowell. Sowell believes lawful citizens should have the right to own and carry concealed weapons because this reduces violent crime.

## Sowell's Conclusion

Sowell uses a hook strategy to return to the contrast he sets up in his introduction between victims of gun violence and the rights of law-abiding citizens: "Statistics on gun accident deaths need to be weighed against statistics on reduced murders where gun ownership is widespread. The latter far more than balance the former—but only if facts matter." This in effect restates his thesis. His essay has led to this conclusion. His last sentence also reinforces his idea that facts should persuade people polarized by the gun-control controversy.

## Albom and Sowell: What Do You Conclude?

Which essay do you find most persuasive: Mitch Albom's "Don't Shoot Holes in Gun Control Bills" or Thomas Sowell's "Mass Shootings and Mass Hysteria"? Perhaps each persuades you somewhat, or each fails to persuade you. Much depends on your own interest, knowledge, and experience with guns.

If you were asked to write an essay supporting a thesis regarding gun control, you could defend or challenge Albom and Sowell. You could look for middle grounds— any ideas that might bridge the extreme positions of being either for or against gun control. You could do research and gather more information on the issue. You could read Lott and Landes's book, More Guns, Less Crime.

## ACTIVITY 6

You have examined two different views on gun control. Here are two more writings on the issue, generated after the Virginia Tech mass shooting: an essay, "Preventing Another Massacre," and an article in Time, "The Gun Lobby's Counterattack." (*Note*: The Time article is more objective and informational than the essay, yet it still contains appeals to logos, pathos, and ethos.) Choose one of these writings and do the following in your notebook. First, write a summary or an outline of it. Then answer the following questions:

1. What is the writing situation and what is the writer's thesis?
2. What strategy does the writer use for the introduction? How well does it work?
3. What insights, assumptions, and overgeneralizations do you notice?
4. How does the writer respond to other or opposing arguments?
5. How does the writer appeal to logos, pathos, and ethos?

6. What is the writer's solution to the problem?
7. What strategy does the writer use for the conclusion? How well does it work?
8. How do you rate the essay or article overall: excellent, okay, weak? Why? ▓

## Preventing Another Massacre

### *Mike Gallagher*

Walking around the campus of Virginia Tech this week, I couldn't shake the feeling that I had been there before. I knew I had never been to Blacksburg, Virginia. So why did I have that unmistakable feeling of familiarity?

Suddenly it hit me. I had been there before. It was 1999. And the place wasn't Blacksburg; it was actually Littleton, Colorado.

This was the "college Columbine."

Like the last time I broadcast my radio show from the scene of a mass killing, the expressions of prayer, grief, anguish and confusion were all demonstrated by the people who lived in this community.

Notable, perhaps, was the absence of total bewilderment over what had happened. I suppose the Columbine massacre was the first in the "instant information" age, so this time around, people sort of knew what to expect, in a morbid kind of way. Hundreds of satellite trucks, the candlelight vigils, the palpable sense of a peaceful little community shattered by ridiculously needless violence.

Tragically, we had all been there before.

Incidentally, I will not say the Virginia Tech killer's name. He was obviously someone who craved notoriety. The media stupidly anointed his videotaped death message a "manifesto" and, thanks to NBC's lack of taste and ethics, force-fed his rambling, evil insanity for hours and hours on end. When I showed up to do my radio show this week, my producer attempted to convince me to play the audio cuts from the horrific video. Sorry, but that just wasn't going to happen. I refused to air one syllable of this vile human being's ramblings.

Did you notice something about the videotape that NBC enthusiastically played over and over again in order to achieve their ratings victory Wednesday night on the Nightly News? The NBC logo, complete with the familiar peacock, was superimposed over the mass murderer's image in the upper left-hand corner so that every single media outlet that played it or printed it on the front page of the newspaper would be sure to give NBC a nice, juicy plug.

How ghastly.

Perhaps NBC could offer the next mass-killer-to-be a free NBC baseball cap or T-shirt that he can wear while videotaping himself killing a bunch of innocent people. That would be a promotional bonanza, too, eh?

I wonder how many Virginia Techs and Columbines are going to have to happen before America wakes up and recognizes that the most effective way to prevent this from happening is right under our noses.

I've heard all the same analysis you have: we need campus lockdowns; let's install air raid sirens; perhaps a couple of armed guards would suffice.

I don't wish to dismiss the well-meaning people who struggle to find a way to make sense of a senseless crime like a madman executing dozens of people. I'm sure their hearts are in the right place.

But I wonder why all these good folks have such a mental block about something as vital as the Bill of Rights?

You see, there is only one way that an evil monster who is intent on killing as many people as he can will be stopped.

He will only stop when he is killed. And the only way to kill him is for an ordinary citizen, someone who is licensed and trained to carry and handle a weapon, to take aim and fire.

It's called the Second Amendment.

Somewhere along the way, we've lost sight of allowing people to have this fundamental right. The very reason people desperately want to protect the right to keep and bear arms is so they can continue to defend and protect themselves—and others.

Can you picture how many lives would have been saved if a faculty member or administrator or even a janitor who is licensed to carry a gun would have been able to take the killer out?

That wasn't going to happen because Virginia Tech is a self-proclaimed, "Gun-free zone." In fact, two years ago, almost two years to the date of this week's killings, a young college student at Virginia Tech was found to have a handgun on campus.

One would have thought he was hiding a nuclear bomb.

Despite having every legal right to carry, and therefore not facing any criminal charges, Virginia Tech nonetheless disciplined him. In fact, the same school spokesman who had to preside over the grim press conferences this week in Blacksburg was the man who told reporters, "We don't feel that the campus is an environment where people should be able to carry guns."

As Dr. Phil would ask, "How's that working for you?"

I was on a panel this week on Fox News Channel which included one of the other guests suggesting that this is "not the time to debate gun control or having guns on campus, this is a time to talk about campus security." I wondered aloud why he didn't understand that having legal guns on campus is precisely the way to improve campus security.

No siren or e-mail campaign or lockdown is going to stop a mass murderer. Just like Columbine, not a single police officer was able to engage this week's killer. He only ended when he was ready to end it. Everything was on his terms.

Let's bring it back to our terms again. Let's embrace the U.S. Constitution, not ignore it. Let's fight evil with might and force.

We have to shoot back.

*Mike Gallagher is a nationally syndicated radio host, Fox News Channel contributor, and author of* Surrounded by Idiots: Fighting Liberal Lunacy in America.

Work Cited

Gallagher, Mike. "Preventing Another Massacre." Townhall.com 20 Apr. 2007. 26 June 2007 <http://www.townhall.com/columnists/MikeGallagher/2007/04/20/preventing_another_massacre>.

# The Gun Lobby's Counterattack

### *Hillary Hylton*

Only two days after a 23-year-old student at Virginia Tech carried out the deadliest mass shooting in U.S. history, the perennial heated debate over gun control has already begun. While gun control advocates have been quick to decry the dangers of lax regulations in Virginia and the rest of the nation, their Second Amendment opponents are already going on a counteroffensive; rather than simply defend their constitutionally protected right to bear arms, many are already treating the campus massacre as a call to arms.

If history is any guide, no one should be surprised at the counteroffensive, which is sure to focus on broadening concealed weapons laws that allow Americans to carry guns beyond their homes or cars. That is precisely what happened in Texas 15 years ago after an unemployed merchant seaman crashed his truck into a Killeen cafeteria, took out his gun and killed 23 in what until Monday was the deadliest mass shooting in American history.

Carrying the banner in 1991 for gun owners' rights was Suzanna Gratia Hupp, a chiropractor, mother and horse rancher who was eating lunch with her parents when the gunman crashed his truck through the cafeteria's windows. The family barricaded themselves behind a table, but as the slaughter went on, Hupp's father said he had to do something and he charged toward the man. Her father was shot in the chest, and as he lay dying, his wife of 47 years crawled towards him to cradle his head. The gunman then shot and killed her.

During the mayhem, Hupp had reached into her purse for her .38 Smith & Wesson, but realized she had left it in her car, afraid that carrying a concealed weapon in public—then against the law in Texas—might endanger her chiropractic license. Having watched helplessly as her parents were killed, Hupp lobbied relentlessly for a 1996 concealed weapons law, now one of 48 such state statutes on the books across the U.S.

Hupp went on to serve as a state representative for 10 years, but she now lays some of the blame for the Virginia killings at the feet of politicians. "I am saddened and sickened, my heart hurts for those people—I've been there," Hupp said. "But at the same time I am angry—even with the sadness—because this was largely preventable on the scale that it happened. The politicians haven't figured it out. They have created gun-free zones, and all of the dreadful things that have happened were in these gun-free zones."

Virginia, like Texas and other states with concealed weapons laws, prohibits gun owners with concealed weapons permits from taking their guns into certain public places—usually bars and restaurants where alcohol is sold, courthouses, schools and campuses; 38 states currently ban weapons on school campuses, and 16 on college campuses. By making some places off-limits, Hupp said, the government is preventing Americans from protecting themselves and their families and has "taken on the responsibility and liability that goes with it."

In fact, in January 2006 the Virginia General Assembly rejected a bill that would have allowed students with concealed weapons permits to carry their guns on campus.

The bill was pushed by the Virginia Citizens Defense League after a Virginia Tech student with a concealed weapons permit was disciplined in 2005 for bringing a gun on campus. The bill, opposed by Virginia police chiefs and the university itself, never made it out of committee. "I'm sure the university community is appreciative of the General Assembly's actions because this will help parents, students, faculty and visitors feel safe on our campus," Virginia Tech spokesman Larry Hinckner told <u>The Roanoke Times</u>.

Hinckner's words are now echoing around the Web, highlighted on gun rights websites and in e-mails, including one Texas State Senator Glenn Hegar received Tuesday morning. Hegar, a Houston-area Republican, is the author of a bill that would allow Texans with concealed weapons permits to leave their guns in their cars at work—something many employers now forbid. The bill is moving through the state legislature and, despite the opposition of the influential Texas Association of Business, may pass thanks to support from another major player, the powerful National Rifle Association (NRA). "There are two types of people who carry guns— those who believe in following the law and those who don't," Hegar said. His bill would give workers with long commute times or late-night hours the protection they want, Hegar said.

Gun control advocates are concerned about the bill. "This is not about personal freedom—getting shot in the workplace by someone who has retrieved a gun from the parking lot is the opposite of freedom," said Paul Helmke, president of the Brady Campaign. "This is about preserving the ability of companies to make workplaces as safe as they can be, and free from gun violence."

The Hegar bill is just one arrow in the NRA's quiver in a national campaign that has focused on state legislatures in recent years. The powerful lobby group has found fertile ground in state capitols where rural and conservative legislators often come from both parties. University of Utah officials just lost their battle with the state's legislature over the geographic scope of its concealed carry law—they had sought to ban weapons on campuses, but the state supreme court said they had to comply with the state law, effectively blocking them from banning permitted guns. By contrast, in Kansas, Gov. Kathleen Sibelius just this week vetoed a law that sought to override local authorities who could put restrictions on carrying concealed weapons at local parks and other public venues.

The gun rights lobby, which has so far refused to comment on the Virginia Tech massacre or its fallout, has been particularly successful in pressing for so-called "castle doctrine" laws, which allow homeowners to shoot intruders, in many cases as long as they simply believe they are in danger of being attacked. Sixteen states have adopted the "castle doctrine," and eight more have it under consideration. The Texas Legislature overwhelmingly adopted the new law last month, which not only allows a homeowner to defend his or her home, but also their vehicle and their workplace.

NRA CEO Wayne LaPierre laid out the group's mission in a message to members last week as they got ready to gather for their annual convention. "When we gather in St. Louis, we're pushing back. We're pushing for Castle Doctrine laws across the country. We're pushing for legislation that ensures the gun confiscations in New Orleans will never be repeated in this country. We're pushing to protect our rights to protect ourselves, even against anti-gun employers who want to leave you defenseless to and from work," LaPierre wrote in the message. "When we gather in St. Louis, we're pushing to protect and promote our freedoms, and we won't stop pushing until we've won."

Both sides of the gun debate expressed their sorrow over the Virginia Tech killings, but when the political debate begins anew proponents of gun ownership feel they will have the momentum. "I think it's a little early," Hupp said, "but my guess is the public has had enough and will demand changes."

*Hillary Hylton is a freelance writer whose work covers business, social issues, politics, and travel.*

Work Cited

Hylton, Hillary. "The Gun Lobby's Counterattack." <u>Time</u> 18 Apr. 2007. 26 June 2007
    <http:// www.time.com/time/nation/article/0,8599,1611939,00.html>.

As you have seen, the gun control controversy is complex—and it matters. Let's close this discussion with an editorial from the <u>New York Times</u>. An editorial has no author identified; rather, it represents the opinion of the publisher and newspaper.

## Guns and More Guns
*Editorial, <u>The New York Times</u>*

By now, the logic is almost automatic. A shooter takes innocent lives, and someone says that if the victims had been armed, this wouldn't have happened. The only solution to a gun in the wrong hands, it seems, is a gun in the hands of everyone.

That's the state of the debate over gun control today. The National Rifle Association and the gun lobby have silenced every legislature in this country. Instead of stricter laws, tighter controls and better background checks, the gun lobby proposes more guns. And what the gun lobby proposes, lawmakers deliver.

Seung-Hui Cho bought his guns illegally, though with the appearance of legality. He slipped through a loophole, through a disconnect between the way Virginia defines a disqualifying mental incapacity and the way the federal government does. After the fact, the loophole is self-evident, and it's tempting to believe that now political leaders will work harder to keep people who are dangers to themselves from becoming dangers to others by buying guns. But the laws are as fragile and imperfect as they are because that is how the gun lobby wants them—and it is paying good money to keep them that way.

Those gun advocates who believe that the Second Amendment confers the right to carry a gun in public are quick to point out that they are law-abiding, decent citizens trying to protect themselves and their families in a world gone mad. But, of course, the guns can't tell the difference. Arming more people would be a recipe for disaster.

True safety lies in the civility of society, in laws that publicly protect all of our rights and in having law-enforcement officers who are trained in the use of deadly force, then authorized to apply it in rationally defined situations. It is the gun lobby's incessant efforts to weaken the gun laws that makes a tragedy like the one at Virginia Tech possible.

Work Cited

"Guns and More Guns." Editorial. <u>New York Times</u> 26 Apr. 2007, late ed.: A24.

## ACTIVITY 7

In your notebook, write a response to the editorial. Given what you have read already in this chapter on gun control, do you agree or disagree with it—or perhaps both? ▆▆

## KINDS OF EVIDENCE FOR ARGUING: EXAMPLES, REASONS, AUTHORITIES, STATISTICS

Whenever you try to support your position on a controversial issue—indeed, on any issue—you need convincing evidence. The following section will help you determine whether evidence is credible and persuasive.

### Using Examples

The example is the most basic kind of evidence. It clarifies the reality behind any idea. You need specific examples and details to show what you mean. Examples—when well chosen and clearly explained—help readers pay attention and understand. They make you seem reasonable, credible, and trustworthy.

Most examples come from real life, based on fact or on what a writer has experienced, witnessed, read or heard.

---

**General:** "My roommates and I survived on fast food."

**Specific:** "In my freshman year, my roommates and I survived on Chinese takeout, express pizzas and taco take-home dinners." (Amy Wu)

**General:** "Teachers should not always think in twos."

**Specific:** "We can make special efforts not to think in twos. Mary Catherine Bateson, an anthropologist at Virginia's George Mason University, makes a point of having her class compare three cultures, not two. Then, students are more likely to think about each on its own terms, rather than as opposites." (Deborah Tannen)

---

Note the difference here: specific examples and details show meaning so readers can see and understand it.

Examples can also be *hypothetical*; that is, they can be imagined in order to suggest or demonstrate an idea. Lee Silver, a biologist at Princeton University, uses hypothetical examples in his book <u>Remaking Eden</u>, which examines the scientific world of reproductive technologies.

> Sometime in the not so different future, you may visit the maternity ward at a major university hospital to see the newborn child or grandchild of a close friend. The new mother, let's call her Barbara, seems very much at peace with the world, sitting in a chair quietly nursing her baby, Max. Her labor was—in the parlance of her doctor—"uneventful," and

she is looking forward to raising her first child. You decide to make pleasant conversation by asking Barbara whether she knew in advance that her baby was going to be a boy. In your mind, it seems like a perfectly reasonable question since doctors have long given prospective parents the option of learning the sex of their child-to-be many months before the predicted date of birth. But Barbara seems taken back by the question. "Of course I knew that Max would be a boy," she tells you. "My husband Dan and I chose him from the embryos we made. And when I'm ready to go through this again, I'll choose a girl to be my second child. An older son and a younger daughter—a perfect family."

Hypothetical examples are useful when an argument concerns future matters, things that have not yet happened but likely could or will.

## Illustration

An illustration is an extended example. You see this in news stories on TV: a reporter focuses on one woman's struggle with cancer and her battle with a health insurance company that refuses to pay for her treatments. If it represents a widespread problem, one in-depth illustration can be more persuasive than brief examples of several people.

What follows is an illustration from the book <u>Flow: The Psychology of Optimal Experience</u> by Mihaly Csikszentmihalyi (pronounced "cheeks sent me high"). Notice how the author uses an extended example to support his topic sentence.

> Some things we are initially forced to do against our will turn out in the course of time to be intrinsically rewarding. A friend of mine, with whom I worked in an office many years ago, had a great gift. Whenever the work got to be particularly boring, he would look up with a glazed look in his half-closed eyes, and he would start to hum a piece of music—a Bach chorale, a Mozart concerto, a Beethoven symphony. But humming is a pitifully inadequate description of what he did. He reproduced the entire piece, imitating with his voice the principal instruments involved in the particular passage: now he wailed like a violin, now he crooned like a bassoon, now he blared like a baroque trumpet. We in the office listened entranced, and resumed work refreshed. What is curious is the way my friend had developed this gift. Since the age of three, he had been taken by his father to concerts of classical music. He remembers having been unspeakably bored, and occasionally falling asleep in the seat, to be awakened by a sharp slap. He grew to hate concerts, classical music, and presumably his father—but year after year he was forced to repeat this painful experience. Then one evening, when he was about seven years old, during the overture to a Mozart opera, he had what he described as an ecstatic insight: he suddenly discerned the melodic structure of the piece, and had an overwhelming sense of a new world opening up before him. It was the three years of painful listening that had prepared him for this epiphany, years during which his musical skills had developed, however unconsciously, and made it possible for him to understand the challenge Mozart had built into the music.

Csikszentmihalyi's illustration shows what he means: although his friend hated music as a boy, in turn he came to love it. Flow is an important concept. You have likely experienced it yourself when your attention is fully engaged by doing some activity you enjoy so much that time seems to disappear and you feel "in the zone."

Well-chosen examples and illustrations are your basic building blocks as a writer. Although they will clarify and energize your writing, they do not necessarily prove an idea—rather, they show and support an idea. Persuasive examples will help readers understand what you mean and appreciate your ability to be clear and interesting. Examples and ethos go together.

## ACTIVITY 8

Using an illustration to show what you mean, write about a time when you experienced flow. Bring this to class to share.  ■■■

## Using Reasons

Reasons are statements that support or explain an opinion. They give coherence to arguments. Without reasons, arguments would have no power: they would be examples and details with no idea to unify or justify them.

Why did you choose the college or university you are attending? To answer this, you would give reasons such as these: (1) *Because* I like State's program in health fitness; I hope to get a job as a physical therapist. (2) *Because* the fitness program has small classes with more hands-on learning than lectures. (3) *Because* the teachers in the program are experts who are not boring. Notice that each of these reasons could be a topic sentence for a paragraph, which you could support with specific examples and details.

To answer questions, you naturally give reasons, which you then explain further with examples and details. Reasons answer the question "why?"

> **Tannen:**
>
> "The argument culture shapes who we are." [Why?] "[Because] it makes us distort facts. . . . It makes us waste valuable time. . . . It limits our thinking. . . . It encourages us to lie."
>
> **Albom:**
>
> "I thought there could be no worse horror, to enter an innocent situation and be looking down the barrel of a gun. Now I realize I was wrong." [Why?] "[Because] the worst horror is to look down the barrel just before it fires."

Reasons go with examples and details to help writers communicate and persuade. Without solid reasons, readers will question your logos as well as ethos. When you present sound reasons, readers find you credible.

## Using Authorities

When you argue, you can use authorities to support your claims. An authority is an expert in a given field who is respected, reliable, and trustworthy. Statements by authorities carry weight and can be persuasive.

Deborah Tannen uses authorities in her article. She cites Deborah Lipstadt, a professor from Emory University, who examined how "deniers" of the Holocaust gain media exposure by presenting themselves as "the other side." Thomas Sowell cites John Lott and his book <u>More Guns, Less Crime</u> for supporting evidence. He also cites a colleague of Lott's, Professor William Landes. Sowell doesn't supply much information about Lott and Landes. But mentioning the University of Chicago, one of the most highly respected universities in the world, lends credence to his claim. The University of Chicago also published Lott's book. Sowell believes that Lott is a credible authority.

As a critical thinker you can cite authorities to support or to challenge opinions. If you write an essay arguing that juveniles who commit murder should receive capital punishment, you can try to find experts with informed opinions to support your position. If you want to show your readers that you are fair-minded and consider various sides of an issue, you can cite experts who disagree with you. Authorities often disagree. Both sides at the infamous O. J. Simpson trial used authorities who claimed they had reliable scientific evidence; both sets of experts tried to persuade the jury with opposing testimony.

Arguing from authority is appropriate when a person is an expert in the field you are discussing; however, part of your job as a critical thinker is to determine whether a person truly is an authority. Consider the scientist Linus Pauling who won two Nobel prizes—for chemistry and for world peace. Although he was a well-respected authority in chemistry, he was not as well respected in medicine and nutrition. Many scientists found Pauling controversial, even crazy, for promoting vitamin C. He argued that people should take 2,000 to 18,000 milligrams per day of vitamin C instead of 60 mg per day as recommended by the National Academy of Sciences. He consumed the maximum dose himself, the equivalent of 240 oranges a day. He lived to be 93 and believed his intake of vitamin C contributed greatly to his longevity.

## GUIDELINES FOR USING AUTHORITIES

1. What are the person's credentials? What achievements make the person well-known? Is the person affiliated with well-respected universities or other organizations? What do other experts say about the person?

2. Is the person an expert in the area you are writing about? If not, using that person as an authority will reflect poorly on your own judgment.

3. Is the testimony from the person relevant? Does the reference or quote you use truly contribute to your argument? If you're using it for padding, to show that you've done "research," then you're jeopardizing your own ethos.

4. Is the authority biased? If you claim that studies show the herb Saint-John's-wort alleviates depression, your claim will have more credibility if the research was done by the Harvard School of Medicine instead of the Saint-John's-wort Institute. (Note that an authority can be an organization.)

5. Try not to overuse authority. If you cite too many experts, your argument may seem like a compilation of their opinions rather than a synthesis of your own understanding.

## ACTIVITY 9

Find at least two authorities who hold different positions on a controversial issue that intrigues you. In your notebook, explain what makes each of them an authority. ▆

## Using Statistics

Statistics are numerical facts. That Linus Pauling took the equivalent of 240 oranges a day is a single statistic—showing his deep conviction in vitamin C's power. As a fact it is objective and verifiable: so much vitamin C equals so many oranges. Statistics are often persuasive; they express information clearly and concisely. Numbers have power. However, because statistics can be easily manipulated to fool readers, critical thinkers need to judge whether the numbers have been used appropriately.

When you find useful statistics to support your argument, you will usually see them expressed by some authority. Jonathan Kozol, an authority on education and literacy, uses many statistics in his book Illiterate America, published in 1985:

> Twenty-five million American adults cannot read the poison warnings on a can of pesticide, a letter from their child's teacher, or the front page of a daily paper. An additional 35 million read only at a level which is less than equal to the full survival needs of our society.
>
> Together, these 60 million people represent more than one third of the entire adult population.
>
> The largest number of illiterate adults are white, native-born Americans. In proportion to population, however, the figures are higher for blacks and Hispanics than for whites. Sixteen percent of white adults, 44 percent of blacks, and 56 percent of Hispanic citizens are functional or marginal illiterates. Figures for the younger generation of black adults are increasing. Forty-seven percent of all black seventeen-year-olds are functionally illiterate.

What is the effect of these statistics? They illuminate the problem, which is why Kozol uses them. He wants to arouse concern in readers. Notice how Kozol carefully classifies illiterate adults. He qualifies his data with "in proportion to population," explaining how more blacks and Hispanic adults are illiterate compared to white adults. Statistics as such appeal to logos and pathos. Kozol's fair-minded use of statistics reinforces his ethos as well.

Statistics rarely stand alone. They usually require someone—not always an expert—to interpret them, to draw inferences from them. In a review of the book The Slave Trade: The Story of the Atlantic Slave Trade: 1440–1870 by Hugh Thomas, Baltimore Sun columnist Gregory Kane cites statistics to catch the attention of readers and to provoke thought about the book:

> Some 11.3 million Africans were transported to the New World during the years 1440–1870. Some 4 million went to Brazil, 2.5 million to countries ruled by Spain, 2 million to the British West Indies and 1.6 million to the French West Indies. Only 500,000 went to the country that eventually became known as the United States of America.

> . . . The figure of 500,000 of Africa's children making it to the United States is especially revealing. For too long egocentric Americans—black and white—have obsessed about the sordid history of slavery as if the scourge were ours alone. . . . But the numbers speak for themselves. Just under 4 percent of the blacks taken from Africa ended up in the United States. So in the guilt department, there are clearly countries that should have much more than the United States.

Although Kane writes that "the numbers speak for themselves," he interprets them. He infers from the facts that Americans should feel less guilt about slavery because compared to other parts of the world we received fewer slaves. You must decide for yourself whether his inference makes sound sense.

Notice how Kane's diction conveys his attitude about the statistics he uses: "Only 500,000" and "just under 4 percent." His use of *only* and *just under* suggests that Kane diminishes the seriousness of the numbers. Although statistics are objective facts, writers usually attach their opinions to them. To infer writers' opinions of the numbers they use, pay attention to words that introduce statistics.

Statistics may be misleading. Most people believe what they hear and read, but as a critical thinker you must learn to question statistics. Numbers often sound believable until you analyze them. What if 50% of young women playing high school football in the United States quit during the last 5 years? This number sounds large, but if only 20 women played football this means that 10 quit but 10 played. These numbers more accurately reflect the truth, while 50% sounds larger—more inflated and dramatic. When you see a percentage such as 50%, you should ask, "Fifty percent of how many?"

As you should question the credentials and bias of an authority, you should also question the source of their statistics. When Wonder Bread claims it builds strong bodies in 12 ways, is this claim based on their own research or on research performed by impartial scientific organizations?

Many advertisers now include online addresses so readers can investigate their claims and statistics in more depth. Consider the nutrition bar Balance—"Tastes too good to be good for you." In an ad Balance uses these statistics: "Based on the clinically proven 40-30-30 nutrition concept (40% of calories from carbohydrates, 30% from protein and 30% from dietary fat), Balance bars provide all the essential nutrients to keep you going for the day." At the bottom of the ad Balance invites readers to inquire for more information about their 40-30-30 formula at <http://www.balance.com>.

Finding statistics usually requires research in a library or online. In his essay "Bigger, But Not Better" in Chapter 1, Ryan Grady Sample reports the following:

> In 1994, it was estimated that the cumulative 30-year value of the fishery, if lake trout were absent, was more than a billion dollars. The estimated value depreciates $640 million if the lake trout remain.

Notice, however, that Sample does not specify who or what organization "estimated" these values. Is it the Yellowstone Park Service? Some federal environmental group? If Sample were writing this essay for a college class, his teacher would probably require that he cite sources for these statistics. Still, Sample presents himself as a credible and knowledgeable person. Because of his ethos, you may surmise that his information is accurate.

## Guidelines for Using Statistics

1. Are the statistics reliable? Do they come from credible, trustworthy sources? Or are they biased, misleading?
2. Are the statistics clear and relevant? If you use too many numbers, readers may soon feel overloaded. To condense statistics, you can present them in tables or charts.
3. Consider your audience. If your statistics are too technical, you will lose not only your readers but your point. Technical statistics are fine if your audience has the knowledge to understand them.

## ACTIVITY 10

Find some statistics concerning a controversial issue that intrigues you. Consider browsing through these federal online sources, Census Bureau (http://www.census.gov/) or Fedstats (http://www.fedstats.gov/). You might look for a chart or table of statistics that interests you. Then in a brief report explain how these statistics are useful or not useful in understanding the controversy. Cite your sources at the end of the paper. (See Chapter 9, "Documentation," for help on citing sources.)  ▬

## Writing an Essay about a Local Issue

Deborah Tannen writes, "There are times when it is necessary and right . . . to argue for your rights or against offensive or dangerous ideas or actions."

## ACTIVITY 11

Do you feel any need "to argue for your rights or against offensive or dangerous ideas or actions"? If so, write about it. You must care about the issue: it must matter to you. If you write about a campus issue, consider submitting your essay to your school newspaper. If you write about an issue concerning your town or state, consider submitting your essay to a local or state newspaper. Strive to use strong examples, reasons, authorities, and statistics. *Note:* Before you write your essay, read the pages on "Organizing an Essay about a Controversy" later in this chapter.  ▬

## Writing a Report to Explore an Argument

Writing a report to explore—analyze and evaluate—an argument enables you to apply fully the critical thinking, reading, and writing skills presented in this chapter.

## ACTIVITY 12

Choose one of the following "Five Essays on Controversial Issues for a Report" and explore it by following the guidelines below. Or you may choose one of the case study readings (further in this chapter) on cheating and success, the drinking age, or same-sex marriage. ▮

## Guidelines for a Report Exploring an Argument

After you decide which selection to write about, read it again more carefully: consider photocopying and annotating it. Use these reading tools: ask questions, and notice insights, assumptions, and overgeneralizations. In a report, first summarize the essay in a paragraph (see Features of Summarizing earlier in this chapter) and then "report" on what you find. For your report please address these questions:

1. What is the writing situation and what is the writer's thesis?
2. What strategy does the writer use for the introduction? How well does it work?
3. What insights, assumptions, and overgeneralizations do you notice?
4. How does the writer respond to other or opposing arguments?
5. How does the writer appeal to logos, pathos, and ethos? Also, what kinds of evidence does the writer use: examples, illustrations, reasons, authorities, statistics? How well are they used?
6. What is the writer's solution to the problem?
7. What strategy does the writer use for the conclusion? How well does it work?
8. How do you rate the essay overall: excellent, okay, weak? Why?

**Notes:**

- Use present tense when you write about an essay. For example, write "Parker argues" rather than "Parker argued."
- Within your report you should quote directly from your selection to demonstrate your points.
- (For information on how to quote, see "Quotation Marks: How to Quote from Sources" in the Handbook toward the end of this book.)
- Your report should be 2 to 4 pages long. Consider your audience to be your class members and your instructor.
- At the end of your report, provide a Work Cited entry to document your source. A citation that you can use (copy) is provided at the end of each reading selection. The Work Cited need not be on a separate page; space down four spaces from the bottom of your report and put the citation there.
- For models of a report, review the discussions of Albom's essay and Sowell's essay in this chapter.

## FIVE ESSAYS ON CONTROVERSIAL ISSUES FOR A REPORT

## Mothers in Combat

### Children Last

#### *Kathleen Parker*

In a world of uncertainty and mayhem, the single constant about which we thought we could be reasonably confident has been that mothers would nurture their children.

We have been disabused of that quaint notion in myriad ways, but nowhere so vividly as in today's military. As a spate of recent news stories reveals, the Pentagon has become complicit in helping thousands of mothers abandon and potentially make orphans of their children.

Since 2002, about 16,000 single mothers have served in Afghanistan and Iraq. What kind of country sends mothers of young children, especially single mothers, to war?

We pretend to nobler notions, of course. Single parents aren't supposed to be accepted for enlistment. But there are ways around inconvenient rules. Single parents can sign up as long as they're willing to sign away their children.

That is, they can enlist if they give up custody to someone else.

Stories about mothers leaving their children for war—in which fathers are almost never mentioned—are both heartbreaking and pathetic. Heartbreaking because the children suffer immensely; pathetic because women have been sold a bill of goods.

A recent <u>Washington Post</u> story featured Sgt. Leana Nishimura, a single mom who left her three children for Iraq. Although she returned eight months ago, her oldest—a 9-year-old boy—still suffers separation anxiety and fears from her deployment. When Nishimura's name was called at a recent ceremony to accept an award for service, the boy clung to her leg and cried.

Said Nishimura: "He went from having one parent to having no parents, basically. People have said, 'Thank you so much for your sacrifice.' But it's the children who have had more of a sacrifice."

Indeed.

Not only do children suffer feelings of abandonment, the consequences of which can be long-term and life-altering, but they live with the daily terror of someone killing their mother. We even have a name for the phenomenon—pediatric postwar syndrome.

While children suffer, some military mothers can't offer much help. Women returning from Iraq are reporting post-traumatic stress disorder in numbers comparable to men, according to the Veterans Administration. One of the reasons cited by analysts is that women are being exposed to combat as never before.

Another recent story—this one in <u>The Hartford</u> (Conn.) <u>Courant</u>—told of Daiana Rivera, whose 16-month-old baby boy has to compete for attention with the demons that followed his mother home from Iraq. Rivera is seeing a therapist weekly, but says she'll never recover the time lost with her son as she deals with treatment and detachment.

In a sane world, mothers do not abandon their children and governments understand that the most important line of defense in the struggle for civilization is the family. Thus, it is urgent that we ask why our government is participating in child abandonment and putting mothers at unnecessary risk.

Women volunteer on their own accord, certainly. But many never anticipated being placed in combat situations, which increasingly has been the case in Iraq. By assigning support personnel to or near combat units, the Pentagon effectively has placed women where, by law and sense, they don't belong.

Otherwise, feminism has succeeded in shaping and presenting the military as just another career option. Young "women" barely out of high school—or single mothers looking to support their families—are vigorously recruited with promises of money, travel and benefits. The military has become "a particular Mecca for single parents," as feminist author Linda Bird Francke put it.

More to the point, the military has become the final frontier for radical feminists, for whom equality won't be complete until the chairman of the Joint Chiefs of Staff has breasts. Putting women into combat is the Maginot Line of the gender wars, which, once crossed, shatters the military's glass ceiling to the highest promotion levels.

In the distorted logic of feminist gender theorists, getting women killed in combat is viewed as "proof" that they're suitable for combat—a sign of progress rather than a tragedy of political idiocy.

But what these trends really prove is that we've lost sight of what matters, not to mention what we fight for. Children need mothers more than wars do, and nations need healthy, well-adjusted children.

If we're willing to sacrifice mothers and abandon the next generation, what sort of civilization, exactly, are we trying to preserve?

*Kathleen Parker is a syndicated columnist with the Washington Post Writers Group. Her column appears in more than 300 papers nationwide. She is also director of the School of Written Expression at the Buckley School of Public Speaking and Persuasion in Camden, South Carolina.*

Work Cited

Parker, Kathleen. "Children Last." <u>Townhall.com</u> 15 Dec. 2006. 26 June 2007 <http://www.townhall.com/columnists/KathleenParker/2006/12/15/children_last>.

## Questions/Topics for Further Thought

1. Do you agree or disagree with Parker—or both? Should women—especially mothers—in the military not see combat duty?

2. Do some research to find two sources that present other views to Parker's argument. Summarize them; then explain whether you agree or disagree with them. Supply Works Cited for them. Add this as an appendix to your report.

# Video Games and Violence

## Video Game Violence and Our Sons

### *Rebecca Hagelin*

"Life is like a video game. Everyone has to die sometime."

If you spent part of your youth playing "Pac-Man" and "Space Invaders," such a statement must seem bizarre. Video games were . . . well, games—innocent diversions that did nothing worse than eat up dotted lines and too much of our allowances. A waste of time? Perhaps. But nobody got hurt.

At least, they didn't used to.

The opening statement above was spoken by Devin Moore, a teenager who murdered three people—two police officers and a 911 dispatcher—in a Fayettesville, Ala., police station in 2003. Arrested on suspicion of car theft, Moore was brought in for booking and ended up on a bloody rampage.

He lunged at Officer Arnold Strickland, grabbed his gun and shot him twice. Officer James Crump, who responded to the sound of the gunfire, was shot three times. And before he ran outside with police car keys he snatched, Moore put five bullets in Dispatcher Ace Mealer. Was this the first time Moore had committed such a heinous crime? Yes and no.

Moore was a huge fan of a notorious video game called Grand Theft Auto. As the title suggests, the goal is to steal cars. If that's all there was to the "game" it would be bad enough, but it gets worse: the way to acquire and hold on to the cars is to kill the police officers who try to stop you. And the sick minds behind the game give you plenty of choices—shooting them with a rifle, cutting them up with a chainsaw, setting them on fire, decapitation.

If you shoot an officer, you get extra points for shooting him in the head. It's no surprise, then, that all of Moore's real-life victims had their heads blown off.

According to court records, Moore spent hundreds of hours playing Grand Theft, which has been described as "a murder simulator."

But this time, his victims weren't a collection of animated pixels on a TV screen. They were flesh-and-blood human beings whose lives were snuffed out in seconds. They had families who continue to mourn their loss—such as Steve Strickland, Officer Strickland's brother. Tomorrow, he will testify before the U.S. Senate Judiciary Committee's Subcommittee on the Constitution, Civil Rights and Property. Chaired by Sen. Sam Brownback, R-Kan., the purpose of the hearing is to examine the constitutionality of state laws regulating the sale of ultra-violent video games to children. Three psychologists will testify about the potential link between playing violent video games and copycat violence, and whether the games contribute to aggressive behavior.

With the ever-expanding use of technology by our children, such hearings are critical. We must determine if Moore and other murderers like him are anomalies or if ultra-violent video games dangerously warp the psyches of our youth. Those tempted to scoff at the connection between video games and behavior should bear a couple of things in mind. First, video games are not passive or spectator media. While playing the game, teenage boys and young men, the largest users of video games, actually become the characters who cut up their victims with chainsaws, set them on fire, or chop off their heads.

According to Dr. Elizabeth Carll of the American Psychological Association (who also will testify tomorrow), this active participation enhances the "learning" experience. And video games are often played repeatedly for hours on end—so, hour after hour, teens playing games such as Grand Theft Auto "learn" how to kill police officers and earn points for their barbarianism.

The second fact to keep in mind is that teenagers' brains are still developing and are extremely impressionable. The parents of teens hardly need reminding that for all their joys, teens often lack judgment, critical thinking skills and foresight.

Some are better than others, yes, but many (like Moore) are startlingly deficient. In short: Put a "murder simulator" in their hands, and you just might be asking for trouble. But don't put words in my mouth—I am not saying that every kid that plays a violent video game will become a criminal.

And as a staunch conservative who believes that "the government that governs least governs best," I'm not advocating a plethora of laws that may have a chilling effect on free speech. I do, however, recognize that it is sometimes necessary to provide special protections for minors from harmful materials—take pornography and alcohol, for example. As a mother, I also believe that our nation must examine how the products of our toxic culture affect the civility and safety of our children and of our society. We owe it to the students who died at Columbine; we owe it to Devin Moore's victims; we owe it to our own children.

*Ethos*

But armed with the truth, and a God-given mandate to train our own children, we must never depend on government to take care of our kids or raise them. Parents must wake up to the fact that our nation's boys are being used and manipulated by an industry making billions of dollars by warping their minds. As I outline in my book, Home Invasion: Protecting Your Family in a Culture That's Gone Stark Raving Mad, it doesn't take an act of Congress to take back your home—it takes active, loving, informed parenting. It takes setting boundaries and sticking with them. It takes understanding our kids, and understanding that our kids need us to guide them. Senator Brownback is taking a bold step and doing his job as an elected official in exploring the effects of video game violence—it's up to parents to use the information to protect our sons and our society.

*Rebecca Hagelin's weekly column, "Heart Beat," appears on WorldNetDaily and Townhall.com. She explores social and cultural issues through the eyes of a mother. She is also a vice president of the Heritage Foundation, whose vision is to"Create an America where freedom, opportunity, prosperity and civil society flourish."*

Work Cited

Hagelin, Rebecca. "Video Game Violence and Our Sons." Townhall.com 28 Mar. 2006. 7 July 2007 <http://www.townhall.com/columnists/RebeccaHagelin/2006/03/28/video_game_violence_and_our_sons>.

**Questions/Topics for Further Thought:**

1. Do you agree or disagree (or both) with Rebecca Hagelin that video games promote real violence in boys and young men? Why?

2. Do some research to find two sources that present other views to Hagelin's argument. Summarize them; then explain whether you agree or disagree with them. Supply Works Cited for them. Add this as an appendix to your report.

# Global Climate Change

## No Change in Political Climate

*Ellen Goodman*

On the day that the latest report on global warming was released, I went out and bought a light bulb. OK, an environmentally friendly, compact fluorescent light bulb.

No, I do not think that if everyone lit just one little compact fluorescent light bulb, what a bright world this would be. Even the Prius in our driveway doesn't do a whole lot to reduce my carbon footprint, which is roughly the size of the Yeti lurking in the (melting) Himalayas.

But it was either buying a light bulb or pulling the covers over my head. And it was too early in the day to reach for that kind of comforter.

By every measure, the UN's Intergovernmental Panel on Climate Change raises the level of alarm. The fact of global warming is "unequivocal." The certainty of the human role is now somewhere over 90 percent. Which is about as certain as scientists ever get.

I would like to say we're at a point where global warming is impossible to deny. Let's just say that global warming deniers are now on a par with Holocaust deniers, though one denies the past and the other denies the present and future.

But light bulbs aside—I now have three and counting—I don't expect that this report will set off some vast political uprising. The sorry fact is that the rising world thermometer hasn't translated into political climate change in America.

The folks at the Pew Research Center clocking public attitudes show that global warming remains 20th on the annual list of 23 policy priorities. Below terrorism, of course, but also below tax cuts, crime, morality, and illegal immigration.

One reason is that while poles are melting and polar bears are swimming between ice floes, American politics has remained polarized. There are astonishing gaps between Republican science and Democratic science. Try these numbers: Only 23 percent of college-educated Republicans believe the warming is due to humans, while 75 percent of college-educated Democrats believe it.

This great divide comes from the science-be-damned-and-debunked attitude of the Bush administration and its favorite media outlets. The day of the report, Big Oil Senator James Inhofe of Oklahoma actually described it as "a shining example of the corruption of science for political gain." Speaking of corruption of science, the American Enterprise Institute, which has gotten $1.6 million over the years from Exxon Mobil, offered $10,000 last summer to scientists who would counter the IPCC report.

But there are psychological as well as political reasons why global warming remains in the cool basement of priorities. It may be, paradoxically, that framing this issue in catastrophic terms ends up paralyzing instead of motivating us. Remember the <u>Time</u> magazine cover story: "Be Worried. Be Very Worried." The essential environmental narrative is a hair-raising consciousness-raising: This is your Earth. This is your Earth on carbon emissions.

This works for some. But a lot of social science research tells us something else. As Ross Gelbspan, author of <u>The Heat Is On</u>, says, "when people are confronted with an overwhelming threat and don't see a solution, it makes them feel impotent. So they shrug it off or go into deliberate denial."

Michael Shellenberger, co-author of <u>The Death of Environmentalism</u>, adds, "The dominant narrative of global warming has been that we're responsible and have to make changes or we're all going to die. It's tailor-made to ensure inaction."

So how many scientists does it take to change a light bulb?

American University's Matthew Nisbet is among those who see the importance of expanding the story beyond scientists. He is charting the reframing of climate change into a moral and religious issue—*see the greening of the evangelicals*—and into a corruption-of-science issue—*see big oil*—and an economic issue—*see the newer, greener technologies*.

In addition, maybe we can turn denial into planning. "If the weatherman says there's a 75 percent chance of rain, you take your umbrella," Shellenberger tells groups. Even people who clutched denial as their last, best hope can prepare, he says, for the next Katrina. Global warming preparation is both his antidote for helplessness and goad to collective action.

The report is grim stuff. Whatever we do today, we face long-range global problems with a short-term local attention span. We're no happier looking at this global thermostat than we are looking at the nuclear doomsday clock.

Can we change from debating global warming to preparing? Can we define the issue in ways that turn denial into action? In America what matters now isn't environmental science, but political science.

We are still waiting for the time when an election hinges on a candidate's plans for a changing climate. That's when the light bulb goes on.

*Ellen Goodman is a columnist for the <u>Boston Globe</u>; her columns appear in more than 375 newspapers. In 1980, she was awarded the Pulitzer Prize for Distinguished Commentary.*

Work Cited

Goodman, Ellen. "No Change in Political Climate." <u>Boston Globe</u> 9 Feb. 2007: A19.

## Questions/Topics for Further Thought

1. Do you agree or disagree (or both) with Goodman's statement "Let's just say that global warming deniers are now on a par with Holocaust deniers, though one denies the past and the other denies the present and future"? Why?
2. Do some research to find two sources that present other views on climate change. Summarize them; then explain whether you agree or disagree with them. Supply Works Cited for them. Add this as an appendix to your report.

# Health Care for All Children

## The Divide in Caring for Our Kids

### *Bob Herbert*

A few weeks ago, Teri Hatcher, one of the stars of the television series <u>Desperate Housewives</u>, was on David Letterman's show, talking very animatedly about a time when her daughter needed emergency dental care.

"It was causing her some pain," Ms. Hatcher said. "And then, of course, it was a Friday night. Overnight the whole thing blew up and it turned out to be an abscess."

Where to get a dentist on a Saturday?

Luckily, Ms. Hatcher's best friend is married to a dentist who was more than happy to open up his office that Saturday. But he needed an assistant. Ms. Hatcher volunteered.

She digressed: "I hate the dentist. Just my whole life, you know. It's the worst. I would do anything to get out of going to the dentist. Really. Anything."

But Ms. Hatcher stood there like a trouper as the dentist examined her daughter's tooth. "He sees it is an abscess, and he has to do surgery," she said. "So you, I'm trying to—I hate it. I'm squeamish. I'm going to throw up, and then I'm trying to pull it together . . .

"So he does the Novocaine and gives her a little of the gas. She is perfectly fine, because she's going, 'I love the dentist. I want to come here every day.' And then, of course, I'm thinking, 'Can I take a tank of that home? Because that is really what I need.' "

And so on. The story, of course, had a happy ending. Ms. Hatcher's daughter was fine. Mr. Letterman got to tell a raunchy dentist joke. The audience was amused, and Ms. Hatcher eventually exited to a robust round of applause.

I was particularly interested in the segment because just a few hours earlier I had filed a column for the next day's paper about health care for children. The column included the story of Deamonte Driver, a homeless 12-year-old from Prince George's County, Md., who also had an abscessed tooth.

Now, if I had been in Ms. Hatcher's position, I would have done exactly as she did. I would have knocked down doors if necessary to get help for a child in distress. So this is no criticism of her. It's an illustration of the kind of stunning differences in fortune that can face youngsters living at opposite ends of America's vast economic divide.

Deamonte needed his tooth pulled, a procedure that was estimated to cost $80. But his mother, Alyce Driver, had no health insurance for her children. She believes their Medicaid coverage lapsed early this year because of a bureaucratic foul-up, perhaps because paperwork was mailed to a homeless shelter after they had left. In any event, it would have been difficult for Ms. Driver to find an oral surgeon willing to treat a Medicaid patient.

Untreated, the pain in Deamonte's tooth grew worse. He was taken to a hospital emergency room, where he was given medication for pain and sinusitis and sent home.

What started as a toothache now became a nightmare. Bacteria from the abscess had spread to Deamonte's brain. The child was in agony, and on Feb. 25 he died.

There's a presidential election under way, but this sort of thing is not a big part of the campaign. American children are dying because of a lack of access to health care, and we're worried about Mitt Romney's religion and asking candidates to raise their hands to show whether they believe in evolution. I'm starting to believe in time travel because there's no doubt this nation is moving backward.

"There can be no keener revelation of a society's soul," Nelson Mandela once said, "than the way in which it treats its children."

There are nine million children who lack health care in the U.S. and millions more who are eligible for coverage but fall through the cracks for one reason or another.

What we need is a national commitment to provide basic health care to all children, not just the children of the well-to-do. This should be a no-brainer. You're a child in the United States? You've got health care. We're not going to let you die from a toothache. We're better than that. We're not going to let your family go bankrupt because you've got cancer or some other disease, or because you've been in a terrible accident.

The cost? Don't fall for that bogyman.

There's plenty of give in America's glittering $13 trillion economy. What's the sense of being the richest nation on the planet if you can't even afford to keep your children healthy and alive?

*Bob Herbert joined* The New York Times *as an op-ed columnist in 1993. He often writes about politics, urban affairs, and social trends. He has taught journalism at Brooklyn College and the Columbia University Graduate School of Journalism.*

Work Cited

Herbert, Bob. "The Divide in Caring for Our Kids." New York Times 12 June 2007, late ed.: A23.

## Questions/Topics for Further Thought

1. Do you agree or disagree (or both) with Herbert's argument that all children should receive "basic health care"? Why?
2. Do some research to find two sources that present other views on universal health care for children in our country. Summarize them; then explain whether you agree or disagree with them. Supply Works Cited for them. Add this as an appendix to your report.

# Capital Punishment

## Expedience No Reason to Kill a Man

### Leonard Pitts Jr.

You don't know what it's like, and neither do I. But we can imagine.

I've always thought it must feel like being buried alive. Lungs starving, lying in blackness, pounding on the coffin lid with dirt showering down, no one hearing your cries.

Or maybe it's like locked-in syndrome, a condition where you lose muscle control—can't move a finger, turn your head, speak. Your body entombs you. You scream within, but no one hears.

Something like that, I think. Something where you're trapped, claustrophobic, unable to believe what is happening, unable to make anyone hear you. That's how it must feel to be an innocent person on Death Row as execution day draws close.

Tuesday was Troy Anthony Davis's scheduled execution day, though I have no idea if he is an innocent person. I do know that he was convicted of the 1989 killing of a police officer, Mark Allen MacPhail, in Savannah, Ga. And I know that he was on the scene, a Burger King parking lot, that fateful night.

But I also know that Davis has always his maintained his innocence. And that no physical evidence—no gun, no fingerprint, no DNA—ever tied him to the crime. And that he was convicted on the testimony of nine key witnesses. And that seven of them have now recanted. They lied, they say. They were scared, they were bullied and threatened, and they said what the cops wanted to hear. Of the two witnesses who have not recanted, one is a fellow named Sylvester "Red" Coles; some witnesses claim he's the one who actually shot MacPhail when the officer tried to break up a parking lot altercation.

Monday, one day before Davis was scheduled to die, the state parole board issued a 90-day stay of execution.

You and I have no idea how that must feel, either, but we can imagine. The buried man gets a sip of air. The paralyzed man moves his toe.

And then back down into the coffin, back down into the tomb of your own skin, back in line to die.

Surely Davis's lawyers have explained to him the 1996 federal law, signed by President Clinton, that is throwing roadblocks in his way. Designed to streamline capital cases, it prohibits the introduction of exculpatory evidence once the state appeals process is done. But just as surely Davis, if he is innocent, must wonder how he could have presented evidence he didn't yet have. And he must wonder, too, how there can be a time limit on truth—especially when a human life is at stake. How can you execute a man when there remain serious questions about his guilt?

That's barbarism, not justice.

What's fascinating is that, though 67 percent of those polled by Gallup pollsters approve of capital punishment in murder cases (and 51 percent say it's not imposed often enough), 64 percent admit it does not deter murder and 63 percent believe an innocent person has probably been executed since 2001.

In other words, the system doesn't work, we *know* it doesn't work, yet we want it to continue—and indeed, expand. What kind of madness is that? It's an intellectual disconnect, a refusal to follow logic to its logical end.

It is, of course, easier to countenance that madness, ignore that refusal, when the issue is abstract, when Death Row is distant, theoretical and does not involve you.

But what must it feel like when it is not abstract, when it is *you* sitting there in the cell watching the calendar move inexorably toward the day the state will kill you for something you absolutely did not do? Is there a suspension of belief? Do you tell yourself that surely people will come to their senses any minute now? Does the air close on you like a coffin lid? Does darkness sit on your chest like a weight?

You and I can only imagine. Some men have no need to try.

*Miami Herald* columnist Leonard Pitts Jr. won the Pulitzer Prize for distinguished commentary in 2004. His 1999 book *Becoming Dad: Black Men and the Journey to Fatherhood* was a bestseller. After the attacks on 11 September 2001, Pitts wrote an impassioned essay headlined "We'll Go Forward from This Moment" that was widely circulated and frequently quoted in the press.

Work Cited

Pitts Jr., Leonard. "Expedience No Reason to Kill a Man." MiamiHerald.Com 18 July 2007. 24 July 2007 <http://www.miamiherald.com/285/story/173895.html>.

### Questions/Topics for Further Thought:

1. Do you agree or disagree (or both) with Pitts's argument? Why?
2. Do some research to find two sources that present other views on capital punishment. Summarize them; then explain whether you agree or disagree with them. Supply Works Cited for them. Add this as an appendix to your report.

## WRITING AN ESSAY WITH SOURCES ABOUT A CONTROVERSY

Writing an essay with sources is similar to writing an opinion essay, as you did in Chapter 1. However, writing an essay with sources requires that you pay close attention to academic style, carefully use direct quotes, and cite page numbers.

## ACTIVITY 13

Write an essay about one of the three case study issues presented in Readings on Controversial Issues forthcoming in this chapter: cheating for success, the drinking age, or same-sex marriage. Or you may choose one of the previous essays in the section on writing a report to explore an argument—however, you must do research and find at least two additional sources. Print those sources and cite documentation for them. The following section gives you advice on how to write an essay with sources about a controversy.

## GUIDELINES FOR WRITING AN ESSAY ABOUT A CONTROVERSY

1. Browse through the readings. Then choose a set of readings that matters to you. Take a stand on the issue—explain whether you are for or against it or whether you take another perspective on it.

2. Examine the set of readings again, more carefully. Select at least three selections you want to use as sources. Either outline or summarize each selection. Use the reading tools presented in this chapter: ask questions, and notice insights, assumptions, and overgeneralizations.

3. Within your paper you should use direct quotes and discuss them. Quote from at least three of the selections. (For information on how to quote, see "Quotation Marks: How to Quote from Sources" in the Handbook toward the end of this book.)

4. Your essay should be 3 to 5 pages long. Consider your audience to be your class members and your instructor.

5. At the end of your paper, make a Works Cited page in which you document the sources you use. (Citations are provided that you can use (copy) at the end of the reading selections.) For your Works Cited page, you will need to put your sources in alphabetical order. For more information on doing Works Cited, see Chapter 9, "Documentation."

**Notes:**

1. Writing this essay is more demanding and complex than writing a report. Pay close attention while you read the following pages on "Organizing an Essay about a Controversy."

2. Use present tense when you write about sources. Use "Allen argues" rather than "Allen argued."

3. Review the previous section on "Kinds of Evidence for Arguing: Examples, Reasons, Authorities, Statistics." This information will help you defend your own position as well as help you analyze and evaluate the evidence other writers use.

## Organizing an Essay about a Controversy

### Present the Other Side First

Most students believe they should present their own side of an argument first, and that the opposing side should come last if at all. But that organization offers little help in establishing a climate in which people can reason together to reconcile their differences. Rather, it seems to say that "my side" is the truth, and your side is inferior. Imagine saying this in a face-to-face confrontation. It would not lead to cooperation, much less reasoning together.

A primary rule of persuasion is to avoid stirring up negative reactions during the discussion. You must not start with assumptions about an opponent's intelligence. You must not send any signal that you think you are superior or that the opponent is inferior. It is important that your readers believe you respect them. At the end of an argument, if you've succeeded, enlightened readers will say, "You're right—I never saw it that way."

To present yourself as fair and unbiased, you must convince others that you understand their side of the argument. Remember that, in fact, it is often impossible to persuade others. The real audience for your discussion, in that case, is the uncommitted, those who haven't made up their minds about the issue. For their sake, you must appear reasonable. Ask yourself, whose mind do you have any chance to reach? Whom can you possibly encourage to see matters as you do?

## Rogerian Argument

Writing an essay about a controversy often takes one of two main forms:

| **Form A** | **Form B** |
| --- | --- |
| Introduction and thesis statement | Introduction and thesis statement |
| Present other view(s) | Present your supporting evidence |
| Present your supporting evidence | Present other view(s) |
| Conclusion and restatement of thesis | Conclusion and restatement of thesis |

Mitch Albom follows Form A; Thomas Sowell follows Form B. Form B involves more risks because the writer, like Sowell, can give the impression that *his* argument is most important. The form reinforces Sowell's tone of harshly judging the arguments of gun-control advocates.

Carl Rogers, a well-known psychologist, developed a method of argumentation that he believed helped his patients communicate in nonthreatening ways. He argues that his method helps opposing groups create bridges of understanding.

The Rogerian method of argument follows Form A in which writers always present an opposing side before presenting their own. The reason for doing this is to reduce the sense of threat an audience might feel. If you show others you understand their position and if you point out what is valid in their reasoning, then you will reduce the level of threat they feel. If you present an opposing view as well as the opponents themselves would present it, they will in turn try to show that they understand your position. The audience will perceive that you are being fair and reasonable and will expect your opponent to do the same. After fully acknowledging each other's positions, you both are more likely to reach some bridge of understanding.

Rogers believes that people have a natural tendency to judge each other—to approve or disapprove what other people say and do. This continual judging threatens most people when they engage in discussions or arguments. Rogers claims that when emotions run high—as with any controversial issue—the tendency to judge others intensifies. To help people avoid this common problem, Rogers advocates "real communication" in which people "listen with understanding" and try to see and feel an idea "from the other person's point of view." For Rogers, communication should involve "understanding *with* a person, not *about*" that person.

Rogers invites readers to do an experiment based on listening to others:

> The chances are very great indeed that your listening has not been of the type I have described. Fortunately I can suggest a little laboratory experiment which you can try to test the quality of your understanding. The next time you get into an argument with your wife, or your friend, or with a small group of friends, just stop the discussion for a moment and, for an experiment, institute this rule. "Each person can speak up for himself only *after* he has first restated the ideas and feelings of the previous speaker accurately, and to that speaker's satisfaction." You see what this would mean. It would simply mean that before presenting your own point of view, it would be necessary for you to really achieve the other speaker's frame of reference—to understand his thoughts and feelings so well that you could summarize them for him. Sounds simple, doesn't it? But if you try it you will discover it one of the most difficult things you have ever tried to do.

If you can listen with understanding to arguments different from yours, and if others can listen with understanding to your argument, then together you may reach a level of cooperation. Such "mutual communication tends to be pointed toward solving a problem rather than toward attacking a person or group."

## ACTIVITY 14

Try Carl Rogers's experiment. Afterwards, in your notebook describe what happened— if the experiment was easy or difficult. Also, when you attend classes, try to notice what happens when people argue. See whether people acknowledge or summarize the position of the person who spoke before them. Take notes on what you observe and bring them to class.

The Rogerian method of argument offers a sensible formula that you can use when you write argument papers or when you argue with someone or some group in person. Again, although most students are eager to present their own arguments first, it is usually wiser to present other arguments first.

Yet, of course, this ideal method of argument is not always used. Michael Moore's documentary <u>Sicko</u> on the health care crisis in our country received much praise from critics, yet many pointed out that Moore does not offer other views different from his own. He does not present arguments or authorities from the health care industry to challenge his own arguments. Some critics accuse Moore of thus being unfair. Other critics argue that Moore doesn't need to present other views—his purpose is to raise questions and a call of alarm: what can we do to give good, basic health care to all citizens of the United States?

## Ending Your Essay

Inexperienced writers tend to use up all their material in the body of their paper and then have nothing left for the end of the paper. The end of the paper, however, should

## ADVANTAGES OF PRESENTING OTHER ARGUMENTS FIRST

1. You cause others who hold different views to pay closer attention to your view.
2. You establish yourself as fair. Your audience can see (hear) that you are not diminishing or distorting anyone's arguments. Your goal is to show the audience how well informed you are about the other side's arguments.
3. You create the grounds for reasoning together by conceding whatever must be conceded. You lose nothing by making concessions, and you imply to others that they should do the same for you. (The audience will see whether they are fair.)
4. The other side will feel the necessity to extend to you the same courtesy (the audience will see whether the other side, too, is courteous). Thus you start off with a positive ethos, instead of trying to "defeat" your "opponent."

be the *point* of the paper. Here you can briefly explain the arguments and points of agreement on both sides. It's good advice to save something significant for the end. Otherwise the end seems unimportant. Both Ryan Grady Sample (in Chapter 1) and Mitch Albom save something for the end. Sample gives two brief examples of environmental problems other readers are probably facing now: "It might be zebra mussels, it might be a coal-mining project . . . ." Albom describes his own close call with a gun. The reason some papers seem not to have any real conclusion is often that the writer has used up the conclusion in the preceding parts of the paper. It is partly a matter of structure.

There is no absolute standard or routine way to write an argument paper (or shouldn't be), but the Form A pattern described earlier is useful for college writers. Instructors of various disciplines know it well:

## GUIDELINES FOR ORGANIZING AN ESSAY ABOUT A CONTROVERSY

1. Present introduction and your thesis statement.
2. Present other view(s): acknowledge briefly, summarize, or present fully and fairly.
3. Present your own supporting evidence: provide examples, reasons, authorities, statistics and direct quotes from sources.
4. Present the conclusion and restatement of your thesis.

When students use this form, instructors can follow an essay's structure easily and concentrate on the meaning expressed and persuasive appeals used: logos, pathos, and ethos.

## ACTIVITY 15

When you have a rough draft of your essay, examine your use of evidence. Evaluate your use of examples: are they specific, important, true? Evaluate your use of reasons: are they clear, sound, logical? Evaluate your use of authorities and statistics. Do you use them carefully? If you don't use any, would your essay be more persuasive if you did? ▮▮▮

Here is a student essay with sources about a controversy. Megan LaPine wrote about affirmative action, a case study in the second edition of <u>Discovering Arguments</u>. Although the text of the sources she uses is not provided, her essay serves as a model to help you write your own essay. As you read, ask yourself whether she follows the advice in this chapter.

Megan LaPine
Professor Chen
English 101
20 October 2007

Equality Created by Inequality

One day a young boy was playing a game of basketball with his father. Knowing there was no way the son could beat him on his own, the father missed all his shots on purpose and turned over the ball many times. Toward the end the father put him on his shoulders so the son could dunk the ball—the winning basket. The father let his son win. But as the son grew older the father stopped letting him win, he stopped holding back, and he stopped treating him like a child. Affirmative action is set up in a way that treats adults like children: it tries to create equality through inequality by giving minorities priority over whites.

Many people believe that affirmative action is good and noble. They argue it is fair and "levels the playing field so people of color and all women have the chance to compete in education and in business" (NOW 125). They say the percentage of white male doctors, business owners, and corporate leaders is too high. "Nearly 27% of the population is black or Hispanic, but few of these minorities are in the upper ranks of most fields" (Bacon 131). They claim that affirmative action gives everyone a fair chance at these positions so dominated by whites. They also argue that with affirmative action, college campuses and the work place are more diverse, thereby creating a better environment for all.

However, in attempting to create diversity, colleges promote racism. Imagine a graduate school looking at two applications; both applicants earned the same GPA and MCAT scores. You would assume they would both be accepted. But they are not. The applicant who checked African-American is accepted over the applicant who checked Caucasian. Colleges can only accept so many students into their graduate programs and when posed with a tie the minority wins. With affirmative action, people are accepted or declined on the pure basis of race.

Colleges demean minorities through affirmative action. This policy insults the minorities by telling them they cannot do it on their own: they are not capable of performing up to par, so the bar is lowered for them. Not all minority members appreciate being treated like this. Shelby Steele, an African American author who was subjected to segregated schools growing up, states in the interview "Shelby Steele: The Content of His Character," "It makes me into someone who cannot move forward unless white people are benevolent and help me move forward. It perpetuates dependency" (123).

Accepting a student to college is not promising him a pot of gold after graduation. Just because someone is accepted does not mean she is ready or able to face the tasks that lie ahead. In "Affirmative Action Doctors Can Kill You," Linda Chavez points out that colleges across the country are accepting "Black and Hispanic students . . . with substantially lower college grades and test scores than whites or Asians" (129). This may raise the percentage of minorities enrolled in college and graduate school, but what happens after school? The GPA earned throughout college, the score on the MCAT or other graduate tests are like glass balls: they foresee how the student will perform in the future. Chavez also indicates that many of the less-qualified students accepted because of race "can't pass their licensing exams" (129). Who then benefits from affirmative action? Few people. Many are not prepared enough to pass their licensing exams, and many are prepared who are not given a chance.

Affirmative action is supposed to be a temporary solution to move our nation towards equality between all races and genders, a way to create more diversified campuses and work places. However, affirmative action creates more *inequality*. Just as you cannot fight fire with fire, you cannot fight inequality with inequality. Affirmative action tries to abolish discrimination by imposing more discrimination. Instead, we should create school systems that are of equal quality from the start for all students. Everyone should be given the same benefits and privileges. Then with time a greater diversity will develop on campuses and in work places. This diversity will occur through equality: everyone being treated the same from the start, and no group receiving higher or lower standards than another group.

Works Cited

Bacon, Perry, Jr. "How Much Diversity Do You Want From Me?" <u>Time</u> 7 July 2003: 108.

Chavez, Linda. "Affirmative Action Doctors Can Kill You." <u>Jewish World Review</u> 21 June 2001. 15 Oct. 2007 <http://www.jewishworldreview.com/cols/chavez.archives.asp>.

National Organization for Women. "Talking about Affirmative Action." 9 Apr. 2002. 15 Oct. 2007 <http://www.now.org/issues/affirm/talking.html>.

Steele, Shelby. "The Content of His Character." <u>Hoover Digest Selections</u> 1996 No. 2. 15 Oct. 2007 <http://www.hoover.stanford.edu/publications/selections/1962/steele.html>.

Notice how Megan uses an analogy in her introduction as a way to both engage readers and to introduce her topic of affirmative action. She ends her introduction with a clear thesis statement. In her second paragraph she presents other arguments on affirmative action in a fair-minded way. Then she defends her thesis by presenting her own arguments and examples, including quotes from her sources. Notice that she doesn't quote too much from the sources she uses: the paper is her own analysis and synthesis of this controversy. She uses sources to help inform her paper. She is careful to cite her quotes accurately and to cite page numbers for them from the readings in the book. In her conclusion Megan restates her thesis and argues that creating equal schools is the best way to achieve the goals of affirmative action. She ends her paper with a Works Cited, listing her sources in alphabetical order. Megan follows the assignment well.

## READINGS ON CONTROVERSIAL ISSUES: THREE CASE STUDIES

## DRINKING AGE

### The Teen Drinking Dilemma

Some parents let their kids use alcohol at home. A most spirited debate.

*Barbara Kantrowitz and Anne Underwood*

In 2002, Elisa Kelly made what she thought was a smart parenting decision. Her son Ryan asked her to buy beer and wine for his 16th-birthday party at the family's Virginia home, promising that no one would leave until morning. Kelly agreed, and to further guard against drunken driving, she collected guests' car keys. But neighbors called police, who arrested Kelly and her ex-husband, George Robinson, for what one official told The Washington Post was the worst case of underage drinking he'd seen in years. Kelly maintained that she was just trying to control drinking that would have gone on whether or not she had bought alcohol for the kids. Both got time in jail; Kelly began her 27-month sentence on June 11.

This graduation season, parents around the country will face a similar dilemma. Should they allow teens to drink under their supervision, or should they follow the law—knowing that their kids are likely to imbibe anyway? Many parents believe teens should learn about drinking at home. Cynthia Garcia Coll, professor of education, psychology and pediatrics at Brown University, grew up in Puerto Rico, where, she says, kids drink at family parties. "Instead, in this country, we go from saying 'No, you can't do it'," and then all at once, we say 'Yes, you can' without really giving them any guidance. It's not like age 21 is a magic time when people become responsible drinkers."

The same reasoning prompted New Yorker Sam Hedrick to offer his three daughters drinks at home. "My youngest is going to be 21 this week," Hedrick says. "She and her friends have had alcohol here with meals." His daughter Lizzie, a student at Bowdoin, agrees with her father. "If your parents are so against alcohol from the start

*"Now, kids, don't look until you're twenty-one."*

**FIGURE 2.3**   Get Serious Cartoon about drinking.
Source: ©2006 Carol Simpson Productions.

when you're younger, you're never exposed and it just becomes this enigmatic, forbidden thing," she says. "I can understand why it seems cool."

But most researchers who study teen substance abuse say that for every family like the Hedricks, there are many more where allowing alcohol causes problems. "The data is quite clear about teen drinking and it has nothing to do with being puritanical," says William Damon, director of the Stanford University Center on Adolescence. "The earlier a kid starts drinking, the more likely they are to have problems with alcohol in their life." The antidrinking message is especially critical in families with a history of alcoholism, which greatly increases the risk.

Even if they don't become alcoholics, teens who drink too much may suffer impaired memory and other learning problems, says Aaron White of Duke University Medical Center, who studies adolescent alcohol use. He says parents should think twice about offering alcohol to teens because their brains are still developing and are more susceptible to damage than adult brains. "If you're going to do that, I suggest you teach them to roll joints, too," he says, "because the science is clear that alcohol is more dangerous than marijuana."

Girls should be particularly careful, says Dr. Mark Willenbring of the National Institute on Alcohol Abuse and Alcoholism. Women generally weigh less than men and have proportionately more fat and less lean body mass. Because blood circulates primarily to lean body mass, the alcohol is distributed to a smaller volume of tissue, which results in higher blood alcohol levels. "We're absolutely seeing more women competing in drinking games," he says. "That's a terribly dangerous thing to do," in part because they become more vulnerable to sexual assault.

It's also widely believed that youngsters in countries with a lower legal age learn to drink responsibly and moderately. There is one problem with that impression: it is not true. "The highest rate of cirrhosis of the liver is in France," where it's legal to drink at 16, says Chuck Hurley, chief executive officer of Mothers Against Drunk Driving. According to a study by the U.S. Department of Justice, fewer American adolescents drink than teens in most other industrialized countries.

Instead of offering teens a beer, parents should present their children with clear rules and expectations. Research shows that involved parents are less likely to raise kids with drinking problems. Give them strategies for avoiding trouble, like telling them to call home for a ride rather than getting into a car with someone who has been drinking. Most important, be a good role model. "Parenting is not supposed to be a popularity contest," says Richard Lerner of the Institute for Applied Research in Youth Development at Tufts University. "If the parent is not modeling honest, safe behavior, it's unlikely the kid will believe that he's supposed to act responsibly. You don't want to be like Tony Soprano, who seemed surprised that his son, A.J., was not a model citizen." Someday, your kids will thank you.

*Barbara Kantrowitz has been an editor and writer at* Newsweek *since 1985. Anne Underwood, a reporter for* Newsweek, *often writes about health issues.*

Work Cited

Kantrowitz, Barbara, and Anne Underwood. "The Teen Drinking Dilemma." Newsweek 25 June 2007: 37.

## There's No Benefit to Lowering the Drinking Age

### *Robert Voas*

After nearly four decades of exacting research on how to save lives and reduce injuries by preventing drinking and driving, there is a revanchist attempt afoot to roll back one of the most successful laws in generations: the minimum legal drinking age of 21.

This is extremely frustrating. While public health researchers must produce painstaking evidence that's subjected to critical scholarly review, lower-drinking-age advocates seem to dash off remarks based on glib conjecture and self-selected facts.

It's startling that anybody—given the enormous bodies of research and data— would consider lowering the drinking age. And yet, legislation is currently pending in New Hampshire and Wisconsin to lower the drinking age for military personnel and for all residents in Vermont. Just as bad are the arguments from think-tank writers, various advocates, and even academics (including at least one former college president) that ignore or manipulate the real evidence and instead rely on slogans.

I keep hearing the same refrains: "If you're old enough to go to war, you should be old enough to drink," or "the drinking-age law just increases the desire for the forbidden fruit," or "lower crash rates are due to tougher enforcement, not the 21 law," or "Europeans let their kids drink, so they learn how to be more responsible," or finally, "I did it when I was a kid, and I'm OK."

First, I'm not sure what going to war and being allowed to drink have in common. The military takes in youngsters particularly because they are not yet fully developed and can be molded into soldiers. The 21 law is predicated on the fact that drinking is more dangerous for youth because they're still developing mentally and physically, and they lack experience and are more likely to take risks. Ask platoon leaders and unit commanders, and they'll tell you that the last thing they want is young soldiers drinking.

As for the forbidden fruit argument, the opposite is true. Research shows that back when some states still had a minimum drinking age of 18, youths in those states who were under 21 drank more and continued to drink more as adults in their early 20s. In states where the drinking age was 21, teenagers drank less and continue to drink less through their early 20s.

And the minimum 21 law, by itself, has most certainly resulted in fewer accidents, because the decline occurred even when there was little enforcement and tougher penalties had not yet been enacted. According to the National Highway Traffic Safety Administration, the 21 law has saved 23,733 lives since states began raising drinking ages in 1975.

Do European countries really have fewer youth drinking problems? No, that's a myth. Compared to American youth, binge drinking rates among young people are higher in every European country except Turkey. Intoxication rates are higher in most countries; in Britain, Denmark, and Ireland they're more than twice the US level. Intoxication and binge drinking are directly linked to higher levels of alcohol-related problems, such as drinking and driving.

But, you drank when you were a kid, and you're OK. Thank goodness, because many kids aren't OK. An average of 11 American teens die each day from alcohol-related crashes. Underage drinking leads to increased teen pregnancy, violent crime, sexual assault, and huge costs to our communities. Among college students, it leads to 1,700 deaths, 500,000 injuries, 600,000 physical assaults, and 70,000 sexual assaults each year.

Recently, New Zealand lowered its drinking age, which gave researchers a good opportunity to study the impact. The result was predictable: The rate of alcohol-related crashes among young people rose significantly compared to older drivers.

I've been studying drinking and driving for nearly 40 years and have been involved in public health and behavioral health for 53 years. Believe me when I say that lowering the drinking age would be very dangerous; it would benefit no one except those who profit from alcohol sales.

If bars and liquor stores can freely provide alcohol to teenagers, parents will be out of the loop when it comes to their children's decisions about drinking. Age 21 laws are designed to keep such decisions within the family where they belong. Our society, particularly our children and grandchildren, will be immeasurably better off if we not only leave the minimum drinking age law as it is, but enforce it better, too.

*Robert Voas is a senior research scientist at the Pacific Institute for Research and Evaluation. He is also on the National Board of Advisors for Mothers Against Drunk Driving.*

Work Cited

Voas, Robert. "There's No Benefit to Lowering the Drinking Age." <u>The Christian Science Monitor</u>
12 Jan. 2007. 6 July 2007 <http://www.csmonitor.com/2006/0112/p09s01-coop.html>.

## The Case Against 21

Lower the drinking age.

### *John J. Miller*

In the first four years of Operation Iraqi Freedom, 563 Americans under the age of 21 were killed in the line of duty. These citizen soldiers were old enough to vote, old enough to put on military uniforms, and old enough to die for their country: They were old enough to do just about anything, except drink a red-white-and-blue can of Budweiser.

Apparently they weren't grown-up enough to enjoy that privilege.

That's because when it comes to alcohol, the United States is more like Indonesia, Mongolia, and Palau than the rest of the world: It is one of just four countries that requires people to be at least 21 years old to buy booze. The only countries with stiffer laws are Islamic ones.

Many public-health advocates regard this latter-day prohibition as a great triumph. Mothers Against Drunk Driving says on its website that setting the legal drinking age at 21, rather than 18, has saved "more than 21,000 lives" from alcohol-related traffic fatalities.

It certainly sounds like a success story. But is it really so simple?

The former president of Middlebury College says that the picture is in fact far more complicated.

"It's just not true," says John M. McCardell Jr. of MADD's assertion. "I'm not going to claim that legal-age 21 has saved no lives at all, but it's just one factor among many and it's not anywhere near the most important factor."

McCardell is the head of Choose Responsibility, a new nonprofit group that calls for lowering the drinking age. He is also the primary author of a draft report on the 21-year-old drinking age.

Three years ago, after stepping down as the head of Middlebury, McCardell penned an op-ed for the <u>New York Times</u> called "What Your College President Didn't Tell You." He criticized tenure and argued that low student-faculty ratios are overrated. He also said that the 21-year-old drinking age "is bad social policy and terrible law."

This last idea sparked the interest of the Robertson Foundation, which encouraged McCardell to write the 224-page paper that Choose Responsibility is now circulating among academics and other interested parties. Although McCardell describes the paper as a "work in progress," it is in fact a devastating critique of the 21-year-old drinking age. (National Review Online obtained a copy; many of its most significant points may be found on the Choose Responsibility website.)

What annoys McCardell most is the recurring claim that the raised drinking age has saved more than 21,000 lives. "That's talking point #1 for modern temperance organizations, but they can't point to any data that show a cause and effect," he says.

As his report reveals, alcohol-related driving fatalities have fallen sharply since 1982, when a presidential commission on drunk driving urged states to raise their drinking ages to 21. That year, there were 1.64 deaths per 100 million vehicle miles of travel; in 2001, there were 0.63 deaths. That's a drop of 62 percent.

This is an important achievement. Yet the drinking age probably played only a small role. The dramatic increase in seat-belt use almost certainly accounts for most of the improvement. The National Highway Transportation Safety Administration says that the proper use of seatbelts reduces the odds of death for front-seat passengers involved in a car crashes by 45 percent. In 1984, when President Reagan linked federal highway funds to the 21-year drinking age, about 14 percent of motorists used seatbelts. By 2004, this figure had shot up to 80 percent. Also during this period, life-saving air bags became a standard feature on cars.

What's more, alcohol-related fatalities were beginning to decline before the movement for a raised drinking age got off the ground, thanks to a cultural shift. "As a society, we've become a lot more aware of the problem of drunk driving," says McCardell. "When I was in school, nobody used the term 'designated driver.'" Demographic forces helped out, too: In the 1980s, following the Baby Boom, the population of young people actually shrank. Fewer young drivers means fewer high-risk drivers, and so even if attitudes about seat belts and drunk driving hadn't changed, there almost certainly would have been a reduction in traffic deaths anyway.

McCardell suggests that one effect of raising the drinking age was not to prevent deaths but merely to delay them. "The most common age for drinking-related deaths is now 21, followed by 22 and 23," he says. "It seems that the minimum drinking age is as likely to have postponed fatalities as to have reduced them."

There's even a case to be made that the higher drinking age has had negative consequences. It encourages disrespect for the law. It usurps the role of parents in teaching their children about the proper use of alcohol, especially in the many states where it's illegal for them even to let their 18-year-old children have a glass of wine at a Thanksgiving dinner.

"There used to be an intergenerational social intercourse that's now completely gone—the law obliterated it," says McCardell. "If you expect adult behavior, you're more likely to get it than if you infantilize people." Is it a coincidence that one of the most commonly cited campus problems is binge drinking?

Despite this, the mythology about the drinking age persists in popular culture and in politics. Three years ago, when Pete Coors ran for the Senate in Colorado, his opponent's campaign dredged up an interview Coors had given to USA Today in 1997. "Maybe the answer is lowering the drinking age so that kids learn to be responsible about drinking at a younger age," said Coors. "I'm not an advocate of trying to get people to drink, but kids are drinking now anyway. All we've done is criminalize them." (He also called for "zero tolerance" for drinking and driving and other alcohol-related crimes, but this was not widely reported.)

Thus was born a mini-scandal over Coors and his candidacy. Was the scion of a famous beer family running for the Senate so he could change the law and expand his customer base? Suddenly and unexpectedly, the drinking age became an issue in the race. "Now it pops up nearly everywhere Coors goes," reported the Denver Post.

Coors's opponent, Ken Salazar, leaned heavily on those bogus MADD numbers: "What would end up happening [if federal government lowered the drinking age] is we'd end up losing as many as 1,000 young people's lives each year." Salazar went on to defeat Coors for several reasons—he was already a popular public official, it was a good year to run as a Democrat in Colorado, and so on—and one of them was this controversy.

An unpopular idea is not necessarily a bad idea, however. McCardell's research makes a strong case against the federally mandated drinking age. Choose Responsibility, which receives no financial support from the beer, wine, or liquor companies, is committed to making sure that we hear it.

I'm convinced: The time has come to lower the drinking age to 18, or perhaps to let states experiment with lowering it. At the very least, shouldn't soldiers who are trusted with M-16s also be trusted with six-packs?

*John J. Miller is a political reporter for* National Review, *a conservative magazine. He also writes essays for the* Wall Street Journal *and the* New York Times. *He has written three books, including* A Gift of Freedom: How the John M. Olin Foundation Changed America *(2005).*

Work Cited

Miller, John J. "The Case Against 21." National Review Online 19 Apr. 2007. 7 July 2007
    &lt;http://article.nationalreview.com/
    ?q=YzU4NTcwMTQ4NTBmYzVlNWMzZjgwYTRjYjgyMzllMjg=&gt;.

## Education

from *Choose Responsibility*

We recommend a new approach to alcohol education. Too often alcohol education either denies the reality of alcohol use amongst its subjects (Just Say No!) or is an intervention measure only after irresponsible alcohol use has been reprimanded (court-ordered alcohol treatment). We envision a program similar to drivers' education in that it will:

- Be taught by a certified alcohol educator, trained specifically to cover the legal, ethical, health and safety issues of the curriculum and skilled in dealing with young adults.
- Consist of at least 40 hours of instruction, with the most time spent in the classroom setting, supplemented by sessions of community involvement—DWI court hearings, safe ride taxi programs, community forums.
- Require a partnership between home and school.
- Entail a final examination that subjects must pass for licensing.
- Provide accurate and unbiased alcohol education for both drinkers and abstainers.

The alcohol education course curriculum must:

- Be a model for reality-based alcohol education.
- Involve collaboration between state, school, and home.

- Create a basis for responsible choices where alcohol is concerned, and wed those expectations of responsible behavior to a system of certification and provisional licensing for 18–20-year-olds.
- Be developed and implemented on a state-by-state basis.
- Provide accurate, truthful, and unbiased alcohol education. It will acknowledge the social reality of alcohol in American society, but will advocate neither abstinence nor consumption. It will seek only to create a basis for responsible choices where alcohol is concerned.

Upon successful completion of the curriculum, each student of the program will receive a license, entitling him or her to all the privileges and responsibilities of adult alcohol purchase, possession, and consumption of alcohol.

*"Choose Responsibility is a nonprofit organization founded [by John M. McCardell Jr.] to stimulate informed and dispassionate public discussion about the presence of alcohol in American culture and to consider policies that will effectively empower young adults age 18 to 20 to make mature decisions about the place of alcohol in their own lives."*

Work Cited

"Education." <u>Choose Responsibility</u> 2007. 7 July 2007 <http://www.chooseresponsibility.org/education/>.

## Drinking Age: Questions/Topics

1. Do you believe the drinking age should be lowered to 18 or should remain at 21? Or do you have another possible solution?
2. What has been your own experience with drinking alcohol? How does this influence your opinion? What has been your observation of the behavior of other young adults who drink?
3. Should young adults be able to drink at home with supervision?
4. Do you support the education proposal by Choose Responsibility? Is it workable? Check their Web site for more information: <http://www.chooseresponsibility.org/education>.
5. To see statistics on the effects of young people drinking, see "A Snapshot of Annual High-Risk College Drinking Consequences" at <http://www.collegedrinkingprevention.gov/StatsSummaries/snapshot.aspx>.
6. Which reading selection do you find most persuasive? Analyze the writer's appeals to logos, pathos, and ethos.

## CHEATING FOR SUCCESS

Personal Survey on Ethics

1. Have you ever shoplifted?                          Yes   No      If yes:   When?   What?
2. Have you ever stolen something from your parents?
                                                      Yes   No      If yes:   When?   What?

*FIGURE 2.4*   Clay Bennett cartoon.

Source: The Christian Science Monitor/Clay Benne.

3. Have you ever lied to your parents?                                          Yes   No
4. Have you ever lied to teachers?                                              Yes   No
5. Have you ever lied to get a job?            Yes   No      If yes:   When?   How?
6. "A person has to lie or cheat sometimes in order to succeed."    Agree   Disagree
7. "When it comes to doing what is right, I am better than most people I know."

                                                                   Agree   Disagree
8. "My parents want me to do the ethically right thing, no matter what the cost."

                                                                   Agree   Disagree
9. "It's important to me that people trust me."            Agree   Disagree
10. "It's not worth it to lie or cheat because it hurts your character."

                                                                   Agree   Disagree

## From <u>Honor Above All</u>

### *Michael Josephson and Melissa Mertz*

Cheating has reached alarming proportions in all segments of American society, creating widespread cynicism and an erosion of trust. The root of the problem can be found in our schools, where academic dishonesty is rampant. Students openly admit to cheating and plagiarism, and openly justify their actions.

According to a 2002 survey of more than 12,000 high school students by the Josephson Institute of Ethics, 74 percent admitted cheating at least once within the past 12 months (48 percent said they cheated at least twice). Things are getting worse; in 1992, 61 percent admitted cheating. When it comes to lying and stealing, the statistics are no more encouraging: 37 percent said they would be willing to lie to get a good job; 46 percent said they sometimes lie to save money and 43 percent agreed with the statement that "a person has to lie or cheat sometimes in order to succeed." Thirty-eight percent said they stole something from a store within the past year (19 percent did so two or more times) and 28 percent said they stole from a parent or other relative. These statistics illustrate the larger problem: a general lack of honesty and integrity.

We are in deep trouble if young people maintain these habits as the next generation of nuclear inspectors and airline mechanics, corporate executives and cops, journalists and generals, legislators and lawyers, and politicians and parents. It is, therefore, a matter of import and urgency that those who have the opportunity to shape the values and attitudes of young people engage in thoughtful, systematic and comprehensive efforts to promote integrity and prevent cheating.

Cheating, though serious in itself, is just one symptom of a lack of integrity. Thus, efforts to combat cheating should be undertaken in the context of a broader positive emphasis on the virtues of honesty and honor. (5)

*Note*: For an updated survey, see "2006 Josephson Institute Report Card on the Ethics of American Youth" at <http://www.josephsoninstitute.org/reportcard>. The Personal Survey on Ethics is adapted from this report.

*Michael Josephson is the founder and president of the Josephson Institute of Ethics, which he named for his parents after retiring from successful careers in business, law and education. Through the Institute, Mr. Josephson founded CHARACTER COUNTS!, the nation's leading character education system that reaches five million young people in schools. Melissa Mertz co-wrote the report.*

Work Cited

Josephson, Michael, and Melissa Mertz. Honor Above All: A Guide to Promoting Integrity and Preventing Academic Dishonesty. Los Angeles: Josephson Institute of Ethics, 2004.

## A Cheating Crisis in America's Schools

*ABCNEWS*

Angelo Angelis, a professor at Hunter College in New York City, was recently grading some student papers on the story of Paul Revere when he noticed something strange. A certain passage kept appearing in his students' work, he said.

It went like this, Angelis told <u>Primetime</u>'s Charles Gibson: "Paul Revere would never have said, 'The British are coming, the British are coming,' he was in fact himself British, he would have said something like, 'the Red Coats are coming.'"

Angelis typed the words into Google and found the passage on one Web site by a fifth-grade class. Half a dozen of his college students had copied their work from a bunch of elementary school kids, he thought.

The Web site was very well done, Angelis said. For fifth graders, he would give them an "A." But his college students deserved an "F."

Lifting papers off the Internet is one of the newer trends in plagiarism—and technology is giving students even more ways to cheat nowadays. Authoritative numbers are hard to come by, but according to a 2002 confidential survey of 12,000 high school students, 74 percent admitted cheating on an examination at least once in the past year.

In a six-month investigation, <u>Primetime</u> traveled to colleges and high schools across the country to see how students are cheating, and why. The bottom line is not just that many students have more temptation—but they seem to have a whole new mindset.

### Get Real

Joe is a student at a top college in the Northeast who admits to cheating regularly. Like all of the college students who spoke to <u>Primetime</u>, he wanted his identity obscured.

In Joe's view, he's just doing what the rest of the world does.

"The real world is terrible," he told Gibson. "People will take other people's materials and pass it on as theirs. I'm numb to it already. I'll cheat to get by."

<u>Primetime</u> heard the same refrain from many other students who cheat: that cheating in school is a dress rehearsal for life. They mentioned President Clinton's Monica Lewinsky scandal and financial scandals like the Enron case, as well as the inconsistencies of the court system.

"Whether or not you did it or not, if you can get the jury to say that you're not guilty, you're free," said Will, a student at one of the top public high schools in the nation.

Mary, a student at a large university in the South, said, "A lot of people think it's like you're not really there to learn anything. You're just learning to learn the system."

Michael Josephson, founder of the Josephson Institute for Ethics, the Los Angeles-based organization that conducted the 2002 survey, said students take their lead from adults.

"They're basically decent kids whose values are being totally corrupted by a world which is sanctioning stuff that even they know is wrong. But they can't understand why everybody allows it."

### An Issue of Expediency

Even if the world were more ethical, students still have reasons for cheating. Some said they cheat because they're graded on a curve—so that their score is directly affected by how other students do.

"There's other people getting better grades than me and they're cheating. Why am I not going to cheat? It's kind of almost stupid if you don't," said Joe.

The pressure for good grades is high. "Grades can determine your future, and if you fail this then you're not going on to college, you're going to work at McDonald's and live out of a car," said high school student Spike.

A business student at a top state university said, "Everything is about the grade that you got in the class. Nobody looks at how you got it." He graduates in a few weeks and will go on to a job with a top investment firm.

Others see it as a sort of moral relativity. Some students feel it is perfectly OK to cheat in some situations and in some courses.

"You'll have an engineer say, 'You know, what do I need to know about English literature? I shouldn't have to take this course,'" said Don McCabe, a professor who heads the center for academic integrity at Rutgers University in New Jersey.

For Mary's classmate Pam, it was a different sort of prioritizing. "You don't want to be a dork and study for eight hours a day. You want to go out and have fun."

And some professors make it easy, students said. They overlook even the most obvious instances.

In fact, McCabe says, a survey of more than 4,000 U.S. and Canadian schools revealed half of all faculty members admitted ignoring cheating at least once.

### Tech War

Still, one of the main elements of cheating is doing it in secret. There are the tried and true methods:

- Many sororities and fraternities maintain a file of term papers for reuse—take one, turn it in.
- The old rubber band trick—stretch one out and write everything you need on it, and when it shrinks back to shape, no one will be the wiser.

But students today also have more technologically sophisticated options open to them:

- A favorite device is the graphing calculator, which most professors allow students to bring in to an exam . . . and into which students can download all kinds of material.
- Another is an iPAQ—a handheld computer similar to a Palm Pilot—which can also download information.
- Cell phones—to take pictures of notes, or among the more wily, to text-message friends for answers.
- Even a two-way pager can be used to cheat. For one student whose campus has wireless Internet access, he used it as a mini-computer to access the entire Internet during his test.
- And then there are Internet-based clearinghouses for term papers, such as Papers4Less, Cheathouse.com and Schoolsucks.com.

Fortunately, educators have technological options too. Schools have been subscribing to a service called Turnitin.com, which can help teachers compare students' papers to all the available literature in its database.

"It's typically 30 percent of all the papers submitted have significant levels of plagiarism," said John Barrie, founder of Turnitin.com.

### Where Is the Tipping Point?

"We are in a crisis," said Josephson. But he added, "I don't think it has to stay that way."

He said he was waiting for the tipping point, like Enron with business ethics, where there would be a sea change in attitudes towards cheating.

An ABCNEWS poll found hopeful signs—but worrying ones as well.

In a random sample of high school students aged 15 to 17, 36 percent admitted to having cheated themselves—fewer than in Josephson's survey.

But seven in 10 kids also say they have friends who cheat, and only one-third of students have ever had a serious talk with their parents about cheating.

"We need to promote integrity. We need to get students to understand why integrity is important—as opposed to policing dishonesty and then punishing that dishonesty. Because they can beat the system," McCabe said.

Josephson emphasized that college teaches students many things: how to learn, behave, overcome challenges, and succeed.

"And if they approach it honestly, they'll learn far more in college than they think they can," he said. "But more than that, they'll come out of it better, stronger people."

Work Cited

"A Cheating Crisis in America's Schools." ABCNEWS.com 29 Apr. 2004. 2 July 2007 <http://abcnews.go.com/Primetime/Story?id=132376page=1>.

## An Educator's Worst Nightmare

### Inside the Life of a Professional Essay Writer and Test Taker

*ABCNEWS*

For the defenders of academic integrity, their nemesis comes in the form of a bright college student at an Eastern university with a 3.78 GPA.

Andy—not his real name—writes term papers for his fellow students, at rates of up to $25 a page. On a busy week, Andy will earn upwards of $1,000.

"In the first few weeks, especially, you make a lot of money writing papers, because kids want to go out and party, not do their schoolwork," he told Primetime's Charles Gibson.

One student writing a paper for another is not new. But the Internet makes it so easy—and allows someone like Andy to work in volume.

He says he's written 500 papers for other students, many of them from schools such as "Syracuse, Penn State, Yale, Michigan State University, Northeastern, Boston University, Cornell."

Andy says he thinks there's nothing wrong with what he's doing. Everybody wins—the writer gets money, the student/client and his parents are happy, and the school doesn't have to fear an expulsion or transfer.

"Before I had a conscience and I was afraid I might get caught," he said. "But now I've been doing it so long that I know I cannot get caught."

### Good Papers, Quick Bucks

Andy says he's so good that he'll ask a student/client for his or her grade point average. If the client generally gets A's, he'll write an "A" paper. Get B's, and Andy will write you a "B" paper. And so on.

"I can tell offhand how good I can do on the paper, depending on the topic itself," he says.

But he doesn't much like writing for women. "Every time a female wants a paper done, it has to be an A. Males don't care what grade they get. And the females are the ones that want their money back if I get an A-minus compared to an A."

Primetime asked Andy to write a paper on one of the theories in Dan Brown's best-selling novel The Da Vinci Code, which he had not read. The process did not seem that hard.

After spending 25 minutes on the Web, he had all the information he needed. Then he spent two hours rewriting each sentence downloaded from the Internet in order to beat Web sites like turnitin.com, a database that teachers use to compare their students' work with others'.

"He's our worst nightmare in a sense," said Hofstra University professor Jean-Paul Rodrigue. "He is a professional writer delivering on-demand papers. There's very little we can do about this, very little."

### Criminal Action?

But Andy is a full-service cheater: For a fee, he'll also take a test for another student.

He says it's easy if the professor doesn't ask for a photo I.D. But he does admit the process makes him a little jumpy.

"Every time I cheat I have like, wracked nerves, I'm nervous, I'm like on the verge of a breakdown, but the moment I see that A on my test . . . I feel like I'm in heaven, you know?"

He also writes admissions essays to get students in college and medical school. A friend gave him a brief outline of his own life, and he says, "I just spiced it up for him." Andy earned $180.

Michael Josephson, founder of the Josephson Institute for Ethics in Los Angeles, calls Andy and his ilk "the money launderers of academia . . . They're laundering grades."

"I hope somebody makes it a crime," he said.

Andy thinks what he's doing is admirable. He wants to become a doctor when he graduates, and says he would have no problem trusting a doctor who had done what he did.

"I think it's an impressive thing to write papers on any subject," he said. "I wouldn't see him as a worse doctor, no."

Josephson said Andy's morals are not an aberration—and that's the scary part. "His morals are becoming the norm," he said. "But they're wrong."

Work Cited

"An Educator's Worst Nightmare." ABCNEWS.com 29 Apr. 2004. 2 July 2007
    <http://abcnews.go.com/Primetime/story?id=132377page=1>.

## Student Comments on the Ethics of Cheating

*Joe Smith*

Is cheating unethical? Hardly, you're not trying if you're not cheating. I'm a recent grad from UNL [University of Nebraska, Lincoln], and there probably wasn't one class that I didn't cheat in. Not because I needed to, or couldn't do the work on my own, but it was the fact that I was smart enough to take care of myself, something NO class can teach you. Looking back on it now, working full time now (in which I've learned more from my job than school) I don't regret a damn thing, and how many people can say they did college in 4 years, not many these days. And my 3.5 GPA wasn't so bad either!!! SUCK-ERS! Words of wisdom, those who are scared of cheating, get caught, don't be scared. One more thing, I did learn what Social Darwinism is, survival, and I survived.

*Mark Pogge*

Cheating is cheating. It doesn't matter if you get a higher grade from cheating. The higher grade is not honest. Cheating is not ethical whether you get caught or not. If you are caught cheating and found guilty after going through the proper channels, then you should be punished. Saying that the benefits of cheating compare to the risks of cheating is simply dumb. One day you might get caught and punished. You will reap what you sow. Don't cheat.

*Jane Doe*

The Joe Smiths of the world are pragmatic and know how to work the system. Like them or not, they are the norm. While it is noble to live a virtuous life, that attitude will set you up time and time again for a fall.

Just consider affirmative action, for example. A white male pre-med student with a 3.96 doesn't stand a chance of qualifying for medical school, yet a minority female is a shoe-in, given the same situation. If Joe Smith doesn't cheat so he gets a 4.0, he doesn't get to become the doctor he wants to be.

I don't condone cheating, but I know too well the cost of integrity. When the government or school or any other system creates rules that help special interest groups get rewards at your expense, don't you feel cheated? And once you have been cheated on, is your integrity so strong that you won't fight back? In this situation I can't condemn cheating any more than I can condone it.

Work Cited

Overmyer, Krystal. "Honor Code, Ethics Questioned When Cheating." Daily Nebraskan 19 Nov.
    2002. 6 July 07 <http://www.dailynebraskan.com/news/2002/11/19>.

## Their Cheatin' Hearts

You call it copying; today's college students call it collaborating.

*Charlotte Allen*

Duke University's business school recently announced that 34 of its first-year M.B.A. students will be expelled, suspended or awarded failing grades for cheating on a take-home examination in a required class. The students were instructed to work through the open-book test individually, but 33 of them were found to have collaborated in groups, producing answers so similar that their professor was alerted to investigate (a 34th student was found guilty of lying, and all are expected to appeal). The incident was the largest ever reported in the history of the business school, currently tied for No. 12 in the nation, according to U.S. News.

Reaction to the scandal has tended to fall into two categories. One might be called the Enron analysis: Business students, like business leaders in capitalist America, see themselves as living in a dog-eat-dog world where competition is cutthroat and any means of succeeding, no matter how unethical by conventional standards, is justified—if they don't get caught. Proponents of this business-is-evil idea point to a survey published in the Academy of Management's journal last fall indicating that 56% of graduate business students had cheated in their academic work, compared with 47% of graduate students in other fields. The obvious implication: M.B.A. programs tend to be incubators of junior Gordon Gekkos, contemptuous of ordinary morality and convinced that, since everyone else is probably cheating, they would be fools not to cheat themselves.

The other reaction might be called "It's Not Really Cheating." An article about the Duke scandal in the current issue of Business Week speculates that getting together with fellow students to produce answers to a take-home exam might be more aptly described as "postmodern learning, wiki style"—a hip academic analogue to the "shared information" and "open source" team projects that bosses in the real-life working world reward. The article quotes Robert I. Sutton, a professor at the Stanford University Design School: "If you found somebody to help you write an exam, in our view that's a sign of an inventive person who gets stuff done."

Nonetheless, you have to be very postmodern indeed to excuse the violation of a professor's order not to share information, an order with which most of the Duke class complied. The Enron analysis is also problematic—for the truth is that cheating on tests and written assignments is at an all-time high, and not just in M.B.A. programs but across the board, at both graduate and undergraduate levels. The Academy of Management's study showed that nearly half of all graduate students on average, in such fields as law, engineering and education, cheated at one time or other in pursuit of their degrees.

Furthermore, the 56% cheating ratio for business-school students is only a few percentage points higher than the 50% of college undergraduates surveyed during the 2006–2007 academic year who reported they had engaged in "serious" forms of cheating—cribbing notes and copying during an exam, performing cut-and-paste plagiarism, submitting someone else's work as their own. So reports Donald L. McCabe, a business professor at Rutgers University who has conducted long-term studies of cheating for the Center for Academic Integrity and who also helped prepare the Academy of Management report. When you factor in forms of cheating that undergraduates don't consider serious—collaborating or getting help on assignments when asked for individual work or learning what was on a test from someone who took it earlier—the percentage rises to 67%, as Prof. McCabe wrote in an e-mail.

Explanations abound. They include: new technology (cell phones, online term-paper mills, wireless Internet access in classrooms) that makes cheating and plagiarism easier than ever; professorial carelessness (giving the same tests year after year and thus feeding the fraternity house old-exams file); bad teaching that renders students cynical and insufficiently inspired to turn in their own work; and a lack of attention paid to the peculiar stresses of student life in the early 21st century.

"The grade is the coin of the realm—it's pegged to the perfect job and the perfect life," says Timothy Dodd, executive director of the Center for Academic Integrity, which is coincidentally headquartered at Duke. "This revs up competition for grades, and when you add that to the community service and leadership skills that are expected of students nowadays, you end up with a time-management problem " Mr. Dodd says. It can tempt students to cut corners.

One disincentive to cheating that he advocates: ease up on tough grading standards. One might wonder whether there isn't enough grade inflation already and also whether today's relatively affluent and leisure-afforded students are really under more pressure than their forebears of the 1930s, 1940s and 1950s who were often the first in their families to attend college and who typically juggled coursework with paying jobs and even family responsibilities. Cheating and plagiarism were problems on campus back then, but there was far less of both. This suggests that the real crisis isn't technological or pedagogical—or ideological, as is charged in the case of business schools—but cultural and moral. Fewer and fewer students seem to believe that academic cheating violates their own internalized standards of honesty and good character. And those internalized standards are exactly what many professors would like to see return.

"Campuses with honor codes have lower levels of cheating," says Prof. McCabe, whose studies of campus cheating involved more than 150,000 students at 150 schools. Yet even schools with honor codes have not been free of cheating scandals, the Air Force Academy and the University of Virginia among them. It should be noted that Duke's business school has an honor code that every student must sign before matriculating.

Which leads to a final observation: One way to instill an internalized standard of honesty is to put in place external standards that discourage dishonesty. Many professors and administrators are quietly doing exactly that: abandoning take-home tests and their temptations and devising cheat-proof exams (multiple versions of the same midterm, for example) or requiring students to submit their term papers through Turnitin.com, a Web-based plagiarism screener. Stanford (its design school notwithstanding) has an honor code dating to 1921, but many professors nonetheless ask students to stash their electronic devices in their backpacks during tests. The Stanford Law School shuts off wireless Internet access at exam time.

Three years ago several business-school professors at the University of Maryland's College Park campus, after hearing reports of cheating on the midterm in a required accounting course, set up a sting operation. For the final exam, the professors posted a set of false answers on their Web site, which students could access via Internet-enabled cell phones as they took the test. The professors uncovered, obtained admissions of wrongdoing from and flunked 12 cheaters among the 400 test-takers. When the professors showed up at the next faculty meeting, they received a standing ovation.

*Charlotte Allen is a contributing editor of Beliefnet and author of* <u>The Human Christ: The Search for the Historical Jesus</u>.

Work Cited

Allen, Charlotte. "Their Cheatin' Hearts." <u>OpinionJournal</u> 11 May 2007. 2 July 2007 <http://www.opinionjournal.com/taste/?id=110010061>.

## Cheating for Success: Questions/Topics

1. Do you justify cheating or lying? Have you had to cheat or lie to succeed? Are you willing to do it again?
2. Do you feel it is all right to cheat in some situations but not in others? Why? When is cheating or lying permissible to you?
3. Is plagiarizing or buying papers okay if you don't get caught?
4. Would it be worthwhile for schools to encourage students to write affirmations? <u>Honor above All</u> by the Josephson Institute of Ethics recommends that students volunteer to write affirmations:

   An Affirmation is written out and signed by students after completing an assignment or exam, as confirmation that they did not cheat on that particular exercise. The Affirmation states:

   > *I affirm on my honor that I have not given or received any unauthorized assistance on this assignment/examination.*

   Such an action promotes reflection about academic integrity, and encourages a personal commitment to integrity.

   > *The . . . Affirmation must not be mandatory.* If students are forced to sign them when they really don't intend to uphold the principles, the act becomes meaningless for everyone.

5. What do you think about Andy, the writer of term papers that students buy?
6. Should you inform on someone who cheats in school or at work?
7. How important is character to you? Do you agree with Ralph Waldo Emerson's statement "Character is higher than intellect"?
8. What should schools do to promote integrity—honesty, truth, trust, responsibility, and fairness?
9. Which reading selection do you find most persuasive? Analyze the writer's appeals to logos, pathos, and ethos.

**Candorville**

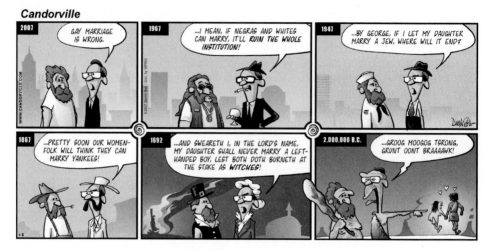

FIGURE 2–5    Candorville cartoon (8 July 2007).

# SAME-SEX MARRIAGE

## Coming Out: Parents Learn True Meaning of Family after Both Son and Daughter Announce They Are Gay

### *Patricia Bertuccio*

*"Imagine that, one day, the Massachusetts Supreme Judicial Court sees what you could not—that your children are entitled to the right and privilege to marry the person of their choosing just as you and your husband did 36 years earlier. You begin to understand how discrimination is perpetuated and feel stupid for having accepted it. The old hopes and dreams for family weddings return."*

*From "Imagine," by* Carole Allen

The fact that Carole and Tom Allen's two children are gay was not what disappointed them when their first child, David, then a junior in high school, "came out" and told his family he was attracted to men. Or when their daughter Abbie, at age 14, discovered she was a lesbian.

It was the dream of weddings and grandchildren that really made their hearts ache.

"It was at a time when [homosexuality] was not out there," Carole said. "It's just realizing and adjusting your expectations. They had to be altered."

"But it turned out a lot less than we thought," Tom added.

That was 15 years ago.

David, 31, wed his partner Michael in 2004, less than a year after Massachusetts Supreme Court made same-sex marriages legal. On New Year's Eve, Abbie, 27, will marry her partner Anna at the Charlestown Navy Yard under Boston's New Year's fireworks.

Carole beamed when asked to see her son's wedding album. Her face radiated with pride like the sun on a perfect beach day as she pointed out her son and son-in-law, her daughter and her fiancée Anna, and other family members in the photos.

"Weddings are for parents, by and large," Tom said.

The Allens felt relief when the state legislature, on June 15, voted 151–45 against a referendum that would let voters decide whether to add a constitutional amendment that defines marriage between a man and woman.

"It would have been really humiliating to have people vote on our children and how much our children were worth," Tom said. "The existing definition of marriage works out very well, thank you very much. It's just letting more people in the club."

Tom said his wife should be a registered lobbyist as she worked with local state representatives and senators, wrote a piece called "Imagine" that describes her experience having gay children and the opportunities same-sex marriage have allowed for her family. She testified at the State House to oppose an amendment to outlaw any same-sex relationship.

"People who claim that their marriage is being hurt by gay marriage are missing the point," Carole said. "It's quite the opposite."

### Out of the Closet

*"Imagine that, when your son is in high school, you discover that he is attracted to men. Even though your brother is gay, you somehow have ignored evidence that your son could be gay, too. Out of fear, you and your husband confront him about this 'dangerous lifestyle,' then spend the next two years anxious and yearning to regain his and each other's trust. You finally find a way to reach out to each other and become even closer than ever before."*

At their home on Beverly Road, Carole and Tom laugh and talk freely about the uncertainty and adjustment that came with learning their children are homosexuals.

Carole calls accepting the sexual orientation of their children a journey. Her brother is gay, but hearing her son was shocked her.

"We didn't handle it well. We confronted him in a way that made him say, 'I don't know yet.'" Carole said of her son's sexuality. "We went through a couple of years of isolation and not talking to each other about it, which was very hard."

Carole said she wanted to learn more about it and went to some PFLAG, Parents, Families and Friends of Lesbians and Gays, support group meetings. She admitted talking about it made her teary-eyed, but after she wrote a letter to David, they reopened the lines of communication.

Tom said he put it aside for a while and it took him years before he could accept and openly talk with coworkers about his children and their sexuality.

"The adjustments are mental. You envision a future for your child and that vision is turned upside down," Tom said. "But as it turns out, it absolutely hasn't been."

After picking David up from college his first year, Tom and David talked it out and they began to rebuild their relationship.

When Abbie came out, Carole said it was a turbulent time in her daughter's life and her being a lesbian was the least of her problems.

"She went through a lot of adolescence stuff," Carole said. "Some of it had to do with that her school placement wasn't correct for her."

Abbie helped found the Gay-Straight Alliance at Arlington High School before she transferred to the Cambridge School of Weston, a more arts-focused secondary school. Carole said a school guidance counselor and a therapist helped get Abbie's sexuality out there and made it easier.

Carole and Tom said some Arlington community members knew David was gay before they did. They didn't face any discrimination and lauded Arlington's tolerance.

"The town has a very active focus on diversity and they're very protective of diversity," Carole said. "[Discrimination] is not tolerated in this town."

The Allens said even though the transition was hard, they loved their children and worked hard to embrace them for who they were, regardless of their sexual preferences. And with state officials moving in favor of acceptance and expanding gay rights, everything was falling into place.

"There's no question that this is the way things are going and anyone trying to resist it is just pulling back against the tide," Tom said of the recent gay marriage rulings. "You get the feeling that society is moving along with you."

### Brides and Babies

*"Imagine that your legislature has the opportunity to oppose discrimination once and for all by defeating the proposed constitutional amendment. You will feel pride and gratitude if they stand up for your family—a family that just wants happiness, togetherness, and standing in the community."*

The Allens are gearing up for a second wedding this winter for Abbie and Anna while waiting for David and Michael to work through the adoption process. David and Michael plan to adopt the child of a woman whose pregnancy they will follow while Abbie and Anna already have talked about adopting a child internationally.

Carole said Abbie and her future daughter-in-law both have bride's dresses and will be back in Arlington this August to continue wedding planning and making arrangements. Carole said wedding planners are excited about organizing a same-sex marriage so they can add it to their portfolios.

Both Tom and Carole called weddings "fun." The excitement and anticipation of the second wedding gleamed in their eyes and smiles.

Though it took years for the Allens to fully accept their children, the journey is over and they look forward to the next phases of their children's lives, particularly grandchildren.

"Neither of us would wish they would be any other way because that would change who they are," Tom said. "You just have to look beyond [sexuality] and embrace your children for the unique and wonderful people they are."

*Quoted material is taken from Carole Allen's "Imagine," a piece she wrote and submitted to legislators to earn their support for gay rights.*

*Patricia Bertuccio is a freelance writer in Massachusetts.*

Work Cited

Bertuccio, Patricia. "Coming Out: Parents Learn True Meaning of Family after Both Son and Daughter Announce They Are Gay." <u>The Arlington Advocate</u> 5 July 2007. 20 July 2007 <http://www.townonline.com/arlington/homepage/x844547859>.

## Marriage Makes a Word of Difference

Why We Can't Call It Something Else

*Evan Wolfson*

"What difference does the word make?"

It's a question often asked of same-sex couples seeking to end their exclusion from marriage—as if these couples had just dreamed up the idea that somehow marriage matters. "Why can't you call it something else?"

As Americans debate the freedom to marry, many are getting to a place of fairness by thinking anew. Others, however, find comfort in way stations, placeholders, and delays. The compulsion to "compromise" the freedom and equality of others is so common, so much a typical feature of civil rights history, that I dedicated an entire chapter of my book, <u>Why Marriage Matters: America, Equality, and Gay People's Right to Marry</u>, to the question, "Why Not Use Another Word?"

Words matter, of course. As the <u>Hartford Courant</u> noted, in a recent editorial urging Connecticut's legislature and high court to move past the 2005 civil union bill to full marriage equality: "Mark Twain famously illustrated the difference between the right word and the almost right word by using as an example the difference between 'lightning' and 'lightning bug'. . . .

What's in a word? For those who want to marry and can't, plenty."

Marriage, as it happens, is not "just" a word. It is a status, created by the law, the very law America pledges equal justice under, to all.

The reason why any other status, call it what you will—civil union, domestic partnership, or schmarriage—is not adequate or fair is that one of the main protections that comes with marriage is, indeed, that status of marriage. When you say, "We're married " everyone knows who you are in relation to the primary person you're building your life with. That clarity, security, and dignity—intangible though they may be—are precious and irreplaceable.

Every legislator debating a marriage bill or its alternative, every judge hearing a case brought by couples and kids excluded from marriage, every American wrestling with this question of fairness, should ask themselves these questions: Either civil unions and marriages are the same—in which case why do we need two lines at the clerk's office?—or they're not the same, in which case what is the government withholding from these couples and their kids, and why? Would you swap your marriage for a "civil union"? And if you say yes, have you checked with your spouse—and your mom?

Not only is there no good reason for the state to create two separate and unequal statuses and shunt some couples around back; in fact, the new legal mechanisms of civil union or domestic partnership fall far short of providing the tangible protections and responsibilities that families need. A recent <u>New York Times</u> story highlighted the ways in which New Jersey's new civil union law is failing to deliver needed security for couples and kids; Garden State Equality, leading the NJ fight for full marriage equality, notes that the law has more than a 10 percent failure rate.

Why give families inadequate and incomplete piecemeal protections instead of the full measure? Why withhold what the one nationwide, universally understood, already existing system of protections and responsibilities would provide? That unique and established system is called marriage.

A record number of state legislatures this year considered bills to end marriage discrimination, and a record number, including Oregon, passed measures en route to marriage equality. Whether such stepping-stones are called civil union, as in New Hampshire and in the bill under consideration now in Illinois, or broad domestic partnership, as in California or here in Oregon, is not all that important. Marriage, after all, is a civil union (a legal status triggered by a civil marriage license), but "civil union" is—deliberately, pointedly—not marriage, with its unique, full dignity and meaning.

Oregon's term "partnership" rather than the now easily invoked "civil union" (coined, amazingly enough, just seven years ago, and now already the default middle ground), perhaps better highlights the incompleteness. But, in fact, both civil union and domestic partnership are intended both to give and to withhold. Both provide some protections for same-sex couples and their children, acknowledged to have parallel needs and dreams, but both deny these families full protection, security, and equality.

A word, a status, a system—marriage is all this and more. Marriage is a commitment, an aspiration, a highly significant personal lived experience, a bundle of personal, social, and spiritual meanings, and, at its best, a strengthener of couples, children, kin, communities, and country. It makes no sense to exclude loving couples already doing the work of marriage in their daily lives from the legal structure intended to reinforce that dedication, those meanings, and, at its heart, commitment and love.

For much of our nation's history, women were denied the right to be lawyers. The Supreme Court itself upheld that exclusion, opining that each sex has its proper sphere and necessary roles, and the "paramount destiny [of women is to] fulfill the noble and benign offices of wife and mother. This is the law of the Creator." Majorities sincerely believed that it was okay to withhold full participation in life choices, including the freedom to marry, based on a person's race or sex. By tradition and "definition" lawyers were men, and that, most believed, is how it had to be.

But when, over the objections of traditionalists, religious leaders, and pandering politicians, our society eventually moved past such discrimination and allowed women to practice law, the sky didn't fall, and we didn't need to come up with a new word for lawyer. The definition of what it means to be a lawyer didn't change; we only needed to end an unfair exclusion. In the same way, marriage is not "defined" by who is excluded, and ending same-sex couples' exclusion will not redefine a word; it will share a precious good.

The right way to end exclusion from marriage is, yes, to end exclusion from marriage. In Oregon, that means undoing the cruel and un-Oregonian state constitutional amendment voters were rushed into enacting in 2004 before getting the full opportunity to meet same-sex couples and hear the personal stories—stories that prompted the legislature this year to enact partnership and get the state back on the road to fairness. Discrimination has no place in the Constitution or the law, no place in Oregon or the rest of America, and no place in marriage either.

We don't need a new word. We don't need a new status. We need to let committed same-sex couples share the same rules, same responsibilities, and same respect. Support the freedom to marry. That's the word. Word out.

*Evan Wolfson is Executive Director of Freedom to Marry, the gay and non-gay partnership working to end marriage discrimination nationwide, and author of Why Marriage Matters: America, Equality, and Gay People's Right to Marry (Simon & Schuster, 2004). In 2004, Time magazine named Wolfson one of the "100 most influential people in the world."*

Work Cited

Wolfson, Evan. "Marriage Makes a Word of Difference." The Portland Mercury, June 14-20
    2007. 5 July 2007 <http://www.portlandmercury.com/portland/
    Content?oid=344646&category=344638>.

## The Homosexual Assault on Traditional Marriage

### Ben Shapiro

There are those who do not believe that the institution of marriage is under assault. There are those who do not believe that same-sex marriage is a knowing attempt to undermine the nature of marriage. There are those who do not believe that many homosexuals bear a particular animus for heterosexual marriage, and have designs beyond mere tolerance.

Then there are those of us who live in the real world.

In Washington, proponents of same-sex marriage, under the banner of the falsely named Defense of Marriage Alliance, have proposed a state ballot initiative that would require straight married couples to have children within three years or face annulment. "For many years, social conservatives have claimed that marriage exists solely for the purpose of procreation," explained DOMA organizer Gregory Gadow. "The time has come for these conservatives to be dosed with their own medicine. If same-sex couples should be barred from marriage because they cannot have children together, it follows that all couples who cannot or will not have children together should equally be barred from marriage."

It seems intensely ironic that same-sex marriage advocates, who proclaim the basis of their politics to be consent, should sponsor such an initiative. But, of course, they are not serious; they are using marriage as a political club to make a point. Their point in Washington is purportedly to prove that traditional marriage is not solely about children— and that if it is not about children, it is about discrimination for its own sake. But even same-sex marriage advocates realize that though traditional marriage sees children as the first priority, it does not rest its legitimacy solely on the basis of child-bearing and rearing.

The goal of same-sex marriage proponents is to elevate homosexuality to the same moral level as heterosexuality. If children are not the sole purpose of marriage, they say, any marriage is merely a grouping of two people who love each other. This is absurd. Marriage is implicitly about the relationship between man and woman. Marriage is codification of the idea that a man and a woman in a committed and sexual union make each other and the surrounding society better.

Women and men are inherently different. They are not interchangeable parts. Men have different strengths and weaknesses than women. A marital relationship between a man and a woman provides spiritual enrichment for each. The union be-tween a single man and a single woman is, as the liturgy says, blessed.

That this blessed union produces the blessing of children demonstrates the Divine origin of such unions. Children are not merely the product of traditional marriage and the beneficiaries of it; they are Divine confirmation that the union of man and woman is special and good. The fact that certain traditional marriages do not produce children does not invalidate the general point that men and women belong together, just as the fact that broken cars exist does not demonstrate that ignition keys ought generally to be put in exhaust pipes.

Advocates of same-sex marriage argue that gender is literally meaningless. It is for that reason that they compare gender to race in legal contexts. Citing *Loving v. Virginia,* the Supreme Court case that ruled anti-miscegenation statutes unconstitutional, advo-cates claim that distinctions based on sex are the same as distinctions based on race.

If gender is meaningless, children do not need both mother and father; a father and a father, two mothers, six fathers and a mother—any or all may suffice. To homo-sexual marriage proponents, the fact that only the sexual union between men and women produces children is an unfortunate accident of nature. Would that nature had made mankind completely androgynous, so as to demonstrate the complete and utter homogeneity of all people!

Gender is not meaningless, of course. The radical individualism that denies all dis-tinction between men and women is deeply pernicious. It denies the spiritual in mankind. It denies the obvious physical and spiritual bounty springing from traditional marriage. It also denies to children the benefits of a mother and father.

In one sense, Washington's same-sex advocates do us a favor: They make clear that in order to deny homosexual marriage, we must uphold the beautiful and natural distinctions between men and women. They also make clear that we must uphold the value of heterosexuality over homosexuality. We must take up the gauntlet and, in doing so, vindicate the possibility of a higher spiritual elevation through the deepest possible human relationship.

*Ben Shapiro, born in 1984, was hired at age 17 to become the youngest nationally syndicated columnist in the U.S. His columns are printed nationwide in major newspa-pers and conservative websites, including Townhall.com. He is the author of Brainwashed: How Universities Indoctrinate America's Youth (2004).*

Work Cited

Shapiro, Ben. "The Homosexual Assault on Traditional Marriage." Townhall.com 7 Feb. 2007. 5
    July 2007 <http://www.townhall.com/columnists/BenShapiro/2007/02/07/
    the_homosexual_ assault_on_traditional_marriage>.

## Dearly Beloved

### *Cal Thomas*

"Dearly beloved, we are gathered together in the sight of God and before these wit-nesses to join this man and this woman in holy matrimony."

So begins most "traditional" marriage ceremonies in Western culture for as long as anyone can remember. Now we are told such exclusivity of preserving marriage for men and women "discriminates" against people of the same sex who wish to "marry" each other. Some forms of discrimination are good, because they send a signal and provide an example that certain behavior is to be preferred over other behaviors for the betterment of society.

That a president of the United States would feel compelled, for whatever reason, to make a public statement that marriage should be reserved for men and women is a leading indicator of the moral state of the union. Imagine Calvin Coolidge saying such a thing, even in the "Roaring '20s." He might as well have stated the equally obvious that the sun rises in the east.

Today, right and wrong, an objective concept rooted in unchanging truth, has been dismissed in favor of the imposed rulings of federal judges guided by their own whims and opinion polls (various polls show the country equally split between those who oppose same-sex marriage and those who would allow it). We are now adrift to sort out our choices based on a weather vane principle: whichever way the wind blows is where we'll go.

When nothing is either true or false and all decisions about life and morals are based on personal choices and whatever new "trend" happens to capture our attention, we lose our moral sense, which, like an immune system, was established to protect us from cultural, as well as biological viruses.

The charge is made that President Bush is "again" using the issue of same-sex marriage to rally his base. But it is not the president who has made this a political issue. Those who would melt the glue of marriage, which has held societies together for millennia, are using the legal and political system for their own ends. In every state where same-sex marriage has been on the ballot, it has been decisively defeated. But like the war in Iraq, the "insurgents" in the culture wars believe all they must do is hang on long enough and the majority will surrender because protracted warfare interferes with our pursuit of pleasure and material consumption.

Some claim that heterosexuals ought to tend to their own marriages before they prohibit people of the same sex from marrying. While it is true that too many heterosexuals divorce (and too many others live together without becoming married), using this as a wedge to undermine a "norm," which, when practiced, serves children and society well, is not a sufficient reason for broadening—and therefore undermining—the traditional definition of what it means to be married.

Allowing same-sex marriage would be the ultimate in social engineering on a scale even grander than the judicial fiat that brought us abortion on demand. And it won't stop there. People whose beliefs about marriage are founded on religious doctrines can expect lawsuits accusing them of "discrimination" should they refuse to hire someone who is "married" to a person of the same sex. Some countries have enacted or are considering laws that prohibit anyone, including ministers, from publicly stating that homosexual practice is wrong, or a "sin." Remember sin? Sinful is what we were before we became "dysfunctional."

Religious groups who operate adoption agencies and schools under government contracts could face lawsuits for opposing same-sex marriages. Under

Massachusetts' anti-discrimination law, for example, the state told Catholic Charities it must place foster children with same-sex couples, or lose its state license to operate its adoption agency. Faced with a choice between its beliefs and the heavy hand of government, Catholic Charities of Boston decided to get out of the adoption business.

We can expect more of this. A Utah polygamist has filed a federal lawsuit demanding that he not be discriminated against for wanting to marry more than one woman. His attorney cites last year's Supreme Court ruling that struck down a Texas sodomy law. Richard G. Wilkins, a law professor at Brigham Young University, notes, "If you can't require monogamy, how in the world can you deny the claims of the polygamists, particularly when it's buttressed by the claims of religion?"

Exactly. When there is no "no" to any behavior, then there must be "yes" to every behavior. If same-sex "marriage" is allowed, no one will ever be able to say "no" to anything again

*Cal Thomas is America's most widely syndicated op-ed columnist appearing in more than 500 newspapers. A conservative, he also hosts a daily radio program syndicated to more than 300 stations nationwide and is a commentator/analyst for the Fox News Channel. Thomas is the author of 10 books, including The Wit and Wisdom of Cal Thomas (2001).*

Work Cited

Thomas, Cal. "Dearly Beloved." Townhall.com 8 June 2006. 5 July 2007 <http://www.townhall.com/columnists/CalThomas/2006/06/08/dearly_beloved>.

## Washington Defense of Marriage Alliance I-957 The Defense of Marriage Initiative

### Gregory Gadow

The Washington Defense of Marriage Alliance seeks to defend equal marriage in this state by challenging the Washington Supreme Court's ruling on *Andersen v. King County.* This decision, given in July 2006, declared that a "legitimate state interest" allows the Legislature to limit marriage to those couples able to have and raise children together. Because of this "legitimate state interest," it is permissible to bar same-sex couples from legal marriage.

The way we are challenging *Andersen* is unusual: using the initiative, we are working to put the Court's ruling into law. We will do this through three initiatives. The first would make procreation a requirement for legal marriage. The second would prohibit divorce or legal separation when there are children. The third would make the act of having a child together the legal equivalent of a marriage ceremony.

Absurd? Very. But there is a rational basis for this absurdity. By floating the initiatives, we hope to prompt discussion about the many misguided assumptions which make up the *Andersen* ruling. By getting the initiatives passed, we hope the Supreme Court will strike them down as unconstitutional and thus weaken *Andersen* itself. And at the very least, it should be good fun to see the social conservatives who have long screamed that marriage exists for the sole purpose of procreation be forced to choke on their own rhetoric.

## Initiative 957

If passed by Washington voters, the Defense of Marriage Initiative would:

- add the phrase, "who are capable of having children with one another" to the legal definition of marriage;
- require that couples married in Washington file proof of procreation within three years of the date of marriage or have their marriage automatically annulled;
- require that couples married out of state file proof of procreation within three years of the date of marriage or have their marriage classed as "unrecognized";
- establish a process for filing proof of procreation; and
- make it a criminal act for people in an unrecognized marriage to receive marriage benefits.

*Gregory Gadow is a computer programmer and founder of the Washington Defense of Marriage Alliance in Seattle.*

Work Cited

Gadow, Gregory. "Washington Defense of Marriage Alliance." 2007. 5 July 2007. <http://www.wa-doma.org/Default.aspx>.

## Lacey Woman Shares Tale of Denial at Bedside of Her Dying Partner

*Venice Buhain*

Four months ago, Lacey resident Janice Langbehn, her partner Lisa Pond and their children Katie, David and Danielle, ages 10 to 13, were set for a relaxing cruise from Miami to the Bahamas.

But Pond, Langbehn's partner for nearly 18 years, was stricken in Miami with a brain aneurysm and died. The family says the way they were treated by hospital staff compounded their shock and grief.

Langbehn, a social worker, said officials at the University of Miami, Jackson Memorial Hospital did not recognize her or their jointly adopted children as part of Pond's family. They were not allowed to be with her in the emergency room, and Langbehn's authority to make decisions for Pond was not recognized.

"We never set out to change the world or change how others accept gay families," Langbehn told the crowd at the Capital City Pride on Sunday. "We just wanted to be allowed to live equally and raise our children by giving them all the same opportunities their peers have."

While Washington is one of a half-dozen states to recognize same-sex partnerships in some fashion, Florida is not.

### Compelled to speak out

Langbehn said that the pain from losing Pond is still fresh, but she spoke at the gay pride event Sunday because the issue of legal recognition of homosexual families was too important to let go.

"I want people to be able to hold their partner's hand in their moment of death," she said.

Pond suffered the aneurysm just before the R Family Vacations cruise ship left Miami for the Bahamas in February, Langbehn said. After Pond was taken to the emergency room, Langbehn said she was informed by a social worker that they were in an "anti-gay state" and that they needed legal paperwork before Langbehn could see Pond.

Even after a friend in Olympia faxed the legal documents that showed that Pond had authorized Langbehn to make medical decisions for her, Langbehn said she wasn't invited to be with her partner or told anything about her condition.

She said she wasn't allowed to see Pond again until a priest arrived to give Pond the Anointing of the Sick, also commonly known as Last Rites.

"I was shocked. It never would have been on my radar that we wouldn't be allowed to say goodbye," Langbehn said. "When I was an emergency room social worker at Mary Bridge (Children's Hospital and Health Center in Tacoma), if someone had said they were an aunt or a partner, I would have let them say their last goodbyes."

Langbehn says she still has not been given Pond's medical records from the hospital nor her death certificate directly from the county or the state, which affected their children's Social Security benefits.

But she has received support from the local community and from former talk show host Rosie O'Donnell, who has e-mailed her to offer support and said she was angry over the way the family was treated. O'Donnell's partner, Kelli O'Donnell, is a co-founder of R Family Vacations.

Capital City Pride co-chair Anna Schlecht said that Langbehn's story drives home the reason why gays and lesbians continue to lobby for national legal recognition of their partnerships and families.

"When Janice told me the story over the phone, I started crying," she said. "Death is hard enough. I can't imagine having my children barred from me in the last moments of my life."

Langbehn said attitudes changed when doctors in charge of organ donation recognized Langbehn and Pond as a couple. They accepted Langbehn's signature on the consent forms, she said. They also allowed the children to visit with their mother, who was kept on life support while organ matches were found.

Pond, who was a volunteer with her church and with the Girl Scouts, as well as a foster mother, wished to donate her organs because she wanted to continue to give to people after her death, Langbehn said.

"I heard from the heart recipient last week," she said. "Now he's able to play with his grandkids again and he definitely would like to meet our family."

*Venice Buhain is a freelance writer for* <u>The Olympian</u> *newspaper in Olympia, Washington.*

Work Cited

Buhain, Venice. "Lacey Woman Shares Tale of Denial at Bedside of Her Dying Partner." The
Olympian 17 June 2007. 5 July 2007 <http://www.theolympian.com/news/story/
138169.html>.

## The Message of Same-Sex Marriage

*Maggie Gallagher*

What message will same-sex marriage send to the next generation?

I got a foretaste recently while taking the shuttle back home from D.C. The young man sitting next to me was a college student, headed home for the holidays. Call him Matthew. We got to talking about the whole SSM thing.

"Why are you against it?" Matthew asked. So I told him.

Marriage is the place where we not only tolerate people having babies and raising children, we positively welcome and encourage it. Same-sex marriage will be a public and legal declaration that the state of Massachusetts believes that children do not need mothers and fathers. Alternative family forms are not only just as good, they are just the same as a husband and wife raising kids together.

"Don't you think that ideally, kids need a mom and a dad?" I asked.

"Not really," Matthew told me. "I don't think so."

He told me knew some kids at school who were being raised by a same-sex couple. They seemed OK to him. Besides, he said, his mom and dad were divorced. His older brother seemed to have some problems with it, he hinted, but that was probably just because his brother was older and knew his dad better before they divorced.

"Kids just accept whatever their family situation is. It doesn't matter," Matthew told me. After all, he was raised by a single mom and doing just fine.

Sure, he was doing fine, in a lot of ways.

But then I pulled out my big gun: "What about you?" I asked him. "Do you think you'll matter to your kids?"

Matthew seemed taken aback by the question. Obviously he had never looked at it from that perspective. He thought for a moment and then followed his train of thought to the only logical conclusion—a train wreck:

"No," he said. "Not really."

Abandon your kids early enough, he implied, and fatherlessness is all they know. They won't need you. Kids adjust.

This has been, of course, the big message of the family diversity crowd since the dawn of the sexual revolution: Adults have awesome intimacy needs that must be met. Family forms, social norms, household arrangements all must be wound, unwound and rewound so the adults get what they need. Kids? Oh, they adjust.

One of the many ways in which same- and opposite-sex couples differ is on this thing called babies. Gays and lesbians can get children only after an enormous amount of effort and deliberate thought: through adoption, buying a baby from a woman (a.k.a. "surrogate motherhood") or artificial insemination. Babies don't just suddenly appear.

By contrast, the things that men and women must do to make sure they do NOT have children outside of marriage are difficult—abstain from sex, have a shotgun wedding, use contraception consistently or have an abortion (in descending order of moral virtue, in my opinion). People won't avoid unmarried childbearing in a society that says what same-sex marriage says: Children don't need mothers and fathers. Alternative family structures are just as good. Young men who are raised to believe that fathers don't matter to their children will not become dependable husbands and fathers themselves.

Marriage is our most basic social institution for protecting children. Same-sex marriage amounts to a vast social experiment on children. Rewriting the basic rules of marriage puts all children, not just the children in unisex unions, at risk. Do not expect boys to become good family men in a society of Matthews who believe, as they have been taught, that men are optional in family life.

Advocates of gay marriage are trying to persuade us that SSM won't affect anyone but the handful of gay and lesbian families. Don't believe it. Listen to Matthew, who has absorbed the message of SSM very well.

Fathers are optional. Children are resilient. Adults are fragile, and their emotional needs come first.

*Maggie Gallagher, a nationally syndicated conservative columnist, is author of four books on marriage, including most recently* The Abolition of Marriage *(2007). She is also president of the Institute for Marriage and Public Policy <http://www. marriagedebate.com>.*

Work Cited

Gallagher, Maggie. " The Message of Same-Sex Marriage." Townhall.com 8 Jan. 2004. 5 July 07 <http://www.townhall.com/columnists/maggiegallagher/mg20040108.shtml>.

## Same-Sex Marriage: Questions/Topics

1. Do you favor or oppose same-sex marriage, or is there another position you could argue?

2. Which label do you prefer for formal same-sex relationships: marriage, civil unions, or domestic partner? Why?

3. Do you agree with Maggie Gallagher that "same-sex marriage amounts to a vast social experiment on children"?

4. Which reading selection do you find most persuasive? Analyze the writer's appeals to logos, pathos, and ethos.

For additional readings on same-sex marriage, see these specific articles: "Same-Sex Marriage–Challenges & Responses" by Gregory Koukl: <http://www.townhall.com/columnists/GregoryKoukl/2007/02/11/same-sex_marriage_%e2%80%94_challenges__responses> and "Family Reunion: The Case Against the Case Against Gay Marriage" by Jonathan Rauch in Democracy: A Journal of Ideas, Issue #5, Summer 2007 <http://www.democracyjournal.org>.

Also, both of these Web sites contain useful information and articles.

Freedom to Marry: <http://www.freedomtomarry.org/>

Institute for Marriage and Public Policy: <http://www.marriagedebate.com>

You may also want to read "President Discusses Marriage Protection Amendment," June 5, 2006 <http://www.whitehouse.gov/news/releases/2006/06/20060605-2.html>.

# Voice and Emphasis

*Understanding sentence structure is like going underneath your writing to see a blueprint of your thoughts.*

## DICTION AND REPETITION

### Repeating Words for Emphasis

Critical thinkers know the value of repetition. By repeating a key word or phrase, you can emphasize an idea as well as your attitude (tone) toward your audience, subject, and self. Such emphasis helps readers hear your voice. For example,

> There are no cheerleaders for readers, *no* front-page pictures, *no* end-zone dance.[1]
> (Leonard Pitts Jr., "No Contest: Books Beat Sport Anytime")

> He's been sent to us because he was *shaken* at a previous foster home, *shaken* hard, *shaken* fast, *shaken* violently until his eyes popped out, whereupon his shaker pushed them back in with his thumbs.
> (Julia Kraus, "If I Told You, Would You Want to Hear?")

> A sentence should contain *no unnecessary* words, a paragraph *no unnecessary* sentences, for the same reason that a drawing should have *no unnecessary* lines and a machine *no unnecessary* parts. (Strunk and White, <u>Elements of Style</u>)

Repeating words is an easy and explicit kind of emphasis. But don't rely on this effect too often. If you emphasize many thoughts this way, you may lose the emphasis. As with most tools of style, the paradox of less is more applies: a tool will usually have more power if you don't overuse it.

---

[1] All italics to indicate emphasis are by the author of this textbook, unless otherwise noted.

## ACTIVITY 1

### REVISION

In your notebook write three sentences in which you repeat a single word or a phrase for emphasis. Also, review your recent writing and see if repeating a word or phrase within a sentence (or group of sentences) will strengthen a point you're trying to make.

## Alliteration

Essayists, poets, politicians—writers of all types—use repetition to create effective sound patterns as well as to emphasize key ideas. The skillful use of sounds can make the difference between powerful, persuasive prose and plain, pale prose.

As a critical thinker you should be aware of *alliteration*: the repetition of consonants at the beginning of words. Sound can reinforce sense (or meaning) and strengthen your writer's voice. In the following sentence from his Inaugural Address, John F. Kennedy repeats two different consonants within a string of words:

> To those people in the huts and villages of half the globe struggling to break the bonds of mass misery, we pledge our best efforts to help them help themselves.

The *b* and *m* sounds of *break the bonds of mass misery* are forceful, calling attention to the words, making the ideas stand out. The repetition indicates that Kennedy cared about the sound of his language in such an important speech. Alliteration used well suggests that a writer has control, and this sense of control inspires credibility.

At his 2005 confirmation hearing to be a member of the Supreme Court, John Roberts said, "I will decide every case based on the record, according to the rule of law, without *fear* or *favor*, to the best of my ability." His clear alliteration of *fear* or *favor* helps him sound credible.

Alliteration usually happens in twos or threes within a sentence.

> Emotional lessons learned in childhood stay with us as *habits* of the *heart* through life.
> (Daniel Goleman, "The New Thinking on Smarts")

*good to have!*

> One man's *trash* is another man's *treasure*.

> I have a dream that my four little children will one day live in a nation where they will not be judged by the *color* of their skin but by the *content* of their *character*.
> (Martin Luther King Jr.)

Well-chosen repetitions can help your ideas sound emphatic and clear, but a little can go a long way.

## ACTIVITY 2

### REVISION

In your notebook practice alliteration by writing three sentences that use it. Try not to overdo it, however. Then review your recent writing to see if you can use some alliteration for emphasis and to improve the sound of a sentence or two. ■

## ACTIVITY 3

Skim "Bigger, But Not Better" by Ryan Grady Sample at the end of Chapter 1. Look for examples of alliteration he uses. How does this tool help convey his voice and tone? ■

## SENTENCE TOOLS

### Joining Complete and Incomplete Thoughts: Subordination

*Subordination* means one thought is not equal to another. It is sometimes explained as dependence: one thought is not complete—it depends on another thought for complete sense.

For example,

> If you never experience sadness, you cannot truly experience happiness.
> (Kelly Battles, student)

The first thought—"If you never experience sadness"—is not complete. That thought is subordinate—not finished. It depends on the other thought to make sense. The word *If* is a signal that the thought is incomplete, even though it has a subject and a verb. Here is a list of *common signal words* (subordinating conjunctions and relative pronouns, technical names you don't need to remember) that connect incomplete thoughts to complete thoughts:

| after | if | until | wherever |
|---|---|---|---|
| although | since | what | which |
| as | that | when | while |
| because | though | whenever | who |
| before | unless | where | whom |

In grammar Kelly's sentence is called a *complex sentence* because it contains one incomplete thought plus one complete thought. The complex sentence gives writers flexibility. For example, Kelly's thought can be reversed so that the complete thought comes first:

You cannot truly experience happiness if you never experience sadness.

The thought is the same, but the incomplete thought now comes last—where *sadness* receives emphasis. Here are other examples of complex sentences that begin with incomplete thoughts. Notice the signal words that begin each incomplete thought.

*If* I could find no word to express what I intended, I made one up.
(Richard Selzer, <u>Mortal Lessons</u>)

*While* we are free to choose our actions, we are not free to choose the consequences of those actions. (Steven Covey, <u>Seven Habits</u>)

"*When* you learn how to die, you learn how to live." (Mitch Albom, <u>Tuesdays</u>)

Here are examples of complex sentences beginning with complete thoughts and ending with incomplete thoughts. Notice the signal words:

Cold often brings on the most spectacular of dreams, *as though* the brain has been incited to fevered activity. (Louis Erdrich, <u>The Blue Jay's Dance</u>)

Educators can help women develop their own authentic voices *if* they emphasize connection over separation. (Belenky et al., <u>Women's Ways of Knowing</u>)

A deeper level of thinking can go on *when* you relinquish your conscious grip on your material. (Peter Elbow, <u>Writing with Power</u>)

*Comma Rule:*   If you begin a sentence with an incomplete thought, place a comma after it.

## ACTIVITY 4

In your notebook write three sentences beginning with an incomplete thought. Then write three sentences beginning with a complete thought followed by an incomplete thought. You may use the same sentences. For example: "*When* I write essays, I drink coffee." "I drink coffee when I write essays."  ▆

You can use complex sentences to revise your writing for variety and clarity. Too many simple sentences can make your thoughts seem all the same weight and emphasis. The result is likely to sound like a list:

The senator is spending his vacation in Africa.
He is taking a break from his many troubles.
His wife is touring the continent with him.
They have been welcomed by the people of Africa.

Instead, you can combine these by using a complex sentence and a compound sentence.

*While* the senator spends his vacation in Africa, he is taking a break from his many troubles. His wife is touring the continent with him, *and* they have been welcomed by the people of Africa.

Here is an example of revising a compound sentence into a complex one:

Many experts claim that thought generates emotion, but others argue that emotion generates thought.

Revision:

*Although* many experts claim that thought generates emotion, others argue that emotion generates thought.

Because subordination emphasizes complete thoughts (such as "others argue that emotion generates thought"), using this pattern will help you better control your thinking.

## ACTIVITY 5

### REVISION

Look at your recent writing. See how often you use complex sentences. Try to combine some simple or compound sentences, making them complex. See if such revision helps you emphasize certain thoughts as well as provide more variety in your writing. ▮

You don't need to identify every sentence you write or read. But if you can see these patterns of coordination and subordination, you will have more control when you revise your writing and when you evaluate other people's writing.

## COLONS AND DASHES AND VOICE

Please actively practice the following tools in your notebook and try to apply them immediately to your current writing.

### Colons

You have already practiced using semicolons to join two complete thoughts in various ways. Using colons and dashes will give your writing more variety and power.

## ACTIVITY 6

In your notebook write a sentence using a colon. (Sentences containing time such as 2:15 P.M. don't count.) If you aren't sure how, don't worry. Just try. ▮

How are colons used in the following sentences?

Writing is important: it helps you think.

Run-on sentences are similar to comma splices: they both involve two complete thoughts not joined properly.

If Professor Morrie Schwartz taught me anything at all, it was this: there is no such thing as "too late" in life. (Mitch Albom, Tuesdays)

Does the sentence you wrote resemble the preceding sentences? When asked to use a colon, most students write a sentence containing a list:

At the bookstore I bought the following: textbooks, legal pads, and LifeSavers.

Colons and lists work well together. They are common. Here is a variation of the colon-list by Anne Lamott:

Here are the two best prayers I know: "Help me, help me, help me," and "Thank you, thank you, thank you." (Traveling Mercies)

However, you can use a colon to clarify your thoughts: the statement before a colon can introduce an explanation that follows it. This sophisticated use of colons shows your reasoning and carries persuasive power.

When you use a colon to introduce an explanation, what follows the colon can be a complete thought (as the previous examples show) or an incomplete thought:

I love one feature most about him: his smile.

To achieve quality in anything, you need this primary emotion: to care.

The fundamental crisis in black America is twofold: too much poverty and too little self-love. (Cornel West, Race Matters)

In formal writing you should not use a colon after forms of the verb *to be* such as *are, is, was,* or *were.*

### Improper

According to Martin Seligman in Authentic Happiness, positive emotions *are*: "satisfaction, contentment, fulfillment, pride, and serenity" (82).

### Proper

According to Martin Seligman in Authentic Happiness, positive emotions are "satisfaction, contentment, fulfillment, pride, and serenity" (82).

If you don't have a complete thought before a colon, you shouldn't use a colon.

Because colons connect closely related thoughts, you may wonder sometimes whether to use a colon or a semicolon in a sentence. Consider this:

Sometimes an outline serves best as a cage to break out of: it makes you think of ideas that won't fit inside but which otherwise wouldn't occur to you. (Peter Elbow, <u>Embracing Contraries</u>)

Elbow could have used a semicolon because both complete thoughts relate to each other. But because the second thought explains the first thought, a colon is a better choice.

*Colon Rule:* To use a colon properly, you need a complete thought before it: whether followed by an explanation, a word or phrase, or a list.

**Improper:** Students in Wright Hall wanted: new mattresses, new carpeting, and free cable for HBO.

**Proper:** Students in Wright Hall wanted new mattresses, new carpeting, and free cable for HBO.

## ACTIVITY 7

### REVISION

In your notebook write three sentences using a colon. At least two of them should introduce explanations. Then look at your recent writing. See if you can use some colons to combine sentences—to introduce explanations. For practice, try to use this tool the next time you write a paper for class or an e-mail. ■

## Dashes

Punctuation marks enable you to set up your thoughts in different ways, as a golfer uses different clubs for different shots. You've already practiced using semicolons (in Interchapter 1) and colons. Now, the dash.

## ACTIVITY 8

In your notebook write a sentence using a dash. If you aren't sure, don't worry. ■

How are dashes used in the following sentences?

I am one of a growing number of students who are completing college in three years instead of four—cramming credits in the summer. (Amy Wu)

I do not shrink from this responsibility—I welcome it. (John F. Kennedy)

> I understand all of a sudden that my family is like this old sweater—it keeps unraveling, but then someone figures out how to sew it up one more time.
> (Anne Lamott, Traveling Mercies)

You can use dashes in various ways. Less formal than colons, dashes are quick connectors—zaps of emphasis.

How do dashes function in the following sentences?

> My white friends want me to act one way—white. My African-American friends want me to act another—black. (Brian Courtney, "Freedom from Choice")

Clearly a single word follows each dash. Set off, each word stands out. The dash emphasizes it with an urgency. A colon could work in each sentence, but colons are more formal and slow than dashes. Notice what Courtney does at the end of his essay:

> Having a separate category marked BIRACIAL will not magically put an end to the pressure to choose, but it will help people to stop judging us as just black or just white and see us for what we really are—both.

His use of a dash followed by *both* is a simple yet beautiful way to restate his essay's thesis. The word represents his synthesis: it's not either white or black but both. Courtney intentionally uses single dashes in his essay to help him express and emphasize key ideas.

Unlike colons, dashes can be used without a complete thought before them:

> Semicolons, colons, dashes—these tools help you connect thoughts.

> Logos, pathos, ethos—writers need to use persuasive appeals intentionally.

> To palm a fevered brow, to feel a thin, wavering pulse at the wrist, to draw down a pale lower lid—these simple acts cause a doctor's heart to expand.
> (Richard Selzer, Down from Troy)

In these examples, a series of three items precedes the dash—but a complete thought follows the dash. Add this pattern to your toolbox of style.

*Dash Rule:* A typed dash is indicated by two hyphens with no space before, between, or after. (However, not all newspapers and magazine follow this rule.) The distinction between a dash and a hyphen is essential for skilled readers. The hyphen connects two words: *ready-peeled, set-off, hand-washed.* In print the dash may look like a single line, but that line is twice the length of a hyphen (dash— hyphen-). When typing, always use two hyphens to indicate a dash.

## ACTIVITY 9

### REVISION

In your notebook write three sentences using a dash. One sentence should contain a dash followed by one word. One sentence should begin with a series of three words or phrases followed by a dash and a complete thought. The other sentence is your free choice. Then look at your recent writing. See if you can use some dashes for emphasis or to combine sentences. For practice, try to use this tool the next time you write a paper for class or an e-mail. ▇▇

## Using Double Dashes

You can use dashes in another way to emphasize thoughts. Consider these examples:

> One measure—and perhaps the best measure—of a person's greatness is the capacity for suffering. (M. Scott Peck, <u>People of the Lie</u>)

> My father—a man with a great sense of humor and no sense of direction—constantly led us on what he referred to as "scenic routes."
> (Ellen Goodman, "In the Male Direction")

> We watched the lightning—quick as a lizard's tongue—from a plastic picnic table at Juanita's. (Verlyn Klinkenborg, "Letter from California")

These double dashes enclose interruptions in thought. The dashes work like parentheses: they set off clarifying or explanatory information not essential to the main meaning of the sentence. Peck's main thought is "One measure of a person's greatness is the capacity for suffering." Although what he encloses in dashes is not essential, Peck's sentence is more conversational and emphatic with his double dashes. His voice is clearer. Ellen Goodman's sentence is more interesting and humorous with her dashes. The last sentence sets off a surprising simile of a lizard's tongue looking like lightning; here also the visual appearance of dashes looks a little like lightning.

Double dashes can also add drama to sentences. Consider these by Al Gore, chairman of the Alliance for Climate Protection:

> We—the human species—have arrived at a moment of decision.

> Our home—Earth—is in danger. ("Moving Beyond Kyoto")

By enclosing *the human species* and *Earth* in dashes at the beginning of these sentences, Gore sets them off in a parallel way, suggesting that there is a close connection between humans and the planet.

Dashes—our most versatile mark of punctuation—can help your voice come alive on the page. *Warning*: Some students become dash happy after learning how to use this tool, whether single dashes or double. The tool loses power if used too often.

## ACTIVITY 10

### REVISION

In your notebook write three sentences using double dashes to set off and enclose information. Then look at your recent writing. See if you can use double dashes for emphasis. For practice, try to use this tool the next time you write a paper for class or an e-mail. ▇▇

## Italics (Underlining) and Voice

How are italics used in the following sentences?

> We must *care* about something to do something about it.
> (Richard Paul, <u>Critical Thinking</u>)

> "Mitch, I *embrace* aging." (Mitch Albom, <u>Tuesdays</u>)

> In the last analysis, what we *are* communicates far more eloquently than anything we *say* or *do*. (Stephen Covey, <u>Seven Habits</u>)

In these examples the italicized words signify emphasis.

When you talk, you often emphasize certain words with the sound of your voice: your tone may deepen or rise with extra feeling; you may put a twist of sarcasm on a word (Oh, I just *love* that new song by the Zebras); you may simply call attention to a word or phrase (The word *quality* is important). In short, using italics is a good way to make your writing sound like a real person—you. As Peter Elbow argues in <u>Writing with Power</u>,

> Writing *without voice* is wooden or dead because it lacks sound, rhythm, energy, and individuality. . . . Writing *with voice* is writing into which someone has breathed.

Sometimes writers will italicize whole sentences to signify their importance. Mitch Albom in <u>Tuesdays with Morrie</u> writes,

> I remembered what Morrie said during our visit: *"The culture we have does not make people feel good about themselves. And you have to be strong enough to say if the culture doesn't work, don't buy it."*

If Albom were to italicize many sentences, the italics would soon lose their effect.

Many writers use italics occasionally. The tool becomes part of their style—to create their writer's voice. Add italics to your stock of stylistic tools as a way to highlight and emphasize certain words or groups of words. But don't use this or any tool of style too much.

*Italics Rule:* Use italics to indicate emphasis of words, phrases, or sentences. Use underlining to indicate titles of long published works such as books, magazines, and newspapers. If you aren't sure whether to use italics or underlining for a class, check your instructor's preferences.

## ACTIVITY 11

### REVISION

*Note:* When you write by hand, use underlining to indicate italics. In your notebook write two sentences that contain italics (or underlining). Use it in a sentence to highlight one word; use it in another sentence to highlight a group of words. Then look at your recent writing for places where you might use italics for emphasis. ■

## Parentheses and Voice

How are parentheses used in the following sentences?

> Evil is in opposition to life (is "live" spelled backwards).
> (M. Scott Peck, <u>People of the Lie</u>)

> Particularly in class or alone with my teachers, I chattered. (Talking seemed to make teachers think I was bright.) (Richard Rodriguez, "Complexion")

> For the writer (prose or poetry) all words rhyme, sort of; that is, all sounded words are more like each other than any word is like silence.
> (William Stafford, <u>Writing the Australian Crawl</u>)

Parentheses are another tool of style you can use to shape your voice on the page. They contain information the writer wants to set off from the main thought of the sentence, yet the information helps to complete the meaning within a sentence. Sometimes parentheses contain secondary information or clarification; sometimes they function as asides—additional comments; sometimes they seem to whisper what writers don't want to say out loud.

## ACTIVITY 12

### REVISION

In your notebook write two sentences using parentheses. Use them in a sentence to enclose a word or phrase; in another sentence use them to enclose a complete thought. Then look at your recent writing to see if you can use parentheses to enclose a comment or information. Try to use this tool the next time you write.

## FINE-TUNING SENTENCES

## Sentence Fragments: Pros and Cons

In academic writing you are expected to write complete sentences. In less formal situations, fragments are more acceptable—to those who accept them at all. You use sentence fragments naturally when you talk as a way to avoid repetition. Professional writers sometimes use fragments intentionally to create certain effects. Consider this fragment by Richard Selzer:

> For the first time we can see into the cavity of the abdomen. Such a primitive place. One expects to find drawings of buffalo on the walls. (<u>Mortal Lessons</u>)

Selzer's fragment express his voice: *Such a primitive place* suggests an aside of surprise; he could have written "It is such a primitive place," but the complete thought is implied. Like short sentences, fragments can help a writer's voice sound authentic; they give writing an oral English (less formal) sound.

In Julia Kraus's essay "If I Told You, Would You Want to Hear?" in Chapter 1, she intentionally uses fragments.

> There's the 3-year-old girl who was stripped, doused with cold water and force-fed. In her front yard. In January.

The two fragments here help shape Kraus's use of pathos (emotional appeal)

When he was a boy, Richard Rodriguez tried to shave off the dark complexion of his skin. How well do his two sentence fragments work here?

> For as I noted with disappointment, the dark would not come out. It remained. Trapped. Deep in the cells of my skin. ("Complexion")

The word *Trapped* and the fragment *Deep in the cells of my skin* have dramatic emphasis.

Depending on your writing situation, sentence fragments may be another stylistic tool for you to use: they can reinforce meaning as well as make your voice sound real. Many modern writers have become increasingly liberal about the use of fragments. However, many instructors forbid all sentence fragments: it isn't always easy to tell whether a fragment is intentional or a mistake.

Here are some sentence fragments written by students.

> I was successful my senior year of track. Specifically in the long jump.

> Plays and symphony concerts are worthwhile. If you participate in them.

> My skin felt hot and sticky. The kind of sticky where your legs peel off from plastic chairs when you get up.

How could you eliminate these fragments? You can connect each fragment to the complete thought before it:

> I was successful in the long jump my senior year of track.

> Plays and symphony concerts are worthwhile if you participate in them.

> My skin felt hot and sticky—the kind of sticky where your legs peel off from plastic chairs when you get up.

When you proofread your writing, look for unintentional sentence fragments. You can usually solve these problems by connecting the fragment to a complete thought before it. You can also use dashes and colons to connect fragments to complete thoughts.

## Conciseness

Writers and editors honor concise writing. Usually, the more concise the better. A good synonym for concise is *succinct*—saying much in little. One of the most concise statements admired around the world is President Lincoln's Gettysburg Address. At that dedication, Mr. Edward Everett, the speaker before Lincoln, took two hours to deliver his address. Historians tell us that Mr. Everett praised Lincoln, saying he wished he had been able to say as much in two hours as the president had in two minutes.

All readers appreciate concise writing. In revision you must try to remove wordy, redundant, loosely written sentences and paragraphs. Reading carefully is a time-consuming task. Your readers will appreciate anything you can do to shorten and lighten their work. Then too, concise language improves your readers' comprehension.

## Omit Needless Words I

Do you often think you're being clear when, in fact, you aren't? Cluttered with excess words, sentences become fuzzy: fuzzy sentences come from fuzzy thinking. If you can remove words without loss of meaning, you should remove them.

These Interchapters have advised you to "omit needless words." Will Strunk advised students to do this in <u>Elements of Style</u>. E. B. White, his former student who revised Strunk's book, says that Strunk's lecture on the importance of brevity was so brief he needed to fill time in class, so he repeated "Omit needless words" three times!

Imagine you wrote the following sentence. Then imagine you revised it.

Up to this point in my life, choosing what I am going to do for the rest of my life has been the biggest decision I have had to make. (30 words)

Choosing what I will do in my life has been my biggest decision. (13 words)

The first sentence is inflated with needless words. The revision is concise and clear, much easier for readers to process.

## ACTIVITY 13

Write each of these sentences in your notebook. Then revise them, omitting needless words.

1. The point that I wish to make is that essentially people learn best what they teach to others.
2. Infants of a young age should not be left alone by themselves.
3. My dad has this way of being able to converse with anyone that he meets on a level that is appropriate to the person he is speaking to at the time. ■

## ACTIVITY 14

### REVISION

Look at your recent writing. Examine your sentences for needless words. Cross them out. ▮▮▮

## Omit Needless Words II

Unnecessary words make your writing sound loose and weak. Avoid adding extra words to reach an assigned paper length. Most teachers would prefer a concise paper to a padded one.

Revise wordy expressions such as the following:

| Wordy | Revised |
|---|---|
| a large number of | many |
| at the present time | now |
| for the reason that | because |
| due to the fact that | because |
| during the time that | while |
| in American society today | in America |
| in light of the fact that | because |
| in order to | to |
| in the event that | if |
| in this day and age | now, today |
| in view of the fact that | because or since |
| the modern world of today | today |

Avoid redundancies like these:

| | | |
|---|---|---|
| advance planning | basic essentials | completely unique |
| disappear from view | disregard altogether | hurry quickly |
| orange in color | rectangular in shape | separate and distinct |

She smiles with phenomenal radiance. [Isn't radiance already phenomenal?]

## ACTIVITY 15

Write each of these sentences in your notebook. Then revise them, omitting needless words.

1. Due to the fact that cigarette smoke irritated his throat, Joe neither smoked nor spent time in places where other people smoked.

2. The game of basketball is a game that is becoming more and more popular in Europe at this point in time.

3. It has been determined by the board of trustees that alcoholic beverages of an intoxicating nature be banned and prohibited in those buildings devoted to housing students. ▉

## ACTIVITY 16

### REVISION

Look at your recent writing. Examine your sentences for any inflated expressions or redundancies like those above. Then try to revise by omitting needless words. ▉

## CHAPTER 3

# Strategies of Argumentation

*As a student of composition, you have to learn how to put . . . natural facilities to work.*
(Ann Berthoff, Forming/Thinking/Writing)

To get people to understand and to respond, wise writers and speakers use various strategies of argumentation—of critical thinking. You have already practiced some of these strategies in Chapters 1 and 2:

---

Using the process of communication: making and supporting a point
Using persuasive appeals: logos, pathos, ethos
Using different kinds of evidence: examples, reasons, authorities, statistics
Using Rogerian argument: presenting other arguments before your own

---

A *strategy* is a plan of action. The word originally referred to generals in armies devising ways to defeat an enemy. But let's consider the word in a more positive way: *a strategy is a plan of action to help you discover, develop, and defend your ideas.* Often this means that logos is the dominant appeal, but you will see that pathos and ethos also play their parts in these strategies.

In this chapter you will explore ten strategies: opposites, comparison, refutation, induction/deduction, narration/description, analogy, classification, cause and effect, humor, and definition. Each strategy is a different pattern of arranging thoughts. Each strategy is also a tool to help you analyze and understand what you write and read. This chapter presents a repertoire of critical thinking tools. They are not ends in themselves. Rather, they are useful means to useful ends—helping you communicate clearly and persuasively.

You have been using these patterns of thinking naturally for most of your life. But have you used them consciously—that is, with awareness? Critical thinkers deliberately choose certain words, sentences, and strategies over others.

## USING OPPOSITES

Many people believe the strategy of opposites cannot be taught directly: it's more like a secret that you discover through your own experience. But these pages will try to help you learn it directly.

To help you discover this principle, let's look at examples of it before exploring what it is. First, here is an excerpt from <u>Herzog</u>, a novel by Saul Bellow. A father is talking with his young daughter:

> "Papa?"
>
> "Yes, June."
>
> "Tell me about the most-most."
>
> For an instant he did not remember. "Ah," he said, "you mean that club in New York where people are the most of everything."
>
> "That's the story."
>
> She sat between his knees on the chair. He tried to make more room for her. "There's this association that people belong to. They're the most of every type. There's the hairiest bald man, and the baldest hairy man."
>
> "The fattest thin lady."
>
> "And the thinnest fat woman. The tallest dwarf and the smallest giant. They're all in it. The weakest strong man, and the strongest weak man. The stupidest wise man and the smartest blockhead. Then they have things like crippled acrobats, and ugly beauties."
>
> "And what do they do, Papa?"
>
> "On Saturday night they have a dinner-dance. They have a contest."
>
> "To tell each other apart."
>
> "Yes, sweetheart. And if you can tell the hairiest bald man from the baldest hairy man, you get a prize."
>
> Bless her, she enjoyed her father's nonsense.

Is the kind of thinking in this passage "nonsense"? You may argue, "Yes, of course it is. It's not logical." Yet you may also argue, "Well, it does make sense in a playful way. It does involve a kind of logic. Words and ideas are reversed, yet both pairs mean the same thing."

Does the following statement by Henry David Thoreau make sense? "The crystal never sparkles more brightly than in the cavern." It seems contradictory. But if a cave were not dark, it would be difficult to notice a bright crystal or light within it. A small light within a dark place is brighter than a candle flame outside at noon. Imagine a photograph in which a black bowling ball rests on a white stool in the center of a totally white room. What would you notice more: the black ball or the white room? You would notice *both* black and white, but your eye would be drawn to the ball, much as your eye would be drawn to a bright crystal in a dark cave. Although these examples are opposites, they suggest the same point: *Contrast produces awareness. When you notice opposites, you think.*

Thinking with opposites may appear not to make sense at first, but upon further analysis, it does. This kind of thinking is as natural as your thumbs. That is, you have *opposable* thumbs, which exist in opposition to your fingers. If you pull your fingers and thumb together as if making a hand shadow talk on a wall, you see that your thumb opposes your fingers. Your opposable thumbs enable you to grab onto things and hold them. Although you don't have fingers and thumbs in your mind, you do have the ability to think of opposites and to consider how they go or don't go together. As novelist F. Scott Fitzgerald wrote, "The test of a first-rate intelligence is the ability to hold two opposed ideas in the mind at the same time—and still retain the ability to function."

Writing expert Ken Macrorie expresses the importance of thinking with opposites:

> Strong writers bring together oppositions of one kind or another. . . . What they choose to present from life—whether it be object, act, or idea—is frequently the negative and the positive, one thing and its opposite, two ideas that antagonize each other. The result is tension. And the surprise that comes from new combinations. . . . The most available and obvious truths are frequently closed to us because we are not open to possible surprise, to seeing the opposite of the common. . . . Make a habit to look for oppositions. You will find suddenly that you are wiser than you thought. Do it automatically. If you find yourself putting down *hot*, consider the possibility of *cold* in the same circumstances; if *simple*, then *complex*; if *loving*, then *hating*; etc. The habit will prevent you from oversimplifying people, processes and ideas.

## ACTIVITY 1

In your notebook, reflect on this strategy of using opposites. Does it make sense to you? Do you recall noticing opposites before? Which opposites? What was the tension between them? What did you realize?

## Using Contradictions and Paradoxes
### Contradictions

Exploring opposites can help you generate ideas and evaluate what you read and hear. Writers often discover ideas by noticing contradictions. Imagine you are talking with your mother about school and you say you don't like English classes. Upon hearing this she says, "But you enjoy reading and writing—how can you not like English classes? This is a contradiction!" Depending on how she vocalizes her last statement, you might interpret it as a criticism or as an invitation for further thought.

Sometimes a contradiction feels like a pickle in baseball: caught between two players, you can be tagged out. But contradictions are useful because they help you think; instead of being called out, you're given an opportunity to keep playing—and the game becomes more interesting. Peter Elbow, in <u>Writing without Teachers</u>, advocates that critical thinkers welcome contradictions.

> Encourage conflicts and contradictions in your thinking. We are usually taught to avoid them; and we cooperate in this teaching because it is confusing or frustrating to hold two conflicting ideas at the same time. It feels like a dead end or a trap but really it is the most fruitful situation to be in. Unless you can get yourself into a contradiction, you may be stuck with no power to have any thoughts other than the ones you are already thinking.

Contradictions spark thought. As a writer you can deliberately look for them, as these students do in their notebooks.

> You can feel close to someone who is very far away. My best friend lives in Switzerland and has had a completely separate life from me for three years. Despite this, through our frequent letters I feel just as close to her as I did when we lived in the same town, let alone the same continent. At times I feel I can relate to Sarah even more than I can to my other friends here in college. When she moved farther away physically we became closer mentally and emotionally because we were forced to evaluate exactly what our friendship meant to each other. (Alison Topham, student)

* * * * * *

> A contradiction is a wise man who is foolish. Consider the biblical story of David and Bathsheeba. David was a wise king who ended up acting very foolishly. He saw Bathsheeba bathing and he gave in to his feelings of lust. He had an affair with her despite the fact he was married. He then proceeded to orchestrate the death of Bathsheeba's husband, so that he could be with her. David was wise but wrong. (Anne Griffith, student)

Critical thinkers notice contradictions. Using his own personal experience and observation, student Mike Slater examines opposites to help him define *pride*:

> Although Grover from <u>Sesame Street</u> tells us "Everybody should be proud of themselves," pride is also one of the seven deadly sins. A contradiction, pride can be a concept of good or evil.
>
> The main benefit of pride is that it gives people a reinforcement for doing good work. This is one reason why there are so many volunteers in America. My Grandpa Matiyow volunteers at St. Mary's hospital in my hometown. Once he told me that even though he doesn't get paid, the feeling of pride he gets in helping others is more than worth the effort. He also creates birdhouses for his family and friends. He spends hours each day perfecting his latest design. Grandpa leads visitors downstairs into the dark corner of his basement where his birdhouses surround them. The gleam in the old man's eyes when he shows off his craft proves to me the importance of pride.
>
> When is pride a harbinger of evil? In medieval times, pride was seen as putting one's self before God, rather than accepting humility as a way to approach religion. For a modern example, turn to any fashion magazine. Women today are made to think they have to be the picture-perfect super model: thin, glamorous, and sexy. I know extremely

good-looking girls who torture themselves and their loved ones in their never-ending desire to achieve what they believe is the perfect weight, look, and body. One of my friends is at her ideal weight, yet she still insists on dieting to lose another *eight* pounds. Another friend who already weighs less than 100 pounds forces herself to throw up each time she consumes a large meal. Unnecessary plastic surgery on breasts, faces, and hips have permanently damaged countless women all because of pride.

Pride is an ambiguous concept because it holds both positive and negative meanings. I suggest we keep the positive meaning of pride but replace the negative meaning with "vanity." I'd amend the seven deadly sins to replace pride with vanity as well. When was the last time you heard someone say, "You should be vain of your accomplishments?" This way, the meaning becomes more clear, and pride can truly be used in a positive way.

By exploring pride's positive and negative meanings, Mike reveals the contradictory nature of the word, and he arrives at an insight by suggesting that *vanity* replace the negative meaning of *pride*.

## ACTIVITY 2

Write a brief essay about a contradiction. First try to generate a list of contradictions that you see in your own life or in your family, friends, school, or society. Then select the contradiction that intrigues you most and write about it. Or explore one of these contradictions: *how someone or something can be strong yet weak, beautiful yet ugly, kind yet cruel, afraid yet brave, happy yet sad.*

## Paradoxes

Critical thinkers notice and examine paradoxes. In his book <u>Modes of Thought</u>, Alfred North Whitehead writes, "We must grasp the topic in the rough, before we smooth it out and shape it." Writers are like artists who work with clay. No one starts out with a finished product (sculpture or essay). Some process must take place first—grabbing an idea and a clump of supporting evidence like a scoop of red clay. The rough idea becomes a precisely stated thesis. Taking away unnecessary words like excess clay, you shape your ideas and polish them.

The words *contradiction* and *paradox* are closely related; both involve a joining of opposites. <u>Webster's New World</u> dictionary defines contradiction as "a condition in which things tend to be contrary to each other" and paradox as "a statement that seems contradictory, unbelievable, or absurd but that may actually be true." If you placed a hand on a hot iron but felt no pain, this would be a contradiction. However, the title of the rock song "Hurts So Good" by John Mellencamp is a paradox.

Although "Hurts So Good" seems contradictory, the test of a paradox is whether it expresses truth. How can anything that hurts be good? Within the song Mellencamp sings that love hurts yet feels good. Does his statement apply to other activities besides love, such as running five miles a day, weight lifting, or writing? Yes, they may hurt while you perform them but you feel good when finished. To distinguish contradiction from paradox, let's conclude that *a paradox is a contradictory statement that involves truth—often a surprising truth*.

Critical thinkers pay attention to paradoxes. They explore them, as the following two students do in their notebooks:

> "The end is the beginning" is a common statement that expresses two opposites in conjunction. This paradox seems to clash unless you look at its true meaning and start to think about your life. After all, each time we end something, there is always something else coming after it. We do not cease to live because one stage in life is over; we move on to the next stage. I never paid much attention to this idea until my great-grandmother clarified it for me. She mentioned that in the natural world another stage always follows the previous one, such as day to night or winter to spring. She spoke of hope, for all things end while bringing fresh starts with them.
>
> Last May, my father and I noticed that half of the people in my graduating class were referring to the upcoming ceremony as "graduation" while the other half called it "commencement." One indicates an ending, the other a beginning, yet both are correct. (Amy Pardee, student)

* * * * * *

> Each bad experience brings with it a chance for hope and joy. Maybe that could be considered "disgusting optimism" or "pathetic happiness." When my car got stuck in a snowbank, I had already had a bad day and was frustrated. As I sat waiting for a tow, my irritation turned to acceptance, and soon I was glad I got stuck there. Right across the street two girls were also stuck. I was strong enough to push their little Hyundai out of the snow. They couldn't help me, but I was glad I was there to help them. Last May when we lost power for a week, it was a nuisance—food spoiled, we cooked oatmeal on the grill—but we had the greatest week of family time we'd had since the kids were little. I saw it as an opportunity to make the best of a bad situation. (Mary Wendt, student)

By exploring paradoxes, these students arrive at insights.

In this brief essay, "Quiet's Noise," student Kelly Betzold shares her discovery of a paradox:

> We think of quiet as being without noise, but it is rarely truly quiet, for there are noises if you listen hard enough.
>
> One night at home, when I couldn't sleep, I listened to the quiet. Within my own room, I could hear my own breathing and the thumping of my heart. The sheets rustled as I turned, and my cat, Yin, purred happily at the end of my bed. My alarm clock ticked with a systematic rhythm, louder than I could recall, and the heater periodically turned on and then off again.
>
> My room was not the only place where quiet let its sounds escape; the rest of the house held its share of noises as well. The refrigerator grumbled every once in a while, the toilet occasionally flushed, and the faint sound of music could be heard from my brother Brian's stereo. A light switch clicked on, a door closed, and a creak came from the floor as someone walked by. Bear, the dog, walked across the linoleum kitchen floor and slurped up

some water. The washing machine churned away at our clothes, and the dryer hummed warmly.

Outside I could hear the wind—seeping through my window and blowing through the leaves. Branches rubbed together and brushed against the roof. A car door slammed. As I lay there listening, a car passed, a garage door squeaked, and a dog barked—thus setting off a chorus of neighborhood dogs!

All of these sounds I heard within the quiet. Most any quiet place you may be, if you really listen, there is still noise. In fact, quiet can contain more noise than loud does; it just contains noises that are seldom noticed. Loudness covers up these usually undetected sounds and so is just one big noise. Therefore, in this paradoxical sense, loud is really quieter than quiet and quiet is really louder than loud! Confused? Merely try to listen once, and you won't be any longer. I listened, and I can see why I couldn't sleep! Shhh! Be very, very quiet . . . and listen.

Kelly's essay builds to a surprising paradox: "loud is really quieter than quiet and quiet is really louder than loud!" By paying close attention, she moves from describing sounds in her bedroom to throughout her house to outside her house in order to collect supporting evidence for her thesis. Kelly risks thinking in an unusual way. Some readers may consider her idea foolish. But critical thinkers take the risk of thinking unusual thoughts if they can support them and if they express truth.

Your life contains many paradoxes, though you may not notice them. You may now be living in a paradox regarding your school. On the one hand, *life at private colleges is more public than private*. True? If you attend a small private college, is there less privacy? On the other hand, *life at large public universities is more private than public*. True? If you attend a large university, do you have more anonymity? Thinking with opposites can help you identify and explore paradoxes.

Do you use both creative and critical thinking? Yes, though you may not be aware of it. Peter Elbow has written insightful books about opposites in the writing process. In <u>Embracing Contraries</u> he explains that writing involves two main kinds of thinking:

> First-order thinking is intuitive and creative and doesn't strive for conscious direction or control. We use it when we get hunches or see gestalts. We use it when we sense analogies or ride on metaphors or arrange pieces in a collage. We use it when we write fast without censoring and let words lead us to associations and intuitions we hadn't foreseen. Second-order thinking is conscious, directed, controlled thinking. We steer; we scrutinize each link in the chain. Second-order thinking is committed to accuracy and strives for logic and control: we examine our premises and assess the validity of each inference. Second-order thinking is what most people have in mind when they talk about "critical thinking."

Does Elbow make sense? When you write rough drafts, do you try to write fast and not care about being logical and grammatical? Or do you try to control your writing right from the start as you generate words and ideas? Elbow advises that it's best to write *carelessly* at first. Then later when you revise a draft you can write *carefully*. But trying to be both careless and careful at the same time is counterproductive, often causing writer's block. Elbow says both kinds of thinking complement each other: the more creative you can be at first, the more critical you can be later when you revise.

## Paradox and Tolerance for Ambiguity

Thinking with opposites helps you develop a high tolerance for ambiguity and a low tolerance for either/or thinking. Being *ambiguous* means "1. having two or more possible meanings 2. not clear; indefinite; uncertain; vague" (Webster's New World). Because paradoxes are ambiguous, they provoke inquiry. Sydney J. Harris, a newspaper columnist, wrote, "The universe is the same for all of us and different for each of us." How can this be so? The universe is the same for us because we are all human beings. But the universe is different for each of us because we are individually different and unique.

As a critical thinker, try not only to tolerate ambiguity but to welcome it. Many problems are too complex to be solved with only one answer. Look for different perspectives from which to see multiple meanings. Roger von Oech, in his playful book A Whack on the Side of the Head, teaches readers to think ambiguously. He asks, "What is half of 8? One answer is 4. But if you assume that the question is ambiguous, you'll look for other answers such as 0, 3 . . . and 'eig,' all depending on how you define 'half.'" He also uses the following figure.

**FIGURE 3.1**   Bird/question mark.

Source: From *A Whack on the Side of the Head* by
Roger von Oech. ©1983, 1990, 1998 by Roger
von Oech. By permission of Warner Books, Inc.

"What is this figure?" von Oech asks? "If you look at it one way, it's a bird; if you look at it another way, it could be a question mark; if you turn it upside down, it looks like a seal juggling a ball on its nose. By assuming an ambiguous attitude, you generate a variety of ideas."

If you saw a bird in the figure and stopped looking for other images, you short-changed your thinking. Through the countless multiple-choice tests and quizzes you have taken in school, you have been conditioned to look for "one right answer." The problem with this, explains von Oech, is that "if you think there is only one right answer, then you will stop looking as soon as you find one." He advises instead that you look for *plural answers* when you explore questions and problems.

## Either/Or Thinking

Using the strategy of opposites can help you avoid either/or thinking, which is seductive. It often sounds good and makes quick, easy sense. For example, in the movie

Harvey with James Stewart, Stewart plays Elwood P. Dowd, an eccentric and lovable man whose best friend is a six-foot imaginary rabbit named Harvey. At one point in the movie Dowd says, "My mother taught me a lesson many years ago . . . that in this world you can be oh so smart or oh so pleasant. I was smart for thirty-five years. I recommend pleasant." Although this may sound nice, it's a false dilemma—another term for simplistic either/or thinking. Why can't Elwood P. Dowd and all of us try to be *both* smart and pleasant?

Thinking with opposites counteracts simplistic either/or thinking, often called dualistic thinking. What you want to do with opposites is examine the tension between them. Thumbs and fingers work together much better than holding something with only thumbs or fingers. Rather than think black *versus* white, you can think black *and* white—and see various shades of gray. Rather than think that scientists are analytical and artists are creative, you can consider that scientists are also creative and artists are also analytical. Rather than stereotype men as fierce competitors and women as nurturers, you can argue that many men are nurturers and many woman fierce competitors—and that it's possible for a person to be both a competitor and a nurturer, depending on the situation.

As a critical thinker, try to notice either/or statements and look for possible middle grounds or "third alternatives" as Stephen Covey calls them in The Seven Habits of Highly Effective People. A little alarm should ring or red flag appear when you hear or read them. Consider either/or statements as invitations for further thought to see what hides between the extremes. If someone says, "It is either day or night," suggest that it may be dawn or dusk. If someone says, "You either write well or you don't," suggest that this assessment depends on each individual paper you write.

Critical thinkers enjoy paradoxes but develop warning signals for simplistic either/or thinking. If you see something paradoxical, if you examine it, you may arrive at an insightful understanding of it.

## ACTIVITY 3

Choose one of the following paradoxes that intrigue you most. Then write about it in your notebook, trying to make sense of it.

1. "An ounce of experience is better than a ton of theory."
   (John Dewey, Democracy and Education)

2. Desire causes suffering; therefore, we should desire not to desire. But how can we desire not to desire? (This paradox is at the center of Buddhism.)

3. "No one can be moral . . . without coming to a working arrangement between the angel in himself and the devil in himself, between his rose above and his manure below. The two forces or tendencies are mutually interdependent, and the game is a working game just so long as the angel is winning, but does not win, and the devil is losing, but is never lost." (Alan Watts, The Book).

## ACTIVITY 4

Write an essay about a paradox. First try to generate some paradoxes that you see in your own life or in your family, friends, school, or society. Select a paradox that means the most to you and write about it. Or explore one of these paradoxes: *Less is more. Winning is like losing sometimes. You must lose yourself to find yourself.* ▪

## Flip It

The book Why Not?: How to Use Everyday Ingenuity to Solve Problems Big and Small recommends that thinkers use opposites to solve problems. Authors Barry Nalebuff and Ian Ayres, professors of economics at Yale University, advise thinkers to keep asking this question: "Would flipping it work?" Turning something around takes courage, they say, but if you can do it, you will see different perspectives you would not have considered otherwise. One of the examples they use to illustrate what they mean involves you as a student.

---

**Volunteering Not to Answer**

Everyone knows that when a teacher asks a question, students signal that they want to answer by raising their hands. What would it mean to flip this around?

Well, of course, it would mean that students who raised their hand *don't* want to answer. Just because you can flip something around doesn't mean that you would want to. In this case, it seems pretty ridiculous to have students who don't want to answer raising their hands in class.

But wait a minute. Changing the meaning of hand-raising could offer some distinct pedagogical advantages. Isn't it better to force the students who aren't prepared to go to the trouble and embarrassment of raising their hands? Maybe, maybe not. . . . As an experiment, Ian tried flipping the meaning of raising your hand and found that it improved the quality of class participation—particularly among shy students.

---

Would you like to try this system of flipping the meaning of silence in class? Hmm, it makes you think. Another example of flipping it concerns organ donation. The policy now is that organ donation is not permitted without prior consent. If you flip this, then organ donation would be permitted "unless prior denial has been given." Would this new idea save more lives?

Doing the opposite or flipping it also worked for Martin Seligman, author of Authentic Happiness. A psychology professor at the University of Pennsylvania, Seligman realized that psychology had long "been consumed with a single topic only—mental illness." He shifted the paradigm and started examining people's "signature strengths" such as originality, goodness, and cooperation. That led him to found

Positive Psychology, a new field of science that studies positive emotions to help people focus on their strengths instead of their flaws to "obtain authentic happiness."

Natalie Angier writes about a flip in her book on science, <u>The Canon</u>:

> In most high schools, students begin with biology in tenth grade, follow it with chemistry, and cap it off in their senior year with physics, a trajectory determined by the traditional belief that young minds must be ushered gently from the "easiest" to the "hardest" science. More recently, though, many scientists have been campaigning for a flip in the educational sequence, teaching physics first, the life sciences last. Leading the charge for change is Leon Lederman, a Nobel laureate in physics. . . . Lederman and others argue that physics is the foundation on which chemistry and biology are built, and that it makes no sense to start slapping the walls together and hammering on the roof before you've poured the concrete base. They also insist that, taught right, physics is no "harder" than any other subject worth knowing.

Is it always best to start with what is "easiest"? Lederman argues no—it depends if a subject is "taught right." Great thinkers like Leon Lederman and Martin Seligman use opposites—the flip—to help them discover new ideas and methods.

## The Wisdom of Opposites

The strategy of opposites—using contradictions and paradoxes to generate and analyze ideas—may be a secret best discovered on your own. Maybe not. Do you have a good handle on it now—with your opposable thumbs? Knowing this strategy can help you as a critical thinker, writer, and reader—and it can help you understand the mystery of life more fully.

Paradox is a common feature of religion and philosophy. That Christ was born from a virgin is a paradox; that he was both human and divine is too. Consider the ancient Chinese philosophy of yin and yang. Yin is "the passive, negative, feminine force or principle in the universe"; yang is "the active, positive, masculine force or principle in the universe" (<u>Webster's New World</u>). The moon symbolizes yin; the sun symbolizes yang. Look at the parallel opposites here: passive/active, negative/positive, feminine/masculine, moon/sun. According to this philosophy, the opposite forces of yin and yang complement each other and create balance in the universe. Now, as a critical thinker you can question yin/yang. Doesn't it stereotype women and men too much? Or perhaps each of us embodies yin and yang in our own ways.

In <u>Tuesdays with Morrie</u>, the wise professor who is dying talks to his student Mitch about the wisdom of opposites:

> *"Have I told you about the tension of opposites?" he says.*
>
> > *The tension of opposites?*
>
> *"Life is a series of pulls back and forth. You want to do one thing, but you are bound to do something else. Something hurts you, yet you know it shouldn't. You take certain things for granted, even when you know you should never take anything for granted.*
>
> > *"A tension of opposites, like a pull on a rubber band. And most of us live somewhere in the middle."*
> >
> > *Sounds like a wrestling match, I say.*

*"A wrestling match." He laughs. "Yes, you could describe it that way."*

*So which side wins, I ask?*

*"Which side wins?"*

*He smiles at me, the crinkled eyes, the crooked teeth.*

*"Love wins. Love always wins."*

*Note*: To learn about how opposites are used in sentences, see Interchapter 4: "Style and Opposites," especially the information on using antithesis.

## USING COMPARISON

A common strategy, comparison is an extremely useful and natural way to present ideas and evidence. If you claim that Bose speakers have superior sound performance, you can demonstrate this by comparing them to Realistic speakers from Radio Shack. If you claim that majoring in biology makes more sense than majoring in English, you can compare both kinds of majors.

The word *compare* means to show similarities and differences. Thus, the phrase *comparison and contrast* is redundant because comparison implies contrast. When you use comparison, you may focus on similarities or on differences, or both. It depends on your purpose. As with all strategies of argumentation, comparison is not an end in itself. Ordinarily you choose comparison because it helps your audience understand a point you're trying to make.

### Organizing Comparison: Block and Alternate Patterns

Consider Princess Diana and Mother Teresa who died within a week of each other in 1997. Diana died at age 36 in a tragic car wreck; Mother Teresa died of natural causes at age 87. They were very different yet both were "famous." Mother Teresa, a nun well known for her charity work for poor people in India and around the world, was awarded the Nobel Peace Prize in 1979. Diana, a beautiful divorced mother of two sons, was largely a socialite yet spoke out on the dangers of land mines.

To compare these women, you could first discuss one and then the other. This is called the *block pattern*: you could discuss Princess Diana's appearance, achievements, and death in that order; then you could discuss Mother Teresa's appearance, achievements, and death. Or you could interweave both. This is called the *alternating pattern*: you can first discuss Diana's and Mother Teresa's appearance, then their achievements, and last their deaths. The previous paragraph uses an alternating pattern.

Which pattern does Richard Selzer use in this excerpt?

Having practiced both surgery and writing, I am struck as much by the similarities between the two vocations as by their differences. A surgeon is apt to think of both in terms of instruments and physical activity. In the carrying out of each, a tool is held in the hand: In surgery this is a scalpel, in writing, a pen. In the use of one, blood is shed; in wielding the other, ink is spilled upon a page. In surgery the tissues of the body are sutured; in writing, words are stitched into sentences. The resemblance is further heightened in that the subject of my writing has so often been my work as a doctor. (<u>Down from Troy</u>)

The alternating pattern enables Selzer to explain and show the close connections he sees between surgery and writing. He uses this strategy because he has intertwined both surgery and writing in his life.

Which pattern does Deborah Tannen use in this excerpt?

More men feel comfortable doing "public speaking," while more women feel comfortable doing "private" speaking. Another way of capturing these differences is by using the terms *report-talk* and *rapport-talk*.

For most women, the language of conversation is primarily a language of rapport: a way of establishing connections and negotiating relationships. Emphasis is placed on displaying similarities and matching experiences. From childhood, girls criticize peers who try to stand out or appear better than others.

For most men, talk is primarily a means to preserve independence and negotiate and maintain status in a hierarchical social order. This is done by exhibiting knowledge and skill, and by holding center stage through verbal performance such as storytelling, joking, or imparting information. From childhood, men learn to use talking as a way to get and keep attention. So they are more comfortable speaking in larger groups made up of people they know less well—in the broadest sense, "public speaking."

Tannen uses the block pattern, discussing women's style of speaking in a separate paragraph and then discussing men's style in a separate paragraph. This approach enables her to discuss at some length each type of talk. You may agree or disagree with Tannen's claims, based on your own experience and observation. She does, however, qualify her generalizations: "more men," "more women," "most women," and "most men."

Although you may choose to use the block pattern or the alternating pattern, often your writing may not neatly fit either pattern but be a kind of combination. Martin Seligman in <u>Authentic Happiness</u> writes about flow (also discussed in Chapter 2), citing a study by Mihaly (Mike) Csikszentmihalyi.

Flow is a frequent experience for some people, but this state visits many others only rarely if at all. In one of Mike's studies, he tracked 250 high-flow and 250 low-flow teenagers. The low-flow teenagers are "mall" kids; they hang out at malls and they watch television a lot. The high-flow kids have hobbies, they engage in sports, and they spend a lot of time on homework. On every measure of psychological well-being (including self-esteem and engagement) save one, the high-flow teenagers did better. The exception is important: the high-flow kids think their low-flow peers are having more fun, and say they would rather be at the mall doing all those "fun" things or watching television. But while all the engagement they have is not perceived as enjoyable, it pays off later in life. The high-flow kids are the ones who make it to college, who have deeper social ties, and whose later lives are more successful. This all fits Mike's theory that flow is the state that builds psychological capital that can be drawn on in the years to come.

As Seligman's paragraph shows, you don't need to use either a block or an alternating pattern. Often when you compare two things, the pattern shapes itself naturally.

## ACTIVITY 5

Write a brief essay in which you use comparison to make a point about two _____ (you fill in the blank). Or using Seligman's paragraph for reference, write about your own observation of high-flow and low-flow young people.

## USING REFUTATION

Refutation means disproving a person's argument. At O. J. Simpson's infamous trial, his defense team succeeded in refuting the prosecution's arguments that he had murdered his ex-wife and her friend Ron Goldman. His lawyers pointed out flaws in the state's case, such as the claim that the bloody glove found by the police was Simpson's. Simpson's lawyers refuted this by having Simpson try on the glove. His lawyer, Johnnie Cochran, repeated a catchy rhyme, "If the glove does not fit, you must acquit." The jury found Simpson not guilty.

Refutation is a useful strategy when sides polarize around a controversial issue such as gun control, same-sex marriage, or legalizing marijuana. It's also useful when you disagree with any claim. However, it's important to keep in mind that refutation does not prove you are right; it only shows that an opponent is probably wrong.

When a group of students read Deborah Tannen's You Just Don't Understand: Women and Men in Conversation, they evaluated the book. Disagreeing with an author and showing weaknesses in an author's arguments requires careful critical thinking. Like all strategies of argumentation, refutation requires making a point and supporting it clearly with specific evidence. This is from student Mike Slater:

> My major complaint about Tannen's methods is that she takes her statement on men's independence and women's intimacy as *the* truth. She assumes that the reader also accepts this claim as instant reality. But Tannen fails to consider any cases where a male is interested in intimacy, or a female toward independence, although she briefly hints that there may be a few scattered incidences. By simply dismissing these cases, Tannen leads me to believe they could prove evidence against her theories. She doesn't want to find herself wrong. Thus, she writes statements such as, "If a man experiences life as a fight for freedom, he is naturally inclined to resist attempts to control him" without offering cases where men do not resist attempts to control them.
>
> From my own experience, I don't believe that more men are interested in independence and women in intimacy. Take break-ups for example. I have known many women who have broken up with men because they felt "smothered" by the male. Is this Tannen's idea of striving for intimacy? Was the initiation of the breakup an example of what Tannen calls

women's "hierarchies more of friendship than of power and accomplishment" (25)? By not addressing cases like these, Tannen seems to pretend they do not exist.

Mike shows keen critical thinking here by questioning Tannen's assumptions and her method of proving her ideas. He cites quotes, gives reasons, and offers examples from his own experience to refute Tannen's claims.

Steven Johnson wrote a book called <u>Everything Bad Is Good for You</u>. Is his title a huge overgeneralization? Absolutely, but he uses it to make readers wonder if it is true. He argue this thesis: "the culture is getting more intellectually demanding, not less." This is a surprising claim—a flip of a traditional view—because many people argue our culture is growing less demanding. Television, video games, and a lack of reading are the usual causes.

To help present his argument, he uses refutation: he imagines a world in which video games have existed for centuries before "page-bound texts" became the popular pastime. (Yes, this requires suspending reason because video games could not exist without electricity.) He asks, "What would the teachers, and the parents, and the cultural authorities have to say about this frenzy of reading? I suspect it would sound something like this:

> Reading books chronically understimulates the senses. Unlike the longstanding tradition of gameplaying—which engages the child in a vivid, three-dimensional world filled with moving images and musical soundscapes, navigated and controlled with complex muscular movements—books are simply a barren string of words on the page. Only a small portion of the brain devoted to processing written language is activated during reading, while games engage the full range of the sensory and motor cortices.
>
> Books are also tragically isolating. While games have for many years engaged the young in complex social relationships with their peers, building and exploring worlds together, books force the child to sequester him or herself in a quiet space, shut off from interaction with other children. These new "libraries" that have arisen in recent years to facilitate reading activities are a frightening sight: dozens of young children, normally so vivacious and socially interactive, sitting alone in cubicles, reading silently, oblivious to their peers.
>
> Many children enjoy reading books, of course, and no doubt some of the flights of fancy conveyed by reading have their escapist merits. But for a sizable percentage of the population, books are downright discriminatory. The reading craze of recent years cruelly taunts the 10 million Americans who suffer from dyslexia—a condition that didn't even exist as a condition until printed text came along to stigmatize its sufferers.
>
> But perhaps the most dangerous property of these books is the fact that they follow a fixed linear path. You can't control their narratives in any fashion—you simply sit back and have the story dictated to you. For those of us raised on interactive narratives, this property may seem astonishing. Why would anyone want to embark on an adventure utterly choreographed by another person? But today's generation embarks on such adventures millions of times a day. This risks instilling a general passivity in our children, making them feel as though they're powerless to change their circumstances. Reading is not an active, participatory process; it's a submissive one. The book readers of the younger generation are learning to "follow the plot" instead of learning to lead.

Johnson cleverly helps readers think about reading and video gaming in new ways.

Using selective evidence—and not being fair-minded, he admits later—he refutes the common assumption that reading bestows great benefits and that video games don't. In his book he explains that he doesn't agree with much of this argument, in part because he reads and writes books himself and knows their value. His aim, rather, is to refute the dominant view that reading is the best way for minds to develop. He argues that video games and television have "increased the cognitive work they demand from their audience, exercising the mind in ways that would have been unheard of thirty years ago."

Refutation is useful. Pointing out counterarguments and flaws requires careful analysis and tact. This strategy, like any other, influences ethos. If your method of refutation seems like an attack on a person, an idea, or an activity, then you may sacrifice your ethical appeal for your logical appeal. If you truly want to persuade readers to change their mind, you need to refute arguments in such a way that they don't feel attacked.

## ACTIVITY 6

Write a brief essay in which you refute one of these claims:

Movies today have no moral value.

Television offers no truly thoughtful shows.

College students are inherently selfish. When they do volunteer work, they do it for themselves and their résumés.

## USING INDUCTION AND DEDUCTION

### Induction

When you use examples and reasons, you can arrange them in two different ways, called induction and deduction. Inductive reasoning means you give your evidence first and then make your point about them—a generalization. You may observe that whenever you walk on campus and pass people they say hello and smile. If it happens often enough, you may generalize that your campus is friendly. This is induction or inductive reasoning. You may have walked on other campuses where passers-by don't greet each other; those campuses feel less friendly. This kind of thinking—observing examples and then generalizing from them—is common. It is also the primary tool of science: scientists observe what happens in their experiments and then draw their conclusions.

Induction, however, seldom absolutely proves a generalization. Although you may have passed by friendly people on your campus, tomorrow you may find that some people ignore you. It's not possible for you to pass by every person at your school to determine whether they are friendly or not. And though you have visited other campuses you find unfriendly, it's possible you didn't spend enough days there to gather enough observations to justify your claim.

The process of induction can fool you if you're not careful. You may think you're drawing logical conclusions from your observations. Suppose you said the following:

---

Aunt Lu smokes and is healthy. Mr. Ronk next door smokes and is healthy. Hey, everyone I know who smokes is healthy. Therefore, smoking isn't really that dangerous.

---

Such thinking shows a leap—called an inductive leap—from observations to a generalization. But just because every smoker you know is healthy does not mean that most other people who smoke are healthy. Your data are insufficient to justify your claim. Plus, you'd be ignoring warnings from the Surgeon General on cigarette packages as well as an abundance of scientific evidence. Induction provides greater and greater (or lesser) degrees of probability.

Induction, then, is an argument that moves from particular examples to an opinion about them. Many reports on television news shows proceed from induction. A report on the dating habits of college students may focus on four young people from one school. Is this sample adequate to form a reliable generalization? Probably not. But if the report includes surveys on dating taken from thousands of students across the country, this would substantiate a generalization. Usually, the more examples you have to support a point, the more reliable that point is. But it is seldom possible to include more than a few examples—except through highly statistical sampling methods, which allow TV forecasters to know on the basis of less than 2% of the voters who is going to win an election.

The search for generalizations we can rely upon is the goal of scientific knowledge. Scientists draw upon their observations to find those "laws of nature" so that they can then use such "laws" in tests and in constructing theories about life and the universe. It is a circle of knowledge. You can try it yourself in a brief experiment:

## ACTIVITY 7

In class, observe what students are wearing and from this draw your conclusions about what other students will be wearing in your next class or wherever you encounter groups of students. If your conclusions are accurate, you will have practiced induction and shown how "probable" your reasoning is. ■

## Deduction

Deduction means that general laws *predict* specific examples or instances. In your travels to various schools, you may conclude that small colleges (of less than 2000 students) are more friendly than large universities (of more than 30,000 students). When you go to a small college, you can predict that the atmosphere will "probably" feel more friendly. When you go to a large university, you can predict that the atmosphere will "probably" feel less friendly. Your predictions may not hold true. You may find a small college unfriendly and a large school friendly. But the process of deduction involves such prediction: drawing out specific cases from a general law. Why use the word *probably*? Very little can be predicted absolutely: science is much more inclined to deal with degrees of probability.

Consider another example of deduction. Because you know from experience that the quality of YumYum restaurants is variable, you can't predict the quality of the next YumYum restaurant you visit. But you can predict that you will probably have good food and service at YumYum in Mt. Pleasant because you have been there many times without being dissatisfied.

Robert Pirsig in Zen and the Art of Motorcycle Maintenance clarifies induction and deduction by providing concrete examples:

> Two kinds of logic are used [in motorcycle maintenance and in living], inductive and deductive. Inductive inferences start with observations of the machine and arrive at general conclusions. For example, if the cycle goes over a bump and the engine misfires, and then goes over another bump and the engine misfires, and then goes over another bump and the engine misfires, and then goes over a long smooth stretch of road and there is no misfiring, and then goes over a fourth bump and the engine misfires again, one can logically conclude that the misfiring is caused by the bumps. That is induction: reasoning from particular experiences to general truths.
>
> Deductive inferences do the reverse. They start with general knowledge and predict a specific observation. For example, if, from reading the hierarchy of facts about the machine, the mechanic knows the horn of the cycle is powered exclusively by electricity from the battery, then he can logically infer that if the battery is dead the horn will not work. That is deduction.

Induction and deduction are another pair of opposites. You use them naturally. But if you can use them more consciously, you will have more power to direct your thoughts. In writing, you can use induction by moving from specific examples to a generalization about them; you can use deduction by moving from a generalization to specific examples.

| **Induction** | **Deduction** |
|---|---|
| Specific example | Generalization |
| Specific example | Specific example |
| Specific example | Specific example |
| Generalization | Specific example |

## ACTIVITY 8

Identify whether you think the following examples show inductive or deductive reasoning:

1. Students who think critically evaluate what they read and write. Seymour thinks critically. Therefore, he evaluates what he reads and writes.
2. Bob reads a lot and gets A's. Roseanne reads a lot and gets A's and B's. Carol does too. Conclusion: Students who read a lot get good grades.
3. Students who take Human Anatomy dissect a cadaver. Franny and Buddy have enrolled in Human Anatomy. Thus, they will dissect a cadaver.
4. My history book cost $50, my sociology book cost $65, and my chemistry book costs $85. Textbooks sure are expensive. ▮▮▮

## ACTIVITY 9

1. Practice induction by writing a paragraph in which you give examples and details of what you see—it may be about this book, the cafeteria, your computer, what you are wearing, the room you are in, what you see outside your window. Conclude by stating a generalization from your examples. For example: "From all these examples I conclude that the cafeteria is as much about socializing as eating."
2. Practice deduction by writing a paragraph in which you state a generalization followed by specific examples or instances:

   *When students laugh in class, they enjoy learning. For example, Professor Davis told a joke (describe joke). . . . On another occasion, my friend Alicia had a terrific sneeze during her speech (describe sneeze). . . .*

# USING NARRATION AND DESCRIPTION

## Narration

Narration means telling events, usually in chronological order. In both formal and informal arguments, stories are useful strategies for stating a claim and supporting it.

Narrative examples often introduce an essay to arouse interest, though they can occur in the body or conclusion of an essay as well. <u>New York Times</u> reporter Nicholas D. Kristof uses a narrative to introduce " A Sister's Sacrifice":

When the janjaweed militia attacked Fareeda, a village here in southeastern Chad near Darfur, an elderly man named Simih Yahya didn't run because that would have meant leaving his frail wife behind. So the janjaweed grabbed Mr. Simih and, shouting insults against blacks, threw him to the ground and piled grass on his back.

Then they started a bonfire on top of him.

But his wife, Halima, normally fragile and submissive, furiously tried to tug the laughing militia members from her husband. She pleaded with them to spare his life. Finally, she threw herself on top of the fire, burning herself but eventually extinguishing it with her own body.

The janjaweed may have been shamed by her courage, for Mr. Simih recalls them then walking away and saying, "Oh, he will die anyway." He told me the story as he was treated at a hospital where doctors peeled burned flesh from his back.

Atrocities like this make up the news and constitute the Sudanese-sponsored genocide here in the region surrounding Darfur, but it is also stories like this—of superhuman courage—that keep me going through my reporting here. Invariably, the most memorable stories to emerge from genocide aren't those of the Adolf Eichmanns, but those of the Anne Franks and Raoul Wallenbergs. Side by side with the most nauseating evil, you stumble across the most exhilarating humanity.

This is a powerful story to show what Kristof means by "exhilarating humanity." The rest of his essay concerns another narrative about an older sister five months pregnant who let herself be beaten and raped by seven janjaweed soldiers so that her younger sister, age 10, could escape. These stories stir emotion in readers, which is why Kristof uses them: emotional stories can provoke thought.

Narratives can be personal experiences as well as historical accounts—stories about important people in history. They can also be objective reports describing how to do something such as conducting an experiment.

However, many narratives are considered testimonial evidence. They are "anecdotal." In these cases, such evidence is considered light or weak, hard to verify. Suppose a friend of yours claims she saw a ghost in her kitchen last night; she tells you all about it. But can you trust her claim? You know she reads many books on the paranormal. One of the reasons for understanding anecdotal evidence is so you can detect it in other people's arguments.

## Description

Description means making visual pictures with words. It means using *concrete details* based on sight, sound, smell, taste, and touch. Such details create images in a reader's mind. Description is a useful strategy of argumentation because, like narration, it can stir an audience's emotions and thoughts.

Consider the following paragraph written by William Laurence, a reporter aboard the flight that dropped an atomic bomb on Nagasaki, three days after the bombing of Hiroshima. This is not fiction. It is the nonfiction account of a journalist describing what he saw for readers without television: the atomic blast is at once horrible and fascinating.

**Descriptive Report**

As the first mushroom floated off into the blue it changed its shape into a flower-like form, its giant petals curving downward, creamy white outside, rose-colored inside. It still retained that shape when we last gazed at it from a distance of about two hundred miles. The boiling pillar of many colors could also be seen at that distance, a giant mountain of jumbled rainbows, in travail. Much living substance had gone into those rainbows. The quivering top of the pillar was protruding to a great height through the white clouds, giving the appearance of a monstrous prehistoric creature with a ruff around its neck, a fleecy ruff extending in all directions, as far as the eye could see.

Today, most of us have seen pictures of atomic blasts. In 1945 almost no one had. Laurence, a working writer, found himself with the job of trying to tell the rest of the world what it was like. As a writer yourself, you can appreciate Laurence's descriptions of the familiar mushroom shape as first a flower and then a monster. Laurence's sentences, full of information and striking detail, form a vivid picture of the atomic cloud as it seemed to him.

Description depends on detail. Through description writers can imply their attitude toward their subject. They can, like Laurence, convey horror and awe without directly using these words. Writers can convey almost any attitude by carefully choosing details that create images.

In his essay "Small Rain," from his book <u>Cold Snap as Yearning</u>, Robert Vivian uses description to help readers imagine being at a lake in summer.

Some river smells or lake smells stay with you forever; just a hint of one of these and we are suddenly thrust back in time. . . . For me they all lead back to Glen Lake in northern Michigan, where I spent many summers as a boy, with the scent of fresh pine and water running their invisible currents through my grandparents' open windows. . . .

I can smell the minnow cages bobbing up and down like human shoulders in the lake. I can smell the fish odors of the dock, scales that shine like open tins, and the water that laps at the underside. I can smell the wet sand and almost taste the salty edge of the bank— all of these are smaller than anything I can hold in my hands. Could it be that standing alone at the end of a dock in fog when you're just a kid is enough to commemorate a whole life in smells? Smelling these just once more, I can suddenly see my grandmother laughing again and the slight gap between her two teeth; I can smell the fabric of her dresses (one faded pattern the color of blood), hear the satisfying sound of cards being shuffled and dealt around the kitchen table, the smooth feel of walnut.

In Glen Lake you can wander out the length of many football fields, and the water will turn a deeper band of blue, rising only to your waist. You can see your own feet on the lake bottom, stirring up shells and small stones.

Notice how Vivian's precise details help you smell, see and feel this lake. His details suggest his awe at the power of smell and how it can open up memory that helps him appreciate being alive.

Description can be used for many purposes and in many ways. Danielle Trussoni writes about her father in an essay "Home Alone." This is her introduction, full of detail.

My father's Army uniform came in three pieces: a jacket, slacks and a button-up shirt. It was made of 50 percent wool and 50 percent polyester and felt strangely resistant to the touch, scratchy, without give. In November 1992, Dad went to his bedroom to put it on, his first time in uniform in 23 years. Ten minutes later, he stood before me in full attire: government-issue ankle-high lace-up black shoes, a black tie and a tight-creased sandwich cap. Two hash marks slashed on the right sleeve of his jacket—one for each six months of overseas duty—and a blue braided ribbon looped his shoulder and chest, signifying infantry. There was a combat infantry badge, a rifleman's badge and patches for rank, unit and division: 25th Infantry "Tropic Lightning" Division.

"How do I look?" he asked, pulling the cap low on his brow. If you didn't know my father, you might never guess how uncomfortable he really felt; he was so good at masking his misgivings. Although pushing 50, he was as trim and soldierly as he had been at 20. He looked dignified, put together. When I hugged him, he did not wrinkle.

That was the year my father walked in his first Veterans Day parade.

In her essay Trussoni explains that her father was drafted to serve in Vietnam and when he came home, with shrapnel in his back and an ulcer, no relatives or friends greeted him. He never wanted to be part of a Veterans Day parade until a friend invited him. "As he marched through downtown Soldiers Grove, people from the crowded sidelines stepped out and shook his hand, looked him in the eye and thanked him for his service. It was remarkable how much those thank yous meant to him. Those were two words he didn't hear in 1969." Trussoni's detailed description of her father's uniform in her introduction gives the end of the essay great power.

Critical thinkers use narration and description for a purpose—to engage readers' interest and to make a point. Readers like stories that demonstrate an idea, and readers like description when it helps them see, hear, feel, smell, and taste what it is you're trying to communicate.

## ACTIVITY 10

Practice narration by writing about an early memory of yours. First make a list of memories that occur to you (from your earliest memory to age 10 or so)—quickly jot them down. For example, crossing a street by yourself or racing with your brother through the house. Then select a memory that fits into a pattern of your life. Crossing a street by yourself and getting scolded for it—you see a parallel in your being a rebel, an adventurer; you realize you've often taken risks. Running through the house—your brother smashed through a glass door, and you have been fascinated with injuries ever since and plan to become a doctor. Write one paragraph in which you describe your early memory (the story) so readers can experience it. Then write another paragraph explaining how the memory fits into a pattern of your life. [1]

---

[1]Activity adapted from Barbara Drake's <u>Writing Poetry</u> and used here with permission (New York: Harcourt Brace Jovanovich, 1983) 15.

## ACTIVITY 11

Write a brief essay in which you describe a place or a person, letting your concrete details suggest your opinion without directly stating it.

## USING ANALOGY

A creative strategy of argument, an analogy is an extended comparison between unlike things; it shows similarities between two ideas or processes that on the surface may appear to have little in common. Critical thinkers use analogies to clarify complex ideas and to persuade audiences. Analogies provide images that help readers visualize and understand meaning. They can be extremely useful in winning an audience's attention. Yet analogies can fool uncritical readers into assuming that important similarities exist when they might not.

Analogies can be short. In her essay "Traveling Mercies," Anne Lamott writes,

> Our preacher Veronica said recently that this is life's nature: that lives and hearts get broken— those of people we love, those of people we'll never meet. She said that the world sometimes feels like the waiting room of the emergency ward and that we who are more or less OK for now need to take the tenderest possible care of the more wounded people. . . .

Does this make sense? It's difficult to explain "life's nature" because this topic is so huge, but Lamott's preacher uses an analogy of a hospital waiting room to simplify and show what she means.

In her book The Canon, Natalie Angier discusses the controversy of evolution and quotes Richard Dawkins, an evolutionary scientist at Oxford University. He uses an analogy to help show and explain what he means.

> "It's often said that because evolution happened in the past, and we didn't see it happen, there is no direct evidence for it," he said. "That, of course, is nonsense. It's rather like a detective coming on the scene of a crime, obviously after the crime has been committed, and working out what must have happened by looking at the clues that remain. In the story of evolution, the clues are billionfold."

Dawkins's detective analogy is readily understandable; it helps clarify the complexity of evolution.

Analogies can be longer as well. Stephen Covey uses analogies to explain how people can transform their professional and personal lives. Here he explains the importance of the "Emotional Bank Account":

> We all know what a financial bank account is. We make deposits into it and build up a reserve from which we can make withdrawals when we need to. An Emotional Bank Account is a metaphor that describes the amount of trust that's been built up in a relationship. It's the feeling of safeness you have with another human being.

If I make deposits into an Emotional Bank Account with you through courtesy, kindness, honesty, and keeping my commitments to you, I build up a reserve. Your trust toward me becomes higher, and I can call upon that trust many times if I need to. I can even make mistakes and that trust level, that emotional reserve, will compensate for it. . . .

But if I have a habit of showing discourtesy, disrespect, cutting you off, overreacting, ignoring you, becoming arbitrary, betraying your trust, threatening you, or playing little tin god in your life, eventually my Emotional Bank Account is overdrawn. The trust level gets very low. Then what flexibility do I have?

None. I'm walking on mine fields. I have to be very careful of everything I say. I measure every word. It's tension city. . . . It's protecting my backside, politicking. And many organizations are filled with it. Many families are filled with it. Many marriages are filled with it. . . .

Our most constant relationships, like marriage, require our most constant deposits. With continuing expectations, old deposits evaporate. If you suddenly run into an old high school friend you haven't seen for years, you can pick up right where you left off because the earlier deposits are still there. But your accounts with the people you interact with on a regular basis require more constant investment.

Does Covey's analogy help you understand trust more clearly? If so, then his analogy is useful. As with all strategies of reasoning, analogy is not an end in itself. Writers use it for a purpose—to help make a point.

Jonathan Haidt, a professor of psychology at the University of Virginia, uses an analogy as a theme throughout his book <u>The Happiness Hypothesis</u>. He says that he and most people are like a rider on an elephant. The rider is small, trying to control the elephant. But the elephant is big, with its own will.

I'm holding the reins in my hands, and by pulling one way or the other I can tell the elephant to turn, to stop, or to go. I can direct things, but only when the elephant doesn't have desires of his own. When the elephant really wants to do something, I'm no match for him.

Haidt says the rider represents a person's "conscious, controlled thought"; the elephant represents the rest of a person: "the gut feelings, visceral reactions, emotions, and intuitions that comprise much of the automatic system. The elephant and the rider each have their own intelligence." What people struggle to do throughout their lives, he maintains, is to help the rider and the elephant work together.

A thought-provoking and useful analogy reflects a writer's persuasive appeals. You may appreciate the writer's ability to use creative reasoning (logos) to help you understand a complex idea; you may enjoy the analogy or feel moved by it (pathos); and you may respect and trust the writer's character and credibility (ethos).

Analogies, however, are not always useful. Although they can help you explain a complex process, they can also weaken arguments. Logically, analogies are not considered strong forms of evidence in argumentation because they involve imagination. They cannot be verified. To make sure important similarities exist in an analogy, you need to evaluate the analogies you and other people use.

If an analogy oversimplifies a subject, or if it contains more important differences than similarities, it is considered a *false analogy* (See fallacies in Chapter 4). For example, consider the idea that arguing is like arm wrestling. Similarities exist. Arguing usually involves two people as arm wrestling does, but arguments often involve several people—such as in heated class discussions. Arguing also involves a show of strength: there is a competition for the strongest arguments, for the most convincing logic and supporting evidence. However, the arm wrestling comparison reduces the real complexity of arguing. Important differences exist. In arm wrestling the object is for one person to win and one person to lose. But arguing need not involve a winner or a loser. In many arguments different sides concede that each side has relevant points. The purpose of argument should be understanding; the aim should be the search for truth. Arguing is more complex than a contest of arm strength.

Analogies often persuade audiences, but analogies do not prove arguments. An analogy is like a map. It's not the exact territory it stands for. But like a map it can be extremely useful. Analogies are one of the most creative tools critical thinkers can use.

## ACTIVITY 12

In a paragraph or brief essay, write an analogy about learning. For example, you could compare writing an essay to driving a car—or to what else? Or write an analogy by developing one of these statements: Reading carefully is like _____. Thinking critically is like _____. ▉

## Explaining the Mind

How would you describe your mind? Because the mind is mysterious and abstract (you can't see, smell, hear, touch, or taste it), it is impossible to describe the mind with total knowledge and accuracy. Thus, comparing the mind with something more concrete and less complex is natural and can be useful. Using an analogy is a way to represent your mind. [2]

It's common for poets to compare the mind to other things. William Carlos Williams compares the mind to a waterfall rushing with thoughts. Our thoughts "forever strain forward." William Stafford writes, "At times in my thinking I take my hands off the handlebars and see what happens. In a poem I do that all the time." He compares his mind to riding a bicycle. Usually people need to hold on well for control, but sometimes we know our mind (bike) so well we can ride without hands and glide. In her poem "The Mind, Like an Old Fish," Diane Wakoski compares the mind to "a rose in a glass paperweight" and "a caterpillar rolled into a ball against prodding." Consider this last image. Have you ever felt like this caterpillar? Have some teachers prodded your mind with a mental stick? Have other teachers encouraged you to move freely and to transform yourself?

---

[2]This section is adapted from D. Gordon Rohman and Albert O. Wlecke, Pre-Writing: The Construction and Application of Models for Concept Formation in Writing, Cooperative Research Project No. 2174 (Michigan State University, 1964) 63–65.

Here are two examples from students who explain how they think:

My mind is like juggling three balls. The balls are constantly being exchanged from one hand to another. My thoughts constantly move through my mind.

Sometimes when I juggle I unexpectedly manipulate the balls or position my body differently and discover a new trick. I'll drop a ball and then kick it up with my foot, continue to juggle, and say to myself, "Wow! I didn't know I could do that." Similarly I'll be sitting in my room or walking down the street and bam—I think of something I hadn't thought of before. I might look at a tree and see a lollipop. I might come up with a solution to a calculus problem I was working on an hour before. Simply by accident I have a realization.

In contrast I will purposefully try some new juggling move, like throwing one of the balls behind my back and catching it as it comes over the opposite shoulder, but I usually fail because of a misguided throw or blink of my eye. Likewise, I often fail with my thoughts. I will try to understand a problem or concept, or think of a topic for an English paper, and nothing will come to my mind. I may already have one thought being juggled in my mind, but no matter how hard I try to think new thoughts or ideas, the same old thought remains there. Sometimes, until a ball happens to come over my shoulder in the right place, my thoughts do not appear. (Bill Antos, student)

******

Last weekend while driving home, I wondered if the mind—or thoughts—can be compared to *anything*.

"Well," I told myself as a raindrop hit the windshield and spattered, "the mind certainly is nothing like a water droplet." But I had to admit that my mind was like that raindrop. Often thoughts—like raindrops—fall down upon me so unexpectedly that I'm unable to turn on my wipers or pull out an umbrella. I'm not ready for them. And they can pelt down making it difficult to see, until I adjust my focus to the change.

As I heard the growing rumble of the engine, I looked at the speedometer and realized I was well above the speed limit. Then it occurred to me that sometimes my thoughts are like my car—they race along without restriction, until I realize my foot is weighing too heavily upon the accelerator.

Well, maybe the mind *is* like all things in *some* way I thought as my hand automatically went to the gold chain around my neck as it does so often when a new thought hits me. As my fingers moved across the smooth metal, I saw my mind as that gold chain: made of many separate thoughts that somehow link together.

Before I knew it I had compared my mind to a clump of grapes, a blank piece of paper and pen, split ends, a ring, a diamond, snowflakes, pavement, traffic signals, a mail box, and a parking lot.

By the time I pulled into my parents' driveway I was quite tempted to accept the notion that the mind is like all matter. But something kept nagging me at the bottom of my mind—like one of those popcorn kernels that never pops. I'll just have to continue working to figure out a way to pop this idea. (Rebecca Dewald, student)

These analogies are maps of the mind—creative representations of an incredibly complex system. Analogies are useful in explaining what seems impossible to explain.

## ACTIVITY 13

Write a brief essay using an analogy to describe your mind or how you think.  ▆▆

## USING CLASSIFICATION

Imagine opening the silverware drawer in your kitchen and finding no tray—the spoons, forks, and knives are all mixed together. Chaos. Hunting for a teaspoon wouldn't be as efficient; it's nice when all the teaspoons are nestled on top of each other in one group. A silverware tray is a system of classification: each utensil is separated according to size and function: teaspoons, tablespoons, forks (large and small), butter knives, and sharp-cutting knives. This way you can easily choose what you need: you can reach for a butter knife for toast and a teaspoon for coffee.

You could not think without classification, as you could not think without comparison or opposites. You naturally divide things and sort them into categories or groups. As a strategy of argumentation, classification enables you to analyze a subject—to break it down into parts or types and to discuss or evaluate them. How you classify something depends on your purpose.

The human mind craves patterns: groupings of related ideas, objects, or events. Richard Coe, in his book <u>Process, Form, and Substance</u>, explains how useful classification is regarding numbers and colors:

> Real-world phenomena exist in overwhelming numbers and complexity. The ordinary human mind can handle approximately seven items (give or take two) in short-term memory. If you try to memorize the series "85490341," you will find it helpful to think of it as "854-903-41." Telephone numbers, credit card numbers, student identification numbers, and so forth, are usually so grouped.
>
> Similarly, when you look at a rainbow, you probably see red, orange, yellow, green, blue, and purple. In other words, you probably divide the spectrum into six basic colors. The human eye is capable of discriminating about 7,500,000 colors; the human mind, however, is not capable of dealing with 7,500,000 distinct colors, so it groups them.

As Coe demonstrates, humans classify numbers and colors to cope with complexity. As such, classification is purposeful.

You argue from classification when you use categories to develop and defend a claim. Like other strategies, classification generates analysis: it helps you see distinctions within a complex topic—an idea, a process, an event, a group of people. Stephen Covey uses this strategy to examine the importance of listening. He argues that for people to listen well, we need a paradigm shift from thinking about ourselves to thinking and feeling the way another person does:

When another person speaks, we're usually "listening" at one of four levels. We may be *ignoring* another person, not really listening at all. We may practice *pretending.* "Yeah. Uh-huh. Right." We may practice *selective listening,* hearing only certain parts of the conversation. We often do this when we're listening to the constant chatter of a preschool child. Or we may even practice *attentive listening,* paying attention and focusing energy on the words that are being said. But very few of us ever practice the fifth level, the highest form of listening, *empathic listening.* . . . The essence of empathic listening is not that you agree with someone; it's that you fully, deeply, understand that person, emotionally as well as intellectually. (Seven Habits)

To define empathic listening, Covey explains how it is different from other types of listening. This prepares readers to follow him. His classification moves in a logical order: from distant to close listening. His categories make sense because readers have experienced them, especially the first four.

This book has classified persuasive appeals: logos (reason), pathos (emotion), and ethos (ethical character). Although these three groupings often work in combination, you can analyze each of them more carefully if you separate them. You can concentrate on one type of appeal at a time when you analyze a piece of writing.

However, if you aren't careful, classification can generate stereotypes. A stereotype is a simplistic generalization about a group of people or an idea: such as "Football players are stupid." It places things in ready-made categories, ignoring individual differences. Aware that some readers might accuse her of stereotyping, Deborah Tannen addresses this problem in the introduction of her book You Just Don't Understand: Women and Men in Conversation:

We all know we are unique individuals, but we tend to see others as representatives of groups. It's a natural tendency, since we must see the world in patterns in order to make sense of it; we wouldn't be able to deal with the daily onslaught of people and objects if we couldn't predict a lot about them and feel that we know who and what they are. But this natural and useful ability to see patterns of similarity has unfortunate consequences. It is offensive to reduce an individual to a category, and it is also misleading. Dividing women and men into categories risks reinforcing this reductionism.

Tannen acknowledges an important paradox about classification: although dividing people (or ideas and objects) into types is useful for analysis, it can be misleading as well. That Tannen is aware of this and discusses it strengthens her ethos—her credibility. She believes that classifying people is worth this risk if it helps people communicate more effectively. Her purpose governs her classification.

Classification can help you think about your future. How important will your work be in your life? It depends on how you view *work.* Martin Seligman in Authentic Happiness writes,

Scholars distinguish three kinds of "work orientation": a job, a career, and a calling. You do a *job* for the paycheck at the end of the week. You do not seek other rewards from it. It is just a means to another end (like leisure, or supporting your family), and when the wage stops, you quit. A *career* entails a deeper personal investment in work. You mark your achievements through money, but also through advancement. Each promotion brings you higher prestige and more power, as well as a raise. . . . A *calling* (or vocation) is a passionate commitment to work for its own sake. Individuals with a calling see their work as contributing to the greater good, to something larger than they are. . . . The work is fulfilling in its own right, without regard for money or for advancement. When the money stops and the promotions end, the work goes on.

Does this classification make sense to you? It is real. Think about the work your parents do or other family members, teachers, bosses. What kind of work best frames their lives?

Seligman adds a paradox: "But there has been an important discovery in this field: any job can become a calling, and any calling can become a job." How can this be? A surgeon can view her work as a job, not a calling; a hospital orderly can view his work as a calling, not a job. Seligman gives an example of such an orderly who told him, "*I bring in new prints and photos every week. You see, I'm responsible for the health of all these patients. Take Mr. Miller here. He hasn't woken up since they brought him in, but when he does, I want to make sure he sees beautiful things right away.*"

Classification is an important strategy of argumentation because the way you divide a topic into categories influences the way you think about that topic. Your categories can also convey your attitude toward the topic—whether you're serious, sincere, or humorous. In sum, you can use classification to argue and to organize your ideas. You can use it to simplify a complex issue; you can use it to show how complex a "simple" issue is. But avoid trivial or obvious classifications: "There are three kinds of cars: small, intermediate, and large." Use classification to help you make a point, not just to show that you can classify things.

## ACTIVITY 14

Write a brief essay using classification to help you communicate an opinion. In your notebook explore various types of thinking, of seeing, of behaving. Consider persuading readers to accept a new way to classify something. Or write about the kinds of work you hope to do in your life.

## USING CAUSE AND EFFECT

Why did it happen? What could have prevented it from happening? What will be the consequences? Or why didn't it happen? These questions concern cause and effect, a type of reasoning you use so often you may not be aware of it.

Most people take causes and effects for granted. Suppose you cram for a biology exam the day before you take it, reading chapters, writing notes. The exam causes you to study. Your procrastination or neglect has also caused you stress and fear. You stay up until 2:00 A.M. and when you go to bed you can't fall asleep. So you lie in bed, restless. The next morning at the exam, you're tired and irritable. You block; you forget some definitions. But you stay and finish and review each of your answers. Later that week you learn you earned a 72%. You know you could have done better; next time you resolve to study earlier for an exam.

Seeing causes and effects—like using comparison and classification—is a natural kind of thinking. Thinking itself is a system of causes and effects. What *causes* thinking? Most experts say that problems do. Something puzzles, intrigues, or bothers you so that you feel tension, which you then want to relieve by solving the problem.

Suppose you're having a problem installing your DVD player. This causes you to read and reread the directions; it causes you to try connecting various wires from the DVD's input and output to the TV's input and output. It's still not working. This causes you frustration, which causes you to sweat. You test each new possible solution to see if it works. Finally, you solve the problem and feel the effect of a hard-earned eureka. You're still not sure what you did that made the DVD work, but you've solved the problem and can now watch the movie you rented.

Writers often use cause and effect as a strategy to present information. In <u>The Happiness Hypothesis</u>, Jonathan Haidt explains what happened when the frontal cortex of a person's brain was damaged:

> There was recently such a case at the University of Virginia's hospital. A schoolteacher in his forties had, fairly suddenly, begun to visit prostitutes, surf child pornography Web sites, and proposition young girls. He was soon arrested and convicted of child molestation. The day before his sentencing, he went to the hospital emergency room because he had a pounding headache and was experiencing a constant urge to rape his landlady. (His wife had thrown him out of the house months earlier.) Even while he was talking to the doctor, he asked passing nurses to sleep with him. A brain scan found that an enormous tumor in his frontal cortex was squeezing everything else, preventing the frontal cortex from doing its job of inhibiting inappropriate behavior and thinking about consequences. (Who in his right mind would put on such a show the day before his sentencing?) When the tumor was removed, the hypersexuality vanished. Moreover, when the tumor grew back the following year, the symptoms returned; and when the tumor was removed again, the symptoms disappeared again.

Haidt's example clearly shows the consequences (effects) that a tumor caused in this man's brain. It further illustrates what happens in medicine: doctors strive to identify causes of their patients' problems. The effects of these problems are often surprising, even shocking.

As a scientist, Jonathan Haidt decided to try taking an antidepressant to see if it might help him be more happy. He took Paxil and describes the effects the drug caused.

> For the first few weeks I had only side effects: some nausea, difficulty sleeping through the night, and a variety of physical sensations that I did not know my body could produce, including a feeling I can describe only by saying that my brain felt dry. But then one day in week five, the world changed color. I woke up one morning and no longer felt anxious about the heavy work load and uncertain prospects of an untenured professor. It was like

magic. A set of changes I had wanted to make in myself for years—loosening up, lightening up, accepting my mistakes without dwelling on them—happened overnight. However, Paxil had one devastating side effect for me: It made it hard for me to recall facts and names, even those I knew well. I would greet my students and colleagues, reach for a name to put after "Hi," and be left with "Hi. . . there." I decided that as a professor I needed my memory more than I needed peace of mind, so I stopped taking Paxil. Five weeks later, my memory came back, along with my worries. What remained was a firsthand experience of wearing rose-colored glasses, of seeing the world with new eyes.

The effects of the drug surprised Haidt, which caused him to stop taking it. Causes and effects are closely related and not always easy to tell apart. By the way, in this passage do you respect Haidt's ethos? He appears honest and forthcoming about his experience with Paxil.

Let's look at one more illustration of cause and effect from Haidt's book. He summarizes a study done by Brett Pelham about the effects of names.

> Whenever you see or hear a word that resembles your name, a little flash of pleasure biases you toward thinking the thing is good. So when a man named Dennis is considering a career, he ponders the possibilities: "Lawyer, doctor, banker, dentist. . . dentist. . . something about dentist just feels right." And, in fact, people named Dennis or Denise are slightly more likely than people with other names to become dentists. Men named Lawrence and women named Laurie are more likely to become lawyers. Louis and Louise are more likely to move to Louisiana or St. Louis, and George and Georgina are more likely to move to Georgia. The own-name preference even shows up in marriage records: People are slightly more likely to marry people whose names sound like their own, even if the similarity is just sharing a first initial. When Pelham presented his findings to my academic department, I was shocked to realize that most of the married people in the room illustrated his claim: Jerry and Judy, Brian and Bethany, and the winners were me, Jon, and my wife, Jayne.

Does this study surprise you? Do you know married couples whose names start with the same letter? Studying causes and effects is what scientists do. Their work can shed light on how we behave.

What would you rather do: have fun or exercise kindness? Martin Seligman writes about this in <u>Authentic Happiness</u>. What gave him the idea for this question was a study Jonathan Haidt had done on *elevation*, when people experience "extraordinarily positive" feelings. Seligman provides an example of a first-year student's experience with elevation:

> We were going home from working at the Salvation Army shelter on a snowy night. We passed an old woman shoveling her driveway. One of the guys asked the driver to let him out. I thought he was just going to take a shortcut home. But when I saw him pick up the shovel, well, I felt a lump in my throat and started to cry. I wanted to tell everyone about it. I felt romantic toward him.

This is interesting in part because the elevation was not based on what the young woman did but on what she saw a fellow classmate do.

Seligman invited one of his classes to do an experiment: to engage in one pleasurable activity and one philanthropic activity and to write about them. He concludes,

> The results were life-changing. The afterglow of the "pleasurable" activity (hanging out with friends, or watching a movie, or eating a hot fudge sundae) paled in comparison with the effects of the kind action. When our philanthropic acts were spontaneous and called upon personal strengths, the whole day went better. One junior told about her nephew phoning for help with his third-grade arithmetic. After an hour of tutoring him, she was astonished to discover that "for the rest of the day, I could listen better, I was mellower, and people liked me much more than usual." The exercise of kindness is a *gratification*, in contrast to a pleasure. As a gratification, it calls on your strengths to rise to an occasion and meet a challenge. Kindness is not accompanied by a separable stream of positive emotion like joy; rather, it consists in total engagement and in the loss of self-consciousness. Time stops. One of the business students volunteered that he had come to the University of Pennsylvania to learn how to make a lot of money in order to be happy, but that he was floored to find that he liked helping other people more than spending his money shopping.

Seligman claims that the *effects* of the experiment were "life-changing." But you might consider that the experiment involved only one fun activity and one act of kindness. Is this enough evidence on which to base a claim? Still, what does your own experience tell you? When you do an act of kindness, does this cause you more gratification than when you do something fun? If this is true, why don't more people act kindly toward others?

You can trace the effects or consequences of a problem in such a way that the effects persuade readers to care about the problem and to address it. Consider the complex problem of illiteracy. Be*cause* of not being able to read, illiterate people experience a chain of effects that severely limits their life. Jonathan Kozol demonstrates this in a passage from Illiterate America:

> Illiterates cannot read the letters that their children bring home from their teachers. They cannot study school department circulars that tell them of the courses that their children must be taking if they hope to pass the SAT exams. They cannot help with homework. They cannot write a letter to the teacher. They are afraid to visit in the classroom. They do not want to humiliate their child or themselves. . . .
>
> Illiterates cannot travel freely. When they attempt to do so, they encounter risks that few of us can dream of. They cannot read traffic signs and, while they often learn to recognize and to decipher symbols, they cannot manage street names which they haven't seen before. The same is true for bus and subway stops. While ingenuity can sometimes help a man or woman to discern directions from familiar landmarks, buildings, cemeteries, churches,

and the like, most illiterates are virtually immobilized. They seldom wander past the streets and neighborhoods they know. Geographical paralysis becomes a bitter metaphor for their entire existence. They are immobilized in almost every sense we can imagine. They can't move up. They can't move out. They cannot see beyond.

Kozol's list of effects is persuasive, building toward his metaphor at the end. His ethos is persuasive because he is knowledgeable and concerned. He understands the problem of illiteracy. He cares about Americans who can't read. This helps readers care, appealing to pathos. Thus, focusing on effects as Kozol does can be an effective way to argue about causes and what should be done to address a complex problem.

Reasoning from cause and effect is extremely useful for critical thinkers. It is another lens through which to see and analyze people, events, and ideas. You can use cause and effect in different ways depending on your purpose. You can focus on causes or on effects, or both. But you don't want to examine so many causes and effects that you tire your audience. Trace major ones.

## ACTIVITY 15

Write a brief essay about one of these suggestions: What causes you to be happy? What has caused you to learn deeply? What has caused you to lose balance in your life? (What were the effects? What caused you to regain balance?) What caused you to have a particular misconception about something? What have been the effects of technology—such as video games, computers, or cell phones—in your life? (Trace some positive and negative effects.) What are consequences (effects) of a major decision you have made? ■

## USING HUMOR

Humor as a strategy of argument not only can cause laughter and delight (a form of pathos, as discussed in Chapter 1) but can also expose serious problems and even suggest surprising ways to solve those problems. It can shed light on issues that matter to many people yet may seem unimportant or silly to others. Although humor can take various forms such as jokes, puns, and editorial cartoons, in this section we will look at humorous tone and satire.

### Humorous Tone

Many writers use humor as a key part of their voice. It helps create the sound of their personality on the page. Readers enjoy and appreciate moments of humor.

When poet Wislawa Syzmborska from Poland accepted the Nobel Prize for Literature in 1996, she said, "They say the first sentence in any speech is always the hardest. Well, that's one behind me, anyway." Her gentle humor here opens a door for listeners, suggesting this speech will not be so bad—it may contain unexpected moments of surprise. If her two sentences made people smile, what a good way to begin.

Natalie Angier in her book <u>The Canon: A Whirligig Tour of the Beautiful Basics of Science</u> uses a humorous tone that conveys her attitude about science and herself. Her purpose in the book is to persuade readers that science matters. She writes, "In sum, I'm not sure that knowing about science will turn you into a better citizen, or win you a more challenging job, or prevent the occasional loss of mental faculties culminating in the unfortunate purchase of a pair of white leather pants." The last part of her sentence about the white pants is a little funny—it's unexpected, like a punch line. Do you have some teachers who use humor this way? If so, is it easier to spend time in their classes, and do you pay more attention and possibly learn more?

Later in her book, Angier writes about winter:

> I hate winter, the whole surgical tool kit of it: the scalpel cold, the retractor wind, the trocar darkness. I hate the snow, whether it's fluffy virginal or doggy urinal. I hate the inevitable harangues about how you lose 30, 50, 200 percent of your body heat through your head, because above all I hate winter hats and refuse to wear one. What happens with a hat? You take it off, and half of your hair leaps up and waves about like the cilia of a paramecium, while the rest lies flat against your skull as though laminated in place.

Angier is having fun here, comparing winter to a kind of surgery, playing with words that sound alike (*virginal* and *urinal*), and using similes to describe what happens to hair when you take off a hat ("like the cilia of a paramecium"). Her use of surprising comparisons contributes to her humorous tone. Here's another simile she uses: "Our universe is like a French pastry: full of air yet unspeakably rich, and really, don't you think one will do?"

When a writer such as Natalie Angier has a humorous tone, she uses it frequently throughout—but not constantly. Not every sentence can be a joke. But some or many can. Her use of humor helps her make the case that science is fun and should be taught in joyful ways.

Anne Lamott in <u>Traveling Mercies</u> also uses humor frequently that causes surprise and delight for many readers. Worried about getting older, she writes,

> I am trying to accept the fact that I am actually m-m-m-m-m-middle age. And even though I am a feminist and even though I am religious, I secretly believe, in some mean little rat part of my brain, that I am my skin, my hair, and worst of all those triangles of fat that pooch at the top of my thighs. In other words, that I am my packaging.

Stuttering on the words *middle age* is funny. The use of *pooch* is surprising. In writing about aging and gaining weight—making fun of herself—Lamott expresses how many older women and men feel.

A humorous tone can help readers have a good time while they consider ideas and arguments. If a writer uses a humorous tone in an essay, it is usually indicated toward the beginning. There are no rules for using humor or how much humor in an essay. It depends on your purpose and your audience.

## ACTIVITY 16

How does Rick Reilly use humor in the following essay? Take some notes on what you notice. Bring them to class to share.

### Swearing Off Swearing

*Rick Reilly*

You and I have the same problem. We swear too goddam much.

Growing up, the worst my mom ever said was, "Crying in the beer bucket!" Still have no idea what it meant, but it was serious. She said cursing was "for the locker room." Man, she wouldn't believe how big the locker room is now.

I realized it a couple of weeks ago at the Colorado–Colorado State football game. The two student sections cursed like teamsters in two-sizes-too-small thongs.

They yelled, "F— 'em up! F— 'em up! Go CU!" They sang, "Bullllls—!" at a ref's call. And they chanted, "F— you, CSU!" (Clap-clap, clap-clap-clap!) And that was their clever stuff.

No student seemed to be able to pass a rival in the concourse without hurling a "F— you!" in the other's ear, accompanied by twin birds and projectile spittle. (And, really, some of the men were just as bad.)

It's not just Colorado. We have become a nation of !@#$%&ers. Michigan hockey fans serenade each opponent sent to the penalty box with a dozen elegant words: "Chump! D—! Wuss! Douche bag! A—! P—! Cheater! Bitch! Whore! Slut! C—!"

Higher education at its finest.

That's why I'm all for what they're doing at Boston University. Beginning this season, anybody who cusses at a BU home athletic event gets pitched out of the arena. "We had to do something," says hockey coach Jack Parker. "People are telling me they're afraid to bring their kids to games."

It's not going to be easy making BU hockey fans give up swearing. It's like asking frogs to give up flies or R Kelly 15-year-olds. Not only that, but how will the Terriers play games with only three players left on the ice? "I just hope an usher doesn't come down and get *me*," says Parker.

Athletic director Mike Lynch and dean of students Kenneth Elmore decided something had to be done after BU fans cursed a blue streak during last spring's NCAA hockey tournament. Now the school will station cuss cops—officials, ushers, even Lynch—all over Agganis Arena's infamous section 118. "They're trying to censor us," says Nick Williams, sports editor of the student paper. "I feel like it limits my freedom of speech."

What the students are mad about is losing their favorite chant, which they yell 25 times a game, no matter whom they're playing: "F— 'em up! F— 'em up! BC sucks!" That's a speech?

Besides, until the last decade, it was "Rough 'em up! Rough 'em up! BC sucks!" according to former BU and Olympic star Mike Eruzione, who asks, "Is it too much to show a little class?"

At least BU has the guts to do something. Maryland's students would make George Carlin blush, but the university still lets them work blue. The best university president C.D. Mote could do was write a sternly worded letter to the student paper that said: "Use of profanity will change when our students decide to change it." Great point, C.D.! Even better, let's make the little darlings drop a nickel in a jar every time they swear!

I'm no better. I'm cursed with cursing. I hate myself for it not just because it's disgusting but also because it's just so *unimaginative.* When I shank one, I yell, "Son of a f— whore!" I wish I could be like my buddy, who yells, "My heinous cousin!" Only his cousin can take offense.

Isn't it more fun to spew something fresher than the same old, "Go f— yourself!"? Any Raiders fan could've scrawled that on his cell wall. Why not, "May you suffer a severe groin injury not covered in your workman's compensation package!"

Thanks to the book <u>Cuss Control</u>, by James V. O'Connor, director of (this is true) the Cuss Control Academy, I'm making progress. According to O'Connor, I should use words that sound like cusses but aren't. I've tried "That was *Bolshevik*, pal!" and "You *nickerfutz*, ref!" and "*Sockchucker*!" People look at you as if they've been stabbed but can't find any blood.

You could always unearth a dead language, like Sanskrit or Latin: *illigitimi*! (Bastards!) Or steal from the 1920s: "Great oogoly moogoly!" Or go edgy Amish: "You son of a biscuit!"

If those don't work, O'Connor says to pretend your grandma is listening. Hey, Michigan students, would you repeat what you just said? Your granny missed it.

Anyway, the world is ugly enough without us turning on each other. So good for you, BU. Because, really, this s— has *got* to stop.

(Oops. Sorry, Mom.)

*Rick Reilly is a popular columnist for <u>Sports Illustrated</u>. Although he usually uses humor, he writes about serious subjects in moving ways as well (see Chapter 1).*

Work Cited

Reilly, Rick. "Swearing Off Swearing." <u>Sports Illustrated</u> 25 Sept. 2006: 80. ▬

## Humor as Satire

A major form of humor is *satire*. Satire helps you see problems in a new perspective. It exposes how foolish, unwise, or immoral something or someone is. <u>Saturday Night Live</u> depends on satire.

One of the most powerful examples of satire is the essay "A Modest Proposal" by Jonathan Swift, written in 1729. He offered a shocking possible solution to overpopulation in Ireland: fatten up poor undernourished children, cook them, and feed them to rich landowners. In this way Swift attacked the landlords who did little to feed and care for their tenants. His essay generated great response, provoking people to think about real reforms to address economic problems. Satire can be lost on undiscerning readers, however. Swift was condemned by many for writing an argument in "bad taste," and many thought he was advocating cannibalism.

For a modern example of satire, consider the following essay by Dave Barry.

## Taking the Manly Way Out

*Dave Barry*

Today we're going to explore the mysterious topic of How Guys Think, which has baffled women in general, and the editors of <u>Cosmopolitan</u> magazine in particular, for thousands of years.

The big question, of course, is: How come guys never call? After successful dates, I mean. You single women out there know what I'm talking about. You go out with a guy, and you have a great time, and he seems to have a great time, and at the end of the evening he says, quote, "Can I call you?" And you, interpreting this to mean "Can I call you?", answer: "Sure!"

The instant you say this, the guy's body start to dematerialize. Within a few seconds you can stick a tire iron right through him and wave it around; in a few more seconds he has vanished entirely, gone into the mysterious Guy Bermuda Triangle, where whole squadrons of your dates have disappeared over the years, never to be heard from again.

Eventually you start to wonder if there's something wrong with you, some kind of emotional hang-up or personality defect that your dates are detecting. Or possibly foot odor. You start having long, searching discussions with your women friends in which you say things like: "He really seemed to like me" and "I didn't feel as though I was putting pressure on him" and "Would you mind, strictly as a friend, smelling my feet?"

This is silly. There's nothing wrong with you. In fact, you should interpret the behavior of your dates as a kind of guy compliment to you. Because when the guy asks you if he can call you, what he's really asking you, in Guy Code, is will you marry him. Yes. See, your basic guy is into a straight-ahead, bottom-line kind of thought process that does not work nearly as well with the infinitely subtle complexities of human relationships as it does with calculating how much gravel is needed to cover a given driveway. So here's what the guy is thinking: If he calls you, you'll go out again, and you'll probably have another great time, so you'll probably go out again and have another great time, and so on until the only possible option will be to get married. This is classic Guy Logic.

So when you say "Sure!" in a bright cheery voice, you may think you're simply indicating a willingness to go out again, but as far as he's concerned you're endorsing a lifetime commitment that he is quite frankly not ready to make after only one date, so he naturally decides he can never see you again. From that day forward, if he spots you on the street, he'll spring in the opposite direction to avoid the grave risk that the two of you might meet, which would mean he'd have to ask you if you wanted to get a cup of coffee, and you might say yes, and pretty soon you'd be enjoying each other's company again, and suddenly a clergyman would appear at your table and YOU'D HAVE TO GET MARRIED AIEEEEEE.

(You women think this is crazy, right? Whereas you guys out there are nodding your heads.)

So my advice for single women is that if you're on a date with a guy you like, and he asks whether he can call you, you should give him a nonthreatening answer, such as: "No."

Or: "I guess so, but bear in mind that I'm a nun."

This will make him comfortable about seeing you again, each time gaining the courage to approach you more closely, in the manner of a timid, easily startled woodland creature such as a chipmunk. In a few years, if the two of you really do have common interests and compatible personalities, you may reach the point where he'll be willing to take the Big Step, namely, eating granola directly from your hand.

No matter how close you become, however, remember this rule: Do not pressure the guy to share his most sensitive innermost thoughts and feelings with you. Guys hate this, and I'll tell you why: If you were to probe inside the guy psyche, beneath that macho exterior and the endless droning about things like the 1978 World Series, you would find, deep down inside, a passionate, heartfelt interest in: the 1978 World Series. Yes. The truth is, guys don't *have* any sensitive innermost thoughts and feelings. It's time you women knew! All these years you've been agonizing about how to make the relationship work, wondering how come he never talks to you, worrying about all the anguished emotion he must have bottled up inside, and meanwhile he's fretting about how maybe he needs longer golf spikes. I'm sorry to have to tell you this. Maybe you *should* become a nun.

Anyway, I hope I've cleared up any lingering questions anybody might have regarding guys, as a gender. For some reason I feel compelled to end this with a personal note: Heather Campbell, if you're out there, I just want to say that I had a really nice time taking you to the Junior Prom in 1964, and I was a total jerk for never, not once, mentioning this fact to you personally.

*Dave Barry is a syndicated humor columnist who worked for 25 years at the <u>Miami Herald</u>. In 1988 he won the Pulitzer Prize for Commentary. He has written more than 30 books.*

Work Cited

Barry, Dave. "Taking the Manly Way Out." <u>Dave Barry Talks Back</u>. New York: Three Rivers Press: 1991.

What makes this essay satirical and funny? Barry offers a new perspective on the gender problem of men not asking women out after the first date. Is this a major problem? Maybe. Is he exaggerating the problem. Yes, likely. *Exaggeration* is a hallmark of much humor. In the first paragraph, Barry suggests that the issue of "How Guys Think has baffled . . . the editors of <u>Cosmopolitan</u> . . . for thousands of years." Is the magazine that old?

How men think is a broad, complex topic, but Barry wisely narrows it down: "How come guys never call?" Is it true that guys never call? Not really. He's exaggerating again, indeed overgeneralizing. But with humor, you can get away with overgeneralizing if it helps you make a point and causes laughter at the same time. When Barry discusses "Guy Logic," he overgeneralizes in a comic way that if a girl wants to go out again with a guy this means she wants to marry him. He claims, "The truth is, guys don't *have* any sensitive innermost thoughts and feelings. It's time you women knew!" Surely this is another funny exaggeration, with a kernel of truth in it for many guys—not all guys.

Besides using exaggeration such as "the guy's body starts to dematerialize," Barry uses specific examples and details to show what he means. He coins a new name: "Guy Bermuda Triangle," mentions "foot odor" as a possible reason guys don't call, and advises girls to say they are nuns so not to make guys afraid.

How does Barry use persuasive appeals? His pathos—he helps readers laugh and enjoy themselves. His logos—he uses humor to exaggerate how guys behave, especially when asking girls on dates. His appeal here is not rational: rather, he turns logic inside out and exaggerates. Yet, if his essay makes you reflect and wonder about your own experience as a girl or a guy with dating, then his logos serves his purpose. His ethos—if you like Dave Barry here for helping you smile and think, then it's hard not to appreciate him as a gifted writer of humor.

Satire is a common feature of humor in the online site <u>The Onion</u>, which labels itself "America's finest news source." This label already is a tip-off suggesting that <u>The Onion</u> is not America's finest news source. This technique of humor is called *irony*: an opposite meaning is intended and causes surprise. Here is a typical "news" item:

> BURLINGTON, VT—University of Vermont junior Becca Davis failed to do anything for the people of Tibet during her summer vacation, disgruntled fellow activists reported Tuesday.
>
> "With class out for the summer, Becca had a valuable window during which she could have pressured the Chinese government to end its tyrannical reign over the Tibetan people," campus activist Sally Coe said. "Instead, she sunbathed in the park and worked part-time at a local bookstore. As a result, the Tibetan freedom cause has been set back months."

What makes this humorous, and what argument is suggested? Would "disgruntled fellow activists" report a student for not working to free Tibet? Not likely. Would the cause be "set back months"? No. But this whole idea is foolish, suggesting perhaps that student activism doesn't really have much effect with certain remote causes.

Here is another news report from <u>The Onion</u>.

> WASHINGTON, DC—Environmental Protection Agency Administrator Stephen Johnson apologized during a press conference Tuesday for what critics called "flagrant oversight and neglect" in monitoring ground- and tap-water quality across the United States, claiming that his department was unaware that citizens were still consuming it. "I can honestly say we had no idea that anyone used faucet water anymore," Johnson said. "Bottled water, sure—I have some here on the lectern. But if there really are people out there still drinking tap water, all I can say is you're better off not knowing what's in there." Johnson added that official EPA policy is that Americans should stick to sports drinks.

Humor in argument is often absurd—untrue and foolish—to make a point. It's funny that an official working for the EPA claims his department "had no idea that anyone used faucet water anymore." He assumes that because everyone is using bottled water, it's not important to monitor the quality of regular tap water. His assumption and his overgeneralization provoke thought, however. What are the effects of bottled water on the environment? How well does the EPA do its job monitoring water?

Not all news items on <u>The Onion</u> are absurd. Some are more serious, though still using satire. Here is an excerpt from Ellen Dunst's op-ed essay, "I Should Not Be Allowed to Say the Following Things about America":

As Americans, we have a right to question our government and its actions. However, while there is a time to criticize, there is also a time to follow in complacent silence. And that time is now.

It's one thing to question our leaders in the days leading up to a war. But it is another thing entirely to do it *during* a war. Once the blood of young men starts to spill, it is our duty as citizens not to challenge those responsible for spilling that blood. We must remove the boxing gloves and put on the kid gloves. That is why, in this moment of crisis, I should not be allowed to say the following things about America:

Why do we purport to be fighting in the name of liberating the Iraqi people when we have no interest in violations of human rights—as evidenced by our habit of looking the other way when they occur in China, Saudi Arabia, Indonesia, Syria, Burma, Libya, and countless other countries? Why, of all the brutal regimes that regularly violate human rights, do we only intervene militarily in Iraq? Because the violation of human rights is not our true interest here. We just say it is as a convenient means of manipulating world opinion and making our cause seem more just.

That is exactly the sort of thing I should not say right now.

This also is not the time to ask whether diplomacy was ever given a chance. Or why, for the last 10 years, Iraq has been our sworn archenemy, when during the 15 years preceding it we traded freely in armaments and military aircraft with the evil and despotic Saddam Hussein. This is the kind of question that, while utterly valid, should not be posed right now.

What is ironic about this? As a citizen of the United States, Ellen Dunst has the right to question our government and speak out about its policies in Iraq. Her essay provides a clever rebuttal to statements President Bush made asking that citizens and Congress support him and the war, and that criticizing the war hurt the morale of the military and our chances to succeed. Humor in this way is smart: it provokes thought, making readers realize that we all have the freedom to question our country and should not apologize for it.

<u>The Daily Show</u> and <u>The Colbert Report</u> both offer satirical views on news events of the day, causing laughter and raising questions. Stephen Colbert introduced a new word, *truthiness*, now defined in <u>Webster's</u>, using Colbert's language, as "truth that comes from the gut, not books" and "the quality of preferring concepts or facts one wishes to be true, rather than concepts or facts known to be true." Here is an excerpt from a transcript of Colbert's first show in which he discusses this new word.

And that brings us to tonight's word: Truthiness.

Now I'm sure some of the word-police, the "wordanistas" over at Webster's, are gonna say, "Hey, that's not a word!" Well, anybody who knows me knows that I am no fan of dictionaries or reference books. They're elitist. Constantly telling us what is or isn't true, what did or didn't happen.

Who's Britannica to tell me the Panama Canal was finished in 1914? If I want to say it happened in 1941, that's my right.

I don't trust books. They're all fact, no heart. And that's exactly what's pulling our country apart today. Because face it, folks, we are a divided nation. Not between Democrats or Republicans, or conservatives and liberals, or tops and bottoms. No, we are divided by those who think with their head, and those who know with their heart.

Consider Harriet Miers. If you think about Harriet Miers, of course her nomination's absurd. But the president didn't say he thought about his selection; he said this:

President Bush: "I know her heart."

Notice he said nothing about her brain. He didn't have to. He feels the truth about Harriet Miers. . . .

Did you know that you have more nerve endings in your stomach than in your head? Look it up. Now, somebody's gonna say "I did look that up and it's wrong." Well, Mister, that's because you looked it up in a book. Next time, try looking it up in your gut. I did. And my gut tells me that's how our nervous system works.

Now I know some of you may not trust your gut . . . yet. But with my help you will. The "truthiness" is, anyone can read the news to you. I promise to feel the news . . . at you.

What makes this satire? Colbert's word *truthiness* causes us to wonder: What is truth? Is truth anything we want it to be? Can we manipulate truth to serve our own ends? He says he's free to change facts if they have "no heart." This is funny and ironic because facts should be objective; *heart* suggests being subjective and not verifiable. He ridicules President Bush for saying he knows the heart of his nominee for the Supreme Court. From this Colbert goes off, suggesting that only heart matters, not critical thought. He says this, but he wants listeners to know he means the opposite. It's not easy using humor as Stephen Colbert does. In criticizing or ridiculing President Bush he can offend many people.

Another form of satire is *parody* in which something or someone is imitated, usually for the purpose of ridicule. The Colbert Report imitates—makes fun of and ridicules—the Fox television news show The O'Reilly Factor. In that show Bill O'Reilly, a conservative commentator known for his combative style, claims his show offers an unbiased presentation of truth based on clear reason and facts. Each show contains a segment called "No Spin Zone." The word *Factor* in the show's title cleverly reinforces his claim that his show doesn't spin facts. On 1 May, 2006 Colbert delivered a monologue at the White House Correspondents Dinner, where he told the audience, "Every night on my show, the Colbert Report, I speak straight from the gut, OK? I give people the truth, unfiltered by rational argument. I call it the 'No Fact Zone.' Fox News, I hold a copyright on that term."

How is Colbert's statement "I give people the truth, unfiltered by rational argument" humorous? It's a contradiction: truth by definition should be filtered by rational argument. He flips the meaning of truth on its head, suggesting that rational argument impedes the search for truth. This is not only funny but it effectively reminds the audience just the opposite of what he says: we need to—especially our leaders in government need to—be truthful and use honest rational argument in our quest for truth.

When you write with humor or examine humor, consider these features:

- Humor often contains something unexpected that causes surprise.
- Humor often involves exaggeration.

- Humor is often illogical, using overgeneralizations and opposites (flips).
- Humor usually depends on details—specific and concrete ones.
- Humor influences logos, pathos, and ethos in interesting ways.

It is easier to analyze and evaluate humor as argument than to write your own argument using humor. But try using humor as a strategy. If you do, keep these guidelines in mind:

## GUIDELINES FOR USING HUMOR AS ARGUMENT

1. Take risks to express the opposite of what is considered normal or status quo.
2. Play with exaggeration.
3. Consider whether your intent is to use humor in a nonoffensive way to help readers laugh at some issue (as Dave Barry does), or whether your intent is to use satire to ridicule something or someone (as Stephen Colbert does).
4. If you use satire for ridicule, evaluate your ethos. Do you want to be mean-spirited like Doug Giles (see Humor as Pathos in Chapter 1) or Ann Coulter, a conservative columnist known for ridiculing liberals and liberal ideas? In her column on 28 June 2007, she wrote, "So for those of you who haven't read any of my five best-selling books: Liberals are driven by Satan and lie constantly." Ridicule can easily damage your ethos, but much depends on your audience. If you present a satire on liberal social policies and your audience is conservatives, you likely won't offend them. If your audience is more general, a combination of various views, you may want to tone down your satire.

## ACTIVITY 17

Explore humor by browsing The Onion online <http://www.theonion.com/content/index>. Select some satirical piece you like, copy it, and annotate it. Bring it to class to share.

## USING DEFINITION

A time-honored strategy is to argue from definition. This strategy is presented last so that you can draw from the previous strategies presented in this chapter to examine and define a word.

Critical thinkers notice unusual words and wonder what they mean—such as "*quiescently* frozen" on the wrapper of a popsicle. They think about important abstract words such as *happiness* and *character*. If you want to communicate and argue clearly, you need to examine the meanings of words. Let's explore *quality* and see if the word contains more meaning than you might think.

## ACTIVITY 18

In your notebook, please complete the following sentence: Quality is _____. You may complete the sentence with a word, a phrase, or a description. ▓

What is *quality*? Is your definition the same as everyone else's? Should you assume this? Suppose you are given two red roses: one is real and freshly cut; the other is plastic. Which rose has more quality? If you think the real one does, fine—but why? You may argue that the real rose once contained life and is more pleasing to your senses of sight, touch, and smell. You might add it is a symbol of love. Surely no one would enjoy receiving a plastic rose on Valentine's Day unless it were a joke, because it would suggest that love was fake. But does the mass-produced plastic rose have quality? Yes. It does not wilt and die.

Suppose you are given two rings: a silver ring with a turquoise stone and a plastic ring shaped like a tiny wristwatch from a bubble gum machine. Which ring has more quality? You might argue that the silver ring has more quality because it is made of precious natural substances and handcrafted. But many children would prefer the toy ring: the novelty of it would give it more quality. Suppose you consider a third ring—a gold wedding band with two names and a date engraved on the inside. Would this have more quality than the other two? You might assume it would mean more to the person who owns it. But if the person is divorced and no longer wears the ring, it may no longer have much quality.

Consider two sentences. Which one has more quality?

1. Nick saw some fish in the water.
2. Nick looked down into the clear, brown water, colored from the pebbly bottom, and watched the trout keeping themselves steady in the current with wavering fins.

Although the first sentence is concise, it does not present any specific images. The second sentence paints a vivid picture. The fish are *trout*, not general *fish*. Also, the sentence contains what appear to be contradictions but aren't: the water is clear yet brown because it's colored from pebbles; the trout keep themselves steady by moving their fins. Some people might argue that the second sentence is *too* descriptive. Is quality in the eye of the beholder? (Ernest Hemingway wrote the second sentence, from his story "Big Two-Hearted River, Part 1.")

Notice that you've been thinking critically about this word *quality*, exploring examples of it (roses, rings, sentences), and analyzing it through comparison. You have seen how the meaning of quality changes depending on where you find the quality.

However, have you as yet reached a clear definition of the term? You have inferred the existence of quality through the particular examples presented. But can you prove—in a more logical way—that quality exists? Robert Pirsig in his book <u>Zen and the Art of Motorcycle Maintenance</u> struggles with the meaning of quality, wondering how people can lead quality lives. After much inquiry he offers this hypothesis, using the strategy of refutation: "A thing exists if a world without it can't function normally. If we can show that a world without Quality functions abnormally, then we have shown that Quality exists, whether it's defined or not."

## ACTIVITY 19

Close your eyes for a minute and think about this question: What would a world without quality be like? Try to imagine how your life would be in such a world. ▬

Without quality, life would contain none of the people, objects, experiences, ideas that you consider valuable. Robert Pirsig explains that without quality what you enjoy would no longer exist. Art would disappear: "There's no point in hanging a painting on the wall when the bare wall looks just as good." Music too, since you would not be able to differentiate music from noise. All sports would vanish because "scores would no longer be a measurement of anything meaningful, but simply empty statistics, like the number of stones in a pile of gravel." Favorite foods and drinks would become bland; supermarkets would sell ungraded meat and milk. People would no longer enjoy "movies, dances, plays and parties." Pirsig concludes that the world *can* function without quality, "but life would be so dull as to be hardly worth living. In fact it wouldn't be worth living. The term *worth* is a quality term. Life would just be living without any values or purposes at all."

For Robert Pirsig the word *quality* carries "a magnitude of importance." Although you encounter the word daily, you may not consider its far-reaching implications—perhaps because the word has lost much of its power from overuse. Advertisers often exploit it. Ford Motor Company's slogan is "Quality Is Job 1." But should you assume Ford products possess quality because their commercials say they do? Any company, college, or corporation can claim it has quality because the word itself is abstract and ambiguous like *family values*. It sounds good. Because *quality* can be used by anyone to elevate almost anything to importance, the word may at last come to mean nothing. This is why defining the word is necessary: the word is too important not to define.

Let's return to your "Quality is _____" completion you wrote at the beginning of this exploration. Does your definition reflect what you think about the word now? Compare yours to this sampling of student responses:

---

Quality is the value a person sees in an object.

Quality is persistent effort.

Quality is a smile coming slowly to your lips because you know the object before you is as good as can be humanly produced short of total perfection.

---

Would a dictionary provide the best definition of *quality*? Webster's New World defines the word as "1. any of the features that make something what it is; characteristic element; attribute 2. basic nature; character; kind 3. the degree of excellence which a thing possesses." The third definition comes closest to what we've examined. Clearly, the dictionary does not provide the best definition. Your definition may mean more because it comes from you.

In <u>Language in Thought and Action</u>, S. I. Hayakawa clarifies the dilemma of definition. He writes, "The meanings of words are *not* in the words; they are in us." As you have seen, the meanings of any abstract word like *quality* depend on what you choose the term to mean. This is why if you wish to communicate the idea clearly you need to give examples—to refer to specific objects, people, events, memories that represent quality to you. Hayakawa adds, "Beware of definitions, which are words about words. Think with examples rather than definitions whenever possible."

Although *quality* does not have a clear definition and its meaning is largely personal, let's delve a little further into the idea of quality, because this directly concerns critical thinking and writing.

## ACTIVITY 20

In your notebook, write a response to this question: How do you achieve quality? Assume you want to achieve quality in some process: a skill or talent of yours, playing a sport or an instrument. When you finish, continue reading. ■

Perhaps you wrote about hard work, skill, determination, practice, concentration. These all indeed help people achieve quality. However, Robert Pirsig concludes that there is one primary force in achieving quality: caring. If you care about what you do, you will do a better job. This sounds simple. But what does *caring* mean? You see, once you start defining words and realize how useful definition is for thinking, it's hard to stop. Pirsig defines the word thus: "When one isn't dominated by feelings of separateness from what he's working on, then one can be said to 'care' about what he's doing. That is what caring really is, a feeling of identification with what one's doing." Do you agree? The times when you have performed at your best, did you care the most? Did you identify deeply with what you were doing?

Let's apply the same question to writing: How do you achieve quality in writing? If Pirsig's claim is true, then when you write well, you don't feel separated from your writing. Indeed, you identify with it: you care about your main idea, your supporting evidence, your organization, your style and voice, your audience and purpose. You care enough to revise, perhaps several times. When you have not written well, did you feel disconnected from your paper? Perhaps you wrote it the night before it was due or didn't care enough to proofread it. Granted, you may care intensely about a paper yet still not produce quality writing. (Perhaps the subject is too close and personal; you need more distance from it.) But—usually—if you care enough about your writing, you will keep working on it until it achieves the quality you and your instructor or supervisor want.

Critical thinkers care about words. They know that meanings are in people, not in words. They know that if they want to communicate clearly they should define key words and provide specific examples. They also know that if they want to understand what somebody means when they use a certain word, they should ask for a definition and an example. Critical thinkers don't assume their audience will automatically know what they mean.

The question of what is *quality* is central to this book's aim in helping you develop yourself as a critical thinker, writer, and reader. Indeed, writing an extended definition of a word is an important skill for critical thinkers.

## Digging for Roots of Words

To help you define words, you can research their origins—their etymology. Like an archaeologist digging for arrowheads, you can find interesting and useful information this way. Suppose a friend told you that you have a lot of *sarcasm* in your voice. His remark bothers you because you don't consider yourself sarcastic. Now puzzled, you start to inquire what your friend means by *sarcasm*. You open your dictionary and read the modern meaning: "a taunting, sneering, cutting, or caustic remark" (Webster's New World). Sometimes you taunt people, you agree—but sneering and cutting? Then, you notice the etymology of the word located in brackets: [LL. *sarcasmos* < Gr. *sarkasmos* < *sarkazein*, to tear flesh like dogs, speak bitterly < *sarx* (gen. *sarkos*), flesh]. You're shocked and wonder if you sometimes talk as if you "tear flesh like dogs." You vow to watch what you say—you don't want to be sarcastic.

As the above etymology reveals, words have histories and you can trace their roots. You can see how *sarcasm* derives from Greek to Latin; you can see how the meaning was extremely concrete (tearing flesh) but now is more general (taunting, sneering, cutting). Digging for roots of words can help you develop arguments. Consider one more example. Suppose somebody calls you *humble*, but you don't know what the word really means. Looking up its modern meaning, you find "1. having or showing a consciousness of one's defects or shortcomings; not proud; not self-assertive; modest 2. low in condition, rank, or position; lowly; unpretentious." Looking at the etymology, you discover "[ME. < OFr.< L. *humilis*, low, small, slight, akin to *humus*, soil, earth]." This concrete description helps you visualize the idea of *humble*: being down-to-earth, being the earth itself like humus—helping things grow. You decide you'd rather be humble than sarcastic.

## ACTIVITY 21

Find and copy the etymology and meanings of three words in a dictionary such as Webster's New World Dictionary, The Oxford English Dictionary, or Dictionary.com. Choose words that puzzle or intrigue you or that pertain to your major interests. Try to find words that have interesting or surprising concrete roots. Cite your source. Some suggestions: *art, science, serendipity, discover*.

As this chapter has shown, you can use various strategies to develop and support an argument. The strategies you use influence your logos, pathos, and ethos. Remember, however, to use strategies not as ends in themselves but as means to achieve your overall purpose—to communicate an idea you care about and to persuade readers to care about it as well.

## ACTIVITY 22

### DEFINITION ESSAY USING VARIOUS STRATEGIES OF ARGUMENTATION

Write an essay (2 to 4 pages) in which you try to persuade classmates and your instructor to accept your understanding of a word. Your essay should contain a title, an introduction with a clearly stated thesis, a body of at least two or three supporting paragraphs, and a conclusion.

Suggestions:

1. Write an essay on *quality*, making what you think quality is the thesis that the rest of your paper will explain and support. Use examples from your experience, observation, and knowledge.

2. Write about a word that you believe is important, a word that intrigues you, a word that bothers you a great deal, a word that has given you problems, or a word over which you experienced a paradigm shift.

3. Think of a word you use a lot. Define what you mean by it in different situations.

For this essay, use some of the strategies presented in this chapter and the previous two chapters:

**Examples, illustrations, and reasons:** showing and explaining what you mean

**Opposites:** examining contradictions or paradoxes

**Comparison:** examining similarities and differences such as crazy/insane or knowledge/ wisdom

**Refutation:** defining a word by explaining what it is not

**Induction or deduction:** arranging evidence from examples to generalization or from generalization to examples

**Description:** using concrete details to show what you mean

**Narration:** telling a story to make a point

**Analogy:** using an extended comparison between unlike things

**Classification:** examining categories, kinds, or types—such as three types of happiness

**Cause and effect:** examining causes and/or effects of a word

**Humor:** using humorous tone or possibly satire while you define a word

**Etymology:** tracing historical roots of a word's meanings

## EXPLORING AN ESSAY

Writers can choose from an array of strategies to help them argue. As a critical thinker, you can explore—analyze and evaluate—any piece of writing by looking at the strategies a writer uses.

## ACTIVITY 23

Choose one of the following essays to explore in a report (2 to 4 pages). Try to write responses to most of these questions and to any questions you raise: What is the writer's thesis and how well does he or she support it? What strategies of argumentation does the writer use, and how are they effective? How do the strategies complement the writer's appeals to logos, pathos, or ethos? Do you agree or disagree with the writer's thesis? How would you describe the writer's voice—the sound of his or her personality? What do you notice about the writer's style—diction and sentence patterns? ▬

### A Feeling of Wildness

#### *David Gessner*

I believe in wildness, both in the natural world and within each of us.

As a nature writer, I have traveled all over the world to experience the wild, but some of my own wildest moments have been closer to home, on the same domestic Cape Cod beach I've returned to all my life. In summer this beach is covered with kids, umbrellas and beach balls, but in the winter the cold clears it of people and its character changes. From the rocks at the end of this beach, I once watched hundreds of snow-white gannets dive from high in the air and plunge into the cold winter ocean like living javelins. Then, as the birds dove down, I suddenly saw something dive up: a humpback whale breaching through the same fish the gannets were diving for.

"In wildness is the preservation of the world," wrote Thoreau, but people often get the quote wrong and use "wilderness" instead. While wilderness might be untrammeled land along the Alaskan coast, wildness can happen anywhere—in the jungle or your backyard. And it's not just a place; it's a feeling. It rises up when you least expect it.

In fact, it was while observing my own species, my own family, that I experienced the two wildest moments of my life. The first happened holding my father's hand while he died. I listened to his final breaths, gasping and fish-like, and I gripped his hand tight enough to feel the last pulsings of his heart. Something rose up in me that day, something deep, animal, unexpected, something that I didn't experience again until nine years later, when my daughter Hadley was born.

Before Hadley's birth everyone warned me that my life was about to change, the implication being that it would become tamer. But there was nothing tame about that indelible moment, during the C-section, when the doctor reached into my wife, and a bloody head appeared, straight up, followed by Hadley's full emergence and a wild squall of life as her little arms rose over her head in victory. And it was somewhere around then that I felt the great rush come surging up. Sure it was physiological—goose bumps and tingling—but it was also more than that: a wild gushing, both a loss and then a return to self,

I believe that these moments of death and life give us a reconnection to our primal selves, a reminder that there is something wilder lurking below the everyday, and that, having tasted this wildness, we return to our ordinary lives both changed and charged. So, while I'll continue to seek out wild places, I know I don't need to travel to the Amazon or Everest to experience the ineffable. It is here on Cape Cod, on the domestic beach where I first walked holding my mother's hand, and where I later spread my father's ashes, that I learned that my wildest moments are often closest to home. And it is where that I now bring my daughter Hadley for our daily walk, secretly hoping that the wild will rise up in her when she least expects it.

*Nature writer David Gessner is the author of six books, including* The Prophet of Dry Hill: Lessons from a Life in Nature *(2005). His essays have appeared in* Orion, The Harvard Review, *and other journals. He teaches creative nonfiction writing at the University of North Carolina at Wilmington.*

Work Cited

Gessner, David. "A Feeling of Wildness." This I Believe 30 July 2007 <http://www.npr.org/templates/story/story.php?storyId=12254393>.

## Here's a Little Tip about Gratuities

### Connie Schultz

If you've ever used a coat check, you probably noticed a tip jar on the counter at evening's end.

You might stick a bill or two into that jar without even thinking about who is getting the tip. You probably assume the person behind the counter, usually a woman, is getting the money.

That's certainly what I always assumed. From now on, I'm going to ask.

In the last year, I have attended three charity events at Windows on the River, a banquet hall at the Powerhouse in the Flats. At the end of each dinner, I picked up my wrap at the coat-check counter.

One of those times, I pointed to the large tip jar bulging with bills and said to the weary clerk, "Well, at least you get a decent amount of tips for standing here."

She shook her head and said, "Oh, we don't get to keep those."

I thought I misheard her. "What?"

"We don't keep the tips."

"Who does?" I asked.

"Management."

When I asked her how that made her feel, she sighed. "They say they use it to give us a Christmas party."

Nowhere was there a sign indicating that the pile of bills in the tip jar was going, not to the clerk, but to management.

Recently, I attended another dinner at Windows on the River. This time, the tips were stuffed into a large, opaque box. I watched as one person after another shoved bills into the slot on the top.

"Who gets these tips?" I asked the coat-check clerk.

She resisted telling me, but I pressed. "Management," she said softly.

"How does that make you feel?" I asked.

She shrugged her shoulders. "Life isn't fair, right?"

This week, I called Kristine Jones, the general manager for Windows.

"Why are you asking about this?" she said. "Why do you care?"

The "girls," she insisted, are happy with the current arrangement. "It's not like they're standing there all night. The girls check the coats and then wait on tables until the last hour. And they're already paid an hourly wage."

Later that same day, two vice presidents—Dave Grunenwald and Pat McKinley—called on speakerphone from Jacobs International Management Co., which owns Windows.

"We're confused," Grunenwald said. "This is newsworthy?"

They were brimming with assurances. Their 30 or so employees—some of the kindest, most professional servers I've ever encountered—are paid more than the minimum wage. How much more, they wouldn't say. The company matches any 401(k) contribution they can make but offers no health insurance because they're all part time.

And they get a free meal. "Some places charge their employees for food," McKinley said.

Grunenwald and McKinley say they collect only $800 a year in that tip jar. Hard to believe, judging from the amount stuffed into the box last Friday night. "We match it for their Christmas party," Grunenwald said.

When I asked if they'd ever let the employees decide between keeping the tips and having a party, they fell silent.

That would be a "no."

"Why does this matter?" they asked.

Dignity is non-negotiable, writes scholar Vartan Gregorian. It is also every human's birthright, and management's blatant rankism at Windows is an assault on the dignity of all involved.

Generous patrons are misled. Hard-working employees must stand silently by as they watch management walk off with hundreds, perhaps thousands, of dollars intended for them.

"Maybe we need to rethink this," Grunenwald said. "Maybe we do," echoed McKinley.

There's no maybe about it. Both union and industry officials say keeping the coat-check tips is unacceptable.

General manager Jones was unrepentant. "I don't ever think about who's getting the tip when I use a coat check," she said. "I don't care."

Then she added, "I don't think anyone else cares who gets the tip, either."

I think she's wrong.

What do you think?

*Connie Schulz, a columnist for* The Plain Dealer *in Cleveland, Ohio, was awarded the 2005 Pulitzer Prize for Commentary "for her pungent columns that provided a voice for the underdog and underprivileged." She was a 2003 Pulitzer Prize finalist in feature writing for her series, "The Burden of Innocence," which chronicled the ordeal of Michael Green, who was imprisoned for 13 years for a rape he did not commit. The week after her series ran, the real rapist turned himself in after reading her stories. He is currently serving a five-year prison sentence.*

### Work Cited

Schulz, Connie. "Here's a Little Tip about Gratuities." The Plain Dealer 1 April 2004.

The Pulitzer Prize Winners 2005 for Commentary. <http://www.pulitzer.org/year/2005/commentary//works/schultz1.html>.

## What Money Can't Buy

### *by Rick Reilly*

The Texas Titans sixth-grade basketball team is on its way to a tournament, so the kids do what they usually do. They board Kenny Troutt's chartered 737 jet (except for the times when they rent the Dallas Mavericks' jet or the San Antonio Spurs'). There's a flight attendant on board, video games and Haagen-Dazs bars. They're going from Dallas all the way to Houston. It will take about 50 minutes.

*The D.C. Assault sixth-grade basketball team is on its way to a tournament, so the players do what they usually do. They pile into assistant coach Ed Powell's 2000 Suburban. Coach Donald Campbell and another parent will also take their cars. They're going from Washington, D.C., all the way to Columbia, S.C. It will take about eight hours.*

On board the private jet is the man who ponies up for everything, the 59-year-old Troutt, whose son is on the team. Troutt is the founder of Excel Communications and, according to <u>Forbes</u>, is worth $1.1 billion. On a lot of the plane trips there'll also be at least one parent of each player, plus the three full-time salaried coaches and the team's general manager. This is nothing. For a tournament in Washington, D.C., last year, the Titans' traveling party numbered 95. Nobody but Troutt spent a dime.

*Crammed into Powell's SW are just the players. Hopefully, none of them will get carsick and throw up like on the trip to Florida last year. Powell's still trying to get the smell out. "A lot of these kids are from the inner city," he says. "They'd never traveled that far in a car before."*

When the Titans arrive in Houston, a luxury bus is waiting for them on the tarmac. They head straight to one of the better hotels in town. Usually it's a Hyatt or an Omni. No hassles at the registration desk—their keys are waiting on a table. It's all been handled by the Titans' advance man.

*The Assault players feel lucky if they get to stay in a Holiday Inn Express. One time they checked into a bargain motel, where the clerk handed them their towels through a slot in the protective glass. The rooms were cold and damp and dirty. The boys refused to get under the covers. They slept on top of the bedspreads or on the floor.*

The Titans meet for dinner in a banquet room set up by the hotel. The food has been selected by the team's trainer-nutritionist.

*The Assault usually gets KFC but occasionally splurges for Chick-fil-A. The coaches pay for the food, the gas and some of the hotel rooms. Powell's a social worker, but he makes more than some of the parents, who sometimes can't afford the $25 a player tournament fee. Then Powell pays that, too.*

The Titans will play about 90 games this year and practice twice a week. They hire private coaches to teach shooting, defense and rebounding. Soon, they'll start practicing at the high-school-sized gym Troutt is adding to his 13,000 square-foot mansion in Dallas.

*The Assault tries to practice twice a week, too, but it's not easy to get court time. The team practices at a rec center unless the high school kids refuse to get off the court.*

The Titans go to great places. Last year they went to Las Vegas for a tournament and stayed at Caesars Palace. Troutt gave each family cash for a nice meal and a Vegas show. A lot of them saw Celine Dion. This summer the team is planning to play in Germany and Lithuania, and each player can bring a parent.

*The Assault goes as far as the parents can drive. They flew one time to a tournament in Oregon. For nearly every kid on the team, it was his first time on a plane.*

A lot of rival coaches and parents would like to dismember the Titans. They think Troutt is spoiling this team as well as the fourth-grade Titans. (He has a son on that team too.) They think 10 is too young to be living like an NBA star. They say Troutt unfairly attracts some of the most talented kids in Dallas with his money. But even rivals say that at least Troutt isn't trying to make money off his players' backs—the scourge of AAU ball—and his players are humble and well behaved. "I'm not spoiling these kids," says Troutt, who co-owns 2003 Kentucky Derby winner Funny Cide. "Any kid that's willing to practice six hours a week and travel three weekends out of four is working hard for what he gets." To which his critics say, "Sounds brutal. Where do we sign up?"

*Powell isn't complaining. His kids are disciplined and well coached. "Sure, we wish we had some of those things they have, but we believe that if you're not handed things, then you're hungrier and you play a little harder. When you're sharing a car for five or six hours, when you're sleeping in the same bed as your teammate, he's not your teammate any longer. He's your brother."*

The Titans played the Assault four times last year. The Assault won all four.

Work Cited

Reilly, Rick. "What Money Can't Buy." <u>Sports Illustrated</u> 12 Mar. 2007: 86.

# Strategies of Repetition

*You can create sentences for meaning and for sound.*

## SENTENCE TOOLS

### Parallelism

What stylistic pattern do the following sentences have in common?

> Losing balance, regaining it, and going on, is the substance of learning.
> (Donald Graves, <u>Writing: Teachers & Children at Work</u>)

> We should be enabling, healing, curing.
> (Christopher Reeve, Democratic National Convention, 1996)

> Making a point, supporting it with specific evidence, and organizing the evidence are basic steps of communication.

Words ending in *-ing* are repeated in each of these sentences. *Parallelism, or parallel structure, is the intentional repetition of a word ending, a single word, a phrase, or a clause.* As a critical thinker, you can use parallelism for emphasis and for making attention-catching patterns of language. By balancing certain words so they have the same structure, you can make sentences clearer, smoother, and easier to read. (Did you notice the repetition of *-er* endings in that sentence?) Parallel ordering of thoughts suggests a careful mind at work.

## ACTIVITY 1

### REVISION

In your notebook write three sentences using a repetition of *-ing* words. Then look at your recent writing, and see if you can improve any sentence by using parallel *-ing* words or phrases. Try to use this tool the next time you write. ■

Notice the stylistic pattern in these sentences.

Your economic security does not lie in your job; it lies in your own power to produce—to think, to learn, to create, to adapt. (Stephen Covey, <u>Seven Habits</u>)

With this faith we will be able to work together, to pray together, to struggle together, to go to jail together, to stand up for freedom together, knowing that we will be free one day. (M. L. King Jr., "I Have a Dream")

We love occasional reversals of established order, both to defuse the tension of inequity and to infuse a bit of variety into our lives. (Stephen Jay Gould, "The Dinosaur Rip-Off")

These sentences repeat phrases that begin with *to*. This repetition provides a clear structure for readers to follow. It also provides a rhythm to the sentences, appealing to your sense of sound. Gould's pair of phrases *to defuse* and *to infuse* are well chosen because of the reversal of thought they convey. A scientist, Gould carefully chooses his words for meaning as well as sound. You can do the same.

Writers sometimes use more than one form of parallelism within a sentence or group of sentences:

"Skilled" thinking can easily be used to obfuscate rather than to clarify, to maintain a prejudice rather than to break it down, to aid in the defense of a narrow interest rather than to take into account the public good. (Richard Paul, <u>Critical Thinking</u>)

Here Paul uses parallel structure by repeating *to phrases* and *rather than*. This double repetition gives the impression that Paul controls his thinking well: he can express a complex idea by fastening it to clear parallel structure. His voice sounds authoritative—persuasive.

**ACTIVITY 2**

## REVISION

In your notebook write three sentences using a repetition of *to* phrases. For one sentence, consider imitating Richard Paul's use of *to* phrases and *rather than*'s. Then look at your recent writing, and see if you can improve any sentence by using parallel *to* phrases. Try to use this tool the next time you write. ▄▄▄

Notice the stylistic pattern in these sentences.

She is a woman of beauty, of wisdom, of grace.

Thinking is a matter of seeing relationships—relationships of parts to wholes, of items in a sequence, of causes and effects. (Ann Berthoff, <u>Forming/Thinking/Writing</u>)

Some of the language of the early [feminist] movement contained an ugly rejection of mothers, of motherhood, of softness, of wanting to be in deep relationships with men. (Anne Lamott, <u>Traveling Mercies</u>)

The *of* phrases smoothly connect different parts of each sentence. They give each sentence a pattern with balance and rhythm. They suggest to readers that the writers know what they are saying and how to say it.

## ACTIVITY 3

### REVISION

In your notebook write three sentences using a repetition of *of* phrases. Then look at your recent writing, and see if you can improve any sentence by using parallel *of* phrases. Try to use this tool the next time you write.

You have practiced three types of parallel structure: repeating *-ing* phrases, *to* phrases, and *of* phrases. Although these types often occur in writing, countless other types occur as well because writers can repeat almost any word ending or word. Here, for example, psychologist Jerome Bruner repeats the familiar *un* prefix:

> Our attention is attracted to something that is unclear, unfinished, or uncertain.
> (Toward a Theory of Instruction)

With style, bits of language can matter a lot. A simple repetition of *un* can make Bruner's sentence easy to read and to consider. Such repetition suggests the work of a critical thinker who carefully guides readers with the structure of his thoughts.

## Anaphora

Notice the stylistic pattern in these sentences.

> We shall fight on the beaches, we shall fight on the landing grounds, we shall fight in the fields and in the streets, we shall fight in the hills; we shall never surrender.
> (Winston Churchill, House of Commons, 4 June 1940)

> We need the arts to express ideas and feelings in ways beyond words. We need the arts to stir creativity and enrich a child's way of knowing. We need the arts to integrate the fragments of academic life. We need the arts to empower the disabled. And, above all, we need the arts to create community and to build connections across the generations.
> (Ernest Boyer, 1994 speech to the National Endowment for the Arts)

This stylistic tool is called *anaphora*, a favorite of many politicians and writers. *Anaphora is the repetition of a single word or phrase at the beginning of clauses or sentences.* As a tool of emphasis, it helps an audience follow along and remember key ideas. It shows an audience that the speaker or writer has control and can steer thoughts in parallel ways. It also helps stir an audience emotionally, as Churchill's sentences did to the people of Great Britain. Anaphora strengthens a writer's voice, capturing a tone of conviction.

Anaphora often occurs toward the end of a speech or essay, but you can use it almost anywhere for emphasis. Anaphora usually shows a writer's passion about an idea or problem. Whenever writers use this tool, they want your attention and usually get it. Notice how Hillary Clinton uses anaphora:

> *Right now*, in our biggest cities and our smallest towns, *there are* boys and girls being tucked gently into bed, and *there are* boys and girls who have no one to call mom or dad, and no place to call home. . . .
>
> *Right now there are* parents worrying: "What if the baby sitter is sick tomorrow?" Or: "How can we pay for college this fall?" And *right now there are* parents despairing about gang members and drug pushers on the corners in their neighborhoods.
>
> *Right now there are* parents questioning a popular culture that glamorizes sex and violence, smoking and drinking, and teaches children that the logos on their clothes are more valued than the generosity in their hearts. (emphasis added)
>
> (Democratic National Convention, 1996)

Clinton's repetition of "Right now there are" serves as a refrain, reinforcing her point that many parents and children in our country experience homelessness, violence, and drugs and that society must address these problems—now.

Lawyers often use anaphora to catch the ear of jury members and to reinforce key ideas. What is the effect of the anaphora used by Daniel Petrocelli (lawyer for the Goldman family whose son O. J. Simpson was accused of murdering) in this passage?

> Petrocelli focused on Simpson's four days of testimony, in which Simpson admitted that he had been unfaithful during his marriage and had been involved in several domestic disturbances.
>
> "What kind of man takes a baseball bat to his wife's car right in front of her and says she was not upset even though she called police for help?
>
> "What kind of man kicks in a door and says it was just a reflex?
>
> "What kind of man says his wife was lying on that tape when she says she was afraid and he was going—in her words—to beat the s— out of her?
>
> "What kind of man says cheating on your wife isn't a lie?
>
> "What kind of man says his wife's most private writings . . . are—quote—a pack of lies? . . .
>
> "What kind of man comes into court and says, I never lied about anything in my life?"
>
> Petrocelli answered his own questions: "A guilty man . . . A man with no remorse. A man with no conscience."

The repetition of "What kind of man" hammers home a question that undermines Simpson's ethos—credibility. Used this way, anaphora can be powerfully persuasive.

One of the most potent stylistic tools writers can use, anaphora can help you as a critical thinker persuade an audience to feel, to think, and to care about a problem. But if you overuse it, anaphora can lose its power and raise questions about your efforts to persuade.

## ACTIVITY 4

Write an example of anaphora in your notebook. It may be one sentence or several sentences. Experiment. Then write another example. For example, "*We learned* to support our ideas with specific evidence; *we learned* to examine paradoxes; *we learned* to argue about what matters to us." Consider using this tool the next time you write or give a speech. ▪

## Epistrophe

Notice the stylistic pattern in these sentences.

> We here highly resolve . . . that government of the people, by the people, for the people, shall not perish from the earth. (Lincoln, Gettysburg Address)

> What education has to impart is an intimate sense for the power of ideas, for the beauty of ideas, and for the structure of ideas. (Alfred North Whitehead, Aims of Education and Other Essays)

> On the wall of my room when I was in rehab was a picture of the space shuttle blasting off, autographed by every astronaut now at NASA. On top of the picture it says, "We found nothing is impossible." That should be our motto. Not a Democratic motto, not a Republican motto. But an American motto. (Christopher Reeve, Democratic National Convention, 1996)

The opposite of anaphora, *epistrophe is the repetition of a single word or phrase at the end of clauses or sentences.* The expression "See no evil, hear no evil, speak no evil" utilizes this tool. Epistrophe creates emphasis at the end of thoughts. Thus, this tool helps an audience focus on and remember key ideas. Lincoln's sentence helps you focus on *people*, Whitehead's on *ideas*, and Reeve's paragraph on *motto*. Epistrophe is not used by writers as often as anaphora, though it is a highly effective tool of style. Used sparingly, epistrophe can give your writing power.

Sometimes writers use both anaphora and epistrophe within the same group of sentences. Notice how Morrie Schwartz uses both tools naturally when he talks with Mitch Albom:

> "There are a few rules I know to be true about love and marriage: If you don't respect the other person, you're gonna have a lot of trouble. If you don't know how to compromise, you're gonna have a lot of trouble. If you can't talk openly about what goes on between you, you're gonna have a lot of trouble. And if you don't have a common set of values in life, you're gonna have a lot of trouble. Your values must be alike." (Tuesdays with Morrie)

You can hear Morrie's voice with the informal *gonna*'s. Notice what Hillary Clinton does here:

> If women are healthy and educated, their families will flourish. If women are free from violence, their families will flourish. If women have a chance to work and earn as full and equal partners in society, their families will flourish. (Hillary Clinton, "Women's Rights Are Human Rights")

Clinton's group of sentences is well crafted, each beginning with *If women* and ending with *their families will flourish*. Her style suggests control, strength, and conviction. It creates her clear and sure voice.

## ACTIVITY 5

Write an example of epistrophe in your notebook. It may be one sentence or several sentences. Experiment. Then write another example. For example, "I value rational people who speak *with their heart*, listen *with their heart*, and act *with their heart*." You may also try combining anaphora and epistrophe. Consider using this tool the next time you write. ▄▄

## THE POWER OF THREES IN SENTENCES

Authentic style is not a collection of tricks you can add to your writing. Style should not be considered gimmicks to give your essays more zip. The tools of diction and sentences presented in these Interchapters will help you communicate more clearly and persuasively. Careful writers and speakers intentionally use these tools. At this point, consider threes.

## ACTIVITY 6

In your notebook, without looking ahead, list as many sayings or phrases as you can think of that contain three main words. For example, *red, white, and blue.* ▄▄

Susan Ager, a columnist for the <u>Detroit Free Press</u>, wrote an essay about threes. As you read it, consider how well she communicates her thesis and supporting evidence. Consider her style: the way she uses words and sentences. Consider her voice (the sound of her personality), her tone (attitude toward her audience, subject, and self), and her use of persuasive appeals—logos, pathos, ethos. Look to see whether she uses any of the stylistic tools you've been learning.

### Baby, Baby, Baby, 3 Has Its Charms

*Susan Ager*

No ifs, ands or buts about it: Three enjoys a magic and rhythm that two and four lack. John and Michelle Engler [former governor and wife of Michigan] will learn what preachers and writers already know: Three is powerful. Memorable. Dramatic. Two is tepid, four overwrought.

Three works.

Had the Engler triplets been boys, they might have been Larry, Mo and Curly. Or Winken, Blinken and Nod. With mixed genders, they might have been Peter, Paul and Mary.

The girls, by birth order, became Margaret, Hannah and Madeleine. Nickname two, and you've got a winning team: Hannah, Maddy and Meg.

Three is magical because we think about much of the world in contrasting pairs: men and women, body and soul, fire and ice.

Couples make the world go 'round, but trios give it zest: Men, women and children. Red, white and blue. Bacon, lettuce and tomato.

## Hop, skip and a jump

The musketeers were three. So were the blind mice and the Magi. So were the witches who chanted around a bubbling cauldron in <u>Macbeth</u>.

The genie gave Aladdin three wishes. We give our friends three guesses. Realtors cite the three most important things to look for in a house: Location, location, location.

Animal, vegetable or mineral? Coffee, tea or milk? Children study readin', 'ritin' and 'rithmetic, and learn their ABCs—not ABs or ABCDs.

What's so wrong with two and four? Think about it geometrically: Two points make nothing but a straight line.

Mork and Mindy. Frick and Frack. Black and white.

Three points make a triangle, elegant and interesting.

The Father, Son and Holy Spirit.

The butcher, the baker, the candlestick maker.

A loaf of bread, a jug of wine and thou.

With four points, you get some variety, but four words or concepts are one too many for graceful recollection.

We can name the Beatles, but each of us chooses a different order. Same with the seasons. I start with winter. My husband starts with summer, because he remembers the Howdy Doody show and Princess Summerfall Winterspring.

## Sun, moon, stars

Whoever named the rock group Blood, Sweat and Tears was wise to the magic of three. The name comes from a Winston Churchill pledge to end World War II with "blood, toil, tears and sweat," but I always have to look up that quote to remember the correct order.

Advice goes down easiest in threes: Eat, drink and be merry. Healthy, wealthy and wise. Jesus told a lame man, "Arise, take up thy bed and walk."

And more: On your mark, get set, go!

Snap, crackle and pop.

Rub-a-dub-dub, three men in a tub.

I could get carried away with this. Like waltzing, the examples are endless and dizzying: *one*-two-three, *one*-two-three, *one*-two-three. So much more mesmerizing than the two-step.

Enough. The Engler triplets will see the magic of three all around them as they grow.

I wish them each a good dose of faith, hope and charity. A safe dose of sex, drugs and rock'n'roll. And opportunities for health, wealth and happiness, every morning, noon and night.

*When strangers ask Susan Ager what her column is about, she says, "Life. It's a big topic."*

Work Cited

Ager, Susan. "Baby, Baby, Baby, 3 Has Its Charms." <u>Detroit Free Press</u>, 15 Nov. 1994: D1.

Susan Ager tries to persuade you that three is a powerful number in thought and style. Not only does she make an insightful point about three, but she makes it humorously. Her voice is inquisitive and honest—she sounds excited in this essay, as if she's having fun with her subject and her language. She writes, "I could get carried away." She does get carried away, and her voice carries readers with her. Through many clear examples of threes, Ager enables readers to consider this number more than they had before.

Elements of three occur often in thought and style. If you can support an idea with three examples, your argument is usually more convincing than if you use only one. Three is satisfying for patterns within sentences too. Browse through the preceding pages on parallel structure and see how many examples contain elements of three. Most do. Your mind easily processes three.

## Using Threes in Sentences: Rising Order or Not

Notice the stylistic pattern in these sentences.

To see, to feel, to discover is all. (Richard Selzer, <u>Mortal Lessons</u>)

*Interdependence* is the paradigm of we—we can do it; we can cooperate; we can combine our talents and abilities and create something greater together. (Stephen Covey, <u>Seven Habits</u>)

Almost all of the world-class athletes and other peak performers are visualizers. They see it; they feel it; they experience it before they actually do it. (Covey)

Notice how Selzer uses three *to* phrases (infinitive phrases). Placing "to discover" last suggests that Selzer believes this is the most important element. *Writers can sequence three elements in rising order of importance.* In Covey's first example he joins three short thoughts with semicolons and anaphora (repetition of "*we* can"); the last thought is longer, explaining more fully the idea of interdependence. His second example is similar: three short thoughts joined with semicolons, with the last one longer, emphasizing the idea of *experience*.

However, many sentences use three elements without rising order, and they too can be effective.

Will Strunk loved the clear, the brief, the bold, and his book is clear, brief, bold.
(E. B. White, <u>Essays of E. B. White</u>)

Science probes the factual state of the world; religion and ethics deal with moral reasoning; art and literature treat aesthetic and social judgment.
(Stephen Jay Gould, "The Dinosaur Rip-off")

While the world celebrated Diana's youth, sense of style and wealth, it was comforted by Mother Teresa's wrinkled face, simple blue-trimmed sari and the vows of poverty her missionary sisters took. (David Crumm, "Lives of Nun and Princess Defined by Differences" )

You can use threes to sequence a rising order of elements; you can join three thoughts by using semicolons; you can simply use three details or examples. The pattern of three is an important tool of style, with many variations.

How many sets of three does Andrew Sullivan use in the introduction to his essay "Life, Liberty and the Pursuit of Happiness" written for the This I Believe project on National Public Radio?

I believe in life. I believe in treasuring it as a mystery that will never be fully understood, as a sanctity that should never be destroyed, as an invitation to experience now what can only be remembered tomorrow. I believe in its indivisibility, in the intimate connection between the newest bud of spring and the flicker in the eye of a patient near death, between the athlete in his prime and the quadriplegic vet, between the fetus in the womb and the mother who bears another life in her own body.

This is a rich paragraph of meaning and of style. Sullivan's use of threes helps it cohere together and give it balance. Three times he repeats "I believe," "as," and "between."

## ACTIVITY 7

### REVISION

In your notebook write three sentences using threes. One of your sentences should contain a rising order of importance. For example, "At our school we know what it means to laugh, to love, and to learn." Write another sentence that contains three complete thoughts joined by semicolons. For example, "It is complete; it is strong; it will last." (Notice how each of the three thoughts contains three words.) Then look at your recent writing. Try to combine and tighten some sentences by using threes. Try to use this tool the next time you write a paper or an e-mail. ■

## Varying Sentence Beginnings: Three Ways
### Using -ing Phrases

Notice the stylistic pattern in these sentences.

Judging by drop-out rates, we see that college does not benefit all students.
(Marisa Proctor, student)

Learning to play the flute, I felt as happy as a butterfly. (Emily Schaeffer, student)

Unbuttoning his shirt, he placed the disc over his heart. (Richard Selzer, <u>Down from Troy</u>)

The above sentences begin with an *-ing* phrase (the -ing verb plus its noun or pronoun). Each *-ing* phrase refers to the subject of the sentence: *Judging* refers to *we*; *Learning* refers to *I*; and *Unbuttoning* refers to *he*.

Beginning a sentence with an *-ing* phrase can help you omit needless words and can give your sentences flexibility and variety. Consider this complex sentence and a revision of it:

> When I studied his arguments, I realized they made sense.
> **Revision:**
> *Studying* his arguments, I realized they made sense.

The revision saves two words. If you find that many of your sentences begin the same way, you can change some of them by using *-ing* phrases. Here's another example:

> As I waited for the plane, I read my book.
> **Revision:**
> *Waiting* for the plane, I read my book.
> Or: I read my book, *waiting* for the plane.

Again you save two words, and you don't need to repeat "I."

You can also use *-ing* phrases to revise compound sentences. Consider this example and two revisions:

> The instructor watched her students write; she wondered if they were prepared.
> **Revision:**
> *Watching* her students write, the instructor wondered if they were prepared.
> Or: The instructor watched her students write, *wondering* if they were prepared.

The *-ing* phrases are flexible; you can often move them around in a sentence. Although commonly used at the beginning or end of sentences, an *-ing* phrase can also be used in the middle:

Campuses, *being* concentrations of young people, are awash with hormones, which are powerful. (George Will, "Sex Amidst Semicolons")

Will could have placed "being concentrations of young people" up front:

> *Being* concentrations of young people, campuses are awash with hormones, which are powerful.

However, breaking up his main thought with the *-ing* phrase, Will uses the phrase as an obvious reminder. Also, Will's original version captures his writer's voice, which is often layered with parenthetical comments.

You can also use an *-ing* phrase after a preposition or other introductory word for even more flexibility and variety.

> *By shepherding, guiding and protecting* our children's souls, we build a better America.
> (Al Gore, Democratic National Convention, 1996)

The *-ing* phrases are extremely useful tools for you as a writer. They provide variety and often save words by combining and compressing thoughts.

## Misusing *-ing* Phrases: Dangling Modifiers

When writers learn how to use *-ing* phrases at the beginning of sentences, they sometimes create unintentional meanings called *dangling modifiers*:

> Using Facebook, my foot fell asleep. [Sounds as if a foot was using Facebook.]

To repair this kind of mistake, you need to supply a logical subject to which the *-ing* phrase refers:

> Using Facebook, *I* realized my foot had fallen asleep.
> Or: While I used Facebook, my foot fell asleep.

Here are two more examples:

> By writing a rough draft, my main idea will come to me.
>     [Sounds as if "my main idea" is writing the draft.]
> *Revision:*
> By writing a rough draft, I will discover my main idea.
> Or: When I write my rough draft, a main idea will appear.
>
> Watching <u>Psycho</u>, goose bumps covered my arms.
>     [Sounds as if goose bumps watched the movie.]
> *Revision:*
> Watching <u>Psycho</u>, I felt goose bumps cover my arms.
> Or: When I watched <u>Psycho</u>, goose bumps covered my arms.

To avoid dangling modifiers, make sure the *-ing* phrase refers to the subject of the sentence—the noun or pronoun it describes.

*Comma Rule:* If you begin a sentence with an *-ing* phrase, place a comma after it.

## ACTIVITY 8

### REVISION

In your notebook write three sentences beginning with *-ing* phrases. In one of your sentences use an *-ing* phrase in the middle or at the end of the sentence. Then look at your recent writing. Try to begin some sentences with *-ing* phrases. See if doing this helps you combine and tighten some sentences. Try to use this tool the next time you write a paper or an e-mail.

## Using *-ed* or *-en* Phrases

Notice the stylistic pattern in these sentences.

> Urged to attend medical school by his father, Keats proved a desultory student.
> (Richard Selzer, <u>Letters to a Young Doctor</u>)

> Offered the same menu, people make different choices.
> (Deborah Tannen, <u>You Just Don't Understand</u>)

> Given a new perspective on the problem, we finally found a solution.

The first two sentences begin with an *-ed phrase* (the *-ed* verb plus its noun or pronoun). Each *-ed* phrase refers to the subject of the sentence: *Urged* refers to *Keats*; *Offered* refers to *people*; the last sentence begins with an *-en phrase*: *Given* refers to *we*.

The *-ed* or *-en* form of a verb (the past participle) can be used like an adjective to describe nouns and pronouns. This sentence tool is similar to using *-ing* phrases (present participles).

## ACTIVITY 9

In your notebook, try to revise each of the following sentences, using an *-ed* or *-en* phrase. Each revision should contain fewer words. For example,

---

Because *I* was tired from writing, I put down my pen. (11 words)
**Revision:** Tired from writing, I put down my pen. (8 words)

1. When I was confused about my philosophy paper, I took a walk. (12 words)
2. They were scared about the lump; they didn't know what the doctor would say. (14)
3. Tim's new monitor was broken beyond repair; it lay in pieces on the floor. (14)

---

These -*ed* and -*en* phrases function like adjectives; they refer to (or describe) the subjects of the sentences. Past participles usually have -*ed* or -*en* endings. In the first two examples you could have used an -*ed* phrase; in the last example you could have used an -*en* phrase. Some other verbs that have an -*en* or -*n* ending for past participle are *chosen, driven, frozen, grown, known, sewn, thrown,* and *woven*.

The -*ed* and -*en* phrases may not occur as often as -*ing* phrases, but they are equally useful in helping writers achieve concise sentences with variety.

*Comma Rule:* If you begin a sentence with an -*ed* or -*en* phrase, place a comma after it.

## ACTIVITY 10

### REVISION

Write three sentences beginning with -*ed* or -*en* phrases. Then look at your recent writing. Try to combine and tighten some sentences by using these phrases. Try to use this tool the next time you write a paper or an e-mail.

## Using *To* Phrases

Notice the stylistic pattern in these sentences.

> To think critically, you must see hidden differences and similarities.

> To polish a rough draft, a writer should evaluate each word and each sentence.

> To understand how pervasive and surreal the violence in our mass media has become, we need to step back and look at our own culture as if we were outsiders.
> (Deborah Prothrow-Stith, <u>Deadly Consequences</u>)

Each sentence begins with a phrase made of *To* and a verb. An *infinitive* is a form of a verb beginning with the word *to*, such as *to think, to polish,* and *to understand*. Each *To* phrase refers to the subject of the sentence, such as *you, a writer,* and *we*. The infinitive is another way to start a sentence: as a tool of style it helps you achieve flexibility and variety.

*Comma Rule:* If you begin a sentence with a *To* phrase, place a comma after it.

## ACTIVITY 11

In your notebook combine the following sentences, using a *To phrase* to begin the sentence. To combine these sentences, you will need to change some of the word order. (Notice that *To* phrase?)

1. Jane Doe hopes to change the image of God as male. She refers to God as female. (17 words)

2. Seymour wanted to learn about love. He decided to do some research on it. (14)
3. Martin Luther King Jr. tried to unite blacks and whites. He delivered his speech before the Lincoln Memorial. (18)

*To* phrases can also function as complete subjects themselves.

To be fair-minded is a hallmark of critical thinking.

To argue well requires paying close attention to logos, pathos, and ethos.

To dwell upon bone is to contemplate the fate of man.
(Richard Selzer, Mortal Lessons)

In each of these sentences the subject is an entire phrase: *To be fair-minded, To argue well*, and *To dwell upon bone*. Thus, infinitive phrases are versatile. They also add formality to your voice, if this is what you want for a particular situation and audience.

## ACTIVITY 12

### REVISION

Write two sentences beginning with a *To* phrase that refers to the subject of the sentence. Then write a sentence beginning with a *To* phrase that functions as the subject of the sentence. Last, look at your recent writing. Try to combine and tighten some sentences by using *To* phrases. Also, try to use this tool the next time you write.

## CHAPTER 4

# The Toulmin Method and Problems in Reasoning

## USING THE TOULMIN METHOD TO ARGUE

Most writers are able to argue from an early age. Even quite young children begin to display the rudiments of argumentation, such as holding adults to their promises (you promised we could go to the movies if we cleaned our rooms . . . ). It is the beginning of a well-known formula in logic: if X then Y: and X therefore Y.

What is new is the analysis of written structures, which tend to be longer and more complex than most oral arguments of youth. Philosopher Stephen Toulmin has simplified the process of analysis in The Uses of Argument. In most arguments, he says, you make some claim that you want others to believe; then you give your reasons. Toulmin's view of most arguments is illustrated as follows:

| **CLAIM:** | **It should be illegal for people to keep dogs in rental apartments.** |
|---|---|
| **GROUNDS:** | (Because = Support for claim): |
| (Reasons, Data, | 1. Dogs are dirty—they slobber, shed hair, and drop waste and urinate on carpets and floors. |
| Evidence, | 2. They carry diseases, ticks and fleas, distemper. |
| *Support,* | 3. They reek, leave dog smell everywhere. |
| for Claim) | 4. They are destructive, dig holes, chew on furniture, scratch doors. |
| | 5. They are noisy, often whine, bark, and howl. |
| | 6. They can be dangerous, especially to small children. |

| **WARRANT:** | What is the connection between your evidence and your claim? What has this to do with apartment living? |
|---|---|
| (Conclusion, inference, Generalization, Principle, "So what?") | *Dogs can be a financial liability.* ("We might lose renters; we could be sued if we allow dogs." "An anti-dog policy could save us money.") |

Whether evidence or "support" comes before or after the claim—that is, whether the reasoning is *inductive or deductive*—the relationship between the claim and the support remains the same. In persuasive arguments you need to know what claim is expressed and what support for the claim is available. And it's possible to start by listing the *grounds*, the reasons for your argument, first.

> **Grounds:** "Because of all these reasons—dogs are dirty, carry diseases, reek, etc."
> **Claim:** "So therefore dogs should be kept out of rental apartments."

Many people looking at the argument about dogs might say, "Yes all those statements are true; therefore, dogs should not be allowed in apartments." But Toulmin asks you not to make up your mind too quickly, not to assume anything is self-evident. He asks the claimant to explain the connection between the claim and grounds even if the connection seems obvious. So what if dogs are dirty, carry diseases, reek, are destructive, and possibly dangerous? What has all this to do with apartment living? Are these statements facts? How do you know? Do they apply to all dogs? The *warrant* is Toulmin's way of asking claimants to analyze the kind of reasoning they are using.

What is new in Toulmin's work is his concept of the *warrant*. The warrant asks, "So what is the connection between the support and the claim?"

## Kinds of Arguments—Kinds of Claims
### Laws and Policies

You can argue about laws and policies—things you believe *should* (could, ought to) be changed. In recent presidential campaigns, *Roe v. Wade* was an important issue. Pro-choice and pro-life advocates argue and re-argue the abortion issue and what role if any the government should play. Here is another policy argument:

### BAN IT?

**Claimant:** Dirty sex pictures should be banned from the Internet.
**Critical Thinker:** Why? What has happened? On what grounds do you make your claim?

> **Claimant:** The *grounds* are that I've discovered children see those pictures.
>
> **Critical Thinker:** So what? What's the connection? What *warrants* the action you want to take?
>
> **Claimant:** Children should not be allowed to see dirty pictures.
>
> **Critical Thinker:** You've already implied as much. We need to know *why* you say that. Besides, your claim would cover adults too—no one would be able to see them.
>
> **Claimant:** No one should see them! But I'll *qualify* my claim: Children should not see dirty pictures on the Internet.
>
> **Critical Thinker:** Why?
>
> **Claimant:** Because they are immoral—they are pornographic.
>
> **Critical Thinker:** So?
>
> **Claimant:** So children should be able to grow up with normal, healthy attitudes about sex. Those pictures damage children's right to a normal childhood. Children are not able to deal with distorted, filthy pornography.
>
> **Critical Thinker:** OK. That might work. Do children have such a right? Note that many of the terms in your warrant are "subjective": *normal, pornography, right.* Can you define these terms?

The critical thinker here is helping the claimant understand that this is a complex argument. The claim that children should not see dirty pictures on the Internet is supported by the claimant's "evidence" (reasons) that such pictures are immoral ("pornographic"). The thinker asks, "So what?" The claimant then offers a warrant, a rule that we might apply to children in general: children have a right to a normal childhood. That's a good warrant if it is true.

## ACTIVITY 1

In your notebook, write three claims based on laws or policies concerning changes. For example: (1) Medical marijuana should be legalized. (2) Prayer should be required in all schools—public and private. (3) The drinking age in all states should be 18, not 21. Then do the following:

1. Select the *claim* you like best and explain why you like it—why you believe it is desirable.

2. Offer at least three good reasons (*grounds*) you could use to support the claim.

3. Try to state the *warrant*—the connection between the claim and the grounds. ▐▌

## Reality, Facts

You can argue about what is real—are there aliens? Is Adolf Hitler dead (or is he still alive somewhere)? How real is the danger of global warming? How can you support such questions? You can "support," though perhaps not "prove," such questions with whatever facts, historical or authoritative data, or other evidence the audience accepts. Factual matters concern what you believe was, is, or will be real.

Philosophers say that *trivial* matters of fact are seldom worth arguing about. You have to decide for yourself what is trivial, but arguing about things for which there are simple tests or readily available proof is the issue here, such as devices that measure temperature, time, and blood pressure. Historic dates like Washington's birthday in 1732 (celebrated every February 22) can be found in encyclopedias, almanacs, and other sources. Most people don't find arguing about such facts interesting.

---

## FACTS

**Claimant:** [claim] The victim died of poisoning.

**Critical Thinker:** On what grounds do you claim this?

**Claimant:** [grounds] The victim began to complain of cramps 20 minutes after dinner. He then began to exhibit convulsions in 60-second intervals. The coroner says the victim died from asphyxiation brought on by distress of respiratory muscles.

**Critical Thinker:** So what?

**Claimant:** [warrant] Such symptoms are characteristic of death by poisoning, namely strychnine.

**Critical Thinker:** How do you know this?

**Claimant:** [backing for warrant] I am an authority in the field of forensic medicine and often called to testify in cases where poisoning is suspected.

---

Sometimes the warrant itself may need additional support. You can use backing to increase the credibility of the warrant. *Backing* can be any sort of evidence or support that will help your readers believe the warrant makes sense. The claimant might have answered, "I'm an undertaker and I've seen lots of corpses that died of poisoning." Or, "I'm a city groundskeeper. We use strychnine often to keep the rodent population under control." As a critical thinker, you need to make sure you have the most authoritative experts you can find.

## ACTIVITY 2

In your notebook write three statements based on reality (facts) you'd like your audience to believe. For example: (1) Not all basketball players need to be seven feet or taller to excel. (2) Students learn better in small classes. (3) Hollywood presents a distorted, unrealistic view of human life. Then do the following:

- Select the *claim* you like best, and explain why you like it—why you believe it is true.
- Offer at least three good reasons (*grounds*) you could use to support the claim.
- Try to state the *warrant*—the connection between the claim and grounds. Use *backing* for the warrant if you can.

### Values, Morals, Taste

You can argue about values: values are whatever you find desirable or not. Values concern your beliefs about morals—your beliefs about good and evil. Values (aesthetics, sometimes called "taste" as in artistic taste) also concern beliefs about what is beautiful and what is not. These are interesting arguments because we all have our own opinions about such matters, and if we include abstract art, it becomes more and more challenging to decide whose opinion makes sense. Can you "prove" Picasso was the greatest modern artist? It's a fascinating question, full of depth and breadth, leading you through the entire world of art. You may or may not be able to "prove" Picasso was the greatest modern artist, but you can offer your reasoning. Here's a different argument based entirely on aesthetic values, or taste:

### AESTHETIC VALUES

**Claimant:** I think that's a hideous house. [claim]

**Critical Thinker:** How so? [request for support for claim]

**Claimant:** The design looks like something out of a cartoon or bad abstract art, and purple and green are violently mismatched colors. [support]

**Critical Thinker:** Do you have some rule or principle about how things should look? [request for warrant]

**Claimant:** Yes. A house should be pleasing to the eye; it should complement the surrounding environment; its lines should be symmetrical, balanced, and designed to give the effect of artistic unity. Its colors should complement the owner's notion of domestic beauty. [warrant]

**Critical Thinker:** So you have a classical view of art!

The Latin expression *de gustibus non disputandum est* (There is no point in arguing about taste) suggests that we all have our opinions, especially about what is or isn't attractive, and therefore it is pointless to argue such things. Do you agree? Do you believe that "my opinion is all that matters to me, regardless of what anyone says"? Do you believe that discussion and argument help you deepen and broaden your understanding of what may or may not be seen as attractive? Claims (opinions) without support are mere opinion. It seems pointless to have "art" if only personal opinion guides us.

## ACTIVITY 3

In your notebook write three claims based on values you'd like your audience to accept. For example: (1) Rap music appeals basically to African Americans. (2) Cheating is a valid way to get ahead if you don't get caught. (3) It was wrong (immoral) for our country to invade Iraq. Then do the following:

- Select the *claim* you like best, and explain why you like it—why you believe it is true.
- Offer at least three good reasons (*grounds*) you could use to support the claim.
- Try to state the *warrant*—the connection between the claim and grounds. Use *backing* for the warrant if you can.

### Warrants

On the surface of it, the dog arguments don't seem limited to apartments. If true, the reasons would be true almost anywhere. If so, why argue against apartments? The *warrant*, Toulmin says, must guarantee the relationship between the *support* (he calls *grounds*) and the *claim*. We are asking the claimant (the landlord) to state the principle that connects the support to the claim. In this case, the landlord's explanation might be something like, "Because dogs are dirty, dangerous animals, they can be a financial liability that may cause landlords to lose renters and/or to be sued."

You could, of course, challenge the data. What makes landlords think dogs are dirty and such a liability? In that case, we would want to see some *backing* for the landlords' data. Most likely we will discover the data are based on personal experience, hearsay (what others have said), and perhaps media reports. No doubt the landlords have seen evidence to cause them to believe the grounds for this claim. Backing for the warrant itself might be court cases: has there ever been a suit? Has anyone ever sued because a renter's dog caused disease, damaged property, or attacked a child? If so, the landlord has a strong case against dogs. If this became a court case, could you find counterarguments (which Toulmin calls *conditions of rebuttal*)?

Perhaps you could raise your *rebuttal*. One set of true facts may be confronted with another. The data may not be wrong but in conflict with other facts. Some pet owners (prospective renters, let's say) will surely object that these facts do not apply to their dog. You can concede that the landlord may have had bad experiences with some dogs, but is it fair to throw out the entire species for a few bad dogs? Not only is it not fair, but you must consider the effect on a jury or on Congress if they hear that these charges are not accurate. They do not apply to little Pookie at all:

### Rebuttal

Our dog is trained. She does not slobber, shed, drop waste, or urinate indoors. Pookie's hair is kept clipped and does not fall off, and we walk her four times a day so that there will be no waste on the rental property. We keep the dog clean—we take her to the Doggy Boutique once a week to be groomed so she doesn't "reek." We take her to the vet every six months for her routine checkup. She isn't destructive, does not dig or scratch. She is not noisy, does not bark or whine day or night. Pookie is a tiny, little toy poodle with the gentlest disposition: she would not attack anyone, and certainly not children, with whom she is especially gentle.

Another argument of rebuttal is that pets are part of the human experience. Certainly most people have learned to put up with some of the inconveniences in order to enjoy the value (the pleasure of) a pet's company. From a renter's point of view the landlord's rules don't sufficiently appreciate dogs. Therefore the renter asks for the landlord's *warrant*, an explanation of the connection between the *support* and the *claim*. And you can challenge a warrant if you don't think it's well made.

There are two ways you can improve a warrant.[1] A well-made warrant should not be too general; it should not use absolute terms where you can only achieve probability. You can show that not *all* dogs fall under the landlord's warrant. Some, like Pookie, are so well behaved that they don't exhibit any of the behaviors the landlord fears and thus represent no threat of any kind. The landlord's fear of "dogs" seems unreasonably broad. It condemns all animals of that species, though not all dogs have the problems the landlord cites.

Also a well-made warrant should not be too specific; it should not be based on only a few individuals, let alone a single individual. If the landlord's argument is based on a single dog encountered once, that's slim evidence on which to condemn the species. Certainly if the warrant is based solely on the landlord's suspicions about our dog Pookie, we can show that not only is the warrant too specific, but the grounds don't apply. (Imagine showing up in court with a little toy poodle feared by the landlord.) It will be helpful if we can cite other cases in which the pet owners (not the landlord) won.

## Stating the Warrant

The warrant should be stated as a law or rule that critical thinkers can apply in other cases. Here you are faced with a problem. Landlords have their reasons, based on whatever their experience has been with dogs. "All dogs" overgeneralizes and makes it easier to show that the "support" really doesn't apply to our dog. But landlords, unfortunately, don't have to listen to reason. Invested with authority for apartments, landlords are likely to refuse to "take a chance" on Pookie. Nobody can give a 100%

---

[1]Adapted from Elaine P. Maimon et al., <u>Writing in the Arts and Sciences</u> (Cambridge, Mass: Winthrop, 1981) 44.

guarantee of a pet's behavior. Sooner or later, the landlord says, there will be a rainy day and the dog will have to stay inside, or there will be an emergency and the dog will be left alone, or a stranger will approach the dog . . . it's just too risky.

Failing all else, it may be helpful if you can cite policy (general rule, law) that applies. For example, it is the nature of renting that landlords must accept certain risks: such as "normal" wear and tear on the property, though how far you can extend that is itself open to debate. Not every renter will meet the landlord's expectations, but there are laws against discrimination, and these may be cited as general policy that supersede the landlord's specific rules.

It's hard enough to argue with landlords when you are standing right in front of them. It's even more difficult to persuade in a letter. Writers are caught in a double bind: to be persuasive you may need to write at length—but the more you write, the more your reader may lose interest and may not finish reading your letter. If the letter must be brief, it will need to be extremely well written. Is there anything you could say in a letter that might persuade landlords to change their mind? Perhaps.

Can you anticipate a landlord's arguments? You might allege that Pookie is "never" out of the apartment without a leash. You could assure the landlord that Pookie is too tiny and too sweet to harm anyone or anything. You might threaten to sue the landlord. You might offer to sign a quit-claim, holding the landlord blameless for any damage the dog might do, and you might offer a financial incentive, an extra charge you would pay for the privilege of having the dog with you (although that seems unfair). Because the underlying concern is financial, you might show that by welcoming pet owners the landlord could find a new clientele that would increase profits. There are many responses renters could make to try to persuade a landlord.

## ACTIVITY 4

For each of the following claims and brief grounds of support, evaluate the warrant and the rebuttal. What warrant or rebuttal would you use instead?

1.  *Claim:* We need stricter laws that restrict gun ownership.
    *Grounds:* Look at Columbine and Virginia Tech.
    *Warrant:* Stricter gun laws will make mass shootings less likely.
    *Rebuttal:* If a few students had a concealed weapon, they might have shot the killers and prevented many deaths. When criminals and crazy people can't assume that nobody has a gun, they will be reluctant to start killing others.
2.  *Claim:* The military should forbid women who are mothers from combat.
    *Grounds:* There are too many negative effects on children and families back home.
    *Warrant:* It's more important for women to be mothers than to fight for our military.
    *Rebuttal:* Should the military also forbid men who are fathers? This is not practical, and it's not fair.

3. *Claim:* Teenagers should not be permitted to play professional sports.

   *Grounds:* They should complete high school and one year of college.

   *Warrant:* Education is more important than the extravagant money a few players can make playing professionally.

   *Rebuttal:* If a pro team wants a teen and that teen can become rich now and help his family, he should have this opportunity. How many teenagers are in this position anyway?

4. *Claim:* A person has to cheat or lie sometimes to succeed.

   *Grounds:* Other people cheat; affirmative action hurts many whites; much of the business world cheats.

   *Warrant:* Cheating is a natural kind of survival in a competitive world.

   *Rebuttal:* People with integrity don't cheat. Cheaters and liars are hard to trust.

5. *Claim:* Same-sex marriage is wrong.

   *Grounds:* Marriage is made for a man and a woman, so they can have children.

   *Warrant:* Traditional marriage by the vast majority of citizens is more important than serving the needs of a minority.

   *Rebuttal:* Old people past child-bearing age often get married. Is having children the best reason?

6. *Claim:* Gays should be allowed to serve openly in the military.

   *Grounds:* Our country faces a shortage of troops; other countries have had no problems with gays serving in the military.

   *Warrant:* It's more important to have a full military than to ban gays from serving.

   *Rebuttal:* Many guys don't want to be around gays; they've learned this from their fathers. If gays serve, they should serve secretly so other men don't know.

7. *Claim:* Marijuana should not be legalized.

   *Grounds:* Pot is psychologically addictive; it makes young people apathetic; it leads to other drugs.

   *Warrant:* It's our government's duty to protect young people from themselves.

   *Rebuttal:* Do you also mean that medical marijuana should not be legal? That has real benefits for people dying of cancer. Isn't pot safer than alcohol?

8. *Claim:* Reading is a wonderful way to improve your mind.

   *Grounds:* Reading helps me think about arguments; I see different perspectives; I realize how small-minded I am sometimes.

   *Warrant:* Reading promotes critical thinking.

   *Rebuttal:* Reading what? <u>National Enquirer</u>? Romance novels? Surely not any kind of reading improves your mind. You should qualify your claim: how about Shakespeare?

*Note:* Notice how it helps to qualify claims. (See Chapter 2 on overgeneralizations.)

# Exploring an Essay Using the Toulmin Method

Let's look at a short essay published in the This I Believe project on National Public Radio. In this project, people from all walks of life write about "core values that guide their daily lives." The essays are read by their authors on the radio and also published online at <http://thisibelieve.org/index.php>. Read this essay carefully, twice, and then see if you can say what the writer wants readers to accept as his claim, support, and warrant.

## The Tense Middle

### Roald Hoffmann

I believe in the middle. Extremes may make a good story, but the middle satisfies me. Why? Perhaps because I'm a chemist.

Chemistry is substances, molecules and their transformations. And molecules fight categorization—they are poised along several polarities. Harm and benefit is one.

Take morphine: Anyone who's had an operation knows what morphine is good for. But it's also a deadly, addictive drug. Take ozone: Up in the atmosphere, a layer of ozone protects us from the harmful ultraviolet radiation of our life-giving sun. But at sea level, ozone is produced in photochemical smog; it chews up tires and lungs.

Chemistry, like life, is deeply and fundamentally about change. It's about substances—say A and B—transforming, becoming a different substance—C and D—and coming back again. At equilibrium—the middle—all the substances are present. But we're not stuck there. We can change the middle; we can disturb the equilibrium.

Perhaps I like the middle, that tense middle, because of my background. I was born in 1937 in southeast Poland, now Ukraine. Our Jewish family was trapped in the destructive machinery of Nazi anti-Semitism. Most of us perished: my father, three of four grandparents, and so on. My mother and I survived, hidden for the last 15 months of the war in a schoolhouse attic by a Ukrainian teacher, Mikola Dyuk.

We were saved by the action of a good man, that schoolteacher. Sad to say, much of the Ukrainian population in the region behaved badly in those terrible times. They helped the Nazis kill us. And yet—and yet—some, like Dyuk, saved us at great risk to their lives.

I couldn't formulate it then, as a child, but I knew from our experience that people were not simply good or evil. They made choices. You could hide a Jewish family or you could choose not to. Every human being has the potential to go one way or the other. Understanding that there was a choice helps me live with the evil that I experienced.

Being a chemist has helped me to see plainly that things—politics, attitudes, molecules—in the middle can be changed, that we have a choice. Being a survivor I can see that choices really matter—all part of this risky enterprise of being human.

The middle is not static . . . my psychological middle as well as the chemical equilibrium. I like that. Yes, of course I also want stability. But I believe that extreme positions—the things you start out with in a chemical reaction, the things you finish with (all people A, bad, all people B, good; no taxes at all, taxed to death)—all of these are impractical, unnatural, boring: the refuge of people who never want to change. The world is not simple, though God knows political forces on every side want to make it so.

I like the tense middle and I am grateful for a life that offers me the potential for change.

*Cornell University professor Roald Hoffmann won the 1981 Nobel Prize in Chemistry. After surviving the Holocaust, he and his mother immigrated to America in 1949. In addition to research and teaching, Hoffmann enjoys writing poetry, plays, and essays.*

Work Cited

Hoffmann, Roald. "The Tense Middle." This I Believe. National Public Radio. 3 July 2006. 22 July 2007 <http://www.thisibelieve.org>.

## Hoffmann's Claim

A *claim* is a writer's thesis (main idea or opinion). A claim can appear anywhere in a paper—it usually appears up front, but it can appear in the middle or the end of an essay. To find the claim, ask yourself: What does the writer want me to believe?

Hoffmann states his claim directly in his first sentence: "I believe in the middle."

By itself, this sentence is an engaging opener because you don't know exactly what he means. To state the claim more clearly, after considering the whole essay, you might conclude that his claim is something like one of these statements:

- Middles are more important than extreme positions.
- Important changes can happen in the tense middle between extremes.
- The tense middle is where change can happen.

Let's choose the last option: it concisely captures Hoffmann's claim. Please know that there is no one right answer here. When you examine an essay using the Toulmin method, you're free to draw your own conclusion as to what the claim is, but your claim should be reasonable and supported by evidence (the grounds). Searching for the claim is a good way to help you understand the essay.

## Hoffmann's Grounds

The term *grounds* basically means supporting evidence: reasons, examples, details, facts. Think of the grounds as the foundation (like earth or cement) upon which a claim is built. Making an informal outline of a writer's supporting evidence can help show you the grounds of an argument:

- He introduces his essay by saying he likes the tense middle because he is a chemist.

—chemistry concerns "transformations"

—specific example: morphine can be both good (relieve pain) and bad (addictive)

—specific example: ozone is also good (protects us) and bad (damages tires and lungs)

—chemistry is like life: about "change," "transforming"

—more general example: substances become a different substance

—the middle provides an equilibrium where change can happen

- He likes the tense middle because of his background.

—specific example: his family was in the Holocaust in southeast Poland

—specific details: most of his family perished, including his father and three grandparents

—he and his mother survived for 15 months because a Ukrainian teacher hid them in a schoolhouse attic

—these personal details appeal to the reader's emotion—pathos

—many Ukrainians helped Nazis kill Jews, yet some saved Jews, risking their own lives

—he knew as a child people were not either good or bad. "They made choices."

—every person can choose to be good or evil; they have a choice

—knowing this helps Hoffmann "live the evil" he experienced

- He relates both chemistry and being a survivor.

—chemistry helps him see the potential for change for things in the middle, including "politics, attitudes, molecules"

—surviving the Holocaust helps him see the necessity of choice in the process of "being human"

- He concludes his essay.

—the middle is dynamic, "not static," including his "psychological middle" and "chemical equilibrium"

—he is not against "stability"

—but "extreme positions . . . are impractical, unnatural, boring"

—people who resist change like extreme positions

—the world is too complex for us to reduce it to simple either/or positions

—yet "political forces on every side" reinforce extreme positions

—he likes "the tense middle" and is grateful that life offers him "the potential for change"

## Hoffmann's Warrant

The term *warrant* means the connection between the claim and the grounds. The warrant asks, "So what? Why is this argument important or useful to know?"

A writer usually doesn't state a warrant. Rather, the reader needs to infer the warrant, which is a key value of Toulmin's method: it pushes readers to analyze a writer's arguments more deeply. But Hoffmann gives part of a warrant at the end: "the potential for change." Here are some other possible warrant statements:

- The potential for change is as vital for people as it is for chemicals.
- The potential for change that the tense middle offers helps people not to think or behave in simplistic either/or ways.

- Thinking critically and being ethical both involve embracing the paradox of the tense middle.

Stating the warrant is not easy, but the effort to do it helps you judge the value of the claim. Hoffmann's claim is insightful, and the warrant is important. He is drawing on the wisdom of opposites discussed in Chapter 3: the wisdom of opposites is seeing what holds the opposites together. Recall that Morrie Schwartz tells Mitch Albom about "the tension of opposites." Perhaps Hoffmann draws the word *tense* from *tension*. Hoffmann's essay is wise: it demonstrates a deep knowing. If people can learn to hold the tension, they can see more sides; they can weigh more options; they can make better choices. Relating chemistry to being a survivor is a leap not many people could make. But it makes sense, profound sense.

## Hoffmann's Backing

The term *backing* refers to any evidence that can support (back up) the warrant. Here, you can discuss Hoffman's ethos. Is he an authority? Is he credible? Does he appear honest and trustworthy? The answer is clearly yes. Hoffmann is a distinguished chemist who won the Nobel Prize in Chemistry in 1981 for his work on how chemicals change and transform themselves. Since 1965 he has taught chemistry at Cornell University, including first-year general chemistry. Thus, his credentials as a chemist and scientist are extraordinary. But his life before chemistry was shaped by being a Holocaust survivor, having first-hand experience with evil and goodness. Hoffman also uses logos well, which reinforces his ethos: his argument is thoughtful and important; he is careful to support his claim with persuasive reasons and specific examples and details. He uses pathos as well, stirring emotion in readers with his information on being a survivor. All this backs up his claim. Knowledge of his background strengthens the backing for the warrant. For more of Hoffmann's life, see <http://nobelprize.org/nobel_prizes/chemistry/laureates/1981/hoffmann-autobio.html>.

## Rebuttal of Hoffmann's Claim, Grounds, and Warrant

Toulmin asks us to perform one more step in his method of analyzing an argument: What counterarguments can be presented?

- Is Hoffmann suggesting that people should be fence-sitters—afraid to take a stand on a controversy or an issue? Good question. Not really. He's suggesting that the middle between extremes is where the most fruitful critical thinking and potential for change can happen. However, being a fence-sitter suggests that a person is neutral or undecided; this doesn't mean the person never changes his mind. Perhaps a fence-sitter is sitting in the tense middle, waiting to process arguments before taking a stand. The image of a fence-sitter also suggests that a person may be stuck on the fence, unable to get off, unable to take a stand. Hoffmann isn't advocating this. He wants us to be unstuck, and exploring the tense middle helps us do this.

- Are extreme positions always bad? Is the tense middle always good? Is "the potential for change" always good? Notice how these questions are stated as extremes. Hoffmann is careful not to use *always* in his essay. Well, what about someone changing from being kind and generous to being mean and selfish? This could happen. But why would it happen? That would be part of the tense middle, the tense mystery. As Hoffmann says, people have a choice to be good or evil. What about a tragedy? Hoffmann uses his own example of the Holocaust. He doesn't go into detail, but prisoners in the camps also had a choice between being evil and good. The tension between good and evil is real: if we are moral, kind, trustworthy, we will choose good. People can choose how they will behave after misfortune or tragedy.
- What does *tense* mean exactly? <u>Webster's New World Dictionary</u> gives this information: "1. stretched tight; strained; taut 2. undergoing or showing mental or nervous strain; anxious; apprehensive; jittery." The etymology also is "to stretch." These connotations are not entirely positive. Yet do they suit Hoffmann's claim, grounds, warrant? He writes, "Being a survivor I can see that choices really matter—all part of this risky enterprise of being human." As humans we can't make free choices unless we can see and know the extremes.

The process of finding and expressing counterarguments can be challenging. But it is worth the effort: doing so will help you appreciate the logical strength of a writer's claim.

## ACTIVITY 5

Look at one of the papers you have written for other chapters in this book. Explore it by using the Toulmin method. What is the claim, grounds, warrant, and backing? Can you find any counterarguments that might rebut your claim, that you could have addressed in your paper when you wrote it?

## ACTIVITY 6

Look at one of the essays on a controversy in Chapter 2. Explore it by using the Toulmin method. What is the claim, grounds, warrant, and backing? Can you find any counterarguments? Consider making an outline, following the outline model presented earlier with "The Tense Middle."

The Toulmin method is worth using: it can help you analyze and evaluate an essay or speech more deeply than you might otherwise. The search for a warrant that explains the connection between a claim and its grounds (supporting evidence) can help you decide how important the claim is. Using backing to back up the warrant is a good way to apply your knowledge of a writer's ethos—credibility and character. Toulmin gives you good tools to explore most anything you read or see that involves arguments and persuasion.

The next time you write an essay or research paper, try to use the Toulmin tools. They can help you, especially when you revise a first rough draft. You can ask yourself: What is my claim? What are my grounds for it? What is the warrant here? What backing do I have? Can I anticipate counterarguments? But trying to use the tools when you first write a draft could be counterproductive. As Peter Elbow says in Chapter 3, writing a first draft is first-order thinking; revising it and analyzing it carefully is second-order thinking. The Toulmin method exemplifies second-order thinking. It can help you strengthen your critical thinking skills.

## ESSAYS TO EXPLORE WITH THE TOULMIN METHOD

After you read the following three essays, choose one to write about in a report (2–4 pages). Explore it by using the Toulmin method. What is the claim, grounds, warrant, and backing? Can you find any counterarguments? You can write your report following the outline model presented earlier with "The Tense Middle." Include a Works Cited section at the end of your report.

### The Lessons I Didn't Learn in College

*Caitlin Petre*

To think there was once a time when I thought nailing the interview was the hardest part of getting a job. I recently applied to be a cocktail waitress at an upscale bowling alley in Manhattan. After a brief interview, the manager congratulated me, saying I'd be a great fit. It was only a momentary victory. She produced a sheaf of papers, and my stomach turned flips. I knew what was coming—the dreaded W-4. I'd filled them out before, for various summer jobs, but I'd always been exempted from taxes because I was a full-time student. Now that I had graduated from college, this was the first W-4 I had to complete fully. The manager watched as I hesitated. "Are you having trouble?" she asked as I squinted at the tiny print. "Oh, no, I'm fine." I stared at the form, trying to figure out how many allowances to claim—or what an allowance was, for that matter. I didn't want to admit that I was stumped, so finally I just took a guess.

Later I asked my friends to shed some light on the matter, but none of them knew any more than I did. Instead, they advised me to do what they did: make it up and hope for the best. So much for being a well-educated college graduate.

Having taken seminars on government, I could hold forth on the relationship between taxation and the federal deficit but was clueless about filling out a basic tax form. I'd graduated with a B.A. in philosophy in May, and had decided against going straight to graduate school. But while countless newspapers claimed that the job market for graduates was the best it had been in years, I had no idea how to take advantage of it. I couldn't imagine myself in an entry-level administrative position staring at a spreadsheet for eight hours a day—partly because it sounded dull, but also because in college I had never learned how to use spreadsheet programs. Cocktail waitressing seemed like a good way to make ends meet.

My friends and I are graduates of Wesleyan, Barnard, Stanford and Yale. We've earned 3.9 GPAs and won academic awards. Yet none of us knows what a Roth IRA is or can master a basic tax form. And heaven help us when April comes and we have to file tax returns.

My friends and I are incredibly lucky to have gotten the educations we have. But there's a discrepancy between what we learn in school and what we need to know for work, and there must be some way for universities to bridge this gap. They might, for example, offer classes in personal finance as part of the economics department. How about a class on renting an apartment? Granted, it might be hard to lure students to such mundane offerings, but the students who don't go will wish they had.

College students are graduating with greater debt than ever before, yet we haven't learned how to manage our money. We can wing it for only so long before employers start wising up to our real-world incompetence. In fact, they already are: a study released last month showed that hundreds of employers have found their college-graduate hires to be "woefully unprepared" for the job market.

All this raises a disturbing question: when I spent a ton of time and money on my fancy degree, what exactly was I buying? The ability to think, some might say. OK, fine, that's important. Still, my résumé would look odd if it read, "Skills: proficient in French, word processing, thinking." The thinking I did in college seems to be of limited utility in the "real world." The fact that I wrote a 30-page critical analysis of the function of shame in society did nothing to ease the sting when I spilled beer on a customer at the bowling alley.

That's not the only time I've found my education incompatible with real life. I had trouble getting used to my new uniform, which consists of a supershort '50s-style bowling skirt, boots and fishnet stockings. As I changed into it for the first time, I had a vision of the feminist philosophers I had read in college hovering over me, shaking their heads disapprovingly.

But it wasn't long before I began to see that the short skirt played a role in boosting my tips—a definite plus now that I was trying to rent an apartment, feed myself and buy the occasional book or new toothbrush.

So which to live by: the philosophers or the skirt? I'm trying to fashion some combination, one that allows me to retain my principles without having to file for bankruptcy. After all, the last thing I want is to be confronted with more confusing government paperwork.

*Petre lives in New York City.*

Work Cited

Petre, Caitlin. "My Turn: The Lessons I Didn't Learn in College." <u>Newsweek</u> 13 Nov. 2006: 20.

## Eating for Credit

*Alice Waters*

It's shocking that because of the rise in Type 2 diabetes experts say that the children we're raising now will probably die younger than their parents—the result of a disease that is largely preventable by diet and exercise. But in public schools these days, children all too often are neither learning to eat well nor to exercise.

Fifty years ago, we had a preview of today's obesity crisis: a presidential council told us that America's children weren't fit—and we did something about it, at great expense. We built gymnasiums and tracks and playgrounds. We hired and trained teachers. We made physical education part of the curriculum from kindergarten through high school. Students were graded on their performance.

Universal physical education is a start, and it's a shame that schools have been cutting back on recess and gym. But in a country where nine million children over 6 are obese we need the diet part of the equation, too. It's time for students to start getting credit for eating a good lunch.

I know from experience that teaching children about food changes their lives. I helped establish a gardening and cooking project in the public schools here in Berkeley called the Edible Schoolyard, and I've come to believe that lunch should be at the center of every school's curriculum.

Schools should not just serve food; they should teach it in an interactive, hands-on way, as an academic subject. Children's eating habits stay with them for the rest of their lives. The best way to defeat the obesity epidemic is to teach children about food—and thereby prevent them from ever becoming obese.

The trouble is that the shared family meal is now a rare experience for most youngsters, with only a third of married couples with children reporting regularly having dinner as a family. We have abdicated our responsibility to these children, placing their well-being in the hands of the fast-food industry, whose products—hamburgers, chicken nuggets, French fries—dominate school lunch programs.

Not only are our children eating this unhealthy food, they're digesting the values that go with it: the idea that food has to be fast, cheap and easy; that abundance is permanent and effortless; that it doesn't matter where food actually comes from. These values are changing us. As a nation, we need to take back responsibility for the health of not just our children, but also our culture.

Our program began at Martin Luther King Jr. Middle School 10 years ago, with a kitchen classroom and a garden full of fruits, vegetables and herbs. A cafeteria where students, faculty and staff members will eat together every day is under construction, and the Edible Schoolyard has become a model for a district-wide school lunch initiative.

At King School today, 1,000 children are involved in growing, preparing and sharing fresh food. These food-related activities are woven into the entire curriculum. Math classes measure garden beds. Science classes study drainage and soil erosion. History classes learn about pre-Columbian civilizations while grinding corn.

We're not forcing them to eat their vegetables; we're teaching them about the botany and history of those vegetables. We're not scaring them with the health consequences of their eating habits; we're engaging them in interactive education that brings them into a new relationship with food. Nothing less will change their behavior.

We can try to improve diets all we want by making school lunches more nutritious and by getting vending machines out of the hallways, but that gets us only partway there. For example, New York City has just banned whole milk in its public schools. It's a courageous first step, but how can we be sure students will drink healthier milk just because it's offered to them, let alone understand what lifelong nourishment is all about?

Indeed, it's too often the fresh fruit and salad that gets tossed in the garbage at school cafeterias. Even if they weren't already addicted to salt and sugar, children tend to be wary of unfamiliar foods—and besides, they can always bring packaged junk in for lunch or buy fast food after school. Healthful food that's offered in a "take it or leave it" way is often, well, left.

But when a healthy lunch is a part of a class that all children have to take, for credit—and when they can follow food from the garden to the kitchen to the table, doing much of the work themselves—something amazing happens. The students want to taste everything. They get lured in by foods that are beautiful, that taste and smell good, that appeal to their senses. When children grow and prepare good, healthy food themselves, they want to eat it, and, what's more, they like this way of learning.

We need a revolution, a delicious revolution, that will induce children—in a pleasurable way—to think critically about what they eat. The study of food, and school lunch, should become part of the core curriculum for all students from kindergarten through high school. Such a move will take significant investment and the kind of resolve that this country showed a half-century ago. It will be costly, but if we don't pay now, the health care bill later will be astronomical.

*Alice Waters is the owner of Chez Panisse Restaurant and Café in Berkeley, California and the founder of the Chez Panisse Foundation. An influential chef worldwide, she believes in using the highest quality, fresh, seasonal ingredients, grown and harvested in an ecologically sound manner.*

Work Cited

Waters, Alice. "Eating for Credit." <u>New York Times</u> 24 Feb. 2006, late ed.: A23.

## Serve or Fail

### *Dave Eggers*

About now, most recent college graduates, a mere week or two beyond their last final, are giving themselves a nice respite. Maybe they're on a beach, maybe they're on a road trip, maybe they're in their rooms, painting their toenails black with a Q-tip and shoe polish. Does it matter? What's important is that they have some time off.

Do they deserve the time off? Well, yes and no. Yes, because finals week is stressful and sleep-deprived and possibly involves trucker-style stimulants. No, because a good deal of the four years of college is spent playing foosball.

I went to a large state school—the University of Illinois—and during my time there, I became one of the best two or three foosball players in the Land of Lincoln. I learned to pass deftly between my rigid players, to play the corners, to strike the ball like a cobra would strike something a cobra would want to strike. I also mastered the dart game called Cricket, and the billiards contest called Nine-ball. I became expert at whiffle ball, at backyard archery, and at a sport we invented that involved one person tossing roasted chickens from a balcony to a group of us waiting below. We got to eat the parts that didn't land on the patio.

The point is that college is too long—it should be three years—and that even with a full course load and part-time jobs (I had my share) there are many hours in the days and weeks that need killing. And because most of us, as students, saw our hours as in need of killing—as opposed to thinking about giving a few of these hours to our communities in one way or another—colleges should consider instituting a service requirement for graduation.

I volunteered a few times in Urbana-Champaign—at a Y.M.C.A. and at a home for senior citizens—and in both cases it was much too easy to quit. I thought the senior home smelled odd, so I left, and though the Y.M.C.A. was a perfect fit, I could have used nudging to continue—nudging the university might have provided. Just as parents and schools need to foster in young people a "reading habit"—a love of reading that becomes a need, almost an addiction—colleges are best poised to create in their students a lifelong commitment to volunteering even a few hours a month.

Some colleges, and many high schools, have such a thing in place, and last year Michael R. Veon, a Democratic member of Pennsylvania's House of Representatives, introduced a bill that would require the more than 90,000 students at 14 state-run universities to perform 25 hours of community service annually. That comes out to more than two million volunteer hours a year.

College students are, for the most part, uniquely suited to have time for and to benefit from getting involved and addressing the needs of those around them. Unlike high school students, they're less programmed, less boxed-in by family and after-school obligations. They're also more mature, and better able to handle a wide range of tasks. Finally, they're at a stage where exposure to service—and to the people whose lives nonprofit service organizations touch—would have a profound effect on them. Meeting a World War II veteran who needs meals brought to him would be educational for the deliverer of that meal, I would think. A college history major might learn something by tutoring a local middle school class that's studying the Underground Railroad. A connection would be forged; a potential career might be discovered.

A service requirement won't work everywhere. It probably wouldn't be feasible, for example, for community college students, who tend to be transient and who generally have considerable family and work demands. But exempt community colleges and you would still have almost 10 million college students enrolled in four-year colleges in the United States. If you exempted a third of them for various reasons, that would leave more than 6 million able-bodied young people at the ready. Even with a modest 10-hours-a-year requirement (the equivalent of two mornings a year) America would gain 60 million volunteer hours to invigorate the nation's nonprofit organizations, churches, job corps, conservation groups and college outreach programs.

And with some flexibility, it wouldn't have to be too onerous. Colleges could give credit for service. That is, at the beginning of each year, a student could opt for service, and in return he or she might get credits equal to one class period. Perhaps every 25 hours of service could be traded for one class credit, with a maximum of three credits a year. What a student would learn from working in a shelter for the victims of domestic abuse would surely equal or surpass his or her time spent in racquetball class—at my college worth one full unit.

Alternatively, colleges could limit the service requirement to a student's junior year—a time when the students are settled and have more hours and stability in their schedules. Turning the junior year into a year when volunteering figures prominently could also help colleges bridge the chasm that usually stands between the academic world and the one that lies beyond it.

When Gov. Gray Davis of California proposed a service requirement in 1999, an editorial in The Daily Californian, the student newspaper at the University of California at Berkeley, opposed the plan: "Forced philanthropy will be as much an oxymoron in action as it is in terms. Who would want to receive community service from someone who is forced to serve? Is forced community service in California not generally reserved for criminals and delinquents?"

First of all, that's putting forth a pretty dim view of the soul of the average student. What, is the unwilling college volunteer going to throw food at visitors to the soup kitchen? Volunteering is by nature transformative—reluctant participants become quick converts every day, once they meet those who need their help.

Second, college is largely about fulfilling requirements, isn't it? Students have to complete this much work in the sciences, that much work in the arts. Incoming freshmen accept a tacit contract, submitting to the wisdom of the college's founders and shapers, who decide which experiences are necessary to create a well-rounded scholar, one ready to make a contribution to the world. But while colleges give their students the intellectual tools for life beyond campus, they largely ignore the part about how they might contribute to the world. That is, until the commencement speech, at which time all the "go forth's" and "be helpful's" happen.

But what if such a sentiment happened on the student's first day? What if graduating seniors already knew full well how to balance jobs, studies, family and volunteer work in the surrounding community? What if campuses were full of under-served high school students meeting with their college tutors? What if the tired and clogged veins of thousands of towns and cites had the energy of millions of college students coursing through them? What if the student who might have become a foosball power— and I say this knowing how much those skills have enhanced my life and those who had the good fortune to have watched me—became instead a lifelong volunteer? That might be pretty good for everybody.

*Dave Eggers, editor of McSweeney's, is the author of A Heartbreaking Work of Staggering Genius and the founder of 826 Valencia, a nonprofit learning center.*

Work Cited

Eggers, Dave. "Serve or Fail." New York Times 13 June 2006: late ed.: WK13.

## PROBLEMS IN REASONING

### Finding the Facts

Finding the *facts*, said Sherlock Holmes, is the beginning of wisdom. What is a fact? A fact is something real, something you can observe or experience. Critical thinkers define facts two ways: first is primary evidence, those things you can discover with your senses or with tests and measurements of various sorts—science. Also, facts can be secondary evidence: beliefs, ideas, information you cannot find with your senses but for which there is historical evidence, documents, testimony, or articles related to the fact in question. Was there ever a man named Jesus? The answer is yes, based on secondary (historical) evidence.

We tend to think of *probability* rather than absolute truth in modern science. Primary evidence usually has a higher probability than secondary evidence—but not always. If you find deer tracks in the soft earth, you can accept this as probable evidence of a fact, evidence of deer (that is, if they really are deer tracks and not some trick). Critical thinkers define facts as things you can discover with your senses, or things you believe are "probable." For example, you believe your history books are probably true, based on both physical and secondary evidence. You believe Adolf Hitler was the German "Führer" during WWII, and most thoughtful people agree he ordered the massacre of millions of Jewish people. Why believe these things? Critical thinkers believe them because people are still alive to attest to them; many historians confirm them; and much physical evidence remains of them. A few people say they don't believe the evidence, but the burden is on them to show how else to explain the probable "facts," including all the newspaper and magazine stories at the time, the books, the pictures, and other more appalling evidence of the Holocaust.

As a thoughtful reader and writer you must resist drawing conclusions until you are sure of all the facts. Critical thinkers know that if you catch someone whose fingerprints are on the murder weapon, you may or may not have found the guilty individual. Reasoning tells you not to seize upon the first available answer: critical thinking tells you to explore, to look for other explanations. Fingerprints on a gun don't automatically solve the problem. "Jumping" to the conclusion, before all the facts are in, isn't reasoning. Reasoning does not start with guessing an answer. First you must collect and evaluate the facts; then you can attempt to put them together to reach your conclusions.

Facts are verifiable reality, truths you can detect with your own senses or with testimony from witnesses or with instruments and rules of science. It is important to determine facts because without them you have only guessing. And in that case, even careful thinkers are likely to make errors. You want to know: did the house burn by accident or was something more deliberate involved? Did the victim die of natural causes . . . or something else? Should you allow developers to build a casino in your town or not? And why? Facts are the foundation of reason.

The purpose of the rest of this chapter is to help you learn to recognize problems in reasoning and to avoid them in your own writing and speaking.

# **I**MPLICATIONS, ASSUMPTIONS, AND INFERENCES

Reasoning requires that you sift and weigh your thoughts and make judgments about evidence. Reasoning has an unpredictable quality. It's like hunting: you seek out the truth by tracking down the facts. Learning principles and techniques of reasoning takes practice. Being able to recognize problems of reasoning will strengthen your critical thinking abilities.

You need to be on the alert for the worst problem of all: self-deception. It's bad enough when you are confronted with faulty evidence; it's worse yet to suspect that you are being deceived by a sly opponent. However, to mislead yourself is the worst problem because it means your own reasoning is not trustworthy. Self-deception means you can never be certain whether you have reached a valid conclusion or are merely accepting the answer you want to hear.

Critical thinkers need to be careful when trying to solve a problem because people don't always spell out everything in clear, logical language. One of the problems of reasoning lies in the fact that what is *not* said can be as significant as what is said. For example, the standard "syllogism" states a major premise, a minor premise, and a conclusion: "All men are mortal; Socrates is a man; therefore, Socrates is mortal." But only logicians talk that way. Most people take shortcuts. You can hop and skip through the language, relying on your reader's ability to follow you. You may use informal reasoning; you may turn things around, skip over the middle part, and sometimes avoid the syllogism altogether: "Of course Socrates was mortal—isn't everyone?"

Therefore, for understanding and interpretation you can rely not only on what you hear or read but also on your ability to use context to supply the missing parts. To analyze problems in reasoning, you need to understand the differences between facts and implications, inferences, and assumptions.

## **Implications**

An implication is a suggestion, an idea expressed with indirect words or an unspoken meaning audiences can detect. For example, you know when your friends don't like your new glasses, even if they say they do like them. Facial expressions, body language, tone of voice (sarcasm, for example) can negate a message, and so can noncommittal responses ("Yeah, okay, I guess"). Such implied messages can mean the opposite of a spoken message: "Your new glasses are . . . very interesting." The speaker seems to say something positive, but most people know this particular message implies something negative. An implication is an unspoken message: "Aunt Bessie has done up her hair, put on makeup, perfume, and earrings. She is wearing her new dress. All this *suggests* (though she doesn't say) she is going somewhere."

Implications, as unspoken messages, may be accurate or inaccurate. When you write 20 pages for your research paper instead of the assigned 10, you may wish to imply (suggest) that you did more work than other students. But length does not equal quality, and most teachers want students to stay within the bounds of the assignment. When you clean your roommate's dishes, you may imply that you are kind. (But the truth might be that you want to borrow your friend's car). When you volunteer at the local soup kitchen, you may imply to others that you have a social conscience. (But the truth may be that you think this will look good on your résumé.)

It's important to be alert to implications because they can lead your reasoning astray. Many people believe the Second Amendment of the Constitution says all citizens have the right to own guns. However, many others believe the amendment implies that only a state militia can be armed.

## Assumptions

An assumption is an idea or belief you take for granted. When you see Aunt Bessie dressed up this way, you take for granted that she is going out. Your assumptions are based on your experiences: you've seen Aunt Bessie dress this way before. Could there be any other reason for her to dress this way? Maybe—but if she isn't going out of the house, why is she wearing her new dress? An assumption is a belief, not necessarily a fact: many religious people assume that Heaven exists and if they lead moral lives they will go there.

You often base your assumptions on prior knowledge: because it's thundering and raining outside, you assume there will be lightning soon. Because the sun just came out, you assume you might see a rainbow.

But some assumptions are hidden and (some people think) destructive. Although the public may assume schools teach reading, writing, and arithmetic, Jonathan Kozol suggests that the true function of public schools is to "weed out" lower-class students, to reconcile them to their low position in society, and to direct them toward "suitable" work. In Savage Inequalities, published in 1991, Kozol writes, "A lot of wealthy folks in Texas think the schools are doing a sufficiently good job if the kids of poor folks . . . had all the necessary skills to do their kitchen work and tend their lawns." Kozol's studies were limited to inner city schools in several large cities. Do such conditions still exist? Are Kozol's conclusions representative of the country at large? If you read his book, might you reach different conclusions?

People assume our schools teach English, math, history, and science, and most people hold the assumption that it is wrong to use schools to teach any sort of ideology. American education is officially "value free," meaning it doesn't preach any religion or doesn't favor any political party or position. Yet critics say that "value free" has come to mean value*less*. If we take the value out of what students learn, what is left? (For more on assumptions, see Chapter 2.)

## ACTIVITY 7

Identify what assumption you think has been made in each of the following statements. Briefly explain your reasoning. (There may be more than one answer.) For example,

After a fine chicken dinner, little Angela became ill. "I'll never serve chicken again," vowed her mother. [Mother assumes the chicken dinner made Angela ill.]

1. The TV ad promised that one bottle of "Feel-Good" would make you feel better. Father immediately rushed out and bought a dozen bottles.
2. Vanessa looked for a new car and finally bought a used Speedster that could go 120 miles per hour.
3. Since the first Gulf War (1991) was relatively easy, victory in the second (2003) should be easier, even with fewer troops, because modern weapons are so much more sophisticated and destructive.
4. Mrs. Harper discovered the joint checking account with her husband was overdrawn. "Darn that man," she exclaimed.
5. The media announced that Iraq possessed weapons of mass destruction and was in violation of United Nations' orders to destroy them or face serious consequences. Protestors immediately began demonstrating against war on Iraq.
6. Al Qaeda is often described as a global terrorist organization loyal to Osama bin Laden, a wealthy Saudi. When New York's Twin Towers (World Trade Center) were destroyed, killing thousands of men, women, and children, many people cursed Al Qaeda.
7. The Three Stooges were a trio of slapstick actors whose brand of rough and tumble comedy became popular in the 1930s. Their films remain popular today, indicating what talented comedians they really were.
8. Violet told her roommate that her doctor had found evidence of anthrax in Violet's blood. Violet's roommate immediately decided to live somewhere else.
9. Madam LaRinda read Nancy's palm, in which she saw "signs" of death. Soon after, Nancy died. "I should never have told her that," Madam LaRinda cried.
10. Spiderman the Movie is based on a scientific phenomenon when a genetically altered spider bites Peter Parker and thus passes on spider attributes to the high school youth.

## Inferences

An inference is a conclusion, a logical deduction. You infer from your friends' comments that they really don't like your new glasses. You infer that Aunt Bessie is going out when she dresses up. If you bring Moby Dick to read at the beach instead of People magazine, some people might infer that you like serious literature. People draw inferences from whatever they notice.

An inference is a conclusion and, therefore, is similar to an assumption, except that an inference is usually based on something you can see or hear, some evidence you can detect with your senses or through premises you believe to be true. Assumptions, however, are usually based on beliefs. For example, Gretchen ended her research paper with the conclusion that there may be Martians, because she could find no evidence against their existence. Gretchen relies on an *assumption*—she assumes that if there had been any Martians she would have found some evidence of them.

An inference is not a guess, such as "Guess what number I'm thinking of?" An inference is a conclusion you reach because you have evidence that leads you to the conclusion. In <u>The Adventures of Huckleberry Finn</u>, for example, Huck makes an important inference based on footprints in the snow: "There was a cross in the left boot-heel made with big nails, to keep off the devil." From this observation he inferred that his father Pap Finn had been around.

Inferences "may be carelessly or carefully made" says S. I. Hayakawa in <u>Language in Thought and Action</u>:

> They may be made on the basis of a broad background of previous experience with the subject matter, or no experience at all. For example, the inferences a good mechanic can make about the internal condition of a motor by listening to it are often startlingly accurate, while the inferences made by an amateur (if he tries to make any) may be entirely wrong. But the common characteristic of inferences is that they are statements . . . made on the basis of what has been observed.

Remember that inferences depend on observation.

It isn't always easy to decide between *implication*, *assumption*, or *inference*, especially when more than one answer seems possible. One helpful technique to use is the "rule of simplicity." When there are competing possibilities, the *rule of simplicity* says to choose the answer that requires the fewest assumptions. That means if you find your pet rabbit dead, the rule of simplicity tells you the rabbit probably wasn't killed by aliens . . . because that answer would require you to introduce an assumption—that there are aliens. You would need additional information before you could reasonably infer that aliens zapped your bunny.

Assumptions, implications, and inferences all rely on your ability to fill in missing information, to make the connection between the information you do have (like the tracks in the snow) and a conclusion, information you don't have. Huck might have been wrong—he lives among superstitious people, and Pap might not be the only man with such a mark. However, in this case, Huck's conclusion was correct, for shortly the man does show up.

## ACTIVITY 8

Use the rule of simplicity—that the simplest explanation is usually the best one—to try to identify which if any of the options is a reasonable inference based solely on the information in the following statements. Select the answer you think is most probable. If none of the answers seems likely to you, select "E. None of the above." Explain your answers.

1. Though no lights showed anywhere, enemy troops began firing into our barracks.

    (A) The enemy assumed we were in our barracks. (B) The enemy was firing blindly in the dark. (C) The darkened barracks were a trap for the enemy. (D) The enemy was trying to frighten us with the noise of gunfire. (E) None of the above.

2. Through the dining room window Mrs. Costello watched her neighbor making gestures over an arrangement of daisies, apparently speaking to them. The next day the flowers appeared dried-up and dead.

    (A) The neighbor's flowers needed water. (B) Mrs. Costello should mind her own business. (C) Mrs. Costello's neighbor is a witch. (D) Mrs. Costello believed daisies were out of season. (E) None of the above.

3. Behind the refrigerator, Aunt Clara found little specks that looked like black rice. "Quick, Mina, get the vacuum," she whispered.

    (A) Aunt Clara whispers because she is unusually nervous and easily frightened by things behind the refrigerator. (B) Mina has been dropping ground pepper behind the refrigerator for a joke. (C) There is something wrong with Aunt Clara's refrigerator. (D) The vacuum is a tool for repairing the refrigerator. (E) None of the above.

4. On 9/11/01, both of New York City's 110-story "Twin Towers" were reduced to rubble in less than 2 hours.

    (A)The Twin Towers housed the World Trade Center. (B) The Twin Towers had been poorly constructed. (C) The Twin Towers were destroyed by terrorists. (D) Between 2,000 and 3,000 people were killed in the destruction of the Twin Towers. (E) None of the above.

5. A customer handed the clerk a new twenty-dollar bill. The clerk examined the twenty on both sides, looking at it carefully, and finally gave it back to the customer, saying, "You better take this to the bank."

    (A) The clerk could not recognize the face on the $20 bill. (B) The clerk was trying to cheat the customer. (C) There are no new twenties and the clerk knew it. (D) The clerk believes the customer is trying to pass on a forged $20. (E) None of the above.

6. The UPS driver found a new sign on the Wilsons' gate: "Beware of Dog." But the driver knew the Wilsons' dog had always been a miniature poodle named Fifi, and so ignored the sign.

    (A) The UPS driver had no fear of dogs. (B) The UPS driver assumed the sign was a joke. (C) The UPS driver assumed the sign referred to Fifi. (D) The UPS driver was unaware that the Wilsons' had replaced Fifi with a pit bull. (E) None of the above.

7. "It is impossible for me to be pregnant, Dr. Stone," said Mary Doe. "I've been 'on the pill' for two years."

    (A) Dr. Stone is kidding Mary Doe. (B) Mary Doe is sexually promiscuous. (C) Mary Doe believes the "pill" is an infallible birth control method. (D) Mary Doe is having an affair with Dr. Stone. (E) None of the above.

8. Over half the audience left before the film ended.

   (A) Those who left did not enjoy the film. (B) Those who stayed were unable to leave. (C) Those who left had already seen the ending. (D) Those who stayed planned to see the film again. (E) None of the above.

9. If we don't provide study questions, many students will fail.

   (A) The students like study questions. (B) The exam is too easy. (C) Students don't need to study. (D) The exam is very difficult. (E) None of the above.

10. The newspaper reported that an old man had been found dead at the foot of a long flight of stairs.

    (A) The stairs had no railing. (B) Someone murdered the old man. (C) A fall down the stairs killed the old guy. (D) The old man had fallen as he started up the staircase. (E) None of the above.

## ACTIVITY 9

Try to find the best answer for each of the following statements based on what you know about facts, assumptions, implications, inferences, or other reasoning. Using the rule of simplicity as a guide, select the answer you think best explains the statement.

1. The contest offered a cash prize to whoever could guess the closest to the number of jelly beans in a large glass jar. The contest required contestants to . . .

   (A) Make an inference. (B) Make an assumption. (C) Make an implication. (D) Count the jelly beans. (E) None of the above.

2. It's useless to try to improve on your natural talents—genetics is destiny. This opinion is . . .

   (A) Scientific evidence. (B) An inference. (C) A question of fact. (D) An assumption. (E) None of the above.

3. Gerhardt heard a noise late at night: he sat up in bed and shouted, "Who's there?"

   (A) Gerhardt believed he was about to be killed. (B) Gerhardt thought the house was creaking. (C) Gerhardt believed someone else was in the house. (D) Gerhardt believed he had been dreaming. (E) None of the above.

4. Kelly used the weight room every day, lifting more and more weight each time on the theory that if lifting 100 pounds was good for him, then lifting 300 must be three times as good.

   (A) An assumption. (B) A fact. (C) Kelly used advanced mathematics to reach this conclusion. (D) An implication. (E) None of the above.

5. One of Magico's best illusions is the Saw Box. An assistant steps into the box, Magico closes the lid and nails it down so that the assistant cannot escape, and then Magico begins to saw the box in half, while the assistant in the box screams and thrashes head and feet. When Magico has completely sawn through, the two halves are separated—with the assistant's feet and head protruding but no longer moving. Members of the audience have been known to faint.

(A) Members of the audience believe Magico's assistant has been cut in half. (B) Those who faint must believe Magic has supernatural powers. (C) Members of the audience believe the assistant in the box has the ability to disengage from her legs. (D) Members of the audience believe Magico uses mirrors to create the illusion. (E) None of the above.

6. The patient had strange symptoms of dark discolorations all over the body, fever, and painfully swollen lymph glands. The patient said he had been bitten by a snake. He died within a day. The best explanation is probably . . .

     (A) The snake venom killed the patient. (B) The patient had contracted the plague. (C) The patient died of some disease unrelated to his symptoms. (D) The patient had been murdered. (E) None of the above.

7. Professor Orson was in his 70s, yet he had long, luxuriant black hair.

     (A) Professor Orson was an old hippie. (B) Professor Orson wore a wig. (C) Professor Orson had his hair dyed each week. (D) Professor Orson came from a long line of ancestors who had long, luxuriant black hair. (E) None of the above.

8. The Quiki store continued to lose money, though sales were strong. "We need to install surveillance cameras to watch the cash register and checkout counter," the manager said.

     (A) The manager assumes the customers are fooling the cashier. (B) The manager's statement implies she believes the cashier may be cheating. (C) The old surveillance cameras no longer work. (D) The accountant may have been reporting incorrect sales figures. (E) None of the above.

9. The marines near the bridge were suddenly under fire. "Return fire," shouted their captain.

     (A) The captain was confused. (B) The captain was out of ammunition. (C) The captain implied the enemy was firing at the marines. (D) The captain assumed the marines might not return fire. (E) None of the above.

10. Day after day the Harelson family mailbox gets appeals for money, irrelevant announcements, inducements to buy "specials" they don't want, and all sorts of colorful catalogs. Ms. Harelson said, "It is safe to predict there will probably be more junk mail in our mailbox today."

     (A) Ms. Harelson believes their mailbox is on some special junk mail list. (B) The Harelsons enjoy all the wonderful things they get in their mailbox. (C) Ms. Harelson is able to predict the future. (D) Mailbox material that tries to get the Harelsons to spend money for things the family doesn't want is called "junk mail." (E) None of the above. ▆

# FALLACIES

To reason well, you must word your statements carefully: you must draw your conclusions according to the rules of logic. If worded properly, a logical statement becomes inescapable, which means the conclusion is as near as you can get to absolute truth.

*fallacie of reasoning.*
*a 'problem's of*

"Worded properly" means with true premises arranged according to some rule of logic that reasonable people can accept. However, without some training, even critical thinkers may accidentally make pseudo statements—statements that may seem logical but which actually contain some error in reasoning.

Most of the errors of reasoning are well known. There may be some exceptions, but on the whole, the fallacies are those presented here. They are listed as "problems" of reasoning because they don't apply automatically.

Some of the fallacies may sound strange to you: a few of them still have their Latin names (such as *ad hominem*). They have English names too, of course, but educated men and women have carried on the tradition of the Latin names for thousands of years. You will have to make up your own mind about that, but once you learn them, you will begin to hear them and see them in print. (Readers tend to skip anything unfamiliar or difficult and thus you may believe that you have never seen or heard these words, but once you learn them you'll discover thoughtful writers have been using them all along.)

## PROBLEMS OF INSUFFICIENT EVIDENCE

Problems of insufficient evidence can result in overgeneralizing, card stacking, ad ignorantium, and post hoc ergo propter hoc. It is the nature of reasoning and research that you rarely have enough evidence. As a result, you can find yourself trying to predict on the basis of small amounts of information. On election night, for example, TV statisticians predict the winners on the basis of only 2 or 3% of the votes. You need general rules and principles when you can't be absolutely sure of the outcome.

> A horse with a winning record is a safer bet than one that has several losses or one that has never raced before.
>
> Red is a relatively uncommon hair color in Asia.

Naturally, you can never be absolutely certain about such generalized conclusions; at best you must assume greater or lesser degrees of probability. You can only say that red is "a *relatively* uncommon hair color" because you really haven't seen many of Asia's billions of people.

If you required 100% certainty before making up your mind about anything, you would live in constant indecision. If a 2-year-old manages to climb to the top of the jungle gym, what might happen? Most adults would become alarmed and would probably get the child down—*probably* because some adults are pretty relaxed and might assume their child was safe. In a court case, you may not have enough information to say absolutely what happened, but you could say the accused is a very small woman weighing less than 100 pounds and has only normal strength and endurance. Is it probable that she could have lifted the victim (a large man who weighs 275 pounds) into a crate, which she then theoretically carried down a flight of stairs and lifted into a truck by herself? It really doesn't seem probable.

However, since you do work with probabilities instead of certainties, you can fall into the habit of casually generalizing without proper sampling and verification techniques. Because you can only predict probabilities, you may develop the attitude that everything is a guessing game and therefore "my guess is as good as anyone's," meaning nothing really matters. But clearly this isn't true. Some opinions can get you in trouble (jail). Random guessing is not the technique of critical thinkers. Guessing is allowed, but an "educated guess" is different from a random "shot in the dark."

Experts who have spent years studying and gaining experience with weapons, ballistics, forensic[2] evidence have expert opinions that are treated differently from yours or ours. They may be giving inferences, but their *educated* guesses carry more influence than those of average citizens (juries). When experts say the victim died of strangulation, you are inclined to believe them.

## Overgeneralizing

*Overgeneralizing* (also called hasty generalizing or faulty generalizing) means drawing a larger conclusion than the evidence supports. Critical thinkers should keep in mind how difficult it is to verify statements about "all" or "most" or even "many" (depending on how many you mean). For example,

> All robins have red breasts.

The statement isn't exactly true. Young robins are usually speckled. The breasts of adult robins can appear to be more orange than red. In any case, it's highly doubtful that anyone could ever claim to have seen "all" robins.

> Many children die before reaching maturity.

That's a difficult statement at best. The word *many* is inherently vague—how "many" are you talking about? Further, both "children" and "maturity" are subject to various interpretations.

> Men don't cry.

---

[2] *Ballistics:* the science of identifying bullets; *forensic:* accepted in courts of law.

This example shows that generalizations can be implicit. The statement doesn't use "all" or "most," but it implies (suggests) a feature of men in general. Depending on how many are included in the statement (some? many? most?), critical thinkers may reject the statement as an overgeneralization. The statement cannot mean that males as a group are biologically incapable of crying: both males and females have functioning tear ducts. It's possible that the statement refers to the quality of being "manly," and therefore it is even less likely to be true (who makes these rules?).

If there are so many exceptions and complications to using generalizations, why use them? The answer is you use them because you must. You will find it difficult to have conversations if you are required to use only scientifically accurate statements. Such information isn't available to most people and would seriously alter our ability to communicate if it were. Imagine, for example, the statement, "Tall men have big feet." In general, many people would agree—it's a handy generalization you can use in appropriate contexts. But if you had to define exactly what you mean by *tall men* and *big feet* you would be unable to proceed with your discussion and instead would begin arguing about the definitions of these general terms. The ability to generalize is an important part of your ability to think and to communicate. However, critical thinkers need to be alert to overgeneralizations.

If you insist on generalizations such as "Pigs will eat anything," you make your statements easy to refute. All you need to refute such a sweeping generalization is to produce something some pig somewhere refuses to eat. A single exception can cast doubt on sweeping generalizations and on your credibility. When you stop to analyze a generalization (one that sounds doubtful to you), you may discover that it means something you can't verify.

However, there is a limit on how far you can trust this. On the whole it is true that pigs are not very picky, and that's an old and accepted truth. If someone shows up at the county fair with a pig that won't eat anything but lilacs, you aren't likely to change that old truism about pigs. You are much more likely to conclude that there is something strange about that lilac-eating pig. Established beliefs are those which have stood the test of time and aren't overturned easily. Despite the rule about big generalizations, it is generally hard to overturn an established rule, and we often require more than a single exception to do it.

Overgeneralizations are one of the most common fallacies of writing and in conversation, for example, "All real men have beards." You know that is not true. Some men do not have beards at all. Many men shave their beards. And, in fact, some women can have surprisingly heavy beards. The generalization about men and beards is too sweeping. It is a fallacy. Be on guard against statements that contain words like *all, everyone, everybody, no one, nothing, everything, anything,* and *always*. Be on guard against statements that imply too many cases, whether they use any of these words or not. Thoughtful writers *qualify* generalizations that seem too sweeping or that are likely to create doubt in the reader's mind. Qualifiers such as *many, some,* or *a few* usually work well.

As a critical thinker you may qualify as much as you need. *Most* children enjoy school until about second or third grade. *Many* of the elderly are more concerned with security than with enjoying life. You need to test your generalizations in your mind before setting them in print. However, too much qualifying can give your writing a tentative, indecisive sound, as if you aren't sure of what you want to say. This is one place where reason and style run into each other, a place where you must make decisions about which way to go. How many "maybe's" and "probably's" can readers encounter before they wish you would just make a good strong statement?

You need to be aware of generalizations—whether they make sense or not, whether they are qualified or not. (For more on overgeneralizations, see Chapter 2.)

## ACTIVITY 10

Read this passage from Richard Paul, author of <u>Critical Thinking: What Every Person Needs to Survive in a Rapidly Changing World</u> (1993). In your notebook, write about these issues: Do you agree with Richard Paul? Evaluate his reasoning (is his reasoning valid?). Does he overgeneralize? How? Bring your response to class for discussion.

> Classroom instruction around the world, at all levels, is typically didactic,[3] one-dimensional, and indifferent, when not antithetical to[4] reason. Blank faces are taught barren conclusions in dreary drills. There is nothing sharp, nothing poignant, no exciting twist or turn of mind and thought, nothing fearless, nothing modest, no struggle, no conflict, no rational give-and-take, no intellectual excitement or discipline, no pulsation in the heart or mind. Students are not expected to ask for reasons to justify what they are told to believe. They do not question what they see, hear, or read, nor are they encouraged to do so. They do not demand that subject matter "make sense" to them. They do not challenge the thinking of other students nor expect their thinking to be challenged by others. Indeed, they do not expect to have to think at all. ▪

## ACTIVITY 11

Analyze the following excerpt from John Gray's book <u>Men, Women and Relationships</u>. What is his thesis and how well does he support it? Do you agree with him? Is his reasoning valid? Does he overgeneralize? How? Write at least a page. Bring it to class for discussion. ▪

---

[3] *Didactic:* boringly moralistic.
[4] *Antithetical to:* against.

## Wallets and Purses

*John Gray*

Contrasts in how men and women confront the world are most visually apparent when we compare a woman's purse with a man's wallet. Women carry large, heavy bags with beautiful decorations and shiny colors, while men carry lightweight, plain black or brown wallets that are designed to carry only the bare essentials: a driver's license, major credit cards, and paper money. One can never be too sure what one will find when looking into a woman's purse. Even she may not know. But one thing is for sure, she will be carrying everything else she could possibly need, along with whatever others may need too.

When looking in a woman's purse the first thing you find is a collection of other, littler purses and containers. It's as though she carries her own private drugstore and office combined. You may find a wallet, a coin purse, a makeup kit, a mirror, an organizer and calendar, a checkbook, a small calculator, another small makeup kit with a little mirror, a hairbrush and comb, an address book, an older address book for really old friends, an eyeglass container, sunglasses in another container, a package of tissue, several partially used tissues, tampons, a condom package or diaphragm, a set of keys, an extra set of keys, her husband's keys, a toothbrush, toothpaste, breath spray, plain floss, flavored floss (her children like mint), a little container of aspirin, another container of vitamins and pills, two or three nail files, four or five pens and pencils, several little pads of paper, a roll of film in its container and an empty film container, a package of business cards from friends and experts in all fields, a miniature picture album of her loved ones, lip balm, tea bags, another package of pain-relief pills, an envelope filled with receipts, various letters and cards from loved ones, stamps, a small package of bills to be paid, and a host of other miscellaneous items like paper clips, rubber bands, safety pins, barrettes, bobby pins, fingernail clippers, stationery and matching envelopes, gum, trail mix, assorted discount coupons, breath mints, and bits of garbage to be thrown away (next spring). In short, she has everything she could need and carries it with her wherever she goes.

To a woman, her purse is her security blanket, a trusted friend, an important part of her self. You can tell how expanded a woman's awareness is by the size of her purse. She is prepared for every emergency, wherever she may find herself.

Ironically, when she is being escorted to a grand ball she will leave this purse at home and bring a little shiny purse with the bare essentials. In this case, she feels that this night is for her. She is being taken care of by her man and she doesn't have to feel responsible for anybody. She feels so special and so supported that she doesn't need the security of her purse.

# Card Stacking

*Card stacking* means selecting only data that supports your own point of view and ignores contradictory data. Card stacking is biased, unfair thinking and writing and should be avoided. For example, consider the following.

> During his time in office, President Clinton was a moral man. He was married to a smart and wise woman, Hillary. He loved his daughter and talked a lot about family values. He went to church each Sunday. He often quoted from the Bible.

These statements are one-sided; there is no reference to the other side of Mr. Clinton's character, his inappropriate behavior with his intern. This little story omits a great deal about the president that critical thinkers need in order to make an informed judgment. Stacking the deck means arranging the cards so that it is possible to know the winner or loser in advance. This little story about the president stacks the evidence to make him seem a winner, but many people know there is more to this story.

Card stacking is especially harmful in research. Researchers who go looking for evidence that supports only one side of an issue—such as evidence that tobacco smoke is harmless—may be able to find an impressive number of people who have smoked all their lives without ill effect and thus the findings will seem to reinforce the preconceived notion of the thesis. But "stacking" the evidence is of course not research at all; it gives only one side of the evidence. Ignoring evidence, whether deliberately or accidentally, can be considered fraud at worst and amateurish at best. No matter how many healthy smokers can be found, you must also account for those who are ill.

As a critical thinker, you must not impose your own bias on the subject or the data. A research paper must examine all sides, all data, and must not be biased toward either side.

## Ad Ignorantium

*Ad ignorantium* is a fallacy based on ignorance, as when a writer tells readers something must be true because they can't prove otherwise. "You can't prove there aren't any leprechauns in Ireland; therefore you should assume there are such creatures." (This is false reasoning. The correct wording should be *there may or may not be* such creatures. In short, the statement is meaningless without evidence one way or the other.) The absence of evidence is not proof.

The "ignorant" argument tells you that something must be true if you cannot prove it false, or that something must be false if you cannot prove it true. "You can't prove your candidate will win the race; therefore I assume your candidate won't." A negative premise is not a good basis for concluding anything. The argument assumes that lack of knowledge, ignorance, can be a source of information.

Except for special cases, most critical thinkers reject the idea that *because* you don't know something, it must be true—or false. The statement is self-contradictory (because you don't know something, you do know something?). Phrase your claims positively when possible.

## Post Hoc Ergo Propter Hoc

*Post hoc ergo propter hoc* translates as "after this, therefore because of this." That is, it's a fallacy based on time. It is often called *post hoc* for short. You assume a later event was caused by an earlier event: "The milk was left out all night and was spoiled the next morning. It should have been put in the refrigerator to keep it fresh." The speaker assumes the first event—leaving the milk out—caused the second event (the milk spoiled). It's a possibility, of course: many people would make that assumption. The milk may have spoiled as a result of being out of the refrigerator all night, but you should reject the notion that one thing must cause another. Could there be any other explanation? Yes, it is possible that the milk never was fresh—that it was spoiled before being left out. Many things are possible but few are necessary, especially where causation is concerned. A young man may fall in love with a young woman after she sprinkles a love potion over his cereal, but critical thinkers would be reluctant to say the potion must have been the cause.

Consider a more difficult example: "Japan became a great industrial nation after its surrender in World War II; therefore the defeat caused this rise in industry." True? Cause-and-effect relationships are seldom as simple as people believe; often there are many indirect as well as direct causes of a single effect. It is certainly not true that one thing must have caused another simply because the two things happened sequentially.

## ACTIVITY 12

### INSUFFICIENT EVIDENCE

Identify the fallacy in each of the following statements. Explain why each statement is called an error of insufficient evidence: overgeneralization, card stacking, ad ignorantium, or post hoc ergo propter hoc.

> **Example:** After he declared an end to our involvement in the Vietnam War, President Nixon was forced out of office: obviously his downfall was the result of his war policy. [Post hoc ergo propter hoc—The later event was not caused by the former. Nixon's downfall was not caused by his war policy.]

1. Some NFL players weigh over 300 pounds; therefore, we can conclude that football makes people fat.
2. It's interesting to speculate about the Loch Ness Monster, Bigfoot, and the Abominable Snowman, but no one has ever proved such things exist. Therefore, it's safe to conclude they don't.
3. Charlie Chaplin was a world-renowned comedian, silent film star, producer, and director. He was surely one of the most creative artists in film history. No wonder so many people throughout the world loved him.
4. Mr. and Mrs. Cartouche sued the Dogs and Beans fast-food hut because after eating there they became ill.
5. "Before amassing his fortune with the enormous royalties from the publication of his hugely popular book <u>Mein Kampf</u>, Hitler earned a living by using his artistic

skills to produce paintings that were sold to the public or used for postcards. Hitler was a great student of the fine arts and studied music, opera, painting, sculpture, and architecture. While living in Vienna under conditions of poverty, he read voraciously and still managed to spend whatever meager income he had to attend lectures, concerts, opera, and the theater. . . . His art continued throughout his leadership of Germany and included detailed building plans, furniture design, city planning, and monuments." (<www.hitler.org/art/>)

6. I have a dozen articles that say AIDS is always fatal; it makes no difference if you can find one or two that say otherwise.

7. After WWII, General Eisenhower became president of the United States. War is good training for the presidency.

8. There was no proof that O. J. Simpson killed his wife. Therefore, he is innocent.

9. Father suffered the terrible pain of arthritis rather than take the codeine pills his doctor prescribed. He feared he might become addicted to the strong opiate in codeine.

10. It is certain that every college student is committed to reading, writing, and diligently studying for years on end to earn a degree. ▬

## ACTIVITY 13

In your notebook write an example of your own for each fallacy: overgeneralization, card stacking, ad ignorantium, and post hoc ergo propter hoc. ▬

## PROBLEMS BASED ON IRRELEVANT INFORMATION

Some writing problems occur when a writer bases ideas on irrelevant information. Here are several fallacies of this kind.

| | |
|---|---|
| Ad baculum | Bandwagon |
| Ad hominem | Plain folks and snob appeal |
| Fallacy of opposition | Ad verecundiam |
| Genetic fallacy | Red herring |
| Guilt by association | Weak opponent |
| Ad misericordiam | Tu quoque |
| Ad populum | Oversimplifying |

The largest group of reasoning problems contains the *irrelevant* arguments. Often these are used by accident, but sometimes they are the result of faulty thinking. "Irrelevant" here means not related to the point at issue. For example, "A packing company is trying to open a new factory in our town. Is it relevant information that the company president has had psychiatric treatment? A new factory would mean jobs; it would be good for the town. What has the president's medical record to do with that?" Essentially this question asks for the warrant, the connection between the evidence and the claim (see the Toulmin method earlier in this chapter). It is the "so what" question. There are several varieties of irrelevance—ways for an argument to stumble over evidence that doesn't clarify but instead muddies the waters of an investigation. You need to know what it would take to persuade people about the president of the new company. Is there some law against people treated for depression holding positions of power and prestige?

Relevance is an important consideration when evaluating evidence. You can lose a lot of time tracking down and/or evaluating evidence that has no relevance to your case. Opponents can create a lot of confusion by introducing irrelevant data. Critical thinkers must remember that the point of reasoning is not to "win" arguments but to find the truth of the matter, to the best of your ability. Using irrelevant information not only confuses the issue but may seriously damage your credibility.

## Ad Baculum

*Ad baculum* comes from the Latin word for a "stick" or "club." The baculum argument is an appeal to force: it may involve threats of physical violence or psychological harm such as public ridicule and loss of reputation. "My gang and I will beat up anyone who doesn't vote our way." Such crude appeals to force may seem laughable today, but even today gangs do make such threats, by implication if not expressly. In the early days of the labor movement, violence was used on all sides—within the unions, between the unions, and between unions and management. Direct threats may be less common today, but the ad baculum "appeal" is alive and well in the form of extortion, blackmail, and other more psychological appeals. For example, opponents are in possession of embarrassing letters and threaten to make them public if you don't comply with their demands.

There are many ways to apply force, threats, and pressure. For example, "If you give our cigarettes a bad report, we may lose our smokers and may even go out of business. Then *you* would lose the source of your grant money!" Here the force is indirect. You are being warned not to give a negative report.

## Ad Hominem

> The Faculty Senate was attempting to decide whether to create a fund for frog-cloning re-search, but the English professors were yelling, "Biomedical researchers are frauds. They don't earn their salaries! They don't do anything productive. They use up all our resources! They're trying to get out of their teaching assignments again! No more money for them!"

*Ad hominem* translates as "to the person." The ad hominem argument ignores the facts entirely and instead attacks the person presenting them. In the example above, nothing is said about the frog-cloning research itself. It is the researchers who are called "frauds" who "don't earn their salaries." Ad hominem arguments are often merely insults; they imply that there is something wrong with speakers, which allows us to ignore their arguments: "There is no point debating this question with Halston, a known pathological liar."

Ideally an argument is a close relationship between a claim and its evidence. You claim that lawyer Fastfoot has embezzled from the company, and the evidence is money found in Fastfoot's vacation cottage. The accountants must be able to show that the numbers don't add up, that the accounting has been altered to make it seem the money is still in the bank. Investigators must show that Fastfoot had the opportunity to siphon off the money and alter the numbers. Anything not related to the claim or the evidence is not relevant. Arguments about Fastfoot's personality or character ("he wouldn't do such a thing") aren't relevant to the question, which is not whether Fastfoot could, but whether he did do such a thing. Calling Fastfoot a thief or worse may make the investigators feel better, but such name calling has no bearing on the question.

Ad hominems are ways to avoid dealing with the question at hand. Insults beget insults; name calling can lead to violence. Avoid such irrelevant tactics and stick to the question at hand. It isn't relevant that Fastfoot may cheat on his marriage partner or may be a tax fraud; not even his virtues are relevant to a question of fact (he may be a conscientious churchgoer). The question is, did Fastfoot take the money?

## Fallacy of Opposition

The *fallacy of opposition* is a specific kind of ad hominem. It is name calling based on the assumption that whatever comes from the opposition must be wrong and harmful. Such an assumption cuts off all reasoned discourse at the outset. If everything an opponent says is condemned just because the opponent says it, then you have no basis for reasoning together.

"Sure, you favor cloning humans because you're an atheist. I am a believer, and I oppose any tampering with God's natural method of conception." The attack is on the idea of cloning because of the person who supports it. In the example, the believer assumes anything an atheist says must be wrong.

## Genetic Fallacy

The *genetic fallacy* is similar to the fallacy of opposition. The genetic fallacy is false because it assumes that *where* an idea comes from affects its validity. For example, "Can . . . any good thing come out of Nazareth?" the Bible asks (John 1:46). People sometimes attach positive or negative qualities to places. Many of these "place" attributes are simply biases.

---

The biomedical research is valid because it was done at Harvard.

You read the <u>Toledo News</u>? I read only the <u>New York Times</u>.

Valedictorians from small midwest towns cannot compete intellectually with valedictorians from New England prep schools.

---

You must examine the evidence in any question and not allow yourself to be influenced by faulty genetic assertions.

## Guilt by Association

*Guilt by association* is an assumption that you choose your friends (or they choose you) because you are similar to them: you are like those you associate with. "Birds of a feather flock together." Parents often become alarmed by their children's friends. Friends who lie and cheat, use vulgar language, or smoke dope alarm parents because they fear their own children may be doing such things under the influence of peers. It is possible that peers *may* influence their friends' decisions, especially among those eager for peer approval.

However, mature people are usually able to withstand pressure to join friends in unwise or illegal activities. Critical thinkers should not make the assumption that people's behaviors must extend to their friends, nor the other way around either. Birds of a feather don't necessarily flock together. A person entering a bar is not necessarily an alcoholic. A person with rowdy friends will not necessarily become rowdy.

## Ad Misericordiam

*Ad misericordiam* is an appeal to pity. Pity is a complex appeal; many people feel it is manipulative. Pity appeals to the emotions (pathos) rather than to the mind (logos). And pathos is frequently used in appeals for charity, for donations to worthy causes. In many cases, pity does seem relevant and does activate thoughtful reasoning.

Aristotle and others have said that pity can be a legitimate appeal—if you can determine that it is really appropriate to the question under consideration. Appeals for veterans wounded in military service, appeals for starving children in impoverished countries, appeals for the aged and the crippled all may be legitimate emotional appeals for help.

But ad misericordiam can sometimes backfire on those who use it:

---

Professor Bertram, please excuse my three absences last week. My grandmother died. She had a horrible stroke two years ago and my mother had to quit her job to care for her. Grandma couldn't talk, eat, or go to the bathroom. But she always smiled when I walked into her room.

---

In the normal course of events, grandparents do tend to pass on, eventually. However this message does not explain what Grandma's death has to do with the three absences. There is an implied claim but no support for it. It's sad, of course, that Grandma had to suffer the stroke, but Professor Bertram may get the idea that all this information is just an attempt to manipulate him. It might have been better if the student had simply asked for permission (before going) to attend Grandma's funeral.

It can be difficult to decide what is *appropriate* to ethos or pathos:

Dad, we need to help my friend Jenny. She is in terrible trouble. She totaled her car last week—a drunk driver ran into her. Her parents refuse to help her. She has no other relatives to turn to. Remember when she went camping with us after her parents' divorce? We all saw how happy she was. Dad, I think it's our ethical duty to help her. She needs a car to get to work.

Would your parents be moved by this appeal? Giving or lending a friend a car is asking for a lot, no matter how tragic the situation. Instead of focusing on the car, your parents—if they really like Jenny—might help by investigating the situation, and they might point out that although you are suggesting an ethical motive, the argument is entirely an appeal to pity.

## Ad Populum

*Ad populum* is an argument "to the people." Ad populum ideas are assumed to be right because they are popular. "Down with big government" is a popular idea, but is it right? Ad populum appeals to biases, prejudices, and slogans. A populist appeal tells people what they want to hear, what they want to believe—such as how great the country is, how wonderful the people are. The populist approach "strokes" the voters with pleasing remarks.

During the Vietnam war a common slogan was "America—love it or leave it." The implication was that if you loved America, you should not criticize the war effort. This was a simplistic ad populum argument because Americans have the right to disagree with the government and the right not to love this country, especially when loving this country really means loving whatever the government does. Many Americans disagreed with the government's war policy and felt we should not be in Vietnam.

Populists appeal to tradition, oppose change, call for a return to the values of the past. Populism often relies more on sound bites than on reasoning. Virtues like "patriotism," "America for Americans," "law and order," and "family values" tend to mean whatever people say they mean. These sound bite slogans subvert the reasoning process: people shouting slogans make it difficult to analyze what is happening. Critical thinkers must remember that one of the traditional rules of the reasoning process is to define terms. Arguments about serious matters are almost never as simple as ad populum slogans would have you believe.

## Bandwagon

*Bandwagon*, a form of ad populum, is an appeal to peer pressure, group identity. An idea is assumed to be valid if many people accept it. "Six million people read the <u>Daily Scandal</u>: it must be an excellent paper."

Bandwagon is an appeal to do things because other people do them. "Get on the bandwagon" comes from the time when big wagons carrying a steam calliope[5] or a

---

[5] *Calliope*: ka-lî-a-pî–a steam-driven pipe (or "whistle") organ, very loud.

band of musicians announced the arrival of the circus in town or some other event. To get on the bandwagon meant to join the parade. Today the expression refers to joining anything that other people are doing. "Twenty million people can't be wrong!" But is that true? Apparently, millions of people still smoke, though research shows the relationship between cancer and smoking. Critical thinkers, obviously, should not do anything just because others do it. Reason is founded on the idea that you can be right no matter how many people oppose you.

*ex.*
*Joe*
*the*
*plumber*

## Plain Folks and Snob Appeal

The plain folks appeal and the snob appeal are variations of the bandwagon appeal. *Plain folks* is an appeal that implies you should follow the ordinary citizen, the man in the street, the simple folk. (Avoid the pretensions of snobs.) There are various ways to indicate plain folks, for example:

> You can pay a fortune for "filet mignon" at some fancy restaurant, but *ordinary people* enjoy the same old steak and potatoes at Downtown Diner.
>
> Your expensive bar of perfumed soap from Paris may make you smell pretty, but good old brown soap will get *folks* just as clean.

*Snob appeal* is the reverse of plain folks. For example, "Your little old Apple II may be workable if you're just using it to type letters. But sophisticated computer users choose the Dynamo Thunderbore VIII." Snob appeal tries to reach the reader's vanity: you should do something because you would then be like one of the beautiful or important people.

> For an automotive experience of real distinction, professional athletes choose the Sportsmobile . . . and so can you.
>
> For a *real* education, you should attend Ivy University.

## Ad Verecundiam

*Ad verecundiam* is the fallacy of inappropriate use of authority. Experts and authorities in one field are inappropriately cited in other fields, as if their expertise were all-encompassing. For example, "Shaquille O'Neal is a great athlete, so he might be a good person to ask about the economy." Inappropriate authorities aren't really authorities at all outside their areas of knowledge and experience. For instance, "Professor Novall knows a great deal about computer technology; she teaches at one of the great universities and has published many books and articles on the subject." However, her expertise on computers doesn't make the professor an authority on other matters, such as which stocks to buy on Wall Street (not even which high-tech stocks), which requires an entirely different expertise.

Another "ad verecundiam" problem concerns the way information is documented in research writing. Readers must be able to find any of the sources you use—to verify your information if they choose. Will your readers be able to find it? (Can *you* find it again?) If not, should you cite it at all? A good rule is to photocopy your sources.

## Red Herring

A *red herring* is an irrelevant point or some side issue leading away from the main point in an argument. According to the legend of the red herring, fleeing prisoners or slaves pursued by dogs would draw a fish across their trail, in the hope that the smell of fish would lead the dogs away from the main path. There is no truth to this legend, but it illustrates the red herring fallacy.

> It's true that tuition fees are rising everywhere, but imagine going to school in some beautiful place like the West Coast.

The issue concerns rising tuition, not the beauty of a school's location. The speaker has introduced a *red herring*, a different subject entirely. Here is another example:

> In order to understand the causes of the Civil War, we must look at the warlike nature of human beings. The history of Europe is full of wars.

Can you explain why this example is called a red herring?

## Weak Opponent

A *weak opponent*, sometimes an imaginary person (or other creature), an opponent made of straw, is someone or something invented for the purposes of an argument, an opponent you can attack without fear of retaliation. For example, many representatives and senators are hard-working, respected government servants, and any unkind or impolite remarks about them could backfire on you. Therefore speakers and writers may invent a weak opponent: "Those no good *politicians* spend their time arguing about how to spend our money. Everyone knows *politicians* have no ethos. All they're interested in is saving their own jobs."

Why is this called a weak opponent? There is no real person involved. "Politicians" are anyone who might fit under that term. We can insult ("throw stones") at this weak opponent or straw person without fearing we will be sued or counterattacked.

The weak opponent isn't merely any group that can be described with a negative label: you must be able to see that the label is unfair, inaccurate, or manufactured just for the sake of the argument. Also, it is possible to have straw people who are those we favor: our *heroic military veterans*, for example, or the *noble immigrants* "who came to this country without money or education or skills and not even speaking English, but despite all that have pulled themselves up by the bootstraps, and in the process have made this country what it is!" No specific individual is indicated. The statement is aimed at a handy, if invented, person we have created and can condemn or applaud without fear of backlash. A good example might be "the modern student": "The modern student needs to study more and drink less," for example.

Stereotypes such as weak opponents just get in the way of critical analysis. Because neither weak opponents nor stereotypes are real, you need to find the true subject of an argument. If there really are people labeled "welfare cheats," who are they, and where are they? Who are the "shiftless slackers" who refuse to work, according to some critics? Where is the "moral majority"? And what is the source of the information about them? Such labels merely obscure the fact that the argument is really about "people we do or don't like," meaning the argument is based on personal prejudice and bias. Critical thinkers should evaluate whether such an argument is worth indulging. You need to dig under the labels to find who or what is really meant.

## Tu Quoque

*Tu quoque* (too-kwó-kway) means "you did it too." It is used as an argument, or an excuse, when accused persons seek to justify their actions by charging that their accusers are "guilty" of the same crime. In effect, the accused person says, "You can't accuse me when you yourself are guilty of the same thing!" For example, "So what if I drink at parties on weekends, Dad. You did the same thing in college." The argument is often used by children: "Why can't I stay up late to watch TV—you do!" However, it is a weak argument. We should be able to make the accusation (providing we have the evidence), no matter how many others have done the same or similar things, including ourselves. For example, "cheating" on one's taxes is said to be nearly universal, yet taxpayers have learned to their sorrow that the tu quoque appeal carries no legal weight with the IRS. It carries little moral weight in any case.

## Oversimplification

*Oversimplification* is the tendency to overlook complexity in an argument. For example, "Students can't write well because they watch too much TV." Television might be one of the reasons that some students don't write well—but it's unlikely to be the only reason for all students. Most serious arguments are more complicated than people know, but people simplify because it makes problems easier to think about and easier to find a quick solution. (If parents turn off the TV, will students then write better?) Consider the abortion issue. Those on either side of the abortion question may reduce the argument to a woman's right to control her own body versus a moral prohibition against murder. Yet when the abortion question is examined critically, you may discover it is more complicated than either side admits. There are legal, moral, financial, philosophical, religious, psychological, racial, and perhaps many other implications of this question, including "the rights of the unborn child" argument. Do you accept the claim that unborn children have rights? Reducing all this to simple pro and con positions is an oversimplification, a failure to understand the complexity of the question.

## ACTIVITY 14

### IRRELEVANT EVIDENCE

Identify the fallacy in each of the following statements. Explain why each statement is called an error of irrelevant evidence: ad baculum, ad hominem, fallacy of opposition, genetic fallacy, guilt by association, ad misericordiam, ad populum, bandwagon, plain folks or snob appeal, ad verecundiam, red herring, weak opponent, tu quoque, or oversimplification. There may be more than one answer for some of these.

1. The Bible says "Thou shalt not kill." Not even the state has the right to take a human life, so therefore capital punishment should be abolished.
2. The exam asked: Is Poe's "The Raven" a good poem? One student wrote: "Poe, who wrote 'The Raven,' is known to have taken drugs like opium. Opium is an addictive narcotic and may cause many physical and psychological disturbances."
3. Senator Estaban was booed and called names like "communist" and "socialist" when she tried to present a bill for a national health program.
4. The union demanded a raise of 11 cents an hour, but management rebuffed them, saying laborers could not dictate the conditions of work.
5. A professor from a small private college complained that she couldn't get her dissertation published because publishers were only interested in work from great institutions.
6. Lloyd's parents berated him for spending time with "that gang of loud-mouthed slackers" they called his friends. "You're becoming as bad as they are," his father said.
7. A young man was permanently paralyzed in a car accident. Unable to move, communicate, or assist himself in any way, he faced a grim life of drugs and machines. His parents petitioned the court to let them turn off the machines that were keeping him alive. In view of his terrible condition and hopeless future, the court granted their appeal.
8. "Those who criticize America's war policy should go and live with the enemy," dissidents were told.
9. Thousands of women were urged to take thalidomide in the early '50s to help with their pregnancy. It was thought to be "completely safe for pregnant women." (Unfortunately, thousands of "thalidomide babies" were born with severe deformities.)
10. Harriet laughed at Miriam's argument until Miriam suddenly looked hostile and made a menacing gesture toward her.
11. Granny Hodgkins pouted and said, "Why shouldn't I go line dancing? You do."

12. Fala announced that she had several friends who were neo-Nazis (fascist groups that admire Hitler and the Nazis following WWII). Ashamed, her parents insisted that she stop associating with these friends for fear that Fala might come to admire the neo-Nazi movement.

13. In the Lacy Peterson case, a pregnant woman's body had been found in the bay where her husband was alleged to have been fishing. TV experts argued that many other terrible things had happened in California recently. Police found that the Peterson home had been broken into. They argued that the Petersons should have had a stronger door with a better lock.

14. Roscoe's friend bought a new 4-door Chevrolet sedan. "You should have bought something better," Roscoe smirked, "like a Corvette, or a Jaguar maybe."

15. Professor Edwina was studying the impact of injuries on athletes. Her plan was to interview authors who had written books on sports.

16. The Second Amendment of the Constitution says all citizens should keep guns for defense of the state; it's as simple as that.

17. Let's return America to greatness by embracing the tradition of true family values.

18. Political advertisements all over town state that if we don't vote for Sitwell, he might have to close his factory and many people would lose their jobs.

19. People can't spell anymore because they use spell-checkers on computers.

20. A student says, "It's true, Dean Potter, that we've been making a little noise on Saturday nights and some neighbors have complained. But have you considered the volunteer work we do for senior citizens each year?"  ▬

## ACTIVITY 15

In your notebook write and label an example of your own for each fallacy in this section: ad baculum, ad hominem, fallacy of opposition, genetic fallacy, guilt by association, ad misericordiam, ad populum, bandwagon, plain folks or snob appeal, ad verecundiam, red herring, weak opponent, tu quoque, and oversimplification.  ▬

## PROBLEMS OF AMBIGUITY

You may find problems of ambiguity in some writing, including amphiboly, begging the question, equivocation, loaded language, and false analogies.

### Amphibole

*Amphibole* (am -'phib-o-ly) comes from a Latin word for "ambiguous" and in English means "ambiguity" or "doubt." An amphibole can be caused by a statement that has more than one meaning. For example, "We had a dog for dinner." In some parts of the world, the sentence may mean serving roast spaniel as the main dinner course. In other parts of the world, the sentence probably means a spaniel was our guest at our evening meal. Or newspaper headlines could announce, "Girl's slip seen by team-mates," suggesting either that the girl fell (slipped) during a game, or she made a mistake (a slip) in some team activity, or some part of her undergarment was exposed.

Sometimes an amphibole may accidentally result from grammatical misplacement (see dangling or misplaced modifier in Handbook):

> The senators were certain the representatives would understand their duty. [Whose duty—the senators or the representatives?]
>
> Doctors sometimes think patients would understand them better if they were in their shoes. [If who were in whose shoes?]

Traditionally, amphiboles arise when sentences are inherently vague, capable of more than one interpretation: "Driving our convertible in the mountains, a bear suddenly appeared at an intersection." The sentence seems to say the bear was driving our car. Modern usage applies amphibole to any ambiguous meaning. For example, statistics, especially percentages, can have more than one interpretation: "Of those asked, 75% said they would vote for the president again." If you don't know how many were asked, percentages can be misleading. The 75% figure suggests three-fourths of the electorate, but in fact it can just as well mean three people out of the four who were asked.

## Begging the Question

*Begging the question* means not answering the question. It is a fallacy in which the conclusion assumes the premise the argument attempts to prove. In effect, the conclusion simply restates one of the premises. One traditional example of begging the question attempts to prove that God exists: "We know that God exists because of all the things that He made!" The answer begs the question. You can't cite anything God made until after you have established that God exists.

Begging the question is sometimes called "circular reasoning." Circular reasoning merely turns the question around. For example, a difficult question for science and religion is, "How can we tell when a fetus is a person?" Nonresponsive, circular answers might include these: A fetus is a person when it is a being, when it is no longer a fetus, when the doctor says it is a person, when it has the attributes of a person. These answers beg the question. You must ask further, when is it a being? When is it no longer a fetus? When does the doctor say it is a person? What are the attributes of a person and when does the fetus acquire them?

The term *begging the question* is sometimes used in court cases:

**Lawyer:** Have you ever been in Mr. Crane's apartment?

**Witness:** I don't know Mr. Crane.

**Lawyer:** Your answer begs the question. You were asked about the apartment, not the person.

## Equivocation

*Equivocation* (e-kwi-vo-ka'-tion) means quibbling over the meanings of words. It can amount to a form of dishonesty, a deliberate misuse of the definitions of words. For example, "I did not steal your pen; I merely borrowed it." Whether the pen was "borrowed" or "stolen" obscures the issue—namely that the pen was taken without permission of the owner. Whether people killed by hand grenades in an Italian airport were killed by "terrorists" or "freedom fighters" depends on point of view—but makes little difference to the material fact[6] that people were killed.

---

> Humboldt lost his job because his supervisor thought he was *obese*. "I'm not obese," Humboldt argued. "I'm a large man, a bit heavy, but not fat."

---

In general, "equivocation" suggests trivial distinctions. Yes, it's important to define your terms, but critical thinkers must recognize the difference between thoughtfully defining terms and merely equivocating, a tactic for delaying or distorting. You need to be clear about the terms of an argument, but at some point, you must stop quibbling over the language and get on with the argument. Whether you call it *euthanasia, death with dignity,* or *assisted suicide,* the question (let us say) is whether the government should pay for it. You need to define your terms (so people know what you are arguing about), but eventually the argument needs to proceed to consideration of the main point.

## Loaded Language

The classic example of *loaded language* is "Do you still beat your spouse?" Assuming you can answer only yes or no, there is no good answer to this question. If you answer yes, you confess you are still a spouse beater; if you answer no, you confess to having been a spouse beater. The question has been "loaded" so that either answer is prejudicial. "Loaded language" is biased language:

---

> Must we listen to more of Harvey's idiotic theories?
>
> Can anyone help us find our way out of this inane problem?

---

Loading the questions with negative, biased words like "idiotic" and "inane" ensures that no matter what answer is given, the impression will have been made that Harvey's theories, and perhaps Harvey himself, are idiotic, and that the problem is "inane." A critical thinker should refuse to offer any answer until the questions have been examined and rephrased without the prejudicial, loaded language.

---

[6]*Material fact*: relevant, important to the case.

Loaded language is slanted language. But language can also be loaded the other way: "The government has come up with another *excellent* strategy for *better* education programs," you are told. You can assume the writer is using a positive load for this statement. Another writer might use a sarcastic load: "The government has come up with another *extraordinary* program for the *useful* distribution of taxpayer money." The writers here may be ironic or sarcastic, depending on readers' interpretations. Writers who use sarcasm suggest that they are superior to the subject matter of the argument. Irony has a slightly better connotation. Sarcasm aims to hurt; irony merely notes the truth in a contradiction. Nevertheless, sarcasm and irony in factual and reasoned essays can easily backfire. Thoughtful writing is not a good place to use words that don't mean what they say.

Usually we expect the claim or thesis of an argument to be as clearly and objectively stated as possible: Should the United States endorse a ban against land mines? When a writer loads the issue or question with prejudicial language, you should challenge the writer's motives: "Let us consider the idiotic proposition that the United States should render its troops defenseless by banning their protective use of land mines." This writer doesn't want to *consider* the proposition: the writer has already decided the proposition is *idiotic*.

## False Analogy

Arguing by analogy assumes that one thing is similar to another, but such comparisons are often faulty. For example, an argument might suggest that smoking tobacco is like drinking poison. But it is often the case that no two events are very similar. Not everyone who smokes suffers ill effects, but everyone who drinks cyanide will almost certainly die. This is not a defense of tobacco but a reminder to critical thinkers that they undermine their own credibility when they use exaggerated comparisons to make a point.

An analogy is a comparison between things that most people think are comparable or that seem reasonable to compare. Ford trucks may be similar to Dodge trucks. But is it reasonable to say "The IRS is an American Gestapo"? That is an extremely harsh criticism, an imagined comparison between American tax collectors (Internal Revenue Service) and the German secret police during WWII, whose ruthless mission was to eliminate Hitler's enemies and to kill all the Jews in Europe. Americans may be unhappy with the IRS, but a comparison with the Gestapo seems excessive and unfair, and undermines the writer's credibility. Even if there may be a few superficial similarities in the comparison, there are many dissimilarities. (The IRS does not have the authority to exterminate taxpayers.) The two do not compare. False analogies usually collapse when examined critically.

Consider this analogy from conservative columnist Gregory Koukl. In his essay "Same-Sex Marriage—Challenges & Responses," he responds to this argument: "They said the same thing about interracial marriage."

> This challenge has great rhetorical force, but it is a silly objection. Consider two men, one rich and one poor, seeking to withdraw money from the bank. The rich man is denied because his account is empty. However, on closer inspection, a clerk discovers an error,

corrects it, and releases the cash. Next in line, the poor man is denied for the same reason: insufficient funds. "That's the same thing you said about the last guy," he snaps. "Yes," the clerk replies. "We made a mistake with his account, but not with yours. You're broke."

In the same way, it simply is not relevant that the same *objection* has been used to deny both interracial and homosexual marriage.

Is what Koukl means here clear? If you need to reread it a few times to see if it makes sense, it likely doesn't. Is it fair to compare gays and lesbians to a poor man who can't withdraw money because of insufficient funds? Do men and women who marry therefore have sufficient funds? Money and marriage are very different. If an analogy is confusing, it can't be persuasive.

Later in his essay Koukl uses another analogy:

Philosopher Francis Beckwith has wryly observed, "Just because you can eat an ashtray doesn't make it food." Linguistic tricks can't change what nature has already determined something to be. Neither ashtrays nor same-sex marriage provide the nourishment intended by food or families, respectively.

Relating ashtrays to same-sex marriage is loaded language. The connotation of an ashtray is smelly, dirty, unhealthy. Is Koukl implying that gays and lesbians are also smelly, dirty, unhealthy? He may, without directly saying so. But an ashtray is too simplistic an image: surely two people are more complex than an ashtray. It's true that ashtrays can't provide nourishment, but countless same-sex marriages do nourish couples, their children, and their families.

Even if you have a good case for a comparison, you can seldom prove a case by comparison. Still, for an analogy to be useful you need some basis for comparison. For example, the common wood saw cuts with its "teeth," so named because they somewhat resemble teeth and serve a similar function. Still, you can see differences between saw teeth and animal teeth. Think of the ways in which saw teeth and human teeth are different and then decide whether they make a convincing analogy.

## ACTIVITY 16

### AMBIGUOUS EVIDENCE

Identify the fallacy in each of the following statements. Explain why each is an error of ambiguous evidence: amphiboly, begging the question, equivocation, loaded language, or false analogy. There may be more than one answer for some of these.

1. "There must be a god," Terry said. "Otherwise, how can we explain all the wonders of earth and the universe?"

2. It is safe to conclude that convicts who have served out their sentences are unlikely to return to crime because it is the purpose of prison to rehabilitate criminals.

3. Three out of four doctors recommend Headache Buster to relieve pain.

4. The farmers had painted plow horses bright pink so that they might be seen as artistic.

5. American presidents have not hesitated to use terms like "Evil Empire" and "Axis of Evil" to demonize certain countries.

6. Thousands of students attend U.S. colleges and universities: many of them are deeply in debt.

7. "Those who criticize our war policy are not *patriots*," the newspaper said. *"They are subversive, filthy communists, traitors!"*

8. Giselle set out her arguments deliberately, one after another, like a bricklayer building a solid wall of reason.

9. Roaring fiercely, "Tigers are becoming an endangered species," the speaker said.

10. The president stood before his audience like a great emperor delivering a powerful warning to the tyrants of the world. ▇

## ACTIVITY 17

In your notebook write an example of your own for each fallacy in this section. Try to explain why each is an error of ambiguous evidence: amphiboly, begging the question, equivocation, loaded language, and false analogy. ▇

## PROBLEMS OF FAULTY REASONING

Some writing may contain problems of faulty reasoning, such as false dilemma (either/or thinking), non sequitur, rationalization, reductio ad absurdum, and slippery slope.

### False Dilemma (Either/or Thinking)

Ordinarily, a *dilemma* is a choice between two alternatives, both of which are (usually) unpleasant: "pay your taxes or go to jail." Dilemmas are often stated as "either/or" alternatives:

> *Either* America must support its allies *or* they will perish.
>
> *Either* we must close our doors to more immigrants *or* see America overrun with foreigners.
>
> *Either* you agree with feminism *or* you don't.

The either/or choice is what makes a dilemma false. You almost always have more than two alternatives. America's allies may find other ways to survive. The notion that America will be "overrun" with foreigners is not only a false dilemma but phrased with loaded language. You may agree with certain aspects of feminism and disagree with others.

Occasionally, however, you may encounter a real dilemma. The car payment is due, but you are out of money. The dilemma is pay up or lose the car. That's a real-life dilemma, but you may be able to resolve it—the car dealer probably doesn't want the car back and may be willing to work out some other alternative. Or you may be able to borrow money to cover the shortage.

A real dilemma may be difficult—too difficult to resolve. But a "false" dilemma is no dilemma at all if your analysis reveals more than just two options. And most reasonable people assume there may be other alternatives, though they might agree that you have a predicament. As a critical thinker, you should assume that few situations can be reduced to only two alternatives.

Either/or statements are forms of oversimplification, and they can be implied without using "either/or":

---

If you don't quit smoking, you'll die of lung cancer.

If you don't study, you won't pass.

Exact change only. [The driver doesn't make change.]

---

Some smokers don't die of lung cancer. Some students pass courses without studying—this dubious achievement depends on what the course is and who the teacher is. The "exact change" dilemma is a predicament for which there does not seem to be an alternative—unless one of the other passengers volunteers to "make change." (For more on either/or thinking see Chapter 3.)

## Non Sequitur

*Non sequitur* (non se'-kwi-ter) means "it does not follow." A "non sequitur" seems unconnected: it is some leap in logic that doesn't make sense. For example, "This photograph appears to show a flying saucer; therefore aliens must have visited earth." The non sequitur often sounds like a faulty conclusion, an error in reasoning: "The president is frequently away from the White House: the vice president must run the country at those times." It doesn't follow that the vice president is in charge just because the president is away. Modern communications keep the president in charge, no matter where he or she is. Here are a few other examples:

---

If e-mail is the future, we might as well stop buying envelopes for mail.
[A non sequitur because there is still much to send via mail, and many people still prefer handwritten or typed messages.]

Because the Internet has so much information, there isn't any need for libraries.
[A non sequitur because many readers prefer actual books, magazines, newspapers, and so on.]

---

## Rationalization

A *rationalization* is an excuse or a self-serving explanation. Some people can "rationalize" their way out of almost any difficulty by inventing some excuse that gets them off the hook:

It's true I don't do well in math, but many creative people have this problem. [Blame a fault on a virtue.]

Yes, I knocked over the crystal vase, but you should have put it away in the cupboard. [Blame the problem on someone else: it's your fault, not mine.]

The Senate passed a new tax bill, but it was only because they knew the president would veto it. [An excuse for a tax bill: blame it on the president.]

## Reductio Ad Absurdum

*Reductio ad absurdum* means to reduce to an absurdity. For example, movie critics said that the film was too long and would be stronger if some scenes were removed. But the producer, director, and writer replied, "What nonsense! If removing scenes made the film stronger, perhaps we should remove a few more to make it even stronger. And perhaps it would be strongest if we removed all of them!" Or, to supply a more modern example, "If one pill is good for me, two should be better, and best of all may be a whole handful!"

The reductio argument uses the opponent's reasoning against itself. By extending the argument, you show some ridiculous conclusion it leads to. Revealing absurdity is a good tactic, if true. However, the tactic can be used merely as a way to ridicule the opponent, and in that case should be avoided by critical thinkers. Example of ridicule:

A friendly critic wrote: "Last night's concert was excellent, even though one of the drummers dropped a cymbal during the second movement." A later critic responded: "Perhaps we should ask other members of the orchestra to drop their instruments at random moments to produce an even better result!"

The reductio fallacy is based on the assumption that more is better or that less is better. For example, "If one piece of pie is a good after-dinner dessert, two is probably better and maybe three or four is the best of all!" (If more is good, more and more may even be better.) The reductio can work in reverse too: "If we can save money by firing one of the secretaries, we should save twice as much if we fire two of them. And maybe we can save even more money by firing all of them." (If less is good, less and less may be even better.)

# Slippery Slope

The *slippery slope* is an assumption that one thing leads to another, especially if the "next step" is in the direction of something forbidden. It is feared, for example, that trying one cigarette may cause youngsters to become addicted to tobacco, or that a single glass of wine will turn you into a wino.

The key to slippery slope isn't just that one thing might lead to another but that one thing *must* lead to another. Much depends on individual personalities. Thoughtful people, especially young people, should evaluate suggestions from peers, particularly concerning dangerous proposals (bungee jumping from bridges perhaps, leading to higher and higher jumps). Russian roulette is a suicidal "game" with a loaded pistol. No matter how much pressure peers exert, thoughtful people know it is a deadly slope to start down. Friends don't let friends drive drunk, and friends don't let friends play with a loaded pistol.

## ACTIVITY 18

### FAULTY REASONING

Identify the fallacy in each of the following statements. Explain why each statement is an error of faulty reasoning: false dilemma, non sequitur, rationalization, reductio ad absurdum, or slippery slope.

1. Thelma refused to experiment with modern expressionism for fear that her art would degenerate to meaningless scribbling.

2. Joe found his car windows smashed and all its tires flat. "It must have been aliens," he said.

3. Many of Dr. Smith's patients have died of cancer, so she must not be a very good doctor.

4. Without a college education many high school seniors must look forward to jobs that are boring, repetitive, and low-paying.

5. You must avoid bungee jumping or face the possibility of a fatal accident.

6. If jogging a mile a day is good for me, it must be even better for me to jog 2 or 3 miles a day.

7. I admit I've gone through the budget too fast this month, but don't forget there have been a lot of birthdays, anniversaries, holidays, and other unexpected events this year.

8. I know I stepped on your earphones, but it was really your fault for leaving them on the floor.

9. Aunt Emma refused to let anyone bring a cooler of beer to the family picnic because, she said, they would all just get drunk and rowdy and crude.

10. Myrna wept while trying to explain her failing grade in chemistry. "It wasn't my fault," she cried. "Professor Reisling just hates me."

## ACTIVITY 19

In your notebook write one good example of your own for each fallacy in this section: false dilemma (either/or thinking), non sequitur, rationalization, reductio ad absurdum, and slippery slope. ▮

## ACTIVITY 20

### REVIEW

Identify the fallacy (there may be more than one) in each of the following statements. Explain your answer.

> **Example:** "Students love their studies, especially research writing." [The statement is an overgeneralization. "Students" implies *all* or *most* students, but it is unlikely that anyone could know what so many students do or don't feel about their studies.]

1. I went to my professor's office to ask him a question about the deadline for research papers, but he wasn't in. Fortunately there was a janitor nearby, so I asked him. *(282) Ad Vere-cundiam*
2. Uncle Fester was a drug addict because he couldn't stop using cocaine. *Post hoc (275)*
3. For the sake of the starving, sickly, dying children of Africa we must send aid immediately. *Ad misericordian (280)*
4. Most college students either love the opera or they hate it. *False dilemma (291)*
5. Since all my friends at the party were drinking, I decided I'd drink too. *Bandwagon 281*
6. Eighty percent of those polled said they would vote for Senator Williams, so it was a good bet that she would probably become our next president. *False Analogy 289*
7. People who study hard usually get good grades, but Bonnie gets poor grades, so she must not study very hard. *Oversimplification 284*
8. The coach asked, "Are you still using steroids?" *Loaded language 288*
9. Since I've never seen anybody faster, Zipper must be the fastest kid in the world. *Ad Verecundian*
10. Sandy was called in as our relief pitcher, but we lost the game anyway. I always knew Sandy was no good. *Oversimplification 284*
11. The coach said, "I don't want men—I want animals, beasts, monsters, meat-eating killers!" *False Analogy 289*
12. The American people are too wise to be fooled by some slick politician: vote for the proven leader. *Weak opponent*
13. I'm just a poor old country boy trying to make an honest living like you, folks; I know what it means to grow up poor and have to struggle to make ends meet. Send me to Washington and I'll take care of the common man. *Plain folks and Snob Appeal 282*

*Tu Quoque*
⌐ 284

14. How can you say I'm a bad driver when you've had five accidents yourself? ⌐

15. I could have done better in the relay race, but it was very hot that day, and the heat cooked the energy out of me. *rationalization* , 28)

16. As high school and college students, many of my friends loved to go to Florida during spring break. Now many of them have developed cancer. They would have done better to stay home and study.

17. The supermodel said she drinks 12 ounces of water a day, so perhaps if I drink 16 ounces a day I'll be a bit more attractive. Maybe if I drink 24 ounces I'll be twice as attractive. If I drink eight glasses a day, as doctors recommend, I should be the most attractive of all!

18. Because this little car, the Chooga, was made in a small Asian country, it can't possibly be any good.

19. Just because we can't prove Elvis is dead doesn't mean he is.

20. I don't know why so many people mistrusted President Clinton: he was tall and good-looking, he came from a Southern state, he was an excellent speaker, he made good grades in college . . . .

21. A "draft dodger" is a criminal. By definition it's against the law to dodge the draft. But a "draft evader" is someone who uses the legal alternatives provided within the law to do something other than go to war.

22. First it's just jumping into leaf piles; then the next thing you know it's jumping out of dorm windows into snow drifts! And where does that lead? To bungee jumping from higher and higher places, until you wear out the thrill . . . and then decide what you really want to do is become a paratrooper jumping out of planes! Don't say you weren't warned!

23. "Buy Diamond Love, the most sophisticated, elegant perfume a beautiful woman can wear. Sold only to the most truly discerning shoppers."

24. The president announced his plan for another tax cut for the voters. As the next election approaches it is time once again for voters to consider whether they really want four more years of the current administration. Perhaps it is time to consider a law limiting a president's reign to a single six-year administration.

25. "Bums, slackers," Mother shouted. "Do any of those louts have a job? Do they help around the house? Do they respect their mothers? No! Bums! Hoodlums! Lying around all day waiting for some way to get in trouble. And *you!* Hanging around with them all the time!" ▪

## ACTIVITY 21

Browse through current magazines and newspapers for any fallacies you can find in advertisements. Copy at least two ads and cite their sources. Bring them to class to discuss. ▪

# Style and Opposites

*Without contraries is no progression.*
(William Blake, <u>The Marriage of Heaven and Hell</u>)

## $\underline{\text{S}}$ENTENCE TOOLS

### Antithesis

What do the following sentences from President John F. Kennedy's Inaugural Address have in common?

> If a free society cannot help the many who are poor, it cannot save the few who are rich.

> Let us never negotiate out of fear, but let us never fear to negotiate.

> Let both sides explore what problems unite us instead of belaboring those problems which divide us.

As a sentence tool, *antithesis combines opposite thoughts, usually arranged in parallel structure.*
   One reason why the following sentence is famous is because of its balanced opposition:

| Ask not | what your country | can do for you; |
| ask | what you | can do for your country. |

This sentence reflects Kennedy's voice. If a president can structure a clear and insightful sentence like that, if he has that kind of control with language, his audience might assume he can govern as well.
   Kennedy's use of antithesis in his inaugural speech is masterful because one of his purposes was to unite the world by forming connections with the Soviet Union. At that time in 1961 the Cold War had produced the real threat of nuclear destruction. Kennedy's use of antithesis suggests that opposites can work together. His style reinforced his message.
   Aristotle valued antithesis. He said:

> This kind of style is pleasing, because things are best known by opposition, and all the better known when the opposites are put side by side. . . . The more concise and antithetical

the saying, the better it pleases, for the reason that, by the contrast, one learns the more, and, by the conciseness, learns with the greater speed.
(Lane Cooper, The Rhetoric of Aristotle)

Politicians and civic leaders like to use antithesis because, as Aristotle says, it appeals to the mind:

Those who have been left out, we will try to bring in.
(Richard Nixon, First Inaugural Address, 1969)

There is nothing wrong with America that cannot be cured with what is right with America.
(Bill Clinton, First Inaugural Address, 1993)

Now is the time to rise from the dark and desolate valley of segregation to the sunlit path of racial justice. Now is the time to lift our nation from the quicksand of racial injustice to the solid rock of brotherhood.
(Martin Luther King Jr., "I Have a Dream")

Setting foot on the moon, Neil Armstrong used antithesis in another statement millions of people know by heart: "That's one small step for a man, one giant leap for mankind." Notice the two major contrasts in this sentence:

| | |
|---|---|
| That's one small step | for a man, |
| one giant leap | for mankind. |

Armstrong's simple sentence with simple diction (ten monosyllabic words, two two-syllable words) is memorable because of its contrasts and the milestone meaning behind them.

Many writers use antithesis. It sparks thought. Shakespeare often used antithesis such as "To be or not to be." Here are a few more examples from other writers:

When we think we are using language, our language is using us.
(Deborah Tannen, You Just Don't Understand)

If thought corrupts language, language can also corrupt thought.
(George Orwell, "Politics and the English Language")

I don't paint to live; I live to paint.
(Willem de Kooning)

Antithesis may require more effort than many other tools of style, but the effect on readers is worth it. Look for antithesis especially when politicians give speeches.

**REVISION**

Write three sentences using antithesis in your notebook. To do this, you might make a list of opposites and then join some together. For example, "Love is constructive; hate is destructive." Or "It is nice to be important, but it is more important to be nice." Then look at your recent writing, and see if you can use an example of antithesis to help make a point. ▪

Newspaper columnist Sydney J. Harris composed a small book of antitheses called <u>Winners and Losers</u>. As you read these selections, consider whether you agree with them. Also, notice how Harris uses a semicolon to separate each pair of opposing thoughts.

**A winner** listens; **a loser** just waits until it's his turn to talk.

**A winner** paces himself; **a loser** has only two speeds: hysterical and lethargic.

**A winner** has a healthy appreciation of his abilities, and a keen awareness of his limitations; **a loser** is oblivious both of his true abilities and his true limitations.

**A winner** takes a big problem and separates it into smaller parts so that it can be more easily manipulated; **a loser** takes a lot of little problems and rolls them together until they are unsolvable.

**A winner** seeks for the goodness in a bad man, and works with that part of him; **a loser** looks only for the badness in a good man, and therefore finds it hard to work with anybody.

**A winner** is sympathetic to weakness in others, because he understands and accepts his own weakness; **a loser** is contemptuous toward weakness in others, because he despises and rejects his own weakness.

Do you think Harris's statements express truth? Which ones? Or do you think some statements are false or stereotypical? Select three of Harris's statements and support and/or challenge them by writing about them in your notebook, giving examples from your own experience to show what you mean. ▪

## Antithesis and Balanced Sentences

How are the following sentences balanced?

**A winner** focuses; **a loser** sprays. (Sydney J. Harris)

The moon symbolizes yin; the sun symbolizes yang.

The sciences are supposed to be objective, intellectual, analytical, reproducible, and useful; the arts are thought to be subjective, sensual, empathic, unique, and frivolous.
(Robert S. Root-Berstein, "For the Sake of Science, the Arts Deserve Support")

If you count the number of words in each complete thought of these sentences, you see they have the same number. Each thought in Harris's sentence contains three words; each thought in the next sentence contains four words; each thought in Root-Berstein's sentence contains twelve. This gives each sentence *balance*, as if both thoughts weigh the same. The semicolon serves as a scale. *Thus, a balanced sentence contains two complete thoughts, each with the same number of words.* The complete thoughts can be opposing as in the above examples, but they don't need to be. You can have a balanced sentence without antithesis:

---

She smiled; I blushed.

I like losing balance; it helps me learn.

Seymour took off his glasses; the book became a blur.

---

Because they contain a careful measurement of thoughts, balanced sentences can suggest to readers that you control your thoughts well.

## ACTIVITY 3

### REVISION

Write two balanced sentences using antithesis in your notebook. Write another balanced sentence with no antithesis. Then look at your recent writing and see if you can use a balanced sentence to help you make a point. ▬

## Loose and Periodic Sentences

You can apply your knowledge of sentence tools to create sentences with more detail. How are the following two sentences similar and different in structure?

A. We caught two bass, hauling them in briskly as though they were mackerel, pulling them over the side of the boat in a businesslike manner without any landing net, and stunning them with a blow on the back of the head.
(E. B. White, "Once More to the Lake")

B. Showing where you found your sources, following a standard method of documentation such as MLA, and providing a list of Works Cited at the end of your paper, you will make readers more likely to accept and trust what you say.

What do you notice? Each sentence contains three *-ing* phrases that refer to the main thought. But where is the main thought in each sentence? This is the major difference. The main thought comes first in White's sentence: "We caught two bass." However, in the other sentence the main thought comes last: "You will make readers more likely to accept and trust what you say."

E. B. White's example is called a loose sentence. *A loose sentence is structured with the main thought first followed by description or explanation.* The loose sentence reflects how the mind often works: you have a thought like an outline and then fill it in with specific thoughts from your memory. Here are two loose sentences with three *-ing* phrases written by students:

> He skated with the puck, looking for an open man, watching for defenders, waiting to put a shot on net. (Michael Krebs)

> She turned the wheel of the car cautiously, looking for oncoming traffic, hoping no one would fly around the corner, deciding to wait for the light to change just in case. (Erica Bachman)

## ACTIVITY 4

### REVISION

In your notebook write three loose sentences using *-ing* phrases. Then look at your recent writing and see if you can combine some sentences into a loose sentence. Try to use this tool the next time you write a paper or an e-mail. ▪

Periodic sentences, such as the one about using sources, are opposite in form from loose sentences. *A periodic sentence is structured so description or explanation comes first and the main thought comes last—toward the period.* This is a useful tool for building up to an idea. The reader has to wait for the main thought in order to understand the entire sentence. Here is a periodic sentence by Alice Walker from her essay "Beauty: When the Other Dancer Is the Self":

> Whirling happily in my starchy frock, showing off my biscuit-polished patent-leather shoes and lavender socks, tossing my head in a way that makes my ribbons bounce, I stand, hands on hips, before my father.

In this sentence Walker uses three-*ing* phrases containing vivid details to show a moment of happiness when she was a young girl. Periodic sentences create suspense. They take you for a ride, and you don't know where you're going. Loose sentences tell you where you're going first and then take you for a ride.

You can often change loose sentences into periodic sentences by reversing their structure:

> Looking for an open man, watching for defenders, waiting to put a shot on net, he skated with the puck.

Looking for oncoming traffic, hoping no one would fly around the corner, deciding to wait for the light to change just in case, she turned the wheel of the car cautiously.

Loose and periodic sentences are useful tools of style; they can help you communicate complex thoughts in interesting patterns that satisfy the mind. However, loose and periodic sentences don't always require a series of *-ing* phrases.

### Loose

In time I learned the strength of words, how they could raise you up high, higher than you deserved, how they could convince others to love you, to do your bidding, how they could deflect wrath. (Richard Selzer, <u>Down from Troy</u>)

### Periodic

Without the ability to think critically, to differentiate verifiable fact from goofball rantings, to understand what is valuable and what is worthless, information in itself means nothing. (George Cantor, "Internet No Substitute for Real Knowledge")

Although these examples do not contain *-ing* phrases, they do contain three parallel groupings of words: Selzer repeats *how they* and Cantor repeats *to* phrases–*to think, to differentiate*, and *to understand*.

Thus, loose and periodic sentences can take various forms. When you use these sentence patterns well, your voice will sound more persuasive.

## ACTIVITY 5

### REVISION

In your notebook write three periodic sentences, two with *-ing* phrases, one with another form. Also, try writing a loose sentence without *-ing* phrases. Then look at your recent writing and see if you can combine some sentences into a periodic sentence. ■

## FINE-TUNING SENTENCES

### False Starts

What do the following sentences have in common?

1. Personally, I feel that both men and women are equally guilty of gossip.
2. There are some arguments that Bruce makes that are not strong.
3. It is through specific examples that we clarify our ideas.

Each of these sentences begins with needless words. You can make them more concise.

1. Men and women are equally guilty of gossip.
   Or: Both men and women gossip.
2. Bruce makes some weak arguments.
3. Through specific examples we clarify our ideas.
   Or: We clarify our ideas through specific examples.

Technically, this problem of beginning sentences with empty words is called *expletive*, from *explere*, to fill. Expletives fill sentences with needless words. A clearer name is *false start*, coined by Stephen K. Tollefson in his booklet <u>Grammar Grams</u>. With ironic humor, Tollefson writes,

> It is true that you should avoid false starts whenever possible. I think that your writing will improve if you do.
> **Revised**: Your writing will improve if you avoid false starts.

The revision contains 9 words as opposed to 21. When you revise, look carefully for any false starts: sentences beginning with *There are, There is, It is, I think, Personally*, or *I feel*. You may not always want to change them: they may sound right. On occasion, to emphasize your conviction, you may want to write "I feel" or "I believe." But usually you should change false starts to omit needless words.

## ACTIVITY 6

Revise the following sentences by omitting false starts and other needless words. Compare your revisions with those of other students in class.

1. Personally I think that it is the combination of fans and team owners that have damaged the game of baseball.
2. There are three options that I am examining the most thoroughly.
3. It is clear that many students' essays are too general.
4. There are too many students who care more about competition than cooperation.
5. The point that I want to express is that too many men abandon their wives and children. ■

## ACTIVITY 7

### REVISION

Look at your recent writing and see if you find any false starts. If so, try to revise them and omit needless words. Then, look through all the writing you've done so far during this course: find false starts and see if revising those sentences makes a difference in your voice. ■

## Active and Passive Verbs

What differences do you notice between these sentences?[1]

1. Vitality can be added to your style through your verbs—but only if they are wisely chosen.
2. You can add vitality to your style through your verbs—but only if you choose them wisely.

The two sentences have the same number of words in them. In fact, the sentences are nearly identical. Both speak of adding vitality to your style by choosing verbs wisely. They differ only slightly in their structure. Most readers and writers prefer the second sentence with *active* verbs.

   In the second sentence *you* add the vitality by choosing the verbs wisely. The first sentence does not say who does the adding or the choosing. In passive sentences, either there is no subject at all or the subject comes at the end of the sentence.

| Active | Passive |
| --- | --- |
| Seymour wrote the essay. | The essay was written by Seymour. |
| The president addressed the nation. | The nation was addressed by the president. |
| We considered the book interesting. | The book was considered interesting by us. |

Not only are active sentences more direct, but they are frequently more concise.

   However, so-called rules of language often turn out to be stylistic choices. For example, some readers insist that writers must always prefer active verbs over passive.

|  | **Subject** | **Verb** | **Object** |
| --- | --- | --- | --- |
| **Active:** | Franny | drove | the bus. |

The verb is called *active* because the subject (Franny) does the acting. The subject is the "doer" of the action. However, writers sometimes turn their sentences around, like this:

|  |  |  |  |
| --- | --- | --- | --- |
| **Passive:** | The bus | was driven | by Franny. |

This kind of sentence seems backwards to many readers who expect the *subject* to come first in a sentence.

   Although active verbs are usually clear, concise, and direct, occasionally you might wish to use a passive sentence to change the rhythm and emphasis of your language. Then too, sometimes you may not know the actor in a situation:

---

[1]These pairs of examples on verbs are adapted from Robert Miles, Marc Bertonasco, and William Karns, <u>Prose Style: A Contemporary Guide</u> (Prentice Hall, 1991) 45–46.

> My car has been broken into three times this year.
>
> The vandals were never identified.

Sometimes you may want to de-emphasize the actor—who did what may not be important:

> The survey was conducted over a two-year period.
>
> The sheep Dolly was cloned in a Scottish laboratory.

Sometimes you may want to hide the actor in a sentence. Instead of naming someone responsible for an error, you may choose to use the passive voice:

> Your check amount was incorrectly doubled.
>
> Mistakes have been made.

Passive verbs aren't always or automatically wrong. Nevertheless, too many passive sentences can make your writing sound abstract and falsely authoritative. Worse than that, you may sound as if you are hiding behind your passive verbs, avoiding responsibility for your own actions, opinions, and conclusions.

> **Weak Passive:** The idea of cloning was not developed in the 1990s. Cloning of plants was known in ancient times. Therefore this experiment will be a continuation of research with a long history. The intention of this study is to show that modern plant clones can be produced with ancient procedures.
>
> **Preferred Active:** Ancient farmers used cloning to develop new fruit trees. Continuing this research, my colleagues and I will show that we can produce modern plant clones with ancient cloning procedures.

Passive verbs tend to weaken sentences and give your voice a distant, impersonal sound. In the past, scientists often used the passive voice to de-emphasize the doer of experiments, to make their writing seem more objective (a practice many editors no longer approve). Today, however, you should use an active voice in your own writing when you can, unless you have a specific need for the passive.

When you revise your writing, fine-tune your sentences by examining your choice of verbs. Writing means anticipating what effects your words might have on your audience. Weak verbs rob your writing of energy, so choose your words carefully. The weakest verbs do not express action at all.

> **Weak Verbs:** *am, is, are, was, were, be, being, been, have, has, had, could, should, would*

When you tie a weak verb to a strong one, you lose some of the strength of your sentence:

**Weak Passive:**    The church glass *had been broken* by the kids.
**Strong Active:**    The kids *shattered* the church glass.
**Weak Passive:**    The party *was organized* to celebrate Dr. Brown's book.
**Strong Active:**    We *organized* a party to celebrate Dr. Brown's book.

You must ask yourself, which of these sentences makes a stronger statement?
How would you describe the differences between the following sentences?

1. Verbs are capable of giving life to your sentences but are also capable of having a deadening effect on them.
2. Verbs can enliven your sentences but can just as easily deaden them.

If you count the number of words in each sentence, you find 20 in the first and 12 in the second. Like good gas mileage in a car, the second sentence works efficiently. If you underline the verbs in both sentences, you find *are capable, are . . . capable*, and *having* in the first sentence and *can enliven* and *can . . . deaden* in the second. The second sentence wins for clarity and conciseness. Also the second sentence contains a nice stylistic touch: *enliven* and *deaden* provide a clear contrast and contain a parallel-*en* ending.
Try your analysis with one more pair. Which is more effective and why?

1. There are some verbs that are able to give a sentence the strength and resilience of a bullwhip; there are other verbs that are likely to bring about the sort of sentence that has no more life than is possessed by a piece of string.
2. The right verbs can give a sentence the snap and sting of a bullwhip; the wrong verbs can render it as lifeless as a piece of string.

Using the same methods of analysis, you can see that the first sentence contains 45 words, the second 27. The first sentence contains six weak verbs: *are, are, are, are, has,* and *is;* the second contains two active verbs: *can give* and *can render.* The conciseness of the second sentence gives it clarity. The first sentence's wordiness drags the meaning. The second sentence works well also because it contains a clear contrast between *the right verbs* and *the wrong verbs.* In addition, the false starts *there are* have been omitted from the second sentence, thus enabling a tighter revision. The alliterative string of *s*'s (*sentence, snap, sting*) of the bullwhip help you hear the sound of the whip. The two images of the bullwhip and piece of string stand out in the second sentence because of the conciseness. Therefore the second sentence more clearly expresses antithesis.

**ACTIVITY 8**

### REVISION

Look at your recent writing. Examine the verbs in your sentences. Underline all the passive verbs you find. Then try to revise sentences by replacing weak passive verbs with strong active ones. See if active verbs help you to omit needless words. You might not figure out how to revise some sentences. Don't worry—some sentences may sound better with passive verbs. But you will be able to revise many sentences. Experiment and see. Then, look through all the writing you've done so far during this course to see how often you use passive verbs; see if revising those sentences makes a difference in your voice.

# Visual Arguments

*Seeing is of course very much a matter of verbalization. Unless I call my attention to what passes be-fore my eyes, I simply won't see it.* (Annie Dillard, "Seeing")

Do you agree? Do words help you see? To notice something clearly, Annie Dillard claims, you use language to call attention to it: in your mind you say the word *moon* when you see it in the sky. Indeed, much of your thinking is sparked by what you see.

Critical thinkers notice what they see—they analyze and evaluate visual images as well as verbal texts. They explore how an image works: what it says, how it says it, and why it succeeds or not. They notice how an image appeals to logos, pathos, and ethos. In this chapter you are invited to think and write critically about photographs, adver-tisements, cartoons, and films.

Visual images are framed moments in time. They take various forms and have various purposes. Like any written text, visual images try to communicate and persuade. They try to be clear and credible. With practice you can learn how to analyze and evaluate them. You can learn how to see more within images and how to help others see what you see.

## PHOTOGRAPHS

Reading a visual image is like reading a paragraph or a small essay: you can read it for its meaning and for the style through which its meaning is expressed. Two common types of photography are news photographs and documentary photographs. There is also a recent genre of Web-posted photographs called Fotolog.

### News Photographs

A news photograph is meant to be a factual image, not imagined nor embellished. It is meant to be objective. Consider this photograph taken September 1, 2005. (Figure 5.1; see color insert.)

The caption under the photo gives you its context, though you could likely infer this yourself. The image was taken by Smiley N. Pool, a member of the staff of <u>The Dallas Morning News</u>, which received the Pulitzer Prize in Breaking News Photography in 2006. Pulitzer Prizes are awarded for distinguished examples of excellence in journalism, letters, and music and serve as an incentive for others to excel. This is a major award. But what makes the photo work so well? What makes it persuasive?

To study a photograph or any visual image, you can make a list of what you notice. A list for this image might include the following notes:

–In the center of the image are four teen boys. Two are standing, looking up perhaps at a helicopter they hope will bring help.

–The biggest boy is holding his right arm up across his forehead. It could be a wave or trying to block sun glare from his eyes. He is holding a stick of some kind in his other hand.

–In the upper left corner a girl waves an American flag.

–There is another American flag loosely rolled up on the ground near the boy holding the stick.

–All the young people on the roof are African-American.

–Two of the boys are lying on the ground; the youngest one is looking up at the helicopter; the other appears to sleep or perhaps is too tired or depressed to look up.

–The word HELP is written in huge white letters on the upper right side of the image.

–The words "The Water is Rising" with the word "Pleas" under it appear in the lower part of the image; they are also written in white.

–The word "pleas" has a double meaning: it can mean "pleas" for help; it might be a misspelling of "please."

–There are a few blankets, bags, and bottles.

–The roof looks black with caking tar; it must be hot and dirty.

–In the lower right corner there is a black iron railing below which there appears to be moving water.

After taking such notes, you can explore three questions to help you analyze the image.

**Question 1**: What is the central purpose of the photo? The purpose is to capture the abandonment these young people experienced in New Orleans after Hurricane Katrina.

**Question 2**: By what means does the photographer achieve his purpose? Here you can use many of the details in your notes to describe the image and to explain a few of the stylistic choices the photographer made. You can also explain how the photo has persuasive appeal. It appeals to **logos**: you think about how long these residents have been held captive by the storm. The storm hit New Orleans on August 29; this photo was taken September 1, three days later. But mostly you think about how wretchedly the state and federal government responded to the crisis. You think how ironic it is for the girl to be waving an American flag. Where did they get those flags, anyway? It appeals to **pathos**: you imagine how these residents must have felt, frustrated, angry, desperately hoping to be rescued from the building, wondering what is taking so long, pleading for help. It appeals to **ethos**: You think that these residents still appear to have hope; despite the heat, and who knows if they've eaten much, they haven't given up. Perhaps they trust that the police, the government, somebody will rescue them. Also, the image is clear and credible. The photographer, Smiley N. Pool, used his expertise to capture this moment clearly and persuasively, especially the irony of the girl waving the American flag.

**Question 3**: Why does the photo succeed or not? It succeeds because it reminds people that Hurricane Katrina was not only a natural disaster but also a disaster of state and federal governments in coming to the aid of hundreds of thousands of residents. It succeeds because it reminds us that when the next natural disaster strikes, we need to be better prepared to help those in need. The image succeeds because it matters.

## Feature Photography

A category of news photography is feature photography, which is not breaking news but rather intimate photo essays—a series of photos that chronicle a personal journey or event. Feature photography often stirs powerful emotions. The 2007 Pulitzer Award for Feature Photography went to Renée C. Byer of The Sacramento Bee; she shows a mother and her young son as he loses his battle with cancer. The 2006 award went to Todd Heisler of the Rocky Mountain News; he shows images of what happened when Colorado Marines returned in caskets from Iraq.

### ACTIVITY 1

Look at two feature photos from the 2007 and 2006 Pulitzer awards. Choose one and follow the "Guidelines for Exploring Images" to write about it. (Figure 5.2, see page 311; Figure 5.3, see color insert.) ▮

### ACTIVITY 2

Go to the Web site for the Pulitzer Prizes and explore photographs that won awards: <http://www.pulitzer.org/>. The site contains winning photos from 1995 to the present that you can click on and view. Choose one photo from any year, print a copy—black and white, or color—and follow the "Guidelines for Exploring Images" to write about it. ▮

*FIGURE 5.2*  Racing barefooted after kicking off her flip-flops, Cyndie pushes her son Derek Madsen, 10, up and down hallways in the UC Davis Medical Center in Sacramento on June 21, 2005, successfully distracting him during the dreaded wait before his bone marrow extraction. Doctors want to determine whether he is eligible for a blood stem cell transplant, his best hope for beating neuroblastoma, a rare childhood cancer, which was diagnosed in November 2004.

Source: ©Renee C. Byer/Sacramento Bee/ZUMA Press.
<http://www.pulitzer.org/year/2007/feature-photography/works/byer01_jpg.html>

## GUIDELINES FOR EXPLORING IMAGES

To analyze a visual image, first make a list of anything you notice about it that catches your eye. What do you notice first? What do you see the more you look at it? How do you feel when you see the image? What questions does the image raise for you? After making a list, explore these main questions:

1. What is the central purpose of the image?                          **(Introduction)**

   *Tell who the artist is and what the title is, if there is one. Also, identify the source of the image: where did you find it—what magazine, newspaper, Web site? When was the image published?*

   *State your thesis about the image. Your thesis can be your answer to the question, "What is the central purpose of the image?"*

*Continued . . .*

**2.** By what means does the artist achieve his or her purpose?   **(Body paragraphs)**

*Describe the image so your readers can see it the way you do.*

*Use present tense when you write about the image.*

*Explain a few of the stylistic choices the artist made.*
   *(See Elements of Images below.)*

*Explain how the image appeals to logos, pathos, and ethos.*

**3.** Why does the image succeed or not?   **(Conclusion)**

*What conclusions do you draw? What is most memorable about the image? Why
   does it matter?*

**Elements of Images**

**subject:** What is the main person or object in the image?

**people:** Who is in the image? What are they doing? What are their facial
expressions—are they looking toward you or away? What is their body
language—standing, sitting, moving, still? What is their clothing—
plain, fancy, dirty, torn? What is their gender, race, ethnicity?

**objects:** What do you see in the image other than people? What are their
shapes, textures?

**actions:** What is happening? If there are no people, what is going on?

**context:** What is the frame of reference for the image? For example, in Dorothea
Lange's photo <u>Migrant Mother</u> (discussed in forthcoming pages), the
context is the Great Depression—the 1930s in the United States.

**setting:** What is the place and time of day?

**background:** What is happening behind the subject?

**focus:** Is it a close-up or wide-distance image? What is clearest in the image?
What is most unclear?

**lighting:** Is the light bright, dark, soft, harsh, natural, artificial, reflected, partial?
Are there shadows?

**color:** Is the image in color or in black and white? How does the color or lack
of color help the image?

**angle:** What is the vantage point of the image? Does the image look down, up,
to a side?

**juxtaposition:** Are there any contrasts operating: light and dark, large and small, or
ironic elements, such as Dorothea Lange's photograph of two poor
hitchhikers during the Depression walking along a dirt road toward a
billboard that reads, "Next time try the train. Relax." ( <u>Toward Los Angeles,
California</u>, 1937) (<http://memory.loc.gov>)

**composition:** How are things arranged in the image—the people, objects, actions?

**framing:** What is placed within the boundaries of the image? How is the image
cropped or cut off?

**Notes for Writing Your Paper:**

1.  Your paper should be 2 to 3 pages.

2.  Make your title, introduction, and conclusion engaging. (See Chapter 1.)

3.  You may use personal experience: if you choose an image to write about because it holds a personal connection for you, you may *briefly* share this in the introduction and/or conclusion, possibly as a hook strategy. (See Chapter 1.)

4.  At the end of your paper, cite the source of your image. This need not be on a separate page—below your conclusion, space down four spaces and put the Work Cited entry there.

5.  Include a copy of the image you write about as the last page of your paper.

# HOW TO CITE A PHOTOGRAPH

**Examples from Electronic Sources:**

Works Cited

Byer, Renée C. 21 June 2005. The Sacramento Bee. The Pulitzer Prize Winners 2007 for Feature Photography. 1 July 2007 <http://www.pulitzer.org/year/2007/feature-photography/ works/byer01_jpg.html>.

Lange, Dorothea. Migrant Mother. 1936. Image and Imagination: Encounters with the Photography of Dorothea Lange. Ed. Ben Clarke. San Francisco: Freedom Voices, 1997. 7 Oct. 2007 <http://www.freedomvoices.org/migrant.htm>.

Pool, Smiley N., and Staff of the Dallas Morning News. 1 Sept. 2005. Dallas Morning News. The Pulitzer Prize Winners 2006 for Breaking News Photography. 27 July 2007 <http://www.pulitzer.org/year/2006/breaking-news-photography/works/dallas11.html>.

**How to Do It:**

1.  Give the photographer's name, last name first.

2.  Underline the title of the photograph if there is a title and use a period.

3.  Give date of the photograph if there is one.

4.  Give the title of the original print source if there is one.

5.  Give title of the online source from which you found the photo and underline it.

6.  Give the date for the online source if there is one.

7.  Give the date you accessed (read and printed) the photograph.

8.  Give the URL in angle brackets. Note that a period ends the citation.

*Continued . . .*

**Example from a Print Source:**

Lange, Dorothea. <u>Texas Panhandle</u>. 1938. The Oakland Museum. <u>An American Exodus: A Record of Human Erosion in the Thirties</u>. By Dorothea Lange and Paul Schuster Taylor. New Haven: Yale U. Press, 1969. 81.

*Note:* The above information on how to cite photographs might not answer all your questions. You may need to adapt your citation the best you can. For more information on citing sources, see Chapter 9 on documentation.

## Staged Images

Each day you are bombarded by so many images in the media that it's hard to tell which images are unstaged or staged. See Figure 5.4.

When media advisors to President George W. Bush orchestrated images, there was much criticism. In a <u>New York Times</u> article, "Keepers of Bush Image Lift Stagecraft to New Heights," Elisabeth Bumillar describes what goes on to create images of the president:

> WASHINGTON, May 15—George W. Bush's "Top Gun" landing on the deck of the carrier Abraham Lincoln will be remembered as one of the most audacious moments of presidential theater in American history. But it was only the latest example of how the Bush administration, going far beyond the foundations in stagecraft set by the Reagan White House, is using the powers of television and technology to promote a presidency like never before.

*Figure 5.4* President Bush profiled beside Mt. Rushmore. This is an AP photo used in the Bumillar article above.

Source: AP World Wide Photos.

Officials of past Democratic and Republican administrations marvel at how the White House does not seem to miss an opportunity to showcase Mr. Bush in dramatic and perfectly lighted settings. It is all by design: the White House has stocked its communications operation with people from network television who have expertise in lighting, camera angles and the importance of backdrops.

On Tuesday, at a speech promoting his economic plan in Indianapolis, White House aides went so far as to ask people in the crowd behind Mr. Bush to take off their ties, WISH-TV in Indianapolis reported, so they would look more like the ordinary folk the president said would benefit from his tax cut.

"They understand the visual as well as anybody ever has," said Michael K. Deaver, Ronald Reagan's chief image maker. "They watched what we did, they watched the mistakes of Bush I, they watched how Clinton kind of stumbled into it, and they've taken it to an art form."

The White House efforts have been ambitious—and costly. For the prime-time television address that Mr. Bush delivered to the nation on the anniversary of the Sept. 11 attacks, the White House rented three barges of giant Musco lights, the kind used to illuminate sports stadiums and rock concerts, sent them across New York Harbor, tethered them in the water around the base of the Statue of Liberty and then blasted them upward to illuminate all 305 feet of America's symbol of freedom. It was the ultimate patriotic backdrop for Mr. Bush, who spoke from Ellis Island.

For a speech that Mr. Bush delivered last summer at Mount Rushmore, the White House positioned the best platform for television crews off to one side, not head on as other White Houses have done, so that the cameras caught Mr. Bush in profile, his face perfectly aligned with the four presidents carved in stone.

## ACTIVITY 3

Do you think it is good for the White House to stage images of the president? Does it present any ethical problems? Is it smart communications? In your notebook please address these debatable questions. ▪▪

## ACTIVITY 4

Photos can hold great power. Exploring—analyzing and evaluating—images can help you determine when images are staged or unstaged. Browse through recent issues of Time, Newsweek, another magazine, or a local or national newspaper. Look at the photos. Which ones work best? Choose one, print a copy, and follow the "Guidelines for Exploring Images" to write about it. ▪▪

## Documentary Photographs

Who we are, to some variable extent, determines what we notice and, at another level of intellectual activity, what we regard as worthy of notice, what we find significant. (Robert Coles, Doing Documentary Work)

Documentary photos capture the lives of real people. Not staged, they serve as witness, as visual proof, as fact. Imagine never seeing any photos of the Holocaust, the September 11 attacks, the tsunami disaster in Southeast Asia, Hurricane Katrina, the Virginia Tech shootings—indeed, without pictures it is hard to imagine these atrocities. Although every photographer makes a picture from his or her own point of view, the purpose of documentary images is to show, usually, a person or a small group of people and the conditions of their life in that moment of time and space.

Robert Coles, a psychologist at Harvard, spent much of his career documenting the living conditions of migrant workers and children. In his book <u>Doing Documentary Work</u>, Coles discusses one of the most famous documentary photographs, <u>Migrant Mother</u> by Dorothea Lange. In this passage he tells about examining some of Lange's photographs and finding "which picture really worked, really got across what the photographer intended for us to contemplate": See Figure 5.5.

> I studied her iconic "migrant mother," a picture known throughout the world. . . . There she sits, her right hand touching her lower right cheek . . . caught gazing, in March of 1936,

**FIGURE 5.5** <u>Migrant Mother</u> by Dorothea Lange.

Source: Courtesy of the Library of Congress.
<http://www.freedomvoices.org/migrant.htm>

one of her children to her left, one to her right, head turned away from us, disinclined to look at the camera and, through it, the legions of viewers with whom it connects. The three figures seem so close, so "tight," it would be said in the South, yet each seems lost to the others: the children lost in the private world they secure by hiding their eyes, the mother lost in a look that is seemingly directed at no one and everyone, a look that is inward and yet that engages with us who look at her, and maybe with her, or through her, at the kind of life she has been living.

Cole's description of the photo lets us see more within it and realize why the image is memorable.

## ACTIVITY 5

Browse one of these Web sites: (1) "A Democracy of Photographs" in the Here Is New York Web site offers thousands of photographs taken on 11 Sept. 2001. See <http://hereisnewyork.org>. (2) The Library of Congress offers a wealth of photographs, including work by Dorothea Lange: see America from the Great Depression to World War II, Photographs from the FSA-OWI, 1935–1945: <http://memory.loc.gov/ammem/fsowhome.html>. (3) Masters of Photography contains images by well-known photographers such as Ansel Adams, Dorothea Lange, Diane Arbus, and Walker Evans and also articles and links: see <http://www.masters-of-photography.com/index.html>. Also, browse the Web for other photograph sites. After you have browsed for an hour, choose one photograph that intrigues you, print a copy, and follow the "Guidelines for Exploring Images" to write about it. ▪

## Fotolog

A recent kind of photography has surfaced on the Internet. Fotolog.com is a Web site showing digital photographs that anyone can post. Although the quality of the photographs may be uneven, many images capture moments of everyday life that are engaging and memorable. Laura Holder is a popular photographer on Fotolog. You can find her images at these Web sites: <http://www.fotolog.com/lauratitian/> and an archive of her work at <http://www0.fotolog.com/all_photos.html?user=lauratitian>.

## ACTIVITY 6

Browse the Web and find some photographs by Laura Holder you like. Choose one that intrigues you, print a copy—color if you can—and follow the "Guidelines for Exploring Images" to write about it. ▪

## STUDENT ESSAYS EXPLORING PHOTOGRAPHS

What do these students do to make their essays clear and persuasive?

### A Window to a Generation

*Duncan Ferguson*

Yes, a picture can say a thousand words, but a picture can also sum up an entire era and describe a generation's attitude toward a war. This photograph, taken by Tim Page on February 25, 1968, depicts a U.S. Marine on a landing strip in Vietnam with both a rifle and a guitar slung around his back. I chose this image because, as a musician, I find more value in a guitar than a gun. This image captures the mixed emotions many soldiers felt during the Vietnam War.

Looking at the photograph, I see the marine facing away from the camera. With his back turned towards the camera, all a person can see of his head is the back of his helmet. Because I cannot see the marine's face, my eye focuses on the surprising contrast between the guitar and the gun slung around the marine's back. I focus on the guitar first because it stands out most on the soldier: it has a light color compared to the dark gray uniform and gun. Also, I focus on the guitar first because it seems out of place for a war photograph. Next I notice the M-16 rifle slung parallel to the guitar on the marine's back. The contrast between the guitar and rifle is vivid.

What does a guitar stand for? Music—a form of communication between people that usually creates positive emotions. What does a gun stand for? Death, ultimately. A tool used to kill people, it also is a form of communication between people but used in the opposite way as a guitar. The guitar's and the rifle's meaning parallel and contradict one another as they rest parallel but opposite each other on the marine's back. This symbolizes the conflicting attitudes many soldiers had during the war. Music, free love, hippies—music was the root of flower power, the opposite of the brutal war in Vietnam.

The marine has a leisurely stance with all his weight on his right leg with his hip cocked out. His helmet, pants, and boots are faded and worn. The fact that he is wearing a flack jacket shows he is prepared for combat. There appears to be a hole in the fabric of his flack jacket indicating that he might have seen combat. The soldier next to the marine, who is cut off by the frame of the image, appears to be hunched over sitting on a box wearing the same faded clothing. The marine is looking upon a landing strip splattered with dirt. Judging by their postures and clothing, I think both soldiers are worn out and tired. To the right of the marine there is a duffle bag with another rifle set on top of it. The rifle seems positioned as if someone just plopped it down. No one is alert. The Marines are just waiting.

This photograph has powerful persuasive elements. The picture's logos captures a time period in history, and it makes you think. It documents the fact that many soldiers did not believe in the cause they were fighting for. The slogan "give peace a chance" was popular. The marine is a product of his time. His ethos is complex: he values his guitar as much or more than his gun. He is not looking back; he is looking ahead to whatever happens. He is still a soldier. This photograph appeals to my pathos because I am a musician, and I cannot imagine being in a jungle-war environment without some form of creative release. I feel how tired he is standing there, but at least he can look forward to playing a song later that day.

The photographer Tim Page captured not only a black and white photograph but a document in history showing the mixed emotions that many U.S. soldiers felt in Vietnam. A picture can say more than a thousand words: it can sum up an entire generation's attitude.

Work Cited

Page, Tim. <u>The Vietnam War.</u> 25 Feb. 1968. 9 Oct. 2007 <http://www.vietnampix.com/hippie.htm>.

***FIGURE 5.6***   Image of Marine with guitar and rifle on his back.

Source: Corbis/Bettmann.
<http://www.vietnampix.com/hippie.htm>

## Talk, Talk, Talk

*Elizabeth Nichols*

A photograph should show life and truth. When looking at Laura Holder's photo of two guys, I see a truth of many Americans today: cell phone junkies. We move too fast; nothing can wait; the littlest detail has to be figured out—now. Cell phones make this lifestyle possible. (Figure 5.7; see color insert.)

The scene is a sidewalk in New York. The street is calm, yet the city buzzes. Two young men stand talking on their cell phones. Neither man looks as if he knows the other. All around them the city is alive with detail. To their left is the blue awning of a party store VERNON WINE & LIQUOR with icicle lights hanging from it. There is a pay phone on the outside wall of the store no one is using. Under the blue awning a green hose lies in a mangled heap on the cement. Water from the hose seeps through cracks in the wide sidewalk toward the street. In the background a chalkboard menu sits on the sidewalk outside its store with a yellow and red sign spelling out the word *Candies*. Just beyond this sign an American flag is present half wrapped around itself because of wind. There is a telephone pole toward the right top corner of the frame. A police car has pulled up to the curb in the background. Bystanders look on: a woman accompanied by two men. The woman's long red coat hangs to her knees; her white purse is hung over her left shoulder, clung to her side as if she protects it. A brown shingled building stands across the street, behind the commotion of the police. The black steel steps of a fire escape hang from the front of the building. Bright yellow letters on a black sign indicate a deli inside. On the middle right of the picture a screen flashes advertisements above the subway station below. These men are not disturbed by the commotion of the city. Cellular phones hold their attention as everything continues around them.

Looking at the ground as he walks, the man in the foreground smiles into the phone as he talks. His brown hair is tousled: his navy blue denim jacket reveals the watch on his left wrist as he holds the tiny silver phone to his ear; the other sleeve covers his right hand completely, as if he might be cold. Like the first man, the second man wears faded blue jeans; his brown button-down shirt is wrinkled. Part of is face is covered from view by his cellular phone. He is right-handed. The first man is left-handed. These positions of the phones offer an interesting contrast in the image.

This photograph appeals to logos because it makes me wonder. What is going on in the lives of these men? The second man may be the manager of the store with the blue awning. He was called into work on his day off. He's outside talking a break, getting some fresh city air. The image of the first man stirs more pathos. Why is he smiling? He looks genuinely happy. He could be talking to his mom, but I feel he is talking to his girlfriend: he called to hear her voice and ask how her day is going. Whomever he is talking to, whatever he is talking about, he is happy. His cell phone keeps him in touch with somebody he cares about. The expression on his face makes me happy too. Does the picture appeal to ethos? I think so. Holder makes our addiction to cell phones not look like so bad. Despite the city bustle around them, these guys on cell phones are all right. They are focused; they look authentic.

Laura Holder's photograph succeeds because it shows how cell phones have become a key part of our daily lives. These men are regular guys, doing their everyday routine. Their day would not be complete without their cell phones. This may be true for most us as well. Through her camera's lens, Holder captures a moment of complex city life that feels very true.

Work Cited

Holder, Laura. Fotolog.net. 11 May 2003. 7 Oct. 2004 <http://www1.fotolog.com/lauratitian/113914>.

## Like a Photograph, a Painting

Paintings, drawings, and sculptures are visual works of art. But what is art? According to <u>Webster's New World</u>, works of art "display form, beauty, and unusual perception." For critical thinkers, works of art offer rich rewards.

### ACTIVITY 7

You can analyze and evaluate a painting the same way you do a photograph. You can give a reading of it to help other viewers increase their understanding of it. Explore Norman Rockwell's famous painting <u>The Problem We All Live With</u> made in 1964. Consider doing research to find some information about the context of the piece: for example, how does Rockwell's painting reflect what was happening in the United States in the 1960s? To find paintings by other great artists, browse the National Gallery of Art site: <http://www.nga.gov/help/index.shtm>. See "Guidelines for Exploring Images" to write about this work of art. (Figure 5.8; see color insert.)

### ACTIVITY 8

To experience a great work of art and a clear, persuasive analysis of it, go to the National Gallery of Art website to view a slide show of Winslow Homer's painting <u>Right and Left</u> about a hunter shooting two ducks: <http://www.nga.gov/collection/rightandleft.htm#trans>.

## ADVERTISEMENTS

Ads promote something. As public displays, they aim to capture your attention—and usually your money. Because ads cost great sums of money to appear in newspapers, magazines, and on the Internet, they are carefully designed to catch your eye. As a critical thinker, you can learn how to analyze and evaluate advertisements so you can better judge what they promote.

Ads come in various forms. Commercial ads sell products such as Lexus, Rolex, or Nike. Ads for social causes try to persuade you to consider an argument such as civil liberties or the ethical treatment of animals. These ads employ the same elements as commercial ads do, but their appeals to logos, pathos, and ethos are often more dramatic. Consider this ad: See Figure 5.9.

To study this ad or any ad, you can make a list of what you notice. A list for this image might include the following notes:

–I see the bullets right away.

–No, they're bullet holes, but I feel the presence of bullets very strongly.

–The bullet holes are spread out toward the center, like the center of a target.

–The holes are in metal that is torn, taking various shapes.

–There are 33 bullet holes—not 41 as mentioned in the text.

–It makes me cringe imagining these bullets in Amadou Diallo.

–Each bullet hole has a word under it, a single word.

–The words say "You have the right to remain silent. Anything you say can be used against you in a court of law. You have the right to speak to an"—the word "attorney" is not there. The sentence is not complete.

–But my eye is drawn to the text at the bottom of the ad which explains the image. The first two sentences appear in dark font to make them stand out: "On February 4$^{th}$, 1999, the NYPD gave Amadou Diallo the right to remain silent. And they did it without ever saying a word." These sentences seem ironic. How could the police give Diallo the right to remain silent without speaking with him? But the next sentence answers this: "Firing 41 bullets in 8 seconds, the police killed an unarmed, innocent man."

–The text at the bottom of the ad continues, this time appealing to all Americans: "Also wounded that night was the constitutional right of every American to due process of law." "Wounded" is an interesting word choice: our right was not killed but wounded.

–The ad gives a call for support: "Help us defend your rights. Support the ACLU." It is important the ad uses "your rights": this addresses each reader.

–The ad also provides a Web address for the ACLU.

–The last four words—"american civil liberties union—are in lower case and dark font. The dark font connects them with the first two sentences of the text.

–The words in between are light gray, less apparent, harder to see easily—perhaps suggesting it's hard to see or remember our constitutional rights.

–There's one bullet hole below the text, near the last word "union."

–There is no frame or box around the ad: it's open, perhaps suggesting that abuse like this cannot be contained unless people actively oppose it.

After taking such notes, you can explore three questions to help you analyze the ad. **Question 1:** What is the central purpose of the ad? To alarm readers with a bullet-ridden image and make them aware of every citizen's constitutional right to due

On February 4th, 1999, the NYPD gave Amadou Diallo the right to remain silent. And they did it without ever saying a word. Firing 41 bullets in 8 seconds, the police killed an unarmed, innocent man. Also wounded that night was the constitutional right of every American to due process of law. Help us defend your rights. Support the ACLU. www.aclu.org **american civil liberties union**

*FIGURE 5.9* Bullet ad by ACLU.
Source: Courtesy of DeVito/Verdi, Inc.
<http://aclu.org/graphics/bullet_ad.jpg>

process of law. **Question 2:** By what means does the ad achieve its purpose? Here you can use many of the details in your notes to describe the image and to explain a few of the stylistic choices the creators of the ad made. You can also explain how the ad has persuasive appeal. It appeals to **logos:** the ad makes you think that what happened to Amadou Diallo was incredibly violent, tragic, and wrong. But the ad doesn't give the view of the police who thought he was reaching for a gun instead of his wallet. Maybe it's not possible to present various sides in an ad. That's good to realize: ads may oversimplify to be more direct and eye-catching. It appeals to **pathos:** the ad makes you feel uncomfortable. The bullet holes are vivid reminders of violence. If bullets do that to metal, what must they do to flesh and bones? The ad's violence repels you, and you feel sad that such tragedies happen to innocent civilians and to police who are trying their best. It appeals to **ethos:** the ad makes you care about due process of law and about legal rights most people take for granted. The American Civil Liberties Union seems an extremely ethical organization to bring this issue to the public's attention. The ad appears well done: the visual and verbal elements go together in a powerful way. The ad is a credible representation of the ACLU. **Question 3:** Why does the ad succeed or not? Its graphic image compels readers to look into it more deeply to understand how it makes sense; it raises questions about whether civil liberties were denied to Amadou Diallo, and if they were, then they could also be denied to others.

---

## SPECIAL CONSIDERATIONS FOR EXPLORING ADS

To analyze and evaluate an advertisement, follow the "Guidelines for Exploring Images" presented earlier. Like photographs, ads may contain the following elements: subject, people, objects, actions, context, setting, background, focus, lighting, color, angle, juxtaposition, composition, and framing. However, ads contain a greater interplay between image and words. Analyzing this interplay will help you determine how well an ad succeeds. Consider these questions:

Where did you find the ad? What magazine, newspaper, or online source? What date? What page number?

Who is the target audience for the ad? Men, women or both? Young adults, children, senior citizens? Wealthy people, middle-class people? People who want to be "successful" or "cool"?

How is language used in the ad? Where is it located: bottom, top, middle, side? How many words are there? How many sentences? What type fonts are used: small, large, capital letters, anything unusual? How much verbal material is there compared to visual material?

How is image used in the ad? What is in the foreground? What does your eye see first? What is in the background? What colors are dominant? Are people beautiful models or ordinary people? Do they appear pleased, happy, sad?

How? What is their nonverbal communication? What are they doing with their faces, hands, legs?

What is the layout of the ad? Where are various elements located? Where is Web site information found? Is the ad easy on your eyes or hard to process?

What does the ad suggest? What does it suggest about ethics—what is right or good? What does it suggest about what men or women desire or need? What might women notice and infer from the ad? What might men notice and infer? What does the ad suggest about social class or status, about values, about family, friendship, competition, luxury, beauty, fun, security, or self-fulfillment?

## HOW TO CITE AN ADVERTISEMENT

**Examples from Print Sources:**

Works Cited

BlackBerry. Advertisement. <u>Newsweek</u> 9 July 2007: 21.

The Fitness Fragrance by Ralph Lauren. Advertisement. <u>GQ</u> Apr. 1997: 111–12.

Honda. Advertisement. <u>Time</u> 26 Mar. 2007: 50.

**How to Do It:**

1. Give the name of the company or product.
2. Write the word Advertisement but don't underline it; follow with a period.
3. Give the title of the magazine or newspaper—underline it; use no period.
4. Give the date of publication.
5. Use a colon followed by page number(s) and end with a period.

**Examples from Electronic Sources:**

American Civil Liberties Union. Advertisement. 26 June 2007. 27 July 2007
    <http://www.aclu.org/safefree/general/30405res20070626.html>.

Hilton. Advertisement. n.d. <u>Billboard.com</u> 27 July 2007
    <http://www.billboard.com/bbcom/index.jsp>.

Verizon. Advertisement. 2007. <u>Newsweek.com</u> 27 July 2007
    <http://www.msnbc.msn.com/id/3032542/site/newsweek/>.

**How to Do It:**

1. Give the name of the company or product.
2. Write the word Advertisement but don't underline it; follow with a period.
3. Give the date of the ad if there is one. If there is no date, write "n.d."

*Continued . . .*

4. Give the title of the Web site if there is one—underline it; use no period.
5. Give the date you accessed (read and printed) the ad.
6. Give the URL in angle brackets. A period ends the citation.

*Note:* The above information on how to cite ads might not answer all your questions. You may need to adapt your citation the best you can.

## ACTIVITY 9

Choose one of the following ads for social causes and follow the "Guidelines for Exploring Images" to write about it. (Figure 5.10, see page 327; Figure 5.11, see page 328.) ▪▪

## ACTIVITY 10

Browse this Web site: People for the Ethical Treatment of Animals (PETA) <http://www.peta.org/mc/printAds.asp>. Choose one ad that intrigues you, print a copy, and follow the "Guidelines for Exploring Images" to write about it. ▪▪

## ACTIVITY 11

Look for commercial advertisements in magazines and newspapers—especially magazines you like to read. Choose one ad that intrigues you, print a copy, and follow the "Guidelines for Exploring Images" to write about it. ▪▪

## ACTIVITY 12

The Tommy "Follow the Flock" ad is from Adbusters, a Web site containing spoofs of ads. (Figure 5.12, see Color Insert.) Follow the "Guidelines for Exploring Images" to write about it. Or choose another spoof ad to write about. See <http://adbusters.org//spoofads/>. Also, Adbusters invites you to create your own print ad and gives you directions: see <http://adbusters.org//spoofads/printad>. ▪▪

## STUDENT ESSAYS EXPLORING ADVERTISEMENTS

What do these students do to make their essay clear and persuasive?

***FIGURE 5.10*** Poster with Martin Luther King Jr. and Charles Manson.

Source: Copyright ©American Civil Liberties Union. Reprinted with permission.

*FIGURE 5.11* PETA ad: "People who are violent to animals rarely stop there."

Source: Courtesy of the People for the Ethical Treatment of Animals.
<http://www.peta.org/pdfs/ADviolenttoanimals.pdf>

## Healthy Hayes

*Kristen Westdorp*

Folic acid. In an advertisement for such a nutrient, you might expect depictions of foods that are sources: orange juice, broccoli, spinach, or fortified cereals. But I doubt you would imagine an adorable baby boy lying there, complete with the words "It's essential for healthy babies." This ad for March of Dimes uses the soft side of almost anyone's heart to catch the attention of its readers. Let's face it: who can pass up reading an ad with a child as the main focus?

This nutrition awareness ad by March of Dimes presents a baby boy—Jordan Hayes—lying on a cream, plush blanket, his big brown eyes staring back with contentment. His pudgy fingers are placed in his mouth, between the cheesy smile on his face. His arms are bent upward, flaunting the "baby fat" in the creases of his arms. The nametag fastened on his wrist with a blue plastic twist tie informs us that this baby is the real thing—someone's child—not just a child for an ad. He is the baby that every mother-to-be hopes for in the heartbeat she hears throughout her pregnancy. (Figure 5.13, see Color Insert.)

Once you take the time to get past the cute baby in the center of the page, you notice the true meaning of the ad. Placed below Jordan is a turkey sandwich and a loaf of bread, depicting the literal interpretation of "the folic acid in enriched white bread may help prevent some birth defects, even before you're pregnant." In stating this, the ad gives advice on how to move forward in getting enough folic acid in your diet, being that "it's essential for healthy babies." Another eye-catching quality about the ad is the fact that "healthy babies" is underlined with the same blue tie that is wrapped around Jordan's wrist. This simple fact makes an important connection between the baby and the point that March of Dimes is attempting to get across.

At first glance, this may seem like an advertisement for Pampers or Gerber, with the world's cutest baby neatly centered between the bottles of lotion or packages of diapers. However, March of Dimes strategically uses the baby to incorporate logos, ethos, and pathos into the ad—which it does quite successfully. The ad informs us that eating white bread can help prevent birth defects, because of the folic acid content; this appeals strongly to logos. Featuring both the symbol for March of Dimes and Grains for Life, as well as the links to their websites, adds strong credibility to the ad. We realize, as readers, that we can go online and check out the information for ourselves, so it is easier to regard the information as factual; this use of ethos makes a big difference. Although logos and ethos are used well, the use of pathos is prominent. Children, no matter what the content, usually have a way of adding emotion to an advertisement. Even the most coldhearted person has a soft spot for a baby. By using the child as the main focus, the ad catches your attention, making you want to read further. Also, by making the connection between the healthy baby shown and the idea of adding folic acid to your diet, the reader is more likely to take the advice into consideration. If readers are not willing to take action for themselves, they will definitely consider it for their baby. Jordan is the straight path to the heart, and March of Dimes has taken advantage of this appeal.

This ad is successful—thanks mainly to the use of pathos. If March of Dimes can simply sell the baby, then it will sell the use of folic acid. In that case, it's a done deal. If nothing else gets you, the brown eyes will.

Work Cited

March of Dimes. Advertisement. <u>Health</u> Jan/Feb. 2008: 111.

## Are You Willing to Endure the Consequences?

### *Mary Kate Lesko*

Cigarettes in a coffin? Bonnie Vierthaler of the BADvertising Company has created an anti-smoking ad that spoofs Merit cigarettes. By "juxtaposing silly, gross, or disgusting images," she makes people realize how tobacco ads glamorize smoking; however, they fail to make people aware of the harsh consequences consumers suffer, with the exception of a small white box in the corner, mandated by the Surgeon General. The central purpose of this image is to alert people to the dangers of smoking, especially death. (Figure 5.14; see color insert.)

This ad first catches the audience's attention by picturing a rather elegant wooden casket with three filter-tipped cigarettes positioned inside it. My attention is drawn to the way that the cigarettes are personified: they are in the casket yet raised a little as if someone has tapped a pack of smokes to lift up a few to select from. The casket is positioned in the center of the ad, against a white background, thus making it the immediate focus. The heading of the image also catches the audience's attention. The words "New crush-proof box" are at the top in large, bold white letters, with the words *crush-proof box* underlined and italicized. It is ironic because a casket is designed to be "crush-proof" to the individual inside. These images are quite morbid as they cause the audience to think about being trapped and dead inside a casket as a result of smoking tobacco.

My attention is further drawn to the words below the picture and the brand name of the cigarettes. It is ironic that the name of the cigarettes is Merit—a word associated with positive meanings such as "something deserving reward or praise" (<u>Webster's New World</u>). This product being advertised is the total opposite. Cigarettes do not warrant reward or praise. Also, the slogan "A world of flavor in a low tar" leaves me in disbelief. After displaying the morbidity of the open coffin and the cigarettes inside, there is still an attempt made at persuading the audience to consider flavor and low tar. The contrast between the continuous effort to push tobacco use and the terrible consequences shown becomes the main theme of the ad.

To achieve its purpose, this ad makes adequate use of the three persuasive appeals. It appeals to logos because it displays the real consequences of tobacco use. It doesn't try to glamorize or glorify the product, but instead displays the truth. It helps the audience think about the real dangers of smoking. The ad appeals to pathos because it makes the audience feel uncomfortable by considering the deadly effects of smoking. If you smoke or someone you love smokes, this ad could make you uneasy. With the open coffin, the ad suggests a funeral parlor and soon a burial. The ad appeals to ethos because it makes the audience question whether it is ethical for tobacco companies to sell their products to consumers if such terrible effects can occur. It makes the audience question tobacco ads in general in that they fail to show the truth; they deceive the consumer in order to make money.

This image succeeds in alerting consumers to the dangers of smoking tobacco. Most memorable about this ad is the image of the open coffin, just waiting for a smoker to occupy that space. As Bonnie Vierthaler, the creator of the ad, writes, "People believe what they see. If what they're seeing is seducing them into a deadly addiction, then we need to counter the seduction by reversing what they see. In other words, fight fire with fire, images with images!" (<http://www.badvertising.org/>.)

### Work Cited

Merit. Advertisement. The BADvertising Institute 2000. 18 Feb. 2004. <http://
www.badvertising.org/pages/04%20BADvertising%20Galleries/thumbnails/pages/19.htm>.

## ACTIVITY 13

In the color insert section, look at Figures 5.15 and 5.16. They show the covers of the first and second edition of Discovering Arguments. How well does each image represent the book? Select the edition image you like most and write about it, following the "Guidelines for Exploring Images." Or compare both the first and second edition cover images. Another option is to compare these images to the cover image of this third edition. Which do you prefer and why? ■

## CARTOONS

Cartoons are drawings that make readers laugh, think, feel, and see different perspectives. Consider this one by Gary Larson.

To study this cartoon or any cartoon, you can make a list of what you notice. A list for this image might include the following notes:

–An artist is painting a woman.

–The woman is posing, not looking at him; she is portly, in her fifties or sixties maybe.

–The artist has painted a big black fly along the left side of the woman's face.

–He appears not to know he has a fly on the left lens of his glasses—I find this funny!

–He appears about the same age as the woman, has a huge nose, a black brush of a mustache, and wears a beret.

–Has he looked at his painting to see how well he's doing?

–Maybe he has or maybe he hasn't—if he has, then because the fly is still on his glasses the image of his painting would reflect the image he actually sees, I think.

–The woman posing is smiling, and her smile appears in the painting even though the legs of this huge spider are pressing closely against her face.

# THE FAR SIDE® By GARY LARSON

*Figure 5.17* The Far Side cartoon by Gary Larson. 19 Dec. 1995.

–This artist must be in the flow of creating: so in the moment he's not aware of his real vision being obstructed. He doesn't see what he doesn't see. It seems ironic because artists are supposed to see more than most of us.

–Perhaps he prides himself on being an artist: he wears a beret, has longish hair below it but is balding at the side; he looks the part, has an easel and a canvas stapled to a frame.

–The smiling woman doesn't know that he is painting a most unflattering portrait of her.

–The tone of the cartoon is comic, absurd, exaggerated to help us see and consider the fly in our own vision.

After taking such notes, you can explore three questions to help you analyze the cartoon. **Question 1:** What is the central purpose of the cartoon? To make you laugh while you realize that you may be similar to this artist. **Question 2:** By what means does the cartoon achieve its purpose? Here you can use many of the details in your notes to describe the image and to explain a few of the stylistic choices the cartoonist made. You can also explain how the cartoon has persuasive appeal. It appeals to **logos:** the cartoon makes you think. You notice the ironic situation: maybe most people are like this painter; maybe we too can't see what impairs our own perspective. So often we assume we're seeing clearly (and writing clearly) when there may be something small obstructing our view in a big way. It appeals to **pathos:** the cartoon makes you laugh at the artist and his model. You may feel guilty for laughing—perhaps because you see yourself in this cartoon. If the humor helps you remember this lesson, the pathos reinforces the logos here. It appeals to **ethos:** you appreciate the creativity and insight of Gary Larson for creating this cartoon—for using an image that helps newspaper readers see a truth clearly, as if he's helping clean your glasses. His cartoon is certainly credible in its ironic details and overall presentation. The woman's and man's faces are humorous to look at: if they were ordinary-looking people it would not be as funny. That he can appeal to logos and pathos the way he does within a cartoon surprises you. **Question 3:** Why does the cartoon succeed or not? It makes you laugh and makes you think about an important lesson: what you don't see affects what you think you see.

Like photographs and ads, cartoons may contain the following elements: subject, people, objects, actions, context, setting, background, focus, lighting, color, camera angle, juxtaposition, composition, and framing. But cartoons usually contain captions or dialogue, an interplay between image and words. Analyzing this interplay helps you determine how well a cartoon succeeds.

## Cartoons and Creativity

> The ordinary mortal thinks most of the time in clichés—and sees most of the time in clichés. (Arthur Koestler, The Act of Creation)

Do you agree with Koestler? Are most of your thoughts unoriginal? His claim is debatable and discouraging. But cartoons try to present original thoughts or fresh perspectives that readers have not considered before.

Creativity has various definitions. Arthur Koestler defines creativity as "the discovery of hidden similarities." His phrase "hidden similarities" describes what usually happens in creativity: someone notices connections that other people don't see. Psychologist Jerome Bruner offers a similar definition: creativity is "the joining of unrelated things" (On Knowing).

Advertisers often try to catch your attention by combining things through hidden similarities. Ads for Absolut vodka show an airplane propeller shaped like the product's distinctive bottles or a lemon cut in half with seeds shaped like the bottles. In the business world advertisers pay great sums of money for creative ads that catch people's attention and help them remember their product.

Does any joining of unrelated things produce creativity? In On Knowing: Essays for the Left Hand, Jerome Bruner argues that genuine creativity contains "effective surprise." He writes:

> Surprise is not easily defined. It is the unexpected that strikes one with wonder or astonishment. What is curious about effective surprise is that it need not be rare or infrequent or

bizarre and is often none of these things. Effective surprises . . . seem rather to have the quality of obviousness about them when they occur, producing a shock of recognition following which there is no longer astonishment. . . . All of the forms of effective surprise grow out of combinational activity—a placing of things in new perspectives.

As a critical thinker you can judge whether a certain "combinational activity" works well or not.

Many cartoons involve "a placing of things in new perspectives." The combinations cause surprise and often laughter. Consider this:

**FIGURE 5.18**    "When Cannonballs Swim" cartoon by Mike Peters.
Source: Reprinted with special permission of King Features Syndicate.

Mike Peters's cartoon "When Cannonballs Swim" is creative because he reverses the usual: human beings in our culture often jump into water yelling "Cannonball!" But cannonballs do not jump into water yelling "HUMAN BEEEEEE-IIINNNGGG!!."

## ACTIVITY 14

Look at the following cartoons. How is each one creative?

**FIGURE 5.19**    Mike Peters' "Mother Goose & Grimm"—"Psst, Leo . . . Your Human's Open."
Source: Reprinted with special permission of King Features Syndicate.

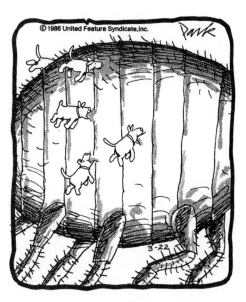

**FIGURE 5.20** W. B. Park's "Off the Leash"—"The Body of a Flea Magnified 215 Times."
Source: Park-Art.

**FIGURE 5.21** W. B. Park's "Off the Leash"—"Fish Drinking at Bar."
Source: Park-Art.

## Creativity and Humor

When cartoons play creatively with opposites, they are similar to many jokes told by comedians. Humor involves the funny joining of unrelated things: an unexpected collision of thoughts occurs, resulting in surprise. Consider this joke by Steven Wright:

I went to a restaurant that serves "breakfast at any time." So I ordered French toast during the Renaissance.

Wright takes a common saying "breakfast at any time" and presents a new way of looking at it. Here are a few more jokes by Wright:

I hate it when my foot falls asleep during the day because that means it's going to be up all night.

A lot of people are afraid of heights. Not me, I'm afraid of widths.

I got food poisoning today. I don't know when I'll use it.

I went to a general store. They wouldn't let me buy anything specific.

I have an answering machine in my car. It says, "I'm home now. But leave a message and I'll call you when I'm out."

Wright thinks with opposites much as Einstein did in conceiving that a person can be falling and at rest at the same time. Such creativity involves, as Arthur Koestler argues, "the ability to break away from the stereotyped routines of thought."

## ACTIVITY 15

Browse through magazines and newspapers or surf the Web for cartoons that strike you as having effective surprise. Find at least one you like and make a copy of it. Consider looking for cartoons by Dave Coverly ("Speed Bump"), Lynn Johnston ("For Better or Worse"), Gary Larson ("The Far Side"), John McPherson ("Close to Home"), Wiley Miller ("Non Sequitur"), and Mike Peters ("Mother Goose & Grimm"). Then follow the "Guidelines for Exploring Images" presented earlier.

### Serious Cartoons

Not all cartoons are meant to make readers laugh. Some may be sad or may be a combination of humor and sadness. Their primary purpose is to make you think and consider a different point of view. But like other cartoons, they contain similar elements, which you can analyze and evaluate. Consider this Non Sequitur cartoon by Wiley Miller. (Figure 5.22, see page 337.)

Does this cartoon succeed? It's not funny; rather, it pays tribute to September 11: the World Trade Center buildings and all the people trapped inside them. The man is hunched over, head bowed as if in prayer. He has just raked piles of leaves into the shape of two towers.

This is his way of mourning—of doing something with this grief. The image of the towers of leaves—that can so easily be blown down—is a surprising symbol. Wiley Miller is creative here by definition. Perhaps some people don't like the cartoon, think-

*FIGURE 5.22*   "Autumn in New York." By Wiley. 8 Oct. 2001.
Source: NON SEQUITUR ©2001 Wiley Miller. Dist. by UNIVERSAL PRESS SYNDICATE.
Reprinted with permission. All rights reserved.

ing it is not a suitable form for reflecting on the 9/11 tragedy. A cartoonist—any creative person or critically minded person—cannot please everyone and should not try.

Cartoons can generate much thought and discussion. Explore the Opus cartoon by Berkeley Breathed (Figure 5.23, see Color Insert.) and then read the essay Kathleen Parker wrote about it.

### Happy Father's Day, Jerk

#### Kathleen Parker

A week before Father's Day, cartoonist Berkeley Breathed did a very cartoonist thing and caused a controversy to be stirred over a comic strip that seemed to slight fathers while celebrating lesbian moms.

More or less. Reaction has been swift and predictable: outrage on the right; smug contempt for the right on the left. In the middle is one happy cartoonist, who got a rise from a jaded nation. Though the message of the strip may be interpreted more than one way—either as advancing an idea or exposing a cultural phenomenon—outrage is not necessarily misplaced.

For those who missed it, the strip—"Opus"—shows two boys talking about third-grader Davie Dinkle having two moms. "Multiple mommies," says one boy. "Cool," says the other. "No dad?" asks Opus Penguin, the existential penguin and namesake of the strip.

In the following frames, the boys wonder how Davie Dinkle will do without a male role model in the house. Whereupon, *CRASH!*—a television set showing a baseball batter on the screen is hurled through a window.

The clever fellow behind this gesture of apparent dissatisfaction is the usual suspect: a beer-slurpin', cigarette-smokin' white guy wearing a three-day beard and a cap festooned with what appears to be a set of mammaries in a bikini top.

"Now THAT was a pitch, you @$%* moron!!" shouts the male role model.

Well, there you go. The gag is a tad threadbare, but cartoonists would be out of business without stereotypes and cliches. We get the point. Maybe. Some see the strip as anti-dad and pro-lesbian; others, including lesbian bloggers, see it as making the point that gender doesn't necessarily predict good or bad parenting. Others might see it as simple recognition that the times, they are a-changin'.

All of which is to say, the comic strip is effective.

It also contains multiple layers of truth. The first truth is that same-sex couples today are raising children, among them one of the grandchildren of the vice president of the United States.

Another truth is that kids are having conversations like the one in the strip. A child who has two mommies (or two daddies) will get noticed and talked about. It is entirely possible that two little boys who love their mothers might think that having two mothers would be twice as good. Sort of like having two candy bars instead of just one. Here's another truth: Children don't know much.

But here's the biggest truth of all: Men and fathers have been on the receiving end of a male-bashing trend for the past 20 years or so, and they've had enough. Breathed's comic strip might have faded into the ethers if it didn't cut so close to the bone, if it weren't one more insult added to a history that long ago ceased to amuse.

On television, men are depicted as boors or buffoons, while in the broader culture, they're deadbeats or wife beaters. In a 1999 study of how fathers were presented in 102 prime-time shows, the National Fatherhood Initiative found only four in which a father was portrayed as present and involved in his children's lives.

At the same time little boys and girls are seeing bad, dumb daddies on TV, more than a third don't live with their own father, owing either to divorce or single motherhood. Despite inevitable exceptions to the rule, it is merely ignorant to say that a father's absence has no effect on children. Study after study shows an association between fatherlessness and a wide range of social pathologies, including drug abuse, promiscuity and delinquency.

---

(Please see biographical notes for Kathleen Parker in *Chapter 3*.)

Two mommies may work out fine for some children. And some men, just like some women, are contemptible slobs or worse. But neither observation diminishes the larger truth that children need fathers, most of whom are not, in fact, the cartoonish characters we love to loathe.

Breathed's comic strip, intended or not, revealed where we have arrived as a society in our attitudes toward male role models, otherwise known as fathers: Two lesbian mommies are cool, while dad is a violent, profane, impulsive, substance-abusing slob. In such a world, we can be grateful for an existential penguin whose voice offers a counterweight to the know-nothingness of children.

Opus Penguin asked the appropriate question: "No dad?"

Work Cited

Parker, Kathleen. "Happy Father's Day, Jerk." <u>Townhall.com</u> 15 June 2007. 28 July 2008.
<http://www.townhall.com/columnists/KathleenParker/2007/06/15/happy_fathers_day,_jerk>.

## ACTIVITY 16

In your notebook, write a response to Kathleen Parker's essay. Do you agree or disagree with her, or perhaps both? Why? Do you notice any insights, assumptions, or overgeneralizations? Does she do a close, accurate reading of the Opus cartoon? Consider doing a Toulmin analysis of her article: what is her claim, her grounds, her warrant (and backing)? Can you produce any counterarguments? (*Chapter 4* gives information on the Toulmin method.) ▤

## Editorial Cartoons

Editorial cartoons, like editorial columns, present particular points of view concerning issues and events happening each day—state, national, world. The purpose of editorial cartoons is to engage readers to think about political, social, or cultural arguments.

Many editorial cartoons such as the one by Walt Handelsman from <u>Newsday</u> showing Larry holding his boarding pass over his privates is funny. And it's simple, not requiring much thought—yet it does generate thought. How far will airport security go? Humorists, as you've seen in this book, often use exaggeration for surprise. (Figure 5.24, see page 340.)

Consider the editorial cartoon by Clay Bennett from <u>The Christian Science Monitor</u>. (Figure 5.25, see page 340.)

This is a simple cartoon with two frames. Each frame contains an overflowing garbage can with a lid almost falling off. The frame on the left says "Television"; the image is somewhat blurry. The frame on the right says "High-Definition Television"; the image is sharp and clear. What is also sharp and clear is Bennett's suggestion that television is basically garbage no matter how much money you pay

**FIGURE 5.24**   "Boarding Pass, Please" cartoon by Walt Handelsman.

Source: ©Tribune Media Services, Inc. All Rights Reserved. Reprinted with permission.
<http://www.pulitzer.org/year/2007/editorial-cartooning/works/cart04_081106_jpg.html>

**FIGURE 5.25**   "High Definition Television" cartoon by Clay Bennett.

Source: ©Clay Bennett/© 1998 The Christian Science Monitor (www.csmonitor.com) All rights reserved.
<http://www.csmonitor.com/news/cartoonClassics.html#>

for a new, technologically advanced set. Is this an overgeneralization? Yes, surely not all television is garbage, but through his contrasting images and his exaggeration, Bennett makes a statement about the quality of what is usually on television: garbage. Readers may disagree or agree or wonder whether it's true.

Millions of people enjoy the feeling of holding open pages of a newspaper and reading, discovering arguments, with a warm cup of coffee or tea nearby. Each day readers look forward to seeing editorial cartoons: the interplay between the visual and verbal in a concentrated form.

Walt Handelsman won the Pulitzer Prize for Editorial Cartooning in 2007; Clay Bennett won the award in 2002. Pulitzer Prizes are awarded for editorial cartooning based on this criteria: "For a distinguished cartoon or portfolio of cartoons published during the year, characterized by originality, editorial effectiveness, quality of drawing and pictorial effect." It's also useful to consider the Pulitzer criteria for distinguished editorial writing: "the test of excellence being clearness of style, moral purpose, sound reasoning, and power to influence public opinion in what the writer conceives to be the right direction." You will often see these qualities in editorial cartoons as well.

## SPECIAL CONSIDERATIONS FOR EXPLORING CARTOONS

To analyze and evaluate an editorial cartoon, follow the "Guidelines for Exploring Images" presented earlier. Analyzing the interplay between image and words will help you determine how well an editorial cartoon works. Consider these questions:

What does the cartoonist do to grab your attention? What do you notice first?

What idea is the cartoon portraying?

Is the image original? Does it present a new perspective? How does it help you consider a certain point of view?

Is the style of the cartoon clear? How is it easy to see and understand? Does it suggest any deeper meanings?

Is there a suggestion of moral purpose? Does the cartoon suggest any arguments for what is right or wrong?

Is the reasoning sound? Does the argument make sense?

Do you sense a "power to influence public opinion in what the [cartoonist] conceives to be the right direction"?

How do the words reinforce the image and the overall message? Look at captions, titles, speech bubbles, or labels in the cartoon.

What symbols are used in the cartoon? What objects in the image represent or suggest certain ideas? Just as the White House is a symbol of our government, in a cartoon an object can symbolize an idea or a problem.

# **H**OW TO CITE A CARTOON

**Examples from Electronic Sources:**

Works Cited

Handelsman, Walt. Cartoon. <u>Newsday</u> 11 Aug. 2006 <u>Pulitzer Prize Winner 2007 Editorial Cartooning</u> 29 July 2007. <http://www.pulitzer.org/year/2007/editorial-cartooning/works/cart04_081106_jpg.html>.

Johnston, Lynn. "For Better or For Worse." Cartoon. 20 June 2007. 29 July 2007 <http:// www.fborfw.com/>.

Peters, Mike. "Mother Goose & Grimm." Cartoon. 20 June 2007. 29 July 2007 <http://www.grimmy.com/comics.php>.

**How to Do It:**

1. Give the cartoonist's name—last name first.
2. If the cartoon has a title such as "For Better or For Worse," give this title in quotation marks. Then write the word Cartoon. If there is no title, just write Cartoon followed by a period.
3. Give the title of the source: newspaper, magazine, book, or Web site. Underline the source. In the Handelsman example, consider <u>Pulitzer Prize Winner 2007 Editorial Cartooning</u> as a second source.
4. Give the date of the cartoon.
5. Give the date you accessed (read and printed) the cartoon if you found it online.
6. Give the URL in angle brackets. A period ends the citation.

**Examples of a Print Source:**

Luckovich, Mike. Cartoon. <u>Newsweek</u> 4 June 2007: 23.

Miller, Wiley. "Non Sequitur." Cartoon. <u>Detroit Free Press</u> 28 July 2007: C7.

*Note*: The above information on how to cite cartoons might not answer all your questions. You may need to adapt your citation the best you can.

## ACTIVITY 17

Browse the Pulitzer Prize site: <http://www.pulitzer.org/>. Choose one of the editorial cartoons between 1995 and the present that intrigues you. Follow the "Guidelines for Exploring Images" to write about it.

## ACTIVITY 18

Look for current editorial cartoons in newspapers, magazines, or on the Web. There are many sites online where you can find them, including <http://www.comics.com/>. You can explore online newspapers where certain cartoonists work: such as Mike Luckovich at the Atlanta Journal-Constitution, <http://www.ajc.com/>. You can explore sites for individual cartoonists: such as Mike Peters's <http://www.grimmy.com/>; his site contains a daily cartoon and an editorial cartoon. Choose an editorial cartoon you like and follow the "Guidelines for Exploring Images" to write about it. ▪

## ACTIVITY 19

Try your hand at creating a cartoon or an editorial cartoon yourself. You don't need to be an expert drawer to do this. Experiment and see. ▪

## Student Essays Exploring Cartoons

What do these students do to make their essay clear and persuasive?

### On the Watch

*Brett Sanborn*

"Always be on the watch," the newspapers read, and we are. Recently I traveled to Europe. Waiting with our group for the return flight home were people dressed in long white robes. Periodically the men of the group got up from their seats and walked to a corner where they huddled into a circle, then opened a small black book. After opening their holy book the men swayed back and forth while reading. This behavior frightened me. What are they going to do, I thought. Are we going to be safe on the plane? Are we going to die? We are always on the watch. But how much is this watch necessary? A cartoon by Pulitzer Prize winner David Horsey titled "Homeland Security: You're Never Too Safe . . . " illustrates this point perfectly. The purpose of this cartoon is to show how the American government has taught us to be in constant fear of attack—and that we can trust no one. (Figure 5.26, see page 345.)

We view the cartoon as if we are a chandelier above illuminating the scene. This black and white cartoon shows a typical American living room. Furnished with a coffee table, several locks on the door, and a small table with a lamp placed neatly on top, the home seems almost familiar. It is dark outside and the door is wide open, letting in the cool night air. A little girl stands off to the right side, her hair in a single ponytail raised high as if on alert. Opened wide, her mouth reveals missing teeth; she is very young. An elderly woman wearing a sunflower skirt stands with her arms outstretched and is near the center of the frame. A small bristly head boy wearing a striped shirt stands behind her. We cannot see his hands. The woman's purse lies next to her on the floor, in front of the coffee table, its contents spread out across the carpeting. Gum, a pen, and lipstick are no longer safe in their leathery surroundings, but exposed. Adorned with large glasses, wrinkles, and gray-white hair, the woman is probably in her late seventies. Behind her glasses, her eyes are wide with surprise.

The little boy has his hands up the back of his great-grandmother's sweater. He has an angry look on his face. As he frisks her in the doorway he says, "Sorry, Great-grandma, but everyone who visits our home is subject to a *RANDOM SEARCH!*" What is he looking for? While the little boy does this, his sister stands rifling through her great grandmother's four-wheeled suitcase, an angry look on her face. The artist draws the looks on the children's faces as if they were airport security people full of extreme suspicion. As she empties its contents one by one, she exclaims, "Aha!! Nail clippers!" I chuckled. I get it, I thought; her grandkids are searching her in their own home, as if she were going through an airport. The people at the airport take away people's nail clippers. It was funny. Then I began to think. Is this really what America is coming to? Can people not feel safe in their own living rooms when relatives come over?

This cartoon appeals to pathos through laughter. The startled look on the grandmother's face allows us to identify with her situation. Anyone who has traveled by air in the past few years knows this truth: you will be searched. In a way, the whole nation is the grandmother, waiting with our arms outstretched for the security person at the airport to establish us as not being terrorists. I remember feeling violated in such a way as I removed my shoes and jacket and placed them into the plastic gray tub while going through airport security. Do my stocking feet make people feel safe, I wonder.

This cartoon appeals to logos by posing an important question: can we truly trust no one? It forces us to think about what our country is coming to for the purpose of security. The Patriot Act has made it legal for law enforcement agencies to search your home, tap your phone line, and monitor your computer use, all without prior notification. This severely circumvents our Fourth Amendment rights against searches and seizures. The question remains: can we truly trust no one? Is our privacy worth the price of this kind of homeland security? This cartoon appeals to ethos by raising the question: to what extreme is security right and good? As a cartoonist Horsey is credible and surprising. He makes it easy for us to identify with the grandmother's situation.

How far will our government go to secure our homeland? In this cartoon David Horsey expresses the feelings of an entire nation: we're always on the watch yet we feel oversearched. One day I hope to stand in line with several white-robed individuals and shrug it off as if it were nothing at all.

Work Cited

Horsey, David. Cartoon. Seattle Post Intelligencer 9 June 2002 Pulitzer Prize Winner 2003 Editorial Cartooning 1 Nov. 2004 <http:/www.pulitzer.org/year/2003/editorial cartooning/ works/20020609.html>.

*FIGURE 5.26*   "Homeland Security" cartoon by David Horsey. <u>Seattle Post Intelligencer</u> 9 June 2002 <u>Pulitzer Prize Winner 2003 Editorial Cartooning</u> 1 November 2004.

Source: ©2002 Seattle Post-Intelligencer/Tribune Media Services.
<http:/www.pulitzer.org/year/2003/editorial-cartooning/works/20020609.html>

## Barbie

### *Elizabeth Nichols*

A person's initial reaction to a comic usually includes a slight grin or even a giggle. Many cartoons, however, have a much deeper meaning. Take this cartoon by David Horsey, found in the May 9, 2002 edition of the <u>Seattle Post-Intelligencer</u>. This cartoon was one of several that won Horsey the Pulitzer Prize. Horsey shows how a woman can go overboard trying to look young and attractive. (Figure 5.27, see page 346.)

The black and white cartoon shows the front porch of a summer home, looking out into the endless horizon of an ocean. Leaves from exotic trees and bushes circle two edges of the frame. Peering out from behind these leaves are two children with wide open eyes. The little boy with spiked hair stands behind his younger sister whose dark hair is pulled tautly into pigtails. The father figure in a checkered shirt stands holding a can of soda or beer. An ordinary, heavyset man, he has dark receding hair, a comb-like mustache and glasses that tint in sunlight resting on the bridge of his large nose. His trusty dog stands by his side.

*FIGURE 5.27*  Botox Cartoon.
Source: David Horsey 5/9/02 ©2002 Seattle Post-Intelligencer.
<http://www.pulitzer.org/year/2003/editorial-cartooning/works/20020509.html>

In the middle of the frame, the center of attention to her family, a Barbie-looking woman sits in a reclining beach chair. Next to her is a bottle of suntan lotion and a glass, perhaps of lemonade or something more stiff like her. Wearing a polka dotted bikini bathing suit and flip-flops, the woman looks artificial. Her waist has a crease, as if two pieces of plastic mold are connected. Long, wavy blonde hair falls past her shoulders; her big round eyes look fake; and her smile is so wide strings must pull it back. Her fingers and toes stick together—one piece of plastic. She is the "perfect" woman.

The caption in this cartoon has the husband saying, "Honey, you'd better cut back on the Botox . . . You're starting to scare the kids!" At first, this cartoon is funny. The woman does look like a Barbie; people get the joke. But looking at it more and thinking about it, I feel sorry for this woman and her family. The cartoon stirs pathos. Why do women put themselves through so much pain in order to look like Barbie?

This cartoon speaks the truth. The media influence a woman's sense of self. If she does not look like the stereotypical beauty, she must change something about herself. Diets, workouts, weight-loss pills—these methods to improve one's appearance don't help every woman. Where can she turn? But should she turn to plastic surgery or to injections of Botox to hide her natural wrinkles? The cartoon appeals to ethos because it asks this important question: how authentic or credible can a woman be if she makes herself into a Barbie?

The logos of this cartoon makes us think about this serious problem. For millions of women the quest to be young and beautiful is an obsession—even an addiction—as it is for the woman in this cartoon. Her children stare at the woman. She has changed her physical appearance and the way she carries herself so much that she is no longer the mother they knew. And she is no longer the woman her husband has known. What can our culture do to address this craze?

Botox injections are a popular way for women and men to look younger and more attractive. But once you take Botox, how far should you go? David Horsey's editorial cartoon shows one woman who took it so far she turned into a Barbie doll, separating herself from her kids, from her husband, and indeed from herself.

Work Cited

Horsey, David. Cartoon. <u>Seattle Post-Intelligencer</u> 9 May 2002 <u>Pulitzer Prize Winner 2003</u> <u>Editorial Cartooning</u> 22 Oct. 2003 <http://www.pulitzer.org/year/2003/editorial-cartooning/works/20020509.html>.

## FILM

Do you watch more movies than you read books? Most people in our culture do. As the most popular art form, films can provide great entertainment and enlightenment. Films can make you think and feel deeply—and care about ethical issues. Thus, films can carry powerful persuasive appeals. As a critical thinker, you can appreciate and understand film more if you read film reviews and write reviews yourself.

A. O. Scott, film reviewer for the <u>New York Times</u>, wrote an essay "Avast, Me Critics! Ye Kill the Fun: Critics and the Masses Disagree about Film Choices" in which he discusses how the film <u>Pirates of the Caribbean: Dead Man's Chest</u> was a tremendous success though most critics did not like it much. After ten days, the film earned $258 million while critics wondered "What is wrong with you people?" Scott writes,

> I don't for a minute believe that financial success contradicts negative critical judgment; $500 million from now, "Dead Man's Chest" will still be, in my estimation, occasionally amusing, frequently tedious and entirely too long. But the discrepancy between what critics think and how the public behaves is of perennial interest because it throws into relief some basic questions about taste, economics and the nature of popular entertainment, as well as the more vexing issue of what, exactly, critics are for.
>
> Are we out of touch with the audience? Why do we go sniffing after art where everyone else is looking for fun, and spoiling everybody's fun when it doesn't live up to our notion of art? What gives us the right to yell "bomb" outside a crowded theater? Variations of these questions arrive regularly in our e-mail in-boxes, and also constitute a major theme in the comments sections of film blogs and Web sites. Online, everyone is a critic, which is as it should be: professional prerogatives aside, a critic is really just anyone who thinks out loud about something he or she cares about, and gets into arguments with fellow enthusiasts.

But it would be silly to pretend that those professional prerogatives don't exist, and that they don't foster a degree of resentment. Entitled elites, self-regarding experts, bearers of intellectual or institutional authority, misfits who get to see a movie before anybody else does and then take it upon themselves to give away the ending: such people are easy targets of populist anger. Just who do we think we are?

There is no easy answer to this question. Film criticism—at least as practiced in the general-interest daily and weekly press—has never been a specialist pursuit. Movies, more than any other art form, are understood to be common cultural property, something everyone can enjoy, which makes any claim of expertise suspect. Therefore, a certain estrangement between us and them—or me and you, to put it plainly—has been built into the enterprise from the start. . . .

The modern blockbuster—the movie that millions of people line up to see more or less simultaneously, on the first convenient showing on the opening weekend—can be seen as the fulfillment of the democratic ideal the movies were born to fulfill. To stand outside that happy communal experience and, worse, to regard it with skepticism or with scorn, is to be a crank, a malcontent, a snob.

So we're damned if we don't. And sometimes, also, if we do. When our breathless praise garlands advertisements for movies the public greets with a shrug, we look like suckers or shills. But these accusations would stick only if the job of the critic were to reflect, predict or influence the public taste.

That, however, is the job of the Hollywood studios, in particular of their marketing and publicity departments, and it is the professional duty of critics to be out of touch with—to be independent of—their concerns. These companies spend tens of millions of dollars to persuade you that the opening of a movie is a public event, a cultural experience you will want to be a part of. The campaign of persuasion starts weeks or months—or, in the case of multisequel cash cows, years—before the tickets go on sale, with the goal of making their purchase a foregone conclusion by the time the first reviews appear. Sometimes it works and sometimes it doesn't, but the judgment of critics almost never makes the difference between failure and success, at least for mass-release, big-budget movies like "Dead Man's Chest" or "The Da Vinci Code."

So why review them? Why not let the market do its work, let the audience have its fun and occupy ourselves with the arcana—the art—we critics ostensibly prefer? The obvious answer is that art, or at least the kind of pleasure, wonder and surprise we associate with art, often pops out of commerce, and we want to be around to celebrate when it does and to complain when it doesn't. But the deeper answer is that our love of movies is sometimes expressed as a mistrust of the people who make and sell them, and even of the people who see them. We take entertainment very seriously, which is to say that we don't go to the movies for fun. Or for money. We do it for you.

Does A. O. Scott help you understand the relationship between film critics and audiences better? It's a complex relationship—and an important one. It's easy to criticize critics and assume they are somehow different from the rest of us. But Scott argues that critics play an essential role: they serve as a rebuttal of sorts against the Hollywood hype created by mass marketing. He claims that art generates "pleasure, wonder and surprise"; a critic can help readers understand how great films do this.

## Writing about a Film

Writing a film review is like writing any argument: you make a point and support it with specific evidence—reasons, examples and details. As with any paper on a visual argument, a film review requires information. Arguing without information is like trying to serve dinner without any food. It takes skill to put your reasons and examples together so that they convince your readers that your opinion of a film is insightful.

## ACTIVITY 20

### FILM REVIEW

Write a 3- to 6-page paper in which you research and synthesize at least three film reviews you find in a library or on the Internet. Try choosing a film that is meaningful in some important way and that strongly appeals to logos, pathos, and ethos. Or you may choose to review a movie whose plot, characters, and theme may be implausible or insignificant—but you enjoy the movie anyway and want to explain why. Try to watch the film twice, and take notes as you do. ▬

## GUIDELINES FOR WRITING A FILM REVIEW

- Good reviews briefly sketch an outline of the plot and inform (perhaps remind) readers about the characters.

- More importantly, good reviews look at both weaknesses and strengths. Consider whether to address weaknesses or strengths first. If you love a film but see some weaknesses in it, it is usually best to present the weaknesses first and then concentrate on the strengths. Presenting weaknesses first will suggest to your readers that you are fair-minded. If you dislike a film but see some strengths in it, present the strengths first and then concentrate on the weaknesses. You can also offer criticisms and then rebuttals within paragraphs.

- Ideally, try to find some insight into the movie that most readers may not have considered before. A good review should help readers have new and deeper understandings.

- What you choose to discuss in your review will depend on your emphasis and purpose. You can discuss the quality of any or some of the following elements:

**Elements of Film**

plot: The sequence of events in a story, what the story is about. The plot involves some conflict or situation the characters must resolve, some problem that causes tension among the characters. Is the plot credible or plausible? How?

*Continued . . .*

**characters:** In serious film the characters are realistic, complex human beings with strengths and weaknesses. Real characters are an important part of the plot. The audience must care about the characters and what happens to them. When characters are too predictable or stereotypical, critics say they are flat, cardboard characters. Are the characters believable? How?

**acting:** The more realistic an actor's actions and reactions, the better the acting. If audiences think an actor is trying too hard to act, they will not value his or her performance. Is the acting natural, believable, credible? Is the acting particularly interesting or distinctive in some way? How?

**theme:** A theme is the main idea the film illustrates. For example, <u>Fargo</u> illustrates that greed can cause lots of unforeseen grief. Is the theme significant? How?

**setting:** The time and place of the story is the setting—anything that helps create the illusion of time and place: clothing, costuming, makeup, buildings, countryside, backgrounds. How does the setting reinforce the plot, the characters, the theme?

**pace:** Few viewers enjoy a movie that takes too long to unfold its story. Does the film's pace work well or drag? How?

**music/sound:** Sound helps create mood. Sound reinforces special visual effects too— the music in <u>Jaws</u> warns you when the shark is coming. You believe what you see in part because of what you hear. How does the music or sound contribute to the film?

**cinematography:** Cinematography refers to camera work. If you think of a movie as a series of still photographs, each "shot" set up perfectly to illustrate the setting, the plot development at that moment in the film, and so on, it may be easier to understand what the photographers and the technical crew contribute to the film. Movies are rarely filmed straight through from beginning to end; therefore, matching lighting and camera angles becomes important. Special effects, too, involve camera work. Many films such as <u>The Polar Express</u> are created with computer graphics. How does the cinematography contribute to the film?

**director:** The director is usually in charge of everything you see and hear on the screen. Camera shots, for example, are usually set up by the director. The actors cannot see what they are doing, but the director can. Has the director done a skillful job? How?

**value:** Does the story have moral, social, psychological, or some other kind of value beyond entertainment? How? Is the entertainment value enough for you to recommend the film?

Consider your audience. Suppose most of your readers have already seen the movie. Thus, they will read your review to see whether they agree with you. But through your review, you must find something to say beyond "I like it."

Although professional reviewers use a variety of methods to present their opinions, the following method will help you organize your paper. It is similar to the method of argument presented in Chapter 2.

## ORGANIZING YOUR FILM REVIEW

1. Present your introduction with a clearly stated thesis.
2. Present an objective summary of the film in one paragraph—without your own opinions in it. Use present tense in your summary.
3. Analyze weaknesses you see in the film—in a paragraph or two. Use present tense.
4. Analyze strengths you see in the film—in three or more paragraphs. Select only those elements of the film that have an impact on you. Support your ideas with reasons, examples and details from the film. Use present tense.

*Note*: Consider discussing three ideas in this section. Your thesis statement could introduce the organization of your paper. For example, "The superb acting, rich cinematography, and moral lessons make The Cider House Rules an outstanding film."

5. Present your conclusion with a brief restatement of your thesis and a call for readers to see or not see the film. Or you might close by addressing one of these questions: Why does the film succeed or not? Why does it matter or not?

*Note:* When many students write film reviews, they spend most of their paper retelling the plot. Try hard not to do this. The purpose of a review is to analyze and evaluate a film. If you concentrate on examining at least three of the elements of film listed in the guidelines, this will help you not retell the plot. Push yourself to critically analyze the characters, acting, theme, setting, pace, music/sound, cinematography, director, or value.

Another way to write about a film is to follow the Guidelines for Exploring Images presented toward the beginning of this chapter. You can examine three main questions:

1. What is the central purpose of the film? Your thesis can be your answer to this question.
2. By what means does the director achieve his or her purpose?

   Present an objective summary of the film in one paragraph—without your own opinions in it. Use present tense in your summary.

   Explain a few of the stylistic choices the director makes—analyze at least three elements of film. (You can discuss weaknesses and strengths here.) Use present tense.

   Explain how the image appeals to logos, pathos, and ethos. (You can discuss weaknesses and strengths here too.) Use present tense.

3. Why does the film succeed or not? Why does it matter or not?

If you wanted to review <u>The Passion of the Christ</u>, for example, you could examine its persuasive appeals. It appeals to logos, provoking much thought. It is hard to watch the film without thinking about ideas of brutality, of forgiveness, of love. It appeals to pathos as well. Many people cry while watching it: as Christ is being flogged, viewers feel flogged too by the graphic violence. It appeals to ethos. Witnessing the violence that Christ endures makes viewers think about his character: his strength and his ability to forgive his betrayers. You can consider the ethos of Mel Gibson. Did it take great courage for him to make the film? Analyzing persuasive appeals can help you think critically about any film.

## Before You Do Research

Before you find reviews by professional film critics, spend some time generating your own ideas about the film. Jot down thoughts about the film's plot, characters, acting, theme, setting, pace, music/sound, cinematography, director, or value. See what you write the most about: this can tell you what to concentrate on in your review. Write down questions you have about the film as well as any insights, assumptions, or overgeneralizations you see in it. Make a list of weaknesses and strengths about the film. Write down your thoughts about how the film appeals to logos, pathos, and ethos.

## Finding and Synthesizing Sources

To write your review, you will do research and find other reviews with which to support and challenge your own arguments. Evaluate these sources. Use the reading tools presented in Chapter 2. Ask questions: try not to assume reviewers are wise and truthful. Examine their point of view. Look for any insights they express. Look for assumptions and overgeneralizations.

Find film reviewers who are *credible* sources—authorities well known and respected for their knowledge and expertise regarding movies. Use Roger Ebert of the <u>Chicago Sun-Times</u> (<http://www.suntimes.com/index/ebert.html>) for one of your sources. Having reviewed films for newspapers and television for over twenty-five years, he has probably reviewed any film you want to write about. You may not agree with him—and that's good. But he will help you think about a film in ways you might not have considered yourself. Also, try to use a review from the <u>New York Times</u>.

Many well-respected film critics belong to the National Society of Film Critics or the New York Film Critics Circle. When you search for critics, consider these: A. O. Scott from the <u>New York Times</u>; Peter Travers from <u>Rolling Stone</u>; Jay Carr from the <u>Boston Globe</u>; Mike Clark, <u>USA Today</u>; David Ansen, <u>Newsweek</u>; Richard Schickel or Richard Corliss, <u>Time</u>. There are many other well-respected and credible critics. You can find reviews by expert critics in most major newspapers such as the <u>Wall Street Journal</u> and <u>Washington Post</u>. You can find worthwhile reviews in many magazines, but consider the magazine. <u>The New Yorker</u> is an excellent source for thoughtful, substantial reviews—far better than <u>People</u> magazine, whose reviews are short and general.

**FIGURE 5.1** New Orleans, LA — Residents sent out a desperate plea for help as they waited to be rescued from the roof of an apartment complex. *(September 1, 2005. Photo by Smiley N. Pool.)*

Source: ©2005 The Dallas Morning News.
<http://www.pulitzer.org/year/2006/breaking-news-photography/works/dalls11.html>

**FIGURE 5.3** After arriving at the funeral home, Katherine Cathey pressed her pregnant belly to her husband's casket, moaning softly. Two days after she was notified of Jim's death in Iraq, she found out they would have a boy. Born on December 23, 2005, he was named James Jeffrey Cathey, Jr.

Source: ©2005 Rocky Mountain News/Polaris Images.
<http://www.pulitzer.org/year/2006/feature-photography/works/heisler14.html>

**FIGURE 5.7** Talking to Mom on Mother's Day.

Source: Laura Holder.
<http://www1.fotolog.com/lauratitian/113914>

FIGURE 5.8    The Problem We All Live With by Norman Rockwell.

Source: Printed by permission of the Norman Rockwell Family Agency. Copyright ©1943 the Norman Rockwell Family Entities.
<http://nrm.org/eyeopener/eye_problem.html>

FIGURE 5.12    "Tommy: follow the flock."

Source: Courtesy of www.adbusters.org.
<http://adbusters.org//spoofads/fashion/tommy/>

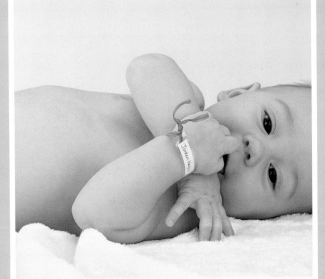

Bread. It's essential for *healthy babies.*

The folic acid in enriched grains, like white bread, may help prevent birth defects*, even before you're pregnant. Learn more at **grainpower.org** or **marchofdimes.com**.

*Birth defects of the brain or spine

**FIGURE 5.13** "Folic Acid: It's Essential for Healthy Babies."

Source: Reprinted by permission of Bernstein & Andrille, Inc. on behalf of Michael Warren, Photographer.

**FIGURE 5.14**

"New Crush-Proof Box."

Source: Courtesy of badvertising.org. <http://www.badvertising.org/pages/ 04%20BADvertising%20Galleries/ thumbnails/pages/19.htm>

**FIGURE 5.15** Cover image of <u>Discovering Arguments</u>, 1st edition. A man and a woman pull a curtain of stars to reveal daylight.
Source: Getty Images, Inc. Artville LLC.

**FIGURE 5.16** Cover image of <u>Discovering Arguments</u>, 2nd edition. A man stands facing a series of huge doors.

Source: CORBIS Images.com.

**FIGURE 5.23** Cartoon by Berkeley Breathed. June 2007.

Although it may be interesting and entertaining to read reviews from questionable sources such as Mutant Reviewers from Hell or The Crackpot Critic, avoid these in your own review. Using sources like these can cause readers to question your credibility as a writer and reviewer.

You can find many sites on the Web for movie reviews. Among the best are these:

**Internet Movie Database:** <http://www.imdb.com>

**Metacritic.com:** <http://www.metacritic.com/>

**Movie Review Query Engine:** <http://www.mrqe.com>

**New York Times Film Reviews:** <http://www.nytimes.com/library/filmarchive>

Consider also searching for reviews in academic journals such as Film Comment, Film Quarterly, Cinema Journal, and Cineaste. You can find many reviews through reference books such as New York Times Film Reviews, Magill's Cinema Annual, Film Review Index, 100 Years of American Film, and The A List: The National Society of Film Critics' 100 Essential Films.

In addition, look for positive and negative film reviews from sources you might not usually consider such as The Advocate, a national LGBT (lesbian, gay, bisexual, transgendered) magazine (<http://www.advocate.com>). How do they review the film I Now Pronounce You Chuck and Larry? Consider the journal The Christian Century for their film reviews (<http://www.christiancentury.org/>). Consider looking for reviews from different countries as well.

## SPECIAL CONSIDERATIONS FOR USING SOURCES IN A FILM REVIEW

1. Whenever you quote directly from a source, you must enclose borrowed language in quotation marks. See "Quotation Marks: How to Quote from Sources" in Handbook.

2. You must be careful not to plagiarize—to act as if borrowed language is your own. See Chapter 9.

3. Use signal phrases to introduce film critics and quotations. For example,

   Jeffrey M. Anderson, of the San Francisco Examiner, claims that A Beautiful Mind sugarcoats mental illness: "This is a precision story as told by filmmakers who are shooting at the side of a barn with water balloons filled with syrup" (2).

   The signal phrase here "of the San Francisco Examiner" is important because it provides the name of the newspaper that published Anderson's review. The reference to it lends credibility to the reviewer. For subsequent quotes by Anderson, you would not repeat the name of the newspaper.

*Continued . . .*

4. Use ellipsis points to condense a quoted passage. An ellipsis indicates that you have omitted words from a quote. An ellipsis is three or four spaced periods. See Handbook for more information on ellipsis.

**Passage with original quote:**

Anderson doesn't hide his criticism of the acting in the film. "Crowe, as directed by the goopy Ron Howard, goes way too far in his performance" (1).

**Passage with ellipsis:**

Anderson doesn't hide his criticism of the acting in the film. "Crowe . . . goes way too far in his performance" (1).

5. If you use a long quote—four or more lines—indent it two tab settings (10 spaces) on the left margin and double-space. Do not put quotation marks around it. See "Quotation Marks: How to Quote from Sources" in Handbook.

6. You need to digest your quotes—do not merely string quotes together. Comment before or after (usually after) each quote you use. This is important. Your job is to synthesize quoted material. Try not to rely on quotes too much. Rather, try to have a conversation with your reviewers.

7. Make sure you provide a page number in parentheses after each quote if your review comes from a print source. See examples in 3 and 4 above. If your review comes from the Internet, you do not need to cite page numbers after quotes (according to guidelines by the Modern Language Association.) For complete information on citing your sources, see Chapter 9.

8. Use present tense when you discuss the film and the reviewers. Use "Ebert writes" rather than "Ebert wrote."

9. Use the Modern Language Association (MLA) style of documentation: parenthetical text references throughout your paper and a complete Works Cited page at the end of your paper. See the information following on "How to Cite Film Reviews."

10. Provide copies of your reviews and *highlight* any direct quotes you use in your paper so your instructor can check them for accuracy. Attach these copies to your film review with a paper clip.

## Note on Underlining Film Titles

When you refer to the title of a film, you should underline it. But often you will find that sources do not do this: they may put the title in quotation marks or simply not use any punctuation at all. When you quote a source, you should quote the film title exactly as you find it.

## HOW TO CITE FILM REVIEWS

**Examples from Electronic Sources:**

Works Cited

Dargis, Manohla. "Smoke 'Em If You Got 'Em; His Career Depends on It." Rev. of Thank You
for Smoking, dir. Jason Reitman. New York Times 17 Mar. 2006. 30 July 2007
<http://movies.nytimes.com/2006/03/17/movies/
17smok.html?adxnnl=1&adxnnlx=1185755601-HAtpbuJfRYyvHWQaNpvIQA>.

Ebert, Roger. "Thank You for Smoking." Rev. of Thank You for Smoking, dir. Jason Reitman.
Chicago Sun-Times 26 Mar. 2006. 7 Mar. 2007 <http://rogerebert.suntimes.com/apps/
pbcs.dll/article?AID=/20060323/REVIEWS/60314009/1023>.

**How to Do It:**

1. Give the reviewer's name, last name first.
2. Give the title of the review in quotation marks.
3. Write *Rev. of*, title of film (underline title). *dir.* and name of the film's director.
4. Give the title of the magazine, newspaper, journal, or Web site. Underline this title.
5. Give the date the review was published.
6. Give the date you accessed (read and printed) the review.
7. Give the URL in angle brackets. End the citation with a period.

**Example from Print Sources:**

Denby, David. "Nailed." Rev. of The Passion of the Christ, dir. Mel Gibson. The New Yorker
1 Mar. 2004: 84–86.

**Notes on Works Cited:**

1. A Works Cited page is arranged alphabetically by the last names of authors. (If a
review has no author, begin with the title of the review in quotation marks.)
2. After the first line of a citation, subsequent lines are indented five spaces.
3. A Works Cited page should be double-spaced. For more information on Works Cited
using MLA style, see Chapter 9.

## STUDENT FILM REVIEWS

Your film review need not sound like a strictly academic research paper; it can be more
informal and lively. Don't be afraid to let your personality show through in your voice.
When you write, you present an ethos—a sense of your own character, which becomes
as much a part of your writing as your appeals to reason (logos) and to emotion (pathos).

## Thank You for Smoking?

*Alex Montoye*

Have you noticed how many movies lately are horror flicks or comedies without deep meaning? Movies in general have been dumbed down. Luckily, Thank You for Smoking (2006) does not follow this trend. While slightly unrealistic at times, the film is well made, with believable characters, good acting, and important insights, all the while being surprisingly funny.

Thank You for Smoking is a satire about a lobbyist named Nick Naylor, who represents Big Tobacco and promotes cigarette smoking. He is a master at his job, using unconventional logic yet convincing arguments. Throughout the movie, Naylor teaches his son how to argue "correctly." In the middle of the movie, Naylor is seduced by an attractive reporter named Heather Holloway who uses Naylor's secrets to write a news article that virtually destroys his career. Naylor, who has given up hope, is convinced by his son that he should still go to the hearing where a senator from Vermont named Ortolan K. Finistirre is trying to pass a bill that would put a skull and crossbones on every cigarette package. Using his uncanny persuasive arguing skills, Naylor prevents this bill from being passed. He is also the victim of a murder attempt because he is so hated for arguing in favor of smoking.

I can see a few reasons why some people would not like this film. Stephanie Zacharek at Salon.com writes, "The chief problem with 'Thank You for Smoking' . . . isn't that it's over the top; it's that it fits so neatly *under* the top . . . . 'Thank You for Smoking' is a winking, inoffensive little movie that doesn't demand deep inhalation . . . . it baits no one, and thus risks offending no one." Zacharek wants this movie to be angrier and to stir controversy. I like her pun that the film "doesn't demand deep inhalation" and agree that the film is not an all-out attack on the cigarette industry. But I've never seen a film about arguing ethically before this one. For this reason I wouldn't call it a "little" movie.

In addition, some parts of the movie are unrealistic. At the beginning of the film Naylor goes to his son's school to speak for a career day. I hope that no teacher would actually let a lobbyist for a tobacco company come to talk to an elementary school class. Also, Naylor actually seems too good at arguing. Sometimes he accomplishes what doesn't seem possible. For example, he has to give the Marlboro Man (Sam Elliott) some money to try to keep him from speaking out against cigarette smoking. The Marlboro Man, who has just been diagnosed with lung cancer, almost shoots Naylor when he pulls up to the house, but Naylor eventually convinces him to take the money. Last, when Naylor falls for Heather Holloway, it is hard to believe that he would tell her incriminating secrets after knowing her only a few days, especially since two of Naylor's good friends had warned him about Holloway. Perhaps the film suggests here that Naylor's grip on logic loosens when he's around a seductive woman.

The first quality I like about the movie is that the characters are for the most part realistic, and the acting is excellent. Played by Aaron Eckhart, Nick Naylor at first seems too perfect, but he shows weakness when he is seduced by an attractive reporter. Also, when he loses his job, he does not bounce right back and get a new job. He sits at home trying to drink away his loss until his son comes over and convinces him to try to get his life back. While being an incredibly good lobbyist, Nick Naylor is only human. Roger Ebert of the <u>Chicago Sun-Times</u> says that Nick Naylor is "not egotistical or conceited so much as an objective observer of his own excellence. It is the purpose of the movie to humble him, but he never grovels, and even in a particularly nasty situation is still depending on his ability to spin anything to his advantage." I like Ebert's idea that Naylor's professional and personal troubles humble him; I had not realized this. Next, I like BR, who is played by J.K. Simmons. He is Naylor's boss and seems realistic, all the time yelling at employees and stressing over cigarettes sales. He fires Naylor when Holloway's story comes out and tries to get Naylor back after Naylor redeems himself, just as any good boss would. Heather Holloway, played by Katie Holmes, is another believable character. It is not uncommon to hear about someone willing to do almost anything to advance his or her career. I am not saying that Holloway is a good person—she is realistic. Gary Thomas, of the <u>Philadelphia Daily News</u>, also likes the characters: "All these characters emerge as strangely sympathetic, even winning. No matter how vile or misleading Naylor's public utterings, we see that in 'real life' he is frank, candid, and actually quite a good father to his son." Ebert and Thomas agree with me that the characters are believable and are played well by the right actors.

This movie also offers some important insights. The entire film is based on the idea that there are at least two sides to every controversy and that arguing correctly can make even an undesirable option seem much better. Glenn Whipp, at the <u>Los Angeles Daily News</u>, captures this movie's theme well when he says, "If Reitman has a message . . . it's that the truth is unimportant—perception is what counts." When Naylor talks with his son about writing an essay for school, he says, "If you argue correctly, you're never wrong." While this sounds like an overgeneralization, it is insightful because it deliberately makes you wonder if this is true. Can we always be right if we argue correctly? No: by arguing correctly we can make others think we are right, but that does not necessarily make us right. A skilled lawyer can persuade a jury that his client did not commit murder (when in fact he did), but that does not make the lawyer right or ethical.

The quality that makes this movie most worthwhile is its surprising humor. Roger Ebert likes it too: "I enjoyed the satire; I laughed a lot because it's a very funny movie." In many scenes, the arguments between Nick and his opponents are funny because Nick uses ridiculous arguments that somehow work. Right at the beginning, Nick appears on a TV show featuring a 15-year-old boy with cancer who used to smoke. There are also some people from anti-smoking associations on the show. Clearly outmatched, Nick argues that the cigarette companies do not want the kid to die because they want to keep him alive and smoking. It is hilarious watching Nick immediately take control and make the others look like the bad guys. Another funny part of the movie occurs when Nick wakes up in the hospital after having nicotine patches put all over his body by the people trying to kill him. The doctor tells him that there is no way that Nick could have survived having all that nicotine in his system if he did not smoke. The doctor then says that smoking saved Nick's life. This is ironic and funny because smoking is not supposed to save lives but hurt or take them. Imagine seeing a claim on cigarette packs "Smoking can save your life." It's absurd, but that's the point.

Thank You for Smoking is a funny satire with good acting and insights. It also offers a good message, which Gary Thompson expresses well when he says, "If you're taking what spinners say at face value, you're inhaling a substance just as dangerous as tobacco, and it's a hard habit to break." It is rare to find a newer movie that is funny and thoughtful, but this one does both well.

Works Cited

Ebert, Roger. "Thank You for Smoking." Rev. of Thank You for Smoking, dir. Jason Reitman. Chicago Sun-Times 26 Mar. 2006. 7 Mar. 2007 <http://rogerebert.suntimes.com/apps/pbcs.dll/article?AID=/20060323/REVIEWS/60314009/1023>.

Thompson, Gary. "'Smoking' a Breath of Fresh Air." Rev. of Thank You for Smoking, dir. Jason Reitman. Philadelphia Daily News 24 Mar. 2006: 40.

Whipp, Glenn. "Thank You' Blows a Lot of Smoke, but Satire Suffers." Rev. of Thank You for Smoking, dir. Jason Reitman. Los Angeles Daily News 16 Mar. 2006. 7 Mar. 2007 <http://www.dailynews.com/filmreviews/ci_3609393>.

Zacharek, Stephanie. "'Thank You for Smoking.'" Rev. of Thank You for Smoking, dir. Jason Reitman. www.salon.com 17 Mar. 2006. 7 Mar. 2007 <http://www.salon.com/ent/movies/review/2006/03/17/smoking/?source=CP=IMD>.

What do you think of Alex's paper? Does it work well? Does he have a clear thesis, an objective summary, supporting evidence? Yes. Does he discuss weaknesses in the film before discussing strengths? Yes. Is he fair-minded? Yes. Does he use too many quotes? No. He uses quotes from his expert reviewers to support or challenge his arguments. He is careful to use signal phrases to introduce each reviewer, and he discusses each quote. He also provides a clear Works Cited section.

Here is another student review about a comedy she finds meaningful.

## A Lighthearted Film with Some Depth

### *Sol Cortez*

Fools Rush In (1997), directed by Andy Tennant, focuses on the hardships that come when opposites fall in love. The film fits into the standard romantic comedy model of two people going through a series of ordeals to discover and defend their union. There are critics who praise the film for its lightheartedness, who dismiss it for lack of credibility, and who find a deep message within it. Overall, it is a worthwhile film that makes you feel good as you watch the two characters overcome their differences for true love.

The story introduces Alex Whitman—played by Matthew Perry—a New York club builder who lives by the rules. He is sent to Las Vegas to oversee a construction site and meets Isabel Fuentes, played by Selma Hayak. She is a free spirited Mexican-American who believes that things happen for a reason. Alex and Isabel immediately connect for one night and unleash their feelings. Alex does not hear from Isabel for another three months until she announces that she is pregnant with his child. After meeting her family, Alex decides that he wants to marry Isabel; without contemplating their action, they get married in a Las Vegas chapel. Soon Isabel and Alex realize that there is more to marriage than just crazy love. Their cultural differences are great and they argue about the future religion of their baby. Their outlook about the meaning of family is even different. Lies, misunderstandings, and fears separate them. However, at the end Alex and Isabel learn that true love lies in understanding and accepting each other's differences. The birth of their baby and their second wedding at the Grand Canyon with their families present conclude the movie. They live happily ever after.

Roger Ebert, of the <u>Chicago Sun-Times</u>, sees value in the film's ability to approach interracial marriages in a lighthearted way. Even though the critic classifies the film as a romance cliché, he acknowledges that it portrays a reality:

> Yes, the movie is a cornball romance. Yes, it manufactures a lot of standard plot twists. But there is also a level of observation and human comedy here; the movie sees how its two cultures are different and yet share so many of the same values, and in Perry and Hayak it finds a chemistry that isn't immediately apparent. . . . In "Fools Rush In," they are opposite, they do attract, and somehow in the middle of the formulaic comedy there is the touch of truth.

Ebert appreciates the message that although Alex and Isabel know that the marriage between them is crazy, they understand that sometimes the best components in life do not make sense but just feel right in the heart. The humorous interaction between the opposite groups shows a lighthearted approach, suggesting that interracial relationships do not have to be as tense as most people view them.

The moral message that love means accepting each other's differences is the greatest quality of the movie. Even though Alex and Isabel find true love with each other, the problems they face are produced from their fear of sacrificing their individual lives. Alex has a life in New York: the city lights, exciting events, and life in the fast lane. Isabel lives in Las Vegas but has the freedom to travel to Mexico when she desires. Her life is free-spirited and laid back, driven by the beauty of the Grand Canyon and fate. Janet Maslin, of the <u>New York Times</u>, questions the credibility of whether a relationship between such different people can work: "But the film never gets past the unlikelihood that its characters have much chance of living happily ever after. Or of finding real heat or humor along the way." Maslin misses the central theme of the movie. It was Alex's and Isabel's differences that attracted them and what will keep them together. The film depicts how people are essentially the same even though they grow up in different ways. Alex and Isabel look at life differently but they seek the same true love and cannot see their lives without each other. Because they are different they complement each other, demonstrating that their differences make up the best component of their relationship.

In most critical reviews of <u>Fools Rush In</u> one can often read about the plot's romantic corniness and the actors' comical performances. Also, many viewers have trouble seeing past the film's central message of love. However, J. Bottum, quoted in an article by Richard J. Neuhaus, in <u>First Things: A Monthly Journal of Religion and Public Life</u>, recognizes the film's deeper pro-life argument. Bottum claims the movie has a strong anti-abortion message. The main reason Isabel goes to see Alex after their one-night stand is because she is pregnant. She informs Alex of this, and even though he is taken back they never consider aborting the pregnancy. Bottum points out the film's subtle way of promoting a "pro-life" message:

> Whether or not the director and the screenwriter intended it, Fools Rush In is astonishingly anti-abortion a modern film. Completely absent are the slogans of the pro-life movement, but present is the truth about how most people actually think when they're not talking abstractly about abortion. Alex falls back in love with his wife when he hears the infant's heartbeat, while Isabel's obstetrician casually asks if they want an ultrasound printout as "the first picture of your baby." (14)

Finding a review of this movie that shares this deeper point is surprising and illuminating. I have seen the movie many times but before now have not viewed the film in this light. This review challenges other reviews that classify <u>Fools Rush In</u> as a typical, unoriginal romance movie.

A movie can be interpreted in many ways. The critics I discussed varied in opinion: Ebert enjoyed its true love plot, Maslin found it hard to believe, and Bottum found a message other than love. Despite these views about <u>Fools Rush In</u>, the movie is humorous and the actors display great chemistry with each other. By the end of the movie you end up with a smile, and it is a film the whole family can watch. The film portrays a story about how love is not something that needs to make sense, but something that feels right.

Works Cited

Ebert, Roger. "Fools Rush In." Rev. of <u>Fools Rush In</u>, dir. Andy Tennant. <u>Chicago Sun-Times</u> 14 Feb.
    1997. 18 Feb. 2003 <http://wwwsuntimes.com/ebert/ebert_reviews/1997/02/021404.html>.

Maslin, Janet. "Fools Rush In." Rev. of <u>Fools Rush In</u>, dir. Andy Tennant. <u>New York Times</u> 14 Feb.
    1997. 18 Feb. 2003 <http://www.nytimes.com/library/film/fools-film-review.html>.

Neuhaus, J. Richard. "A Woman's Choice." Rev. of <u>Fools Rush In</u>, dir. Andy Tennant. <u>First Things:</u>
    <u>A Monthly Journal of Religion and Public Life</u> 79(1998): 69+. Jan. 1998. 18 Feb. 2003
    <http://www.firstthings.com/ftissues/ft9801/public.html#Woman's>.

Sol's review works well. She has a clear thesis, an objective summary, and supporting evidence. Her organization is different from Alex's. She analyzes the film's lighthearted approach to interracial marriage (using Ebert for support), the moral message that one critic does not find credible (Maslin), and the film's pro-life message (using Bottum, quoted in Neuhaus, for support). Sol is careful to use signal phrases to introduce each reviewer, and she discusses each quote. She also provides a clear Works Cited section.

# Exploring Style

*Style is ethos.*

Which is more important: *What* you say or *how* you say it? This is a false dilemma: the issue is not either/or. *Both* what you say and how you say it are important. They are inseparable. *How you say your message is part of what you say.* Each time you write, your style creates your appeals to logos, pathos, and ethos. Your style creates your voice—the sound of your personality. Style gives your writing credibility—or not—depending on how well you can manage your stylistic choices.

## PRESENTING YOURSELF IN E-MAIL

If it is true that style is ethos, then the way you present yourself in e-mail messages reflects your character. Ordinarily this is not a problem when you correspond with close friends. But it is a problem when you correspond with teachers, employers, or anyone else with whom you want to make or maintain a good impression.

Here is a series of e-mails between a teacher and his student. Notice the way the student presents herself through her use of words, sentences, and grammar.

---

**From Julie:** Thank you for getting back to me I cant believe that I answered only 9 of the questions right. I felt like I did better then that. I will have the revisions of papers 3 and 4 at class, I do want to meet with you though for the film paper. You said I didnt do the assignment right, and I would like some information on how to make it better. Monday is my most hectic day so any other day besides that works for me, Wednesday is good for me!

**From Professor Holden:** Julie, let's meet on Wednesday before class. (May I point out that your e-mail contains several serious problems with grammar such as run-on sentences, comma splices, and missing apostrophes for contractions? Should these problems matter?)

**From Julie:** Sorry, whenever I write an email I dont really look at my grammer. I always write what is on my head, rather then spending so much time on getting a little message out. I will try to work on it for you.

---

**From Professor Holden:** I was reluctant to mention it, Julie. This grammar business does matter: you can develop stronger writing habits if you proofread and edit your e-mails. Even in this one (and again I'm reluctant to point this out, but being your English teacher I feel I should), you're missing an apostrophe in "don't"; you misspell "grammar"; and you use "then" rather than "than." What can I do to help you proofread your e-mails better?

What do you think? Is Professor Holden being too picky? Is Julie being too lazy to proofread her messages and revise? Professor Holden tries not to offend his student; he hesitates to bring up the problem of Julie's poor grammar in e-mails. Should he be more blunt? "Julie, you should be ashamed of yourself. Don't bother to send me any e-mail unless you make sure it is carefully proofread and edited. If you don't respect me as your teacher here, you should drop this course—and soon." Using shame as a method to help students is not usually productive—is it?

The way you write depends on your situation, audience, and purpose. If you want to write without regard to rules of grammar with your friends, so be it: if you all play by these rules, no harm done. But whenever you write to a teacher or an employer, use your most carefully proofread language. It's important for you not to lose credibility. This doesn't mean you can't use an informal voice. Let your writing sound like you, but be careful to present yourself well when your writing situation and audience call for it.

## TOOLS OF STYLE

You can use what you've learned in these Interchapters to explore—analyze and evaluate—the style of other writers.

When you explore a writer's style, select what you consider the writer's dominant tools of style. Here is a list of stylistic tools presented in previous Interchapters.

## TOOLS OF STYLE

**Patterns of Diction**

Monosyllabic (strings of one-syllable words for emphasis) or multisyllabic

Literal or figurative—metaphors and similes

Specific or general

Concrete or abstract

Precise words (such as strong or surprising verbs)

**Patterns of Repetition in Diction**

Key words

Phrases

Alliteration

**Patterns of Punctuation**

Semicolons

Colons

Dashes

Italics (or underlining)

Parentheses

**Patterns of Sentences**

Short

Compound (coordination)

Complex (subordination)

Intentional sentence fragments

Antithesis

Balanced

Loose

Periodic

Varying sentence beginnings (-ing phrases, -ed or -en phrases, -to phrases)

**Patterns of Repetition with Sentences**

Parallelism (-ing phrases, -to phrases, -of phrases)

Anaphora

Epistrophe

Using threes in sentences

Knowing these tools of style will help you write an essay in which you analyze and evaluate any writer's style.

## GUIDELINES FOR WRITING AN ESSAY TO EXPLORE STYLE

1. When you analyze and evaluate a writer's style, use this pattern of organization for your essay:

   A. Introduce the essay and state your thesis about the writer's style.

   B. Summarize the selection (essay or speech) objectively to show readers you understand it. Use present tense in your summary.

*Continued . . .*

C. Analyze and evaluate a few tools of style the writer uses. Support your analysis with reasons, examples, and details—and direct quotations to illustrate your points. Use present tense: "King writes" rather than "King wrote."

D. Conclude and restate your thesis.

2. Choose patterns of style to analyze and evaluate that stand out for you, that you can explain by citing at least three examples to show what you mean. Don't argue that a writer uses a lot of antithesis if you find only one example of it.

3. Ask yourself questions when you discuss an element of style, such as these:

Why does King use such an extraordinarily long sentence in his paragraph?

Why does Louise Erdrich use periodic sentences when she describes birth?

Why does Rick Reilly use anaphora so much in his <u>Sports Illustrated</u> essay?

Ask yourself: How does a particular tool of style contribute to the writer's meaning (thesis and support); to the writer's appeals of logos, pathos, or ethos; and to the writer's voice and tone? If you can't find any significant answers, look for another element of style to analyze. Write about whatever you find most interesting that sheds light on relationships between meaning and style.

4. When you analyze and evaluate elements of style, take up one element at a time. You may need to use more than a single paragraph for each element. Try to build up to what you consider is the most important element.

5. Give *examples* of elements of style to show what you mean: quote from the selection. If you quote a passage of fewer than four lines, incorporate it within a paragraph of yours. If you use a long quote—more than four lines—set it off: indent it 10 spaces (two tabs) on the left side and double space.

6. When you refer to words or letters, italicize them:

E.B. White repeats the word *same* five times within one sentence.

You can hear the long *o* sound in the words *home* and *soul*.

7. When you quote, be responsible and accurate. Proofread each quote carefully.

8. The MLA style requires that you cite page numbers for material you quote; these should appear in parentheses before the sentence period. For example,

Orwell argues that "ready-made phrases . . . think your thoughts for you" (405).

See Chapter 9 for additional rules about this kind of "in-text" documentation.

9. If you write about a whole essay or speech (not an excerpt), cite its source at the end of your paper. This need not be on a separate page—below your conclusion space down four spaces and put the Work Cited entry there. For information on how to do Works Cited, see Chapter 9 on documentation.

## EXPLORING THE STYLE OF A PASSAGE

The purpose of stylistic analysis is to show that style is a part of meaning. They are inseparable, like the singer and the song.

## ACTIVITY **1**

To practice analyzing and evaluating style, read the following paragraph by Martin Luther King Jr. from his "Letter from Birmingham Jail" written on April 16, 1963. In this long and famous letter King writes to fellow clergymen who are white. After you've examined King's paragraph, write a short essay (1 to 2 pages) in which you present and support a clearly stated thesis about King's long periodic sentence. In your analysis, consider addressing one or more of these questions: Why is the sentence effective? What does King do within the sentence to give it power? How does the style of King's periodic sentence help express his meaning and his appeals to logos, pathos, or ethos? How does it help express his voice and tone (his attitude toward his audience, subject, and self)? To help you in your analysis and evaluation, look for any patterns of diction and sentence tools presented in the Interchapters of this book—see the list of Tools of Style. Also, consider typing and annotating the selection to help you notice more.

We have waited for more than 340 years for our constitutional and God-given rights. The nations of Asia and Africa are moving with jetlike speed toward gaining political independence, but we still creep at horse-and-buggy pace toward gaining a cup of coffee at a lunch counter. Perhaps it is easy for those who have never felt the stinging darts of segregation to say, "Wait." But when you have seen vicious mobs lynch your mothers and fathers at will and drown your sisters and brothers at whim; when you have seen hate-filled policemen curse, kick and even kill your black brothers and sisters; when you see the vast majority of your twenty million Negro brothers smothering in an airtight cage of poverty in the midst of an affluent society; when you suddenly find your tongue twisted and your speech stammering as you seek to explain to your six-year-old daughter why she can't go to the public amusement park that has just been advertised on television, and see tears welling up in her eyes when she is told that Funtown is closed to colored children, and see ominous clouds of inferiority beginning to form in her little mental sky, and see her beginning to distort her personality by developing an unconscious bitterness toward white people; when you have to concoct an answer for a five-year-old son who is asking: "Daddy, why do white people treat colored people so mean?"; when you take a cross-country drive and find it necessary to sleep night after night in the uncomfortable corners of your automobile because no motel will accept you; when you are humiliated day in and day out by nagging signs reading "white" and "colored"; when your first name becomes "nigger," your middle name becomes "boy" (however old you are) and your last name becomes "John," and your wife and mother are never given the respected title "Mrs."; when you are harried by day and haunted by night by the fact that you are a Negro, living constantly at tiptoe stance, never quite knowing what to expect next, and are plagued with inner fears and outer resentments; when you are forever fighting a degenerating sense of "nobodiness"—then you will understand why we find it so difficult to wait. There comes a time when the cup of endurance runs over, and men are no longer willing to be plunged into the abyss of despair. I hope, sirs, you can understand our legitimate and unavoidable impatience. ▬

## ACTIVITY 2

For a stylistic challenge, try to write a long periodic sentence, using King's sentence as a model. Bring it to class to share. Here is an example from student Megan Crawford:

When you have experienced the mix of passion and pain that comes from being so far away from the one who has your heart; when you have spent an entire day crying and wishing there was no such thing as college or responsibility; when you have felt overwhelming hatred towards complete strangers when you see them walking down the street, fingers intertwined, stealing kisses as they pass; when you have found yourself driving 150 miles for a mere five hours together; when you live for the weekends you see each other because you know that for 48 amazing hours you will be inseparable; when you don't even bother to put on makeup in the morning because, really, you have no one around to impress; when you find yourself unable to concentrate in math class because all of a sudden you miss him so much that it hurts; when the little things—a ticket stub, a cell phone ring, a certain type of cologne—remind you of him during the most inconvenient times; when you give yourself a stiff neck taking a second look at anyone who looks even vaguely similar, just on the small chance that maybe, just this once, he has come to surprise you; when you cherish the memories of previous weekends together, of days spent forsaking all other human contact, walking hand in hand around campus and waking up early to watch him as he sleeps on the futon next to you; when you've memorized everything about him—his face, his walk, the sound he makes when he breathes— in the desperate hope that these features will stay with you when you're apart; when you lock your dorm room, telling your friends that you want to take a nap, when really you just want to sneak in a phone call between classes; when the first thing you hear in the morning and the last thing you hear at night had better be his voice or else the entire day goes awry; when you find yourself staring at pictures and old letters, daydreaming rather than studying; when you know the emotion of feeling so loved, yet so incredibly alone, all at the same time—then you will understand what it is like to be in a long-distance relationship. ▬

## ACTIVITY 3

For further practice analyzing and evaluating style, read the following passage by Louise Erdrich from her book *The Blue Jay's Dance*. Then write a short essay (2 to 3 pages) in which you present and support a clearly stated thesis about her style. Explain how two or three of her stylistic choices help create her meaning, her appeals to logos, pathos, or ethos, or her voice and tone (her attitude toward her audience, subject, and self). Look for any patterns of diction and sentence tools presented in the Interchapters of this book—see Tools of Style. Consider typing and annotating the selection to help you notice more.

> Rocking, breathing, groaning, mouthing circles of distress, laughing, whistling, pounding, wavering, digging, pulling, pushing—labor is the most involuntary work we do. My body gallops to these rhythms. I'm along for the ride, at times in some control and at others dragged along as if foot-caught in a stirrup. I don't have much to do at first but breathe, accept ice chips, make jokes—in fear and pain my family makes jokes, that's how we deal with what we can't change, how we show our courage.
>
> Even though I am a writer and have practiced my craft for years, and have experienced two natural childbirths and an epidural-assisted childbirth, I find women's labor extremely difficult to describe. In the first place, there are all sorts of labor and no "correct" way to do it. I bow to the power and grandeur of those who insist on natural childbirth, but I find the pieties that often attend the process irritating. I am all for pain relief or caesareans when women want and need these procedures. Enduring pain in itself doesn't make one a better person, though if your mind is prepared, pain of this sort—a meaningful and determined pain based on ardor and potential joy—can be deeply instructive, can change your life. . . .
>
> The first part of labor feels, to me anyway, like dance exercises—slow stretches that become only slightly painful as a muscle is pulled to its limit. After each contraction, the feeling subsides. The contractions move in longer waves, one after another, closer and closer together until a sea of physical sensation washes and then crashes over. In the beginning I breathe in concentration, watching Michael's eyes [her husband]. I feel myself slip beneath the waves as they roar over, cresting just above my head. I duck every time the contraction peaks. As the hours pass and one wave builds on another there are times the undertow grabs me. I struggle, slammed to the bottom, unable to gather the force of nerve for the next. Thrown down, I rely on animal fierceness, swim back, surface, breathe, and try to stay open, willing. Staying open and willing is difficult. Very often in labor one must fight the instinct to resist pain and instead embrace it, move toward it, work with what hurts the most.
>
> The waves come faster. Charlotte [a midwife] asks me to keep breathing *yes, yes.* To say yes instead of shuddering in refusal. Whether I am standing on the earth or not, whether I am moored to the dock, whether I remember who I am, whether I am mentally prepared, whether I am going to float beneath or ride above, the waves pound in. At shorter intervals, crazy now, electric, in storms, they wash. Sometimes I'm gone. I've poured myself into some deeper fissure below the sea only to be dragged forth, hair streaming. During transition, as the baby is ready to be pushed out into life, the waves are no longer made of water, but neons so brilliant I gasp in shock and flourish my arms, letting the colors explode from my fingertips in banners, in ribbons, in iridescent trails—of pain, it is true, unendurable sometimes, and yet we do endure. ▬

## EXPLORING THE STYLE OF AN ESSAY OR A SPEECH

In an essay or a speech, you can examine more fully relationships between a writer's meaning and style, between what is expressed and how it is expressed.

## ACTIVITY 4

Writing an essay analyzing and evaluating an essay or speech is challenging. It is important for you to choose a text that you enjoy and find worthwhile. The end of this Interchapter contains Essays for Exploration. You may choose one of those three. Or you may choose to explore one of the essays you have already read in this book, such as any of the My Turn essays in Chapter 1, essays on controversial issues in Chapter 2, or essays at the end of Chapter 3.

For your analysis, follow the Guidelines for Writing an Essay to Explore Style presented earlier. Your paper should be 3 to 6 pages long. Choose one of these options:

1. Explain how three of a writer's stylistic choices help create the meaning of his or her essay or speech. (See the student paper, "Analyzing Rhetoric with a Swoosh.")
2. Explain how three of a writer's stylistic choices help create the writer's appeals to logos, pathos, and ethos.
3. Explain how three of a writer's stylistic choices help create the writer's voice and tone (attitude toward audience, subject, and self).

Here are suggestions for finding your own essay or speech to analyze:

1. Look at a magazine you like to read and try to find an essay there. If you read <u>Sports Illustrated</u>, look for an essay by Rick Reilly.
2. Consider browsing through issues of <u>Vital Speeches of the Day</u> in a library. Look for a speech delivered by a recent presidential candidate or by someone at a recent Democratic or Republication national convention.
3. Browse the Internet looking for commencement addresses. Find one you like and analyze it. <u>Newsweek</u> columnist Anna Quindlen delivered an address at Mount Holyoke College on May 23, 1999 that has become well known. See it at <http://www.mtholyoke.edu/offices/comm/oped/Quindlen.shtml>. Quindlen has delivered several commencement addresses. To see what she said at Barnard College in 2005, go to <http://www.beliefnet.com/story/167/story_16749.html>. Or consider reading what Steve Jobs, CEO of Apple Computer, said in his address at Stanford University in 2005: <http://news-service.stanford.edu/news/2005/june15/jobs-061505.html>.

Here is an essay, "The Swooshification of the World," by <u>Sports Illustrated</u> columnist Rick Reilly. After you read it, read the student analysis of it. This analysis provides you with a model to help you with your own paper.

## The Swooshification of the World

### Rick Reilly

*Cracking in the face of a marketing behemoth, the author goes loco over a logo*

I must get more Swoosh in my life. More, more, more. It's not enough to have the Swoosh on every jersey and scoreboard and dugout roof. It's not enough that the Swoosh is on basketballs, footballs, soccer balls and volleyballs. It's not enough that the Swoosh is slapped all over more than 40 universities, eight NFL teams, six NHL teams (two more next season) and five Major League Soccer teams.

I want the eye black under baseball and football players' eyes to take the form of a Swoosh. I want hockey sticks, nine-irons and yardage markers to be made in the shape of a Swoosh. I want to know who's in the on-deck Swoosh. I want to watch the Swoosh Channel. I want Swoosh condoms (Just Do It).

It's not enough that the Swoosh is on Michael Jordan's beret and Mary Pierce's headband and Gabrielle Reece's beach volleyball top. It's not enough that the center on the Hawaii basketball team had his sideburns shaped into Swooshes. I want a Swoosh tattoo. I want a Swoosh lasered onto my retinas. I want to name my son Swoosh. (If it's a girl, Swooshie.)

I want these things because the Swoosh is the most ubiquitous symbol in sports history. The Swoosh is so huge that the name of the company that goes with the Swoosh doesn't even appear anymore. In the ads, on the shoes, even on the company letterhead, all you get is the Swoosh, and you just *know*. Try that with Keds, pal.

Happiness is a warm Swoosh. Do you see the way it *swooshes* upward, a snappy little check mark, letting you know that everything in your life is A-O.K.? It's airy, windswept, uplifting. It's the delighted little final stroke your pen makes when endorsing the biggest check of your life.

But there is not enough of it in our lives yet. From here on in, instead of H-O-R-S-E, I want kids to play S-W-O-O-S-H. I want skis to go *Swoosh!* I want to get the autograph of Sheryl Swoosh.

Woe to you who underestimate the Swoosh. Tiger Woods, the coolest athlete on Planet Swoosh, has the Swoosh on the front of his hat and the side of his hat and the back of his hat and on his turtleneck and on his shirt and on his sweater and on his vest and on his pants and on his socks and on his shoes. But when Woods arrived in Thailand two weeks ago, he found that his luggage had been misplaced, and he had to play a program without his usual complement of Swooshes. He lasted just 13 holes before heat and exhaustion got to him. Don't you see? The Swoosh is the source of all his powers!

I wasn't always like this. I used to rage against the Swoosh. "Why?" I yelped at strangers. "Why must the Swoosh run the world?" Why, I asked, after almost 30 years, did the Denver Broncos let the Swoosh people redesign the team's uniforms and logo so that they were suddenly uglier than the jerseys of a meat-market softball team? I cried out against the subliminal Swooshing all over the new Denver uniform.

"Don't you see it?" I railed, pointing to the Broncos' new logo. "The horse's nostril! It's a Swoosh!"

In protest I determined to go an entire day without getting Swooshed. I made it 14 minutes, just past my Eggo, when my wife came down in her Swoosh sports bra. Something snapped in me that morning. I gave in. You cannot fight the Swoosh.

I want my kids to attend the University of California at Swoosh. I want to get up in the morning and eat a big bowlful of chocolate Swooshios as part of a nutritionally balanced breakfast. I want to meet Carolyn Davidson. She's the graphic designer who, after graduating from Portland State in 1972, came up with the Swoosh for Phil Knight, Zeus of Swoosh, for $35. Thirty-five dollars! When she handed it to Knight, she remembers, he said, "I don't love it, but maybe it'll grow on me." Twenty-five years and a zillion dollars later, you think it's all right now, Phil? (Davidson, who in 1983 was given some Nike stock by Knight and who recently retired, says her second most famous work is the wallpaper she designed for a motel in Yakima, Wash.) Carolyn Davidson, stand up and take your place in world history!

Some experts believe the Swoosh is better known than the McDonald's golden arches. Nine national soccer teams, including Brazil's, wear the Swoosh. The Tour de France leader wears the Swoosh. When the U.S. played Russia in hockey's recent World Cup, both teams were wearing the Swoosh.

The Swoosh is like Jell-O: There's always room for the Swoosh. I want Swoosh on the periodic table of the elements, right next to boron. I want Swoosh to be the 27th letter of the alphabet. I want to order raw eel at a Swooshi bar.

Do not fight it, brothers and sisters. Trust in the Swoosh. The Swoosh is good and powerful. If our government leaders would only let it, the Swoosh could bail us out of this deficit thing like *that*. Of course, we would have to make a few small concessions.

*Al, does the presidential seal look different to you?*

## Analyzing Style with a Swoosh

### Gavin McMacken

In his <u>Sports Illustrated</u> essay, "The Swooshification of the World," published February 24, 1997, Rick Reilly questions the overuse of Nike's Swoosh image—a small logo generating such big business it's almost overtaking the world. Reilly's exaggerated style reflects Nike's exaggerated marketing campaign for the Swoosh to appear practically everywhere. Reilly's use of italics, simple yet creative diction, and anaphora enable him to create a playfully ironic voice to question the excess of the Nike Swoosh.

Reilly believes the Nike Swoosh logo has grown out of control not only in the world of sports but in the whole world. He repeatedly says he wants to see more Swooshes than there already are. Citing various facts, he claims "it's not enough" that many universities and professional sporting teams use the logo. He wants the image to enter his personal life more. The Swoosh is so omnipresent that Nike doesn't need to use its Nike name. Reilly even warns that the Swoosh has supernatural power: Tiger Woods is a great golfer because he wears so many Swooshes. Although Reilly used to question the proliferation of the Swoosh, he no longer fights it. He wants more of it. He celebrates the graphic designer who created it for $35 in 1972. After citing some more facts about how teams around the world use the Swoosh, Reilly concludes by telling readers to worship the logo because it "is good and powerful." It could also, he suggests, solve our country's deficit problem—and even help run our country.

Reilly's voice is playfully ironic in this essay. He sounds obsessed with the logo to show how our country is obsessed with it. Although he keeps saying he wants more Swoosh, he does not think the logo "is good." He really does not want "a Swoosh lasered onto [his] retinas." He does not want to name his child Swoosh. He does not want "Swoosh condoms." What he wants is for readers to wake up and stop buying into the Swoosh craze. Because his examples are often extreme and foolish, Reilly succeeds in making readers think more about Nike's advertising blitz. Through his playful irony, he appeals to pathos and logos; he helps readers laugh and think. Because he does this so well, readers appreciate Reilly's ethos: he is clever yet insightful, and he uses style to reinforce his sense.

Reilly's use of italics contributes to his voice. They help readers hear his voice: "Do you see the way it *swooshes* upward . . . ?" "I want skis to go *Swoosh*!" "The Swoosh could bail us out of this deficit thing like *that*." These italics help Reilly exaggerate his point about Swooshification. In one paragraph in which he drops his persona and seems somewhat serious, Reilly writes, "The Swoosh is so huge that the name of the company that goes with the Swoosh doesn't even appear anymore. In the ads, on the shoes, even on the company letterhead, all you get is the Swoosh, and you just *know*." The word *know* resonates, and we know what Reilly means. In addition, the last sentence is completely italicized: *"Al, does the presidential seal look different to you?"* That Reilly italicizes his last sentence is noteworthy because he raises a question that seems both absurd yet reasonable: Is Nike so rich it could influence or buy the federal government?

Reilly's use of simple yet creative diction is also effective. Overall Reilly's diction is informal with easy words. Many are monosyllabic as seen in his first two sentences: "I must get more Swoosh in my life. More, more, more." These sentences begin the train of Reilly's exaggeration and playful irony. His heavy use of one-syllable words is fitting because the Swoosh itself is so simplistic in appearance. Throughout his essay Reilly uses eleven sentences containing all monosyllabic words and ten sentences containing all but one monosyllabic word such as "But there is not enough of it in our lives yet."

Reilly maximizes the monosyllabic *and* in the essay's longest sentence:

> Tiger Woods, the coolest athlete on Planet Swoosh, has the Swoosh on the front of his hat and the side of his hat and the back of his hat and on his turtleneck and on his shirt and on his sweater and on his vest and on his pants and on his socks and on his shoes.

The sentence contains 64 words, 57 of which are monosyllabic. That Reilly repeats *and* nine times is effective because the word makes the sentence sound slow and tired. The repetition reinforces Reilly's idea that the Swoosh is ridiculously everywhere—especially on star athletes like Tiger Woods whom millions of sports fans emulate.

Yet two important multisyllabic words resonate in the essay. The title contains the five syllable *Swooshification*. This complex yet playful word suggests Reilly's thesis that the Nike logo has grown out of control. The other word is *ubiquitous* used in this sentence: "I want these things because the Swoosh is the most ubiquitous symbol in sports history." Here Reilly drops his persona of a Swoosh-crazed guy. He's serious. *Ubiquitous* is a serious word, one that forces many readers to look at it twice and then possibly run for a dictionary. It means "seeming to be present everywhere at the same time" (Webster's New World). This intellectual word is perfect for describing the Swoosh, and it conveys Reilly's thesis.

Reilly's creative use of diction helps create his voice of playful irony. He says he wants to name his son Swoosh but "(If it's a girl, Swooshie.)" Making a pun on Cheerios, he says he wants to "eat a big bowlful of chocolate Swooshios." And he makes a pun on the word *boron*: "I want Swoosh on the periodic table of the elements right next to boron." This word works well because it sounds like *boring* or *bore on*: Reilly is bored with the Swoosh and thinks we all should be. Reilly's use of assonance (repetition of vowel sounds) also contributes to his playful voice. Notice the long *u* sound he repeats three times in this sentence: "Woe to *you* who underestimate the Sw*oo*sh." The assonance reinforces his exaggeration that the Swoosh has magical power. Later he refers to Phil Knight who founded Nike as the "Zeus of Swoosh," again playing on the long *u* vowel. Reilly uses some alliteration as well, playing on *s* sounds: "It's not enough that the center on the Hawaii basketball team had his *s*ideburns *s*haped into *S*wooshes." "I want to get the autograph of *S*heryl *S*woosh" and "I cried out against the *s*ubliminal *S*wooshing all over the new Denver uniform." Reilly doesn't overuse these sound devices; he doesn't need to because of his strong use of anaphora through the essay.

Reilly's use of anaphora is extreme but highly effective. By repeating the same beginning words in many sentences, he shows how obsessed he and the country are about the Swoosh. He uses two forms of anaphora. One is "It's not enough":

> It's not enough to have the Swoosh on every jersey and scoreboard and dugout roof. It's not enough that the Swoosh is on basketballs, footballs, soccer balls and volleyballs. It's not enough that the Swoosh is slapped all over more than 40 universities, eight NFL teams, six NHL teams (two more next season) and five Major League Soccer teams.

This repetition at the beginning of the essay enables Reilly to show his exaggerated obsession—the Swoosh is not "on every jersey and scoreboard and dugout roof," although it may seem like it. The three repetitions echo and prepare readers for his theme: the endless repetition of the Swoosh logo. He uses the same anaphora in two more sentences in paragraph three.

Reilly uses his second form of anaphora "I want" seventeen times throughout the essay. This pattern helps create Reilly's playfully ironic voice:

> I want the eye black under baseball and football players' eyes to take the form of a Swoosh. I want hockey sticks, nine-irons and yardage markers to be made in the shape of a Swoosh. I want to know who's in the on-deck Swoosh. I want to watch the Swoosh Channel. I want Swoosh condoms (Just Do It).

Reilly not only wants to see more Swoosh in the world of sports but also in his personal world: "I want a Swoosh tattoo. I want a Swoosh lasered onto my retinas. I want to name my son Swoosh." Toward the end of the essay his exaggeration reaches climactic heights: "I want Swoosh on the periodic table of the elements, right next to boron. I want Swoosh to be the 27th letter of the alphabet." The logo has taken over Reilly's imagination. He has seen it so often that he obsessively wants to see it more.

It has taken over the sports world. By repeating that he wants to see more of it, he causes readers to wonder if the logo is good to see at all.

Reilly's anaphora serves two main purposes. One, the Swoosh exists for people to buy Nike products. Nike wants consumers to say, "I want that baseball cap with the Swoosh." Reilly's refrain of "I want" echoes this. Two, the anaphora skillfully voices Reilly's exaggerated obsession—and the obsession at large in our culture. This is effective because after a while he sounds like a child: the Swoosh has become something to nurse on, which feeds us. But it's not nutritious, Reilly implies; rather, it's full of empty calories that cost consumers too much money. Without anaphora, the essay—and Reilly's voice—would lose much of its power.

"The Swooshification of the World" is a hole-in-one, a three-pointer basket, a grand-slam essay. To achieve his playfully ironic voice, Reilly uses italics, simple yet creative diction, and anaphora. Although his essay is fun to read, he raises a serious question: when is enough Swoosh enough? He wants readers to think about whether the Swoosh logo is good for sports and for people who keep buying Nike products. Reilly cleverly implies his answer: It's not good. It's boring. It's spinning out of control. Through his style, Reilly communicates clearly. Maybe I'll subscribe to Sports Illustrated so I can read more Reilly.

Work Cited

Reilly, Rick. "The Swooshification of the World." Sports Illustrated 24 Feb. 1997: 78.

## ESSAYS FOR EXPLORATION

### The Abiding Legacy of My Mother—the Listener

*Ellen Goodman*

Long, long ago, I wrote a column describing my mother this way: "My mother is someone who will listen to your problems until you are bored with them."

*Reader's Digest* wanted to use it and a fact-checker called me for my mother's telephone number. She actually wanted to ask my mother whether it was true.

I told this tale for years as a funny story about fact-checkers. But now, of course, I know it was really a story about my mother. About Edith Weinstein Holtz, who died last month at age 92, just two days after Thanksgiving, on what would have been the 70th anniversary of her wedding.

It had been a long, long time since my mother was able to listen to my problems. Dementia, that terrible thief, stole her memory and then her personality, one piece at a time. Obituaries rarely list dementia as a cause of death. But she was a victim of its burglary until, at last, she let go of food, of fear, of need, of life.

My mother, born before suffrage, before World War I and World War II, before the feminine mystique and feminism, taught me everything I know of family values.

She taught me that family came first. She taught me to make cheesecake and keep peace. She taught me that a real home was a place where you were welcome for Sunday brunch and conversation. She taught me to accept your children's life choices without criticism and with confidence in their judgment. She taught me patience—although I am afraid I never passed the finals in that class.

When my sister and I went to the funeral home, the director asked us how to list her "occupation." Together, we said, "homemaker." Making a home was all she ever wanted to do. My mother, beautiful and vulnerable, also taught us—not on purpose—the risk of having love as your only job.

When my father died, she was only 50. She didn't worry about how to live without this vital, funny, loving center of her life because, I found out later, she didn't think she would survive a year. She lived 42 more years.

I think my mother regarded "independence" as a synonym for "loneliness." She tried to create a second life. She tried school. She tried a job or two. She tried another marriage. Nothing really worked. But over these years she was also the one who nourished her granddaughters and nephews with peppermints and attention. She listened to their problems until they were bored with them.

Old age is not for sissies. My mother's long slow terrible decline lasted over a decade. There was the television she could no longer work and then the telephone. There were the small spiral notebooks whose pages were covered with names from a past she struggled to retain. One page listed her favorite movie star: Cary Grant. Another listed my father's best friend: Lou Novins.

In the last year, what mattered to my mother? The $3 faux pearl stud earrings, final artifacts of her femininity, bought by the dozen and lost by the dozen. The boxes of chocolate and the family photos. My mother never lost the taste for chocolate nor did she lose the smile with which she welcomed her family.

We were gathered for Thanksgiving weekend when she died. That would have mattered to her. It mattered to us. Together, we were able to rewind the tape to the days when our mother, aunt, grandmother, sister was our listener.

There is little that is harder in life than watching the slow disappearance of someone you love. Dementia is a contagious disease that spreads its suffering to anyone within the range of love. Millions of families have caught it. Ours is just one. And yet here, too, she taught us more than simply how to bear a burden.

Not long before her death, my daughter and I took my 3-year-old grandson to visit. We outfitted him with a bag of doughnuts to pass out to my mother and everyone on her floor. Though she no longer knew his name, she watched him with joy.

The next morning at a breakfast table covered with cereal and Play-Doh, he looked up and asked me, "Grandma, is your mommy going to die soon?"

Taken aback, I answered, "I'm afraid she is, Logan." He thought for a moment and said, "But, Grandma, then you won't have any mommy."

After the silence filled only with my tears, this little, little boy turned and said, "Grandma, when I grow up, I'll be your daddy."

So my mother's gift for family, my mother's talent for empathy, was passed down from one generation to the next and the next. It is her abiding legacy.

*Ellen Goodman is a columnist for the <u>Boston Globe</u>; her columns appear in more than 375 newspapers. In 1980, she was awarded the Pulitzer Prize for Distinguished Commentary.*

Work Cited

Goodman, Ellen. "The Abiding Legacy of My Mother—the Listener." <u>Boston Globe</u> 8 Dec. 2006: A21.

## Growing Old with Dave

### *Dave Barry*

Call me a wild and crazy guy if you want, but recently, on a whim, I decided to—Why not?—turn 48.

It's not so bad. Physically, the only serious problem I've noticed is that I can no longer read anything printed in letters smaller than Shaquille O'Neal. Also, to read a document, I have to hold it far from my face; more and more, I find myself holding documents—this is awkward on airplanes—with my feet. I can no longer read restaurant menus, so I fake it when the waiter comes around.

> **ME (pointing randomly):**  I'll have this.
>
> **WAITER:**  You'll have your napkin?
>
> **ME:**  I want that medium rare.

It's gotten so bad that I can't even read the words I'm typing into my computer right now. If my fingers were in a prankish mood, they could type an embarrassing message right in the middle of this sentence HE'S ALWAYS PUTTING US IN HIS NOSE and there is no way I'd be able to tell.

I suppose I should go see an eye doctor, but if you're 48, whenever you go to see any kind of doctor, he or she invariably decides to insert a lengthy medical item into your body until the far end of it reaches a different area code. Also, I am frankly fearful that the eye doctor will want me to wear reading glasses. I have a psychological hang-up about this, caused by the fact that, growing up, I wore eyeglasses for 70,000 years. And these were not just any eyeglasses: These were the El Dork-O model, the ones that come from the factory pre-broken with the white tape already wrapped around the nose part. As an adolescent, I was convinced that my glasses were one of the key reasons why the opposite sex did not find me attractive, the other key reason being that I did not reach puberty until approximately age thirty-five.

Anyway, other than being functionally blind at close range, I remain in superb physical condition for a man of my age who can no longer fit into any of his pants. I have definitely been gaining some weight in the midriff region, despite a rigorous diet regimen of drinking absolutely no beer whatsoever after I pass out. The only lower-body garments I own that still fit me comfortably are towels, which I find myself wearing in more and more social settings. I'm thinking of getting a black one for funerals.

Because of my midriff situation I was very pleased to read recently about the new Miracle Breakthrough Weight Loss Plan For Mice. In case you missed this, what happened was, scientists extracted a certain chemical ingredient found in thin mice, then injected it into fat mice; the fat mice lost 90 percent more weight than a control group of fat mice who were exposed only to Richard Simmons. The good news is that this same ingredient could produce dramatic weight loss in human beings; the bad news is that, before it becomes available, it must be approved by the Food and Drug Administration (motto: "We Haven't Even Approved Our Motto Yet"). So it's going to take a while. If you're overweight and desperate to try this miracle ingredient right away, my advice to you, as a medical professional, is to get hold of a thin mouse and eat it. It can't be any worse than tofu.

But getting back to aging: Aside from the vision thing, and the weight thing, and the need to take an afternoon nap almost immediately after I wake up, and the fact that random hairs—I'm talking about *long* hairs, the kind normally associated with Cher—occasionally erupt from deep inside my ears—aside from these minor problems, I am a superb physical specimen easily mistaken for Brad Pitt.

Not only that, but I have the mind of a steel trap. Of course very few things in the world—and I include the Home Shopping Network in this statement—are as stupid as a steel trap. What I'm saying is, I have definitely detected a decline in some of my mental facilities. For example, the other day I was in my office, trying to perform a fundamental journalistic function, namely, fill out an expense report, and I needed to divide 3 into a number that, if I recall correctly (which I don't; that's the problem), was $125.85, and *I couldn't remember how to do long division.* I knew I was supposed to put the 3 into the 12, then bring something down, but what? And how far down? And would I need the "cosine"?

I was starting to panic, when all of a sudden—this is why you youngsters should pay attention in math class—my old training came back to me, and I knew exactly what to do: Ask Doris. Doris works in my office, and she has a calculator. I guess I should start carrying one around, along with some kind of device that remembers (a) people's names, (b) where I put the remote control, and (c) what I had planned to do once I got into the kitchen other than stand around wearing a vacant expression normally associated with fish.

But so what if my memory isn't what it used to be? My other mental skills are as sharp as ever, and I'm confident that I can continue to do the kind of astute analysis and in-depth research that have characterized this column over the years, which is why today I want to assure you, the readers, that my advancing age will in no way change the fact that MAINLY HE SCRATCHES HIMSELF.

*Dave Barry is a syndicated humor columnist who worked for 25 years at the Miami Herald. In 1988 he won the Pulitzer Prize for Commentary. He has written more than 30 books.*

Work Cited

Barry, Dave. "Growing Old with Dave." <u>Dave Barry Is from Mars and Venus</u>. New York: Ballantine, 1997: 254–257.

Dr. Martin Luther King Jr. delivered the following classic speech at the Lincoln Memorial in Washington, D.C., on 28 August 1963, climaxing the civil rights demonstration of that day.

## I Have a Dream

### *Martin Luther King Jr.*

I am happy to join with you today in what will go down in history as the greatest demonstration for freedom in the history of our nation.

Five score years ago, a great American, in whose symbolic shadow we stand today, signed the Emancipation Proclamation. This momentous decree came as a great beacon light of hope to millions of Negro slaves, who had been seared in the flames of withering injustice. It came as a joyous daybreak to end the long night of their captivity.

But one hundred years later, the Negro still is not free. One hundred years later, the life of the Negro is still sadly crippled by the manacles of segregation and the chains of discrimination. One hundred years later, the Negro lives on a lonely island of poverty in the midst of a vast ocean of material prosperity. One hundred years later, the Negro still languishes in the corners of American society and finds himself in exile in his own land.

So we've come here today to dramatize a shameful condition. In a sense we've come to our nation's capital to cash a check. When the architects of our republic wrote the magnificent words of the Constitution and the Declaration of Independence, they were signing a promissory note to which every American was to fall heir. This note was the promise that all men—yes, black men as well as white men—would be guaranteed the unalienable rights of life, liberty, and the pursuit of happiness.

It is obvious today that America has defaulted on this promissory note insofar as her citizens of color are concerned. Instead of honoring this sacred obligation, America has given the Negro people a bad check, a check which has come back marked "insufficient funds." But we refuse to believe that the bank of justice is bankrupt. We refuse to believe that there are insufficient funds in the great vaults of opportunity of this nation. So we've come to cash this check—a check that will give us upon demand the riches of freedom and the security of justice.

We have also come to this hallowed spot to remind America of the fierce urgency of "now." This is no time to engage in the luxury of cooling off or to take the tranquilizing drug of gradualism. Now is the time to make real the promises of democracy. Now is the time to rise from the dark and desolate valley of segregation to the sunlit path of racial justice. Now is the time to lift our nation from the quicksand of racial injustice to the solid rock of brotherhood. Now is the time to make justice a reality for all of God's children.

It would be fatal for the nation to overlook the urgency of the moment. This sweltering summer of the Negro's legitimate discontent will not pass until there is an invigorating autumn of freedom and equality. Nineteen sixty-three is not an end, but a beginning. Those who hope that the Negro needed to blow off steam and will now be content will have a rude awakening if the nation returns to business as usual. There will be neither rest nor tranquility in America until the Negro is granted his citizenship rights. The whirlwinds of revolt will continue to shake the foundations of our nation until the bright day of justice emerges.

But there is something that I must say to my people who stand on the warm threshold which leads into the palace of justice. In the process of gaining our rightful place we must not be guilty of wrongful deeds. Let us not seek to satisfy our thirst for freedom by drinking from the cup of bitterness and hatred. We must forever conduct our struggle on the high plane of dignity and discipline. We must not allow our creative protest to degenerate into physical violence. Again and again we must rise to the majestic heights of meeting physical force with soul force. The marvelous new militancy which has engulfed the Negro community must not lead us to a distrust of all white people, for many of our white brothers, as evidenced by their presence here today, have come to realize that their destiny is tied up with our destiny. And they have come to realize that their freedom is inextricably bound to our freedom. We cannot walk alone.

As we walk, we must make the pledge that we shall always march ahead. We cannot turn back.

There are those who are asking the devotees of civil rights, "When will you be satisfied?" We can never be satisfied as long as the Negro is the victim of the unspeakable horrors of police brutality. We can never be satisfied as long as our bodies, heavy with the fatigue of travel, cannot gain lodging in the motels of the highways and the hotels of the cities. We cannot be satisfied as long as the Negro's basic mobility is from a smaller ghetto to a larger one. We can never be satisfied as long as our children are stripped of their selfhood and robbed of their dignity by signs stating "For Whites Only." We cannot be satisfied as long as a Negro in Mississippi cannot vote and a Negro in New York believes he has nothing for which to vote. No, no, we are not satisfied, and we will not be satisfied until justice rolls down like waters and righteousness like a mighty stream.

I am not unmindful that some of you have come here out of great trials and tribulations. Some of you have come fresh from narrow jail cells. Some of you have come from areas where your quest for freedom left you battered by the storms of persecution and staggered by the winds of police brutality. You have been veterans of creative suffering. Continue to work with the faith that unearned suffering is redemptive.

Go back to Mississippi, go back to Alabama, go back to South Carolina, go back to Georgia, go back to Louisiana, go back to the slums and ghettos of our northern cities, knowing that somehow this situation can and will be changed. Let us not wallow in the valley of despair.

I say to you today, my friends, even though we face the difficulties of today and tomorrow, I still have a dream. It is a dream deeply rooted in the American dream.

I have a dream that one day this nation will rise up and live out the true meaning of its creed: "We hold these truths to be self evident: that all men are created equal." I have a dream that one day on the red hills of Georgia the sons of former slaves and the sons of former slave owners will be able to sit down together at the table of brotherhood.

I have a dream that one day even the state of Mississippi, a state sweltering with the heat of injustice, sweltering with the heat of oppression, will be transformed into an oasis of freedom and justice. I have a dream that my four little children will one day live in a nation where they will not be judged by the color of their skin, but by the content of their character.

I have a dream today.

I have a dream that one day, down in Alabama, with its vicious racists, with its governor having his lips dripping with the words of interposition and nullification, one day right there in Alabama little black boys and black girls will be able to join hands with little white boys and white girls and walk together as sisters and brothers. I have a dream today.

I have a dream that one day every valley shall be exalted, every hill and mountain shall be made low, the rough places will be made plain and the crooked places will be made straight, and the glory of the Lord shall be revealed, and all flesh shall see it together.

This is our hope. This is the faith that I go back to the South with. With this faith we will be able to hew out of the mountain of despair a stone of hope. With this faith we will be able to transform the jangling discords of our nation into a beautiful symphony of brotherhood. With this faith we will be able to work together, to pray together, to struggle together, to go to jail together, to stand up for freedom together, knowing that we will be free one day.

And this will be the day . . . this will be the day when all God's children will be able to sing with new meaning. "My country, 'tis of thee, sweet land of liberty, of thee I sing. Land where my fathers died, land of the Pilgrims' pride, from every mountainside, let freedom ring." And if America is to be a great nation this must become true.

So let freedom ring! From the prodigious hilltops of New Hampshire, let freedom ring! From the mighty mountains of New York, let freedom ring, from the heightening Alleghenies of Pennsylvania!

Let freedom ring from the snowcapped Rockies of Colorado!

Let freedom ring from the curvaceous slopes of California. But not only that.

Let freedom ring from Stone Mountain of Georgia!

Let freedom ring from Lookout Mountain in Tennessee!

Let freedom ring from every hill and molehill of Mississippi. From every mountainside, let freedom ring, and when this happens . . . when we allow freedom to ring, when we let it ring from every village and every hamlet, from every state and every city . . . we will be able to speed up that day when all of God's children, black men and white men, Jews and Gentiles, Protestants and Catholics, will be able to join hands and sing in the words of the old Negro spiritual: "Free at last! Free at last! Thank God Almighty, we are free at last!"

Work Cited

King, Martin Luther, Jr. "I Have a Dream." Address Delivered at the March on Washington for Jobs and Freedom. Washington, D.C. 28 Aug. 1963.

## CHAPTER 6

# Critical Thinking About Poetry, Fiction, and Literary Nonfiction

*The poet's job is not to tell you what happened, but what happens: not what did take place, but the kind of thing that always does take place.* (Northrop Frye, The Educated Imagination)

Reading literature is a time-honored way to develop critical thinking skills. Because poems, stories, and literary essays are artistic, they resist easy analysis. Yet they are persuasive because they *move* you: literary writers create certain effects that cause you to think, to feel, and to consider ethical issues. These forms challenge you to question what you read. They require you to slow down and pay close attention to *meaning* (what is being expressed) and to *style* (how it is being expressed).

To read critically means to think while you read. The object is not how many facts you can remember but how well you can understand. Critical reading means

- *Analyzing*—noticing appeals and arguments, strategies of thinking, insights
- *Questioning*—wondering why, how, what if, so what?
- *Inferring*—drawing conclusions from what is suggested or implied in a text
- *Interpreting*—explaining your own understanding of a text
- *Evaluating*—judging the value or worth of a poem, story, essay, any text

In sum, critical reading matures your ability to think.

## READING AND WRITING ABOUT POETRY

Critical thinking helps you understand poetry. Let's begin with the following poem, "My Papa's Waltz":

## My Papa's Waltz

### *Theodore Roethke*

The whiskey on your breath
Could make a small boy dizzy;
But I hung on like death:
Such waltzing was not easy.

We romped until the pans
Slid from the kitchen shelf;
My mother's countenance
Could not unfrown itself.

The hand that held my wrist
Was battered on one knuckle;
At every step you missed
My right ear scraped a buckle.

You beat time on my head
With a palm caked hard by dirt,
Then waltzed me off to bed
Still clinging to your shirt.

## ACTIVITY 1

In your notebook write a paragraph in which you support one of the following interpretations of this poem: (1) "My Papa's Waltz" is a poem about connection and love.
(2) "My Papa's Waltz" is a poem about child abuse. (3) Offer another interpretation.
Try to cite details from the poem to support your points. ▪

Poetry—all art—challenges you *to feel and to think*. To think about what a poem
means, you need to pay attention to its words. Usually there is more than one way to
interpret a poem. An interpretation relies not directly on what a poem says but on
what it implies through its use of language. Critical thinkers should be able to explain their interpretations. This does not mean, however, that there are right and
wrong interpretations—only reasonable and not so reasonable ones, depending on
your evidence.

You don't need to know a lot about reading poetry to enjoy Roethke's poem. "My
Papa's Waltz" is a favorite in American literature. The image of father, a little drunk,
"waltzing" roughly with his child is easy to visualize. And mother's disapproving
"countenance"—the look on her face that shows her feelings—that "Could not

unfrown itself" is also easy to see. You may recall a childhood moment when your father's behavior with children caused your mother to frown.

Why does she frown? After all, father seems in good spirits. Maybe a little too good? She doesn't say it, but many mothers might think it: "Someone's going to get hurt." When drunk, father becomes unpredictable, a little rowdy. Then too, something is shared between father and child from which mother is excluded.

If you enjoy the poem, you might ask yourself questions about the way it's constructed. Why is the poem addressed to "you" for example? Why is it written in the past tense? Why does it contain words that rhyme? To understand the poem fully, you must see Papa, smell "the whiskey on [his] breath," enough to "make a small boy dizzy." The poet is telling you something—or rather the narrator in the poem ("I hung on") is—and you must imagine it in your mind if you are to understand the poem.

Whether you can see the images depends on your understanding of the language. Although Roethke's poem is not usually considered difficult (except perhaps for *countenance* in line 7), the poem can present problems of interpretation. Words like *whiskey, dizzy, death* may carry negative connotations, as do *hand that held my wrist, battered, scraped, beat time on my head, palm caked hard by dirt*. All these negative words or connotations of words seem to make the poem itself negative. But against the negative ideas, there are three key ideas, unfamiliar to many students: waltzing, romping, and beating time.

Suppose a student claims the poem concerns child abuse, the drunken father "beating" the child while the mother does nothing. In part this interpretation is the result of media campaigns against child abuse, wife abuse, and drunkenness. The student's interpretation may be less her own understanding of the poem than an interpretation that fits what she has heard about "beating."

Is child abuse a good interpretation? Why isn't it sufficient for the student to say, "Well, that's the way I see it—that's *my* interpretation"? Although the student believes she has a good understanding of the poem, this reading could be the result of hurrying through it. The child abuse interpretation weakens when readers consider the positive connotations in the poem. The key word is *beat* in line 13. That word can mean physical abuse, but here the context suggests something else: "You beat *time*." A waltz is a formal dance, requiring much twirling in circles—dancers must move in time to the music. The other word that might lead a reader to infer child abuse is *battered* in line 10. Yet it isn't the child but the adult who is "battered on one knuckle." (Well, maybe his knuckle got battered from beating the child? Possibly, but that requires you to make an assumption based on the interpretation you are trying to defend.)

When you interpret a poem, your job is to make a point and to support it with specific evidence from the poem—examples of words, details, lines. If you believe the poem is about child abuse or about love or something else, you need to defend this view by citing and analyzing parts of the poem that show this. But keep in mind that poems, being works of art, tend to hold some mystery. Poems rarely contain clear topic sentences or thesis statements. Poems suggest meaning: you infer meaning from a poem, and a poem can hold various meanings, even contradictory meanings. Your job is to think about and feel a poem, sorting out what it suggests to you.

Might "My Papa's Waltz" concern both love and terror? Might the speaker feel closely connected to his father in the waltz yet feel terrified too—terrified of the father's show of love, his unsteady movements, of the mother's frown and fear, of his own complex feelings toward his father? When he holds on "like death," this could mean that he doesn't want to let go of his father physically or let go of his father's love. Thus, the way you interpret this poem depends on the details you cite to support your idea. A "simple" poem, "My Papa's Waltz" is more complex than many readers first think. This is true of most excellent poetry.

## The Language of Poetry

Critical reading requires two people—the poet on one end and the reader on the other. Between them is the poem, made of language. But this is true of all reading. Why should poetry be different, harder? Why can't you skim through poetry the way you can skim through a newspaper? Think of champion skaters who do complex yet beautiful twirls—should you forbid them from doing anything extraordinary? Can you insist they stick to *plain* skating? Poets are artists of language. As a critical reader you should try to stay with them, try to appreciate and understand their efforts. If you look for *meanings* in a poem, you may find different levels of meaning. Poetry often expresses ambiguous truth.

Many poems present images and music to help you feel and comprehend some strong emotion. Read, for example, the following poem. (If you don't understand it at first, that's okay, but don't give up on it—it has some surprises.)

### A narrow Fellow in the Grass

**Emily Dickinson**

A narrow Fellow in the Grass
Occasionally rides—
You may have met Him—did you not
His notice sudden is—

The Grass divides as with a Comb—
A spotted shaft is seen—
And then it closes at your feet
And opens further on—

He likes a Boggy Acre
A floor too cool for Corn—
Yet when a Boy, and Barefoot—
I more than once at Noon

Have passed, I thought, a Whip lash
Unbraiding in the Sun
When stooping to secure it
It wrinkled, and was gone—

Several of Nature's People
I know, and they know me—
I feel for them a transport
Of Cordiality—

But never met this Fellow
Attended, or alone
Without a tighter breathing
And Zero at the Bone—

How might you read this poem to appreciate it as well as to interpret it? In his classic book on poetry, <u>Sound and Sense</u>, Laurence Perrine offers three useful questions to help critical thinkers: (1) Who is the speaker and what is the occasion of the poem? (2) What is the poet's central purpose? (3) How does the poet achieve this purpose?

In "A narrow Fellow in the Grass" Emily Dickinson refers to the speaker as a boy: "Yet when a Boy, and Barefoot—." Poets often create the speaker of their poems; you shouldn't assume the poet is the speaker. The speaker of this poem may be a man who looks back at being a boy and mistaking a creature as being a "Whip lash." The occasion? The speaker tells about noticing a certain creature of nature.

What is Dickinson's central purpose in the poem? Although she never uses the word *snake*, you can infer from Dickinson's images and details that this poem concerns a snake: "narrow Fellow," "spotted shaft," "a Whip lash / Unbraiding in the Sun." The speaker seems in awe of snakes: they are wonderful creatures yet stir great fear in the speaker and in most people. Dickinson's central purpose may be to capture this contradictory feeling of awe and fear—and to help readers feel this same way.

How does Dickinson achieve this purpose? This third question involves analyzing how a poet uses language. You could argue that Dickinson achieves her purpose through using the second person pronoun *you*, vivid images, and figures of speech. She involves you as a reader by including you in the poem: "You may have met Him—did you not." Most of us have met snakes unexpectedly. Her second stanza also involves the reader: "And then it closes at your feet / And opens further on" as if a snake in the grass has come near you but left you alone. But after the references to "you," the speaker refers to himself as "I." The poem focuses on the speaker's feelings and thoughts.

Dickinson's images of the snake are visual: "narrow Fellow," "spotted shaft," "a Whip lash / Unbraiding in the Sun." The snake "wrinkled, and was gone"; it seems supernatural. Her simile—"The Grass divides as with a Comb"—conveys the snake's latent power. You can see grass dividing. The whiplash metaphor suggests the snap of a whip like a snake bite. These images create a rising fear in the poem. The speaker does not feel cordial with snakes.

You could analyze other aspects of Dickinson's language such as her unusual capitalization (is it for emphasis?), her unconventional punctuation (no periods, and why so many dashes—because they look like snakes?). If you did some research on Dickinson's poem and writing style, you could probably find answers to these questions.

To address the third question of how the poet achieves her purpose, you could also analyze the poem's persuasive appeals to logos, pathos, and ethos. She appeals to logos or reasoning by moving you to think about snakes and nature and your complex reactions. You may question whether other creatures are like "Nature's People" and whether humans are sometimes like snakes. Dickinson uses pathos by rousing emotions—you may feel awe at imagining a snake riding and dividing the grass; you may feel fear at imagining a whiplash moving and then "stooping to secure it." You may have felt cold fear—"a tighter breathing" at seeing a lone snake. Dickinson stirs your feelings of awe and fear, enabling you to identify with the speaker. She also helps readers appreciate the ethos of the speaker. Highly observant and thoughtful, he seems to care about nature, even referring to creatures as "Nature's People." His frank admission of fear makes the speaker honest and credible. You can trust the speaker; you sense he is sharing a truth about snakes and nature with you. Indeed, you might conclude that Dickinson's appeals to the speaker's character and to your own feelings combine to provoke you to think about snakes and your complex relationship with nature.

## Elements of Poetry

Here is a brief introduction to some of the major elements of poetry, most of which exist in essays, stories, and plays, too.

### Diction

Diction means word choice. To analyze a poem, you notice the poem's words and think about what the words do to create meanings and to appeal to your reason, emotion, and character.

Words have denotation and connotation. The *denotation* is the dictionary meaning of the word, what most people mean by it. Denotation comes from *denote*—to "note" the meaning of. *Home* denotes where a person lives when not working.

*Connotation* is implied meanings and attitudes attached to a word; it is suggestions and associations that color a word with certain meanings. *Home* usually carries connotations of warmth, security, and love. But *home* can carry negative connotations if it calls to mind physical or emotional abuse for somebody. In determining the meanings of poetry, you must be alert to both denotations and connotations of words. The way many readers view Roethke's line "You beat time on my head" depends on whether they consider "beat" as physical violence or making music.

As with any form of writing you read carefully, when you see a word in a poem you don't know or understand, such as *countenance*, look it up in a dictionary after you read the complete poem. This bit of research is necessary—and another hallmark of critical thinking. Certain words can unlock a poem for you when you reread it. Certain words hold meanings you aren't aware of until you look them up in a dictionary. This research and discovery of word meaning is part of the pleasure of reading poems—and stories and essays. Of course, if you need to look up many words in a poem to understand it, you may quickly feel overburdened. But most poems don't require such work.

Diction also refers to whether words are simple or complex, specific or general, concrete or abstract, literal or figurative. (See Interchapter 1.)

## Imagery

An image is a sensory experience made of words—a detail based on one or more of your senses: sight, smell, sound, taste, touch. Through images a writer attempts to evoke some sensory event so you can imagine waltzing in a kitchen or witnessing a snake in the grass. Not all poems contain images, but most do. Look at the images in "Root Cellar," another poem by Theodore Roethke:

### Root Cellar

*Theodore Roethke*

Nothing would sleep in that cellar, dank as a ditch,
Bulbs broke out of boxes hunting for chinks in the dark,
Shoots dangled and drooped,
Lolling obscenely from mildewed crates,
Hung down long yellow evil necks, like tropical snakes.
And what a congress of stinks!—
Roots ripe as old bait,
Pulpy stems, rank, silo-rich,
Leaf-mold, manure, lime, piled against slippery planks.
Nothing would give up life:
Even the dirt kept breathing a small breath.

## Figures of Speech: Metaphors, Similes, and Symbols

Metaphors and similes are kinds of comparisons, and poets use them often. A metaphor is an implied comparison without the word *as* or *like*. Consider the metaphors in this poem:

### Metaphors

*Sylvia Plath*

I'm a riddle in nine syllables,
An elephant, a ponderous house,
A melon strolling on two tendrils,
O red fruit, ivory, fine timbers!
This loaf's big with its yeasty rising.

> Money's new-minted in this fat purse.
> I'm a means, a stage, a cow in calf.
> I've eaten a bag of green apples,
> Boarded the train there's no getting off.

To what do Plath's metaphors refer? (You will soon see.)

Similes are explicit comparisons containing the word *as* or *like*. Roethke describes shoots dangling "like tropical snakes" and "Roots ripe as old bait." Dickinson describes the grass dividing "as with a Comb."

Through metaphors and similes, poets join unrelated things to spark your imagination and consider new thoughts. (For more on metaphors and similes, see Interchapter 1.)

Symbols are visible objects that suggest or represent other things, often ideas. You know many common or conventional symbols: a dove suggests peace; a red rose suggests love; a cross suggests Christ; darkness suggests ignorance; light suggests knowledge. In Dickinson's poem "A narrow Fellow in the Grass," the snake might symbolize a loss of innocence or the presence of evil.

## Tone

Tone is a writer's attitude toward the subject. Tone can be serious, humorous, playful, sad, loving, caring, angry, annoyed, and much more. How would you describe Roethke's tone in "Root Cellar"? Perhaps mock-serious or full of awe? After his earthy images he ends the poem by suggesting the cellar is incredibly full of life. The speaker seems in awe of nature in a confined space. How would you describe Plath's tone in "Metaphors"? She describes being fully pregnant, using extreme comparisons to help readers feel this condition. Her tone seems playful, yet the tone of the last line shifts into a serious realization: the speaker has "Boarded the train there's no getting off."

## Speaker

Determining who speaks or narrates a poem can help you understand and interpret it. In "My Papa's Waltz" the speaker addresses his or her father. Although Theodore Roethke, a man, wrote the poem, the speaker could be a son or daughter. You shouldn't always assume that the speaker of a poem is the author of that poem because poets often invent speakers—they adopt personas. In "Root Cellar," the speaker is an observer; you don't know what relationship he has to the cellar, although students doing research on Roethke would find that his family owned a greenhouse in Saginaw, Michigan. In "Metaphors" Sylvia Plath is an exasperated woman fully pregnant. Plath may have been that woman; she did have two children. But she does not announce that she is the woman—the speaker could be any woman close to bearing a child. Analyzing the speaker of a poem helps you analyze the appeal to ethos in a poem—the character of the speaker.

## Sound Patterns

Poems often contain sound patterns. In "Root Cellar" Roethke uses *alliteration*:

> "*d*ank as a *d*itch," "*B*ulbs *b*roke out of *b*oxes," "*S*hoots *d*angled and *d*rooped," "*R*oots *r*ipe as old bait"

Alliteration is the repetition of initial consonants of words. Roethke's thick alliteration suggests the thickness of vegetation in the cellar. The sound reinforces the sense or meaning of the poem.

In her snake poem Emily Dickinson uses *assonance*: the repetition of vowel sounds in words. The long *o*'s in Dickinson's poem echo the fear the speaker feels:

> But never met this Fell*o*w,
> Attended, or al*o*ne
> Without a tighter breathing
> And Zer*o* at the B*o*ne—

Assonance often reinforces emotion in a poem.

What sound do you hear in this Dickinson line about a snake: "His notice sudden is—"? A hiss sound? Yes. Using words that echo the sound they denote is called *onomatopoeia*. The word "cricket" makes the sound of the insect; say the word a few times to hear it. But this sound device occurs much less often than alliteration and assonance. Sound patterns create the musical quality of poetry and much of the pleasure of listening to poetic language.

## Structure

Considering a poem's physical structure can help you understand the poem. In "Metaphors" Plath cleverly structures her poem on the number *nine*: the title word has nine characters; each line contains nine syllables; the poem contains nine lines. This pattern is not readily apparent, but once you see it, it helps the poem make sense: a woman nine months pregnant is full-term; perhaps such a woman naturally thinks of nines. The number becomes a clue to the poem's meaning. "My Papa's Waltz" contains four-line stanzas, each with two rhymes such as "breath" / "death" and "dizzy" / "easy." These rhymes create a waltzing rhythm in the poem. This structure reinforces the interpretation that the speaker feels connected in a joyful dance with the father.

Poems usually contain stanzas. A stanza is a group of lines in a poem. A poem may contain one long stanza with no breaks, or it may contain several stanzas of same-numbered lines such as two-line stanzas, three- or four-line stanzas, or longer, depending on the poet's purpose. A poem about two lovers might work well with two-line stanzas to reinforce the idea of two. Yet many poems have irregular stanzas: two lines in one, five in another, three in the next. When this happens, the poet doesn't want to create the impression of order in a poem's structure.

## Line Breaks

One of the most distinguishing features of poetry is that it contains line breaks. Poets deliberately choose where to end their lines to cause certain effects. They might end a line with a key word for emphasis or end a line in such a way that causes surprise. Consider these lines:

When I called
Dad mumbled out
of sleep, asking
"Who's there?"

The second line "Dad mumbled out" causes a little surprise because you might assume he mumbled out words, but he "mumbled out / of sleep." Poets might end a line to break a rhythm or to make a rhyme. A line in a poem can run on to the next line like turning a corner, or it can stop. Thus, when you read poems, noticing line breaks will help you appreciate and understand a poem more.

When you analyze poems, you may not need to consider all of these elements. Certain elements will stand out for you. You can focus on these. But an awareness of all the elements of poetry will help you understand and appreciate any artistic use of language.

## READING NOTEBOOK

A reading notebook is especially worthwhile when you read literature. Your own notebook allows you to stop a few moments during or after your reading to reflect, to pull together your own thoughts about a poem, story, or essay, to make some record of how it affects you. Reading is most rewarding when you reflect on it. Your personal response to the work of other writers will help you clarify your own ideas and emotions. Reading and writing in this way connects you with an author.

Think of your notebook as your own approach to reading. As you respond to what you read, the notebook contains whatever you notice that catches your attention, puzzles you, or connects with you personally. When you begin more formal writing, you can draw upon your notebook reflections.

## ACTIVITY 2

After you read the following poem, in your notebook write a page or so about what you notice in it. ■

### Traveling through the Dark

**William Stafford**

Traveling through the dark I found a deer
dead on the edge of the Wilson River road.

It is usually best to roll them into the canyon:
that road is narrow; to swerve might make more dead.

By glow of tail-light I stumbled back of the car
and stood by the heap, a doe, a recent killing;
she had stiffened already, almost cold.
I dragged her off; she was huge in the belly.

My fingers touching her side brought me the reason—
her side was warm; her fawn lay there waiting,
alive, still, never to be born.
Beside that mountain road I hesitated.

The car aimed ahead its lowered parking lights;
under the hood purred the steady engine.
I stood in the glare of the warm exhaust turning red;
around our group I could hear the wilderness listen.

I thought hard for us all—my only swerving—
then pushed her over the edge into the river.

Here is an entry about Stafford's poem from Zac's notebook:

Stafford describes a really sad event—or a terrible event, or a non-event, depending on how you feel about nature, I guess. Are we supposed to "enjoy" this poem? I read that Aristotle said tragedy was good for us—it purges the soul. If this is true, I wonder how Stafford's poem purges my soul.

At first "Traveling through the Dark" seems like a routine event, something we can easily deal with. The deer is dead on the road, but she's pregnant—there's a live fawn inside. If Stafford just wanted to make us happy, maybe he could have produced a hunting knife, opened the doe, and delivered the fawn. Maybe he could have driven the fawn into town, where the local vet would have cared for it. This would have made a happy Disney ending.

Instead though the speaker pushes the doe over the edge into the river. It's a shock ending; I didn't expect it. Why does it happen? There's no mention of a hunting knife in the poem, nothing to suggest the speaker might have a hunting knife. Is it hunting season? Even if the speaker could deliver the fawn, there's no guarantee any vet could be found who would care for it. A fawn requires a lot of attention, feeding several times a day. Without its mother, the fawn would almost certainly die.

Perhaps Stafford is trying to shock us into thinking about a serious problem—civilization's intrusion into the deer's habitat. The speaker tells us this is not the first deer killed on this road: "It is usually best to roll them into the canyon." This suggests he has done this before or knows about it. As cities expand in urban sprawl, what happens to the wilderness? What happens to the creatures of the wilderness? What happens to *us*?

The speaker "hesitates" but at last decides what must be done. I wonder what I would have done in the same situation.

The more I think about this poem, the more questions come to mind. If the doe had not been "huge in the belly," would I respond differently? Suppose the deer had been a stag? And does it make a difference whether the speaker is male or female?

Do I feel purged? I don't know. But I do feel as if I just had this experience with the deer on the road.

I do notice some neat details in the poem. The image "By glow of tail-light"—perhaps it suggests blood. Maybe it's a kind of foreshadowing too. I like how the speaker "stumbled," not sure of what to do. This seems honest—I'd stumble. I really feel emotionally caught up in the third stanza. I can imagine my fingers touching the deer—"her side was warm." I like too how the poem builds in tension and how Stafford gives the car human qualities—"The car aimed ahead its lowered parking lights." And the engine "purred" like an animal. He refers to the deer and fawn and car and himself as "our group." They are all united in this awful and somehow precious moment. How can "the wilderness listen"? Maybe it can—maybe trees and hidden animals listen when there's tragedy—as if they care. I really like this suggestion.

I think maybe this is what Stafford wants us as readers to do—to care too. Maybe his poem helped purge me of indifference. Interesting.

## WRITING AN ESSAY ABOUT A POEM

Explore—analyze and evaluate—a poem: state a thesis about the poem and defend it. You may discover that after you write about a poem, you will understand and appreciate it much more.

## ACTIVITY 3

Choose a poem you like a lot or that intrigues or puzzles you. Your job is to look for clues that show a writer's intended effects—this will help you analyze and evaluate how the poem works. After the following guidelines and a student's essay about a poem, you will find "Poems to Consider for Writing an Essay."

# GUIDELINES FOR WRITING AN ESSAY ABOUT A POEM

1. Analyze and evaluate a poem by addressing these three questions:

   *Who is the speaker and what is the occasion?* Is the speaker someone different from the poet? If so, how? The occasion refers to when and where the poem takes place, as far as you can tell.

   *What is the central purpose of the poem?* What do you think the poet is trying to do in the poem—to express some emotion or truth, to describe a scene so vividly you never forget it, to help you appreciate what you have . . . ?

   *By what means does the poet achieve this purpose?* What does the poet do with elements of poetry: diction, imagery, figures of speech, tone, speaker, sound, structure, or line breaks? Focus on at least three elements of poetry. You may also analyze how the poem appeals to logos, pathos, and ethos. Analyze whatever stands out to you that the poet does to achieve his or her purpose.

2. Before you write your rough draft, type the poem you want to analyze, double-spaced. This will help you notice details about the poem. Proofread carefully against the original to catch any errors. Also, on the right margin, number the lines by 5's: 5, 10, 15, and so on. You will need to refer to line numbers when you quote from the poem in your essay.

3. Annotate the poem you typed—write notes on it. In the margins or between the lines write down anything you notice, feel, or think about. Draw arrows or question marks or stars—use whatever system you want to interact with the poem. Annotation helps you see more into the poem to find connections and ideas to write about. As you annotate, ask yourself questions: Why this word? Why this image? Why this structure? Why do I feel this way here in the poem? and so on.

4. Proceed to write a rough draft following this format for your essay:

   **A.** *Title:* Give readers an idea about the poem you will analyze, and try to arouse interest. Which of these titles is more effective?

   > Kindness in the "Blueblack Cold" or An Analysis of a Poem

   **B.** *Introduction:* Draw readers into your essay. Identify the author and the poem you will analyze. Then state a carefully worded thesis—your main idea—as the last sentence of your introduction.

   **C.** *Body:* Defend and demonstrate your thesis.

   1. Present a brief summary of the poem you will analyze, using your own language. Within your summary answer question one: Who is the speaker and what is the occasion? Use present tense in your summary.

   2. Proceed into your analysis, answering questions two and three: What is the central purpose of the poem, and by what means does the poet achieve this purpose? Use brief quotations—and a long quotation or two if appropriate—for supporting evidence. Cite line numbers after quoting from the poem. The

body section will likely be at least three or more paragraphs. Use present tense: "Plath writes" rather than "Plath wrote."

D. *Conclusion:* Reassert and clarify your thesis, and briefly discuss the overall quality of the poem.

E. *Work Cited:* Provide a complete Work Cited entry for the poem. This need not be on a separate page—below your conclusion space down four spaces and put the Work Cited entry there. In the forthcoming Poems to Consider for Writing an Essay, Work Cited information is provided for you to use. (For more information on Works Cited, see Chapter 9.)

F. *A Typed Copy of the Poem:* This should be a clean and accurate copy of the poem you analyze, with line numbers indicated on the right margin. Option: Present the poem toward the beginning of your essay.

5. Your essay should be 3 to 5 pages. Consider your audience for this paper to be your fellow classmates and instructor.

### How to Quote from a Poem

You can quote a word, a phrase, or a stanza—it depends on your purpose. According to the MLA style of documentation, if you quote part or all of a single line from a poem, put it in quotation marks within your text.

> Stafford gives the car animal-like qualities such as "under the hood purred the steady engine" (14).

You may also incorporate two or three lines within your text, using a slash with a space on each side ( / ) to indicate line breaks:

> Stafford's speaker expresses his dilemma in the poem's last lines: "I thought hard for us all—my only swerving— / then pushed her over the edge into the river" (17–18).

The numbers at the end of the quotes refer to the line numbers in the poem, not page numbers. You should use line numbers when you quote.

Quotations of more than three lines should be treated like a long quote of prose: indent each line 10 spaces (two tabs) from the left margin and double-space between lines, adding no quotation marks that do not appear in the original.

## Student Essay Exploring a Poem

What follows is a poem, "Those Winter Sundays," and a student's analysis and evaluation of it that serves as a model on how to write about a poem.

### Those Winter Sundays

**Robert Hayden**

Sundays too my father got up early
and put his clothes on in the blueblack cold,

then with cracked hands that ached
from labor in the weekday weather made
banked fires blaze. No one ever thanked him.

I'd wake and hear the cold splintering, breaking.
When the rooms were warm, he'd call,
and slowly I would rise and dress,
fearing the chronic angers of that house,

speaking indifferently to him,
who had driven out the cold
and polished my good shoes as well.
What did I know, what did I know
of love's austere and lonely offices?

*Robert Hayden grew up in a Detroit ghetto called Paradise Valley. At eighteen months, he was given to next-door neighbors William and Sue Ellen Hayden, who raised him. William "Pa" Hayden is immortalized in "Those Winter Sundays." Robert Hayden was the first African American to be appointed "Consultant in Poetry to the Library of Congress"; this position was later called the Poet Laureate.*

## Kindness in the "Blueblack Cold"

### *Ryan Lampman*

Have you ever felt regret for not thanking someone for the kindness he showed you? Robert Hayden's poem "Those Winter Sundays" concerns such regret. Through his careful diction, sound, and imagery, Hayden helps readers feel a mix of regret and gratitude.

"Those Winter Sundays" is told through first-person. Someone—it may be Hayden himself but doesn't need to be—is telling about how his father woke early in their cold house and got a fire started to heat the place. The speaker is reflecting back on what happened those days. When the house was warm, the father called to wake him. The speaker says as he dressed he "fear[ed] the chronic angers of that house." The speaker spoke "indifferently to him," even knowing that his father had polished his "good shoes," suggesting that the family or the speaker would be going to church on those Sundays. The poem ends with the speaker questioning his behavior—the way he reacted to his father's kindness.

To enable readers to feel and think about regret and gratitude, Robert Hayden uses carefully chosen words that suggest the character of the father. "Sundays too" (1) suggests that the father got up early other days as well in the winter to heat the house for his family. He didn't sleep in; he wasn't selfish. He "put his clothes on in the blueblack cold" (2). The word *blueblack* is surprising: it suggests that the morning was early dawn; Hayden joins the two words together into one and we can hear the *b* sounds of alliteration. The father was a laborer who worked outside. He had "cracked hands that ached / from labor in the weekday weather"

(3–4). His life was not easy. But he "made / banked fires blaze" (4–5). Hayden's word choice in this first stanza holds sounds that echo: the hard rhymes of *black* and *cracked* (2–3), more *b* sounds of alliteration in *banked* and *blaze*, and long *a* sounds of assonance in *ached* (3), *made* (4) and *blazed* (5). All these sounds help weave the poem's feeling and meaning together. The first stanza ends with a powerful statement: "No one ever thanked him" (5)—not only the speaker of the poem, but no one else in the family.

How cold is *cold*? The second stanza says the speaker could "hear the cold splintering, breaking" (6). These images suggest the house was cold as ice. The father didn't call until "the rooms were warm" (7). He demonstrates his love this way. When the speaker says he "fear[ed] the chronic angers of that house" (9), we don't know what he means. The father doesn't seem angry in his early morning kindness. Perhaps the speaker's parents fought, or there were siblings who fought. The poem doesn't give details about "the chronic angers." But these words suggest the family was not happy.

The third stanza expresses the speaker's regret for "speaking indifferently to him, / who had driven out the cold / and polished my good shoes as well" (10–12). Why was the speaker so indifferent? Why didn't he thank his father? These questions stir personal questions for readers as well. Why have we been indifferent at times to the kindness given to us? Why have we not thanked others for their sacrifice?

The last two lines deepen the speaker's regret and dawning awareness. His repetition of "What did I know" resonates with the long *o* sounds in *know*. The long *o* is an emotional sound, like a cry of regret, "Oh, why didn't I thank him?" The long *o* in *lonely* carries this sound too. The last line, however, complicates yet enriches the poem with the word *austere*: "love's austere and lonely offices" (14). Webster's New World Dictionary defines *austere* as "showing strict self-discipline and self-denial." This meaning clearly applies to the selfless father; he certainly possessed "strict self-discipline and self-denial." But why does Hayden end with the word *offices*? Although we don't usually use the word this way, Webster's New World says it means "something performed or intended to be performed for another" and "a function or duty assigned to someone, esp, as an essential part of his work or position." The job of being a loving parent involves performing kind, good acts for children, such as heating up the house and cleaning their shoes for church.

This poem has persuasive appeals. In terms of logos, the poem helps us think about kindness and those times we have taken it for granted. It helps us think about regret: if we could only thank those people now who were so kind to us. Perhaps the speaker's father has died; he can no longer thank him. In terms of pathos, the poem helps us feel the speaker's sorrow for "speaking indifferently" (10) to his father. It can help us feel sorrow for not thanking someone who sacrificed for us. It's easy to feel this sorrow, and it's a useful sorrow if it can help us be grateful and express gratitude in the future. In terms of ethos, the poem showcases the character of a loving father who generated warmth in the house through his literal and symbolic actions. The man was trustworthy and credible. The family could count on him. The poem also suggests the character of the speaker: he is very human in being a selfish child and taking his father's kindness for granted. But the poem's tone suggests that the speaker is sorry for this and wishes he could have expressed his loving thanks to his father.

One of the purposes of poetry is to humanize us: to help us see ourselves and how we might be better. Robert Hayden's poem "Those Winter Sundays" achieves this noble purpose. His careful use of words, sounds, and images helps us feel both regret and gratitude. For this, we can thank him.

Work Cited

Hayden, Robert. "Those Winter Sundays." Angle of Ascent: New and Selected Poems. New York: Liveright, 1975. 113.

## POEMS TO CONSIDER FOR WRITING AN ESSAY

### The Summer Day

#### Mary Oliver

Who made the world?
Who made the swan, and the black bear?
Who made the grasshopper?
This grasshopper, I mean—
the one who has flung herself out of the grass,
the one who is eating sugar out of my hand,
who is moving her jaws back and forth instead of up and down—
who is gazing around with her enormous and complicated eyes.
Now she lifts her pale forearms and thoroughly washes her face.
Now she snaps her wings open, and floats away.
I don't know exactly what a prayer is.
I do know how to pay attention, how to fall down
into the grass, how to kneel down in the grass,
how to be idle and blessed, how to stroll through the fields,
which is what I have been doing all day.
Tell me, what else should I have done?
Doesn't everything die at last, and too soon?
Tell me, what is it you plan to do
with your one wild and precious life?

*Mary Oliver, winner of the Pulitzer Prize for Poetry and the National Book Award, is one of the most celebrated poets in America. Her poems often express interconnections between nature and people.*

Work Cited

Oliver, Mary. "The Summer Day." New and Selected Poems. Boston: Beacon Press, 1992. 94.

## Student

### Ted Kooser

The green shell of his backpack makes him lean
into wave after wave of responsibility,
and he swings his stiff arms and cupped hands,

paddling ahead. He has extended his neck
to its full length, and his chin, hard as a beak,
breaks the cold surf. He's got his baseball cap on

backward as up he crawls, out of the froth
of a hangover and onto the sand of the future,
and lumbers, heavy with hope, into the library.

*Ted Kooser worked as an insurance executive for many years before becoming an English professor at the University of Nebraska–Lincoln. His poetry is known for showing the extraordinary in ordinary things. Kooser won the Pulitzer Prize for Poetry in 2005 and was our country's Poet Laureate from 2004 to 2006.*

Work Cited

Kooser, Ted. "Student." <u>Delights & Shadows</u>. Port Townsend, WA: Copper Canyon Press, 2004. 8.

## To Be of Use

### Marge Piercy

The people I love the best
jump into work head first
without dallying in the shallows
and swim off with sure strokes almost out of sight.
They seem to become natives of that element,
the black sleek heads of seals
bouncing like half-submerged balls.
I love people who harness themselves, an ox to a heavy cart,
who pull like water buffalo, with massive patience,
who strain in the mud and the muck to move things forward,
who do what has to be done, again and again.

I want to be with people who submerge
in the task, who go into the fields to harvest

and work in a row and pass the bags along,
who are not parlor generals and field deserters
but move in a common rhythm
when the food must come in or the fire be put out.
The work of the world is common as mud.
Botched, it smears the hands, crumbles to dust.
But the thing worth doing well done
has a shape that satisfies, clean and evident.
Greek amphoras for wine or oil,
Hopi vases that held corn, are put in museums
but you know they were made to be used.
The pitcher cries for water to carry
and a person for work that is real.

*Marge Piercy was raised in a working-class neighborhood of Detroit. She has published many novels and books of poetry and essays, including* Colors Passing Through Us: Poems *(2003) and* Three Women: A Novel *(2001).*

Work Cited

Piercy, Marge. "To Be of Use." The Art of Blessing the Day: Poems with a Jewish Theme. New York: Knopf, 1999. 73–74.

## Vocations Club

### Paula Sergi

We met on Tuesdays after school
with Sister Mary Agnes,
the two Mary Lous, Julie, Kay and me
to learn about being nuns.
The convent sounded good;
a room of my own, a single bed,
time to think and pray, no fighting
over what we'd watch—Bonanza versus Dragnet,
or who would get the couch.
I dug those crazy nun outfits, and hated hand me-downs
with too long sleeves and too tight waists.
I'd take the smell of polished wood and incense
over burnt grilled cheese and sour milk.

I'd have a good job, teaching kids
and all the chalk I'd want,
long, unbroken pieces that echoed off the board,
all eyes on me as I'd tap directions,
conducting my classroom all day.
People, I'd begin, today we're talking about . . .
whatever I want to!
Nuns got great rosaries with fancy beads
and lots of gifts at Christmas.
And the solitude of celibacy sounded pretty good,
better than worrying about French kissing
like my sister, better than pining for men,
like mom, whose men left anyway.

*Paula Sergi is co-editor of* Boomer Girls: Poems by Women from the Baby Boom Generation, *University of Iowa Press, 1999. She lives in Wisconsin. One of her interests is the intersect of science and poetry, informed by her BS in nursing and experience as a nurse.*

Work Cited

Sergi, Paula. "Vocations Club." Family Business. Georgetown, KY: Finishing Line Press, 2005. 7.

## May

### Bruce Weigl

I wanted to stay with my dog
when they did her in
I told the young veterinarian
who wasn't surprised.
Shivering on the chrome table,
she did not raise her eyes to me when I came in.
Something was resolved in her.
Some darkness exchanged for the pain.
There were a few more words
about the size of her tumor and her age,
and how we wanted to stop her suffering,
or our own, or stop all suffering
from happening before us
and then the nurse shaved May's skinny leg

with those black clippers;
she passed the needle to the doctor
and for once I knew what to do
and held her head against mine.
I cleaved to that smell
and lied into her ear
that it would be all right.
The veterinarian, whom I'd fought
about when to do this thing
said through tears
that it would take only a few minutes
as if that were not a long time
but there was no cry or growl,
only the weight of her in my arms,
and then on the world.

*Bruce Weigl served in Vietnam for two years and received the Bronze Star. In The Circle of Hanh: A Memoir, he writes, "The war took away my life and gave me poetry in return." He was nominated for the Pulitzer Prize in 1988 for his collection of poems Song of Napalm. He is a professor of English at Lorain County Community College in Ohio.*

Work Cited

Weigl, Bruce. "May." What Saves Us. Evanston: Northwestern U. Press, 1994. 57.

## A Blessing

### James Wright

Just off the highway to Rochester, Minnesota,
Twilight bounds softly forth on the grass.
And the eyes of those two Indian ponies
Darken with kindness.
They have come gladly out of the willows
To welcome my friend and me.
We step over the barbed wire into the pasture
Where they have been grazing all day, alone.
They ripple tensely, they can hardly contain their happiness
That we have come.
They bow shyly as wet swans. They love each other.
There is no loneliness like theirs.

At home once more,
They begin munching the young tufts of spring in the darkness.
I would like to hold the slenderer one in my arms,
For she has walked over to me
And nuzzled my left hand.
She is black and white,
Her mane falls wild on her forehead,
And the light breeze moves me to caress her long ear
That is delicate as the skin over a girl's wrist.
Suddenly I realize
That if I stepped out of my body I would break
Into blossom.

*James Wright (1927–1980) was born in the steel-producing town of Martins Ferry, Ohio. Wright, a student of poet Theodore Roethke at the University of Washington, received the Pulitzer Prize for his* Collected Poems *in 1972. He taught at Hunter College in New York.*

Work Cited

Wright, James. "A Blessing." Above the River: Complete Poems. New York: Farrar, Straus and
 Giroux, 1990: 143.

## homage to my hips

### Lucille Clifton

these hips are big hips
they need space to
move around in.
they don't fit into little
petty places. these hips
are free hips.
they don't like to be held back.
these hips have never been enslaved,
they go where they want to go
they do what they want to do.
these hips are mighty hips.
these hips are magic hips.
I have known them
to put a spell on a man and
spin him like a top!

Lucille Clifton was raised in Buffalo, New York. She has published many books of poetry including the National Book Award winner <u>Blessing the Boats: New and Selected
Poems 1988–2000</u> and many children's books, including a series about a young African
American boy, Everett Anderson. Her poetry is noted for saying much in few words. In
2007 she received the Ruth Lilly Award for Lifetime Achievement.

Work Cited

Clifton, Lucille. "homage to my hips." <u>Good Woman: Poems and a Memoir 1969–1980</u>.
    Brockport, NY: BOA Editions, 1987. 168.

## The Gift

### Li-Young Lee

To pull the metal splinter from my palm
my father recited a story in a low voice.
I watched his lovely face and not the blade.
Before the story ended, he'd removed
the iron sliver I thought I'd die from.

I can't remember the tale,
but hear his voice still, a well
of dark water, a prayer.
And I recall his hands,
two measures of tenderness
he laid against my face,
the flames of discipline
he raised above my head.

Had you entered that afternoon
you would have thought you saw a man
planting something in a boy's palm,
a silver tear, a tiny flame.
Had you followed that boy
you would have arrived here,
where I bend over my wife's right hand.

Look how I shave her thumbnail down
so carefully she feels no pain.
Watch as I lift the splinter out.
I was seven when my father
took my hand like this,
and I did not hold that shard
between my fingers and think,

*Metal that will bury me,*
christen it Little Assassin,
Ore Going Deep for My Heart.
And I did not lift up my wound and cry,
*Death visited here!*
I did what a child does
when he's given something to keep.
I kissed my father.

*Born in Indonesia, Li-Young Lee moved with his family to the United States to escape a regime that had imprisoned his father, who was Mao Zedong's personal physician. Lee lives in Chicago with his wife and children. He has published four books of poetry: Rose (1986), The City in Which I Love You (1990), Book of My Nights (2001), and Behind My Eyes (2008). He also published a memoir, The Winged Seed (1995).*

Work Cited

Lee, Li-Young. "The Gift." Rose. Rochester, NY: BOA Editions, 1986. 15–16.

*Note:* If you'd prefer to analyze a poem not in this book, please ask your instructor for permission. It's important to choose a poem you enjoy and that intrigues you in some way.

## READING AND WRITING ABOUT FICTION

*A story is good when you continue to see more and more in it, and when it continues to escape you. In fiction two and two is always more than four.* (Flannery O'Connor, Mystery and Manners)

Short stories and novels contain an artistic use of language—most of the same elements of poetry presented in the previous section: diction, imagery, figures of speech, tone, speaker, sound patterns, and structure. Fiction, however, isn't usually as musical as poetry because it doesn't employ stanzas and line breaks, which emphasize sound patterns more than paragraphs do. Like meaning in poetry, meaning in fiction is usually suggested, not readily explained. Readers infer meanings from a story based on what characters do, say, and think—and on connotations, details and images a writer uses.

Like poetry, serious or literary fiction requires a slower and more careful kind of reading than skimming through a newspaper or report. Such deliberate reading carries rewards: moments of entertainment and enlightenment.

## ACTIVITY 4

Consider the following vignette—a short literary sketch. After you read it, reflect on it in your reading notebook. What do you notice? What do you like? What questions does it raise for you? What does the vignette mean to you?

### Lights

*Stuart Dybek*

In summer, waiting for night, we'd pose against the afterglow on corners, watching traffic cruise through the neighborhood. Sometimes, a car would go by without its headlights on and we'd all yell, "Lights!"

"Lights!" we'd keep yelling until the beams flashed on. It was usually immediate—the driver honking back thanks, or flinching embarrassed behind the steering wheel, or gunning past, and we'd see his red taillights blink on.

But there were times—who knows why?—when drunk or high, stubborn, or simply lost in that glide to somewhere else, the driver just kept driving in the dark, and all down the block we'd hear yelling from doorways and storefronts, front steps, and other corners, voices winking on like fireflies: "Lights! Your *lights*! Hey, lights!"

This is a "light" little scene—not heavy, with no definite characters. But there is a conflict. Why does the speaker say that he or she and others yelled "Lights!"? Although the answer is not stated, it is implied: a car without lights on at dusk poses a danger—a driver might not see clearly, and other people might not see a car clearly. A driver without lights on could hit a child; an elderly person could step in front of such a car. Thus, yelling "Lights!" is a community call for caution.

This vignette is taken from Stuart Dybek's book <u>The Coast of Chicago</u>, the city where he grew up. How would you describe Dybek's tone or attitude? He recalls this ritual with fondness: "we'd pose against the afterglow on corners, watching traffic cruise through the neighborhood." The words *pose* and *cruise* suggest a time of ease, of relaxation on these summer evenings. But if a car didn't respond by turning on its lights, the callers kept calling until a driver honked "back thanks" or "his red taillights" would "blink on." Dybek's images enable you to see, to hear, and to experience this setting and situation. The simile "voices winking on like fireflies" is surprising. It suggests that out of concern for others, the people's voices became lights.

## ACTIVITY 5

Here is another vignette by Stuart Dybek. When you finish, write about it in your notebook. Try to reflect on what it means and on how Dybek uses language to create certain effects. ■

### Maroon

*Stuart Dybek*

—for Anthony Dadaro, 1946–58

A boy is bouncing a ball off a brick wall after school. The bricks have been painted maroon a long time ago. Steady as a heartbeat the ball rebounds oblong, hums, sponges back round. A maroon Chevy goes by.

Nothing else. This street's deserted: a block-long abandoned factory, glass from the busted windows on the sidewalk mixed with brown glass from beer bottles, whiskey pints. Sometimes the alkies drink here. Not today.

Only the ball flying between sunlit hands and shadowed bricks and sparrows brawling in the dusty gutters. The entire street turning maroon in the shadow of the wall, even the birds, even the hands.

He stands waiting under a streetlight that's trying to flicker on. Three guys he's never seen in the neighborhood before, coming down the street, carrying crowbars.

What do you notice about Dybek's use of language? How does his language create his meaning? Here is an entry from Monica's notebook:

I notice right away the color "maroon" and how it foreshadows blood and the violence that seem implicit in the vignette. The bricks of a wall are painted maroon and so is a car that drives by. Toward the end the "entire street" turns maroon-colored as dusk falls.

I notice too that the dedication provides an important clue to the vignette's meaning: "For Anthony Dadaro, 1946–58." This boy lived only twelve years; he could be the boy in the vignette that the three "guys," not boys, victimize. Why they hurt the boy we readers don't know. Dybek doesn't give any details about their race or if the boy had offended the guys in some way. Perhaps the guys kill the boy for some kind of pleasure, as the boy plays catch for pleasure. But the boy is not a rubber ball.

This is a sad vignette, just the opposite of Dybek's "Lights." There is no concern in this—except the tone. Dybek's tone seems concerned—his dedication suggests this. I like his ethos in this.

I'm surprised by Dybek's ability to describe the scene. He notices so much yet uses so few words. I used to play catch with a rubber ball against a wall at school: "the ball rebounds oblong, hums, sponges back round." That's exactly what happens. But the boy doesn't bounce back, and we don't know why people sometimes commit such brutal acts.

## ACTIVITY 6

Read the following from Anne Caston, the title piece from her book <u>Flying Out with the Wounded</u>. This vignette is a prose poem, a combination of prose and poetry: the author intentionally breaks lines and indents in certain ways. Then in your notebook, write about your reactions: what you notice, feel and think, what questions the piece stirs within you. ■

### *Flying Out with the Wounded*

**Anne Caston**

When the lightning struck, trees blackened against
a silver sky and the river bruised, the undersides of clouds
wounding its surface. But this was not my work. My work,

pressed into the dark hold of the chopper, was a drunk
man—foul and fuming, restrained against his drunkenness,
his abdomen packed with gauze to staunch the bleeding—and
his head-on victims: a woman and a girl whose head had been
bandaged to keep the brain intact.
The girl was dead.
                We lifted off with our cargo. There
were scant inches in which to crouch. Jack had to ride in
front. I was airsick and praying that the snarl of blades
overhead wouldn't snag in the electric night.
                      Somewhere
between that stretch of sky and Birmingham, the man caught
sight of the woman and girl. "Goddamn," he said, "Goddamn.
*Gooks*." And then, to me, "In 'Nam we used to throw 'em
out, watch 'em splatter." He laughed and laughed to himself.
The woman flinched. She turned her face from him, went
back to stroking the girl's cheek. The girl's gaze was fixed.
Still the woman was making the shushing sound. I leaned
over the man. "Shut up," I said close to his ear so he would
hear me over the noisy blades; "Shut up or I will push *you*
out." He quieted then and I sat back to ride the airsickness in
me out.
    Can I tell you I liked thinking about pushing him
out? Can I say I was imagining how easy it would be for me to
roll the man out into the rumble of thunder and the whirring
blades? I was.
    But then he seized. He arched against his bonds. His
eyes rolled back to white. I straddled the man; I called out for
help. Jack grabbed the ambu bag and started the count. I
placed my hands, palms down, against that spot two fingers'
breadth from the tip of the sternum. I pushed: the man's
wound gushed, wet and warm, against my thighs. The smell
of blood thickened. I wanted to lift myself from him. Still I
pushed the man's heart to respond. Still Jack counted. Still
the ambu bag wheezed in and out.
                   We worked like that the
whole way in, and when we landed someone else took over.
They lifted him away; I stepped out to catch a mouthful of
wet, clean air, to drive the blood-drunk smell of him from my
lungs. I looked down then and saw myself: bloodied, where I
had straddled the man, as if I had just given birth.

*Anne Caston, a former nurse, teaches English at the University of
Alaska-Anchorage. Her first collection of poems, <u>Flying Out with
the Wounded</u>, won the 1996 New York University Prize for Poetry.
Her second book of poems is <u>Judah's Lion</u> (2007).*

Work Cited

Caston, Anne. "Flying Out with the Wounded." <u>Flying Out with the Wounded</u>. New York: NYU Press, 1997. 18–19.

# ACTIVITY 7

After writing in your notebook about Caston's vignette, write a brief essay (2 pages) in which you analyze Caston's use of persuasive appeals. How does she appeal to logos, pathos, and ethos? Which of these appeals does she draw on most? State a thesis and defend it with reasons and specific evidence from the piece. ■

## Elements of Fiction

Although fiction contains elements of poetic language, it contains other elements that characterize fiction as well as plays and movies. Essentially, a story involves *a main character* who experiences *a conflict* of some kind, minor or major. How the character reacts to the conflict moves the story forward. Usually the character undergoes a change of some kind during a story. This change creates much of the meaning in the story. For serious fiction, character and conflict must be credible and convincing—believable; otherwise, readers will not care what happens.

In Anne Caston's vignette, the speaker is an emergency medical technician. Her character is convincing because she battles to save the life of a drunk man who, in a head-on car accident, has injured a Vietnamese woman and killed her daughter. The major conflict is the speaker's contradictory desire to push the man out of the helicopter and to save his life.

### Plot and Conflict

The plot is what happens in a story—the sequence of cause and effect events. The plot hinges on some conflict a main character finds him or herself in. A story may have a single conflict or several conflicts, even layers of conflict operating at the same time. Usually a story's conflict rises in tension and becomes resolved or not resolved by the end. Keep in mind also that there are degrees of conflict: conflict can be dramatic and graphic as in Anne Caston's vignette. It can be more quiet, as in Dybek's "Lights."

### Character

In analyzing serious fiction, you can evaluate whether characters are *round* (complex, contradictory, real) or *flat* (stereotypical, one-dimensional, artificial). For fiction to work well, the main character must be not only credible but also worth caring about for you to keep paying close attention. Also, what characters say and what they wear reveal their personalities. If a character says "I seen that movie before," you can infer the character may be poorly educated.

But "character" also refers to the ethos or morality of a person in a story. Is the person good, evil, or a mixture of both? Does the person do right, wrong, or both? In short, does the main character have *good character*?

## Point of View

Who is telling the story? In fiction, the "narrator" is generally not the "author"—narrators are characters. Narrators can be

| | |
|---|---|
| First person ("I" or "We"): | I yelled, "Lights!" We yelled, "Lights!" |
| Second person ("You"): | You yelled, "Lights!" |
| Third person ("He," "She," "They" or "It"): | He yelled, "Lights!" She yelled, "Lights!" They yelled, "Lights!" |
| Omniscient: | The narrator knows the thoughts and feelings of one, some or all of the characters. |

First person, says fiction writer Stuart Dybek, is by nature the most intimate point of view, capable of producing lovable characters such as Holden Caulfield or Huck Finn. First person encourages the reader to identify with the main character, and to identify is to believe the story. A story needs to be both emotionally and physically credible. When details are specific, concrete (appealing to the senses), and precise, a reader finds it easier to identify and to participate in the story.

## Setting

Setting is where the story takes place. It is where a conflict is set in motion. In Dybek's "Maroon" the setting is a rough city street that appears abandoned where a boy plays catch with a rubber ball until three ominous guys approach. In "Flying Out with the Wounded" the story happens within a helicopter and outside the copter when it lands. A story may contain several different settings or scenes and different times of day or year. It may include flashbacks to the past and flash forwards to the future.

## Moral Issues

Serious fiction deals with moral issues, questions of value. Dybek's vignettes concern caring about people not getting hurt. Caston's vignette concerns questions such as "Is it right to help a drunken man whose recklessness has caused irreparable harm?" As a nurse the speaker is obligated to help; as a person she is tempted to push the man out of the chopper. The way characters struggle to deal with moral issues is part of their conflict and a story's meaning.

## WRITING AN ESSAY ABOUT A STORY

Explore—analyze and evaluate—a short story: state a thesis about the story and defend it.

## ACTIVITY 8

Choose one of the following stories: "Popular Mechanics," "Shotgun Wedding," or "The Undeclared Major" to explore in an essay.

## GUIDELINES FOR WRITING AN ESSAY ABOUT A STORY

1. Analyze and evaluate a story by addressing these three questions:

   *Who is the narrator and what is the occasion?* The occasion refers to when and where the story takes place, as far as you can tell.

   *What is the central purpose of the story?* What do you think the writer is trying to do and say in the story?

   *By what means does the writer achieve this purpose?* What does the writer do with elements of fiction such as plot and conflict, character, point of view, setting, and moral issues? What does the writer do with elements of language such as diction, imagery, figures of speech, and tone? Focus on at least three elements of fiction or language. You may also analyze how the story appeals to logos, pathos, and ethos. Analyze whatever stands out to you that the writer does to achieve his or her purpose.

2. Make a copy of the story and annotate it. Write notes on it in the margins or between the lines. Write down anything you notice, feel, or think about. As you annotate, ask yourself questions: Why is this character doing that? Why did the character say that? Why do I feel this way here in the story?

3. Proceed to write a rough draft following this format for your essay:

   **A.** *Title:* Give readers an idea of what story you will analyze, and try to arouse interest.

   **B.** *Introduction:* Draw readers into your essay by engaging them somehow. Identify the author and the story you will analyze. Then state a carefully worded thesis—your main idea—as the last sentence of your introduction.

   **C.** *Body:* Defend and demonstrate your thesis.

   **1.** Present a brief summary of the story you will analyze, using your own language. Within your summary answer question one: Who is the narrator and what is the occasion? Use present tense in your summary.

   **2.** Proceed into your analysis, answering questions two and three: What is the central purpose of the story, and by what means does the writer achieve this purpose? Use brief quotations—and a long quotation or two if appropriate—for supporting evidence. The body section will likely be at least three or more paragraphs. Use present tense: "Dybek writes" rather than "Dybek wrote."

   **D.** *Conclusion:* Reassert and clarify your thesis, and briefly discuss the overall quality of the story.

   **E.** *Work Cited:* Provide a complete Work Cited entry for the story. This need not be on a separate page—below your conclusion space down four spaces and put the Work Cited entry there. At the end of each story Work Cited information is provided for you to use. (For more information on Works Cited, see Chapter 9.)

*Continued . . .*

**4.** Your essay should be 3 to 5 pages. Consider your audience for this paper to be your fellow classmates and instructor.

### Note on Quoting from a Story

To communicate clearly, you will need to refer to the story itself. Use some quotations—brief or long—to provide supporting evidence for your points, to show what you mean. With fiction as with nonfiction, a long quote is four or more lines and should be set off 10 spaces (two tabs) from the left margin and double spaced. After each quote you use, cite the page number where you found the quote in parentheses.

## STORIES TO CONSIDER FOR WRITING AN ESSAY

### Popular Mechanics

#### *Raymond Carver*

Early that day the weather turned and the snow was melting into dirty water. Streaks of it ran down from the little shoulder-high window that faced the backyard. Cars slushed by on the street outside, where it was getting dark. But it was getting dark on the inside too.

He was in the bedroom pushing clothes into a suitcase when she came to the door.

I'm glad you're leaving! I'm glad you're leaving! she said. Do you hear?

He kept on putting his things into the suitcase.

Son of a bitch! I'm so glad you're leaving! She began to cry. You can't even look me in the face, can you?

He looked at her and she wiped her eyes and stared at him before turning and going back to the living room.

Bring that back, he said

Just get your things and get out, she said

He did not answer. He fastened the suitcase, put on his coat, looked around the bedroom before turning off the light. Then he went out to the living room.

She stood in the doorway of the little kitchen, holding the baby.

I want the baby, he said.

Are you crazy?

No, but I want the baby. I'll get someone to come by for his things.

You're not touching this baby, she said.

The baby had begun to cry and she uncovered the blanket from around his head.

Oh, oh, she said, looking at the baby.

He moved toward her.

For God's sake! she said. She took a step back into the kitchen.

I want the baby.

Get out of here!

She turned and tried to hold the baby over in a corner behind the stove.

But he came up. He reached across the stove and tightened his hands on the baby.

Let go of him, he said.

Get away, getaway! she cried.

The baby was red-faced and screaming. In the scuffle they knocked down a flowerpot that hung behind the stove.

He crowded her into the wall then, trying to break her grip. He held on to the baby and pushed with all his weight.

Let go of him, he said.

Don't, she said. You're hurting the baby, she said.

I'm not hurting the baby, he said.

The kitchen window gave no light. In the near-dark he worked on her fisted fingers with one hand and with the other hand he gripped the screaming baby up under an arm near the shoulder.

She felt her fingers being forced open. She felt the baby going from her.

No! she screamed just as her hands came loose.

She would have it, this baby. She grabbed for the baby's other arm. She caught the baby around the wrist and leaned back.

But he would not let go. He felt the baby slipping out of his hands and he pulled back very hard.

In this manner, the issue was decided.

*Raymond Carver (1938–1988), born in Oregon, is best known for his short stories concerning the toll of alcoholism and breakups. His books include* What We Talk about When We Talk about Love *(1989) and* Where Water Comes Together with Other Water: Poems *(1986).*

Work Cited

Carver, Raymond. "Popular Mechanics." What We Talk about When We Talk about Love: Stories. New York: Vintage, 1989. 123–126.

## Shotgun Wedding

### Bonnie Jo Campbell

Clearly this groom is more accustomed to lugging hay bales and veal calves, but with those big hands he manages to lift my sister's veil and smooth it back prettily over her hair, revealing her face and shoulders. I feel vaguely shameful about this ritual undressing, though I myself have stripped naked in all sorts of places with men whom I've no intention of marrying. Now, as the groom bends toward my sister's face, the bought flowers vibrate in the vases, and my hands shake. My sister, who has a tiny waist and who is an honest-to-goodness virgin, absorbs the moment before the kiss and pulls all the energy from the room, leaving the rest of us feeling dull.

The softness of their kiss gives me the seasick feeling that I'm with my sister and the groom on the honeymoon bed. After all, I shared a room with her until I left for college. I look away, to the pastor who looms over this procedure with the gravity of a hangman, then up to the electric chandelier, which gleams motionless. No longer do I fear that my dress will come unzipped or that the brass fixture will fall and crack open my sister's skull; instead I fear that this kiss will not end, that time will freeze and abandon me in this orbit. My sister's eyes are closed, her lashes spread out over her cheeks. Even after they've opened again, her eyes remain in the sleep of that kiss as though covered with a milky effluent, something the fairies would make in their mouths and spit onto those they favor.

In the upholstered front-row pew, my parents' eyes seem covered with the milky substance as well. My mother dabs her face with a Kleenex; in the garden she wipes the sweat off her forehead with the bottom of her T-shirt. My father, who didn't even wear a suit to my aunt's funeral last year, is dressed like Fred Astaire and has got his legs crossed. The change in my parents frightens me more than walking on carpeting in three-inch heels, and I'm wishing that I had carried my own weedy bouquet of wild phlox or had neglected to shave my legs or had worn a necklace of stones, done anything that would make me feel more like myself. I'm letting my sister down by being sucked into her fairy tale. Someone should always remain vigilant.

My job now is to follow the bride and the groom down the aisle. My sister's gown is something out of a 1940s movie, sleeveless and crusted with embroidery, front and back—I wouldn't let her tell me what she paid for it. Her gloves extend past her elbows, to tiny biceps unbefitting a farm girl. Though we are not a touchy family, my father reaches out from the pew and squeezes my free hand with his calloused palm. He taught me to shoot, my father, by pressing his index finger over my own to squeeze the trigger the first time. As I shuffle behind the bride and groom, I let my father's hand drop and look away so he doesn't see that I've started to cry.

When my father taught me to shoot, I was ten. First I shot at a target placed against a side of the hill in the pasture, and then at raccoons who tried to get into the chicken house. My sister refused even to touch the shotgun; she did not want to be Annie Oakley or Laura on the prairie. She wanted to be Cinderella or Snow White, passive and pure at heart. Like the princess who couldn't bear the pea beneath the mattress, when my sister started her period, she spent three days in bed without speaking—she had seen the health movies in school, but she had honestly not believed that her own body would betray her in this way. My father always worried about my sister not learning to shoot; he told my mom that a girl like her especially needed to be able to defend herself.

From now on she has her husband to defend her, I suppose. And who knows? Maybe the two of them will have one of those lives of enduring bliss you hear about on the radio. I remain six feet behind my sister so I don't step on her train, and I take the hand of the flower girl, my cousin's daughter, who has emptied the basket of rose petals and is now fidgeting at having to walk so slowly. Suddenly, in the first unchoreographed move of this ceremony, just before passing through the double doors beneath the " Exit" sign, my sister turns and looks back toward the altar. Had I anticipated that she would then look at me, I'd have straightened out my face and smiled, but she catches my eyes full of tears and my mouth set grimly in the memory of shooting my first raccoon dead outside the chicken house, of the shot picking its body up off the ground and slamming it against the barn wall.

My sister wears all kinds of waterproof mascara and eye shadow, so her eyes appear especially white and alert; but the fairy milk clears the instant her gaze meets mine, leaving the naked look of a girl in the water who can't swim. She stares at me for one second, two seconds. Why doesn't the groom notice my sister's distress? He should turn her around and kiss her hard, crushing those flowers in his pocket if necessary. Kiss her,

I want to yell. Instead, I collect myself into a half-smile which does not fool her. There's nothing I can do except reach down and straighten her embroidered train which I have almost just stepped on. The flower girl bends and helps, grateful for something to do. Through the back of my head I feel my parents watching.

When I was thirteen, my sister was nine. That was one of the winters both my father and my mother worked at the Halko plant making automotive armrests and glove boxes on third shift, leaving the house at ten-thirty at night. Though the area is starting to get built up, our house then was a half-mile from the next neighbor; the police might take half an hour to get to us, so my father told me to sleep with the shotgun against the wall beside my bed. He placed it there before he left each night. "If you hear anyone outside, you get that gun," he had instructed me. "If anyone comes into this house without your permission, you blow 'em away, honey."

My sister always slept soundly—Sleeping Beauty, my mother called her because she was lost to our world for ten or twelve hours a night. I have never needed that much sleep, but I could read without disturbing her in the bed next to mine, or reorganize the shells and polished stones on the top of my dresser by shape or color or size. After my parents went to work, I sometimes got up and walked the floors of all the rooms, including what would have been my sister's room if she'd been willing to move into it. We'd cleared it out and painted it for her; she could have put up filmy curtains instead of living with the burlap ones Mom helped me make. Mom began to store boxes of our outgrown clothes in the room that my sister did not occupy, and eventually she put her sewing machine and ironing board back in.

One night just after Mom and Dad left for work, when the oil burner kicked off and left the house silent, I heard the crunching of driveway gravel, steps in a man's cadence, so that I thought it must be my father returning. I looked out from the window in the landing and did not see his truck, but saw a tall stranger walking toward our porch, glancing side to side, his hands in his pockets. He wore a quilted, red-checked flannel shirt without a jacket though it was below freezing out. I descended the stairs and moved toward the front door as the man ascended to the porch, so that we approached one another, he with his laced-up workboots, and myself barefoot with the shotgun loaded and pointed forward, safety off. The man did not knock, but the doorknob turned halfway. I touched it to assure myself that my parents had locked the door on their way out. The brass conducted cold from outside. I stepped back and pointed the gun at the latch.

"Wait until an intruder's in the house," my father had said, "or else you'll have to drag him inside and tell the cops that's where you shot him." He had said this as if joking, but now I envisioned myself dragging that man's body across the threshold by one limp arm or a belt loop. My father had told me to shoot a man anywhere on the abdomen, because I couldn't miss at close range, and the twelve gauge at close range would tear a man apart. When I'd shot that first raccoon outside the chicken house its body turned inside out.

The man stood on the other side of the door, perhaps deciding which window to break, or deciding how much force it would take to destroy the front door hardware. It never occurred to me that the man might have come for warmth or merely to steal money or the television. My sister sleeping upstairs no longer seemed a regular flesh-and-blood girl, but had become a rare treasure like a unicorn or a living swan made of white gold, and it made sense that our house would be under siege.

The gun grew heavy against my shoulder, but the weight felt natural, and the metal of the barrel and the trigger gradually warmed to my body temperature. Whenever I'd actually pulled the trigger, I'd been bruised by the recoil; now I looked forward to that burst of pain again, the price I would pay for exploding this man's stomach or heart. One blast should take him down, but if he was still standing, I'd load and shoot again. After the first, there were four shots in the magazine, enough to kill a bull, or even a vampire. After I shot that raccoon, my father dug a hole and buried it right here; he said the other raccoons would smell it and stay away.

The man stepped to the side and looked in through the skinny single-paned window beside the door. Most likely he saw first the identifiable roundness of the end of the shotgun barrel, the size of a nickel, which I had moved to point straight at him. Then he cupped his hands against the glass and let his eyes adjust to the darkness, in which he gradually made out my face, my strawberry blond hair which has darkened in the years since, my freckles, my ray eyes. My face gave away nothing, and in the several seconds during which the man stared into my eyes, he might have seen his own self turned inside out.

His face seemed surprisingly delicate except for a day's growth of beard; his skin was pale and his eyes dark, quiet, and dilated. I had not expected an intruder to be beautiful. I let the gun slide forward slightly, so the tip of the barrel kissed the window, clinked against the glass like the turning of a key. The pretty gaze dissolved. His jaw fell loose. As the man's face disintegrated, I stood unearthly still, not even blinking, poised to fire. I felt no fear, standing in a flannel nightgown which was both too large and too short, whose pattern of galloping horses had faded, and whose frayed ruffle moved back and forth across my legs, brushing the bare skin just below my knees. I felt no fear, though my legs were thin, hardly bigger than the barrel of the gun, and my arms were strained. I felt no fear at the prospect of shooting this man, of watching his body crumple, then dragging the corpse inside, quickly so the heat didn't escape from the house.

I held the gun up long after the man turned and walked down the steps and ran across our frozen lawn toward the road. His hands were still in his pockets, but he held his arms tight against his sides now. When he looked back over his shoulder at the house, he tripped over an apple tree stump my father had been meaning to dig out with the backhoe. He briefly lay prone before he took his hands out of his pockets to push himself up and continue to the road at a jog. The electricity in the air dissipated, but still I held that gun up, even after my arms began to shake, pointing it at the front door where now only the ghost of the man remained. The house air seemed dusty and suffocating. A screech owl cried broken heartedly from the woods across the road. The furnace kicked on and kicked off twice before I lifted that gun off my shoulder and let my arms hang free. I would not sleep that night but would walk the rooms of the house until morning. Under my weight the floorboards creaked in a thousand places. I returned again and again to the room where my sister slept. Hour after hour, while I kept watch, her princess hair curled onto her pillow, and all night her long dark lashes rested against her cheeks, beneath eyes clenched firmly in dreams.

*Bonnie Jo Campbell lives on a farm near Kalamazoo, Michigan. After earning a master's degree in mathematics, she started writing fiction. Her book* <u>Women and Other Animals</u> *won the Associated Writing Programs Award for short fiction. She*

*practices Kouburyo karate and also created a microbrew, Q Brew, to go with her
novel <u>Q Road</u> (2002).*

Work Cited

Campbell, Bonnie Jo. "Shotgun Wedding." <u>Women and Other Animals</u>. New York: Scribner,
2002. 56–61.

## The Undeclared Major

### *Will Weaver*

In his gloomy periods Walter Hansen saw himself as one large contradiction. He was
still twenty, yet his reddish hair was in full retreat from the white plain of his forehead.
He had small and quick-moving blue eyes, eyes that tended skyward, eyes that noted
every airplane that passed overhead; his hands and feet were great, heavy shovels. As
Walter shambled between his classes at the University of Minnesota in Minneapolis, he
sometimes caught unexpected sight of himself in a tall glass doorway or window. He always stopped to stare: there he was, the big farm kid with a small handful of books.
Walter Hansen, the only twenty-year-old Undeclared Major on the whole campus.

But even that wasn't true. Walter Hansen had declared a major some time ago;
he just hadn't felt up to telling anyone what it was.

At present Walter sat in the last, backward-facing seat of the Greyhound bus,
reading <u>The Collected Stories of John Cheever</u>. Occasionally he looked up to stare at
the blue-tinted fields, which in their passing pulled him, mile by mile, toward home.
Toward his twenty-first birthday this very weekend.

By the third hour of the trip Walter had a headache from reading. He put away
Cheever and began to watch the passing farms. It was a sunny, wet April in central
Minnesota. Farmers were trying to spread manure. Their tractors left black ruts in the
yellow corn stubble, and once Walter saw two tractors chained together straining, the
big rear wheels spinning, throwing clods in the air, as they tried to pull free a third
spreader sunk to its hubs beneath an overenthusiastic load of dung.

At the end of the fourth hour Walter's hometown came onto the horizon. It was
low and scattered, and soon began to flash by in the windows of the slowing bus like
a family slide show that was putting to sleep even the projector operator. A junkyard
with a line of shining hubcaps nailed on the fence. A combination deer farm and
aquarium with its stuffed black bear wearing a yellow hula skirt, and wheels that stood
by the front door. Then the tall and narrow white wooden houses. The square red brick
buildings of Main Street, where the bus sighed to a stop at the Shell station. Ducking
his head, Walter clambered down the bus steps and stood squinting in the sunlight.

Main Street was three blocks long. Its two-story buildings were fronted with
painted tin awnings or cedar shake shingles to disguise the brick and make the buildings look lower and more modern. At the end of Main Street was the taller, dull gray
tower of the feed mill. A yellow drift of cornmeal lay on its roof. A blue wheel of pi-
geons turned overhead. At the stoplight a '57 Chevy chirped its tires, accelerated rapidly for half a block, then braked sharply to turn down Main Street.

Which Walter planned to avoid. On Main Street he would have to speak to people. They would ask him things.

"Walt—so how's the rat race?"

"Walt—where does a person park down there?"

"So Walt, what was it you're going into again? Business? Engineering? Vetinary?"

Carrying his small suitcase, and looking neither left nor right, Walter slipped undetected across Main Street. He walked two blocks to the railroad crossing where he set out east.

The iron rails shone blue. Between the rails, tiny agates glinted red from their bed of gravel, and the flat, sun-warmed railroad ties exhaled a faint breath of creosote. On Walter's right, a robin dug for worms on the sunny south embankment; on the north side, the dirty remnant of a snowbank leaked water downhill. Walter stopped to poke at the snowbank with a stick. Beneath a black crust and mud and leaves, the snow was freshly white and sparkling—but destined, of course, to join the muddy pond water below. Walter thought about that. About destiny. He stood with the chill on his face from the old snowbank and the sun warm on his neck and back. There was a poem buried somewhere in that snowbank. Walter waited, but the first line would not visit him. He walked on.

Walter was soon out of town and into woods and fields. Arms outstretched, suitcase balanced atop his head, he walked one rail for twenty-two ties, certainly a record of some sort. Crows called. A redheaded woodpecker flopped from east to west across the rails. The bird was ridiculously heavy for the length of its wings, a fact which made Walter think of Natural Science. Biology. Veterinary Medicine and other majors with names as solid and normal as fork handles.

Animal Husbandry.

Technical Illustration.

Mechanical Engineering.

Ahead on Walter's left was a twenty-acre field of new oat seeding, brown in the low spots, dusty chartreuse on the higher crowns of the field.

Plant Science.

He could tell people he was developing new wheat strains for Third World countries, like Norman Borlaug.

He walked on, slower now, for around a slight bend he could see, a half mile ahead, the gray dome of his father's silo and the red shine of the dairy barn. He neared the corner post of the west field, where his father's land began. Half the field was gray, the other half was freshly black. He slowed further. A meadowlark called from a fence post. Walter stopped to pitch a rock at the bird.

Then he heard a tractor. From behind a broad swell in the field rose his father's blue cap, tan face, brown shirt, then the red snout of the Massey-Ferguson. The Massey pulled their green four-row corn planter. His father stood upright on the platform of the tractor. He stood that way to sight down the tractor's nose, to keep its front tires on the line scuffed in the dirt by the corn planter's marker on the previous round. Intermittently Walter's father swiveled his neck for a glance back at the planter. He looked, Walter knew, for the flap of a white rag tied around the main shaft; if the white flag waved, the main shaft turned, the planter plates revolved, pink kernels fell—Walter knew all that stuff.

He stopped walking. There were bushes along the fencerow, and he stooped to lower his profile, certain that his father hadn't seen him. First Walter wanted to go home, talk to his mother, have a cup of coffee. Two cups, maybe. A cinnamon roll. A bowl of bing cherries in sauce, with cream. Maybe one more splash of coffee. Then. Then he'd come back to the field to speak with his father.

Nearing the field's end, his father trailed back his right arm, found the cord, which he pulled at the same moment as he turned hard to left. Brakes croaked. Tripped, the marker arms rose, the Massey came hard around with its front wheels reaching for their new track, the planter straightened behind, the right arm with its shining disk fell, and his father, back to Walter, headed downfield.

Except that brakes croaked again and the tractor came to a stop. His father turned to Walter and held up a hand.

Walter waved once. He looked briefly behind him to the rails that led back toward town, then crossed the ditch and swung his suitcase over the barbed wire.

His father shut off the tractor. " Hey, Walt—" his father called.

Walter waved again.

His father waited by the corn planter. He smiled, his teeth white against the tan skin, the dust. Walter came up to him.

"Walt," his father said.

They stood there grinning at each other. They didn't shake hands. Growing up, Walter believed people shook hands only in the movies or on used-car lots. None of his relatives ever shook hands. Their greeting was to stand and grin at each other and raise their eyebrows up and down. At the university Walter and his circle of friends shook hands coming and going, European style.

"How's it going?" Walter said, touching his boot to the corn planter.

"She's rolling," his father said. " Got one disk that keeps dragging, but other than that."

People in Walter's family often did not complete their sentences.

"A disk dragging," Walter said.

"Yep," his father said. He squinted at Walter, looked down at his clean clothes. "What would you do for a stuck disk?" he asked.

"I'd take out the grease zerk and run a piece of wire in there. That failing, I'd take off the whole disk and soak it in a pan of diesel fuel overnight," Walter said.

Father and son grinned at each other.

His father took off his hat. His forehead was white, his hair coppery. " So how's the rat race, son?"

"Not so bad," Walter said.

His father paused a moment. " Any . . . decisions yet?" his father said.

Walter swallowed. He looked off toward town. " About . . . a major, you mean?" Walter said.

His father waited.

"Well," Walter said. His mouth went dry. He swallowed twice.

"Well," he said, " I think I'm going to major in English."

His father pursed his lips. He pulled off his work gloves one finger at a time. "English," he said.

"English," Walter nodded.

His father squinted. "Son, we already know English."

Walter stared. "Well, yessir, that's true. I mean, I'm going to study literature. Books. See how they're written. Maybe write one of my own some day."

His father rubbed his brown neck and stared downfield.

Two white sea gulls floated low over the fresh planting.

"So what do you think?" Walter said.

His father's forehead wrinkled and he turned back to Walter. "What could a person be, I mean with that kind of major? An English major," his father said, testing the phrase on his tongue and his lips.

"Be," Walter said. He fell silent. "Well, I don't know, I could be a . . . writer. A teacher maybe, though I don't think I want to teach. At least not for a while. I could be . . . " Then Walter's mind went blank. As blank and empty as the fields around him.

His father was silent. The meadowlark called again.

"I would just be myself, I guess," Walter said.

His father stared a moment at Walter. "Yourself, only smarter," he added.

"Yessir," Walter said quickly, " that's it."

His father squinted downfield at the gulls, then back at Walter. "Nobody talked you into this?"

Walter shook his head no.

"You like it when you're doing it?" his father asked. He glanced across his own field, at what he had planted.

Walter nodded.

His father looked back to Walter and thought another moment. "You think you can make a living at it?"

"Somehow," Walter said.

His father shrugged. " Then I can't see any trouble with it myself," he said. He glanced away, across the fields to the next closest set of barns and silos. "Your uncles, your grampa, they're another story, I suppose."

"They wouldn't have to know," Walter said quickly.

His father looked back to Walter and narrowed his eyes. "They ask me, I'll tell them," he said.

Walter smiled at his father. He started to take a step closer, but at that moment his father looked up at the sun. "We better keep rolling here," he said. He tossed his gloves to Walter. " Take her around once or twice while I eat my sandwich."

Walter climbed onto the tractor and brought up the RPMs. In another minute he was headed downfield. He stood upright on the platform and held tightly to the wheel. The leather gloves were still warm and damp from his father's hands. He sighted the Massey's radiator cap on the thin line in the dirt ahead, and held it there. Halfway downfield he remembered to check the planter flag; in one backward glance he saw his father in straight brown silhouette against the chartreuse band of the fencerow bushes, saw the stripe of fresh dirt unrolling behind, the green seed canisters, and below, the white flag waving. He let out a breath.

After two rounds, Walter began to relax. He began to feel the warm thermals from the engine, the cool breath of the earth below. Gulls hovered close over the tractor, their heads cocked earthward as they waited for the disks to turn up yellow cutworms. A red agate passed underneath and was covered by dirt. The corn planter rolled behind, and through the trip rope, a cotton cord gone smoothly black from grease and dusty gloves, Walter felt the shafts turning, the disks wheeling, the kernels dropping, the press wheel tamping the seed into four perfect rows.

Well, not entirely perfect rows.

Walter, by round four, had begun to think of other things. That whiteness beneath the old snowbank. The blue shine of the iron rails. The damp warmth of his father's gloves. The heavy, chocolate-layer birthday cake that he knew, as certain as he knew the sun would set tonight and rise tomorrow, his mother had hidden in the pantry. Of being twenty-one and the limitless destiny, the endless prospects before him, Walter Hansen, English Major.

As he thought about these and other things, the tractor and its planter drifted a foot to the right, then a foot to the left, centered itself, then drifted again. At field's end his father stood up. He began to wave at Walter first with one hand, then both. But Walter drove on, downfield, smiling slightly to himself, puzzling over why it was he so seldom came home.

*Will Weaver writes fiction for adults and young adults. Born in northern Minnesota, he grew up on a dairy farm. His recent book is* Sweet Land: New and Selected Stories *(2006). There is also a film based on his book called* Sweet Land *(2005). Weaver teaches writing part-time at Bemidji State University in Minnesota.*

Work Cited

Weaver, Will. "The Undeclared Major." *A Gravestone Made of Wheat*. New York: Simon & Schuster, 1989. 169–175.

## READING AND WRITING ABOUT LITERARY NONFICTION

Some readers assume stories occur only in fiction. But that isn't true. Biography and autobiography, history, even news events are often presented as stories. They share chronological organization to tell readers *what happened* and *what happened next*. Some of our finest nonfiction writers have learned not only to tell what happened but also to tell it with techniques normally found only in fiction—dialogue, setting, and character development. Literary nonfiction, or creative nonfiction as it is commonly called, usually involves poetic description: a rich use of imagery, metaphors, and similes. Like poetry and fiction, literary nonfiction works by implication: your job as reader is to infer meaning.

You can think critically whenever you read. But how you read depends on your purpose. Often you may want to skim a news article to get the gist of the information. Or you may read purely for pleasure, as many people do with romance novels. Sometimes you may read for spiritual comfort, as with the Bible. But the purpose of this book is to help you develop yourself as a critical thinker, reader, and writer. The selections in this book were chosen to stir questions within you, to puzzle you, to surprise or shock you, and to cause you to consider a writer's appeals to logos, pathos, and ethos.

The following essay, "Brute," was written by Richard Selzer. Taken from his book <u>Letters to a Young Doctor</u>, first published in 1982, the essay has stirred controversy for Selzer. Selzer was a surgeon for many years who also taught surgery at Yale University until he retired to write full-time. "Brute" is a narrative essay based on an experience of his in an emergency room. As you read "Brute," consider why you think many people have judged this essay as controversial. When you finish the essay, write your reactions to it in your notebook.

## Brute

### *Richard Selzer*

You must never again set your anger upon a patient. You were tired, you said, and therefore it happened. Now that you have excused yourself, there is no need for me to do it for you.

Imagine that you yourself go to a doctor because you have chest pain. You are worried that there is something the matter with your heart. Chest pain is your Chief Complaint. It happens that your doctor has been awake all night with a patient who has been bleeding from a peptic ulcer of his stomach. He is tired. That is your doctor's Chief Complaint. I have chest pain, you tell him. I am tired, he says.

Still I confess to some sympathy for you. I know what tired is.

Listen: It is twenty-five years ago in the Emergency Room. It is two o'clock in the morning. There has been a day and night of stabbings, heart attacks and automobile accidents. A commotion at the door: A huge black man is escorted by four policemen into the Emergency Room. He is handcuffed. At the door, the man rears as though to shake off the men who cling to his arms and press him from the rear. Across the full length of his forehead is a laceration. It is deep to the bone. I know it even without probing its depths. The split in his black flesh is like the white wound of an ax in the trunk of a tree. Again and again he throws his head and shoulders forward, then back, rearing, roaring. The policemen ride him like parasites. Had he horns he would gore them. Blind and trussed, the man shakes them about, rattles them. But if one of them loses his grip, the others are still fixed and sucking. The man is hugely drunk—toxic, fuming, murderous—a great mythic beast broken loose in the city, surprised in his night raid by a phalanx of legionnaires armed with clubs and revolvers.

I do not know the blow that struck him on the brow. Or was there any blow? Here is a brow that might have burst on its own, spilling out its excess of rage, bleeding itself toward ease. Perhaps it was done by a jealous lover, a woman, or a man who will not pay him the ten dollars he won on a bet, or still another who has hurled the one insult that he cannot bear to hear. Perhaps it was done by the police themselves. From the distance of many years and from the safety of my little study, I choose to see it thus:

The helmeted corps rounds the street corner. A shout. "There he is!" And they clatter toward him. He stands there for a moment, lurching. Something upon which he had been feeding falls from his open mouth. He turns to face the policemen.

For him it is not a new challenge. He is scarred as a Zulu from his many battles. Almost from habit he ascends to the combat. One or more of them falls under his flailing arms until—there is the swing of a truncheon, a sound as though a melon has been dropped from a great height. The white wedge appears upon the sweating brow of the black man, a waving fall of blood pours across his eyes and cheeks.

The man is blinded by it; he is stunned. Still he reaches forth to make contact with the enemy, to do one more piece of damage. More blows to the back, the chest and again to the face. Bloody spume flies from his head as though lifted by a great wind. The police are spattered with it. They stare at each other with an abstract horror and disgust. One last blow, and, blind as Samson, the black man undulates, rolling in a splayfooted circle. But he does not go down. The police are upon him then, pinning him, cuffing his wrists, kneeing him toward the van. Through the back window of the wagon—a netted panther.

In the Emergency Room he is led to the treatment area and to me. There is a vast dignity about him. He keeps his own counsel. What is he thinking? I wonder. The police urge him up on the table. They put him down. They restrain his arms with straps. I examine the wound, and my heart sinks. It is twelve centimeters long, irregular, jagged and, as I knew, to the skull. It will take at least two hours.

I am tired. Also to the bone. But something else . . . Oh, let me not deny it. I am ravished by the sight of him, the raw, untreated flesh, his very wildness which suggests less a human than a great and beautiful animal. As though by the addition of the wound, his body is more than it was, more of a body. I begin to cleanse and debride the wound. At my touch, he stirs and groans. "Lie still," I tell him. But now he rolls his head from side to side so that I cannot work. Again and again he lifts his pelvis from the table, strains against his bonds, then falls heavily. He roars something, not quite language. "Hold still," I say. "I cannot stitch your forehead unless you hold still."

Perhaps it is the petulance in my voice that makes him resume his struggle against all odds to be free. Perhaps he understands that it is only a cold, thin official voice such as mine, and not the billy clubs of half-a-dozen cops that can rob him of his dignity. And so he strains and screams. But why can he not sense that I am tired? He spits and curses and rolls his head to escape from my fingers. It is quarter to three in the morning. I have not yet begun to stitch. I lean close to him; his steam fills my nostrils. "Hold still," I say.

"*You* fuckin' hold still," he says to me in a clear, fierce voice. Suddenly, I am in the fury with him. Somehow he has managed to capture me, to pull me inside his cage. Now we are two brutes hissing and batting at each other. But I do not fight fairly.

I go to the cupboard and get from it two packets of heavy, braided silk suture and a large curved needle. I pass one of the heavy silk sutures through the eye of the needle. I take the needle in the jaws of a needle holder, and I pass the needle through the center of his right earlobe. Then I pass the needle through the mattress of the stretcher. And I tie the thread tightly so that his head is pulled to the right. I do exactly the same to his left earlobe, and again I tie the thread tightly so that his head is facing directly upward.

"I have sewn your ears to the stretcher," I say. "Move, and you'll rip 'em off." And leaning close I say in a whisper, "Now *you* fuckin' hold still."

I do more. I wipe the gelatinous clots from his eyes so that he can see. And I lean over him from the head of the table, so that my face is directly above his, upside down. And I grin. It is the cruelest grin of my life. Torturers must grin like that, beheaders and operators of racks.

But now he does hold still. Surely it is not just fear of tearing his earlobes. He is too deep into his passion for that. It is more likely some beastly wisdom that tells him that at last he has no hope of winning. That it is time to cut his losses, to slink off into high grass. Or is it some sober thought that pierces his wild brain, lacerating him in such a way that a hundred nightsticks could not? The thought of a woman who is waiting for him, perhaps? Or a child who, the next day and the week after that, will stare up at his terrible scars with a silent wonder that will shame him? For whatever reason, he is perfectly still.

It is four o'clock in the morning as I take the first stitch in his wound. At five-thirty, I snip each of the silks in his earlobes. He is released from his leg restrainers and pulled to a sitting position. The bandage on his head is a white turban. A single drop of blood in each earlobe, like a ruby. He is a maharajah.

The police return. All this time they have been drinking coffee with the nurses, the orderlies, other policemen, whomever. For over three hours the man and I have been alone in our devotion to the wound. "I have finished," I tell them. Roughly, they haul him from the stretcher and prod him toward the door. "Easy, easy," I call after them. And, to myself, if you hit him again . . .

Even now, so many years later, this ancient rage of mine returns to peck among my dreams. I have only to close my eyes to see him again wielding his head and jaws, to hear once more those words at which the whole of his trussed body came hurtling toward me. How sorry I will always be. Not being able to make it up to him for that grin.

*Richard Selzer is a former surgeon and Yale School of Medicine professor. He started writing stories and essays when he was 40. He has received many honors for writing including a Guggenheim fellowship. Among his several books are Mortal Lessons: Notes on the Art of Surgery (1996) and The Exact Location of the Soul: New and Selected Essays (2002).*

Work Cited

Selzer, Richard. "Brute." Letters to a Young Doctor. New York: Simon & Schuster, 1982. San Diego: Harvest, 1996. 59–63.

"Brute" is based on an event that happened to Richard Selzer twenty-five years before he wrote about it. With the book published in 1982, this means the event took place in 1957. It is a personal story, not fiction. But for critical thinkers the essay raises at least two important questions. First, who is the brute? Is the brute the patient or the doctor? Or are there other possibilities—both men? Neither? Second, do you think Selzer is possibly racist in this essay?

## ACTIVITY 9

What is your position regarding either of the two main questions that "Brute" raises? Write a response in your notebook. ▪

## WRITING ABOUT A LITERARY NONFICTION ESSAY

Explore—analyze and evaluate—a literary nonfiction essay: state a thesis about the essay and defend it.

## ACTIVITY 10

Option 1. You may write about "Brute" by using a two-sided argument (as presented in Chapter 2). Write about whether you believe Selzer or the patient is a brute—or that both are or neither. Or write about whether you think Selzer is possibly racist in the essay. To determine your thesis, you need to read closely—to infer Selzer's position based on his description and narration.

1. Introduce your essay and state your thesis (your position) as the last sentence.
2. In one paragraph summarize "Brute" objectively to show readers you understand it. Use present tense. "Selzer writes" rather than "Selzer wrote."
3. In one paragraph, summarize the view (or views) opposing your position. Be fair-minded. Use present tense.
4. In at least three paragraphs defend your position with reasons, examples, details, and direct quotations. Use present tense. Cite page numbers for quotes.
5. Conclude and restate your thesis.

Option 2. To write about one of the following essays, follow the Guidelines for Writing an Essay about a Story presented in Activity 8. ▪

### Field Trip

#### *Naomi Shihab Nye*

Only once did I take a large group of children on a field trip. A summer creative writing class journeyed by bus to a printing shop to see how pages were bound together to make books and our cheerfully patient guide chopped her finger off with a giant paper cutter.

I had not prepared the children for anything beyond typefaces, camera-ready copy, collation. Standing toward the rear of our group like a shepherd, I felt their happy little backs stiffen at the moment of severance. A gasp rose from their throats as the startling blot of blood grew outward, a rapid pool staining all the pages. The woman pressed forward through our frozen crowd, cupping her wounded hand against her chest, not screaming, but mouthing silently, " Hospital—now—let's go."

A flurry of motion erupted among the other workers, much like the flurry of feathers when anyone steps too quickly into a chicken coop. Two people dialed phones, then asked aloud why they were dialing—couldn't they drive her to the hospital themselves? A voice at the emergency room said to place the severed finger on ice and a man who had been pasting up tedious layouts ran for ice. One boy tugged at my shirt and croaked, "The last thing she said was—you have to be very careful with this machine."

Someone dropped a ring of keys and I crawled under a desk to retrieve them. It felt good to fall to my knees. For a second the stricken woman loomed above me and I stuttered, apologizing for our visit, which had inadvertently caused this disaster, but she was distracted by something else.

"Honey, *look* at that thing!" she exclaimed, staring into the cup of ice where the index finger now rested like a rare archival specimen. " It's turning white! If that finger stays white, I don't want it on my body!"

We laughed hard and loudly, and the children stared at us, amazed. Had we lost our senses? That she could joke at such a moment, as the big fans whirred and the collating machines paused over vast mountains of stacked paper . . . I wanted to sing her blackness, to call out to those girls and boys, " This, my friends, is what words can do for you—make you laugh when your finger rests in a Styrofoam cup!"

But she went quickly off toward the hospital and I shuffled an extremely silent group of children back onto our bus. I wanted to say something promising recovery, or praising our guide's remarkable presence of mind, but my voice seemed lost among the seats. No one would look at me.

Later I heard how they went home and went straight to their rooms. Mothers called me. Some of the children had nightmares. Molly's mother said, " What in the world happened on that field trip? Sarah came over today and she and Molly climbed up on the bed and just sobbed." At our next meeting we made get-well cards. Come-together-again cards. May the seam hold. May the two become one. They thought up all kinds of things. I had been calling the printing shop to monitor her progress and the reports sounded good. The students had been gathering stories; someone's farmer-uncle whose leg was severed in a cornfield, but who lived to see it joined, someone's brother's toe.

I went to her home with a bundle of hopeful wishes tied in loops of pink ribbon. She was wearing a terry cloth bathrobe and sitting in a comfortable chair, her hand hugely bandaged. She sighed and shook her head. "I guess none of those cute kids will ever become printers now, will they? Gee, I hope they don't give up reading and writing too! Oh, I feel just terrible about it. They were such an interested little audience." She'd been worrying about the children while they'd been worrying about her.

Reading their messages made her chuckle. I asked what the doctors had said about the finger turning black again. She said they thought it would, but it might be slightly paler than the rest of her hand. And it would be stiff for a long time, maybe forever.

She said she was missing being at work. Vacations weren't much fun when they came this unexpectedly. But wasn't it great what medicine could do? I decided she might be one of my heroes. The pain was a lot better than it had been last week, and could I please thank those kids for their flowers and hearts?

After that I took my workshops onto the schoolyard but no farther. I made them look for buttons and feathers. I made them describe the postures of men and women waiting for a bus. Once I'd dreamed of visiting every factory in town, the mattress factory, the hot sauce factory, the assembly line for cowboy boots, but I changed my mind.

By the time our workshop ended that summer, we felt more closely bonded than other groups I'd known. We hugged each other tightly. Perhaps our sense of mortality linked us, our shared vision of the fragility of body parts. One girl went on to become one of the best young writers in the city. I'd like to think her hands were blessed by our unexpected obsession with hands.

And I continued to ruminate over field trips in general, remembering the time my high school health class visited the state mental hospital where our teacher unwittingly herded us into a room of elderly women who'd recently had lobotomies, after telling us people didn't do that to one another anymore. Or the absolutely inappropriate ventures—to the Judson Candy Factory on the day Robert Kennedy was shot. Our home economics teacher had planned this day as an end-of-school celebration.

My classmates and I stood staring numbly at vats of creamy chocolate brew. The air hung heavy around us. He was dead and an Arab had killed him. I couldn't mention the second part out loud, but it made me feel sick to my stomach. And the candy factory seemed less sensible now than ever—all that labor to make something that wasn't even good for you. A worker joked that a few of his friends had ended up in those bubbling vats and nobody smiled. How could we?

As a child I finally grew brave enough to plot a trip out into the fields years after my friends had first done it—to Camp Fiddlecreek in Missouri, for Girl Scouts. I'd postponed such an adventure due to an unreasonable fear of spiders. I felt certain a giant furry spider would crawl into my bedroll the minute I got there and entangle itself in my hair. The zipper on the sleeping bag would stick and I would die, die, die. Finally I decided a life without courage might be worse than death, so I packed my greenest duds and headed to the hills.

The first night I confided my secret fear to the girl who slept next to me. She said she'd always been more scared of snakes than spiders. I said, " Snakes, phooey!"

The next day while we were up in the hills hiking, a group of donkeys broke out of a nearby field and ran at us. One knocked me down and trampled me. My leg swelled into three large, hard lumps. I could not walk. I would have to be driven home to the city for X-rays. My friend leaned over, smoothing back my bangs and consoled me. "Donkeys! Can you believe it? Who would ever believe a donkey could be so mean?"

I had never, ever thought about a donkey with any fear. But here began a lifetime of quirks suspended on a single thread: the things we worry about are never the things that happen. And the things that happen are the things we never could have dreamed.

*Naomi Shihab Nye was born to an American mother and a Palestinian father. She lives in San Antonio, Texas. Known mostly for her poetry that celebrates humanity, she also writes children's books and essays. Her books include <u>A Maze Me: Poems for Girls</u> (2005), <u>19 Varieties of Gazelle: Poems of the Middle East</u> (2002), and <u>Habibi</u> (a novel for teens, 1999).*

Work Cited

Nye, Naomi Shihab. "Field Trip." <u>Never in a Hurry: Essays on People and Places</u>. Columbia, SC: U. of South Carolina, 1996. 198–202.

## Living Like Weasels

### *Annie Dillard*

A weasel is wild. Who knows what he thinks? He sleeps in his underground den, his tail draped over his nose. Sometimes he lives in his den for two days without leaving. Outside, he stalks rabbits, mice, muskrats, and birds, killing more bodies than he can eat warm, and often dragging the carcasses home. Obedient to instinct, he bites his prey at the neck, either splitting the jugular vein at the throat or crunching the brain at the base of the skull, and he does not let go. One naturalist refused to kill a weasel who was socketed into his hand deeply as a rattlesnake. The man could in no way pry the tiny weasel off, and he had to walk half a mile to water, the weasel dangling from his palm, and soak him off like a stubborn label.

And once, says Ernest Thompson Seton—once, a man shot an eagle out of the sky. He examined the eagle and found the dry skull of a weasel fixed by the jaws to his throat. The supposition is that the eagle had pounced on the weasel and the weasel swiveled and bit as instinct taught him, tooth to neck, and nearly won. I would like to have seen that eagle from the air a few weeks or months before he was shot: was the whole weasel still attached to his feathered throat, a fur pendant? Or did the eagle eat what he could reach, gutting the living weasel with his talons before his breast, bending his beak, cleaning the beautiful airborne bones?

I have been thinking about weasels because I saw one last week. I startled a weasel who startled me, and we exchanged a long glance.

Near my house in Virginia is a pond—Hollins Pond. It covers two acres of bottom-land near Tinker Creek with six inches of water and six thousand lily pads. There is a fifty-five mph highway at one end of the pond, and a nesting pair of wood ducks at the other. Under every bush is a muskrat hole or a beer can. The far end is an alternating series of fields and woods, fields and woods, threaded everywhere with motorcycle tracks—in whose bare clay wild turtles lay eggs.

One evening last week at sunset, I walked to the pond and sat on a downed log near the shore. I was watching the lily pads at my feet tremble and part over the thrusting path of a carp. A yellow warbler appeared to my right and flew behind me. It caught my eye; I swiveled around—and the next instant, inexplicably, I was looking down at a weasel, who was looking up at me.

Weasel! I had never seen one wild before. He was ten inches long, thin as a curve, a muscled ribbon, brown as fruitwood, soft-furred, alert. His face was fierce, small and pointed as a lizard's; he would have made a good arrowhead. There was just a dot of chin, maybe two brown hairs' worth, and then the pure white fur began that spread down his underside. He had two black eyes I did not see, any more than you see a window.

The weasel was stunned into stillness as he was emerging from beneath an enormous shaggy wild-rose bush four feet away. I was stunned into stillness, twisted backward on the tree trunk. Our eyes locked, and someone threw away the key.

Our look was as if two lovers, or deadly enemies, met unexpectedly on an overgrown path when each had been thinking of something else: a clearing blow to the gut. It was also a bright blow to the brain, or a sudden beating of brains, with all the charge and intimate grate of rubbed balloons. It emptied our lungs. It felled the forest, moved the fields, and drained the pond; the world dismantled and tumbled into that black hole of eyes. If you and I looked at each other that way, our skulls would split and drop to our shoulders. But we don't. We keep our skulls.

He disappeared. This was only last week, and already I don't remember what shattered the enchantment. I think I blinked, I think I retrieved my brain from the weasel's brain, and tried to memorize what I was seeing, and the weasel felt the yank of separation, the careening splashdown into real life and the urgent current of instinct. He vanished under the wild rose. I waited motionless, my mind suddenly full of data and my spirit with pleadings, but he didn't return.

Please do not tell me about "approach-avoidance conflicts." I tell you I've been in that weasel's brain for sixty seconds, and he was in mine. Brains are private places, muttering through unique and secret tapes—but the weasel and I both plugged into another tape simultaneously, for a sweet and shocking time. Can I help it if it was a blank?

What goes on in his brain the rest of the time? What does a weasel think about? He won't say. His journal is tracks in clay, a spray of feathers, mouse blood and bone: uncollected, unconnected, loose-leaf, and blown.

I would like to learn, or remember, how to live. I come to Hollins Pond not so much to learn how to live as, frankly, to forget about it. That is, I don't think I can learn from a wild animal how to live in particular—shall I suck warm blood, hold my tail high, walk with my footprints precisely over the prints of my hands?—but I might learn something of mindlessness, something of the purity of living in the physical senses and the dignity of living without bias or motive. The weasel lives in necessity and we live in choice, hating necessity and dying at the last ignobly in its talons. I would like to live as I should, as the weasel lives as he should. And I suspect that for me the way is like the weasel's: open to time and death painlessly, noticing everything, remembering nothing, choosing the given with a fierce and pointed will.

I missed my chance. I should have gone for the throat. I should have lunged for that streak of white under the weasel's chin and held on, held on through mud and into the wild rose, held on for a dearer life. We could live under the wild rose wild as weasels, mute and uncomprehending. I could very calmly go wild. I could live two days in the den, curled, leaning on mouse fur, sniffing bird bones, blinking, licking, breathing musk, my hair tangled in the roots of grasses. Down is a good place to go, where the mind is single. Down is out, out of your ever-loving mind and back to your careless senses. I remember muteness as a prolonged and giddy fast, where every moment is a feast of utterance received. Time and events are merely poured, unremarked, and ingested directly, like blood pulsed into my gut through a jugular vein. Could two live that way? Could two live under the wild rose, and explore by the pond, so that the smooth mind of each is as everywhere present to the other, and as received and as unchallenged, as falling snow?

We could, you know. We can live any way we want. People take vows of poverty, chastity, and obedience—even of silence—by choice. The thing is to stalk your calling in a certain skilled and supple way, to locate the most tender and live spot and plug into that pulse. This is yielding, not fighting. A weasel doesn't "attack" anything; a weasel lives as he's meant to, yielding at every moment to the perfect freedom of single necessity.

I think it would be well, and proper, and obedient, and pure, to grasp your one necessity and not let it go, to dangle from it limp wherever it takes you. Then even death, where you're going no matter how you live, cannot you part. Seize it and let it seize you up aloft even, till your eyes burn out and drop; let your musky flesh fall off in shreds, and let your very bones unhinge and scatter, loosened over fields, over fields and woods, lightly, thoughtless, from any height at all, from as high as eagles.

*Annie Dillard, raised in Pittsburgh, Pennsylvania, won the Pulitzer Prize for Nonfiction in 1975 for A Pilgrim at Tinker Creek. Known for her poetic description about natural events, she values the process of noticing the concrete world. Her other books include The Writing Life (1990) and The Maytrees: A Novel (2007).*

Work Cited

Dillard, Annie. " Living Like Weasels." <u>Teaching a Stone to Talk: Expeditions and Encounters</u>. 1982. New York: HarperPerennial. 65–70.

## CHAPTER 7

# Research Strategies

## **R**ESEARCH WRITING OPTIONS

Research starts with a genuine desire to investigate and to understand some problem or issue that intrigues you, that matters to you. This desire will pull you through the hard work research involves. But you can make the work easier if you treat it like a process, one that you divide into stages or phases.

Writing a research paper is more like following a spiral than a straight line. As you find sources in the library and on the Internet, you may form a rough outline or start writing brief notes. Later, after you have found information that relates to your purpose and your arguments, you can start adding to your notes. Then you may find yourself returning to the library to find more sources, some you found mentioned in your reading. You may reread various chapters in this book; you may need to reread parts of this chapter. Although you are likely to read Chapters 7 to 10 in chronological order, you may also need to look back to previous chapters, to check information available in online indexes, to check MLA or APA form for documenting journal or magazine articles, and so on. Keep the spiral idea in mind: return to different chapters to answer questions as you do your research and write your paper.

## The Report

Research papers can take various forms. Two common forms are the report and the argument paper.

In a report, you examine a problem or an issue because you want to know more about it and you think readers can benefit from knowing about it too. For this paper you can explain what something is; explain how something was formed, created, discovered; or explain how something works. You can offer possible solutions for solving a problem or help readers understand an issue better.

Do you know anyone who could benefit from your research? A relative or a friend? Yourself? Suppose a health problem runs through your family: breast cancer, hemophilia, aneurysms. You can do research to find out more about it. What treatment options can you find for combating the problem? A report like this could be useful and meaningful—worth doing.

Whatever topic you choose for a report, however, you need to be impartial and fair-minded. You need to weigh the information you gather and decide which is the clearest and most helpful. For an example of a report, see "Saturated by Color" in Chapter 10.

## The Argument Paper

In an argument paper, the key strategy is to present other or opposing views before you evaluate the evidence and draw conclusions. This option requires more research and analysis; it is more challenging than a report.

In discussing any issue on which there is more than one position, you should present various sides of it—especially the side most contrary to your own. Presenting the opposing sides of an issue will show your audience that you are fair-minded. If you have presented both sides well, readers should be able to see which side has the stronger support. If you have been fair, your readers will listen more carefully to what you have to say. (See Chapter 2 for more on writing about arguments and controversies.) For an example of an argument paper, see "Grain or Grass: What's the Beef?" in Chapter 10.

## ACTIVITY 1

In your notebook, explore possible research questions you would like to investigate for your research paper. The questions must intrigue you or matter to you in some way. Choose three questions that you could explore in a report. Consider writing about a health problem that affects you or someone close to you. Then choose three possible questions involving controversies that you could explore in an argument paper. Keep all of these possible research topics tentative. You cannot decide for sure what your topic will be until you see what information is available. Bring your notebook to class to share ideas with classmates. ▪

These research chapters include process notes from a student, Ryan. Use process notes to explore problems while doing research and writing a paper—and possible solutions to them, including eurekas.

## MODERN RESEARCH

I usually have to do five times the amount of research that I will need. . . .

When I wrote the book about Buffalo Bill (<u>This Old Bill</u>), I had to read four or five books about the Pony Express because Bill rode the Pony Express when he was 14. I had to find out what kind of spurs he wore as a teenager. One little detail like that can cost you a day or two. (Loren Estelman)

Modern libraries store many kinds of information: books, newspapers, magazines, journals, government documents, manuscripts, artworks, film, music, videos, photographs, historic artifacts . . . nearly anything that can be stored, protected, and retrieved. Researchers must work harder than ever to keep up with the constant flow of new research: you barely have time for all the reading you must do. There is so much information that researchers must specialize. Instead of all medicine, for example, medical researchers and doctors specialize in various divisions and subspecialties of medicine. Many doctors specialize in only one organ or one system or one disease. It's not exactly a joke to say that modern scholars know more and more about less and less.

No matter what subject you choose, you are likely to find dozens of books, magazines, journals, and newspapers with articles about your subject. You may rightly feel appalled at the thought of so many books and articles confronting you: "Must I really read all that?" The answer seems to be yes and no. Most researchers say it's a good rule to read everything you can; therefore, the best tactic is to narrow your research to the smallest question you can. Fortunately not everything you find is required reading. Much of it is simply repetitious. When one researcher publishes a significant paper, dozens of newspapers, magazines, television and radio news broadcasts repeat the findings, often without adding insight or criticism. For that reason, researchers attempt to find the "significant" or "reliable" sources, and you may be able to weed out some of the items in your working bibliography: the list of possible sources you will consider using in your paper.

To reduce the amount of work you must do, you need to become knowledgeable about your subject. As you read the research, you will discover what is important and what isn't. It takes only a little reading about the safety of mass-produced meat, for example, to come across the name of Eric Schlosser and his well-documented book <u>Fast Food Nation</u>. Your research itself will reveal the significant and reliable sources.

## START IN THE LIBRARY

The library can help you decide what your project should be. Before making too many important decisions, you need to see what information is available. The library can guide you to material that will help you find a worthwhile project. Research writing starts with research reading. Fortunately, modern libraries have many sources of information that can provide you with ideas: encyclopedias, indexes, or the main computer catalog.

A brief search of the online catalog can reveal how many sources—especially recent sources—are available, and the search can suggest whether the subject contains enough research for your purposes.

Information isn't piled up in warehouses. If that were true you'd never have much chance to find anything. Most sources in the library have a specific address called a "call" number that matches a shelf address. And powerful "search engines" can help you find material on the Internet. Google is one of the fastest, and Alltheweb claims to be the most comprehensive search engine, covering the entire Web, hence its name.

Librarians are an essential resource for you. Trained information specialists, they are available and eager to answer your questions and to help you find sources. Academic libraries can be intimidating; it can save you much time and frustration to get help from a librarian. You may find that a librarian can direct you to sources you otherwise might not have found. The reference desk is usually the best place to find a librarian.

## Preliminary Reading

The clearer and simpler your research question, the more you are likely to find an answer. Part of any project is the search for your thesis. Thus, you need a plan for finding your research question. The best procedure is to find your question in the research itself. No matter what your project is, you should start by reading the research. The issue of eating healthy food, for example, may include many topics.

---

**Ryan's Process Notes**

As I did my research—floundering around to find a topic I most wanted to write about—I made a list of possible topics for my paper: diets low in meat; risks and benefits of vegetarianism; risks and benefits of eating meat; ethical problems of slaughtering and eating animals; animal rights; factory farms; vegetarian nutrition; plant-only diets; CAFO's (Concentrated Animal Farming Operations); environmental issues with meat: contributes to global warming, methane, depletion of rainforests; antibiotics in meat; growth hormones in meat; protein in meat vs. plants; food additives; organic foods; genetically modified foods; meat from cloned animals; mad cow disease; chicken—Tyson Foods; seafood—wild-caught fish vs. farm fish; family farms; cage-free eggs vs. caged-hen eggs; treating animals humanely; processed foods; animal rights extremists and eco-terrorists; grain-fed meat vs. grass-fed meat; sustainable practices with meat.

There are so many topics here! But I think I know now which one it will be: grain-fed meat vs. grass-fed meat. I've decided not to examine vegetarianism because I know I don't want to give up all meat. I like an occasional steak too much.

---

Before you can make any meaningful decisions as a researcher, you must read. You must teach yourself the background of your project, as Ryan did.

It's a mistake to try to decide in advance exactly what point to make—what question to examine or thesis to argue—before you have done the necessary background reading. It's too easy just to accept the conventional ideas everyone hears, like deciding to write on the dangers of smoking.

Preliminary reading will give you a background that will help you to evaluate where each new bit of evidence fits into your research. You need a *context* that will help you to understand the relative importance of the data you find. Preliminary reading gives you an overview of your subject, a context for your research, and an indication of the size of your project.

## Locating Your Research Question

You need some question to guide your research and your writing. But you need to skim/browse/read a great deal before you decide on your research question. Strategy One is reading. That is where you will find your research topic and question.

---

**Ryan's Process Notes**

As I read various sources, I made a list of possible research questions:

Is a meat-centered diet worth the effects on our bodies and the environment?
Should we eat less meat?
Should we eat less fast food?
Should we stop eating fast food?
Is a vegetarian diet healthier than a diet including meat?
How can we eat more humanely?
Grain-fed vs. grass-fed meat—which is better?
Grain-fed vs. grass-fed meat—which is better for humans and the earth?
Grain-fed vs. grass-fed meat—which is better for animals, humans, and the environment?

Okay—I think this last question might be the one. I'm not positive but it feels like it might work. It concerns what I'm most interested in exploring.

---

## STRATEGY ONE: FINDING BACKGROUND MATERIAL

A search strategy will give order to your work. Not all researchers work the same way, of course; eventually you'll work out your own procedures, but at the outset you'll find it helpful to proceed from general to more specific sources.

Look for background material before getting into more serious research. Background material creates a rough map: it doesn't show all the details, but it shows you the area and gives you an idea of how to get where you're going. Background reading can help you evaluate and make informed selections among all those library sources.

### General Encyclopedias

In print or online, the general encyclopedias provide summary backgrounds and histories. A quick look at an encyclopedia like the <u>Britannica Online</u> will show articles on factory farms, ethics of raising and eating animals, and Peter Singer, a leading philosopher and advocate of animal rights. <u>Britannica Online</u> contains not only its own articles but links to many other Internet sites including journal and magazine articles as well as video and media links. With an article on factory farms, other subject headings were listed such as industrial farming and services.

One of the virtues of encyclopedias is that they often contain bibliographies that will help you find reliable sources for your project. Encyclopedias can give you an authoritative background. Then too, other researchers may assume you have certainly read the encyclopedia material. You should read the encyclopedias, of course, but how you use this material is a different question. Most college instructors will expect you not to cite information from a general encyclopedia. *Note*: You will likely need to use your school's library to have access to <u>Britannica Online</u>. This source is well worth investigating.

Should you use Wikipedia, "the free encyclopedia"? Is it a trustworthy source of information? See Chapter 8 on this dilemma.

## ACTIVITY 2

Consider one of the subjects you'd like to research. Find two or three general encyclopedias with articles related to this subject. In your notebook write a page explaining your judgment on how these encyclopedia articles compare with each other and which you think would be most useful for your background understanding. ▮

## Specialized Encyclopedias

In addition to the general encyclopedias, most libraries also contain specialized encyclopedias that focus on particular subjects. Note that libraries often use the words *encyclopedia* and *dictionary* interchangeably.

<u>Encyclopedia of American History</u>
<u>Dictionary of American History</u>
<u>Encyclopedia of Bioethics</u>
<u>Encyclopedia of Life Sciences</u>
<u>Encyclopedia of Psychology</u>

Specialized encyclopedias and dictionaries deal with the subjects indicated in their titles. The information they contain can give important background material for that subject. However, if specialized encyclopedias and dictionaries are outdated, they will not be useful.

Research is connected to research: you don't have to start from scratch. Background material in encyclopedias will connect you to the work of other researchers so that your project can grow from a context of information. You need to be able to answer questions about your project: Why do it? What is the point? How can readers know your information is reliable? When your project is connected to the work of other researchers, you will be able to answer such questions with confidence.

## ACTIVITY 3

Find one or more specialized encyclopedias related to your research area. Write a page of summary notes on the relevant information that might be useful. ▪

## THE GROWTH PHENOMENON: A RESEARCH PROBLEM

It's important to keep your thesis restricted. You need to start small and simple because no matter how simple an idea seems when you start, you may soon discover that your project is growing all by itself. As you delve into the research, you will discover that each new idea leads to others. Good researchers don't skip over all the new ideas they encounter. New ideas can help you refine your project and lead you into unexpected areas of research. For example, you might start by investigating "healthy diets" in general. However, soon other questions will arise.

### Critical Thinking in a Research Notebook

Collecting and synthesizing information isn't critical thinking. Summarizing, paraphrasing, and outlining are all useful kinds of note-taking activities, but they don't require much of your own "thinking." In fact, notes often require you to reduce someone else's words to main- and subpoints, while keeping your own ideas out. Critical thinking requires analysis and evaluation. At the outset in your research, before you get very far into your subject, the research notebook is a useful tool. The notebook will help you to think about what you are reading.

To think critically, you must react to your reading: respond, agree, disagree, challenge the reasoning, find contradictions and exaggerations. Ask questions: Why does the author say that? What gives her the authority? Is this true? Look for insights, assumptions, and overgeneralizations (see Chapter 2). Notebooks are like dialogs between you and the authors you are reading.

In the following example from Ryan's research notebook, notice how he cites quotes and discusses them. This helps him interact more closely with the source.

22 August 2007
Lappé, Frances Moore. <u>Diet for a Small Planet</u>. New York: Ballantine, 1991.

When I found this book, I didn't know if it would be useful. The 1991 publication date is the book's 20th anniversary edition. So, it's somewhat old. But I have seen the book mentioned in other sources several times.

Lappé was one of the first writers to examine the importance of diet—especially the effects of eating meat on people and the planet. When she first became interested in this issue, she was considered a revolutionary. "Anyone who questioned the American diet's reliance on beef—since cattle are the most wasteful converters of grain to meat—was perceived as challenging the American way of life (especially, when that someone came from Forth Worth, Texas—'Cowtown, USA')" (xvi). But she found herself compelled to examine the issue—there was a great need for people to rethink their eating habits.

I woke up to this problem after seeing the film <u>Fast Food Nation</u> this summer. I never thought about the quality of the hamburger at McDonald's. Now I do. I'm interested in what wakes people up to problems. Lappé writes, "In one sense, what motivated me to write *Diet for a Small Planet* was simple outrage. We feed almost half the world's grain to livestock, returning only a fraction in meat—while millions starve. It confounds all logic. Yet the pattern has intensified" (xvii). I feel a mild outrage, if there is such a thing, about fast food meat, but I want to keep an open mind. I want to be fair and see what the research tells me. Even though I plan to focus on beef in my argument paper, I've read a lot about how chicken and pigs are mistreated (one writer, Michael Pollan, said *brutalized*) and pumped full of growth hormones and antibiotics.

Lappé says that only until recently in human history have people had a "meat-centered diet" (13). Before, it was always a plant-centered diet. Meat was not the main dish—it was a supplement, if there was any meat at all. She advocates that we return to plant-centered diets because it's better for our own health and the health of the planet. This will be tough for most of us who are addicted to meat.

At the end of her introduction, Lappé quotes from a Chinese writer, Lu Hsun:

> Hope cannot be said to exist, nor can it be said not to exist.
> It is just like the roads across the earth.
> For actually there were no roads to begin with,
> but when many people pass one way a road is made. (xliii)

I love the last line. Maybe more people should change their eating habits by relying less on meat—especially meat from fast food restaurants. If enough people do this, a new major road will be made.

Example from a Research Notebook

This notebook entry illustrates an active, critical response to reading. Critical thinkers *react* to information. A research notebook will encourage you to explore, to question, to think about and write about what you read. Your notebook can also help you find a worthwhile thesis.

*Note*: If you borrow ideas, quote, or paraphrase from your reading, always give a full bibliographic reference, including page numbers. See the example from a research notebook.

## ACTIVITY 4

As you research, you need to assimilate information and respond to it. Start a reading notebook for your research. It will help you write your paper. ▬

## Keeping Notes

Research notes, by contrast with notebook entries, usually stick to the subject, though digressions are possible now and then. In your notes (versus your notebook) record information from the source material. "Notes" are summaries, paraphrases, quotes, and always the one absolute rule, the bibliographic information for each and every source you write about: no bibliography, no research. Notes will be of little use if you can't say where they came from. You may add a brief comment or two as a reminder about the source, but usually "notes" indicate what the source says. The rule for notes is read much, write little.

Many researchers prefer to take notes on note cards. Cards can be numbered and easily organized. Other researchers prefer to take notes on legal pads, for example, and carefully record information from one source at a time. However, sheets of paper are likely to encourage more writing than is necessary or good. Still, if you do take notes that way, make sure you document your sources: write down all bibliographic information, even if you probably won't use things like volume and issue numbers, and be careful to quote accurately and cite page numbers. Also, when you print source material, make sure it contains all bibliographic information; if it doesn't, you will need to go back and find the information again.

## STRATEGY TWO: LOOKING FOR BOOKS

One function of your early reading is to help you identify the significant research. The more you read, the more you will understand which books and articles you should read, and which ones you can weed out. In the beginning your bibliography should contain too much rather than too little. A working (or preliminary) bibliography isn't the same as the "Works Cited" that will accompany your paper: you probably won't use all the sources you collect or read.

You may discover that an outstanding book will help you more than any other kind of source. If the author is credible and an authority in the field, if the book itself is well documented, and if the book is so well written that you find yourself carefully reading it instead of skimming it, you know you have a valuable source for your paper.

---

**Ryan's Process Notes**

When I read <u>The Omnivore's Dilemma</u> by Michael Pollan, I suddenly felt I was on solid ground. I enjoyed the process of reading this book so much more than browsing encyclopedias or articles online. I didn't have time to carefully read each page, but I read most of the book, driven by a desire to know more about meat and whether we should eat it. I liked reading about Pollan's in-depth research of his own—how he visited factory farms and farms where animals were humanely treated and where beef grazed on pasture grass, how he described preparing his own meals, how he bought a cow and traced its journey from birth to slaughter, how he hunted for boar, shot one, and prepared a meal from it. Also, Pollan's list of sources is more than 15 pages—he did so much research for this book!

Then I got a copy of <u>Fast Food Nation</u>, the book that the film is made from. I enjoyed reading this too, seeing again how fast food affects not only the meat we eat but also the workers (who are mostly underpaid, poor, often illiterate immigrants) and our environment. Eric Schlosser has 60 pages of notes based on his research and a bibliography of 5 pages—single spaced, small font. He also did a great amount of research for his book.

Doing a short research paper seems like nothing compared to what Pollan and Schlosser did. But for me, this is hard work. It makes me nervous—yet I enjoy the challenge too.

## The Library Catalog

You can find books by searching your library's online catalog by author, title, key word, and subject. When you locate a book online, check to see if it is available. If it's not, check with a librarian to request that the book be returned soon, if possible.

Cards from an online catalog may have information you can use to evaluate whether a source might be useful to you. The online card can provide you with the name of the author and title, whether there is a bibliography, the publisher, date of publication, and subject headings.

The library card in Figure 7.1 shows that the book by Peter Singer and Jim Mason contains "bibliographical references," which means you can find sources they

---

Library Catalog

Call Number TX357 .S527 2006                                    Status: Available

| | |
|---|---|
| Author | Singer, Peter, 1946- |
| Title | The way we eat : why our food choices matter |
| Bibliography | Includes bibliographical references (p. 302–324) and index. |
| Pub Info | [Emmaus, Pa.] : Rodale; [New York] : Distributed to the trade by Holtzbrinck Publishers, c2006 |
| Description | viii, 328 p.; 24 cm. |
| Subject | Food—Moral and ethical aspects. |
| | Diet—Moral and ethical aspects. |
| | Food industry and trade—Moral and ethical aspects. |
| | Gastronomy. |
| | Food preferences. |
| Add Author | Mason, Jim. |

---

*FIGURE 7.1*  Example of a library access catalog card.

used. The screen also gives you the call number you would need to find this book in the library (note "Status: Available").

When you find a book in the library online catalog, check the subject headings listed. Notice that the Singer and Mason book lists five subjects. These are links you can go to automatically. Such links may prove helpful.

If you use the online catalogs as well as the print indexes for books, you will soon have a large number of items for your working bibliography. Must you read all these books? No—as a researcher you can learn to skim effectively. A brief overview can tell you a lot: look through the table of contents, the index, any topical headings. An overview can help you decide which books merely repeat information you already have, which are only shallow treatments of the subject, which are authoritative but not too technical to be useful. You can expect to do a great deal of reading, and you must try to find the best sources available.

When you find an unfamiliar book, try the index test: think of three things you believe should be in the index of a good book on your topic; then check to see whether any of them are listed. See if you can find the author listed anywhere—to check if the author has published other works. A little preliminary work can help you identify which books you need to read.

*Note:* Your library probably offers interlibrary loan services; if your library does not have a certain book you need, you may order it through interlibrary loan. A disadvantage of this service is that it may take more time than you can spare to receive the book.

## Online Databases for Book Lists

On the Internet, you will find many places such as FirstSearch, WorldCat, and Pro-Quest where you can search for book publications by subject, title, author, and sometimes key words. Finding book lists isn't the same as finding the books themselves, of course, but you do need to make a list before you go hunting.

### ACTIVITY 5

Try to locate a few books on your research topic. Use your library catalog to see what books are at your school. Use another source such as WorldCat to find other books on the topic. ▨

## STRATEGY THREE: LOOKING FOR ARTICLES

In the library you can find popular magazines, scholarly journals, and newspapers, collectively referred to as serials or periodicals, meaning published periodically. In addition to print indexes, most libraries subscribe to online databases such as InfoTrac, FirstSearch, or ProQuest to find articles. You can also use search engines such as Google, MSN Search, and Yahoo! to find articles. The online indexes are fast and easy to use, but the print indexes may contain articles from farther back in time.

---

**Ryan's Process Notes**

When I was assigned this research paper, I didn't know exactly what my focus would be. There were so many options. At first I thought about researching vegetarianism—because that would be the most extreme reaction to eating meat. I did a Google search, and this was probably a mistake because I quickly found myself lost: the more I read, the more I didn't know what my focus would or should be. I didn't want to write about how vegetables are good for you—we all know that. There was so much information that I felt exhausted and depressed after a few hours. I printed sources that might be useful, and I bookmarked them on my computer, but as I was doing this I wondered if I was wasting my time and paper. I don't think that doing a Google search is the best method for doing research. It's not focused enough—it doesn't distinguish the quality of sources well at all.

---

## Readers' Guide to Periodical Literature

The Readers' Guide to Periodical Literature is a useful index to popular magazines and newspapers, starting with the year 1900. It is now online as Readers Guide Abstracts; you can access it through FirstSearch. Readers Guide Abstracts lists articles by author, by subject, and by title. The Guide is also cross-indexed under many different descriptors. This index will soon lead you to many useful articles.

You will find that many magazines and newspapers have their own Web sites and maintain online archives; however, the archives can differ considerably, and some require a small fee for downloading articles. Time magazine (<http://www.time.com/time/magazine/archives/advanced>) archives go back to 1923. The New York Times archives go back to 1996, and through its link with ProQuest Archiver has articles (not the entire paper) as far back as 1851; the Washington Post archives go back to 1887.

Ryan used the Readers Guide Abstracts to search for articles on grass-fed cattle and found these entries:

---

**Grass-Fed Cattle**

A Cut Above. Author: Lothstein, Jessica. In: Best Life, v.4 no4 (May 2007), p. 46–7

The Grass-Fed Revolution. Author: Roosevelt, Margot. In: Time v. 167 no24 (June 12 2006) p. 76–8

Better Beef. Author: Smith, Nancy. In: The Mother Earth News no212 (October/November 2005) p. 81–9

Cattle Futures? Author: Pollan, Michael. In: The New York Times Magazine (Jan 11 2004) p. 11–12

Power steer. Author: Pollan, Michael. In: The New York Times Magazine (Mar. 31 2002) p. 44–51

Factory farming is fouling our food. Author: Long, Cheryl. In: Organic Gardening (1998) v. 47 no5 (Nov./Dec. 2000) p. 12–13

---

FIGURE 7.2   Excerpt from Readers Guide Abstracts.

## Newspaper Online Archives

Many newspaper sites can be accessed directly online in full text. However, online archives differ considerably in their holdings. InfoTrac contains 150 full-text newspapers from which to search for articles. Most leading newspapers maintain their own Web sites that you can search:

**New York Times** <http://www.nytimes.com>

**Wall Street Journal** <http://online.wsj.com/public/us>

**Washington Post** <http://www.washingtonpost.com>

## ACTIVITY 6

Use at least two different newspaper archives and Readers Guide Abstracts to find half a dozen articles on your research topic. ▪▪▪

## Searching Databases

Databases will help you find magazine and journal articles. Your library has access to various databases such as FirstSearch, InfoTrac, Lexis-Nexis, and ProQuest. For example, FirstSearch offers access to "dozens of databases and more than 10 million full-text and full-image articles" (<http://www.oclc.org/firstsearch/>). FirstSearch will allow you to find material in newspapers, magazines, and books and will then allow you to print out copies of the articles you find.

ProQuest is a comprehensive newspaper database, containing the New York Times archives from 1999 to current and the Wall Street Journal from 1982 to current. It also features ProQuest Research Library with collections of journals, magazines, and newspapers of general reference subjects.

To use a database, you can do a keyword search such as "grass-fed cattle." If you use a general key word such as "diet," you will get too many hits. Narrow your terms when you can, and try different terms such as "grain-fed cattle" or "mad cow disease." You can also search for an article that you found a reference to in a book. Try to track it down through a database.

Databases often contain full articles that you can view. Many articles can be printed as a PDF (portable document format) from the original journal with original page numbers.

## To Use Popular Sources or Not

Some instructors believe that students should use only scholarly sources for research, not popular magazines. Others believe that certain popular sources are acceptable. Ask your instructors for their policies.

News sources like <u>Time</u>, <u>Newsweek</u>, <u>U.S. News and World Report</u> are often considered responsible and credible. If you were examining recent public attitudes toward global warming, it would be appropriate to search these magazines.

Scientific and technical sources like <u>Scientific American</u> and <u>Nature</u> are nearly always considered authoritative publications that you can rely on for scientific information. As always, when you read, evaluate your sources: consider whether the authors are well qualified, fair-minded, and logical. (See Chapter 8, "Evaluating Evidence" for more on distinctions between magazines and journals.)

## Divide Your Work into Steps or Phases

Just as with books, you can reduce the time and effort you need in finding articles by first using the periodical indexes. Make yourself a working bibliography of periodical articles. Preliminary reading or skimming can help you reduce the number of articles you must read. Follow the researchers' rule that the broader, more general the subject, the more articles you will find, possibly thousands on a broad subject like "global warming." Researchers, especially students, need to find a small subdivision of a subdivision. You may start out thinking about a general subject, but you must keep reading and thinking critically until you find a small, specific research question. (See "The Growth Phenomenon" earlier in this chapter.)

Research librarians can help you find lists of articles pertaining to your research subject as well as the articles themselves. If your library doesn't have all the magazines and journals you require, you may need to go to another library or order what you need through interlibrary loan. However, much use of interlibrary loan is probably a clue that you need to rethink your subject or thesis or both.

## Look for the Most Recent Sources First

Research can be a big job, and many students want to know "Where should I start?" In general, the rule is start where you are. Look for the most recent sources first and then work your way back to earlier research. How far back you need to go depends on your project. You will find that recent sources rely on older research. Older data may no longer be valid. Research tends to age. Unless you are doing something historical such as research about Adolf Hitler, you should seek the most recent information.

### ACTIVITY 7

Use at least three different databases to find half a dozen articles on your research topic. Don't take all your articles from the same database (don't take them all from <u>FirstSearch</u>, for example). ▪

## PROFESSIONAL, TECHNICAL, AND SPECIALTY JOURNALS

In addition to using indexes and databases for magazine, newspaper, and journal articles, there are many specialized indexes covering professional journals and other information not generally found in popular magazines. Many academic disciplines have one or more indexes in which you can find articles written for an audience of well-educated readers. Often journals are intended for members within the profession. For example, College English is intended for an audience of college English instructors. The following list shows some of the special indexes available in libraries.

**ART:** Art Index, Humanities Index

**BIOLOGY:** General Science Index, Bibliography of Bioethics, Biology Digest

**BUSINESS:** Social Sciences Index, Business Periodicals Index

**CHEMISTRY:** General Science Index, Chemical Abstracts

**COMMUNICATION:** Social Sciences Index, Communication Abstracts

**COMPUTER SCIENCE:** ACM Guide to Computing Literature

**DANCE:** Humanities Index, Art Index, Physical Education Index

**ECONOMICS:** Social Sciences Index, EconLit

**EDUCATION:** Education Abstracts, ERIC

**GEOLOGY:** General Science Index, GEOBASE

**HISTORY:** Humanities Index, Historical Abstracts, GPO (Government Publications Office)

**HUMANITIES:** Humanities Index

**LANGUAGES AND LITERATURE:** Humanities Index, MLA International Bibliography Series

**MATHEMATICS:** General Science Index, ACM Guide to Computing Literature, Mathematical Reviews

**MUSIC:** Humanities Index, Music Index

**PHILOSOPHY:** Humanities Index, Philosophers Index

**PHYSICS:** General Science Index

**POLITICAL SCIENCE:** Social Sciences Index, GPO, Public Affairs Information Service Bulletin, Vital Speeches of the Day

**PSYCHOLOGY:** Social Sciences Index, General Science Index, PsychINFO

**RELIGION:** Humanities Index, ATLA Religion

**SOCIOLOGY:** Social Sciences Index, Sociological Abstracts

**THEATER:** Humanities Index, Social Sciences Index

**WOMEN'S STUDIES:** Women Studies Abstracts

Find out as much as you can about your library's indexes. The indexes can give you many articles on practically any subject. Pay particular attention to cross-referencing, such as "See also" under subject headings. Ask your librarian for suggestions of additional databases or indexes on your subject.

## ACTIVITY 8

Use the indexes for professional journals to find articles related to your research topic. Compile a preliminary bibliography of half a dozen journal articles. Don't take all your references from the same index. █████

## STRATEGY FOUR: LOOKING FOR SPECIALIZED INFORMATION

### Government Documents, Statistics, Reports

Census Bureau (<http://www.census.gov/>) provides data about the nation's people and households, business and industry, geography (including maps), and other information. This site includes the Statistical Abstract of the United States—facts and figures about America and Americans (<http://www.census.gov/compendia/statab/>).

Fedstats (<http://www.fedstats.gov/>) provides access to a full range of official statistical information produced by the federal government on such topics as economic and population trends, crime, education, health care, aviation safety, energy use, farm production and more.

GPO Access (<http://www.gpoaccess.gov/>) is a service of the U.S. Government Printing Office that provides free electronic access to a wealth of important information produced by the federal government. You can view legislative resources such as congressional bills and the *Congressional Record* as well as the Supreme Court Web site.

USA.gov (<http://www.usa.gov/>) provides information on a wide variety of topics such as the environment, energy, and agriculture. Links to many governmental organizations are included.

*Note:* The World Almanac and Book of Facts, though not affiliated with the government, is a reference book containing information you may find useful in your research writing.

### Biographical Sources

You may need to identify authorities, experts, specialists, and researchers in order to determine whether they are true authorities in their fields. You can find many biographical sources online. For example, suppose you use an essay from New York Times columnist Nicholas D. Kristof and you want to check his credentials. The New York Times provides a biography for him and for its other major writers: see <http://www.nytimes.com/ref/opinion/KRISTOF-BIO.html>.

Academy of Achievement <http://www.achievement.org/>

American Men and Women of Science

Biographical Dictionary

Biography Index

Directory of American Scholars

Directories of Scientists

4000 Years of Women in Science <http://www.astr.ua.edu/4000WS>

PBS History: Biographies <http://www.pbs.org/history/history_biographies.html>

Suppose you want to find information on Lee Silver, author of Remaking Eden: Cloning and Beyond in a Brave New World. Does Professor Lee Silver have solid credentials? Yes, you can see where he graduated (University of Pennsylvania and Harvard), where he has taught (Cornell and Princeton), and some of his areas of research. He is an authority on genetics. (See Figure 7.3)

This information also provides Lee Silver's postal and e-mail addresses at Princeton in case you want to contact him. *Note:* Abbreviations and symbols in directories like American Men and Women of Science are usually explained in the front of the directory: "Res fel" (Research fellow.) This biographical information doesn't include a list of Silver's books or publications.

If you did a Web search on Silver, you would find a link to his recent book, Challenging Nature: The Clash of Science and Spirituality at the New Frontiers of Life, published by Ecco in 2006. This Web site (<http://www.leemsilver.net/challenging/top/biosketch.htm>) contains reviews of this book and his other books. It also contains a long biography as well as his curriculum vitae—his official résumé.

It's fairly easy to find biographical information on major authorities you use in your research writing. The ordinary researcher, who has published an article but has yet to achieve a major distinction, can be harder to find. Scholarly journals frequently give a brief identification of authors of articles.

---

**Silver, Lee Merrill.** Personal Data: b Philadelphia, Pa, Apr 27, 52; m 74; c 2. Education: Univ Pa, BA & MS, 1973; Harvard Univ, PhD(biophys), 1978. Prof Experience: Ed, Mammalian Arome, 89–; PROF MOLECULAR BIOL & PUB AFFAIRS, PRINCETON UNIV, 1984–; asst prof genetics, Med Sch, Cornell Univ, 1979–1980 & State Univ NY Stony Brook, 1980–; sr staff investr, Cold Spring Harbor Lab, 1980–84; vis asst prof genetics, Albert Einstein Col Med, 1980; assoc, Sloan Kettering Cancer Inst, 1979–1980; Fel, Pop Coun, 1977–1978 & NIH, 1978–1979; Res fel genetics, Sloan Kettering Cancer Inst, 1977–1979. Memberships: Am Soc Cell Biol; AAAS; Int Soc Differentiation; Genetics Soc Am. Mailing Address: Dept Molecular Biol, Princeton Univ, 404 Roberston Hall, Princeton NJ 08544–1013. Fax: 609–258-7122. E-mail: lsilver@princeton.edu.

Figure 7.3　Excerpt from American Men and Women of Science, 22 edition, 2005 (821).

## ACTIVITY 9

Use two or three sources to find biographical information on an authority in your research. In your notebook, write a page describing and explaining his or her credentials. Be sure to include where you found your information. ▄▄

## Book Reviews

Book reviews can help you identify research material. Newspapers and magazines often contain reviews. Check major newspapers like the New York Times (including the New York Times Book Review), and search the Readers Guide Abstracts under the title or the author's name. You can also use special reference works devoted to book reviews:

> Book Review Digest, 1905
>
> Book Review Index, 1965–
>
> Book Reviews Online (Best sellers) <http://www.bookspot.com/reviews/>

You can access Book Review Digest through FirstSearch. You can use other databases such as Academic Onefile (through InfoTrac) and ProQuest to find reviews as well: simply type the book's name and see if any reviews appear.

---

**Ryan's Process Notes**

Because I learned so much from Fast Food Nation, I thought I'd check out some book reviews of Eric Schlosser's next book, Reefer Madness: Sex, Drugs, and Cheap Labor in the American Black Market, to see if I might want to read it. It wasn't too hard finding reviews. I had the best luck with using Academic OneFile through InfoTrac.

---

### Pot, Porn and Prison; America's Black Economy

*The Economist*

How free is the free market? Not very, insists Eric Schlosser, an American journalist, in his new book, "Reefer Madness," the follow-up (and in some ways a companion volume) to his 2001 bestseller, "Fast Food Nation." Witness the booming black market. In 1998 Americans neglected to report an estimated $1.5 trillion of income. In Los Angeles County an estimated 28% of the workers are paid in cash; black-market activity may represent as much as 30% of the city's economic activity.

"Reefer Madness" comprises three previously published essays. Each is a deftly woven tale of corruption and desperation. In the title essay Mr. Schlosser explores how a country that once required colonists to grow hemp became one of the harshest prosecutors of marijuana offenders in the world, and ponders the myriad social and economic consequences of that transformation.

Mr. Schlosser shines a light on the dramatic changes in drug laws over the years. In 1981, for instance, Newt Gingrich introduced a bill to legalise the use of marijuana for medical purposes; 15 years later he sponsored legislation making the punishment for bringing more than two ounces of pot into the country life in prison or the death penalty. In America today—a society Mr. Schlosser describes as being "caught in the grip of a deep psychosis"—a person convicted of selling marijuana can be sentenced to more time than a murderer.

The second essay follows Mr. Schlosser's investigations into illegal migrant farmers in California; the third tells the story of America's $10 billion pornography industry. He concludes that there is a connection between the black market and falling personal incomes, a widening gap between rich and poor, and an overall slowdown in the nation's economic development. Mr. Schlosser puts forward his thesis with great passion, though to be completely convincing it would need to be argued more thoroughly.

Though less obviously of a piece than "Fast Food Nation," fans will nevertheless find that Mr. Schlosser's telling of the rise and fall of Reuben Sturman, Cleveland's king of porn, is alone worth the price of "Reefer Madness."

Work Cited

"Pot, Porn and Prison: America's Black Economy." <u>The Economist</u> 10 May 2003: 88. Academic OneFile. Gale. Alma College Lib. Alma, MI. 29 Aug. 2007 <http://infotrac.galegroup.com>.

## ACTIVITY **10**

Find three different reviews of a book central to your research. Print out one and annotate it. Bring it to class to discuss briefly. ▬

## STRATEGY FIVE: USING ELECTRONIC SOURCES AND MICROFORM READERS

Modern libraries contain many electronic aids to help you with research. Seated at a computer, you can search databases by subject headings, and in many cases you may be able to download or print complete texts of the articles you need. If you have your own computer and have access to your school's library, you can do much research at home, though you will still need to spend time in the library to find many of the books and articles you want.

When you do research in a library, ask librarians for help when you have problems finding a source. They will help you—and help you save time. Most libraries have printed instruction sheets for their standard procedures—especially in the reference library—so that students can find available services.

## Microform Readers

Not all information is available on the Internet or in print. Much older information is stored on microform. *Microform* is a general term for microfilm and microfiche.

Microfilm looks somewhat like photographic film: it's wound on a spool or reel. Microfiche (pronounced "micrafeesh") is a small sheet of film material, about the size and shape of a postcard. An entire issue of a newspaper or magazine can be reproduced on a single spool of microfilm or a single microfiche.

Microforms store back issues of newspapers and some magazines. To find information on microform, you usually need the date of publication. For example, the New York Times Index will give you the dates on which articles appeared. Using dates from an index, you can locate the microforms you need.

## ACTIVITY 11

Using the date of your birth, find the appropriate microform issue of the New York Times. Write a brief synopsis of newsworthy events on the day you were born.

## STRATEGY SIX: USING INTERVIEWS

Along with your library and Internet research, consider doing field research such as conducting personal interviews. You might interview a professor knowledgeable about your topic, a local doctor, or a government official. If you are doing a report on breast cancer because it runs in your family, you could interview your mother or grandmother. Consider interviewing anyone who has experience with your topic. This kind of research is more personal, but this doesn't make it not valuable. As long as you treat the information fairly and objectively, it can add to your paper—make it more engaging and real.

## CHAPTER 8

# Evaluating Evidence

## THE WIKIPEDIA DILEMMA

Do you use Wikipedia? If so, has it been useful? This site is so popular and is used so often that when you do a Web search, the Wikipedia site often comes up first. But does this mean the site is reliable and trustworthy? No. Does this mean the site is not useful? No. Hmmm. A contradiction? Yes.

Wikipedia is a controversy in higher education. Read this article to see why. As you read it, ask yourself whether you agree or disagree—or both.

### A Stand Against Wikipedia

*Scott Jaschik*

As Wikipedia has become more and more popular with students, some professors have become increasingly concerned about the online, reader-produced encyclopedia.

While plenty of professors have complained about the lack of accuracy or completeness of entries, and some have discouraged or tried to bar students from using it, the history department at Middlebury College is trying to take a stronger, collective stand. It voted this month to bar students from citing the Web site as a source in papers or other academic work. All faculty members will be telling students about the policy and explaining why material on Wikipedia—while convenient—may not be trustworthy.

"As educators, we are in the business of reducing the dissemination of misinformation," said Don Wyatt, chair of the department. "Even though Wikipedia may have some value, particularly from the value of leading students to citable sources, it is not itself an appropriate source for citation," he said.

The department made what Wyatt termed a consensus decision on the issue after discussing problems professors were seeing as students cited incorrect information from Wikipedia in papers and on tests. In one instance, Wyatt said, a professor noticed several students offering the same incorrect information, from Wikipedia.

There was some discussion in the department of trying to ban students from using Wikipedia, but Wyatt said that didn't seem appropriate. Many Wikipedia entries have good bibliographies, Wyatt said. And any absolute ban would just be ignored. "There's the issue of freedom of access," he said. "And I'm not in the business of promulgating unenforceable edicts."

Wyatt said that the department did not specify punishments for citing Wikipedia, and that the primary purpose of the policy was to educate, not to be punitive. He said he doubted that a paper would be rejected for having a single Wikipedia footnote, but that students would be told that they shouldn't do so, and that multiple violations would result in reduced grades or even a failure. "The important point that we wish to communicate to all students taking courses and submitting work in our department in the future is that they cite Wikipedia at their peril," he said.

He stressed that the objection of the department to Wikipedia wasn't its online nature, but its unedited nature, and he said students need to be taught to go for quality information, not just convenience.

The frustrations of Middlebury faculty members are by no means unique. Last year, Alan Liu, a professor of English at the University of California at Santa Barbara, adopted a policy that Wikipedia "is not appropriate as the primary or sole reference for anything that is central to an argument, complex, or controversial." Liu said that it was too early to tell what impact his policy is having. In explaining his rationale—which he shared with an e-mail list—he wrote that he had "just read a paper about the relation between structuralism, deconstruction, and postmodernism in which every reference was to the Wikipedia articles on those topics with no awareness that there was any need to read a primary work or even a critical work."

Wikipedia officials agree—in part—with Middlebury's history department. "That's a sensible policy," Sandra Ordonez, a spokeswoman, said in an e-mail interview. "Wikipedia is the ideal place to start your research and get a global picture of a topic, however, it is not an authoritative source. In fact, we recommend that students check the facts they find in Wikipedia against other sources. Additionally, it is generally good research practice to cite an original source when writing a paper, or completing an exam. It's usually not advisable, particularly at the university level, to cite an encyclopedia."

Ordonez acknowledged that, given the collaborative nature of Wikipedia writing and editing, "there is no guarantee an article is 100 percent correct," but she said that the site is shifting its focus from growth to improving quality, and that the site is a great resource for students. "Most articles are continually being edited and improved upon, and most contributors are real lovers of knowledge who have a real desire to improve the quality of a particular article," she said.

Experts on digital media said that the Middlebury history professors' reaction was understandable and reflects growing concern among faculty members about the accuracy of what students find online. But some worry that bans on citing Wikipedia may not deal with the underlying issues.

Roy Rosenzweig, director of the Center for History and New Media at George Mason University, did an analysis of the accuracy of Wikipedia for <u>The Journal of American History</u>, and he found that in many entries, Wikipedia was as accurate or more accurate than more traditional encyclopedias. He said that the quality of material was inconsistent, and that biographical entries were generally well done, while more thematic entries were much less so. Like Ordonez, he said the real problem is one of college students using encyclopedias when they should be using more advanced sources.

"College students shouldn't be citing encyclopedias in their papers," he said. "That's not what college is about. They either should be using primary sources or serious secondary sources."

In the world of college librarians, a major topic of late has been how to guide students in the right direction for research, when Wikipedia and similar sources are so easy. Some of those who have been involved in these discussions said that the Middlebury history department's action pointed to the need for more outreach to students.

Lisa Hinchliffe, head of the undergraduate library and coordinator of information literacy at the University of Illinois at Urbana-Champaign, said that earlier generations of students were in fact taught when it was appropriate (or not) to consult an encyclopedia and why for many a paper they would never even cite a popular magazine or nonscholarly work. "But it was a relatively constrained landscape," and students didn't have easy access to anything equivalent to Wikipedia," she said. "It's not that students are being lazy today. It's a much more complex environment."

When she has taught, and spotted footnotes to sources that aren't appropriate, she's considered that "a teachable moment," Hinchliffe said. She said that she would be interested to see how Middlebury professors react when they get the first violations of their policy, and said she thought there could be positive discussions about why sources are or aren't good ones. That kind of teaching, she said, is important "and can be challenging."

Steven Bell, associate librarian for research and instructional services at Temple University, said of the Middlebury approach: "I applaud the effort for wanting to direct students to good quality resources," but he said he would go about it in a different way.

"I understand what their concerns are. There's no question that [on Wikipedia and similar sites] some things are great and some things are questionable. Some of the pages could be by eighth graders," he said. "But to simply say 'don't use that one' might take students in the wrong direction from the perspective of information literacy."

Students face "an ocean of information" today, much of it of poor quality, so a better approach would be to teach students how to "triangulate" a source like Wikipedia, so they could use other sources to tell whether a given entry could be trusted. "I think our goal should be to equip students with the critical thinking skills to judge."

*Scott Jaschik, an editor for <u>Inside Higher Ed</u>, is a leading voice on higher education issues. He regularly publishes articles in the <u>New York Times, Boston Globe,</u> and <u>Washington Post</u>.*

Work Cited

Jaschik, Scot. "A Stand Against Wikipedia." Insidehighered.com 26 Jan. 2007. 8 Aug. 2007
<http://www.insidehighered.com/news/2007/01/26/wiki>.

## ACTIVITY 1

Does this article stir your thinking? How? Do you find any surprises in it? Where? What is your opinion of the history department at Middlebury College barring students from citing Wikipedia as a source of information in research papers? Write a response in your notebook. ▪

What are some key ideas from "A Stand Against Wikipedia" that can help you as a researcher? Consider these:

- Resist using Wikipedia as a source in a paper. Expect that most of your teachers will expect you not to cite it; they will not regard it as a legitimate source.
- Because many Wikipedia sources are unedited and unchecked for accuracy, how do you know if a source is credible and trustworthy? You don't know, unless you do research to determine if the source's information is accurate. But do you want to spend your time doing this? Sandra Ordonez, a spokeswoman for Wikipedia, claims her site "is the ideal place to start your research." But if you can't rely on sources being credible, then it is likely not an *ideal* place. An ideal place might be to check Britannica Online.
- Yet Wikipedia can be useful: it can give you an overview on a topic, but more importantly it can provide a bibliography of legitimate sources that you can find and read.

Your job as a researcher is to be a critical thinker: to ask questions, to search for insights, assumptions, and overgeneralizations (see Chapter 2). Evaluating sources requires keen critical thinking. But perhaps, as already suggested, the Wikipedia dilemma should not be framed in either-or ways.

T. Mills Kelly wrote a response to "A Stand Against Wikipedia" and posted it in the comment section of Insidehighered.com. See if you agree with his argument.

## Why I Won't Get Hired at Middlebury

### T. Mills Kelly

Oh my.

It's a good thing I'm not a finalist for a job at Middlebury College, because my decision to assign the Wikipedia as the textbook in my Western Civ course this semester flies in the face of a decision the History Department there has made to ban students from citing Wikipedia in any of their work. In a January 26 article in Insidehighered.com, Don Wyatt, chair of the department, is quoted as saying, "Even though Wikipedia may have some value, particularly from the value of leading students to citable sources, it is not itself an appropriate source for citation."

To me this seems like such an odd position for historians to take, given that so many of the sources we work with every day are highly contested as to their veracity, their meaning, their provenance. Every time I open a folder in the archives and look at a source, I reflexively ask myself "Who created this?", "Why did he/she/they create it?", "Is this an original, a copy, or even a forgery?", "Is this the complete source or was it edited and if so who might have edited it and why?" Responsible historians *must* ask these (and many more) questions every time we look at a source. But apparently, if we are to follow the policy of our colleagues at Middlebury, we do not need to teach this same reflexive skepticism to our students.

Instead, we should just tell them that some sources of information simply are too unreliable to use.

I wish someone in my graduate program had told me the same thing about the Habsburg secret police reports that I spent months sorting through as part of my attempt to understand as much as I could about late-Habsburg Czech political figures. How much easier it would have been to just say, "Even though secret police reports may have some value, particularly from the value of leading researchers to citable sources, they are in themselves not appropriate sources for citation." After all, those Habsburg spies made up all sorts of things about Czech politicians, fabricating evidence of disloyalty, drunkenness, and other misdeeds.

Oh well, the book is written now, so it's too late for me. But maybe I can save some of my students from making the same mistakes I made and ban them from citing unreliable sources in their work.

I wonder what the folks at Middlebury (and some of the others who chimed in in the comments below the *Insiderhighered.com* article) will think of me now that I'm assigning Wikipedia as my textbook?

You're doing *what*?!? Ah, but there's a method to my depravity.

You see, I'm a firm believer that we can deny, deny, deny that new forms of content delivery are undermining all that we find comfortable, but denial just never seems to work in the end. I know (and so do you) that students are going to use Wikipedia regardless of what I tell them they can and can't do. Even the folks at Middlebury admit this—students there are allowed to *use* Wikipedia for their research—they just can't *cite* Wikipedia in their papers (explain that one to me). So, it seems to me that as educators we have an obligation to teach our students how to make *appropriate* use of the resources they are using and I'm not sure how a ban on citation will teach them anything worth knowing.

To address this problem, I've required each student in my class to create or substantially edit one historical entry in Wikipedia, complete with bibliography, link to other entries, an image (where appropriate), and so on. Then they must track what happens to their entry during the 14 weeks they are enrolled in my class and at the end of the semester they will write an essay in which they (a) analyze what happened to their entry and (b) analyze what they learned about the creation of historical content from the experience. Along the way we'll be discussing all the things that make us squeamish about Wikipedia—the constant ebb and flow of facts in the entries, the problems of vandalism, and so on.

I may be going out on a limb here, but I'm willing to bet at least a few dollars that at the end of the semester my students will be much better consumers of digital historical content than those enrolled at Middlebury.

*T. Mills Kelly is a professor in the Department of History and Art History at George Mason University in Fairfax, Virginia. He is also the associate director for the Center for History and New Media there.*

Work Cited

Kelly, T. Mills. "Why I Won't Get Hired at Middlebury." <u>Edwired</u> 26 Jan. 2007. 8 Aug. 2007 <http://edwired.org/?p=126>.

## ACTIVITY 2

Imagine yourself as a student in Mills's history class. What do you think of his method of using Wikipedia as a textbook and assigning students "to create or substantially edit one historical entry"? Write a response in your notebook.

Begun in 2001, Wikipedia, "the free encyclopedia," was founded by Jimmy Wales. One of the major problems with the site is that entries can be changed at will by anonymous sources, or people can make up names and credentials and post their own articles. Someone can spread lies about someone else. John Seigenthaler, a journalist, discovered that Wikipedia contained a false biography about him. He called it "character assassination." He wrote about it in <u>USA Today</u>, quoting from the biography: *"John Seigenthaler Sr. was the assistant to Attorney General Robert Kennedy in the early 1960's. For a brief time, he was thought to have been directly involved in the Kennedy assassinations of both John, and his brother, Bobby. Nothing was ever proven."* He did work for Kennedy, but the suggestion that he was involved with their deaths is ludicrous and defaming, he argued. For four months Seigenthaler tried to track down the source of his "biographer" but couldn't. Wikipedia founder Jimmy Wales eventually removed the biography from the Web site (<http://www.usatoday.com/news/opinion/editorials/2005-11-29-wikipedia-edit_x.htm>).

How important are credentials? Would you want a bogus doctor operating on you? Clearly not. But what about scholarly credentials? Well, what exactly is a *scholar*? <u>Webster's New World Dictionary</u> defines *scholar* as "a learned person, a specialist in a particular branch of learning." It defines *scholarly* as "having or showing much knowledge, accuracy, and critical ability." The words *accuracy* and *critical ability* are key here: these skills generate knowledge; they develop a scholar. When you do research, when you write a research paper, you are being a scholar—or trying to be, to the best of your ability. It is essential that your information be accurate.

Wikipedia faced a scandal in 2006 when it was discovered that a person named Essjay claimed to be a tenured professor with a doctorate. He was in fact Ryan Jordan, a twenty-four-year-old fraud with no advanced degree who had never taught. Essjay, according to an exposé in <u>The New Yorker</u> ("Know It All: Can Wikipedia Conquer Expertise," 31 July 2006) had "written or contributed to sixteen thousand entries."

Using Wikipedia is like asking people you don't know for directions. They might know where you want to go and tell you the best way to get there. Then again, they might not know yet pretend to know. Or they might give you wrong directions because they like mischief or are mean-spirited. The dilemma of Wikipedia is useful if it helps you think more intentionally about the sources you use, whether they are credible, trustworthy, honest, and whether the people who wrote them are indeed experts—scholars.

## RESEARCH AND THE INTERNET

The Internet is information without limit: a vast virtual library of books, magazines, newspapers, pictures, recordings, and videos related to human knowledge and curiosity. There is no end to the additions to the Net, day after day, year after year. As search engines get faster and more powerful, our ability to find useful information also increases. So far, the Internet is largely uncontrolled and unregulated. There are few rules about what is available or what you can find. Along with useful information, you can also find hate sites preaching various forms of bigotry. Skillful researchers can usually tell reliable from unreliable information, but as a student encountering unfamiliar subjects you may have difficulty.

Certainly you can find excellent sources on the Internet, but there can also be important differences among sites. Just as with printed sources, Internet researchers need to be alert to problems of evaluation and verification. Because the Internet is open to everyone, it isn't always easy to determine whether material is valid, reliable, nor even placed on the Net in good faith. There are guidelines for evaluating Net material, but few guarantees.

The "Web" or World Wide Web ("www" in site addresses) is a network of computers throughout the world connected somewhat like a spider web. There is no central connection or control over the Web. It was deliberately conceived as a web of so many connections that (in case of war or terrorist attack) the communication system cannot be disrupted by destroying any central or controlling site.

## WHAT IS A RELIABLE SITE?

### Evaluating Web Sites

The more you rely on Internet material, the more you must consider the reliability of the sources. Many sites are meant for entertainment, not research. Reliability is a key criterion in research: it is a judgment you must make. You must use critical thinking.

Sources that researchers use with confidence are called *reliable*. In general, you should use sources that other researchers use. Suppose you wanted to submit your paper to an undergraduate science conference. Should you use supermarket tabloids like the National Enquirer as sources? No, they are not intended for research. But if you were writing about developments in stem cell research, could you use Reader's Digest as a source of information? Possibly. Michael Kinsley published an essay there, "Cure Me If You Can," in which he argues that stem cell research is necessary because many people, like him, have diseases that could be cured through research (August 2003). Kinsley has been a journalist for many years and is widely considered reliable and trustworthy. Still, it's not always clear what student researchers should or should not use. A paper on contemporary music could cite Rolling Stone, for example.

If you find an opinion piece, should you use it? One answer could depend on where you find the piece. If an article on stem cell research appears in The New England Journal of Medicine, that fact could help you accept the article more than if it appears in a local newspaper, The Evening Star. This comparison isn't a question of good, bad, or better: periodicals are aimed at different audiences for different purposes. The NEJM is a highly respected journal that medical researchers read.

You can look for reliable information in government sources, university sources, and professional organizations such as the National Education Association. In addition, of course, there is the Library of Congress and many other excellent databases (such as WilsonSelectPlus) that specialize in journal articles. Still, you must use a reasonable degree of common sense and caution on the Net.

Critical thinkers should also consider this question: which sites are probably not relevant or significant for your research? You can quickly eliminate much of the Web if you are only interested in a specific subject, but that still leaves a lot to evaluate. If you were to exclude all popular sources (nontechnical) you would further narrow the search, but not all researchers would wish to do that. Anything published on a "professional site" (professional journals, for instance) should be, by definition, reliable, but some popular sites like Time and Newsweek may also be considered authoritative by some researchers.

## Criteria for Web Sites

1. *Whose site is it?* Who has put the site on the Web? The author? A political group such as People for the American Way (<http://pfaw.org>), MoveOn.org (Democracy in Action), or the National Rifle Association (<http://www.nra.org/>)? Harvard University <www.harvard.edu>? Some commercial enterprise? Is there any way to tell?

   The final suffix of URLs gives you a good clue about sites: .com (commercial); .edu (educational institution); .gov (government agency); .net (network); .org (nonprofit organization).

   Does the site contain a mission statement that explains its purpose, its slant (such as conservative or liberal), and its intended audience?

Does the site indicate the source of its information: authors, dates, links? If you can't find identifying information, should you use the material? Probably not. If such information is available, what do you learn from it?

## ACTIVITY 3

Select a Web site that you particularly want to explore. What does the site reveal about itself? What do you notice? Evaluate what the site reveals (or doesn't).  ▪

2. *How credible is the site? Has it been refereed?* Do you find any sort of review or reference to criteria for the site? A refereed or reviewed site is one that has been examined by authorities and experts. Books are previewed by publishers, editors, professional readers, and reviewers. Manuscripts don't become books until they have been carefully read by knowledgeable editors and readers, and they don't get into a school library until librarians or instructors recommend them. The Internet, however, has no such restrictions. Some sites have been rated by various groups, but most sites haven't been rated by anyone other than their authors.

## ACTIVITY 4

Find an Internet site that has been reviewed or verified in some way. What in the site suggests that it is legitimate, authoritative research? Report in your notebook what you find.  ▪

3. *How current is the site?* How recently has it been updated? If a site hasn't been updated for a few years, this suggests it has been neglected. It may no longer contain accurate, useful information. Don't use undated material—it is likely not reliable.

4. *Can you communicate with the site manager, the author, or whoever sponsors the site?* Is there an e-mail address or phone number? Reliable researchers usually assist their readers and welcome questions or comments about their work. Is there a link to an author that shows his or her credentials? If there is no site manager or author, be wary of using the site.

## ACTIVITY 5

Find a site that identifies its sponsor or permits you to communicate with the site sponsor or manager. Explain in a brief notebook entry what you find.  ▪

5. *How easy is it to use the site, move around in it, read its information, copy or print from the site?* Can you move from the home page to various directories or indexes and

from there to useful information, and then back to the home page? Is the organization of the site reasonable and logical? Does the site appear to have been set up for the reader's convenience?

## ACTIVITY 6

Choose a Web site related to your research topic. In your notebook, analyze and evaluate the site: how easy is it to use, to read, and to copy or print from? ■■■

6. *Does the site provide links to other sites?* Finding a reliable site is like finding a door to the world of information: one discovery usually leads to another in research. Specialists, experts, and authorities are often aware of other sources on the Web and can help you find them. However the mere presence of links doesn't guarantee reliability (there are no guarantees in research): the links must lead to reliable, verifiable information. If you need help with the site, is there a HELP button, or some way to get assistance?

## ACTIVITY 7

Search for sites on the Web dealing with your research subject. Look for a site that offers links or other indicators of reliability as well as concern for readers. Report in your notebook what you find. ■■■

7. *Is there a problem with advertising?* There may not be anything wrong with advertising per se, but finding advertising in the objective, scientific, scholarly world of reliable information raises serious questions. Advertisements might mean that the information is partially or entirely paid for by the advertisers and, therefore, may not be objective. Advertisers may feel less obligation to be entirely truthful.

Advertising is part of the business world: it makes radio, TV, and the Web apparently free to consumers. However, thoughtful writers and researchers need to work without the pressures that corporate sponsors can create. Readers need to believe they are reading reliable information. Advertising on the Web suggests that information exists as a lure—to deliver consumers to the advertiser.

Is there anything researchers can do about advertising? You can be alert to the problem while you attempt to find reliable information for your project. Too many intrusive ads (color, sound, animations) may mean that the site is too compromised to be useful. Even subtle, unobtrusive ads (the manufacturer's name discreetly tucked away in some corner) may alert you to a possibility of conflict between what you need and what the source offers. Critical thinkers should examine carefully the relationship between advertisers and Web sites. You need to be aware of biases—slants, exaggerations, distortions, partial truths, "spin" (spinning the truth until it sounds the way someone likes).

## ACTIVITY 8

Select two or three Web sites that appeal to you. Describe any use of advertising you find. Look for evidence of spin. Report what you find in your notebook. ▆

---

**Ryan's Process Notes**

Doing my research on grain-fed or grass-fed beef, I encountered many different Web sites. The beef industry sites such as Beef.org, run by the National Cattlemen's Beef Association, are definitely pro-beef. It's an easy site to navigate, with many links. The .org suffix is interesting because this site really seems to be pro beef business. The site is very biased toward the virtues of eating beef and how safe beef is.

I found Eatchicken.com, which is a commercial site advocating eating chicken. I'm not sure what the difference is between that site and Beef.org.

Most vegetarian sites have the .org suffix. They are biased the other way, such as The Vegetarian Resource Group (<http://www.vrg.org/>). Farm Sanctuary is a site for animal rights and vegetarianism. "Farm Sanctuary was founded in 1986 to combat the abuses of industrialized farming and to encourage a new awareness and understanding about 'farm animals.' At Farm Sanctuary, these animals are our friends, not our food" (<http://www.farmsanctuary.org/about/index.htm>). There are links to other sites that Farm Sanctuary sponsors, such as VegForLife.org and BanCruelFarms.org.

An extreme Web site for animal rights is People for the Ethical Treatment of Animals. It's fascinating. Just today I found a story about a new PETA ad showing Al Gore eating a drumstick with the tagline "Too Chicken to Go Vegetarian." Gore is the target because of his advocacy in fighting global warming. Says PETA, "The meat industry is the leading source of greenhouse gas emissions, but Gore has repeatedly refused even to discuss the issue." PETA cites a United Nations' report claiming that "raising animals for food generates more greenhouse gasses than all the cars and trucks in the world combined" (<http://www.peta.org/MC/NewsItem.asp?id=10208>). I wonder if this is true. I'm not sure I can trust PETA. It seems so extreme.

---

# WHO IS THE AUTHOR?

In evaluating information on Web sites, the question of authorship is an important consideration. Who is the author? How is that person credible? What are the person's credentials?

## Identifying Authors

Avoid unidentifiable, unverifiable information. The Internet's basic characteristic derives from the First Amendment of the Constitution: freedom of speech. The Net, so far, is a public medium: Web pages are not policed; people can post anything they like, making it difficult for you to determine what is reliable information and what isn't. A general rule for critical thinkers is to be suspicious in relation to the amount of information a site offers (or doesn't offer) about itself. An essay with only an author's name for identification isn't necessarily unreliable, but be cautious.

Depending on how recently researchers have been published, you should be able to find clues to their identities that can then help you infer the reliability of their information. You may be able to find biographical information in one of the biographical reference works, one of the large encyclopedias, the archives of a reliable newspaper, magazine, or professional journal, and sometimes from a simple Web search such as Google.

## ACTIVITY 9

Based on your research so far, who would you say are two or three important researchers in your project? Select two and see what you can find about their credentials. ▪▪▪

## Watch Out for False Authorities

The Internet is wide open to everyone, and therefore it isn't always easy to identify authors on the Net. Albert Einstein may have written the article you are reading, but it's also possible that someone else has borrowed Einstein's name. As a researcher you must avoid articles that appear out of the blue—with no indication of who wrote them or who sponsors them or why. While researching "Black Holes," for example, suppose you find a Web site by Professor Vayout in which he presents his own essay on black holes as the home of aliens who manage to travel in and out of them.

| Whose site is this? | **Black Holes: Home of Aliens**<br>**Professor Vayout** | Who is this author? |
|---|---|---|
| | Nature's great mystery, the black hole has been a favorite tool of science fiction writers. However, science now reveals that the gravitational fields which were thought to prevent anything from escaping a black hole are not so | **Source of this information?** |
| **Assumption: "aliens"?** | powerful as previously thought. And that fact coincides with another great mystery. Where is the home of the aliens we call UFOs? How is it so many UFOs can be reported within the earth's atmosphere, but none can ever be | |
| **Assumption: "would have powers"?** | tracked leaving? Where do they go, where are they from?<br>    Black holes are one possible answer. Creatures that can travel the universe would have powers beyond our knowledge, perhaps enough power to enter and leave black holes. | **Source of this information?**<br><br>**Credibility of this article?** |

**FIGURE 8.1**  Illustration of Doubtful Web Site.

A "black hole" is an area of the universe whose gravitational pull is so powerful that not even light can escape, according to modern science. If this author doesn't identify him- or herself, you must examine the Web page for clues to identity. Without a university, a research institute, or some other identifiable reliable sponsor for Professor Vayout, you will find identification difficult. You might try some of the links the professor suggests (if any), but it's possible that those sites may also be doubtful. Without documentation in the essay, without identifying information on the author, and without some kind of sponsorship for this page (The Black Hole Society of America?), nothing about this essay resembles the way authorities publish their work.

Before you spend much time trying to identify hard-to-find people or verifying their expertise, look for those who may be easier to find. The more you read about your subject, the more you will discover the important figures. Then when you come across someone hard to identify, like Professor Vayout, you will have a context for judging both the author and the information.

The Web is highly accessible. By contrast, print journals have room for only so many articles. Editors receive hundreds of submissions but usually have room to publish only a dozen or so. This state of affairs is difficult for researchers: it can be extremely difficult to get published in the print journals; however, articles in print have at least been read by an editor and may have been submitted to reviewers before publication. Furthermore, journals frequently give brief biographical descriptions of authors.

## ACTIVITY 10

Keep a file of doubtful or ridiculous sources that you find during your research journey. Print out one and bring it to class to share as an example of what not to use in scholarly research writing.

## Authority

Authorities are expert witnesses. But what makes an *expert* witness? There are no easy answers to that question. Experts are usually (but not always) people with advanced degrees and years of experience. By definition, the expert witness is one we can turn to when we need highly specialized, technical information. But if the technical information is reliable, it can count more than advanced degrees. Suppose you plan to be an elementary school teacher and decide to do research on teaching writing. Who would be an expert witness—a fourth-grade teacher who has taught writing for 20 years or a professor of education with a PhD who has never taught in an elementary school? You might assume the fourth-grade teacher would be. But how reliable is the testimony of one teacher? And much depends on whether that teacher enjoys or dreads teaching kids how to write.

Expert testimony can contain problems. The only real solution is to continue reading and studying until you can find authorities whose judgments you trust.

## Questionable Ethos

Can you trust all doctors, all scholars, all experts? You might want to, but you shouldn't. The following editorial from the <u>New York Times</u> shows how unethical some doctors are when they receive money for promoting certain drugs.

### Generic Smear Campaign

*Daniel Carlat*

That pharmaceutical companies pay doctors to say good things about their drugs is no longer newsworthy. Two former editors of <u>The New England Journal of Medicine</u>, Jerome P. Kassirer and Marcia Angell, have documented the drug industry's use of doctors to promote new medicines through professional articles and at medical conferences.

But in a move that may astonish even the most jaded critics of ethically challenged pharmaceutical marketing, makers of sleeping pills are now paying doctors to publish bad things about competing drugs.

The market for sleeping pills is huge—42 million prescriptions were filled last year—and it is more competitive than ever, thanks to the recent introduction of Sepracor's Lunesta (the one with the butterfly commercials), Sanofi-Aventis's Ambien CR (a controlled-release version of Ambien) and Takeda Pharmaceuticals' Rozerem. Ads have made most of these drugs household names. Yet many people have never heard of one of the most widely prescribed hypnotics in the United States: trazodone.

First approved by the Food and Drug Administration 25 years ago, trazodone is categorized as an antidepressant. Nonetheless, psychiatrists prescribe it off label to treat insomnia, because it works so well. Trazodone carries no risk of addiction; its half-life is long enough to keep patients asleep all night; it has a long safety record; and it is cheap, costing as little as 10 cents a pill. (Ambien and Lunesta can cost $3 a pill or more.) And in the only sizable study to compare trazodone with Ambien as a sleep aid, the two drugs performed equally well.

But each time a psychiatrist prescribes trazodone, a potential sale of Lunesta or Ambien is lost. No doubt that is why, in the past few years, several articles have been published in professional journals that can only be described as trazodone-bashing. With titles like "The Use of Trazodone as a Hypnotic: A Critical Review" (published in <u>The Journal of Clinical Psychiatry</u>), these articles purport to present balanced reviews of the scientific literature on sleeping pills. But the authors, psychiatrists with university affiliations, have been paid by Sepracor, Sanofi-Aventis or Takeda, the companies that stand to gain from trazodone's downfall.

A disclosure statement at the top of one such paper, "A Review of the Evidence for the Efficacy and Safety of Trazodone in Insomnia," also in <u>The Journal of Clinical Psychiatry</u>, states that Sepracor "assisted in the preparation" of the article, and paid the author a fee for "the services he provided in support of the development" of the manuscript.

A careful reading of these articles reveals a pattern of rhetorical techniques: a minimization of trazodone's advantages and an emphasis on its negative qualities.

Trazodone is criticized as lacking high-quality research data on its ability to help people sleep. What is left unmentioned is that because trazodone is no longer patented, no pharmaceutical company stands to profit from doing such research.

The authors also dust off older studies highlighting side effects from trazodone, like cardiac arrhythmias or priapism (prolonged painful erections). But these side effects are extremely rare: priapism has been found to occur in one in 5,000 men who take the drug, and the incidence of cardiac arrythmias is even lower.

Case reports of such side effects inevitably surface when a drug has been on the market for 25 years. In the case of Ambien, the oldest of the newer drugs, we are already seeing a flurry of reports of problems like drug abuse, sleepwalking, night eating and car accidents that may be associated with its use.

The way to discourage this practice of negative marketing disguised as legitimate scientific commentary is to mandate fuller disclosure of links between drug companies and authors. Several states now insist that drug makers report the gifts they give doctors.

These same companies should be required to disclose the exact nature of a doctor's involvement in preparing a sponsored article, as well as the dollar amount of his or her fee. I suspect it would be the rare doctor who would want such information to come to light.

*Daniel Carlat, a professor at Tufts Medical School, is the editor-in-chief of* The Carlat Psychiatry Report.

Work Cited

Carlat, Daniel. "Generic Smear Campaign." New York Times 9 May 2006, late ed.: A27.

Carlat's editorial provides outsiders with insider information on what happens with some unethical doctors. It rings a bell of warning: don't assume that all scientific studies are legitimate.

---

## GUIDELINES FOR EVALUATING AUTHORS

1. Is the author credible? What clues in the writing make you believe the author is trustworthy and fair-minded? What is your sense of the author's ethos?

2. Is the author a well-known authority? If so, information on him or her should be easy to locate online.

3. Does the author provide strong persuasive evidence: examples, reasons, statistics, other scholarly studies? Does the author sound knowledgeable?

4. Does the author's information fit with the body of research you have been collecting? If it disagrees or differs very much, does the author offer believable reasons why it does?

5. Does the author cite sources—authoritative information—and provide a bibliography of "Works Cited" or "References"?

## RELIABLE INFORMATION: ON THE WEB AND OFF

*Caveat emptor* is an ancient warning ("let the buyer beware"): in the computer age, let the *researcher* beware. A good rule for critical thinkers is to avoid anything you can't identify or verify. Continue searching until you find data you can rely on.

Step one is to read information and decide what you think of it. There is little to gain by spending much time on information you don't think is good, useful, relevant, or reliable for your project—such as much information from Wikipedia. Background reading can help you to skim through new material and make your judgments about it. While you are building your list of books and articles, you need to start reading, developing a context with which to evaluate material.

### Context

Without some *context* for information, your evaluations must remain general and not very useful. You need a background of fundamental information, a preliminary understanding that can serve as a context for evaluations.

A brief reading or skimming can suggest whether an Internet article might be useful for your research. Other aids can help, if you find them: titles, labels, and headings can give you a quick indication of an article's usefulness. Introductory statements typically contain the thesis or some statement of intent, if there is one: a quick read through the first paragraph or two should give you a fair idea of an author's purpose. Many researchers skim through the introduction and then hop to the conclusion to see whether a report may be useful. A context of preliminary readings and a common-sense application of guidelines should help you decide whether an article is likely to be relevant or useful for your project, and whether you should print it.

### Timely Data

Researchers tend to believe that newer data are better than old, but that depends on what you are researching. Research about works of art like Shakespeare's <u>Hamlet</u> can be useful even if it's more than a hundred years old.

Most scientific research, however, requires the most recent data. Recency alone doesn't necessarily carry the day: some data may only confirm instead of contradict earlier data. Studies published in the year 2008 don't automatically mean more than those published in 1995 or 2000. But you should always try to find the most recent data. As a researcher, you have to justify much use of old research. Information tends to age rapidly, online or off. You needn't completely ignore older material, but if you use material from the 1980s or '90s, for example, you must look for recent material as well. Omissions or other problems in your documentation must be explained. Some material may not be available at first, but you should keep after it until eventually your research does cover the most recent material, without raising questions or creating problems.

### Documentation and Credibility

In-text references (as well as footnotes and endnotes) show readers where your information came from and assist readers in finding relevant material. Research is connected to research, and reliable researchers will help you to find those connections. Documentation is a significant component of scholarly writing. Thus, an important criterion for reliable information is whether the author has provided documentation.

Documentation helps critical thinkers produce thoughtful research, no matter what their credentials may be. For example, the Journal of the American Medical Association (JAMA) published the science project of a sixth-grade girl concerning "therapeutic touch." Some people believe there is a "human energy field" that can be manipulated without touching a patient. The technique is taught in some nursing schools.

Emily Rosa devised a test for this "energy field." A cardboard screen with hand holes obstructed subjects' view. The subjects put their hands through the holes. Emily held one of her own hands above one of theirs and then asked whether they could "feel" which of their hands she was near. Subjects answered correctly in 44% of 280 trials, a score less than chance. (The significance level for such experiments is typically 95%.) With a little help, Emily's paper "A Close Look at Therapeutic Touch" was published in JAMA 279 (1998): 1005–1010, and then online.

Whether the work of a scientist or a student, research writing—online or in print—becomes credible when it states a clear thesis and presents clearly documented information on that thesis. Good researchers tell readers where to find that information.

If researchers follow the traditions of academic writing, critical readers can be optimistic about the validity of the research. (Serious researchers don't usually resort to humor, sarcasm, satire, or other "light" tones, but once in a while they may.) As a critical thinker you must remain objective and impartial regardless: it's difficult to challenge carefully documented research, but you should attempt to verify the documentation, especially online references.

## Hoaxes and Frauds

Critical thinkers don't expect scientific research to rely on dubious or obviously fraudulent sources of evidence, but errors can happen, even today. In the 19th century, the "Cardiff Giant" was a 10-foot fraud: a "petrified man" was planted in the ground until it was discovered and proven a fraud (Britannica Online). "Piltdown Man," discovered in the 20th century, turned out to be "disguised" fragments from a modern human skull as well as pieces of orangutan and chimpanzee teeth. No one knows the motives behind these hoaxes, but today there is great pressure on scientists and professors to produce successful experiments. Consider this example from a New York Times article, "In a Scientist's Fall, China Feels Robbed of Glory" (15 May 2006):

> Not very long ago, China saw itself as a nation on the verge of a technological breakthrough.
>
> But today, China appears shocked and shamed by a scandal that has already begun to tarnish that vision. It involves a top computer scientist, Chen Jin, who became a national hero in 2003 when he said he had created one of China's first digital signal processing computer chips, sophisticated microchips that can process digitized data for mobile phones,

cameras and other electronic devices. His milestone seemed to hold the promise of helping close the enormous gaps with the West in science and technology.

On Friday, however, the government said it was all a fraud.

The distinguished scientist, the government said, had faked research conducted at Jiaotong University and simply stolen his chip designs from a foreign company, then passed them off as his own.

Mr. Chen, who has not admitted wrongdoing in the case, declined to comment when he was reached on Sunday by telephone. "This is not the right moment to talk," he said.

In a society where honor is particularly important and where the fear of public shame runs especially deep, the story of Mr. Chen has a profound resonance. Now, after all the honors and accolades bestowed on this 37-year-old favorite son, who returned home to China from the United States with a Ph.D. from the University of Texas at Austin six years ago, people here are beginning to question whether China is pushing its leading thinkers too hard to innovate and catch up with the West. Could Mr. Chen's downfall, they ask, represent an example of how even smart and successful people in China are being forced to cut corners to meet the nation's hyper-ambitious goals?

"There's now a national competition going on in China, and there are very high expectations on scholars returning from the West," said Bai Ruoyun, a media specialist from China who is now a researcher at the University of Illinois at Urbana-Champaign. "They're paid very handsome salaries and given lots of incentives to achieve. And in return, these scholars are expected to produce some concrete results."

A fraud such as this represents fatally bad ethos on the part of Chen Jin. Scientific research is founded on objective accuracy and absolute honesty. But pressures are enormous to achieve results, even if the results are bogus. Thus, critical thinkers must evaluate evidence.

## Guidelines for Reliable Information

1. Use reputable sources and Web sites. Avoid sites you're not sure about.
2. Use sources that other researchers use.
3. Identify researchers when possible. Avoid those you can't identify.
4. Look for documentation of sources. Avoid information you can't verify.
5. Seek confirmation of evidence. Avoid data you can't confirm.

For additional information on evaluating Internet sources, visit these Web sites:

<http://www.library.cornell.edu/olinuris/ref/research/webeval.html>
<http://www.library.jhu.edu/researchhelp/general/evaluating/>
<http://www3.widener.edu/Academics/Libraries/Wolfgram_Memorial_Library/Evaluate_Web_Pages/659/>

# UNDERSTANDING EVIDENCE

Some readers accept everything they read as true. "After all," they say, "who am I to question the authorities? If it's in the newspapers, it must be true." However, not everything in print is correct. As a critical thinker, you *should* challenge what you find online or in print. Maybe writers are right, maybe not. But relying only on experts, closing your own mind to discovery, isn't good research. Besides, you may soon discover that the "experts" do not agree.

## Claim

A research "claim" is a thesis, a proposition to be inferred or supported with evidence. What does the author want you to believe: what is the claim? Can you find the author's thesis? Critical thinkers take as much care in reporting their work as in doing the research in the first place. You should be able to find a thesis clearly stated at the beginning of most research papers, though it can sometimes appear elsewhere. If the author's claim is not clear, it will be difficult, perhaps impossible, to evaluate the effectiveness of the research.

## Persuasion

*examples*
*documentation*

How does the writer attempt to persuade you? Consider logos. If there is factual data, is it documented? If not documented, should you accept it? If the reasons are theoretical, speculative, do they sound logical, convincing? Can you think of exceptions to the reasons, contradictions, or equally persuasive but contrasting reasons? If you can think of exceptions, how does that affect your judgment of the article? Consider pathos. Does the writer attempt to move you? Although journal articles rely less on emotional appeals *Empathy* than magazine articles do, pay attention to any attempts writers use to stir your feelings. Also, consider ethos. Remember that any piece of research you read implies a writer's ethos or credibility of character. If you infer that a writer is unfair or not trustworthy in any way, you should doubt that writer's presentation of information.

→ *Credibility*

## Questioning Evidence

Evidence is the heart of research. Thinking about evidence is a critical thinker's most important task. Collecting dozens and dozens of sources means little until you analyze them and decide their relevance or significance. Some evidence may be good, but some may be light and of doubtful value. Facts make good evidence; theories and arguments can also be good evidence. But how can you tell what the evidence means? How can you know whether evidence is significant? Before you answer such questions, you need to know some basics about evidence.

## Primary and Secondary Evidence

*Primary evidence is firsthand.* If you are the first one who finds the evidence, through your own investigations, in the lab, in the field, and so on, it is "primary evidence." (Often the first to discover something new gets to name it, like Halley's Comet.) Can students do primary research? Yes—consider Emily Rosa's experiment. Students might do interviews, surveys, questionnaires, simple experiments in human behavior.

Doing research can be fun. One student, Lauren Hunt, investigated how many licks it takes to get to the center of a Tootsie Roll Pop. She established rules for eight participants in her study—no biting or sucking—and instructed them on how to lick a pop. She examined variations in tongue size, age, and saliva. The average number of licks was 393. Lauren's younger sister licked her pop 585 times before breaking through to the candy inside; her mother took 883 licks, and her father took 255 licks. Also using secondary sources in her paper, including information from Tootsie Roll Industries, Lauren enjoyed writing her paper, and fellow students in class enjoyed reading it.

*Secondary evidence means you rely on the work of others*. As a critical thinker, you must remember that primary research requires secondary research. Most research starts in the library. Generally it includes library material and information you can find on the Internet. Nearly all research requires at least some secondary material, even if you intend to conduct a primary research experiment. Suppose you plan a project to explore this question: How important is character development to college students? But before starting any kind of survey at your school, you must go to the library to find out what research has already been done, to examine the projects of other researchers, and to read their conclusions. In research, secondary evidence often comes first, before primary evidence.

At the library or on the Internet you can discover what other researchers already know about your subject. You will discover what to read, whose projects are important, and what critics have said about your topic. However, suppose you don't find any information. Does that mean no one knows anything about your topic? Can you then just skip the secondary research and start making a questionnaire and interviewing students? No. If you can't find what you need, seek out a reference librarian. Perhaps a librarian will tell you about a source he found recently: the <u>Journal of College and Character</u> (<http://www.collegevalues.org/index.cfm>). If the librarian can't find anything, then you need to alter your question or try an altogether different subject.

In secondary research you will discover what other researchers have said. You probably won't find just one definitive answer to your question; instead, you will find various answers. To analyze secondary research, you must weigh the evidence, analyze the data, and interpret the findings. After all that, you must decide what your evidence is telling you. Often the evidence is inconclusive: you may conclude that there isn't enough data or that the evidence isn't good enough to give a clear, final conclusion. Such research can be valid; it reveals what you don't know. Those results aren't considered failures. Most researchers say it's better to find the mistakes and flaws in research than to believe you know the answers when you don't.

## The Weight of Evidence

The "weight" of evidence really means the "amount." But is it true that whoever has the most evidence wins? That notion disregards the kind and quality of evidence.

Dragging in dozens of character witnesses who swear Old Joe is incapable of crime won't override the bank's security videotape, which clearly shows Old Joe pointing a bazooka at the bank teller. Still, all other things being equal, we tend to accept the weight of evidence as an important factor in research.

It's human nature to believe in the weight of evidence. We have laws that try to protect the public, but a single test of a new product is never enough to satisfy the Food and Drug Administration (FDA), which requires many tests before giving its stamp of approval, especially for drugs. Nevertheless, you need to know what the weight of evidence does suggest. Is all your evidence of the same quality? Are some facts more convincing than others? Is there more evidence on one side than the other?

## Magazines and Journals

Popular magazines like <u>People</u> contain colorful pictures and advertisements. They provide entertaining, often short, pieces about celebrities, people recently in the news, and simplified articles about recent events and interesting issues. Popular magazines are often printed on glossy paper and feature large, eye-appealing pictures on the cover, sometimes with bizarre, provocative headlines. Magazines aren't usually too difficult to read, but the reliability of such publications varies. News magazines such as <u>Time</u> and <u>Newsweek</u>, and others aimed at educated readers, are considered reliable by many researchers.

A few periodicals like <u>Nature</u> and <u>Scientific American</u> look like magazines but are well respected among scientists and other highly educated readers. These periodicals attempt to present valid, accurate articles, but—as they will freely admit—they must have advertisers and subscribers in order to survive. Information they present is generally considered accurate but "popularized," meaning written at a level nonspecialist, educated readers can understand. "Popularization" is frequently considered a negative term, meaning "dumbing-down" the information, but without such publications many readers would be uninformed about developments in fields of knowledge other than their own.

## What Are Professional Journals?

Journals report research and developments in the academic and technical professions; they don't often use glossy paper, color, or pictures, and they don't usually have advertisements, although that is changing. As the cost of publishing has increased, many journals have had to rely on ads—often from publishers, sometimes from professional organizations. Traditionally journals have been easy to distinguish from magazines. Magazines look lively, attractive, inviting; journals, at best, look businesslike, plain, more like reports than entertainment.

The writing itself—serious, formal, objective—can suggest that you are reading a journal. Journal authors are usually professors who specialize in a certain academic area or scientists. Opinions are usually labeled "editorial" or are otherwise designated so that readers will know, especially in scientific writing, that the information is not intended as fact. Often journals are intended only for their own professional membership; thus they can be more technical and difficult to read than students are prepared for. Professional journals do not usually "dumb down" their articles.

The more you read, the more you will be able to identify which publications are considered reliable and informative and which are designed for entertainment and profit.

ACTIVITY 11

Try to find three journal articles for your project. In your notebook evaluate whether they are useful or not and why. ▬

## Researchers' Rule

Researchers use the sources that other researchers are likely to read. You should avoid sources designed as entertainment for mass audiences, gossip magazines, picture magazines, or sources aimed at children. Researchers do not usually look for information in children's editions of adult magazines like <u>Sports Illustrated for Kids</u> or <u>Time for Kids</u>. That's not absolute, of course; you might use such sources if your project concerns values and biases in children's magazines. Too many "popular" sources can raise questions about the credibility of your research. Avoid "digests" and other sources in which information has been summarized, condensed, or in some other way altered. Try to make sure you're reading the original source of information. *Note:* as discussed with the Wikipedia dilemma, most instructors prefer that students not cite information from a general encyclopedia in their research. Although encyclopedias are helpful for you to first understand a subject (see Chapter 7), college instructors expect you to use more specific sources of information.

## "Best" Sources of Evidence

You should use the best sources available, but there may be problems if you rely too much on only the "best" sources. (See Genetic Fallacy in Chapter 4.) Critical thinkers shouldn't assume that the source of evidence always provides unconditional credibility. Researchers at great institutions like Duke, Johns Hopkins, and Stanford, for example, are not automatically more reliable than researchers at humbler institutions. The research that produced "Dolly," the first cloned animal, was conducted at the Roslin Institute in Scotland, an institute unknown to most Americans. Nor are the larger newspapers such as the <u>New York Times</u>, the <u>Wall Street Journal</u>, and the <u>Washington Post</u> necessarily always more authoritative than smaller papers.

The great institutions—universities, government agencies, research institutes—are generally reliable and authoritative, but there is no such thing as "automatic" or "constant" authority. No place has a permanent lock on the truth. It helps when researchers find evidence from big and powerful institutions with big research grants and Nobel Prize–winners on the staff, but you must not disregard evidence just because it comes from a humble source. On the whole, research should be impartial, based on facts and evidence, regardless of its source.

## Remaining Impartial

Researchers must remain unbiased. You must not let your own emotions influence your judgment. It can be difficult to research alcoholism, drug addiction, or any serious diseases or disorders if someone you know is afflicted. But starting out with an attitude for or against the subject would mean your research is biased from the very beginning.

Bias can also creep into a project through unconsciously over- or underresearching one side or the other. If you find much data on one side of your question but little on the other, you will of course conclude in favor of the side with the most data. Any bias for one side or the other will cause you to lose your impartiality.

## Information without Attribution

Unfortunately, not all experts are careful about documentation. Experts writing to other experts can (and often do) take much for granted. They may assume much information to be common knowledge among the well-informed members of their specialty. However, these aren't permissible assumptions for those who aren't yet specialists. You need to find supporting evidence for information you use, whether it was documented where you found it or not.

It's a convention (a custom) in journalistic writing that readers must accept the journalist's word that everything has been checked and verified, usually by more than one source. Published news articles are presumed to be true (columns and editorials follow a different rule, since by definition they are opinion pieces). Nevertheless, for students, any use of information without attribution (documentation) is a mistake, despite the fact that professionals don't always document fully. For example, consider this excerpt from Mark Schoofs's essay "Fear and Wonder":

> Tests for drug abuse are now commonplace, but they were first introduced in professions where public safety is at stake. Should genetic tests be used in a similar way? Should someone with a predisposition to, say, Alzheimer's be allowed to become president? Fly an airplane? Drive a school bus? Take custody of a child after a divorce? Genetic fitness has already arisen in a custody battle.

You should ask, where did Mark Schoofs get the information concerning a custody battle in which genetic fitness was an issue? His last statement is used as a fact, but he supplies no source for this fact, not here nor at the end of his article. Mark Schoofs is a journalist who received the Pulitzer Prize in 2000 for International Reporting; he writes for the <u>Village Voice</u> and the <u>Wall Street Journal</u>. Readers may accept his word as accurate. However, as a careful researcher, you should not rely on this statement unless you can find a valid source for it.

## Evaluating Statistical Data

The first law of statistics is beware of statistics. Much research today uses statistics, but many people don't understand statistics and have only a limited ability to do the math required in statistics. Be critical of statistics. When you encounter them in your research, you may need to find someone who can help you understand them. For example, "If 50% of students have a 30% chance of scoring at 80% or above on the final exam . . . "—such statements soon get beyond most readers' ability to calculate.

Statistics can also bias research simply because of the power of numbers. Numbers tend to carry more weight than other kinds of data. Specific numbers are often more convincing than generalizations about "more" or "less" of anything.

## GUIDELINES FOR UNDERSTANDING EVIDENCE

1. Don't assume everything you read by authorities is true or accurate. It may be biased. Question what you read.

2. Evaluate an author's claim, supporting evidence, and use of persuasive appeals to determine if a source is credible and worthwhile.

3. Determine if evidence is primary (firsthand information from interviews, surveys, experiments) or secondary (based on the work of others in libraries or Internet).

4. Determine the weight of evidence: how much makes a convincing case? Is all your evidence of the same quality? Are some facts more convincing than others? Is there more evidence on one side than the other?

5. Understand the differences between the evidence in magazines (full of advertising) and in journals (formal investigations of topics, including references).

6. Follow the researcher's rule: read the important sources other researchers will read.

7. The most prestigious sources are not always the most credible. Humble sources can matter too.

8. Determine if evidence is reliable: accurate, impartial, approved by other scholars. Be familiar with the experts that other experts know.

9. Check to see if an author cites documentation for claims. Don't readily accept a writer's evidence until he or she cites a source for it.

10. Be careful when you read statistics. Numbers have power. Don't accept statistics unless you understand them.

## GOING BEYOND THE INFORMATION GIVEN

Let's see how you might explore a topic by doing some research on it and evaluating evidence for it. One way to do this is to take an article from a newspaper or magazine and research it to go beyond the information given. The process of exploring it and evaluating its evidence is the same process you follow when doing a report or an argument paper. Suppose, since you've started college, you read the New York Times each day to see more about what's going on in the world. You discover this article.

*(handwritten margin note: Do not believe everything is said.)*

# Save the Darfur Puppy

*Nicholas D. Kristof*

Finally, we're beginning to understand what it would take to galvanize President Bush, other leaders and the American public to respond to the genocide in Sudan: a suffering puppy with big eyes and floppy ears.

That's the implication of a series of studies by psychologists trying to understand why people—good, conscientious people—aren't moved by genocide or famines. Time and again, we've seen that the human conscience just isn't pricked by mass suffering, while an individual child (or puppy) in distress causes our hearts to flutter.

In one experiment, psychologists asked ordinary citizens to contribute $5 to alleviate hunger abroad. In one version, the money would go to a particular girl, Rokia, a 7-year-old in Mali; in another, to 21 million hungry Africans; in a third, to Rokia—but she was presented as a victim of a larger tapestry of global hunger.

Not surprisingly, people were less likely to give to anonymous millions than to Rokia. But they were also less willing to give in the third scenario, in which Rokia's suffering was presented as part of a broader pattern.

Evidence is overwhelming that humans respond to the suffering of individuals rather than groups. Think of the toddler Jessica McClure falling down a well in 1987, or the Lindbergh baby kidnapping in 1932 (which Mencken described as the "the biggest story since the Resurrection").

Even the right animal evokes a similar sympathy. A dog stranded on a ship aroused so much pity that $48,000 in private money was spent trying to rescue it— and that was before the Coast Guard stepped in. And after I began visiting Darfur in 2004, I was flummoxed by the public's passion to save a red-tailed hawk, Pale Male, that had been evicted from his nest on Fifth Avenue in New York City. A single homeless hawk aroused more indignation than two million homeless Sudanese.

Advocates for the poor often note that 30,000 children die daily of the consequences of poverty—presuming that this number will shock people into action. But the opposite is true: the more victims, the less compassion.

In one experiment, people in one group could donate to a $300,000 fund for medical treatments that would save the life of one child—or, in another group, the lives of eight children. People donated more than twice as much money to help save one child as to help save eight.

Likewise, remember how people were asked to save Rokia from starvation? A follow-up allowed students to donate to Rokia or to a hungry boy named Moussa. Both Rokia and Moussa attracted donations in the same proportions. Then another group was asked to donate to Rokia and Moussa together. But donors felt less good about supporting two children, and contributions dropped off.

"Our capacity to feel is limited," Paul Slovic of the University of Oregon writes in a new journal article, "Psychic Numbing and Genocide," which discusses these experiments. Professor Slovic argues that we cannot depend on the innate morality even of good people. Instead, he believes, we need to develop legal or political mechanisms to force our hands to confront genocide.

So, yes, we should develop early-warning systems for genocide, prepare an African Union, U.N. and NATO rapid-response capability, and polish the "responsibility to protect" as a legal basis to stop atrocities. (The Genocide Intervention Network and the Enough project are working on these things.)

But, frankly, after four years of watching the U.N. Security Council, the International Criminal Court and the Genocide Convention accomplish little in Darfur, I'm skeptical that either human rationality or international law can achieve much unless backed by a public outcry.

One experiment underscored the limits of rationality. People prepared to donate to the needy were first asked either to talk about babies (to prime the emotions) or to perform math calculations (to prime their rational side). Those who did math donated less.

So maybe what we need isn't better laws but more troubled consciences—pricked, perhaps, by a Darfur puppy with big eyes and floppy ears. Once we find such a soulful dog in peril, we should call ABC News. ABC's news judgment can be assessed by the 11 minutes of evening news coverage it gave to Darfur's genocide during all of last year—compared with 23 minutes for the false confession in the JonBenet Ramsey case.

If President Bush and the global public alike are unmoved by the slaughter of hundreds of thousands of fellow humans, maybe our last, best hope is that we can be galvanized by a puppy in distress.

*Nicholas D. Kristof, an op-ed writer for the* New York Times, *often writes about global health, poverty, and gender issues in the developing world. In 2006 he won the Pulitzer Prize for his work focusing on genocide in Darfur.*

Work Cited

Kristof, Nicholas D. "Save the Darfur Puppy." New York Times 10 May 2007, late ed.: A33.

If you wanted to do some research, how might you go beyond the information given in the article? First, you can reread the article—*actively* read it with a pencil: write down questions and mark insights you notice as well as assumptions and over-generalizations (see Chapter 2). Write briefly in your own words what you think about the information. Why does it matter?

When you do research, it's useful to keep a notebook. Let's suppose Ryan writes an entry about Kristof's article in his notebook:

Interesting—this makes sense. We don't seem to care about mass suffering as much as one person's suffering—or one animal's suffering. But why? Kristof says that "we respond to the suffering of individuals rather than groups." Take breast cancer. We all know it causes great suffering for many women, but until my grandmother had breast cancer last year, I didn't really care about this issue. Now I do. I even participated in a Relay for Life walk raising money for cancer research.

There is a paradox in this article: "the more victims, the less compassion." This is a contradiction with a profound truth. It reinforces what we've been learning about logos, pathos, and ethos. Appeals to emotion (pathos) can trigger thinking (logos) and action—

studies show people donate more money for one child than for thousands of children. Such humane action reflects good character (ethos). But we don't care much unless we can feel compassion for an individual child or animal. One photograph of a starving child with a bloated stomach moves us more than a photo of a thousand starving children whose eyes we cannot see and feel.

In his second paragraph Kristof refers to "a series of studies by psychologists," and later he refers to a journal article by Paul Slovic. Kristof says Slovic "argues that we cannot depend on the innate morality even of good people. . . . we need to develop legal or political mechanisms to force our hands to confront genocide." This is a major insight because genocides keep happening. Compassion is not enough, though such "mechanisms" would not develop, it seems, without compassion. "More troubled consciences," Kristof says, might help solve the problem. And it would help if major news sources like ABC spent more time covering these stories in more depth. But, again, one child, JonBenet Ramsey, who was murdered seems more important than "the slaughter of hundreds of thousands of fellow humans."

Ryan has written a thoughtful reaction to Kristof's article. But to go beyond the information given, suppose he checks the sources in Kristof's article. He does some research online, evaluates the evidence he finds, and then writes the following:

To find out more information, I did a Web search to find Paul Slovic's journal article. It was the first link, one of 200 results (<http://journal.sjdm.org/7303a/jdm7303a.htm>). It turns out that his title is longer than the one Kristof mentions. The full title of Slovic's article is " 'If I Look at the Mass I Will Never Act': Psychic Numbing and Genocide." Slovic explains in his introduction: "My title is taken from a statement by Mother Teresa: 'If I look at the mass I will never act. If I look at the one, I will.'" This is an excellent quote—it conveys wisdom simply put.

There is a powerful photograph under the title of the article, showing a young black child, a boy I think, crying as he lies on his mother's lap. The mother is in grief; her left hand holds her head and covers her face. The image strongly appeals to pathos, which reflects Slovic's thesis.

The article appears in the journal <u>Judgment and Decision Making</u>, vol. 2, no. 2, April 2007, pp. 79–95. Kristof doesn't provide this information in his <u>New York Times</u> article, but he doesn't need to. It was easy to find Slovic's article.

Slovic's article contains an abstract before the introduction which summarizes his article. It's a long article with an introduction, nine divisions in the body, and a postscript for a conclusion. After the postscript there is a quote in bold: **"Are we all human?"** by Romeó Dallaire, 2005. (Dallaire, Slovic writes earlier in his article, was "the commander of the tiny U.N. peacekeeping mission in Rwanda," where genocide happened in 1994.) What a question! It really makes me wonder. Then there are three colorful photographs: two of individual children looking directly at the viewer, and one photo of a group of mothers and children also looking at the viewer. No one is crying in these images. Rather, the faces implore us to do something. Slovic uses visuals well as persuasive appeals.

Within the body of his article he also uses tables, including a list of genocides in the last century; figures, including Figure 2 that shows how imagery and attention both generate feeling, which then generates helping; and a painting of the rescue of Baby Jessica from a well. While Kristof mentions only Slovic, Slovic himself includes many sources for his supporting evidence. He cites a study by D. A. Small, G. Loewenstein, and himself, "Sympathy and Callousness: The Impact of Deliberative Thought on Donations to Identifiable and Statistical Victims" in <u>Organizational Behavior and Human Decision Processes</u> (2007). This study includes the examples of Rokia and Moussa, the children Kristof writes about in his article. Slovic's list of references includes over 50 sources—articles and books. It's clear that this is an incredibly well-researched article, and that Slovic himself is a scholar.

I went to the home page of the journal in which Slovic's article appears. <u>Judgment and Decision Making</u> is the journal of the Society for Judgment and Decision Making. This journal began in 2007 and publishes six times a year online (<http://journal.sjdm.org/>). But you can also download a PDF version of the article, so you can cite page numbers if you want. The online journal appears very academic and nonflashy with muted, dull colors. The home page provides information which helps give the journal credibility: the editor is Jonathan Baron, from the University of Pennsylvania. Three associate editors work at the University of Arizona, University of California–Berkeley, and Hebrew University of Jerusalem. There is also a list of consulting editors from universities all over the world. Although I had never heard of this journal before doing this research, it's clear the journal is important and credible.

Ryan has evaluated Paul Slovic's article well, discovering that Kristof uses a shortened version of the title. After examining the journal's Web site and list of editors, Ryan concludes that the journal is a scholarly publication. But to practice doing more research that goes beyond Kristof's article, Ryan probes further.

Who exactly is Paul Slovic? I know he wrote this important article that Nicholas Kristof draws from. The journal <u>Judgment and Decision Making</u> doesn't give biographical information on him, though it does mention that Slovic is affiliated with Decision Research and the University of Oregon.

I've never heard of Decision Research before. But on the same first page of the Web search where I found Slovic's article, there is a site, <http://www.decisionresearch.org/>, which says about itself,

> Decision Research is a nonprofit research organization investigating human judgment, decision-making, and risk. We conduct both basic and applied research in a variety of areas including aging, aviation, environmental risk, finance, health policy, medicine, and law. Founded in 1976, Decision Research is dedicated to helping individuals and organizations understand and cope with the complex and often risky decisions of modern life.
>
> We receive funding from US government agencies (including the Environmental Protection Agency, National Science Foundation, National Institutes of Health, and the National Aeronautics and Space Administration) and from private companies and philanthropic organizations.

I can infer from its funding sources that this organization is important.

I found a link to the 2007 Princeton Colloquium on Public and International Affairs that featured a keynote address by Paul Slovic, with the same title as his journal article (<http://www.wws.princeton.edu/pcpia/keynote.html>). It gave this information on Slovic:

> Paul Slovic is president of Decision Research and a professor of psychology at the University of Oregon. He studies human judgment, decision making, and risk analysis, and has published extensively on these topics. Dr. Slovic received a B.A. degree from Stanford University, M.A. and Ph.D. degrees from the University of Michigan, and honorary doctorates from the Stockholm School of Economics and the University of East Anglia. He is past president of the Society for Risk Analysis and in 1991 received its Distinguished Contribution Award. In 1993, Dr. Slovic received the Distinguished Scientific Contribution Award from the American Psychological Association, and in 1995 he received the Outstanding Contribution to Science Award from the Oregon Academy of Science.

It clearly appears that Paul Slovic is an outstanding scholar with excellent credentials and achievements.

When I read Kristof's article, I wondered about the dog stranded on the ship. I found a Web site, Kidsnewsroom.com, but figured this isn't a good college-level source, yet it did confirm the dog story. Another source with a corny name, Dogsinthenews.com, ran a story about a two-year-old dog left on an Indonesian tanker for 18 days. The tanker had burned and the crew left. The dog, named Forgea, belonged to the captain. The Humane Society of the United States along with the Hawaiian Humane Society organized a $50,000 rescue effort for the small white dog (<http://www.dogsinthenews.com/issues/0204/articles/020422a.htm>). This further verifies that what Kristof wrote about the dog is true. Although this dog is not the "Darfur puppy" that Kristof refers to in his title or his introduction, the dog serves as a symbol that more people will care about a single dog's suffering than the mass suffering of thousands and thousands of people.

One more discovery I want to point out about my research is that Slovic's article contains a reference to Jonathan Haidt, the author of The Happiness Hypothesis, which is discussed several times in Chapter 3 of our book Discovering Arguments. Slovic cites Haidt's article "The Emotional Dog and Its Rational Tail: A Social Intuitionist Approach to Moral Judgment" published in Psychological Review in 2001. Nice title—it makes me wonder if the tail (reason) leads the dog (emotion) or emotion leads reason. Maybe I'll read this Haidt article next.

As Ryan shows, examining an article to explore information from it is a useful kind of research. It's what you should do as you work on your report or argument paper. Doing research is a system of opening doors: you open one door (Kristof's New York Times article) that leads to another door (Slovic's article) that leads to another door (the journal Judgment and Decision Making) that leads to another door (the 2007 Princeton Colloquium on Public and International Affairs) that leads to another door (Dogsinthenews.com) and so on. Going through these doors, reading information and evaluating it can help you see whether information is credible, accurate, trustworthy.

# EXPLORING AN ARTICLE BY DOING RESEARCH FROM IT

## ACTIVITY 12

Choose one of the following newspaper articles and explore it in a similar way that Ryan explores Nicholas Kristof's article "Save the Darfur Puppy." Actively read the article by annotating it: write down questions it raises for you such as Why? How is that so? Who says? What is the truth here? Is this person a credible authority? Note insights, assumptions, overgeneralizations. Then write an informal report on what you find.

Explore—analyze and evaluate—your choice of article by following this structure:

1. *Discuss the main article:* what you notice about it, what you think about it. Quote from it at times to show what you mean.

2. *Do research from the article—go beyond the information given.* Make notes of what sources or studies are mentioned in the article that you could research—find more information on. Find *at least three* of the studies or sources mentioned. Make copies of them and annotate them. Analyze and evaluate what you find. See whether the sources help you understand, disagree with, or verify information in the article. Quote at times to show what you mean.

3. *Probe further by evaluating the credentials of the main author* and any other authors you find in your research. What are the credentials of the author? What are the credentials of some of the people quoted? Quote at times to show what you mean.

4. It's important for you to get into the habit of citing your sources. Thus, at the end of your report include a Works Cited list, including the article from which you do your research. Here is a list for the sources Ryan used, in MLA format (see Chapter 9).

Works Cited

"Cast Away Dog Rescued at Sea." <u>Dogsinthenews.com</u> 22 Apr. 2002. 12 Aug. 2007
    <http://www.dogsinthenews.com/issues/0204/articles/020422a.htm>.

Decision Research Home Page. <u>Decision Research</u> 2007. 12 Aug. 2007
    <http://www.decisionresearch.org/>.

"From Passion to Politics: What Moves People to Take Action." <u>2007 Princeton Colloquium on</u>
    <u>Public and International Affairs</u> 20 Apr. 2007. 12 Aug. 2007
    <http://www.wws.princeton.edu/pcpia/keynote.html>.

Kristof, Nicholas D. "Save the Darfur Puppy." <u>New York Times</u> 10 May 2007, late ed.: A33.

Slovic, Paul. "'If I Look at the Mass I Will Never Act': Psychic Numbing and Genocide."
    <u>Judgment and Decision Making</u> 2. 2 (Apr. 2007)
    <http://journal.sjdm.org/7303a/jdm7303a.htm.

Small, D. A., G. Loewenstein, and P. Slovic. "Sympathy and Callousness: the Impact of Deliberative
    Thought on Donations to Identifiable and Statistical Victims." <u>Organizational Behavior and</u>
    <u>Human Decision Processes</u> 102 (2007): 143-153.

**Notes on Works Cited:**

1. A Works Cited page is arranged alphabetically by the last names of authors. (If a source has no author, begin with the title of the review in quotation marks.)

2. After the first line of a citation, subsequent lines are indented five spaces.

3. A Works Cited page should be double-spaced. For more information on Works Cited using MLA style, see Chapter 9.

## Teens Can Multitask, But What Are Costs?

Ability to Analyze May Be Affected, Experts Worry

### *Lori Aratani*

It's homework time and 17-year-old Megan Casady of Silver Spring is ready to study.

She heads down to the basement, turns on MTV and boots up her computer. Over the next half hour, Megan will send about a dozen instant messages discussing the potential for a midweek snow day. She'll take at least one cellphone call, fire off a couple of text messages, scan Weather.com, volunteer to help with a campus cleanup day at James Hubert Blake High School where she is a senior, post some comments on a friend's Facebook page and check out the new pom squad pictures another friend has posted on hers.

In between, she'll define "descent with modification" and explain how "the tree analogy represents the evolutionary relationship of creatures" on a worksheet for her AP biology class.

Call it multitasking homework, Generation 'Net style.

The students who do it say multitasking makes them feel more productive and less stressed. Researchers aren't sure what the long-term impact will be because no studies have probed its effect on teenage development. But some fear that the penchant for flitting from task to task could have serious consequences on young people's ability to focus and develop analytical skills.

There is special concern for teenagers because parts of their brain are still developing, said Jordan Grafman, chief of cognitive neuroscience at the National Institute of Neurological Disorders and Stroke.

"Introducing multitasking in younger kids in my opinion can be detrimental," he said. "One of the biggest problems about multitasking is that it's almost impossible to gain a depth of knowledge of any of the tasks you do while you're multitasking. And if it becomes normal to do, you'll likely be satisfied with very surface-level investigation and knowledge."

Megan's parents, Steven and Donna Casady, might have their worries about the iPod/IM/text messaging/MTV effect on Megan's ability to retain the definition of "biochemical similarity," but they say it's hard to argue with a teenager who boasts a 3.85 unweighted grade-point average.

"To me, it's nothing but chaos," Steven Casady said. "But these kids? It seems to work for them. It seems to work for [Megan]. But it's hard for me to be in the same room when this is going on."

Thanks to the Internet, students say, facts are at their fingertips. If they get stuck on a math problem, they say, help is only an IM away.

"I honestly feel like I'm able to accomplish more during an hour if I multitask," said Christine Stoddard, 18, a senior at Yorktown High School in Arlington County. "If it's something like English or history that comes easily to me, then I can easily divide my attention. It's the way I've always been."

In fact, Christine sheepishly confessed that she was filling out a college scholarship application while being interviewed for this story.

Whatever the consequences of multitasking, they're going to be widespread. A recent report from the Kaiser Family Foundation found that when students are sitting in front of their computers "studying," they're also doing something else 65 percent of the time. In 1999, 16 percent of teenagers said they were "media multitaskers"—defined as using several type of media, such as television or computers, at once. By 2005, that percentage had increased to 26 percent. The foundation also found that girls were more likely to media multitask than boys.

The current generation of teens "is trying to do lots of multitasking because they think it's cool and less boring and because they have lots of gadgets that help them be more successful at this," said David Meyer, director of the Brain, Cognition and Action Laboratory at the University of Michigan. "The belief is they're getting good at this and that they're much better than the older generation at it and that there's no cost to their efficiency."

Meyer, a psychologist and cognitive scientist who studies multitasking, has doubts.

"Kids who grow up under conditions where they have to multitask a lot may be developing styles of coping that would allow them to perform better in future environments where required to do a lot, but that doesn't mean their performance in the workplace would be better than if they were doing one thing at a time."

Researchers say there isn't any answer yet to whether multitasking helps, hurts or has no effect on teens' development.

"Given that kids have grown up always doing this, it may turn out that they are more skilled at it. We just don't know yet," said Russell Poldrack, an associate professor of psychology at the University of California at Los Angeles, who co-authored a study that examined multitasking and brain activity.

In Poldrack's study, volunteers in their 20s were given stacks of cards and asked to sort them. Then they were told to listen to a series of tones and identify the high-pitched ones while they sorted the cards. Researchers found that although there were similar success rates between the two groups when it came to sorting, when interviewed later, those who did not multitask were able to describe the cards in more detail.

Poldrack said imaging showed that different parts of the brain were active depending on whether the subjects did single or multiple tasks. When subjects were focused on sorting, the hippocampus—the part of the brain responsible for storing and recalling information–was engaged. But when they were multitasking, that part of the brain was quiet and the part of the brain used to master repetitive skills—the striatum—was active.

Multitaskers "may not be building the same knowledge that they would be if they were focusing," Poldrack said. "While multitasking makes them feel like they are being more efficient, research suggests that there's very little you can do that involves multitasking that you can be as good at when you're not multitasking."

Meyer said if parts of the brain are less active when someone is multitasking, it could be especially detrimental for teenagers, who are still developing their ability to think and analyze information.

"They develop a more superficial style of study and may not learn material as well. What they get out of their study might be less deep," he said.

They might be getting goods grades, Meyer said, but there's a chance they could be getting better grades if they learned to focus on a single task or academic subject at a time.

Teens say they know there are limits.

Blake student Priscilla Tiglao, 17, is a multitasking blur when she sits down at her desk in the evening. But she says she will often forgo IM chats when it comes to AP chemistry or AP psychology—topics she finds more taxing. She might, however, bend the rules for AP statistics.

Nane Tiglao, Priscilla's mother, is a nurse who is used to juggling multiple tasks. She talks on the phone while cooking and doing other chores. But when she watches her daughter—oy.

Still, she thinks, in the end this will be good for Priscilla.

"I think it's necessary for the future," Tiglao said. "This generation needs to multitask and to do it right. It's a good trait for anyone."

Meyer, a multitasker himself, agrees with some of that sentiment. Many jobs demand, even require, people to be multitaskers: air traffic controllers, bond traders, commodities brokers, to name a few.

"In that case, possibly the future's bright for these kids," he said. "But I think what's really needed in the future is a fairly heavy emphasis on learning and performing in different situations. If they want to be learning and performing under conditions of multitasking, then fine. But don't let them get away with just doing just that and completely losing out on other forms of learning."

*Lori Aratani is a <u>Washington Post</u> staff writer.*

Work Cited

Aratani, Lori. "Teens Can Multitask, But What Are the Costs?" <u>Washington Post</u> 26 Feb. 2007: A01.

## Flame First, Think Later: New Clues to E-Mail Misbehavior

### *Daniel Goleman*

Jett Lucas, a 14-year-old friend, tells me the kids in his middle school send one another a steady stream of instant messages through the day. But there's a problem.

"Kids will say things to each other in their messages that are too embarrassing to say in person," Jett tells me. "Then when they actually meet up, they are too shy to bring up what they said in the message. It makes things tense."

Jett's complaint seems to be part of a larger pattern plaguing the world of virtual communications, a problem recognized since the earliest days of the Internet: flaming, or sending a message that is taken as offensive, embarrassing or downright rude.

The hallmark of the flame is precisely what Jett lamented: thoughts expressed while sitting alone at the keyboard would be put more diplomatically—or go unmentioned—face to face.

Flaming has a technical name, the "online disinhibition effect," which psychologists apply to the many ways people behave with less restraint in cyberspace.

In a 2004 article in the journal CyberPsychology & Behavior, John Suler, a psychologist at Rider University in Lawrenceville, N.J., suggested that several psychological factors lead to online disinhibition: the anonymity of a Web pseudonym; invisibility to others; the time lag between sending an e-mail message and getting feedback; the exaggerated sense of self from being alone; and the lack of any online authority figure. Dr. Suler notes that disinhibition can be either benign—when a shy person feels free to open up online—or toxic, as in flaming.

The emerging field of social neuroscience, the study of what goes on in the brains and bodies of two interacting people, offers clues into the neural mechanics behind flaming.

This work points to a design flaw inherent in the interface between the brain's social circuitry and the online world. In face-to-face interaction, the brain reads a continual cascade of emotional signs and social cues, instantaneously using them to guide our next move so that the encounter goes well. Much of this social guidance occurs in circuitry centered on the orbitofrontal cortex, a center for empathy. This cortex uses that social scan to help make sure that what we do next will keep the interaction on track.

Research by Jennifer Beer, a psychologist at the University of California, Davis, finds that this face-to-face guidance system inhibits impulses for actions that would upset the other person or otherwise throw the interaction off. Neurological patients with a damaged orbitofrontal cortex lose the ability to modulate the amygdala, a source of unruly impulses; like small children, they commit mortifying social gaffes like kissing a complete stranger, blithely unaware that they are doing anything untoward.

Socially artful responses emerge largely in the neural chatter between the orbitofrontal cortex and emotional centers like the amygdala that generate impulsivity. But the cortex needs social information—a change in tone of voice, say—to know how to select and channel our impulses. And in e-mail there are no channels for voice, facial expression or other cues from the person who will receive what we say.

True, there are those cute, if somewhat lame, emoticons that cleverly arrange punctuation marks to signify an emotion. The e-mail equivalent of a mood ring, they surely lack the neural impact of an actual smile or frown. Without the raised eyebrow that signals irony, say, or the tone of voice that signals delight, the orbitofrontal cortex has little to go on. Lacking real-time cues, we can easily misread the printed words in an e-mail message, taking them the wrong way.

And if we are typing while agitated, the absence of information on how the other person is responding makes the prefrontal circuitry for discretion more likely to fail.

Our emotional impulses disinhibited, we type some infelicitous message and hit "send" before a more sober second thought leads us to hit "discard." We flame.

Flaming can be induced in some people with alarming ease. Consider an experiment, reported in 2002 in <u>The Journal of Language and Social Psychology</u>, in which pairs of college students—strangers—were put in separate booths to get to know each other better by exchanging messages in a simulated online chat room.

While coming and going into the lab, the students were well behaved. But the experimenter was stunned to see the messages many of the students sent. About 20 percent of the e-mail conversations immediately became outrageously lewd or simply rude.

And now, the online equivalent of road rage has joined the list of Internet dangers. Last October, in what <u>The Times of London</u> described as "Britain's first 'Web rage' attack," a 47-year-old Londoner was convicted of assault on a man with whom he had traded insults in a chat room. He and a friend tracked down the man and attacked him with a pickax handle and a knife.

One proposed solution to flaming is replacing typed messages with video. The assumption is that getting a message along with its emotional nuances might help us dampen the impulse to flame.

All this reminds me of a poster on the wall of classrooms I once visited in New Haven public schools. The poster, part of a program in social development that has lowered rates of violence in schools there, shows a stoplight. It says that when students feel upset, they should remember that the red light means to stop, calm down and think before they act. The yellow light prompts them to weigh a range of responses, and their consequences. The green light urges them to try the best response.

Not a bad idea. Until the day e-mail comes in video form, I may just paste one of those stoplights next to my monitor.

*Daniel Goleman is the author of* <u>Social Intelligence: The New Science of Human Relationships</u> *(2007) and* <u>Emotional Intelligence: Why It Can Matter More Than IQ</u> *(1997). He has taught at Harvard University where he received his PhD.*

Work Cited

Goleman, Daniel. "Flame First, Think Later: New Clues to E-Mail Misbehavior." <u>New York Times</u> 20 Feb. 2007, late ed.: F5.

## F.D.A. Dismisses Medical Benefit from Marijuana

### *Gardiner Harris*

The Food and Drug Administration said Thursday that "no sound scientific studies" supported the medical use of marijuana, contradicting a 1999 review by a panel of highly regarded scientists.

The announcement inserts the health agency into yet another fierce political fight.

Susan Bro, an agency spokeswoman, said Thursday's statement resulted from a past combined review by federal drug enforcement, regulatory and research agencies that concluded "smoked marijuana has no currently accepted or proven medical use in the United States and is not an approved medical treatment."

Ms. Bro said the agency issued the statement in response to numerous inquiries from Capitol Hill but would probably do nothing to enforce it.

"Any enforcement based on this finding would need to be by D.E.A. since this falls outside of F.D.A.'s regulatory authority," she said.

Eleven states have legalized medicinal use of marijuana, but the Drug Enforcement Administration and the director of national drug control policy, John P. Walters, have opposed those laws.

A Supreme Court decision last year allowed the federal government to arrest anyone using marijuana, even for medical purposes and even in states that have legalized its use.

Congressional opponents and supporters of medical marijuana use have each tried to enlist the F.D.A. to support their views. Representative Mark Souder, Republican of Indiana and a fierce opponent of medical marijuana initiatives, proposed legislation two years ago that would have required the food and drug agency to issue an opinion on the medicinal properties of marijuana.

"Mr. Souder believes that efforts to legalize medicinal uses of marijuana are a front for efforts to legalize all uses of it," said Martin Green, a spokesman for Mr. Souder.

Tom Riley, a spokesman for Mr. Walters, hailed the food and drug agency's statement, saying it would put to rest what he called "the bizarre public discussion" that has led to some legalization of medical marijuana.

The Food and Drug Administration statement directly contradicts a 1999 review by the Institute of Medicine, a part of the National Academy of Sciences, the nation's most prestigious scientific advisory agency. That review found marijuana to be "moderately well suited for particular conditions, such as chemotherapy-induced nausea and vomiting and AIDS wasting."

Dr. John Benson, co-chairman of the Institute of Medicine committee that examined the research into marijuana's effects, said in an interview that the statement on Thursday and the combined review by other agencies were wrong.

The federal government "loves to ignore our report," said Dr. Benson, a professor of internal medicine at the University of Nebraska Medical Center. "They would rather it never happened."

Some scientists and legislators said the agency's statement about marijuana demonstrated that politics had trumped science.

"Unfortunately, this is yet another example of the F.D.A. making pronouncements that seem to be driven more by ideology than by science," said Dr. Jerry Avorn, a medical professor at Harvard Medical School.

Representative Maurice D. Hinchey, a New York Democrat who has sponsored legislation to allow medicinal uses of marijuana, said the statement reflected the influence of the Drug Enforcement Administration, which he said had long pressured the F.D.A. to help in its fight against marijuana.

A spokeswoman for the Drug Enforcement Administration referred questions to Mr. Walters's office.

The Food and Drug Administration's statement said state initiatives that legalize marijuana use were "inconsistent with efforts to ensure that medications undergo the rigorous scientific scrutiny of the F.D.A. approval process."

But scientists who study the medical use of marijuana said in interviews that the federal government had actively discouraged research. Lyle E. Craker, a professor in the division of plant and soil sciences at the University of Massachusetts, said he submitted an application to the D.E.A. in 2001 to grow a small patch of marijuana to be used for research because government-approved marijuana, grown in Mississippi, was of poor quality.

In 2004, the drug enforcement agency turned Dr. Craker down. He appealed and is awaiting a judge's ruling. "The reason there's no good evidence is that they don't want an honest trial," Dr. Craker said.

Dr. Donald Abrams, a professor of clinical medicine at the University of California, San Francisco, said he had studied marijuana's medicinal effects for years but had been frustrated because the National Institutes of Health, the leading government medical research agency, had refused to finance such work.

With financing from the State of California, Dr. Abrams undertook what he said was a rigorous, placebo-controlled trial of marijuana smoking in H.I.V. patients who suffered from nerve pain. Smoking marijuana proved effective in ameliorating pain, Dr. Abrams said, but he said he was having trouble getting the study published.

"One wonders how anyone" could fulfill the Food and Drug Administration request for well-controlled trials to prove marijuana's benefits, he said.

Marinol, a synthetic version of a marijuana component, is approved to treat anorexia associated with AIDS and the nausea and vomiting associated with cancer drug therapy.

GW Pharmaceutical, a British company, has received F.D.A. approval to test a sprayed extract of marijuana in humans. Called Sativex, the drug is made from marijuana and is approved for sale in Canada. Opponents of efforts to legalize marijuana for medicinal uses suggest that marijuana is a so-called gateway drug that often leads users to try more dangerous drugs and to addiction.

But the Institute of Medicine report concluded there was no evidence that marijuana acted as a gateway to harder drugs. And it said there was no evidence that medical use of marijuana would increase its use among the general population.

Dr. Daniele Piomelli, a professor of pharmacology at the University of California, Irvine, said he had "never met a scientist who would say that marijuana is either dangerous or useless."

Studies clearly show that marijuana has some benefits for some patients, Dr. Piomelli said.

"We all agree on that," he said.

*Gardiner Harris, a reporter for the* <u>New York Times</u>, *often writes about the politics of health issues.*

## Work Cited

Harris, Gardiner. "F.D.A. Dismisses Medical Benefit from Marijuana." <u>New York Times</u> 21 Apr. 2006, late ed.: A1.

## CHAPTER 9

# Documentation

Documentation refers to the method by which you tell your readers where you found your information. Because other researchers must be able to evaluate the quality of your work, it's important to be accurate and consistent in the way you give references.

A reference is information, such as a name and page number in parentheses, referring to an entry in your Works Cited or References bibliography at the end of your paper. Writers use various documentation styles today: MLA, APA, traditional footnotes, endnotes, and several others.

If some problem should arise that isn't covered by the models in this chapter, you should make a reasonable adaptation from the most appropriate model. Although documentation is essential in research writing, you must not let it overwhelm or distract from your text.

## USING SOURCES

Writing a report or an argument paper is like writing an opinion essay. You have a thesis, which you support with specific evidence. You organize the evidence so it's easy for readers to follow. You engage readers with your title, introduction, and conclusion. You work on writing clear sentences with variety in structure and punctuation—you pay attention to style. You proofread, edit, and polish your writing.

You also pay attention to persuasive appeals: logos, (thinking), pathos (emotion), and ethos (credibility of your character). Although research papers may use examples, illustrations, and visuals to stir emotion in readers, research papers emphasize logos and ethos. Using clear reasoning to explain what you mean is crucial. Your ability to use good reasoning reflects your character—whether readers can trust your information and your presentation of it.

What also reflects your character in research writing is your ability to use and cite sources carefully. If you show where you found your sources, if you follow a standard method of documentation such as MLA, if you provide a list of Works Cited at the end of your paper, readers will more likely accept and trust what you say. If you don't cite every source you use, if you don't use quotations marks around each direct quote, if you don't follow the conventions of a Works Cited list such as alphabetizing your sources, then readers will not accept what you say and will not trust you. Your credibility will take a major hit.

## Citing Information from Sources

Rules—there are many formalities you must follow when you use sources. This is partly why research writing is hard work. But you don't need to memorize these rules; rather, you need to know how to use them. Remember that you can review this chapter any time.

The Modern Language Association uses a system of in-text citations. Suppose this sentence appears in a report on happiness:

### In-Text Citation

In his book <u>The Happiness Hypothesis</u>, Jonathan Haidt writes, "Pleasure comes more from making progress toward goals than from achieving them" (84).

Notice the following about this example:

---

- A signal phrase is used to introduce the author. Readers know that Haidt wrote this book; this lends him some credibility right away.
- At the end of the quote, a page number is cited in parentheses, telling what page this quote appears in Haidt's book.
- From this example, readers can expect to find Haidt's book listed among the Works Cited at the end of the report.

---

### Entry in Works Cited

Haidt, Jonathan. <u>The Happiness Hypothesis: Finding Modern Truth in Ancient Wisdom</u>.
  New York: Basic Books, 2006.

But citing information gets more complicated because there are so many variables, as you'll see.

## Using Direct Quotes

Whenever you use information directly from a source, you need to let readers know this. Ordinarily you do this by using quotation marks around any quote you use or any information you borrow but put in your own words (summarize or paraphrase).

| | |
|---|---|
| *Quoting a word:* | Morrie Schwartz emphasizes "detachment" when he talks to Mitch (119). |
| *Quoting a phrase:* | Morrie discusses the importance of "being fully present" (135). |
| *Quoting a sentence:* | Morrie tells Mitch, "Without love, we are birds with broken wings" (92). |

*Quoting a long passage:*

Haidt writes that there are various methods that help people be more happy.

> Suppose you read about a pill that you could take once a day to reduce anxiety and increase your contentment. Would you take it? Suppose further that the pill has a great variety of side effects, all of them good: increased self-esteem, empathy, and trust; it even improves memory. Suppose, finally, that the pill is all natural and costs nothing. Now would you take it? (35)

What is this magic pill? It's simply meditation. Many people would not need to take antidepressants if they practiced meditation, Haidt claims.

## How to Cite Long Quotes

1. MLA style requires writers to indent (set off or block display) quotations of *four or more lines.*

2. Indent all lines of a long quotation *10 spaces* (or two tabs) from the left margin and type the quote double-spaced. Do not indent from the right-hand margin; do not attempt to make all the lines the same length. Also, do not double-double space before or after a long quote.

3. Do not use quotation marks around a long quote. The fact that the quote is set off indicates it is a direct quote. To use quotation marks around a long quote is redundant. Use quotation marks for shorter quotes only.

4. Discuss a long quote after you use it. If you don't comment on it, the quote hangs there. Think of a sandwich: you introduce a long quote (the top slice of bread); the quote is the peanut butter and jelly (or meat); you close with a comment (the bottom slice of bread).

5. Parenthetic page references for long quotations come after the final sentence period.

6. Long quotations should be copied exactly as you find them, including any quotation marks you find *within* them.

7. When using a long quote (four or more lines), do not indicate the beginning of a single quoted paragraph with indentation. However, if you display more than one full paragraph in your long quote, indent the first line of each subsequent paragraph *three spaces* (not five).

## Using an Ellipsis Mark to Indicate Omission of Words

Use three ellipsis dots to indicate you have omitted one or more words from quoted matter.

Suppose you wanted to omit the words underlined in the following quote from
<u>Tuesdays with Morrie</u>.

### Quoted Matter in a Long Quote

Mitch Albom provides a clear description of Morrie:
> He is a small man who takes small steps, <u>as if a strong wind could, at any time,</u>
> <u>whisk him up into the clouds. In his graduation day robe, he looks like a cross</u>
> <u>between a biblical prophet and a Christmas elf.</u> He has sparkling blue-green
> eyes, thinning silver hair that spills onto his forehead, big ears, a triangular
> nose, and tufts of graying eyebrows. Although his teeth are crooked <u>and his</u>
> <u>lower ones are slanted back—as if someone had punched them in</u>—when he
> smiles it's as if you'd just told him the first joke on earth. (3–4)

It's easy to visualize this man who became Albom's mentor.

### Quoted Matter with Ellipsis

Mitch Albom provides a clear description of Morrie: "He is a small man who takes small
steps. . . . He has sparkling blue-green eyes, thinning silver hair that spills onto his forehead, big ears, a triangular nose, and tufts of graying eyebrows. Although his teeth are
crooked . . . when he smiles it's as if you'd just told him the first joke on earth" (3–4). It's
easy to visualize this man who became Albom's mentor.

The ellipsis requires a space before and after each of its three periods. Do not let
your computer move one or more of the dots to the next line. Move all three, prefer-
ably with the word that precedes them. When the ellipsis comes at the end of a sentence, the sentence period becomes the fourth dot. The ending ellipsis can indicate a
few words omitted, or it can indicate several sentences have been omitted.

*Note*: When you quote a single word or phrase, do not use ellipsis dots; readers will infer that
material has been omitted. Ordinarily, you do not need to use the ellipsis at the beginning of a
quotation. But if you omit words at the end of a final quoted sentence, you should use ellipsis
before the closing quotation mark and parenthetical citation. For example,

> Morrie "has sparkling blue-green eyes, thinning silver hair that spills onto his forehead. . ."
> (3–4).

*Note*: the final period comes after the citation.

## Using Brackets to Add Your Own Words in a Quote

Square brackets set off clarifying material you insert into quotations.

> Four score [80] and seven years ago our fathers brought forth on this continent a new
> nation . . .

*good explanation!*

President Lincoln did not have the word *80* in his speech, and you do not have the right to alter his words without some signal to readers. Therefore, you call attention to the fact that you are adding something to his speech, to clarify a term that is no longer familiar to many readers.

## Using "Sic" to Indicate Errors in Quotes

To indicate an error in material you quote, use the word *sic*, meaning "thus the error was" in the original. In MLA style of documentation, use parentheses around *sic*.

> "Lincoln delivered his famous Gettysburg Address in 1963 (sic); one eyewitness said it lasted only two minutes." [sic tells readers that the date is incorrect.]

## When It Is Appropriate to Use Direct Quotes

If you are fairly new to doing research writing, you will experience problems deciding when to quote a source and when not to.

You might be tempted to use too many direct quotes. This is a mistake. Avoid the *string of pearls effect*: stringing one quote after the other without intervening explanation. Rarely do you want to follow one quote with another quote from a different source. It's important to discuss your quotes as you use them, especially afterwards. Your job as a writer is to synthesize your research: to weave it in and out of your own language so it feels natural and smooth.

### GUIDELINES FOR USING DIRECT QUOTES

1. To show an authority's clear reasoning.
2. To show someone's unclear or suspicious reasoning.
3. To use vivid details and examples from an authority.
4. To capture the tone (attitude) and ethos (character) of an authority.
5. To cite facts and statistics that are too complex for you to paraphrase.

## Using Signal Phrases with Direct Quotes

A signal phrase is a group of words giving information about a source; the phrase lends credibility to the source.

> In his book <u>Stumbling on Happiness</u>, Daniel Gilbert, a professor of psychology at Harvard, argues that happiness is caused by the choices we make.

In this example, there are two signal phrases: Gilbert's book title and his being a professor at Harvard. These two bits of information suggest that Gilbert is an expert; thus, if you quote from him, you are likely using a well-respected, credible source. You could use one signal phrase:

> In his book <u>Stumbling on Happiness</u>, Daniel Gilbert argues that happiness is caused by the choices we make.

This would be fine. But the fact that Gilbert teaches at Harvard is impressive, though you can't assume that this automatically makes him credible. He needs to prove it in his book, and you need to prove it by the way you use him as a source.

So, signal phrases introduce your sources. They name sources and establish credibility. They are essential tools for you to use as a writer.

You can use various verbs within your signal phrases. Consider these:

Smith *argues . . . claims . . . acknowledges . . . points out . . . states . . . notes . . . writes . . . contends . . . refutes . . . suggests . . .* There are many more. Try not to rely on or overuse the same verbs for signal phases such as *argues* or *writes.*

## PLAGIARISM, SUMMARIZING AND PARAPHRASING

The etymology (root) of the word *plagiarism* is *kidnapper* (<u>Webster's New World</u>). Plagiarism is kidnapping someone else's words or ideas (or both) and acting as if they are your own. Research papers often involve problems with plagiarism because it is hard work to put ideas and information into your own words. It is hard work not to use too many direct quotes. Also, many students are not familiar with summarizing and paraphrasing information and thus may plagiarize unintentionally.

But, you may ask, does it really matter? Plagiarism represents dishonesty and profoundly damages a writer's ethos: it makes a writer automatically lose credibility, reliability, and trust. How exactly does a writer feel whose work has been plagiarized? Leonard Pitts Jr. shares his experience in the following essay.

### Chris Cecil, Plagiarism Gets You Fired

#### *Leonard Pitts Jr.*

Dear Chris Cecil:

Here's how you write a newspaper column. First, you find a topic that engages you. Then you spend a few hours banging your head against a computer screen until what you've written there no longer makes you want to hurl.

Or, you could just wait till somebody else writes a column and steal it. That's what you've been doing on a regular basis.

Before Tuesday, I had never heard of you or the <u>Daily Tribune News</u>, in Cartersville, Ga., where you are associate managing editor. Then one of my readers, God bless her, sent me an e-mail noting the similarities between a column of mine and one you had purportedly written.

Intrigued, I did a little research on your paper's website and found that you had "written" at least eight columns since March that were taken in whole or in part from my work. The thefts ranged from the pilfering of the lead from a gangsta rap column to the wholesale heist of an entire piece I did about Bill Cosby. In that instance, you essentially took my name off and slapped yours on.

On March 11, I wrote: *I like hypocrites. You would, too, if you had this job. A hypocrite is the next best thing to a day off. Some pious moralizer contradicts his words with his deeds and the column all but writes itself. It's different with Bill Cosby.*

On May 12, you "wrote": *I like hypocrites. You would, too, if you had this job. A hypocrite is the next best thing to a day off. Some pious moralizer contradicts his words with his deeds and the column all but writes itself. It's different with Bill Cosby.*

The one that really got me, though, was your theft of a personal anecdote about the moment I realized my mother was dying of cancer. "The tears surprised me," I wrote. "I pulled over, blinded by them." Seven days later, there you were: "The tears surprised me. I pulled over, blinded by them on central Kentucky's 1-75."

Actually, it happened at an on-ramp to the Artesia Freeway in Compton, Calif.

I've been in this business 29 years, Mr. Cecil, and I've been plagiarized before. But I've never seen a plagiarist as industrious and brazen as you. My boss is calling your boss, but I doubt you and I will ever speak. Still, I wanted you to hear from me. I wanted you to understand how this feels.

Put it like this: I had a house burglarized once.

This reminds me of that. Same sense of violation, same apoplectic disbelief that someone has the testicular fortitude to come into your place and take what is yours.

Not being a writer yourself, you won't understand, but I am a worshiper at the First Church of the Written Word, a lover of language, a student of its rhythm, its music, its violence and its power.

My words are important to me. I struggle with them, obsess over them. Show me something I wrote and like a mother recounting a child's birth, I can tell you stories of how it came to be, why this adjective here or that colon there.

See, my life's goal is to learn to write. And you cannot cut and paste your way to that. You can only work your way there, sweating out words, wrestling down prose, hammering together poetry. There are no shortcuts.

You are just the latest in a growing list of people—in journalism and out—who don't understand that, who think it's OK to cheat your way across the finish line. I've always wanted to ask one of you: How can you do that? Have you no shame? No honor or pride? How do you face your mirror knowing you are not what you purport to be? Knowing that you are a fraud?

If your boss values his paper's credibility, you will soon have lots of free time to ponder those questions.

But before you go, let me say something on behalf of all of us who are struggling to learn how to write, or just struggling to be honorable human beings:

The dictionary is a big book. Get your own damn words. Leave mine alone.

P.S.: Chris Cecil was fired Thursday by <u>Daily Tribune News</u> Publisher Charles Hurley, immediately after he learned of the plagiarism.

*<u>Miami Herald</u> columnist Leonard Pitts Jr. won the Pulitzer Prize for distinguished commentary in 2004. For more information on him, see his essay "Expedience No Reason to Kill a Man" in Chapter 2.*

Work Cited

Pitts Jr., Leonard. "Chris Cecil, Plagiarism Gets You Fired." <u>Miami Herald</u> 3 June 2005: B1.

## ACTIVITY 1

Write a summary of Pitts's essay. To help yourself avoid plagiarizing, read the essay again. Then close your book and write down what you remember, starting from the beginning of Pitts's essay if you can. Use a signal phrase: "Leonard Pitts Jr., a columnist for the <u>Miami Herald</u>, writes . . . ." Write down the gist of what happened to him, how he felt, and what happened to Chris Cecil. ▮

## ACTIVITY 2

Compare your summary to Pitts's original essay. If you see strings of words you wrote directly from his essay, put quotation marks around them to signal that they are his words, not yours. ▮

It's not uncommon for journalists to plagiarize and to get caught for it and fired. In April 2007, Katie Couric, anchor for <u>CBS Evening News</u>, had an embarrassing experience with this problem. Couric presented a daily essay called "Katie Couric's Notebook" on radio and video. But she didn't write the essays. It turned out that her producer had plagiarized an essay by Jeffrey Zaslow of <u>The Wall Street Journal</u> in which he discusses how few kids use libraries. Several sentences were verbatim or closely matched Zaslow's. For example, Zaslow wrote, "It's a last ditch place to go if they need to find something out." Couric's essay contained the exact sentence. Couric's producer was fired.

Can you be fired if you are caught plagiarizing at school? It depends. As a student, your job is to do the work teachers ask you to do and to do it as well and honestly as you can. If you cheat by plagiarizing, a teacher has various options: give you a failing grade for the paper, give you a failing grade for the course, and/or send you to the Academic Standards Committee, which may decide to expel you from school.

Thus, plagiarism is usually the result of improper or missing documentation. It amounts to stealing an author's work. Failure to document properly makes a problem for your readers. There is no research when readers can't verify your sources. Let's examine a few cases.

## CASE 1

### The Original Material

What follows is a paragraph from the book <u>Why Not?</u> by Barry Nalebuff and Ian Ayres, page 5.

> Wayne Gretzky invented a new offense for ice hockey. He stood behind the opponent's goal and thereby forced all the defenders—including the goalie—to swivel their heads back and forth to keep an eye on him and his teammates. Blind spots were created upon which Gretzky quickly capitalized. He would shovel a quick pass to an open teammate in front of the net or, if an opponent skated behind the net to attack him, Gretzky would dart out the other side to score himself. Gretzky's innovation remains one of the hardest plays in hockey to defend against.

### Correct Use of Borrowed Information in a Research Paper

> In their book <u>Why Not?</u> Nalebuff and Ayres explain that innovation occurs in sports as well as in the marketplace. For example, Wayne Gretzky discovered that if he positioned himself behind the defending goalie's net, then players, as well as the goalie, would turn to watch him. This weakened their defense, enabling Gretzky to "shovel a quick pass to an open teammate" or for him to skate to the side of the net and score (5).

This writer correctly paraphrases by using her own words, using quotation marks to show what was borrowed, and giving a page reference to show the page from which the borrowed material came. The original authors, Nalebuff and Ayres, are mentioned, and a signal phrase naming their book is given. Their names need not be repeated in the parenthetic reference. In the Works Cited section at the end of her paper, the writer would provide a full reference to their book, like this:

> Nalebuff, Barry, and Ian Ayres. <u>Why Not?: How to Use Everyday Ingenuity to Solve Problems Big and Small</u>. Boston: Harvard Business School, 2006.

### Plagiarism, Careless

> Innovation occurs in sports as well as in the marketplace. For example, Wayne Gretzky discovered that if he positioned himself behind the defending goalie's net, then players, as well as the goalie, would turn to watch him. This weakened their defense, enabling Gretzky to "shovel a quick pass to an open teammate" or for him to skate to the side of the net and score.

One purpose of reference notes is to help readers find the material you have used. The other purpose is to give writers credit for their work. Here a student has correctly quoted from source material but omitted any reference to Nalebuff and Ayres or any page reference to their book. This looks like an accidental omission (maybe), but it's a serious omission.

## Plagiarism, Deliberate

One source explains that Wayne Gretzky invented a new offense for ice hockey. He stood behind the opponent's goal and thereby forced all the defenders—including the goalie—to swivel their heads back and forth to keep an eye on him and his teammates. Blind spots were created upon which Gretzky quickly capitalized. He would shovel a quick pass to an open teammate in front of the net or, if an opponent skated behind the net to attack him, Gretzky would dart out the other side to score himself. Gretzky's innovation remains one of the hardest plays in hockey to defend against.

This is a deliberate theft of an author's property. Nalebuff and Ayres's exact words have been used, and this writer provides neither a citation nor quotation marks around the borrowed material. The writer admits the material is borrowed from "one source," but without quotation marks readers cannot tell which are the borrowed words and which aren't. It looks as if the writer wants to take credit for these words. The basic crime of plagiarism is failure to document.

## CASE 2

## The Original Material

What follows is an excerpt from the book <u>Authentic Happiness</u> by Martin Seligman, page 5.

College yearbook photos are a gold mine for Positive Psychology researchers. "Look at the birdie and smile," the photographer tells you, and dutifully you put on your best smile. Smiling on demand, it turns out, is easier said than done. Some of us break into a radiant smile of authentic good cheer, while the rest of us pose politely. There are two kinds of smiles. The first, called a Duchenne smile (after its discoverer, Guillaume Duchenne), is genuine. The corners of your mouth turn up and the skin around the corners of your eyes crinkles (like crow's feet). The muscles that do this, the *orbicularis oculi* and the *zygomaticus*, are exceedingly difficult to control voluntarily. The other smile, called the Pan American smile (after the flight attendants in television ads for the now-defunct airline), is inauthentic, with none of the Duchenne features. Indeed, it is probably more related to the rictus that lower primates display when frightened than it is to happiness.

When trained psychologists look through collections of photos, they can at a glance separate out the Duchenne from the nonDuchenne smilers. Dacher Keltner and LeeAnne Harker of the University of California at Berkeley, for example, studied 141 senior-class photos from the 1960 yearbook of Mills College. All but three of the women were smiling, and half of the smilers were Duchenne smilers. All the women were contacted at ages twenty-seven, forty-three, and fifty-two and asked about their marriages and their life satisfaction. When Harker and Keltner inherited the study in the 1990s, they wondered if they could predict from the senior-year smile alone what these women's married lives would turn out to be like. Astonishingly, Duchenne women, on average, were more likely to be married, to stay married, and to experience more personal well-being over the next thirty years. Those indicators of happiness were predicted by a mere crinkling of the eyes.

Questioning their results, Harker and Keltner considered whether the Duchenne women were prettier, and their good looks rather than the genuineness of their smile predicted more life satisfaction. So the investigators went back and rated how pretty each of the women seemed, and they found that looks had nothing to do with good marriages or life satisfaction. A genuinely smiling woman, it turned out, was simply more likely to be well-wed and happy. (5)

## Correct Use of Borrowed Information in a Research Paper

In his book <u>Authentic Happiness</u>, Martin Seligman writes about a study done at the University of California, Berkeley in which researchers studied the smiles of graduating seniors at Mills College. The smiles were classified as either "genuine" (Duchenne) or "inauthentic" (Pan American, or phony stewardess). Duchenne smiles involve involuntary facial muscles. Out of 141 photos of the seniors, half had genuine smiles, half didn't, and three did not smile. The Mills students "were contacted at ages twenty-seven, forty-three, and fifty-two and asked about their marriages and their life satisfaction." The researchers found that the women who had smiled genuinely in college were more happy throughout their life, and more happy in their marriages, than the women whose smiles were not genuine. "A mere crinkling of the eyes"—a sign of Duchenne's smile—predicted life satisfaction. The researchers also studied the photos to see if there was a correlation between being pretty and smiling. They found this was not so. Duchenne smilers were no more pretty than Pan Am smilers. "A genuinely smiling woman, it turned out, was simply more likely to be well-wed and happy" (5).

This writer properly summarizes and paraphrases by using his own words, using quotation marks to show what was borrowed, and giving a page reference to show the page from which the borrowed material came. The author, Seligman, is mentioned, and a signal phrase naming his book is given. In the Works Cited section at the end of his paper, the writer would provide a full reference to the book, like this:

> Seligman, Martin E. P. <u>Authentic Happiness: Using the New Positive Psychology to Realize Your Potential for Lasting Fulfillment</u>. New York: Free Press, 2002.

## Plagiarism, Deliberate

Martin Seligman writes about a study done at the University of California in which researchers studied the smiles of graduating seniors at Mills College. The smiles were classified as either genuine (Duchenne) or inauthentic (Pan American, or phony stewardess). With Duchenne smiles the corners of your mouth turn up and the skin around the corners of your eyes crinkles (like crow's feet). Out of 141 photos of the seniors, half had genuine smiles, half didn't, and three did not smile. The Mills students were contacted at ages twenty-seven, forty-three, and fifty-two and asked about their marriages and their life satisfaction. The researchers found that the women who had smiled genuinely in college were more happy throughout their life, and more happy in their marriages, than the women whose smiles were not genuine. "A mere crinkling of the eyes"—a sign of Duchenne's smile—predicted life satisfaction. The researchers also studied the photos to see if there was a correlation between being pretty and smiling. They found this was not so. Duchenne smilers were no more pretty than Pan Am smilers. A genuinely smiling woman, it turned out, was simply more likely to be well-wed and happy.

Although the author's name is used at the beginning, this paraphrase contains several direct quotes with no quotation marks around them, yet one quote does contain quotation marks. It is thus difficult to determine which words are the student's and which are Seligman's. This is irresponsible research writing. The student has not worked hard enough to cite quotes properly and carefully, and also has not cited a page reference.

As you've seen in this section already, writing research papers involves summarizing and paraphrasing information. Through this book you have been asked to write summaries: in Chapter 2—to summarize an essay to understand it; in Chapter 5—to summarize a film before you review it; in Chapter 6—to summarize a poem, story, or literary essay before you analyze and evaluate it.

## ACTIVITY 3

Review "Features of Summarizing" in Chapter 2. Then in your notebook write a summary of the following excerpt by Lee Silver. Begin your summary by identifying the author and providing a signal phrase that points out his book: for example, According to Lee Silver, author of <u>Remaking Eden</u>,

### Weeks 6—14: The Embryo Becomes A Fetus

Between six and eight weeks after fertilization, the embryo turns into—what appears to be—a miniature human being with arms, legs, hands, feet, fingers, toes, eyes, ears and nose. It is these external humanlike features that cause a shift in terminology from embryo to fetus. By twelve weeks, the inside of the fetus has also become rather humanlike with the appearance of all the major organs. The first trimester of pregnancy is now completed.

Although looks alone can have a powerful effect on how we view something, it is important to understand what is, and what is not, present at this early stage of fetal development. While most major organs can be recognized, they have not yet begun to function. Although the cerebral cortex—the eventual seat of human awareness and emotions—has begun to grow, the cells within it are not capable of functioning as nerve cells. They are simply precursors to nerve cells without the ability to send or receive any neurological signals. Further steps of differentiation must occur before they even look like nerves or develop the ability to make synaptic contacts with one another. And in the absence of communication among nerve cells, there cannot be any consciousness. . . . (53–54)

Look over your summary and check it against the original text to see if you copied any phrases or sentences directly from it. If you did, you must put quotation marks around them; without using quotation marks, you have plagiarized. For example,

---

**Incorrect (Includes Plagiarism)**

During this stage, the embryo has developed arms, legs, hands, feet, fingers, toes, eyes, ears and nose. Now the embryo is referred to as a fetus.

**Correct**

During this stage, the embryo has developed "arms, legs, hands, feet, fingers, toes, eyes, ears and nose" (53). Now the embryo is referred to as a fetus.

**Or**

During this stage, the embryo has developed visual human qualities such as hands, toes and eyes. Now the embryo is referred to as a fetus (53).

---

The second correct version is better because it does not rely on quoting words directly from the source. *Note*: Because the first correct version uses a direct quote, a page reference is cited. However, because the second correct version uses Silver's idea—even though the student has paraphrased it—a page reference is also given because this information is not common knowledge.

Thus, summarizing includes paraphrasing: using your own words to explain an author's information. This is not easy, but it's essential work for a critical thinker and researcher. When you summarize information, it helps to read the source first and then cover it: try to write your summary without relying on the text because the temptation to use words directly is strong. But if you do use direct wording from a source, remember to put quotation marks around it to avoid plagiarism.

## Guidelines to Avoid Plagiarizing

1. Use signal phrases to establish the credibility of authors and to introduce quotes and information you use. Signal phrases help remind you to give credit where credit is due.
2. Use quotation marks around any words and sentencess you take directly from a source.
3. Make sure you cite a source of information even if you paraphrase the information. If you use ideas and information that are not common knowledge, you must indicate your source for it.
4. Whenever you use facts (not commonly known) or statistics, you must cite your source.
5. Whenever you use a visual illustration such as a photograph, map, or chart, you must cite your source for it.

## Common Knowledge

Common knowledge is information that most educated people are expected to know. You learn information from your friends, television, radio, movies, newspapers, magazines, and so on. You are surrounded by information. President Clinton was impeached but not convicted in 1999. That's common knowledge—most people know it, and you don't need a source for it.

Still, it may be difficult for you to know what is or isn't common knowledge. What is or isn't common is largely the result of the audience to whom you are writing and your own expertise in the matter. If you aren't sure whether information you use is common knowledge, give a source for that information. When in doubt, document.

# MLA STYLE: IN-TEXT RULES

The Modern Language Association (MLA) style of documentation presented here prefers references in the body of your paper itself. Give enough information in your paper so that readers can find the source in your Works Cited list. This in-text style is meant to keep documentation accurate but unobtrusive. Learn to incorporate documentation smoothly into your writing just as you learn to incorporate the words and ideas of your sources.

## Using Author's Name and Signal Phrase

Most of your references should give the author's last name in the text of your paper instead of in a parenthetical note at the end of a sentence, but place page numbers at the end. Also, use a signal phrases to introduce the author. For example,

> In <u>The Happiness Hypothesis</u>, Jonathan Haidt writes, "Human thinking depends on metaphor" (2).

The signal phrase "In <u>The Happiness Hypothesis</u>" identifies Haidt as an authority. If you were to quote from Haidt again, you would not need to mention his book.

*Note*: A period follows the parenthetic page reference. If a quote ends with a question mark, add the period after the parentheses: Haidt asks, "Now would you take it?" (35).

## Using Author's Name in Parentheses

You can vary the way you cite your sources, just as you vary your sentence structure. Instead of using a signal phrase at the beginning of a sentence, you can cite an author's name and page number in parentheses at the end of a sentence, as in this paraphrase:

> Thinking depends on the ability to see connections between unlike things (Haidt 2).

*Note*: No punctuation is used between the author's last name and the page number.

## Using Sources with Two or Three Authors

For more than one author, give the names in the order you find them on the title page, whether or not they are in alphabetical order:

> Nalebuff and Ayres write, "The why-not attitude lets you see potential improvements that are just waiting to happen" (3).

In your bibliography, if a source has two or three authors, reverse the name of the first author only. Give all other authors' names in normal order.

> Miller, Judith, Stephen Engleberg, and William Broad. <u>Germs: Biological Weapons and America's Secret War</u>. New York: Simon, 2001.

> Nalebuff, Barry, and Ian Ayres. <u>Why Not?: How to Use Everyday Ingenuity to Solve Problems Big and Small</u>. Boston: Harvard Business School, 2006.

In your paper, if you refer to a source with three authors, separate the names with commas: (Miller, Engleberg, and Broad 251).

## Using Sources with Four or More Authors

If there are four or more authors, include only the first author's name followed by *et al.*, which in Latin means "and others." Or you may list all authors' names. (Second and subsequent names would appear in normal order.)

The title page of <u>Fields of Writing: Reading Across the Disciplines</u> lists five authors: Nancy R. Comley, David Hamilton, Carl H. Klaus, Robert Scholes, and Nancy Sommers. In your Works Cited list, give the first author's name, followed by "et al."

> Comley, Nancy R., et al. <u>Fields of Writing: Reading Across the Disciplines</u>. 8th ed. Boston: Bedford/St. Martin's, 2007.

In your paper, if you refer to a source with four or more authors, use *et al.* (Comley et al. 42), or separate the names with commas. For simplicity and brevity, use *et al.*

## Using a Committee or Group Author

Use the name of the committee or group when referring to a source in your paper.

> The USDA approves of meat irradiation ("Industry Food Safety").

USDA stands for the United States Department of Agriculture. In your Works Cited, you would list this source beginning with the group's full name: United States Department of Agriculture.

## Using Authors with the Same Last Name

If you use two sources who share the same last name, differentiate them by providing information in a signal phrase or by using their first initial in the parenthetic citation.

> In his book <u>Happiness and Unhappiness</u>, Smith claims that . . .

One cannot know happiness without knowing its opposite (K. Smith 10).

## Using an Unknown Author

Many newspaper and magazine articles do not have names of authors. In such a case, refer to the source by the title of the article:

The war in Iraq has generated more potential for terror in the United States ("Terror's New Depths" 24).

In a Works Cited, this source would begin with its title and look like this:

"Terror's New Depths." The Economist 11 Sept. 2004: 23–25.

Disregard articles *a*, *an*, *the* when alphabetizing authorless titles in your Works Cited:

"An Idea Worthy of Consideration." Journal 21 Aug. 2004: 10.

"The Man in the Middle." Evening Standard 27 Sept. 2004: 14.

"A Stonehenge of Sorts Lies in the Sahara." New York Times 2 Apr. 1998, late ed.: A5.

## Using a Source Quoted in Another Source

If you use a quote that is quoted in a source, use *qtd. in* to signify this.

Richard Selzer marvels at the human body the way poet Marianne Moore marveled at a cherry: "What sap went through that little thread to make the cherry red!" (qtd. in Down from Troy 132).

## Using Shortened Titles

To keep references brief, you should shorten titles, but keep them unambiguous so that the reader can recognize the titles in your Works Cited. For example, suppose your paper contains a source from Sharon Begley of Newsweek. References to her article "Little Lamb, Who Made Thee?" could be shortened:

Begley asks, "Will it take a few human-clone disasters to bring about a ban?" ("Little Lamb" 57).

## Using a Web Source with No Page Numbers

Because most Web sources do not have page numbers, MLA advises that you don't cite a page reference for a quote. Even if you print out a Web article, your printer may break pages differently than another printer. However, if a source contains a PDF (portable document format) file—which is a copy of an article from a magazine or journal with original page numbers—use it so you can cite those page numbers.

## Using a Source That Is One Page

If you use a source that is one page long, you may omit the page number when you quote from it, says MLA. However, many instructors prefer that you use the page number. It's a good idea to use it when you can because it can clarify for readers what information is from the source and what is not.

## Citing Page Numbers

When making reference to a specific part of a source, you must give a page number in the reference (unless it is an online source). When the reference note comes at the end of your sentence, the sentence period should be placed after the parenthesis. In MLA style, page numbers are not identified with *p.*, *pp* or the word *page*. If additional references are made to the same source, you need only the page number.

Don't precede page numbers with a comma:

**Incorrect:**        (Smith, 97).

**Correct:**          (Smith 97).

## Using Works with Numbered Sections or Lines

For references to plays, poetry, or other works with numbered sections or lines, give all the relevant numbers that would help a reader find the source: section, part, act, scene, line. Don't use *l.* or *ll.* for *line*.

"I must be cruel, only to be kind" (<u>Hamlet</u> III.iv.178).

This line is from Shakespeare's <u>Hamlet</u>, act three, scene four, line 178. In general avoid roman numerals, but the use of roman numerals for plays is an exception.

When you quote from a poem, cite line numbers:

"Sundays too my father got up early / and put his clothes on in the blueblack cold" (1–2).

These are the first two lines from Robert Hayden's poem "Those Winter Sundays." References to the Bible should use standard abbreviations and numbers:

"Why do you look at the speck that is in your brother's eye, but do not notice the log that is in your own eye?" (Matt. 7.3)

## Using Publishers' Names

Use a shortened form of a publisher's name. Words and abbreviations like *Company*, *Co.*, and *Inc.* can be dropped. Names formed from two names (Harcourt Brace, Houghton Mifflin, Prentice Hall, etc.) need only the first name: Harcourt, Houghton, Prentice. You can use UP for University Press, as in Oxford UP.

Some publishers have divisions with different names. Anchor is a division of Doubleday. Use a hyphen to separate division names from the parent company: Anchor-Doubleday.

## Using Copyright Date

The copyright date is listed on the back of the title page. If you find more than one date on the copyright page, use the most recent date.

## Using Content Notes

A content note is a note from you to your readers. The note gives additional information or clarification. There is some bias against using notes; many researchers feel that any relevant or important information ought to be included in the body of the paper, and anything else should be omitted. The best advice is to use notes only when they are truly important but would seem intrusive in your paper. A content note should appear as a footnote at the bottom of a page.

## BASIC WORKS CITED MODEL, BOOK (MLA)

This basic bibliography form for books is standard for the MLA.

A                BC            D                                              E F

Goleman, Daniel.  Social Intelligence: The New Science of Human Relationships.
        New York: Bantam, 2006.

G      H       I J          K

A.  Author's name in inverted order (only the first author's name is inverted)
B.  Period after author's name
C.  Two spaces (after all end marks)
D.  Full title, underlined
E.  Period
F.  Two spaces
G.  Second line double-spaced, indented five spaces
H.  Place of publication
I.  Colon
J.  Publisher's name, followed by comma
K.  Copyright date followed by period

### BASIC WORKS CITED MODEL, PERIODICAL (MLA)

   A         BC    D                     E F   G    H   I        J K L

Quindlen, Anna.  "Disinvited to the Party."  Newsweek 3 Sept. 2007: 68.

A.  Author's last name first
B.  Period
C.  Two spaces

D. Title of article in quotation marks

E. Period within quotes

F. Two spaces

G. Title of magazine underlined (no period used)

H. One space

I. Date in military order: day, month, year; no commas within

J. Colon after date

K. Page number without "p." or "pg." or other label

L. Period

## BOOKS: MLA WORKS CITED MODELS

### One Author

> Begley, Sharon. <u>Train Your Mind, Change Your Brain: How a New Science Reveals Our Extraordinary Potential to Transform Ourselves</u>. New York: Ballantine, 2007.

### More Than One Book by Same Author

When you use two or more books (or articles) by the same author, after the first book, use a string of three hyphens in place of the author's name.

> Elbow, Peter. <u>Embracing Contraries: Explorations in Learning and Teaching</u>. New York: Oxford UP, 1986.

> ---. <u>Everyone Can Write: Essays Toward a Hopeful Theory of Writing and Teaching Writing</u>. New York: Oxford UP, 2000.

Any different information about the authorship of subsequent books must be indicated. If, in a subsequent book, the author is an editor, translator, or served in any capacity different from that in the previous book, this new information must be included (---, ed.)

Note that this convention doesn't apply to coauthors. If Smith has written one book and coauthored another, don't use hyphens for Smith's name with the coauthored book. See next category.

### Author of One Book, Coauthor of Another

> Goleman, Daniel. <u>Emotional Intelligence: Why It Can Matter More Than IQ</u>. New York: Bantam, 1995.

> Goleman, Daniel, Richard E. Boyatzis, and Annie McKee. <u>Primal Intelligence: Learning to Lead with Emotional Intelligence</u>. Boston: Harvard Business School Press, 2004.

## Committee or Group Author

American Civil Liberties Union. <u>Freedom under Fire: Dissent in Post-9/11 America</u>.
New York: ACLU, 2003.

*Note*: When the author is a government agency, begin with its full name.

## Book with Editor(s)

Bly, Robert, ed. <u>The Soul Is Here for Its Own Joy: Sacred Poems from Many Cultures</u>. Hopewell,
NJ: Ecco, 1995.

Schwehn, Mark R., and Dorothy C. Bass, eds. <u>Leading Lives That Matter: What We Should Do
and Who We Should Be</u>. Grand Rapids, MI: William B. Eerdmans, 2006.

## Article or Chapter in an Edited Work

Boyle, Joseph. "The Bioethics of Global Medicine: A Natural Law Reflection." <u>Global Bioethics</u>.
Ed. H. Tristram Engelhardt Jr. Houston: Rice U, 2006. 300–334.

Paley, Grace. "Here." <u>Good Poems</u>. Ed. Garrison Keillor. New York: Penguin, 2002. 429.

## Translation

Include the translator's name if it appears on the title page.

Allende, Isabel. <u>Inés of My Soul: A Novel</u>. Trans. Margaret Sayers Peden. New York: Harper
Collins, 2006.

## Multivolume Work

Cornell, Vincent J., ed. <u>Voices of Islam</u>. 5 vols. Westport, CT: Praeger, 2007.

If you cite one of the volumes, put the volume number after the title, and end with
the total number of volumes.

Cornell, Vincent J., ed. <u>Voices of Islam</u>. Vol. 4. Westport, CT: Praeger, 2007. 5 vols.

## Reprint of Older Work

Give the original publication date first (after title) and then the reprint date (after the
publisher's name).

Morrison, Toni. <u>Beloved</u>. 1987. New York: Vintage, 2004.

## Publisher Imprint

A book may be published by a division (imprint) of a publisher. When this happens, join the name of the imprint and the name of the publisher with a hyphen. Put the imprint first.

> Selzer, Richard. <u>Letters to a Young Doctor</u>. 1982. New York: Harvest-Harcourt, 1996.

## Edition

> Meyer, Michael. <u>Poetry: An Introduction</u>. 5th ed. Boston: Bedford, 2006.

*Note*: Point out an edition number only if it is not the first edition.

## Introduction, Preface, Foreword

> Levine, Noah. Foreword. <u>Wide Awake: A Buddhist Guide for Teens</u>. By Diana Winston. New York: Perigee, 2003. xi–xii.

> Palmer, Parker J., and Tom Vander Ark. Introduction. <u>Teaching with Fire: Poetry That Sustains the Courage to Teach</u>. By Sam M. Intrator and Megan Scribner, eds. San Francisco: Jossey-Bass, 2003. xvii–xxiv.

## Bible, Sacred Works

> <u>Holy Bible: The New King James Version</u>. Nashville: Thomas Nelson, 1994.

> <u>The Koran</u>. Trans. N. J. Dawood. New York: Penguin Classics, 2004.

## Dictionary

> Agnes, Michael E., ed. <u>Webster's New World College Dictionary</u>. 4th ed. New York: Wiley, 2004.

## Specialized Encyclopedia

> Ross, James F. "Analogy in Theology." <u>Encyclopedia of Philosophy</u>. 2nd ed. Detroit: Thomson-Gale, 2006. 138–144.

# PERIODICALS: MLA WORKS CITED MODELS

## Weekly Magazine Article

> Begley, Sharon. "The Truth about Denial." <u>Newsweek</u> 13 Aug. 2007: 20+.

> Kantrowitz, Barbara, and Anne Underwood. "The Teen Drinking Dilemma." <u>Newsweek</u> 25 June 2007: 37.

> Reilly, Rick. "Swearing Off Swearing." <u>Sports Illustrated</u> 25 Sept. 2006: 80.

*Note:*

1. Magazine (or other periodical) titles don't end with periods (while book titles do end with periods).
2. No punctuation separates the date from the magazine title.
3. Abbreviate months (except May, June, July): Jan., Feb., Mar., Apr., Aug., Sept., Oct., Nov., Dec. Use a period after each abbreviation. Note too that the day precedes the month, and no comma is needed to separate the date from the title or the month from the year.
4. The plus sign (+) indicates that there is more to the article following on discontinuous pages. The article "The Truth about Denial" appears on pages 20 to 27, is interrupted by a full-page ad on page 28, and concludes on page 29.
5. Page numbers aren't identified by "page" or "p" or any other designator in MLA style.

## Magazine Article, No Author Given

"Terror's New Depths." The Economist 11 Sept. 2004: 23–25.

## Monthly Magazine Article

Fallow, James. "China Makes, the World Takes." Atlantic July/Aug. 2007: 48+.

## Newspaper Article

Goodman, Ellen. "No Change in Political Climate." Boston Globe 9 Feb. 2007: A19.

Kristof, Nicholas D. "Save the Darfur Puppy." New York Times 10 May 2007, late ed.: A33.

Robinson, Lori. "Pressure Builds to End Abuse of Black Women." Chicago Tribune
19 Aug. 2007, sec. 2: 5.

*Note:*

1. Omit an initial *The* in a newspaper title such as The New York Times.
2. If an article appears in a newspaper with sections that begin with letters (as in the Goodman and Kristof examples), cite the letter followed by the page number. If a newspaper identifies its sections with numbers instead of letters (as in the Robinson example), use the abbreviation "sec." followed by the section number, a colon, a space, and the page number: for example, "sec. 2: 5."

## Newspaper Article, Unsigned

"FDA Tighter on Drug Approvals." Chicago Tribune 19 Aug. 2007, sec. 1: 4.

"Two Galactic Clusters Are Colliding Millions of Light Years Away." Washington Post 24 Sept.
2004: A9.

*Note*: You will often find titles of newspaper articles in lowercase letters except for the first word, such as "Lawyers ready to split tobacco billions." When you use the MLA style, you should regularize the capitalization: "Lawyers Ready to Split Tobacco Billions."

## Editorial

"Guns and More Guns." Editorial. <u>New York Times</u> 26 Apr. 2007, late ed.: A24.

## Letter to the Editor in Magazine or Newspaper

Ehrlich, Paul R. Letter. <u>Newsweek</u> 3 Sept. 2007: 17.

McCleery, Sheryl. Letter. <u>Detroit Free Press</u> 1 Sept. 2007: A14

Letters don't usually have titles, though editors may supply them. Unless you know for certain that the title was part of the original letter, you should not use it.

## Book Review

Gates, David. "Road Rules." Rev. of <u>On the Road</u>, by Jack Kerouac. <u>Newsweek</u> 13 Aug. 2007: 51+.

Proctor, Robert N. "Material Metaphors." Rev. of <u>Origins and Revolutions: Human Identity in Earliest Prehistory</u>, by Clive Gamble. <u>Nature</u> 448 (2007): 752+.

## Film Review

Denby, David. "War Wounds." Rev. of <u>The Bourne Ultimatum</u>, dir. Paul Greengrass. <u>The New Yorker</u> 6 Aug. 2007: 76–77.

Scott, A. O. "Open Wide and Say 'Shame.' " Rev. of <u>Sicko</u>, dir. Michael Moore. <u>New York Times</u> 22 June 2007, late ed.: E1.

*Note*: For more information on citing film reviews, see Chapter 5.

## Music Review

Lewis, Miles Marshall. "Purple Drizzle." Rev. of <u>Planet Earth</u>, by Prince. <u>Village Voice</u> 25–31 July 2007: 84.

## Journal Article, Each Issue Starting with Page 1

Baker, Douglas W. "When English Language Arts, Basketball, and Poetry Collide." <u>English Journal</u> 96.5 (2007): 37–41.

The volume and issue numbers are 96.5. These typically distinguish journals from magazines. (For magazine citations, don't use volume and issue numbers; use the date instead: day-month-year.)

## Journal Article, Pages Numbered Continuously Throughout Year

Hacker, Jacob S. "Healing Our *Sicko* Heath Care System." <u>New England Journal of Medicine</u> 357 (2007): 733–735.

"Pages numbered continuously" means that if the first issue ends on page 155 the next issue will start on page 156. These examples use only the volume number because issue numbers are not needed when pages are numbered continuously.

## Titles and Quotes within Titles

Hinton, Rebecca. "Steinbeck's The Grapes of Wrath." The Explicator 56.2 (1998): 101–03.

To write about Hinton's article concerning John Steinbeck's novel The Grapes of Wrath, you should underline Steinbeck's title in the title of her article.

# OTHER SOURCES: MLA WORKS CITED MODELS

## Handout or Unpublished Essay

Yin, Roseanne. "English 320: Critical Theory." Course Syllabus. Alma College. Alma,
MI: 8 Jan. 2008.

## Lecture, Speech, Public Address

Albright, Madeleine. "Responsible Leadership." Alma College, Alma, MI. 12 Sept. 2007.

Jobs, Steve. Commencement Address. Stanford University, Stanford, CA. 14 June 2005.

If there is no title, use an appropriate descriptive label—such as Address, Lecture, Reading, Speech—not underlined nor enclosed in quotation marks.

## Film

The Godfather. Dir. Francis Ford Coppola. Perf. Marlon Brando, Al Pacino, and James Caan.
Paramount, 1972.

## Video Recording: Film or Television

Antwone Fisher. Dir. Denzel Washington. Perf. Derek Luke and Denzel Washington. 2002. DVD.
20th Century Fox, 2003.

"The Field of Time." Bill Moyer's The Language of Life. Dir. David Grubin. Videocassette.
Newbridge Communications, 1995.

## Play, Performance

King Lear. By William Shakespeare. Dir. Trevor Nunn. Perf. Ian McKellen.
Brooklyn Academy of Music's Harvey Theater, New York, 12 Sept. 2007.

## Musical Performance

Bob Dylan. Concert. Ryman Auditorium. Nashville, TN. 20 Sept. 2007.

## Musical Composition

Beethoven, Ludwig van. Symphony no. 7 in A, op. 92.

## Musical Recording

Carpenter, Mary Chapin. <u>The Calling</u>. Zoe Records, 2007.

London Chamber Orchestra. <u>LCO2</u>. Virgin Classics, 1989.

## Individual Selection from a Recording

Carpenter, Mary Chapin. "Twilight." <u>The Calling</u>. Zoe Records, 2007.

London Chamber Orchestra. "The Lark Ascending." By Ralph Vaughan Williams. <u>LCO2</u>. Virgin Classics, 1989.

## Television Show

"Imagining Other Dimensions." Narr. Brian Greene. <u>The Elegant Universe</u>. PBS. 21 Dec. 2004.

"More Fries, Please . . . Filmmaker on McDonald's Diet Gains Weight and Praises." Narr. John Stossel. <u>20/20</u>. ABC. 18 June 2004.

## Work of Art

<u>Aphrodite</u> (the "Venus de Milo"). The Louvre, Paris.

Hopper, Edward. <u>Cape Cod Morning</u>. National Museum of American Art, Washington, DC.

## Poem Published Separately

Olds, Sharon. "Easter, 1960." <u>The New Yorker</u> 19 Feb. 2007: 158.

## Poem in a Collection

Collins, Billy. "Introduction to Poetry." <u>Sailing Alone Around the Room</u>. New York: Random, 2001. 16.

## Letter, Personal

Cavalieri, Grace. Letter to the author. 15 Dec. 2007.

## Letter(s), Published

Van Gogh, Vincent. <u>The Complete Letters of Vincent Van Gogh</u>. 3 vols. Greenwich, CT.: New York Graphic Society, 1958.

Van Gogh, Vincent. Letter to Theo, No. 358. <u>The Complete Letters of Vincent Van Gogh</u>. Vol. II. Greenwich, CT: New York Graphic Society, 1958. 265–69.

Use the date of a letter, when it's present, along with any identifying number. If there is an editor, add (for example) "Ed. George Smith." after the title of the collection. To cite more than one letter from a collection, give a reference to the collection in your Works Cited and cite the various letters in your paper itself (Van Gogh 265–69).

## Personal Interview

Clifton, Lucille. Personal interview. 23 May 2006.

## Telephone Interview

Daniels, Jim. Telephone interview. 20 Jan. 2006.

## Published Interview

"10 Questions for Al Pacino." Time 25 June 2007: 6.

Wagenvoord, Helen. "The Cheapest Calories Make You the Fattest: Interview with Michael Pollan." Sierra Sept./Oct. 2004: 34–35.

## A Chart, Diagram, Map, or Table

"What Happens in the Brain?" Diagram. Time 16 July 2007: 45.

## A Cartoon

Miller, Wiley. "Non Sequitur." Cartoon. Detroit Free Press 28 July 2007: C7.

Vey, P.C. Cartoon. The New Yorker 5 Feb. 2007: 54.

## An Advertisement

Honda. Advertisement. Newsweek 3 Sept. 2007: 28.

Norwegian Cruise Line. Advertisement. The New Yorker 12 Feb. 2007: 17.

## ELECTRONIC SOURCES: MLA WORKS CITED MODELS

This MLA form (for online magazines and journals) shows common elements for most electronic sources.

A        BC        D              E F  G H        I        J        K            L

Kluger, Jeffrey. "Rewiring the Brain." Time 30 Aug. 2007. 4 Sept. 2007
       <http://www.time.com/time/magazine/article/0,9171,1657822,00.html>.

M                                                                          N

A. Author's last name first
B. Period
C. Two spaces
D. Title of article between quotation marks
E. Period within quotes
F. Two spaces
G. Title of magazine or journal underlined
H. One space
I. Date in military order: day, month, year; no commas within
J. Period, then two spaces
K. Date you accessed (examined) the site
L. One space
M. URL (Web address) enclosed in angle brackets
N. Period

Because Internet sources are subject to updating and editing, it is important to give both the date the source was posted and the date you accessed the source. Note that when Internet addresses are too long to fit on a single line of your paper, divide them only after a slash. Do not add hyphens to make arbitrary breaks.

## Article from an Online Magazine

Friedman, Carrie. "Stop Setting Alarms on My Biological Clock." Newsweek 23 July 2007. 4 Sept. 2007 <http://www.msnbc.msn.com/id/19762056/site/newsweek/>.

"Researchers Find Link Between Education, Smartness." The Onion 3 Sept. 2007. 10 Oct. 2007 <http://www.theonion.com/content/news_briefs/researchers_find_link>.

## Article from an Online Newspaper

Stephens, Heidi. "Your Assignment: Be Happier." Chicago Tribune 2 Sept. 2007. 10 Oct. 2007 <http://www.chicagotribune.com/features/lifestyle/q/ chi-mxa0902qcoverhappiersep02,0,5782532.story>.

## Article from an Online Journal

Hacker, Jacob S. "Healing Our *Sicko* Heath Care System." *New England Journal of Medicine* 357.8 (2007). 10 Oct. 2007 <http://content.nejm.org/cgi/content/full/357/8/733?query=TOC>.

*Note*: For online journals, cite both the volume and the issue numbers before the date in parentheses.

## An Entire Web Site

The Purdue Online Writing Lab. 2008. Purdue University. 8 Feb. 2008 <http://owl.english.purdue.edu/>.

## Chapter or Section from a Web Site

Stolley, Karl, and Kristen Seas. "MLA Formatting and Style Guide." The OWL at Purdue. 20 Aug. 2007. 10 Oct. 2007 <http://owl.english.purdue.edu/owl/resource/557/09/>.

## Article from a Web Site

"Protein." Harvard School of Public Health. 2007. 22 Aug. 2007 <http://www.hsph.harvard.edu/nutritionsource/protein.html>.

## E-Mail

Bender, Carol. "Memoir questions." E-mail to author. 15 May 2007.

## Online Book

Chopin, Kate. The Awakening. Chicago: Herbert S. Stone, 1899. Electronic Text Center. Ed. Judy Boss. U of Virginia Library. 1997. 10 Oct. 2007 <http://etext.virginia.edu/toc/modeng/public/ChoAwak.html>.

Increasingly, entire books are being scanned onto the Net. Depending on your own software and the capacity of your computer, a book in your computer can be relatively quickly and easily searched, analyzed, and compared.

See links to other full-text sites: <http://www.bartleby.com/>, <http://www.gutenberg.net/>, and <http://digital.library.upenn.edu/books>.

## Part of an Online Book

Emerson, Ralph Waldo. "Compensation." Essays and English Traits. New York: P. F. Collier, 1909. Bartleby.com: Great Books Online. 2001. 10 Oct. 2007 <http://www.bartleby.com/5/105.html>.

## Online Government Publication

National Commission on Terrorist Attacks Upon the United States. The 9-11 Commission Report: Final Report of the National Commission on Terrorist Attacks Upon the United States, Official Government Edition. 2004. 10 Oct. 2007 <http://www.gpoaccess.gov/911/index.html>.

United States. Environmental Protection Agency. Climate Change. 24 July 2007. 10 Oct. 2007 <http://www.epa.gov/climatechange/>.

## CD-ROM

Corey, Gerald, Marianne Schneider Corey, and Robert Haynes. Ethics in Action. 2nd ed. CD-ROM. Belmont, CA: Wadsworth, 2003.

## Work from an Online Database

Libraries subscribe to databases such as <u>FirstSearch</u>, <u>InfoTrac</u>, and <u>ProQuest</u>. You can find abstracts and full-text articles through them. If you use a library database, you should provide information in your citation.

> Moore, David L. "Happiness That Sleeps with Sadness." <u>Studies in American Indian Literature</u> 18.3 (2006): 41–42. ProQuest. Alma College Lib., Alma, MI. 4 Sept. 2007 <http://www.proquest.com>.

> Spitzer, Peter. "Hospital Clowns—Modern-Day Court Jesters at Work." <u>The Lancet</u> 368.9554 (2006): S34+. <u>Expanded Academic Index</u>. InfoTrac. Alma College Lib., Alma, MI. 4 Sept. 2007 <http://infotrac.galegroup.com>.

> Wadyka, Sally. "Don't Have a Cow: Advantages of Meatless Diets for Runners." <u>Runner's World</u> 41.12 (2006): 51. <u>General OneFile</u>. InfoTrac. Alma College Lib., Alma, MI. 17 Aug. 2007 <http://infotrac.galegroup.com>.

## Weblog Site

If you cite a Weblog, ask yourself whether the site and author are credible.

> Sullivan, Andrew. <u>The Daily Dish</u>. Weblog. 5 Sept. 2007. Atlantic.com. 10 Sept. 2007 <http://www.andrewsullivan.com/>.

## Weblog Entry

> Sullivan, Andrew. "Thinking Through the Surge." Weblog post. <u>The Daily Dish</u>. 5 Sept. 2007. Atlantic.com. 10 Sept. 2007
> <http://andrewsullivan.theatlantic.com/the_daily_dish/2007/09/thinking-throug.html>.

*Note*: For more help on MLA style see <http://owl.english.purdue.edu/owl/resource/557/01/>.

## **A** PA STYLE: NAME AND DATE METHOD OF DOCUMENTATION

The name and date method of documentation is based on the style of the American Psychological Association (APA). This method is often used in science, education, and business. Some researchers feel that references in the text are helpful because readers can identify authorities and dates of research immediately; the full references can be found at the end of the paper when additional source information is desired. If you plan to cite whole books and articles without quoting directly from them, this may be the preferred form of documentation, especially when the age of the research is an important consideration:

> At least three books on happiness written by well-respected professors have become popular (Gilbert, 2006; Haidt, 2006; Seligman, 2002).

Such documentation indicates that all three sources are about the same subject.

# GUIDELINES FOR REFERENCES IN YOUR TEXT: APA STYLE

## Using Author's Name

At the most appropriate place in the text (often the end of a sentence), give the author's name, followed by comma, space, date, and page number if necessary.

Thinking depends on the ability to see connections between unlike things (Haidt, 2006, p. 2).

*Note*: Within the parentheses, the date of year is given and a *p.* is used before the page number.

*Option*: As an alternative, the author's name can be given in the text, with only the date and pages (when needed) supplied in parentheses.

According to Haidt (2006), thinking depends on the ability to see connections between unlike things (p. 2).

You must give a full description in your reference list for a note like this:

Haidt, J. (2006). *The happiness hypothesis: Finding modern truth in ancient wisdom.* New York: Basic Books.

## Using Sources with Two Authors

For two authors, always give both authors' last names.

Nalebuff and Ayres (2006) write, "The why-not attitude lets you see potential improvements that are just waiting to happen" (p. 3).

Or

Asking "Why Not?" generates possible solutions to problems (Nalebuff & Ayres, 2006, p. 3).

*Note*: Use the ampersand (&) in parenthetical citations, but not otherwise in your paper.

## Using Sources with Three to Five Authors

For three to five authors, give all authors' names in the first reference; thereafter use only the first author's name with "et al."

### First Reference

(Campbell, McWhir, Ritchie, & Wilmut, 1996)

### Subsequent References

(Campbell et al., 1996)

## Using Sources with Six or More Authors

For six or more authors, give only the first author's name and "et al." for all references.

(Sagan et al., 1978) [6 authors]

## Using an Unknown Author

If there is no author's name, use either the title or an abbreviated (but recognizable) form of the title in a signal phrase toward the beginning of a sentence or in parentheses at the end.

> The war in Iraq has generated more potential for terror in the United States ("Terror's New Depths," 2004, p. 24).

## Using a Committee or Group with a Long Name

You may shorten or abbreviate lengthy names of committees (USDA, 2001) or groups so long as the reader will be able to recognize the name in your References list: United States Department of Agriculture.

> Our federal government approves of meat irradiation (USDA, 2001).

## Using Two Authors with Same Last Name

Use initials to identify authors with the same last name:

> (G. Kennedy, 2003), (J. Kennedy, 2006).

## Using Same Author, Same Year

Two or more works by the same author published in the same year should be further identified with lowercase letters in parentheses: . . . (Watts, 1999a, 1999b) . . .

In your References list these titles should be listed alphabetically by the title, after the date.

> Watts, Jonathan. (1999a). Experiment sparks cloning debate in Japan. *The Lancet, 354,* 1801.

> Watts, Jonathan. (1999b). Japan set to make first legal prohibition on life-sciences research. *The Lancet, 354,* 1885.

*Note*: Volume numbers and commas that follow are italicized for periodicals.

## Using Multiple References

If you have more than one author in a reference, follow the order in your References list, usually alphabetical (Clauer, 2004; Henderson, 2005; Lopez, 2002). References to the same author also follow the order in the References list—chronological rather than alphabetical (Davis, 2002, 2003, 2005).

## Using a Source Quoted in Another Source

If you use a quote that is quoted (cited) in another source, follow this model.

> Marianne Moore marveled at a cherry: "What sap went through that little thread to make the cherry red!" (as cited in Selzer, 1992, p. 132).

## Using a Long Quote

In APA style, a long quote is 40 or more words. Indent a long quote 5 spaces or one tab from the left margin. Use double-spacing. Use no quotation marks around the long quote: because it is set off, this signifies it is a direct quote. Use a sentence to introduce the quote, ending with a colon.

> Haidt (2006) writes that there are various methods that help people be more happy:
>> Suppose you read about a pill that you could take once a day to reduce anxiety and increase your contentment. Would you take it? Suppose further that the pill has a great variety of side effects, all of them good: increased self-esteem, empathy, and trust; it even improves memory. Suppose, finally, that the pill is all natural and costs nothing. Now would you take it? (p. 35)
>
> What is this magic pill? It's simply meditation. Many people would not need to take antidepressants if they practiced meditation, Haidt claims.

*Note*: As with MLA style, when you use APA you should use signal phrases to establish the authority and credibility of your sources. You can use ellipses and brackets as well.

## REFERENCES LIST IN APA STYLE

Your References list should contain only those sources you actually cite in your paper. When you use the name and date style, the list is always called "References" (not "Bibliography," which might include sources not cited). The purpose of the References list is to help other researchers find the materials you have used, and you should provide complete and accurate information from the title page of a book (not the cover) or as the information appears in a journal, magazine, newspaper or other source, not the table of contents or indexes. However, use only the initials of authors' first and middle names, even if spelled in full in the source.

Reference models given here are the ones most often needed by students. Others may be inferred from those given here. Occasionally you may find a source for which there is no exact model; in that case you must invent a reasonable application of these general principles.

## BASIC REFERENCE FORM, BOOK (APA)

    A  B      C  D  E                       F

Nalebuff, B. & Ayres, I. (2006). *Why not?: How to use everyday ingenuity to solve problems big and small*. Boston: Harvard Business School.

G         H  I J       K        L

A. Author(s) name(s), last name first (note that all authors' names are inverted). Use only initials for first and middle names, even if full name is given on title page.

B. Ampersand in place of *and* (but use *and* when referring to authors in your paper: "Nalebuff *and* Ayres show that . . .").

C. One space between name and date. (Use one space after any end mark.) Period after initial serves as end mark.

D. Date of publication in parentheses (frequently given as "copyright" on title page), followed by period and one space.

E. Capitalize only the first word of the title and any proper names. The first word of a subtitle after a colon or dash should be capitalized: *Women, men, and gender: On-going debate.*

F. Italicize the titles of books.

G. Indent subsequent lines five spaces.

H. Period ending book title. Any explanatory information, such as (ed.) for edition is usually set off in parentheses.

I. Place (city) of publication.

J. Colon and one space between place and name of publisher.

K. Publisher's name: shorten publisher's name—Boynton instead of Boynton/Cook Heineman. Drop redundant information like "Co." and "Inc."

L. Period at end of reference.

## BASIC REFERENCE FORM, PERIODICALS (APA)

Periodicals include journals, magazines, newspapers, and other publications that are published "periodically." What follows is an example of a Reference form for a journal.

    A      B C   D                          E

Daley, G. O. (2004). Missed opportunities in embryonic stem-cell research.

    *The New England Journal of Medicine, 351,* 627–628.

  F                 G            H I    J    K

A. Author's last name, first and middle initials (even if full name is spelled out in the source).

B. One space between author's name and date.

C. Date in parentheses, followed by period.

D. Title of journal article given without quotation marks. Capitalize only first word, proper names, and first word of subtitle after colon. End with period or other end mark.

E. One space between title of article and title of journal.

F. Indent subsequent lines five spaces or one tab.

G. Capitalize first and all significant words of periodical title, and italicize it.

H. Comma after periodical title, italicized.

I. Italicize volume number and the comma that follows; add one space.

J. Give page numbers last. (Use "p." or "pp." for newspaper entries.)

K. Period at end of reference.

## **B**OOKS: REFERENCE LIST MODELS, APA STYLE

### One Author

Clinton, H. R. (2003). *Living history*. New York: Simon.

Hawking, S. W. (2001). *The universe in a nutshell*. New York: Bantam.

Hersh, S. M. (2004). *Chain of command: The road from 9/11 to Abu Ghraib*. New York: Harper.

*Note*: List items in reference list in alphabetical order.

### More Than One Book by Same Author

Treat these books as if they were written by different authors with the same name. Don't use a string of hyphens. Chronological order is required, earliest year first.

Kennedy, G. A. (1963). *The art of persuasion in Greece*. Princeton, NJ: Princeton University Press.

Kennedy, G. A. (1972). *The art of rhetoric in the Roman world, 300 B.C.–A.D. 300*. Princeton, NJ: Princeton University Press.

Kennedy, G. A. (1980). *Classical rhetoric and its Christian and secular tradition from ancient to modern times*. Chapel Hill: University of North Carolina Press.

Identify most states except those very well known or those identified in the publisher's name. Do not use U and P for University and Press.

### Author of One Book, Coauthor of Another

Goleman, D. (1995). *Emotional intelligence: Why it can matter more than IQ*. New York: Bantam.

Goleman, D., Boyatzis, R. E., & McKee, A. (2004). Primal intelligence: Learning to lead with *emotional intelligence*. Boston: Harvard Business School.

Coauthored books should be listed after books with one author.

### Two or More Authors

Kass, L., & Wilson, J. Q. (1998). *The ethics of human cloning*. Washington, D.C.: Agi Press.

Belenky, M. F., Bond, L. A., & Winestock, J. S. (1997). *A tradition that has no name: Nurturing the development of people, families, and communities*. New York: BasicBooks-Harper.

Sagan, C., Drake, F. D., Druyan, A., Ferris, T., Lomberg, J., & Sagan, L. S. (1978). *Murmurs of earth: The Voyager interstellar record*. New York: Random.

For APA style, your References list must give all authors' names, no matter how many. Don't use "et al." in your References list. However, to cite such a work in your paper use only the first author's last name, et al., and the date: (Belenky et al., 1997). Add page numbers if needed: (Belenky et al., 1997, p. 25).

## Committee or Group Author

American Civil Liberties Union. (2003). *Freedom under fire: Dissent in post-9/11 America*. New York: ACLU.

President's Council on Bioethics (U.S.). (2002). *Human cloning and human dignity: The report of the president's council on bioethics*. New York: PublicAffairs.

Group authors and unsigned works are alphabetized according to the first significant word in the name: don't alphabetize under *A*, *An*, or *The*. The Zuider Report would be alphabetized as if it started with Zuider.

## Book with Editor(s)

Schwehn, M. R., & Bass, D. C. (Eds). (2006) *Leading lives that matter: What we should do and who we should be*. Grand Rapids, MI: Eerdmans.

## Article or Chapter in an Edited Work

Bayley, C. (2004). The challenge of physician education in genetics. In G. Magill (Ed.), *Genetics and ethics: An interdisciplinary study* (pp. 176-185). St. Louis: Saint Louis University Press.

Note that editor's name is not inverted, in contrast with the preceding "Book with Editor(s)" and no period appears between the book title and parenthetical reference to pages.

## Translation

Allende, I. (2006). *Inés of my soul: A novel*. (M. S. Peden, Trans.) New York: HarperCollins.

## Multi-volume Work

Cornell, V. J. (Ed.). (2007). *Voices of Islam*. (Vols. 1–5). Westport, CT: Praeger.

## Reprint of Older Work

Morrison, T. (1987). *Song of Solomon*. New York: Plume-Penguin. (Original work published 1977).

Selzer, R. (1996). *Letters to a young doctor*. New York: Harvest-Harcourt. (Original work published 1982).

Parenthetic references to reprints should give both dates in your paper: (Selzer, 1982/1996) or (Selzer, 1982/1996, p. 35).

## Edition Other Than the First

Meyer, M. (2006). *Poetry: An introduction* (5th ed.). Boston: Bedford.

## Introduction, Preface, Foreword

Robe, L. Y. (2004). Foreword. In M. Weinberg, *The real rosebud: The triumph of a Lakota woman* (p. xi). Lincoln: University of Nebraska Press.

## Dictionary

Agnes, M. E. (Ed.). (2004). *Webster's new world college dictionary* (4th ed.). New York: Wiley.

## PERIODICALS: REFERENCE LIST MODELS, APA STYLE

## Weekly Magazine Article

Lemonick, M. D. & Park, A. (2007, July 16). The science of addiction. *Time, 170*, 42–48.

With APA style you should give volume numbers for magazines as well as for journals.

## Magazine Article, No Author Given

Picturesque charm: All two blocks of it. (1998, February 9). *U.S. News & World Report, 124*, 58.

## Monthly Magazine Article

Riddle, R. D., & Tabin, C. J. (1999, February). How limbs develop. *Scientific American, 280*, 74–79.

Significant words in the titles of the periodicals are capitalized, but not words in the titles of articles themselves. Also, months are not abbreviated (by contrast with MLA).

## Newspaper Article

Broder, D. S. (2003, May 25). A call for service. *The Washington Post*, p. B7.

Goodman, E. (2007, February 9). No change in political climate. *Boston Globe*, p. A19.

Note that the comma after a newspaper title should be italicized along with newspaper title. Newspaper articles and sections of books require "p." and "pp." for "page" and "pages." For newspaper articles with discontinuous pages, separate the pages with commas:

> Suskind, R. (1990, September 6). A lady lawyer in Laramie writes landmark letter. *The Wall Street Journal*, pp. A1, A6.

*Note*: With APA style, do not omit *The* from the title of a newspaper or magazine.

## Newspaper Article, Unsigned

> FDA tighter on drug approvals. (2007, August 19). *Chicago Tribune*, sec. 1: p. 4.

## Editorial, Signed and Unsigned

> Stem cell battles. (2004, 15 August). [Editorial.] *The New York Times*, sec. 4, p.10.

> Zabludoff, M. (1998, September). [Editorial]. Fear and longing. *Discover, 19*, 6.

## Letter to the Editor

> Crochet, K. (16 July 2007). Unfailing bravery [Letter to the editor]. *Time, 170*, 9.

## Book Review

> Proctor, R. N. (2007). *Material metaphors.* [Review of the book *Origins and revolutions: Human identity in earliest prehistory*]. *Nature, 448*, 752.

## Film Review

> Scott, A. O. (2007, June 22). Open wide and say "shame." [Review of the film *Sicko*]. *The New York Times*, p. E1.

*Note*: With reviews, use brackets to describe the article. When there is no title, use the bracketed information and the brackets as the title.

## Music Review

> Lewis, M. M. (2007, July 25–31). Purple drizzle. [Review of the CD *Planet Earth*]. *Village Voice*, p. 84.

## Journal Article, Each Issue Starting with Page 1

> Baker, D. W. (2007). When English language arts, basketball, and poetry collide. *English Journal, 96*(5), 37–41.

Note that volume numbers are italicized, but issue numbers are enclosed in parentheses. Since each volume usually has several issues in it, readers need to know the issue number in order to find pages 37–41. There is no space between volume and issue numbers. Page numbers aren't preceded with "p." or "pp." for journal references.

## Journal Article, Pages Numbered Continuously Throughout Year

Hacker, J. S. (2007). Healing our *Sicko* heath care system. *New England Journal of Medicine, 357,* 733–735.

## OTHER SOURCES: REFERENCE LIST MODELS, APA STYLE

## Lecture, Speech, Public Address

Albright, Madeleine (2007, September 12). *Responsible leadership.* Lecture presented at Alma College, Alma, MI.

*Note*: Titles of handouts, unpublished essays, and public addresses are italicized in APA style.

## Motion Picture: Film, Video, or DVD

Coppola, F. F. (Director). (1972). *The Godfather.* [Motion picture]. United States: Paramount.

Washington, D. (Director). (2002). *Antwone Fisher.* [DVD]. United States: 20th Century Fox.

## Television Broadcast

Smiley, T. (Producer). (2007, September 28). *PBS presidential primary forum with Tavis Smiley.* [Television broadcast]. New York: PBS.

Stossel, J. (Producer). (2004, June 18). More fries, please . . . filmmaker on McDonald's diet gains weight and praises. *20/20* [Television broadcast]. New York: ABC.

## Play, Performance

Shakespeare, W. (2007). *King Lear.* (T. Nunn, Director). Brooklyn Academy of Music's Harvey Theater, New York.

## Individual Selection from a Recording

Carpenter, M. C. (2007). Twilight. On *The Calling* [CD]. New York: Sony.

## Work of Art

Hopper, E. (1950). *Cape Cod morning.* [Painting in oil]. Washington, DC: National Museum of American Art.

## A Chart, Diagram, Map, or Table

A figure is a chart, map, or diagram, or any visual information other than columns of numbers (a table). Figures should have a citation at the bottom of the same page as the figure. The citation should appear as a footnote.

Begley, S. (1997, March 10). [Diagram of Dolly cloning]. In little lamb, who made thee? *Newsweek, 129,* 56–57.

## ELECTRONIC SOURCES: REFERENCE LIST MODELS, APA STYLE

### Internet Articles Based on a Print Source

Because most articles online are the same as their print versions, APA style requires that you follow the documentation style for print sources, but add "Electronic Version" inside brackets after the article title. However, if you use an article from an online source with a different format and page numbering system than the original print source, add the date you retrieved the document and the URL.

### Article from a Journal, Print Source

> Daley, G. Q. (2004, August 12). Missed opportunities in embryonic stem-cell research. [Electronic Version]. *The New England Journal of Medicine, 351*(7), 627–628.

### Article from an Online Journal, No Print Source

> Price, R. H. (2003, October 1). Systems within systems: Putting program implementation in organizational context. *Prevention & Treatment, 6*(1). Retrieved October 4, 2004, from http://journals.apa.org/prevention/volume6/pre0060020i.html

*Note*: For APA style, use no angle brackets around the URL and no final period unless a period belongs at the end of the URL.

### Article from a Magazine

> Krauthammer, C. (2004, August 23). Why lines must be drawn. *Time, 164*, 78. Retrieved October 4, 2004, from http://www.time.com/time/columnist/krauthammer/article/0,9565,683012,00.html

### Article from an Online Newspaper

> Fumento, M. (2004, August 15). Adult cell lines already cure a variety of diseases; embryonic cells treat no one, can result in cancer. *The Detroit News*. Retrieved October 10, 2004, from http://www.detnews.com/2004/editorial/0408/15/a17-242314.htm

### Online Book

> Chopin, K. (1899). *The Awakening*. Ed. Judy Boss. 1997. University of Virginia Library. Retrieved October 4, 2004, from the *Electronic Text Center* http://etext.virginia.edu/toc/modeng/public/ChoAwak.html

### Online Government Publication

> National Commission on Terrorist Attacks upon the United States. (2004). *The 9-11 Commission report: Final report of the National Commission on Terrorist Attacks Upon the United States, official government edition.* Retrieved October 2, 2004, from http://www.gpoaccess.gov/911/index.html

## Work from an Online Database

Moore, D. L. (2006). Happiness that sleeps with sadness. *Studies in American Indian Literature 18*(3), 41-42. Retrieved September 4, 1007, from *ProQuest* database.

Wadyka, S. (2006). Don't have a cow: Advantages of meatless diets for runners. *Runner's World 41*(12), 51. Retrieved 17 August 2007, from InfoTrac database.

## Weblog Entry

Sullivan, A. (2007, September 5). Thinking through the surge. Weblog post. *The Daily Dish*. Retrieved September 10, 2007, from http://andrewsullivan.theatlantic.com/the_daily_dish/2007/09/thinking-throug.html

## CHAPTER 10

# Writing Your Research Paper

## RESEARCHERS AS WRITERS

Research and writing are closely connected. Both researchers and writers have a responsibility to their readers, not only to be fair-minded and accurate but to be concise and readable.

At the outset, when you are learning to deal with technical subject matter, the task can be intimidating. For that reason, when you write a research paper, it's best to follow a logical sequence: a procedure in which prewriting, collecting, drafting, organizing, synthesizing, and rewriting follow one another. In practice, these stages of research often overlap. As said in Chapter 7, writing a research paper is more often a spiral than a straight line.

You should organize your research paper in a standard form. This shortens the time for readers who expect to find your thesis early in the paper so that they don't have to hunt for it. Research papers are written in plain English because most readers don't have time for artistic language. Nor do readers have time for dull, plodding language that anesthetizes the analytical mind. Readers are grateful to find the parts of your paper where they expect to find them. Some readers may choose to skip to the end, to read the conclusion first, to see whether the research has any useful findings for their own work. They will find the conclusion readily when you follow a standard arrangement and label the parts of your paper.

## WRITING A REPORT

Various forms of writing require you to present information in a clear, concise, and coherent way. Such writing can include proposals, explanations of projects or events, and reports.

## A Model Report

The following student paper is a report using research. As you read it, try to notice how Mary Wendt introduces her paper, uses specific supporting evidence, uses sources and quotes, organizes her evidence, and presents her Works Cited. Notice her appeals to logos, pathos, ethos. Notice her voice and style. Notice anything you have learned in Discovering Arguments that she succeeds at doing.

Wendt 1

Mary Ellen Wendt

Professor Chen

English 101

20 November 2007

Saturated by Color

We do not see things as they are; we see things as we are.

~ saying from the Talmud

Science tells us that dogs see in black and white, a world in shades of gray. Bees, on the other hand, see colors of the spectrum beyond what humans see, into the ultraviolet, so they can locate pollen in flowers. Humans fall somewhere in the middle. We see red bricks, red roses, tired red eyes. We see blue skies and blue waters. We see green and know it is spring. But unlike any other animal, we do much more than *see* color: we make it very much a part of who we are. Our lives are saturated by color.

Designers know about the power and psychology of color, how to sway an audience in a particular direction. As Cailin Boyle in his book <u>Color Harmony for the Web</u> explains it, "Designers use colors to ignite certain emotions in their target audiences or facilitate brand recognition. Who doesn't recognize the bright orange of the Tide box or the signature red of Coca-Cola?" (11). They know, too, about "cool" colors and "warm" colors, terms used by decorators and painters to describe the implied "temperature" of a color (Horton 171). A room painted a warm color—yellow with a hint of orange, for example—is supposed to give the room a cozy, harmonious feeling, while a room painted light blue will give it a cheerful and open feeling. Designers also know that most shades of blue are con-sidered professional, black connotes seriousness and sensuality, and white is pure and fresh. Businesses often use color to create a very specific persona, as in UPS, which recently spent $20 million on the new brown and gold shield logo (Griswold). Sometimes, though, businesses use color for other purposes.

Until it was pointed out to me, I was unaware of the color palette for fast-food chains: they almost always use red and/or yellow. McDonald's famous golden arches and red sign, Wendy's yellow sign with the little red-haired girl, Burger King's red letters sandwiched in a yellow bun—these choices are anything but arbitrary. It turns out that red and yellow are food colors: when we see them, we think of warmth and fullness and satisfaction. Apparently the combination of red and yellow taps into our psychic need to eat. According to Boyle, red "has the most energy" of all colors (23). When you combine this with warm yellow, the most attention-getting color, you have not only a sign that grabs the attention of those driving by, but a winning combination of warmth and an urgency for food—unless you live outside the United States.

We are used to the colors that surround us and assume that everyone thinks as we do. But this is not true, and this has become more important than ever with the ubiquity of the Internet; Web designers often have to appeal to a global market. For example, Oliu, Brusaw, and Alred in their book <u>Using Graphics to Communicate Internationally</u> tell us:

> Red commonly indicates warning or danger in North America, Europe, and Japan. In China, however, red symbolizes joy. In Europe and North America, blue generally has a positive connotation; in Japan, the color represents vil-lainy. In Europe and North America, yellow represents caution or cowardice; in Arab countries, yellow generally means fertility or strength. (543)

In addition to these contradictions, some Asian cultures think of black as pure and holy, while white symbolizes evil. In their culture, the good guy would not be wear-ing white.

Wendt 3

Despite the various meanings of some colors between cultures, other colors seem to cross cultures. Green, for example, is the sign of life and health nearly everywhere, unless you desaturate it—add grey, white, black, or some yellow. A drab yellowish green called avocado green hardly looks lively. If your grandmother has an avocado green stove, you'll know what I mean.

Those avocado green appliances were not a mistake, though some people today might have trouble believing it. In the seventies, gold and avocado green were popular. Boyle explains the colors associated with the last five decades of the 20th century: "The 1950s were pink," he says, pastels of innocence that covered homes and cars and lipsticks (22). In the '60s, bright colors like oranges, yellows and reds rebelled against the softness of the fifties, while the '70s shifted once again, this time into earthy tones (22). The golds and browns and rusts of the seventies, the era of environmental awareness, led to the '80s, what Boyle says was "billed as the Color Conscious Decade" as our culture professionalized with navy and khaki and muted mauve (22). By the '90s, green—but not avocado green—was in style along with more muted tones of yellows and reds. Boyle doesn't get to this century, but as I walk through the mall, look at a parking lot, or drive down the street in my neighborhood, it seems clear that this decade is in love with bright colors: bright blue houses, primary red and yellow clothing, even purple and bright yellow cars. While I notice some still clinging to the professional look of the '90s, our parking lots and streets are looking more like rainbows every day. IKEA even has a new slogan, "Be brave, not beige." Their new TV ad boasts rooms of furniture and accessories in loud colors that contrast vividly with montages of beige furniture and shoes, beige food and a beige brain. The message seems to be that we are done toning things down.

This brightening of the 21st century says much about the mood of our lives these days. We are busy—too busy, most would say—and depressed more than ever before. We need bright hues and deep saturation to keep us from losing perspective. William Horton in <u>The Icon Book</u> lists people's reactions to color. For example, red is associated with aggression, impulsiveness, and optimism, to name a few. We react to green by associating it with freshness, hope, health, and prosperity. Purple creates strong reactions: people tend to either love it or hate it, perhaps because purple is associated with vanity, wit, and spirituality. On the other hand, colors like gray make us think of restraint, barrenness, grief, and indifference, black of death, grief, and gloom, and brown of duty, reliability, and poverty (175). This explains the need for such bright colors—and perhaps those who surround them-selves with more depressing colors like black.

Feng shui, the Chinese art of creating balance through your surroundings, is be-coming increasingly popular in the United States. Not surprisingly, feng shui relies heavily on color. According to <u>The Spiritual Feng Shui</u>, "Feng shui uses [the] natural magic of colors to transform your life" (Wang). Feng shui divides colors into yin col-ors and yang colors. Yin colors—blue, black, purple, and white—are supposed to bring about relaxation and healing, while yang colors—yellow and orange and other "fire and wood" colors like red and brown—provide energy and motivation (Wang). Feng shui is often very specific about how to use color; for example, houses facing the south should be painted white, blue, or grey.

Whether we work toward total feng shui harmony in our homes or just want to make sure we like our walls, color saturates our lives, from what clothes to wear for a date to the billion-dollar campaign of Pepsi to "own" royal blue. UPS now "owns" their brown color, a color of dependability and simplicity. Celebrities like Johnny Cash, "The Man in Black," and Prince with his obsession with purple frequently use color to define themselves, sometimes, like the musician Pink, even making their signature color also their name. However we look at it, color has significance and meaning.

Wendt 5

### Works Cited

Boyle, Cailin. Color Harmony for the Web. Gloucester: Rockport Publishers, 2001.

Griswold, Alicia. "Martin Presents a New Look: UPS." Adweek.com 25 Mar. 2003. 12 Nov. 2007

    <http://www.adweek.com/aw/national/article_display.jsp?vnu_ content_id=1848494>.

Horton, William. The Icon Book: Visual Symbols for Computer Systems and Documentation.

    John Wiley and Sons, 1994.

Oliu, Walter E., Charles T. Brusaw, and Gerald G. Alred. "Designing Effective Documents and

    Visuals." Writing That Works: Communicating Effectively on the Job. 7th ed. Boston:

    Bedford/St. Martin's, 2004. 542–546.

Wang, Mike Z. "Significance of Colors in Feng Shui Practice." The Spiritual Feng Shui. n.d.

    12 Nov. 2007 <http://www.thespiritualFengShui.com/Feng-Shui-color.php>.

Mary's report represents a popular research assignment: an objective presentation or analysis of an issue. Her report explains how important color is in our lives: in our own moods and preferences as well as in business. Color indeed saturates our lives: we make it a part of who we are. She helps readers become more aware of this. Increasing readers' awareness of an idea or issue is a hallmark of good research writing—of most excellent writing.

Mary's paper doesn't present an argument: that is, she does not examine two or more positions on a controversial issue. Thus, she doesn't need to present counter-arguments or make concessions. Instead, her paper answers an implied question: how important is color in our lives?

Yet is Mary's report persuasive? Does she use the appeals of logos, pathos, and ethos? Regarding logos, Mary presents ideas and information clearly. Her reasoning is easy to follow because she uses specific examples readers can relate to. Granted, she is not reporting on extremely technical aspects of color. She chose not to do this. Yet she stirs curiosity and satisfies it. Pathos? Mary doesn't use examples or illustrations to move readers emotionally. However, she tries to present evidence that readers can relate to their own moods and preferences. Not all papers—especially research papers—need strong appeals to pathos. If she were writing a report on Darfur, she likely would have used stronger emotional appeals. Ethos? Do you find Mary credible, trustworthy, honest? She is careful to present information in an engaging way that doesn't bore readers. She is careful to use sources responsibly, to quote directly, to cite page numbers when she can, to provide a clear Works Cited page, in short, to use MLA style well. She has proofread and edited her paper. She cares about her writing, and this helps readers trust her presentation of information.

In her report Mary tries to engage her audience with her title, her epigraph from the Talmud, her introduction, and her conclusion. She applies information presented in Chapter 1 of this book. In her supporting evidence, she uses clear examples and concrete details (details referring to our senses) such as "We see red bricks, red roses, tired red eyes. We see blue skies and blue waters. We see green and know it is spring." She offers examples of colors used by fast-food restaurants and explains why these colors activate appetites. For most readers, this may be new information—something they didn't know before. Mary also uses clear sentences with variety in structure and punctuation, applying tools of style presented in the Interchapters of this book.

## Organizing Reports

Consider using the following outline to structure a report of your own:

### GUIDELINES FOR ORGANIZING REPORTS

I.  Introduction

   **A.** Catch your reader's interest. (See "Introductory Strategies" in Chapter 1.)

   **B.** Present your thesis: the answer to the question that generated your search.

II.  Body

   Present—in some organized way—the information you have found. There is no one right way to do this: you need to discover a way that best suits your purpose. Consider using chronological order or order of importance. Consider using any of the strategies of development explained in Chapters 2 and 3: examples, details, illustrations, reasons; authorities, statistics; opposites, comparison, refutation, induction/deduction, description, narration, analogy, classification, cause-effect, definition.

III. Conclusion

   **A.** Re-present your thesis.

   **B.** Explain why the information in your report is important for readers to know. Answer the "So what?" question: So why does this information matter?

Keep in mind that research writing isn't like cooking or carpentry in which step by step you complete each act and then go on to the next. Writing is more like gardening: you must keep after it, returning to it again and again to water, fertilize, weed, hoe, prune, and, finally, to harvest the outcome. Many writers find themselves returning again and again to earlier thoughts, making changes, revising and editing, adding more information.

## WRITING AN ARGUMENT PAPER

### Shaping Your Thesis

A thesis is an implied promise to your readers. For example, this is Ryan's thesis: "If you read my paper, you'll know why grass-fed beef is better for animals, humans, and the environment." If Ryan's paper succeeds, readers will feel satisfied that he has kept his promise.

# Discovering Order

As you collect your notes (on notecards or on paper), you can begin sorting them in different ways. Label key ideas and main points. At this point in the process you shouldn't concern yourself too much about the final plan for your paper. These early explorations should be tentative and experimental; look for whatever order may reveal itself in your notes. Even if you happen upon a reasonable-looking plan at the outset, you should still experiment with other possibilities. A "good enough" plan isn't the goal. You need the best plan—but you may not discover this until you start writing your paper.

You needn't be committed to an iron-fast decision about organization. Keep sorting and thinking, working with your notes until you find the strategy that works best for the material you have and the audience you anticipate. Work with a rough outline, your data, and your rough draft until they all begin to jell. At first, the early work controls your time—reading, note-taking, outlining. But as you make progress, the later work begins to control your time—drafting and polishing. From your rough draft you can give more consideration to your readers. You can start to check the logic of your paper, your use of persuasive appeals, and the readability of your writing.

# Working through Your Project

Although you could go on and on collecting sources, reading, taking notes and revising, at some point you must make a decision: your research is finished when you have enough material, enough to establish your thesis, enough to persuade your readers. Knowing when to stop is part of the process. A good rule is to stop when you are not finding anything new, when the material gets repetitive, but beware of making that judgment too soon.

# Understanding Audience

Usually the audience for school papers is your instructor and sometimes other students. Your readers will not wish to read a thin overview of your subject. The more experienced your audience is, the more they will expect you to follow standard procedures for research writing. The best advice is to take your assignment seriously, but don't overdo it.

# Controlling Your Voice

Use your own voice in your research paper. You shouldn't attempt to sound as if you were one of the authorities in the research. Avoid pretentious writing, which occurs when writers pretend to be more important than they really are. Avoid slang. In general your paper should sound like you. The sound of your personality should not be very different from your ordinary voice when you are being polite. An academic voice should be objective. You should stick to the subject in research writing, use clear reasoning, and present factual evidence including statistics and testimony from authorities. With an argument paper, you need to appeal to your readers' logos, pathos, and ethos so you can persuade them to consider or accept your thesis.

Through your voice, your readers hear your attitude toward them, toward the subject you are investigating, and toward yourself. You don't want to sound superior to your audience (and thus condescending). You don't want to sound indifferent. If you are bored, your readers will be bored too.

In sum, clear, plain, simple English is the best approach. Research writers don't usually try to be amusing or entertaining. Refrain from using creative word plays. Avoid jargon when possible, and be as concise as you can. It's permissible at times to use the pronoun "I." What is not recommended is artificial, inflated language used to impress "one's" readers. (For more on voice see Interchapter 1.)

## Taking Your Time

You can lose everything in a hastily written paper. Like other aspects of research, writing the paper takes time and patience. As your project begins to take shape, the components will begin to influence each other. As your data begin to pile up, your rough outline begins to take shape (usually altered from your first conception of it), and the paper too begins to form in your mind. The last-minute syndrome, in which writers attempt to throw together a paper the night before it is due, can have predictably unfortunate results. Plus, you need incubation time when you write a research paper: you need to work on your writing over a period of days or weeks so your subconscious mind can work on various problems. (See "The Process of Thinking" in Chapter 1.)

## Substantiating Your Data

You must help readers find your sources and check your facts if need be. Substantiation makes the difference between research and other kinds of writing. Library research is a compilation of the available information, and somewhere between not enough and too many is an appropriate number of sources. You need as many references as is necessary to establish your thesis.

Citing research shows that you are well read in your subject and therefore have authority for your work. Substantiation answers the questions "Who said so? How do you know this? Where did you get this information?" Substantiation is the reason for your documentation—your Works Cited or your References. (See Chapter 9, "Documentation.")

## THE FORMAL OUTLINE

Many research papers require a formal outline. The outline is useful to your readers: it shows at a glance the structure and development of your paper and reveals whether your material is clearly organized. Preliminary outlines can let your instructor (or a classmate) offer advice and assistance. Most of all, the outline focuses your attention on the logic of your paper, whether your ideas are arranged in sequence and follow a plan that leads to your conclusion.

As you collect your sources, you can begin to sort and organize them into major and minor points. Your outline isn't usually a simple plan that you can fill in with details from your reading. Like your paper itself, your outline should grow and develop until you begin to understand your data in terms of categories, points and subpoints.

The outline should not become an arbitrary blueprint you impose on the data. Instead of forcing data to fit into your outline, you should alter the outline to accommodate the data. Even while you are writing the first draft of your paper, you may find yourself working back and forth, first shaping the paper to fit the outline and then altering the outline to fit the paper. This kind of creative give and take makes the outline a useful tool—it helps you understand what you are doing. When you finish, your paper and outline will agree with each other.

Not all writers benefit from making a preliminary outline and revising it as they write their paper. Another way is to outline after you have written a rough draft. Some writers prefer to discover their organization as they write. When a rough draft is finished, then they make an outline to check the logic of their paper's organization.

## Revising the Preliminary Outline

A formal outline should go beyond listing the main points. The finished outline that accompanies your paper should contain enough detail so that readers can see your main and minor points and the structure of your paper.

The following is a preliminary outline for a paper on grain or grass-fed beef.

    I.  Thesis Statement

   II.  Advantages of Grain-Fed Beef

  III.  Advantages of Grass-Fed Beef

  IV.  Disadvantages of Grain-Fed Beef

   V.  Disadvantages of Grass-Fed Beef

  VI.  Evaluation of Arguments

 VII.  Works Cited

This is a satisfactory outline, but it doesn't have enough detail yet to tell much about the paper. It shows the main parts of the paper, but it doesn't tell anything about the research. This outline isn't much more than headings from the paper. Still, it is enough to get a writer started. It is consistent in its use of topics. Best of all, it shows a careful balance of viewpoints. With more writing and revising of the argument paper, the writer can produce a more detailed and helpful outline.

## ACTIVITY 1

After you have done most of your research—reading, note-taking, gathering ideas and data—prepare a preliminary outline for your research paper. Follow the form of the preceding example. Remember that your outline will be tentative—not finished until after you have completely written your paper.

# THE FORMAL OUTLINE MODEL

## Grain or Grass: What's the Beef?

*by Ryan Lampman*

Thesis: Although grain-fed beef is an efficient method of mass production, grass-fed beef is better for animals, humans, and the environment.

I. Advantages of Grain-Fed Beef

    A. Grain is mostly corn, which is cheap.

    B. People enjoy the taste and dependability of taste.

    C. Beef production is big business.

    D. Beef is an excellent source of protein.

    E. The cattle industry argues that its animals are treated well.

    F. The cattle industry also argues that the beef it produces is safe.

II. Advantages of Grass-Fed Beef

    A. Grass-fed beef represents an alternative to grain-fed beef.

        1. A *Time* article profiles rancher Jon Taggart.

        2. Michael Pollan profiles Joel Salatin.

    B. Grass-fed beef is a small but growing business.

    C. Eating grass-fed beef may have more health benefits beyond protein.

    D. Small grass-fed cattle businesses do not have a record of harmful health effects.

    E. Small grass-fed cattle businesses have a different work force than factory farms.

    F. Small grass-fed cattle businesses are environmentally friendly and sustainable.

III. Disadvantages of Grain-Fed Beef

    A. *Fast Food Nation* describes contamination in mass-produced beef.

    B. Meat is often irradiated to kill bacteria.

    C. Poor immigrants are the main labor force.

        1. They typically don't know English.

        2. They aren't given health benefits.

        3. They work the most dangerous jobs.

    D. Factory farms harm the environment.

        1. A major problem is the amount of manure produced.

        2. The smell is overpowering.

        3. CAFOs produce manure lagoons, contaminating local water.

        4. Methane from cattle is a potent gas contributing to global climate change.

IV. Disadvantages of Grass-Fed Beef

    A. Grass-fed beef is harder to find and more expensive than grain-fed beef.

    B. Grass-fed beef tastes differently than mass-produced beef.

        1. The meat is more lean and may taste stronger.

        2. The meat may not be as tender.

        3. A study in 2005 shows that consumers prefer grain-fed beef.

V. Evaluation of Arguments

    A. As omnivores, we need to ask "What should we eat?"

    B. We need to know that grass-fed beef offers more health benefits.

    C. We should know what happens in the production of our food.

    D. Pollan questions the reliability of Temple Grandin and her efforts to improve animal handling at factory farms.

    E. She is the only authority the National Cattlemen's Beef Association regularly cites.

    F. Schlosser of <u>Fast Food Nation</u> claims consumers have power to effect change.

    G. Pollan claims that habits of raising, killing, and eating animals would change if consumers saw what happens at factory farms and slaughterhouses.

VI. Works Cited

Anyone reading this outline will get a clear understanding of the subject, the thesis, the major and minor points, and the structure of the paper.

A formal outline like this helps you (and your readers) to think about the overall structure and coherence of your paper. A well-organized paper can also help your credibility—your ethos: it shows that you are a careful researcher-writer.

---

## GUIDELINES FOR MAKING AN OUTLINE

1. Begin with the thesis statement.
2. Make items as parallel as possible. It's helpful to use topic sentences from your paper when you can.
3. Using sentences helps readers understand an outline more readily, although you may choose to use phrases instead. But be consistent: use either all sentences or all phrases.

*Continued . . .*

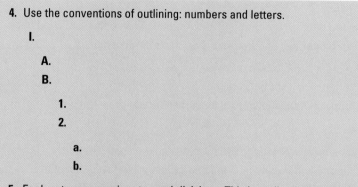

4. Use the conventions of outlining: numbers and letters.

    **I.**

        **A.**
        **B.**

            **1.**
            **2.**

                **a.**
                **b.**

5. Each category requires two subdivisions. This is outline logic: you shouldn't have a *I* without a *II*, an *A* without a *B*, a *1* without a *2*, an *a* without a *b*.

6. Try not to do an exhaustive outline, including every point and subpoint in your paper. Present the main divisions and points as well as some subpoints. (See Ryan's outline.)

---

**Ryan's Process Notes**

*Making an outline did help me. At first I did a simple prelim outline of advantages and disadvantages of grain-fed beef and grass-fed beef. It wasn't until I finished my paper that I went back and fleshed out the outline. This was interesting to do because I noticed that the outline itself showed that grain-fed beef presents more problems for animals, people, and the environment than grass-fed beef. I tried to be balanced. But in the research I did there was way more information on the disadvantages of grain-fed beef. The evidence toward the end becomes kind of lopsided—but this helps prove my thesis.*

*I wondered if I should have used another organization for the paper—the method presented in Chapter 2 where you present the opposing side before you present your side. This method works well for shorter papers. I could have divided my research paper in half: discuss advantages and disadvantages of grain-fed beef first, and then advantages and disadvantages of grass-fed beef. I guess this could still work. But alternating the advantages and then the disadvantages felt better, more carefully balanced. I'm hoping it might be easier for readers this way too, to process the information this way instead of processing two big opposing chunks of information and arguments.*

## ACTIVITY 2

After you have done most of your research—reading, note-taking, gathering ideas and data—prepare an outline for your research paper. Follow the form of the preceding example—a sentence outline. Remember that your outline will be tentative—not finished until after you have completely written your paper. ▪

# THE ABSTRACT

The abstract is a summary of your paper. Though not every paper requires an abstract, the longer and more technical your paper is, the more an abstract will help your readers. For casual readers, an abstract serves as a quick preview. For more serious readers, your abstract indicates the quality and significance of your work; it tells other researchers whether your paper may have relevance to their own research. An abstract helps you examine your project objectively. Though the abstract appears first—either before or after your outline—it is written last.

Here is an abstract written by student Caitlin Donegan for Honors Day at Alma College, a day when students attend presentations by other students who have done research projects. Her paper is titled "Borrowed Legends: Investigating the Histories of Catholic Saints":

> The ancient Celtic tribes knew Brigid as a goddess, patroness of healing, fertility, and inspiration; to Catholics, Bridget is a saint, best known for founding religious communities in Ireland and acts of startling generosity. In truth, a comparison shows that the two women are one and the same. At some point in history, Brigid underwent a transformation from a pagan fertility goddess to a virgin Catholic saint. This raises questions: How did such a transformation occur? What qualities did Brigid possess that made her so invaluable to two such different religions? To consider these issues, this paper examines three other deities that have undergone similar metamorphoses.

Before Honors Day, all students receive a program of abstracts of the research projects, which helps them decide which presentations to attend.

Because research must be indexed and catalogued, scholars need to follow procedures for clarity and accuracy in their abstract, using concise language. APA guidelines, for example, are highly restrictive, limiting the abstract to no more than 120 words.

## ACTIVITY 3

Write an abstract for your research paper. Assume you will present your paper at a conference on undergraduate research, and the conference director wishes to compile abstracts into a program for the conference. Or, write your abstract for a professional journal that interests you. Follow the journal's guidelines for abstracts (usually in the front of the journal). If you can't find journal guidelines, limit your abstract to a page, double spaced. ▬

## USING WHAT YOU HAVE LEARNED IN EARLIER CHAPTERS

An argument paper provides a good opportunity for you to apply ideas and skills you have learned throughout this book.

- Work on engaging your audience with your title, introduction, and conclusion. Review Chapter 1 for this information.
- Consider your use of persuasive appeals: logos, pathos, ethos. Review Chapter 1.

- Examine your paper looking for problems such as overgeneralizations and assumptions that suggest poor thinking. Look also for any insights you have generated that you hope readers will notice and appreciate. Review Chapter 2.
- Review Chapter 2 for information on kinds of evidence for arguing: using examples, reasons, authorities, and statistics.
- Review Chapter 3 to see if you might use certain strategies of argumentation such as description, narration, opposites, comparison, refutation, analogy, classification, cause and effect, definition.
- Review Chapter 4 to see if the Toulmin method can help you analyze and evaluate your argument and opposing arguments better.
- Review Chapter 5 to see if you might include a visual of some kind in your paper: a photograph, a chart, a table. (Remember that you will need to document these.)
- Review Interchapters 1–5 as you proofread and edit your writing. Apply what you've learned. Use punctuation variety to present your thoughts with more power: semicolons, dashes, colons. Use sentence variety to show that you can control the structure of your thoughts in different ways for different purposes. Go through your writing to omit needless words.

## ACTIVITY 4

Evaluate the title, introduction, and conclusion in your research paper. Do they work well? If not, revise them to give them more power. Then evaluate your use of persuasive appeals: logos, pathos, ethos. ▉

## WORKS CITED OR REFERENCES

Different instructors may require different formats for documentation. Before handing in your research papers, make sure you know which format is preferred. The two most widely used formats for in-text references are the Modern Language Association style and the American Psychological Association style (name and date). Both are illustrated in Chapter 9.

Your bibliography is a useful and necessary part of your paper: it lets your readers see how recent your research is and shows whether you are aware of important publications. It's a measure of how thorough your research is.

### The Bibliography Rule

You must not include any sources in your Works Cited or Reference lists that you haven't actually used in your paper: the bibliography must match your in-text references. Use only those works actually cited in your paper.

## A MODEL ARGUMENT PAPER

One of the most challenging tasks of research writers and readers is the evaluation of research. On what criteria can you determine the value of this kind of writing?

## ACTIVITY 5

Read the following argument paper using research. Then in your notebook, evaluate the paper by using "A Critical Thinker's Guide for Evaluating Writing" at the end of Chapter 1. Evaluate the paper's title, introduction, body, and conclusion. Evaluate the writer's persuasive appeals: logos, pathos, and ethos. Evaluate the writer's use of evidence and documentation. Evaluate the writer's voice and style. What are the paper's strengths and weaknesses? What feedback would you give this writer?

Lampman 1

Ryan Lampman

Professor Chen

English 101

26 November 2007

Grain or Grass: What's the Beef?

Imagine no summer barbeques—your dad or mom not standing behind a grill cooking hamburgers, laying slices of cheese on them, lifting them onto a platter, then everyone grabbing a bun and adding whatever they like: tomato, onion, relish, mustard, ketchup. It's hard for most Americans to imagine this. We love beef. However, most of us take for granted how beef is produced. There are important differences between beef raised for fast food and other kinds of beef. Although grain-fed beef is an efficient method of mass production, grass-fed beef is better for animals, humans, and the environment.

### Advantages of Grain-Fed Beef

The fast food industry depends on grain-fed beef. The primary ingredient of such beef is corn. Because corn is cheap to grow and farmers are subsidized by our government to grow it, mass-produced cattle are fed corn to fatten them up as fast as possible. The more quickly cattle are produced, the more beef can be ground up into hamburger.

People who eat hamburgers at McDonald's or Burger King enjoy the taste and how easy it is to eat a meal—especially in a car. In his book The Omnivore's Dilemma, Michael Pollan describes his experience as a boy: "I loved everything about fast food: the individual portions all wrapped up like presents . . . the pleasingly sequenced bite into a burger—the soft, sweet roll, the crunchy pickle, the savory moistness of the meat" (111). Haven't most of us experienced this same pleasure with fast food? The National Cattlemen's Beef Association states, "U.S. grain-fed beef has earned a worldwide reputation for its quality, consistency and taste" ("Feedlot Finishing"). Consumers like knowing that a Quarter Pounder will taste like a Quarter Pounder every time.

Beef production is big business. Beef.org, sponsored by the U.S. Department of Agriculture, states there are  most of which are small family businesses with herd sizes of 40 or so cattle ("Beef from Farm to Fork"). After cattle are raised on pasture or range land for 12–18 months, they go to huge feed lots for 3–6 months where they are fed grain from corn and gain "between 2.5 and 4 pounds per day" ("Feedlot Finishing"). Cattle are also given growth hormones, and because they share close quarters, they are given antibiotics to control outbreaks of disease. According to Beef.org, "Total beef production during 2005 was 24.7 billion pounds" ("Beef Industry at a Glance").

Many people eat mass-produced beef because it is an excellent source of protein, which is essential for our bodies. The Harvard School of Public Health explains online that protein is "in muscle, bone, skin, hair, and virtually every other body part or tissue. It makes up the enzymes that power many chemical reactions and the hemoglobin that carries oxygen in your blood." Proteins are complex. Not all are equal. Some are considered *complete* when they contain "all the amino acids needed to build new proteins." Beef, and other animal sources, contain complete proteins, but vegetables and fruits do not. This is why many people fear becoming vegetarian: they will need to find other sources of protein.

The cattle industry argues that its animals are treated well. Animalhandling.org is a Web site developed by Temple Grandin, PhD, of Colorado State University; it is sponsored by the American Meat Institute in Washington, D.C. In 2001 McDonald's hired Grandin to create a system of humane animal handling. Eric Schlosser, in his book <u>Fast Food Nation</u>, writes that for many years production lines at meat processing plants ran at "excessive" speeds, and "improper stunning" methods resulted in some cattle "being dismembered while fully conscious" (282). Grandin told Schlosser that after McDonald's threatened to stop buying beef from companies that mistreated cattle, these inhumane practices changed within a year. In her Web site, Grandin explains that the cattle industry cares about "animal welfare": it is im-portant that "meat is derived from animals raised and processed according to scientific standards and state and federal regulatory requirements."

The cattle industry also argues that the beef it produces is safe. Although there have been famous cases of *E. coli* microbes contaminating beef, such as in 1993 when four people died from eating undercooked hamburgers from Jack in the Box, the industry maintains it has addressed this problem. It also maintains that it has addressed the "mad cow disease" problem, caused when cattle were fed parts of other cattle (such as brains and spinal cords) and developed BSE (bovine spongiform encephalopathy). The National Cattlemen's Beef Association sponsors a Web site, BSEInfo.org, "to share scientific information about BSE and the systems in place to ensure U.S. beef remains the safest in the world" ("About BSE").

**Advantages of Grass-Fed Beef**

Grass-fed beef represents an alternative to grain-fed beef. The alternative seems radical now in our "fast food nation," but it was the traditional method of raising cattle until the mid 20th century. Cattle are ruminants, so called because their stomachs contain four compartments which can digest the cellulose of grass. People cannot digest grass, though we can eat many grains.

Lampman 4

In a <u>Time</u> magazine online article, "The Grass-Fed Revolution," Margot Roosevelt profiles rancher Jon Taggart. He used to graze his cattle on pastures sprayed with "weed killers and fertilizers"; when they were half-grown he shipped them to feedlots where they ate pesticide-treated corn, were "implanted with synthetic hormones to make them grow faster," and given antibiotics to resist disease; then they were trucked to huge slaughterhouses and butchered. Taggart has changed his operation:

> Today his 500 steers stay home on the range. And they're in the forefront of a back-to-the-future movement: 100% grass-fed beef. In the seven years since Taggart began to "pay attention to Mother Nature," as he puts it, he has restored his 1,350 acres in Grandview, Texas, to native tallgrass prairie, thus eliminating the need for irrigation and chemicals. He rotates his cattle every few days among different fields to allow the grass to reach its nutritional peak. And when the steers have gained enough weight, he has them slaughtered just down the road. Finally, he and his wife Wendy dry-age and butcher the meat in their store, Burgundy Boucherie. Twice weekly, they deliver it to customers in Fort Worth and Dallas happy to pay a premium for what the Taggarts call "beef with integrity—straight from pasture to dinner plate."

Taggart is not alone in paying attention to Mother Nature. Michael Pollan in <u>The Omnivore's Dilemma</u> profiles cattleman Joel Salatin who insisted that Pollan lie on his pasture with him to see firsthand the variety of grasses his cattle eat, including orchard grass, red and white clover, timothy, and sweet grass (187).

Grass-fed beef is a small but growing business. Roosevelt writes, "Within the past five years, more than 1,000 U.S. ranchers have switched herds to an all-grass diet." Yet grass-fed beef "still represents less than 1% of the nation's supply." The business is bound to stay small compared to huge factory farms because grass-fed cattle "take longer to reach slaughter weight," writes Pollan (71). Pollan adds that raising cattle on grass contains too many variables to be an efficient system on a

Lampman 5

mass scale. Different farmers raise different kinds of cattle, and unlike corn used as grain "grass is not a commodity" (202).

Yet eating grass-fed beef may have more health benefits for people beyond its source of protein. Grass is high in fiber while corn is not. Roosevelt claims that "grass-finished meat is higher than grain-finished meat in vitamin A and vitamin E, two anti-oxidants thought to boost resistance to disease." Pollan notes that grass-fed cattle "also contain conjugated linoleic acid (CLA), a fatty acid that some recent studies indicate may help reduce weight and prevent cancer, and which is absent from feed-lot animals" (267). He points out the value of omega-3 fatty acids found in grass-fed beef: they "play an indispensable role in human health, and especially in the growth and health of neurons—brain cells. . . . Researchers report that pregnant women who receive supplements of omega-3s give birth to babies with higher IQs" (267).

Small grass-fed cattle businesses do not have a record of harmful health ef-fects. Because cattle are raised locally on grass and grown at natural rates, because they are not trucked hundreds of miles to gorge on grain and to be pumped with hormones and synthetic antibiotics, because they are slaughtered locally, there is less chance for cattle to become diseased and to spread disease.

Small grass-fed cattle businesses are environmentally friendly and sustainable, based on traditional methods of raising cattle on pastures where the manure they produce is natural fertilizer. With such farming, pesticides are rarely used; no "nitrogen runoff or growth hormones [are] seeped into the watershed" (Pollan 182). Water to grow corn is not as depleted. Less petroleum is used for massive trucking of animals to factory farms. The air quality is cleaner. Without huge concentrations of cattle, there is less dust from dried manure carrying harmful microorganisms.

### Disadvantages of Grain-Fed Beef

Eric Schlosser's book <u>Fast Food Nation</u> presents a graphic indictment of cattle con-fined at factory farms. "The cattle now packed into feedlots get little exercise and live amid pools of manure" (202). He cites a USDA study in 1996 that found that "78.6 percent of the ground beef [sampled at processing plants] contained microbes that are spread primarily by fecal matter." While critics may point out that this USDA study was done in 1996, Michael Pollan argues the problem persists. Because animals are processed at industrial plants so quickly, up to 400 animals an hour, "sooner or later some of the manure caked on these hides gets into the meat we eat" (81–82). Bacteria in the manure includes *E. coli.* Although our stomachs contain strong acids that destroys most bacteria, some of it continues to live.

For this reason mass-produced beef is often irradiated, a controversial method of using x-rays or gamma rays to kill bacteria in meat. The USDA approves of meat irradiation, claiming, "Extensive scientific research has indicated that irradiated food is safe to eat" ("Industry Food Safety"). However, according to the Web site Sustainable Table, irradiation has not been proven safe. "The long-term health consequences of eating irradiated food are still unknown. Irradiation creates a complex series of reactions that literally rip apart the molecular structure of the food." The process can also change the "flavor, odor, texture, color and nutritional value" of beef ("Food Irradiation").

Huge processing plants that make the ground beef used at McDonald's and other fast food restaurants typically employ poor immigrants who don't know English and aren't given health benefits. Immigrants who have crossed the border from Mexico take jobs no one else wants. They live in poor housing, often run-down trailers or motels. To keep up with the fast pace of production, many workers use methamphetamine. Communities experience more crime (Schlosser 162).

Schlosser points out that immigrants work extremely dangerous jobs at the slaughterhouses. They wear "chain-mail" on their bodies as a protection from cutting themselves and from being cut accidentally by other workers (169). But many workers make mistakes because the line moves so fast. Schlosser declares, "Meatpacking is now the most dangerous job in the United States" (172). Citing data from

Lampman 7

the Bureau of Labor Statistics, he reports that the rate of traumatic injuries "is roughly thirty-three times higher than the national average in industry" (173). To make his point vivid, Schlosser uses these specific examples:

> At a National Beef plant in Liberal, Kansas, Homer Stull climbed into a blood-collection tank to clean it, a filthy tank thirty feet high. Stull was overcome by hydrogen sulfide fumes. Two coworkers climbed into the tank and tried to rescue him. All three men died. Eight years earlier, Henry Wolf had been overcome by hydrogen sulfide fumes while cleaning the very same tank; Gary Sanders had tried to rescue him; both men died; and the Occupational Safety and Health Administration (OSHA) later fined National Beef for its negligence. The fine was $480 for each man's death. (178)

That the fatal problem was repeated shows that the National Beef plant did not consider the issue important. That the fines were so small suggests that OSHA didn't consider these deaths significant.

Another major problem at factory farms or Concentrated Animal Feeding Operations (CAFOs) is the amount of manure produced by cattle and what is done with it. Michael Pollan, in an interview on PBS's <u>Frontline</u>, said the smell at factory farms is "overwhelming. . . . And it's not the smell of a cow on a farm. This is the smell of the bus station men's room. It's fierce. And you wear it in your clothing for days afterward" ("Industrial Meat"). Madeline Drexler, author of <u>Secret Agents: The Menace of Emerging Infections</u>, writes,

> The site of modern meat production is akin to a walled medieval city, where waste is tossed out the window, sewage runs down the street, and feed and drinking water are routinely contaminated by fecal material. Each day, a feedlot steer deposits 50 pounds of manure, as the animals crowd atop dark mountains composed of their own feces. ("Animal Farms")

Lampman 8

The main way CAFOs deal with their manure problem is to mix it with urine and water to produce manure lagoons ("Factory Farming"). Contaminants from this waste often leech into groundwater, streams, rivers, and lakes. Drinking water can be affected. Methane is another problem from manure. According to the Environmental Protection Agency, "Methane, produced as part of the animals' normal digestive process, is a potent greenhouse gas that contributes to global climate change" ("Animal Feeding Operations").

**Disadvantages of Grass-Fed Beef**

Grass-fed beef is harder to find and more expensive than grain-fed beef. Although there are many small grass-fed cattle operations around the country, customers need to locate them or to order beef online. One such place is Alderspring Ranch in Idaho where "beef is dry-aged 18–21 days, the old fashioned way" ("Dry-aging"). There are also larger companies such as Wild Oats (<wildoats.com>), which says on its Web site, "We guarantee that the all-natural meat products we carry from our long-term suppliers are raised without antibiotics, artificial hormones and growth-promoting drugs. The result is pure, delicious flavor and superior quality you can trust" ("Meat & Poultry").

Grass-fed beef tastes differently than mass-produced beef. Because the meat is more lean, the taste may be stronger. Doug Helman, the local butcher in Alma, says that grass-fed meat is not as tender as grain-fed beef; it contains less marbling, which affects texture and taste. Yet Alderspring Ranch claims its dry-aged beef contains more flavor and is more tender: "Dry-aging is very time consuming and expensive, requiring extra effort, storage, excellent facilities, and high-quality beef. . . . This is why dry-aged steak is offered only in fine restaurants, upscale grocery stores and gourmet steak companies." The <u>Journal of Animal Science</u> published a study in 2005 on consumer preferences of grain-fed beef versus grass-fed beef. It concluded that grain-fed beef rated higher for "flavor, juiciness, tenderness, and overall accept-ability." Yet it also acknowledged that consumers in the United States "might have become accustomed to the flavor of corn-fed beef and therefore prefer it" (Sitz et al.).

## Evaluation of Arguments

An *omnivore* is a person or animal that eats plants and animals. The dilemma that Michael Pollan addresses so fully in his book is this question: what should we eat? He argues that we should be smart with our choices. We should know, for example, that grass-fed beef offers more health benefits such as omega-3 fatty acids that help grow brain cells. We should know what happens in the production of the food we eat. We should know what the fast-food industry doesn't want us to know: how its factory farms treat animals, workers, and the environment.

However, Pollan and other proponents of grass-fed beef do not discuss at least two problems with this traditional method of raising cattle. If there were no factory farms, how much land would be required to feed cattle on pastures? What problems would this cause? Also, wouldn't the methane generated from cows on pastures continue to be a greenhouse gas contributing to climate change? These questions should be addressed.

Instead Pollan focuses on the extreme problems with meat produced for fast food. He explains how difficult it will be to make people aware of these problems. "Eating industrial meat takes an almost heroic act of not knowing or, now, forget-ting" (84). Indeed, after reading The Omnivore's Dilemma, Fast Food Nation or see-ing the film version of it, people will need to forget what they have learned in order to eat a Big Mac. But perhaps such forgetting is easier than Pollan suggests because most Americans are addicted to fast food.

Pollan also questions the reliability of Temple Grandin whose efforts reportedly have made animal handling at factory farms more humane. He says, "I realize I'm

relying on the account of its designer" (330). It is curious that she is the only authority that the National Cattlemen's Beef Association regularly cites. It is also curious
that little, if anything, is mentioned in the NCBA's Web sites about immigrant workers and the dangerous jobs they do at industrial meat packing plants.

Schlosser believes that consumers have more power than we think. We can
stop buying fast food. If enough people demand that McDonald's sell hamburgers
made with grass-fed beef, it will (269). But how many people will demand it, and
what will persuade enough people to demand it? Schlosser's and Pollan's books
will help, but it is doubtful they will have great impact. Most Americans love their
fast-food burgers too much to give them up. Pollan, however, has a possible
solution. We need to see more clearly what is happening to animals on a mass
scale in our country:

> Sometimes I think that all it would take to clarify our feelings about eat-
> ing meat, and in the process begin to redeem animal agriculture, would
> be to simply pass a law requiring all the sheet-metal walls of all the
> CAFOs, and even the concrete walls of the slaughterhouses, to be re-
> placed with glass. . . . Were the walls of our meat industry to become
> transparent, literally or even figuratively, we would not long continue to
> raise, kill, and eat animals the way we do. (332–333)

Lampman 11

Works Cited

"About BSE." BSEInfo.org 2007. 10 Nov. 2007 <http://www.bseinfo.org/AboutBSE.aspx>.

"Animal Farms." <u>Modern Meat</u>. <u>Frontline</u>. Public Broadcasting System 2005. 14 Nov. 2007

    <http://www-c.pbs.org/wgbh/pages/frontline/shows/meat/industrial/farms.html>.

"Beef from Farm to Fork." 2007. 10 Nov. 2007 <http://www.beef.org/resoBeefProduction.aspx>.

"Beef Industry at a Glance." 2007. 10 Nov. 2007 <http://www.beef.org/resoBeefProduction.aspx>.

"Dry-aging." Alderspring Ranch. n.d. 16 Nov. 2007

    <http://www.alderspring.com/cooking/html/dry_aging.html>.

Environmental Protection Agency. "Animal Feeding Operations." 14 Aug. 2007. 15 Nov. 2007

    <http://www.epa.gov/oecaagct/anafobmp.html>.

"Factory Farming." <u>Sustainable Table</u>. n.d. 15 Nov. 2007

    <http://www.sustainabletable.org/issues/factoryfarming/>.

"Feedlot Finishing." 2007. 11 Nov. 2007 <http://www.beef.org/resoBeefProduction.aspx>.

"Food Irradiation." <u>Sustainable Table</u>. n.d. 15 Nov. 2007

    <http://www.sustainabletable.org/issues/irradiation/>.

Grandin, Temple. "Animal Welfare 101." <u>Animalhandling.org</u>. n.d. 12 Nov. 2007

    <http://www.animalhandling.org/animalwelfare101.htm>.

Harvard School of Public Health. "Protein." 2007. 11 Nov. 2007

    <http://www.hsph.harvard.edu/nutritionsource/protein.html>.

Helman, Doug. Personal Interview. 12 Nov. 2007.

"Industrial Meat." <u>Modern Meat</u>. <u>Frontline</u>. Public Broadcasting System 2005. 16 Nov. 2007

    <http://www-c.pbs.org/wgbh/pages/frontline/shows/meat/industrial/consolidation.html>.

"Meat & Poultry." Wild Oats Marketplace 2007. 16 Nov. 2007

    <http://www.wildoats.com/u/Department/meat_&_poultry/>.

Pollan, Michael. <u>The Omnivore's Dilemma: A Natural History of Four Meals</u>. New York:

    Penguin, 2006.

Roosevelt, Margot. "The Grass-Fed Revolution." <u>Time</u> 11 June 2006. 11 Nov. 2007

    <http://www.time.com/time/magazine/article/0,9171,1200759,00.html>.

Lampman 12

Schlosser, Eric. <u>Fast Food Nation: The Dark Side of the All-American Meal</u>. New York: Harper-

Perennial, 2005.

Sitz, B. M., C. R. Calkins, D. M. Feuz, W. J. Umberger, and K. M. Eskridge. "Consumer Sen-

sory Acceptance and Value of Domestic, Canadian, and Australian Grass-Fed Beef

Steaks." <u>Journal of American Science</u> 83.12 (2005): 2863–2868. ProQuest. Alma Col-

lege Lib., Alma, MI. 16 Nov. 2007 <http://www.proquest.com>.

United States Department of Agriculture. "Industry Food Safety." 22 Feb. 2001. 14 Nov.

2007 <http://www.ers.usda.gov/Briefing/IndustryFoodSafety/unconventech.htm>.

**Ryan's Process Notes**

This argument paper was more challenging and difficult than I thought it would be. For example, it's hard to write with sources without using too many direct quotes. Who am I to say something any better than an expert like Michael Pollan? I tried not to use strings of direct quotes. I tried to paraphrase information yet still cite sources for it. I also discovered this method: while writing my draft, I used direct quotes whenever I felt I had to. Then when I revised my draft, I was able to take many of these quotes out—I was able to use my own language to express the information, much of which was common knowledge found in most of my sources. This helped.

I could tell that when I revised my rough draft, my paper was stronger. I realized a few paragraphs didn't have a clear topic sentence. So I worked on that. I didn't end up using some of the sources I thought I would. I had read a book, <u>The Way We Eat: Why Our Food Choices Matter</u>, by Peter Singer and Jim Mason. It was insightful, and I know it helped inform me, but I never needed to quote from it. Yet I wanted to. Singer is such a renowned expert in animal rights. I'm afraid I might rely too much on Pollan's book. But that's the way my paper worked out. Pollan was an excellent source for me. So was Schlosser. I trusted them as writers, researchers, and authorities. I've realized I can't control everything that happens when I write a draft. Maybe subconsciously choices are being made that I can't control. I need to let them happen. A lot of incubation happens when you write a research paper over a few weeks.

All in all, I'm satisfied with my argument paper. It took lots of hard work and time. I never figured I'd learn so much. Also, from writing this I now know how to do research and how to write a decent paper. I know the process. I know how much commitment it takes.

# MLA GUIDELINES FOR MANUSCRIPT FORMAT

To understand current MLA guidelines (6th edition), please review the report and argument paper presented in this chapter. Follow the format of those papers and this information:

**Professional appearance:** Use standard white typing paper. If you don't have a good printer, copy your work to a disk and take it where you can use a good printer. Use one side of the paper only. Laser print is the highest quality and is recommended. Use standard size type (about 12 point or "pica"); avoid smaller type sizes.

Most instructors prefer that pages be stapled together. Don't pin, fold, or tear corners to fasten the pages together. Covers are not recommended: check with your instructor.

**Identification and title:** Title pages are optional for MLA. Ask your instructor. If no title page is desired, put your name, your professor's name, the course number, and the date in the upper-left (not right) corner of the first page of your paper. Center your title. See examples of the report and argument paper in this chapter. Don't underline or put quotation marks around the title of your paper.

If your instructor requires an outline, use a title page first, followed by the outline, then your paper. For a title page, center all information. Place the title one-third down the page. Center your name in the middle of the page. Near the bottom of the page, center the course name, professor's name, and date.

To paginate your outline, use small roman numerals: in the upper right-hand corner type Lampman i, Lampman ii . . .

After your outline, the text of your paper will begin on page one: Lampman 1. Repeat your title and center it.

**Pagination:** Number *every* page, including your Works Cited pages. For MLA style, number each page with an arabic numeral (1, 2, 3 . . . ) in the upper right-hand corner. Use your last name as a header: Lampman 1. Don't write "page" or "p." or use anything other than your own name as a header.

**Line Spacing and Margins:** All text should be double-spaced, including indented quotes. Don't add extra line spaces above or below long quotes. Double-space your Works Cited pages, too.

Use a one-inch margin on all edges of your paper, except for the top of pages where you may use a half-inch margin to accommodate your last name and page numbers in a header. Indent each paragraph five spaces.

**Long Quotations:** Set off a long quote if it is longer than four typed lines. Indent it 10 spaces (or two tabs). Double-space it, and don't add spacing above or below it. Don't use quotation marks around a long quote; that would be redundant.

**Headings:** MLA provides no guidelines on using headings or subheadings. Headings are useful, however, in long research papers: they provide visual breaks and help readers quickly identify sections of the paper. See the argument paper in the chapter for an example of using headings.

Proportional Contribution to Premature Death

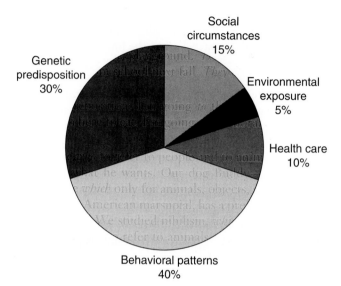

*FIGURE 10.1* Determinants of Health and Their Contribution to Premature Death.
Source: Schroeder, Steven A. "We Can Do Better—Improving the Health of the American People." New England Journal of Medicine 357 (2007): 1222.

| *TABLE 1* Percent of Students Reporting Illicit Drug Use, 2005–2006 | | | | | | |
|---|---|---|---|---|---|---|
| | **8th Grade** | | **10th Grade** | | **12th Grade** | |
| | **2005** | **2006** | **2005** | **2006** | **2005** | **2006** |
| Past month | 8.5% | 8.1% | 17.3% | 16.8% | 23.1% | 21.5% |
| Past year | 15.5 | 14.8 | 29.8 | 28.7 | 38.4 | 36.5 |
| Lifetime | 21.4 | 20.9 | 38.2 | 36.1 | 50.4 | 48.2 |

Source: "Juveniles and Drugs." Office of National Drug Control Policy. 22 Mar. 2007. 12 Sept. 2007 <http://www.whitehousedrugpolicy.gov/drugfact/juveniles/index.html>.

**Visuals:** Visual material includes charts, drawings (including cartoons if appropriate), graphs, maps, and photographs. They should be labeled as figures or tables.

Label and number all visuals consecutively throughout your paper. If you have both figures and tables in your paper, label figures *Figure 1*, *Figure 2*, and so on; tables *Table 1*, *Table 2*, and so on. (You may abbreviate Fig. 1, Fig. 2 . . . ) The label and number for a figure or any kind of visual material are usually placed below the figure, followed by a caption on the same line (see Figure 10.1). The label and number for a table are usually placed *above* the table. All figures and tables should be numbered consecutively throughout your paper.

A table is usually columns of numbers. Capitalize all significant words in the title of a table. A table requires a caption that identifies the subject of the table. Below the table, cite the source for it.

Visuals should be introduced at the place in your paper where you mention them, if that is possible, or as close thereafter as practical. If there are too many such figures, or if it's impossible to position them close to your mention of them, place them at the end of your paper in an appendix.

**Works Cited:** Your Works Cited should begin on a new page. Follow the format you see in the report and argument paper in this chapter.

Works Cited should be in alphabetical order. Use the last names of authors. If a work has no author, use the first word of the title (not including *A*, *An*, or *The*).

The first line of each work cited is not indented, but subsequent lines are. This enables any reader to quickly locate the last name of authors or titles of works with no authors.

Web addresses (URLs) must be divided at the end of a line only where there are slashes in the address. MLA requires that each URL be enclosed in angle brackets: <http://www.time.com>. If your computer highlights and underlines URLs, try to undo this.

# APA GUIDELINES FOR MANUSCRIPT FORMAT

**Professional Appearance:** Use standard white typing paper. If you don't have a good printer, copy your work to a disk and take it where you can use a good printer. Use one side of the paper only.

**Title Page and Identification:** The title page is required. Page headers as well as running heads should be abbreviations of your title. For the title page, center all information. Place the title in the middle of the page. Near the bottom of the page, center the writer's name, course name, professor's name, and date.

**Pagination:** Every page, starting with the title page, should be numbered. The title page should be numbered i; if you use an abstract page, it should be numbered ii.

The upper left corner of each page of text should contain a running head: an abbreviated title of your paper, followed by five spaces and then the page number.

**Line Spacing and Margins:** Type all text double-spaced only. Do not single-space indented quotations. Double-space your Reference pages, too. Footnotes, however, are single-spaced. Indent each paragraph five spaces.

**Long Quotations:** Set off a long quote if it is longer than 40 words. Indent it five spaces (or one tab) from the left margin. Double-space it, and don't add spacing above or below it. Don't use quotation marks around a long quote.

**Headings:** Center major headings, and capitalize all major words.

**Visuals:** Visual material includes tables and figures (charts, drawings, graphs, and photographs). Label and number all visuals consecutively throughout your paper: *Figure 1*, *Figure 2*, and so on; tables *Table 1*, *Table 2*, and so on.

The label and number for a table are placed *above* the table. The label and number for a figure are placed *below* the figure, followed by a caption on the same line.

Visuals should be introduced at the place in your paper where you mention them, if that is possible, or as close thereafter as practical. If there are too many visuals, or if it's impossible to position them close to your mention of them, place them at the end of your paper in an appendix.

**References:** References should begin on a new page. See the following model APA paper.

References should be in alphabetical order. Use the last names of authors. If a work has no author, use the first word of the title (not including *A, An,* or *The*).

Check Chapter 9, "Documentation," for more information on how to do References.

## A MODEL RESEARCH PAPER USING APA STYLE

The following paper is the report used earlier in this chapter, but it is written here using APA style.

Saturated i

Saturated by Color

Mary Ellen Wendt

English 101

Professor Chen

November 20, 2007

Saturated 1

*We do not see things as they are; we see things as we are.*

~ *saying from the Talmud*

Science tells us that dogs see in black and white, a world in shades of gray. Bees, on the other hand, see colors of the spectrum beyond what humans see, into the ultraviolet, so they can locate pollen in flowers. Humans fall somewhere in the middle. We see red bricks, red roses, tired red eyes. We see blue skies and blue waters. We see green and know it is spring. But unlike any other animal, we do much more than see color: we make it very much a part of who we are. Our lives are saturated by color.

Designers know about the power and psychology of color, how to sway an audience in a particular direction. As Boyle (2001) explains it, "Designers use colors to ignite certain emotions in their target audiences or facilitate brand recognition. Who doesn't recognize the bright orange of the Tide box or the signature red of Coca-Cola?" (p. 11). They know, too, about "cool" colors and "warm" colors, terms used by decorators and painters to describe the implied "temperature" of a color (Horton, 1994, p. 171). A room painted a warm color—yellow with a hint of orange, for example—is supposed to give the room a cozy, harmonious feeling, while a room painted light blue will give it a cheerful and open feeling. Designers also know that most shades of blue are considered professional, black connotes seriousness and sensuality, and white is pure and fresh. Businesses often use color to create a very specific persona, as in UPS, which recently spent $20 million on the new brown and gold shield logo (Griswold, 2003). Sometimes, though, businesses use color for other purposes.

Until it was pointed out to me, I was unaware of the color palette for fast-food chains: they almost always use red and/or yellow. McDonald's famous golden arches and red sign, Wendy's yellow sign with the little red-haired girl, Burger King's red letters sandwiched in a yellow bun—these choices are anything but arbitrary. It turns out that red and yellow are food colors: when we see them, we think of warmth and fullness and satisfaction. Apparently the combination of red and yellow taps into our psychic need to eat. According to Boyle (2001, p. 23), red "has the most energy" of all colors. When you combine this with warm yellow, the most attention-getting color, you have not only a sign that grabs the attention of those driving by, but a winning combination of warmth and an urgency for food—unless you live outside the United States.

We are used to the colors that surround us and assume that everyone thinks as we do. But this is not true, and this has become more important than ever with the ubiquity of the Internet; Web designers often have to appeal to a global market. For example, Oliu, Brusaw, and Alred (2004) tell us:

> Red commonly indicates warning or danger in North America, Europe, and Japan. In China, however, red symbolizes joy. In Europe and North America, blue generally has a positive connotation; in Japan, the color represents villainy. In Europe and North America, yellow represents caution or cowardice; in Arab countries, yellow generally means fertility or strength. (p. 543)

In addition to these contradictions, some Asian cultures think of black as pure and holy, while white symbolizes evil. In their culture, the good guy would not be wearing white.

Despite the various meanings of some colors between cultures, other colors seem to cross cultures. Green, for example, is the sign of life and health nearly everywhere, unless you desaturate it—add grey, white, black, or some yellow. A drab yellowish green called avocado green hardly looks lively. If your grandmother has an avocado green stove, you'll know what I mean.

Those avocado green appliances were not a mistake, though some people today might have trouble believing it. In the seventies, gold and avocado green were all the rage. Boyle (2001) explains the colors associated with the last five decades of the 20th century: "The 1950s were pink," he says, pastels of innocence that covered homes and cars and lipsticks (p. 22). In the '60s, bright colors like oranges, yellows, and reds rebelled against the softness of the fifties, while the '70s shifted once again, this time into earthy tones (p. 22). The golds and browns and rusts of the seventies, the era of environmental awareness, led to the '80s, what Boyle says was "billed as the Color Conscious Decade" as our culture professionalized with navy and khaki and muted mauve (p. 22). By the '90s, green—but not avocado green—was in style along with more muted tones of yellows and reds. Boyle doesn't get to this century, but as I walk through the mall, look at a parking lot, or drive down the street in my neighborhood, it seems clear that this decade is in love with bright colors: bright blue houses, primary red and yellow clothing, even purple and bright yellow cars. While I notice some still clinging to the professional look of the '90s, our parking lots and streets are looking more like rainbows every day. IKEA even has a new slogan, "Be brave, not beige." Their new TV ad boasts rooms of furniture and accessories in loud colors that contrast vividly with montages of beige furniture and shoes, beige food and a beige brain. The message seems to be that we are done toning things down.

This brightening of the 21st century says much about the mood of our lives these days. We are busy—too busy, most would say—and depressed more than ever before. We need bright hues and deep saturation to keep us from losing perspective. Horton (1994) lists people's reactions to color. For example, red is associated with aggression, impulsiveness, and optimism to name a few. We react to green by associating it with freshness, hope, health, and prosperity. Purple creates strong reactions: people tend to either love it or hate it, perhaps because purple is associated with vanity, wit, and spirituality. On the other hand, colors like gray make us think of restraint, barrenness, grief, and indifference, black of death, grief, and gloom, and brown of duty, reliability, and poverty (p. 175). This explains the need for such bright colors—and perhaps those who surround themselves with more depressing colors like black.

Feng shui, the Chinese art of creating balance through your surroundings, is becoming increasingly popular in the United States. Not surprisingly, feng shui relies heavily on color. According to Wang (2007), "Feng shui uses [the] natural magic of colors to transform your life." Feng shui divides colors into yin colors and yang colors. Yin colors—blue, black, purple, and white—are supposed to bring about relaxation and healing, while yang colors—yellow and orange and other "fire and wood" colors like red and brown—provide energy and motivation. Feng shui is often very specific about how to use color; for example, houses facing the south should be painted white, blue, or grey.

Whether we work toward total feng shui harmony in our homes or just want to make sure we like our walls, color saturates our lives, from what clothes to wear for a date to the billion-dollar campaign of Pepsi to "own" royal blue. UPS now "owns" their brown color, a color of dependability and simplicity. Celebrities like Johnny Cash, "The Man in Black," and Prince with his obsession with purple frequently use color to define themselves, sometimes, like the musician Pink, even making their signature color also their name. However we look at it, color has significance and meaning.

*References*

Boyle, C. (2001). *Color harmony for the web.* Gloucester: Rockport Publishers.

Griswold, A. (2003, March 25). Martin presents a new look: UPS. *Adweek.com.* Retrieved November 12, 2007 from

http://www.adweek.com/aw/national/article_display.jsp?vnu_content_id=1848494

Horton, W. (1994). *The icon book: Visual symbols for computer systems and documentation.* John Wiley, 163–181.

Oliu, W. E., Brusaw, C. T., & Alred, G. G. (2004). Designing effective documents and visuals. *Writing that works: Communicating effectively on the job* (7th ed.). Boston: Bedford/St. Martin's, 542–546.

Wang, M. Z. (n.d.). Significance of colors in feng shui practice. *The spiritual Feng Shui.* Retrieved November 12, 2007 from

http://www.thespiritualFengShui.com/Feng-Shui-color.php

## ACTIVITY 6

The beginning of Chapter 1 contains a quote by Eckhart Tolle: "When you give more attention to the doing than to the future result . . . your doing then becomes not only a great deal more effective, but infinitely more fulfilling and joyful." Through using this book have you given more attention to the process of doing? Has this in turn helped you generate papers showing clear and persuasive critical thinking? I hope you have learned more than you expected and that, as in the Buddha parable, you found unexpected grapes or eurekas along the way that helped you keep going. Keep looking for them. They are there.

Throughout this book you have been asked to notice details, ideas, and arguments; to notice appeals to logos, pathos, and ethos; to notice insights, assumptions, and overgeneralizations; and to notice words and sentences: how you say your message is part of what you say. Noticing leads to discovery: your job as a critical thinker is to discover. In doing so you become more aware of yourself and the world.

Please write in your notebook a page or two about your growth since the semester began. Give a candid analysis of changes you have noticed in your ability to think, write, and read.

# Concise Handbook of Grammar, Mechanics, and Usage

HANDBOOK
Sentences

HANDBOOK
Punctuation

HANDBOOK
Mechanics

HANDBOOK
Sentences

## SENTENCES

Sentences are units of thought. A popular definition of a sentence is "a complete thought." You may write in paragraphs, essays, and longer units of text, but you create text one thought at a time, one sentence at a time.

Thoughts and ideas, like sentences, are composed of a subject—for example, "Thomas Edison." But what about Thomas Edison? To make a sentence, you need a statement about this subject. Here is one: "Thomas Edison *inspired Henry Ford.*" If you wanted to support this sentence with specific evidence, you would then produce more sentences, such as this: "Ford admired Edison so much he obtained Edison's last breath bottled up in a test tube." (The story of "Edison's Last Breath" is available on-line at <http://members.tripod.com/yakich/palmer.html>.)

There are many possibilities for sentences and ideas, some better than others. In this section of the book, you will examine some of the common problems that distort writers' ideas and sentences.

## What Is a Sentence?

When language is simple, it is easy to identify sentences, but in more complex language, the identification can be more difficult. When your thoughts are clear, your sentences should be too, but complicated thoughts and complex language can pose difficulties for writers.

A sentence is "complete" when it has a subject and a verb and when its patterns meet our expectations. The importance of the subject is that it establishes what the verb can be, whether the verb must be *is* or *are*, for example. Finding the subject is an important step in achieving agreement between the subject and its verb.

## Finding the Subject of a Sentence

How can you find the subject of a sentence, and why is that important?

## ACTIVITY 1

See if you can underline the subject(s) for each of the following sentences.

1. Seymour cleaned his glasses.
2. Scientists are now able to produce identical animals through a process known as cloning.
3. Although eurekas may be big or small, they give us energy when we write.

You can usually find the subject of a sentence by asking *who* or *what* is the actor in the sentence: who is (or was) doing the action of the sentence? The subject is often first or early in the sentence, but not always. For example: "Last night because of all the noise outside, I read <u>Moby Dick</u> until nearly dawn." Ask yourself, *who* is or was doing the action in the sentence (who was reading <u>Moby Dick</u>)?

However, not all subjects need to be creatures that can "act" in the sense of doing something like singing. Some "actions" may be purely mental. Sentence "subjects" can be anything people talk about. For example, "*Intelligence* was once thought to be entirely genetic." A subject such as "Intelligence" isn't really an actor, but if you rely on the test for subjects (ask who or what "were once thought to be genetic") you can find even abstract subjects like this one.

### Why Is Finding the Subject Important?

It is important for writers and readers to find the subject in a sentence because of the relation of the subject to the verb. The reader needs to know what you are writing about, and also the subject and verb must "agree." Whether the verb should be *were* or *is* depends on the subject. Plural subjects need plural verbs. The verb states what the subject is or was or will be "doing." Many verbs express action or behavior such as *go, speak, see, feel, think.* Other verbs express a state of being such as *am, is, are, was, were.* But regardless of the kind of verb you use, it must agree with the subject of your sentence.

### Subject and Verb Agreement Problems
### Any Verb Must "Match" Its Subject

A singular subject requires a singular verb; a plural subject requires a plural verb.

> The *sound* of the waves *puts* me to sleep. [singular]
> *Seymour wants* to clean his glasses. [singular]
> *Seymour and Buddy hope* to go hiking in Vermont. [plural]

How can you tell whether a verb is singular or plural? Most verbs (but not all) follow the same pattern for singular and plural. Study the following lists for a moment. Can you tell which are the singular and which are the plural verbs?

| | |
|------|-------|
| go | goes |
| have | has |
| think | thinks |

A simple test will reveal which are the singular and which are the plural verbs. Say *we* before the verb. *We* is a plural pronoun (so is *they*) and the verbs *go*, *have*, and *think* are plural verbs. They go together: we go, they have, we think. To find a singular verb, say *he*, *she* or *it* before the verb: he goes, she thinks, it has. Only these three pronouns—*he*, *she*, *it*—take a different verb form. All other pronouns take the same verb form: I go, you go, we go, they go. Only *he*, *she*, or *it* changes the verb to *goes*. Therefore, use only *we* or *they* to find plural verbs (in the little verb test). Use only *he*, *she*, or *it* to find singular verbs.

Finding the correct subject and verb can be difficult enough with simple subjects, but agreement problems can be more difficult when the subjects are compound, that is, when they are joined by *or* and *nor*; or when joined by *either/or*, *neither/nor*, or *not/but*, or the indefinite pronouns such as *each*, *everyone*, and *everybody*.

## ACTIVITY 2

See if you can select the correct verb for the subjects in these sentences. Try to say whether the verb is singular or plural. If you're not sure, give your best answers.

1. George and Franny (plans/plan) to develop their own software company.
2. Brazil or Argentina (is/are) where we would like to take our vacation.
3. The cheeses or the crackers (was/were) the cause of so much diarrhea at the party.
4. Neither the eel nor the glass snake (is/are) a true snake.
5. Everybody (is/are) entitled to (her/their) own opinions.

Why is "agreement" so important? One answer to that is simply that there are many ways for subjects and verbs to go wrong. The other part is that many people believe agreement mistakes are serious grammatical errors, serious enough to lead readers astray and to cast doubt on the writer's credibility. Your sentences should flow along without hitches or sudden confusion that might cause your reader to stop and possibly back up to reread . . . trying to figure out what you are saying.

### Agreement with Compound Subjects

*Subjects Joined by Or or Nor.* Singular subjects joined by *or* or *nor* take a singular verb. Plural subjects joined by *or* or *nor* require a plural verb.

> *Lori or Takisha is* available to take Sharon's place.
> *Neither he nor she has* been infected by the flu bug.
> Either the *women* or the *men are* supposed to decide the homecoming theme.

*Using Either . . . Or, Neither . . . Nor, or Not . . . but.* When *either . . . or*, *neither . . . nor*, or *not . . . but* joins a singular subject to a plural subject, the verb should agree with the closer one.

> *Neither* the dog *nor* the cats were responsible for the mess in the garage.
> *Not* the cats *but* the dog *was* responsible for the mess in the garage.

*Each, Every, Everybody Require Singular Verbs.* *Each*, *every*, *everybody* and most other indefinite pronouns require singular verbs. (See Pronoun Agreement Problems.)

*Each* of the students *writes* an essay in an hour. [not *write*]
*Everyone* in the deal *is* concerned about the financial loss. [not *are*]
*Neither* of the book reviews *gives* a fair analysis. [not *give*]

*Verbs and Who, Which, or That.* After *who*, *which*, or *that*, the verb agrees with the word the pronoun identifies.

She is one of those *lawyers who earn* high salaries.
[*who* refers to *lawyers*; the verb *earn* must be plural]
Jerry is one of those *students who excel* in every class.
[who refers to students; the verb excel must be plural]
Jerry is a student who excels in every class.
[*who* refers to a *student*; thus the verb *excels* must be singular]



## Pronoun Agreement Problems

Readers expect subjects and verbs to agree. And pronouns too can have agreement problems, both before and after the verb. Pronouns must agree with the words to which they refer.

## ACTIVITY 3

Try to determine whether the pronouns and verbs in these sentences agree. Underline anything that seems like an error. Try to give a brief explanation of the error, such as "needs plural verb" or "needs singular subject."

1. Everyone has a hobby or some special activity they love to do.
2. When someone eats in a restaurant, they may need to worry about secondhand smoke.
3. None of the boys on the team was older than 13.
4. Everybody needs some kind of engine to provide drive in their life.
5. Everyone in the major cities were notified of the possible threat.

Words such as *all*, *another*, *any*, *anybody*, *anyone*, *few*, *each*, *either*, *everyone*, *everybody*, *many*, *most*, *neither*, *none*, *no one*, *one*, *several*, *some*, *somebody*, *someone*, and *something* are called indefinite pronouns. In formal writing situations, these pronouns are generally used as singular words that require singular verbs and singular pronouns for agreement.

Incorrect: *Everyone* needs positive reinforcement in their lives.
[*Everyone* is singular but *their* is plural]

Revised: *All people* need positive reinforcement in *their lives.*
or *Everyone* needs positive reinforcement in *his life.*
or *Everyone* needs positive reinforcement in *her lif*
or *Everyone* needs positive reinforcement in *his* or *her life.*

(The Modern Language Association recommends against these *his/her, him/her,* and other split constructions. Try to rephrase your sentence instead: "We all need positive reinforcement.")

Incorrect: Love makes a *person* who they are.
[*person* is singular, but *they* is plural]
Revised: Love makes *people* who they are.
or Love makes a *person* who *she* is.
or Love makes a *person* who *he* is.

In some cases, the correct sentence may sound awkward or unnatural. In that case, you need to revise your sentence until it sounds both correct and natural.

Incorrect: *Everybody* will have *their* moment of fame.
[*Everybody* is singular, but *their* is plural]
Revised: "We will *all have* our moment of fame."

*Exception to the Rule:* The following pronouns agree with singular *or* plural verbs and other pronouns: *all, half, any, more, part, none,* and *some.* They agree with singular verbs when they refer to singular words but agree with plural verbs when they refer to plural words.

All *patriots* are ready to surrender *their lives* for *their* country.
*More women and children live* on welfare than any other people.
*Some* of the *recruits were* in the service less than six months.
*Some vandal has* broken the window to the storeroom.

Other agreement problems concern collective nouns, clauses, pronouns as objects, and choices between *who* and *whom.*

## Agreement with Collective Nouns

Though collective nouns identify groups (the *troop is* [not *are*] ready), treat them as singular, requiring singular verbs and pronouns for agreement: the *army,* the *band,* the *faculty,* the *corporation.* Words like these require singular pronouns and verbs.

The *company knows* what *it is* doing.
[Not: The *company* knows what *they are* doing.]
The *band* will record *its* first song next week.
[Not: The *band* will record *their* first song next week.]
*Scotland College* claims *its* athletes are scholars and *its* scholars are athletes.
[Not: *Scotland College* claims *their* athletes are scholars and *their* scholars are athletes.]

## Clauses, Dependent and Independent

Before you can go much further with subjects and objects, you need a brief look at clauses. A clause is a group of words containing a subject and a verb—and it may have other components, such as objects. What pattern do you see in these clauses?

When it snows . . .
If it rains . . .
Until we meet again . . .
. . . because no one said we couldn't.
. . . even if we must stay home.

Every clause has a subject and verb. Each dependent clause is less than a complete sentence. Clauses may start a sentence, end a sentence, or appear anywhere within a "complex" sentence, but dependent clauses alone are not full sentences. They do not make complete thoughts. They are called "dependent" clauses because they depend on some other clause to make the thought complete. The main clause contains the main subject and verb. Dependent clauses contain secondary subjects and verbs.

A sentence is also a clause because it has a subject and a verb. The difference between a clause and a sentence is this: a sentence is a clause that makes sense by itself; a sentence is a complete thought that can stand on its own—it is an *independent* clause. "When *it rained* . . ." is a clause because it has a subject and a verb, but it isn't a sentence—it is incomplete. It is called a dependent clause because it *depends* on the rest of the sentence: "When it rained, *we all went home*." The clause "we all went home" is an *independent* clause because it can stand by itself. It contains the main subject and verb.

## ACTIVITY 4

In the following activity, try to determine how many clauses each sentence contains and whether they are dependent or independent. Try to draw a line under the main clause(s).

1. If it snows, we must stay home.
2. If it snows, we must stay home until it quits.
3. Though he was quite a young man, George Washington proved to be an able soldier, and he was also a superior politician, though he preferred the agrarian work of his home, Mount Vernon.  ▓

Sentences can have more than one independent clause and more than one dependent clause, each with its own subject and verb. For example, here are two dependent clauses: *"When the rain stopped* but *before the sun appeared . . . ."*

Sentences may also have more than one independent clause (both of which could stand alone as an independent sentence):

The rain finally stopped, and we all went home.
After the rain stopped, *we decided* to go to the theater, but *we changed* our minds later when the rain started again.

In theory, there is no limit to the number of clauses a sentence might have. The second example above has four clauses.

## Pronouns as Subjects and Objects in Clauses

Pronouns can be troublesome because they change spelling depending on how they are used in a sentence. Often your ear will tell you when a pronoun is incorrect: "Him is cleaning out the garage." But in more complicated sentences, it can be difficult to determine which is the correct form of a pronoun.

## ACTIVITY 5

Select the pronoun you would use in each of these sentences, and then in a few words explain your selection: for example, *subject pronoun* or *object pronoun*.

1. (We/Us) guys were getting ready for a game of softball later in the day.
2. The general expected (we/us) new recruits would learn the drill quickly.
3. After conquering the Turks, Dracula ordered (they/them) to build (he/him) a fortress.
4. The police were certain it was "Light Fingers Maria" (who/whom) had opened the safe.
5. (Whoever/Whomever) has the loot is probably the one who stole it.

Pronouns can serve as subjects or objects in clauses. Which form of a pronoun is correct depends on how the pronoun is used in its clause. But if the correct form sounds awkward, even though "correct," you should revise your sentence.

Because only Jeremy would go, we sent *him*.
It was *he whom* we sent.
  [Technically this sentence is "correct," but it sounds so unnatural that you should revise it until it sounds both correct and natural: "We sent him."]
Merriam discovered the new puppy was for *her,* a birthday gift.

*Using Subject Pronouns. I, we, you, he, she, it, they, who,* and *whoever* are subject pronouns. In addition to using them as subjects, you should use these pronouns after the "being" verbs of *am, is, are, was, were, be, being,* and *been,* including the future and perfect forms: *It will be she. It has been I.* After one of the "being" verbs, nouns and pronouns are technically not objects because being verbs express no action. Therefore, after a "being" verb you should use a *subject* pronoun.

It is *I*. [not *me*]
The one they wanted was *she*. [not *her*]
When the voice on the phone asked for Phil, he said, "This is *he*." [not *him*]
This is *who*? [not *whom*]

*Using Possessive Pronouns. My, mine, our, ours, your, yours, his, her, hers, its, their, theirs,*
and *whose* are possessive pronouns. Note that pronouns do not use apostrophes: they
indicate possession with a change in spelling.

I once had a dog; it was *my* dog.
Many people of poor countries are struggling for *their* survival.
I gave my friend a cat: "Now that cat is *yours*," I said.

*Using Object Pronouns. Me, us, you, him, her, it, them, themselves, whom, whomever* are
object pronouns. The "object" receives the action of the verb:

We saw *him*. We admired *her*.
The theater sent *them* tickets for the concert.

You can usually find the *object* (if there is one) by asking "what" after the verb. "I read
the book."—read what? (the book).

Prepositions too can have objects. In general, prepositions are followed by object
pronouns:

There were no secrets *between him* and *me*. [not *him* and *I*]
He wrote, "Let's just keep this *between you* and *me*." [not *you* and *I*]
She waved *at* Shannon and *me*. [not *Shannon* and *I*]

You can find the object of a preposition by asking "what" after the preposition:

Benny fell into the well. [Into what? the *well*]
We found a box of coins beneath the floor of the attic.
[Beneath what? the *floor*]

As the name implies, most prepositions (but not all) are words of position. The following is a list of prepositions. Although you already use these naturally when you speak and
write, it is helpful for you when constructing sentences to become more aware of them.

| | | | |
|---|---|---|---|
| above | behind | inside | since |
| about | below | in spite of | through |
| according to | beneath | instead of | throughout |
| across | beside | into | to |
| after | between | like | toward |
| against | beyond | near | under |
| along | but | next to | underneath |
| amid | by | of | until |
| around | despite | on | up |
| as | except | on behalf of | upon |

| | | | |
|---|---|---|---|
| aside from | for | out of | with |
| as to | from | outside | within |
| at | in | over | without |

## Who and Whom

The most difficult pronoun agreement problem is using *who* and *whom, whoever* and *whomever*. *Whom* and *whomever* are slowly passing out of American English. Especially in oral English many people use only *who* for both subjective and objective case. However, because *whom* and *whomever* are still recognized as correct objective case by educated readers and writers, you need to know the differences between *who* and *whom*.

## ACTIVITY 6

Try to select the correct pronouns in the practice sentences here. Try to explain why you selected your answer (i.e., "who" is the subject; "whom" is the object). If you're not sure, don't worry; write down your best answers.

1. Trudy was not the person (who/whom) we expected to have the answer.
2. Anyone (who/whom) gives illicit drugs to a child should be punished.
3. (Whoever/whomever) wants to go on the picnic should sign up before June 10.
4. (Whoever/whomever) smokes should be aware of the serious dangers in tobacco.
5. (Who/whom) we should send on the cruise is not easy to decide. ▬

*Who* acts like a subject: *Who* ate the pizza? *Who* knows why the sky is blue? *Whom* acts like an object: *Whom* will I go to for help? To *whom* is this addressed? To test whether to use *who* or *whom*, convert the question into a statement using another pronoun. If a subject pronoun (like *he* or *she*) is appropriate, the sentence requires *who*. If an object pronoun (like *him* or *her*) is appropriate, the sentence requires *whom*.

Who/Whom made that noise? [*He* made that noise. Thus, choose *Who* here]
Who/Whom did you invite? [You did invite *her*. Thus, choose *Whom* here]

## ACTIVITY 7

For practice, select the correct who/whom pronouns in these sentences. Try to explain your answer, for example: "*who* is the subject of *goes*"; or "*whom* is the object of *found*."

1. We knew the old man (who/whom) lived across the street.
2. The ones (who/whom) left the place in such a shambles never paid their bill.
3. The workers (who/whom) we asked to do the work were late.
4. The picture revealed (who/whom) was the one in the background.
5. (Who/Whom) we wanted for president we were reluctant to say. ▬

**HANDBOOK Sentences**

## Appropriate Verb Tenses

Verb tenses indicate time. The simple tenses indicate past, present, and future events: *I go, I went, I will go.* The "perfect" tenses indicate ongoing or customary action: past perfect time indicates one action was completed before another, and future perfect indicates events that will be completed before some other in the future:

| | |
|---|---|
| Present Perfect: | I have talked about this for years. |
| Past Perfect: | I had talked for an hour before the exit bell rang. |
| Future Perfect: | After today, I will have talked to this group 20 times. |

There are also "progressive" forms for ongoing actions. You can see at once the pattern of progressive forms.

| | |
|---|---|
| I am talking | I have been talking |
| I was talking | I had been talking |
| I will be talking | I shall have been talking |

## ACTIVITY 8

Before you examine various problems with verbs, try to underline the correct verbs in these sentences. Try to explain your choices.

1. Hiram's well-respected book on stem cell research (gave/gives) a terse response to critics: "Nuts to them," he (says/said).

2. This researcher (finds/found) that animals kept in below zero temperatures quickly die.

3. It is essential that everyone (attend/attends) the meeting on resources and expenses.

4. The data (seem/seems) persuasive.

5. If it (was/were) possible to increase our budget by a million dollars, I would certainly attempt to do so.

6. Our experiments were not successful until we (begin/began) to include some ancient secrets.

7. It was clear that we lost all the ongoing experiments because the lab (burned/had burned) down.

8. <u>Time</u> magazine (presented/presents) one of the best articles on the life of zebras.

9. The financiers asked, "Suppose the experiment (was/were) to fail, how would we get our money back?"

10. I first (introduce/introduced) a quart of highly acidic solution and then (allow/allowed) it to give off toxic fumes until the experimental subjects (die/died). ▮

The following problems or examples can help you understand verb usage.

## Use the Past Tense to Describe What Happened in Your Research

We *implanted* hundreds of cells before producing one live embryo.
I *kept* oocytes alive in petri dishes.

*Exceptions to the rule.* You may sometimes address the reader in the present tense, as if explaining your reasoning or speculating aloud:

If we [meaning researchers, or the reader and the writer] *produce* 277 failures before we *get* one live sheep embryo, what *is* the implication for human cloning?

## Use Present Tense to Quote from Books and Articles or to Refer to Source Material

Michael Pollan's book <u>The Omnivore's Dilemma</u> gives a clear argument on knowing more about the food we eat.
Leonard Pitts Jr. explains how it feels to have someone plagiarize his writing.

## Use Past Tense to Identify Source Material

Michael Pollan's book <u>The Omnivore's Dilemma</u> was published in 2006.

## When Some Events Occur Further Back in Time Than Others, Use *Had*

When some events occur further back in time than others, use *had* (the past perfect tense) for the earlier event:

Incorrect: We knew the bird escaped when we saw its cage door open.
Revised: We knew the bird *had* escaped when we saw its cage door open.

## Use *Were* and *Be* to Express Doubts, Wishes, Probability, Conditions Contrary to Fact, or Hypothetical Statements

If I *were* you, I would not get there too early.
He wished he *were* an astronaut.
If we *were* to do it, we might regret it.
We insist that you *be* present.

## Avoid Unjustified Shifts in Tense

Make sure all other verbs in your sentences match tenses.

Incorrect: In the play, Susan *is waiting* for the proper moment, but John suddenly *announced* he *was* leaving. [present and past tense mixed]
Revised for Consistent Tense:
In the play, Susan *waits* for the proper moment, but John suddenly *announces* he *is* leaving. [all in present tense]
or: In the play, Susan *waited* for the proper moment, but John suddenly *announced* he *was* leaving. [all in past tense]

## Lie and Lay

Most verbs have four distinct forms. Some have alternate forms; a few have repeated forms. Regular verbs form their past and past participle with *-d*, or *-ed*: *seized, wanted, sailed*. Irregular verbs usually form their past and past participle with a spelling change: *swim, swam, swum, swimming*. The forms of a few verbs are listed here:

| Present | Past | Past Participle | Present Participle |
|---------|------|-----------------|--------------------|
| awaken | awakened | awakened | awakening |
| begin | began | begun | beginning |
| break | broke | broken | breaking |
| draw | drew | drawn | drawing |
| drink | drank | drunk | drinking |

*Lie* and *lay* are three different verbs, each with its own four forms:

| lay | laid | laid | laying |
|-----|------|------|--------|

*Lay* means "to put" or "to set" as in *lay* the plates on the table, and I *laid* the flowers on the table an hour ago. We *have laid* the plates for dinner.

| lie | lay | lain | lying |
|-----|-----|------|-------|

*Lie* means "to recline" as in *lie* down and rest awhile. I *lay* in bed all this morning. I *have lain* there for hours.

| lie | lied | lied | lying |
|-----|------|------|-------|

*Lie* here means "to falsify" as in "to tell a lie."

The first two verbs, *lay* and *lie*, confuse people, especially writers. (You can disregard the third verb for now, since few people are confused about lying.) It may be helpful to remember that *lie* and *lay* are different in meaning and they are also different in usage. The first one, *lay*, always takes an object: you must lay *something* somewhere. The second, *lie*, never takes an object; it is usually followed by a place expression—down in bed, on the ground, on the floor.

## ACTIVITY 9

In this activity you can ignore the verb that means falsify. The activity concerns only *lie* (recline) and *lay* (put). Underline the correct verb in these sentences. Try to explain your answer, for example, "past tense of lie" or "present tense of lay."

1. Rover had (laid/lain) in the culvert for most of the day, hiding from the sun.
2. The newspaper had been (laying/lying) on the front steps all through the rain.

3. I (lay/laid) my best shotgun on the gun rack after every use.
4. All day we (laid/lay) the tools in the shed and cleaned them.
5. Auntie Em had (laid/lain) Dorothy's blue dress on the bed. ▬

## Revise Faulty Parallelism

What pattern(s) do you see in the following sentences?

Many people today enjoy swimming, scuba diving, and surfing.
As a student I like to read, to write, and to think.
So far we have read novels, histories, short stories, and biographies.

The pattern in each sentence above concerns "parallel construction." Sentence elements should be parallel if possible. Parallel construction means that elements in the sentences are structured the same way, using the same form for each item in the pattern. For example:

Incorrect: I like reading and to write.
Revised:   I like *reading* and *writing.*
Incorrect: The laboratory needed new equipment to improve instruction and which
           would expose students to new technology.
Revised:   The laboratory needed new equipment *to improve* instruction and *to expose*
           students to new technology.
Incorrect: Dr. Brown is a person of beauty, of grace, and she is wise.
Revise:    Dr. Brown is a person *of beauty, of grace,* and *of wisdom.*
           Or, for the sake of rhythm: . . . a person of *beauty, grace,* and *wisdom.*

*Note*: For more on parallelism, see Interchapter 3.

## Dangling or Misplaced Modifiers

Watch for modifiers that have nothing to modify or that seem to modify the wrong thing in your sentence: "Sleeping all afternoon, the cot was as comfortable as a bed." The writer knows what is intended, but for the reader, the sentence seems to say the cot was sleeping all afternoon.

## ACTIVITY 10

What is a "dangling" or "misplaced modifier"? Even if you are not sure, give your best guess. Try to explain the errors (if any) in the following sentences.

1. Don't bite into apples with your teeth when they are dirty.
2. We had brought toys for the children in the trunk of our car.
3. We asked the waitress with the menus standing at our table to give us a minute.
4. Coasting without a sail, the shoreline soon came into sight.
5. Feeling a sour stomach, the medicine Irene took was proving effective. ▬

The misplaced modifier is similar to the *-ing* dangling modifiers in items 4 and 5. If a modifier has no subject, it is called a "dangling modifier." Who or what is "coasting without a sail"? Who or what is "feeling a sour stomach"?

When the modifier is aimed at an improper or inappropriate subject, it is called "misplaced." Who or what is the subject of "when they are dirty" in item 1?

If writers lose the sense of their sentences, words for people and objects can get misplaced. You may know what you are trying to say: your ideas may seem obvious to you, but your readers have only the words on the page to guide them. For example

Incorrect: We hid our gifts to surprise the assistants in our lab coats.

By placing the phrase *in our lab coats* next to *assistants*, the writer has made it seem that the assistants were wearing the coats. The sentence makes better sense if you get the coats away from the assistants:

Revised:       To surprise the assistants, we hid our gifts in our lab coats.
Other examples:
Incorrect:    The audience applauded Franny's playing with enthusiasm.
              [Who or what is enthusiastic in this sentence: the audience or Franny's playing?]
Revised:       The audience enthusiastically applauded Franny's playing.
              or The audience applauded Franny's enthusiastic playing.
Incorrect:    People shouldn't eat fish when they smell bad.
              [Who smells bad here, the people or the fish?]
Revised:       Never eat fish that smell bad.

The main rule to remember is this: find or supply an appropriate subject for your modifiers. Place modifiers next to—or as close as possible to—the thing they modify. When they are placed next to some other word, the "misplacement" results. To revise these sentences you may need to supply an appropriate subject.

Incorrect: Sleeping without a heavy blanket, the room began to get cold.

The problem here is that there is no person who is "sleeping without a heavy blanket." The only noun your readers can find is "the room." You must supply an appropriate subject for these "dangling" modifiers.

Revised: Sleeping without a heavy blanket, *Jenny* began to feel cold.
      or Jenny began to feel the room getting cold.

## Avoid Sexist Language

Sexism is inappropriate. Writers should avoid a bias in words that indicate gender. For example, when a class contains both men and women, you should indicate that fact: *Each student* should bring *his* or *her* book to class.

## Write in the Plural if Possible

*Students* should bring *their* books to class.

Sexist:  *A researcher* needs endurance if *he* hopes to finish *his* work on time.
[Don't assume all researchers are male.]

Revise:  *Researchers* need endurance if *they* hope to finish *their* work on time.

Sexist:  Ask personnel to send an extra *workman* over.
[Don't assume all workers are male.]

Revised: Ask personnel to send an extra *worker* over.

## Substitute Neutral Words When Either Gender Is Implied

*humankind* instead of *mankind*

*spokesperson* instead of *spokesman*

*chairperson* instead of *chairman*

*mail carrier* instead of *mailman*

*postal worker* instead of *postman*

*personnel* instead of *manpower*

Unless there are other clues to suggest you are talking about only one gender or the other, you should substitute neutral words.

## ACTIVITY 11

Revise these sentences to remove gender bias.

1. Whoever is manning that ship is about to wreck it.
2. If you need a good lawyer, try someone new—he'll try harder.
3. Make sure the surgeon gets his hands clean before putting on his gloves.
4. The idea must have come from some very creative young guy.
5. A secretary who can't spell won't keep her job for long. ▉

## PUNCTUATION

In Interchapters 1 and 2, you learned about semicolons, colons, dashes, italics (*underlining*), and parentheses as punctuation tools that help create your voice—the sound of your personality on the page. Used well, these various ways to join thoughts give your writing more power. They clarify your meaning and add emphasis. Imagine if you could use only periods—no other forms of punctuation. The possibilities for joining and emphasizing certain thoughts would shrink. This section presents other matters of punctuation that you can refer to as you edit your writing, trying to make it clear and free of errors.

## Period
## Use a Period at the End of a Complete Statement

Writing generates thinking.

*Note*: Failure to end a sentence with a period makes a writer look careless.

## Use a Period for Each Item in a Sentence Outline or List of Full Sentences

The student employees had a few minor complaints:

1. The working hours were too long.
2. The pay was too low.
3. The working conditions were uncomfortable.

In a list or outline of words or phrases rather than sentences, do not use periods.

The students had only these minor complaints:

1. Long working hours
2. Low pay
3. Uncomfortable working conditions

## Use Periods with Most Abbreviations and Initials

e.g.   Inc.   pp.   Ms.   Mr.   Dr.   J.F.K.

Do not add an additional period when an abbreviation or initial comes at the end of a sentence.

We were set to go at 8:00 p.m.
Our list server is listserv@eff.org.

Many abbreviations of well-known organizations do not require periods.

FBI   NAACP   NFL   NOW   NRA

## Comma Splices and Run-on Sentences

Comma splices and run-on (or fused) sentences are common sentence problems. (See Interchapter 1).

*Comma splice*: A comma splice is a sentence error. A comma divides two complete thoughts without any connecting word (such as *and, but, or*).

Seymour noticed a mistake, he told his friend who fixed it

*Run-on*: A run-on sentence is a rear-end collision. One complete thought runs into another with no punctuation between them.

Seymour noticed the mistake, he told his friend who fixed it.

Comma splices and run-ons can be repaired various ways:

- By connecting both complete thoughts with a semicolon
- By connecting both complete thoughts with a comma and connecting word

- By connecting both complete thoughts with a dash (or a colon if the first thought introduces the second)
- By separating both complete thoughts with a period and starting a new sentence
- By combining into one concise complete thought

## ACTIVITY 12

Try to revise the errors in these sentences. Then try to identify the errors (comma splice or run-on sentence).

1. Madeleine Albright was Secretary of State in the Clinton administration, she was the first woman ever to hold that position.
2. The F-22 Raptor Stealth Fighter was hailed as a great advance in modern weaponry it was virtually invisible to enemy radar.
3. Tchaikovsky's <u>Swan Lake</u> remains one of his popular ballets it features graceful and beautiful swanlike movements.
4. The boa constrictor is a fearsome snake, often huge, the powerful snake kills prey by tightening its muscles around the doomed animal, preventing it from breathing.
5. The kangaroo is the world's largest marsupial, it is native to Australia. ▪▪▪

### Comma (see also Interchapter 1)
### Use Commas to Separate Sentences Joined by *And, But, Or, Nor, For, Yet, So*

The film made me laugh, *and* I felt better after seeing it.
The book weighed five pounds, *but* it was useful.
Thousands of fans packed the stadium, *yet* they made hardly a sound as the performer sang.

*Note*: The comma comes *before* the connecting word, not after.

## ACTIVITY 13

Try to correct any comma errors (if any) in these sentences. See if you can explain the errors.

1. Hundreds of shoppers hurried through the mall starting their Christmas shopping early but they seemed too preoccupied to enjoy the holiday season.
2. Too many reporters began asking many tough questions so the senators ended their televised session immediately.

3. Urban and suburban development increasingly encroaches on wildlife havens yet people are surprised to discover wild animals wandering through city streets.

4. A set of the new biology texts arrived and we quickly placed them on bookshelves.

5. Computers can already take dictation and, now many are wireless. ▨

## Use a Comma to Join Very Short Complete Thoughts if Similarly Constructed

I came, I saw, I left.
We sang, we laughed, we danced all night.

## Use a Comma after Most Introductory Elements

Yes, happiness is a complicated subject.
First, we must organize a committee.
Besides Carol, Chih-Ping and Bob are going.
To think critically, you must see hidden differences and similarities.
Looking at the deep blue sky, I noticed a hawk.
Whenever you write, you also think.

**HANDBOOK
Punctuation**

## ACTIVITY 14

Decide whether these sentences are properly punctuated. If you see any punctuation problem(s) try to correct them and to explain why they are problems.

1. Reaching for the gravy Bud accidentally spilled it all over the table.

2. After the mixture comes to a boil you must carefully add the sodium.

3. When the bell rang the two boxers staggered toward each other.

4. Although apparently sober Jeeter was unable to convince the officers that he should be allowed to drive his car home.

5. Looking at a morning glory I saw a bumblebee back out of it. ▨

## Use a Comma to Separate Items in a Series

I had stopped on my way from the airport at a nearby supermarket and purchased some turkey, potato salad, macaroni salad, and bagels. (Mitch Albom, <u>Tuesdays</u>)

When a series of items is the subject of a sentence, do not insert a comma after the last item—do not separate the subject from its verb.

Newspapers, magazines, and books covered Don's floor.
[Not: Newspapers, magazines, and books, covered Don's floor.]

## Use a Comma between Movable Adjectives

If adjectives describe the same word and can be rearranged without loss of meaning, separate them with commas. A good test is to ask whether the word *and* could be inserted between them. If so, use commas.

> It was an entertaining, unusual experience.
> (It was an entertaining [and] unusual experience.)

## Use Commas to Set Off a Group of Nonessential Words

> Ernest Hemingway, author of <u>The Old Man and the Sea</u>, spent many years fishing off the coast of Havana.

This sentence is complete without the words "author of <u>The Old Man and the Sea</u>." Other examples:

> The young woman, who had just turned eighteen, entered MIT.
> Katie, on the other hand, loved to dance.
> The idea, it occurred to me, just might work.

*Note*: You can use dashes for more emphasis instead of commas.

## Use Commas to Set off Contrastive Elements

> The issue concerns people, not politics.
> He's a great guy, but spoiled.
> Most students volunteered, yet some did nothing.

## Use Commas to Separate Dialogue from the Rest of a Sentence

> She asked, "How can you distinguish between the dancer and the dance?"
> "It's not who wins," he said bitterly, "but how much you get paid."

*Note*: Commas and periods go inside quotation marks.

## Use Commas Correctly in Dates and Addresses

> Amber was born on May 16, 2000, at Greenville General Hospital.
> Ann Arbor, Michigan, is still Spencer's permanent address.

(Notice especially the commas after *2000* and *Michigan*)
When the day precedes the month, no commas are required:

> She was born 16 May 2000.

## Use a Comma after Openings and Closings of Any Letter

| | | |
|---|---|---|
| Dear Mark, | Dear Mom, | Hi Honey, |
| Sincerely, | Love, | Best wishes, |

**HANDBOOK**
**Punctuation**

## Use Commas for Clarity

Sometimes you may need to use a comma to prevent ambiguity or misreading.

| | |
|---|---|
| Confusing: | Those who can teach the rest of us. |
| Revised: | Those who can, teach the rest of us. |
| Confusing: | Having eaten the children went quietly to bed. |
| Revised: | Having eaten, the children went quietly to bed. |

## Overuse of Commas

Use a comma before a word like *and, but, or* only if the word joins two complete thoughts. The comma is a signal to readers. But with a compound verb, use no comma. For example: "She *wrote* and *proofread* her paper." Without the comma you tell your readers that you have written one sentence with two verbs: *wrote* and *proofread*.

Bob typed his paper carefully and handed it in the next morning.
   [Not: Bob typed his paper carefully, and handed it in the next morning.]
She shrugged her shoulders and walked away.
   [Not: She shrugged her shoulders, and walked away.]
We found our way to the train station and called our host family.
   [Not: We found our way to the train station, and called our host family.]

## ACTIVITY 15

**HANDBOOK
Punctuation**

Try to fix punctuation errors, if any, in these sentences, and try to explain any errors you find.

1. Time, Newsweek, USA Today, were our favorite news sources.
2. The campus police impounded Rachelle's car, and took her to the Public Safety building.
3. Shakespeare the great English playwright wrote Hamlet and King Lear.
4. The politicians each asserted "My opponent is mistaken about the facts."
5. The children were told to send their letters to Mrs. Morgan at 665 Green Street, Saginaw Michigan.
6. There's no sense in using the bed for eating bread crumbs get all over the place.
7. The school was used for many other community activities not just education.
8. "Not me" Aaron insisted "I'm not going in there for anything!"
9. The Snack Shop promised a soul-lifting simply divine malted milkshake.
10. Japanese aircraft attacked Pearl Harbor on December 7 1941 "A day that will live in infamy" according to President Franklin Delano Roosevelt. ▮

## Semicolons and a Complex Series

Use semicolons to separate items in a series containing commas:

The United States has several observatories, such as the Palomar, near San Diego, California; Mount Wilson, near Pasadena, California; McDonald, near Fort Davis, Texas; and Kitt Peak, near Tucson, Arizona.

A report from the National Center for Clinical Infant Programs makes the point that school success is not predicted by a child's fund of facts or a precocious ability to read so much as by emotional and social measures: being self-assured and interested; knowing what kind of behavior is expected and how to rein in the impulse to misbehave; being able to wait, to follow directions, and to turn to teachers for help; and expressing needs while getting along with other children. (Daniel Goleman, <u>Emotional Intelligence</u>)

Using semicolons to divide elements in a complex list can involve phrases or complete thoughts between the semicolons.

*Note*: For more on semicolons, see Interchapter 1. For information on colons and dashes, see Interchapter 2.

## Exclamation Mark

The exclamation mark is seldom used in formal writing. But for informal writing it can be used—usually in dialogue—to indicate excitement, shouting, or extreme emphasis.

What a disgusting thing to say!

Using more than one exclamation mark at a time is not appropriate in formal writing.

## Parentheses (see also Interchapter 2)
### Use Parentheses to Set Off Clarifying Information

Parentheses set off clarifying information or information not grammatically connected to the sentence.

The affliction (anorexia nervosa) is an eating disorder.
Repeating *people* for emphasis, Lincoln wanted "a government of the *people*, by the *people*, for the *people*." (emphasis added).

The phrase (emphasis added) tells readers that you italicized the word *people* in the quote.

### Use Full Parentheses to List or Outline

The processes of writing can be grouped into (1) generating ideas, (2) using specific evidence, (3) organizing the evidence, and (4) revising and editing.

*Note:* The half-parenthesis is not used in MLA or APA styles.

Incorrect: We knew that 1) there was too much salt, and 2) we could not account for it.

## Brackets (See Chapter 9)

### Use "Sic" to Indicate Errors in Quotes (Also see Chapter 9)

To indicate an error in material you quote, use the word *sic*, meaning "thus the error was" in the original. In MLA style of documentation, use parentheses around *sic*.

**MLA Style**

"Many people are anxious to continue with cloning research because they believe cloning will allow them to become immoral" (sic).

[*sic* tells readers "immoral" was not your mistake; it was in the original.]

The APA style requires *sic* to be underlined or italicized and enclosed in brackets: [*sic*]. APA's rule is that if you find an error in something you are quoting, you are required to copy the error, but immediately after the error, in square brackets give [*sic*]. Note the placement inside the sentence period for both MLA and APA.

**APA Style**

Our expedition found itself standard [*sic*] on the Galapagos islands until they realized we were late and sent a boat for us.

[*sic*] tells readers "standard" was not your error; it was in the original.

### ACTIVITY 16

HANDBOOK Punctuation

Try to correct any punctuation errors in these sentences; then give a brief explanation for each error.

1. It is likely many scientists agree that a retrovirus is responsible for acquired immune deficiency syndrome (AIDS).
2. Wieners, burgers, potato salad, were the picnic food.
3. Art worked night and day to finish his Ph.D..
4. The Connecticut Cooking Club prepared pies, and cakes for the workers repairing the old church.
5. Until the children stop making so much racket the TV remains off.

## Quotation Marks: How to Quote from Sources

Quoting from sources is a serious activity, especially in research writing. It's important to get your quotations accurate by applying quotation marks properly.

### ACTIVITY 17

Try to fix errors concerning quotation marks in the following sentences. Don't worry if you feel uncertain about your answers. See if you can give brief explanations for any errors you find, for example, "poem title."

1. "Newsweek" carried an article on the positive psychology.
2. Amy Wu, in her essay, Stop the Clock, asserts that she "is a failure at housework.
3. In his article on gun control, Mitch Albom writes that 'we live in an age of hair trigger-tempers—and that is no place for hair-trigger weapons'.
4. My favorite poem is Robert Frost's Stopping by Woods on a Snowy Evening.
5. Ms. Remington asked the eighth graders, What is Poe's poem The Raven really about. ▨

## Copying and Quoting
### Use Quotation Marks for Any Words You Copy from a Source

| | |
|---|---|
| Quoting a word: | Seymour repeats "notice" three times in his essay. |
| Quoting a phrase: | Tannen argues that we live in an "argument culture" (8). |
| Quoting a sentence: | Tannen writes, "The argument culture urges us to approach the world, and the people in it, in an adversarial frame of mind" (9). |

### Some Exceptions to the Quotation Rules

Indirect quotes give a report of what someone said, not the actual speech by that person.

| | |
|---|---|
| Indirect: | The boss told us we would have to start looking for new jobs. |
| Direct: | The boss said, "You will all have to start looking for new jobs." |

Rhetorical questions are questions asked for effect, not intended to elicit answers. They can sometimes be a way to avoid harsh statements.

| | |
|---|---|
| Harsh statement: | "No one can get a new job now." |
| Rhetorical question: | "Who can find new jobs under these conditions?" |

Internal thoughts, monologues, conversations with yourself need quotation marks:

"I wonder what they meant by that? Should I say something back? No, better just to let it pass, I think."

### Long Quotations Do Not Use Quotation Marks (See also Chapter 9)

MLA style requires writers to indent (set off or block display) quotations of four or more lines. APA style requires writers to set off (indent) any quotation longer than 40 words.

Indent all lines of a long quotation *10 spaces* (or two tabs) from the left margin (APA says five spaces), and type the quote double-spaced. Do not indent from the right-hand margin; do not attempt to make all the lines the same length. To indent 10 spaces and to use quotation marks around a long quote is redundant: use quotation marks for shorter quotes only. Also, add no extra space above or below the quote.

Long quotations should be copied exactly as you find them, including any quotation marks you find *within* them. Parenthetic references for long quotations come after the final sentence period in both MLA and APA styles. Here is an example of a long quote in a student paper on cloning:

---

#### Indented Quote

Cloning would provide reproductive options for people other than married heterosexual couples. Lee Silver in <u>Remaking Eden</u> explains:

> Lesbian couples, in particular, would have a new way to share biological parentage of a child. One member of the couple could provide the donor cell, and either one could provide the unfertilized recipient egg. The newly formed embryo could then be introduced into the uterus of the genetically unrelated woman. The child that is born would be related by genes to one mother, and related by birthing to the other, so that both women could rightly call themselves biological parents. (116)

Other possibilities are equally interesting. Single women could have one of their own cells cloned and fused with one of their own unfertilized eggs. Older women past menopause could bear children who were cloned. Men could also clone themselves by providing their own donor cell—but they would need to use a woman's unfertilized egg and a woman to serve as a surrogate mother.

---

*Note*: When using a long quote (four or more lines), do not indicate the beginning of a single quoted paragraph with indentation. However, if you display more than one full paragraph in your long quote, indent the first line of each subsequent paragraph three spaces (not five).

## Vary the Way You Use Direct Quotes

Here is a quote from Richard Selzer's book <u>Mortal Lessons</u> (9):

"The truth is at least as accessible in ugliness as it is in beauty."

You can vary the way you present a quote. In the following, note the placement of commas inside all quote marks and the placement of citation inside the period.

### Direct Quote Ends a Sentence

Selzer writes, "The truth is at least as accessible in ugliness as it is in beauty" (9).

### Direct Quote Begins a Sentence

"The truth is at least as accessible in ugliness as it is in beauty," Selzer writes (9).

### Direct Quote Interrupted

"The truth," Selzer writes, "is at least as accessible in ugliness as it is in beauty" (9).

*Note*: Where to interrupt Selzer's sentence is not a random decision. You need to consider what the interruption will do to Selzer's style: the effect on the flow of his sentence, the distortion or emphasis on his thought, and the possible distraction for your reader.

## Use Quotation Marks around Material Incorporated into Your Own Sentences

In a <u>Newsweek</u> essay, "Burned Out and Bored," Professor Ronald Dahl says one of the more disturbing problems for parents today may be the "rising rates of psychiatric problems among children and adolescents in our society" (18).

The quotation has been incorporated or blended into the grammar of the sentence and does not require a comma. Incorporated means it is part of the sentence; if you didn't see it printed this way, you wouldn't hear where the quote marks go. There is no signal for the quotation.

## Use Quotation Marks around Words Used in a Special Sense or Misused Intentionally

My teacher is an optimist; he likes to call November "Yesvember."
Seymour wondered if college ever involved "lower" education.

## Use Quotation Marks to Indicate Dialogue

"Papa?"
"Yes, June."
"Tell me about the most-most."
For an instant he did not remember. "Ah," he said, "you mean that club in New York where people are the most of everything."
"That's the story." (Bellow 295–96)

*Note*: Each change of speaker requires a new line and a paragraph indentation.

## Use Quotation Marks for Titles of Short Works and Divisions within Longer Works

Essays: "Stop the Clock" by Amy Wu

Poems: "A Dream Deferred" by Langston Hughes

   (Titles of long poems such as <u>The Odyssey</u> are underlined.)

Short stories: "A Good Man Is Hard to Find" by Flannery O'Connor

Newspaper articles: "A Call for Service" by David Broder, <u>Washington Post</u>

Magazine articles: "The Swooshification of the World" by Rick Reilly,

   <u>Sports Illustrated</u>

Book chapters: "Different Words, Different Worlds"—Chapter 1 in <u>You Just Don't</u>

   <u>Understand</u> by Deborah Tannen

Popular songs and specific works on albums (record, tape, cassettes, CDs):

   "The Scientist" by Coldplay

   (Titles of longer musical compositions such as operas and ballets should be underlined or italicized.)

## Commas and Periods Go Inside the Quotation Marks

Commas and periods always go inside the quotation marks—unless you cite a page number.

> Morrie did not want to be "useless."
> Morrie did not want to be "useless," but he needed help from a live-in nurse.
> Morrie did not want to be "useless" (Albom 12).

## Using Other Punctuation with Quotation Marks

Colons and semicolons always go outside quotation marks:

> *Affect* means "to influence": e.g., the weather *affects* my mood.
> Kay called her poem "Autumn Moonlight"; it was sweet and romantic.

Question marks and exclamation marks go either inside or outside the quotation marks, depending on the quoted matter.

### Quoted Matter Is Not a Question

> Are we going to follow the example of history: "If we *can* do it, we *will* do it"?

### Quoted Matter Is a Question

> The scientists wondered, "Is it possible to stop this madness?"

### Both Quoted Matter and Not-Quoted Matter Are Questions

> Do you know the song "Oh Where Has My Little Dog Gone?"

### Exclamation

> "No, the name of the Beatles reflects music, not insects!" I said.

**HANDBOOK
Punctuation**

## Using Single Quotation Marks

Use single quotation marks around a word or group of words quoted within double quotation marks:

> Mitch Albom writes that Morrie "was intent on proving that the word 'dying' was not synonymous with 'useless' " (12).
> Cathy asked, "Have you read Salinger's story 'A Perfect Day for Bananafish'?"
> "Harry is really being difficult," Lori complained. "He said, 'Do it yourself,' when I asked him to help me clean the room."

Theoretically, by alternating double and single marks, there might be no end to the number of embedded quotes you could write. But as a practical matter, you should probably rethink your sentence rather than have more than two or three sets of marks.

## Question Marks
### Use a Question Mark after a Direct Question

Did you cite page numbers after your quotes?

Indirect questions require no question mark:

She wondered why nobody liked her.
He asked whether she could help him with physics.

### Use a Question Mark for a Question Embedded in a Statement

A democracy needs citizens who can understand complex political issues (how else can we decide questions about abortion, equality, and civil liberties?).

## Ellipsis (See Chapter 9)

## Slash

Use a slash to incorporate two or three lines of poetry within your text: with a space on each side ( / ) to indicate line breaks. It is often better to "incorporate" a line or two than to set them off as a block quote. Incorporating them into your own sentence makes for smoother reading and less distraction for your readers.

He had "cracked hands that ached / from labor in the weekday weather" (3–4).

## ACTIVITY 18

Try to correct any errors of quotation marks or other associated punctuation errors (if any) in these sentences, including end-of-sentence errors. Add needed marks; underline unneeded marks. Try to explain your corrections.

1. One of Robert Frost's early poems is 'The Road Not Taken'.
2. Most Americans know President Kennedy's sentence ask not what your country can do for you, ask what you can do for your country?
3. On the witness stand, Lamar swore I have never met Noreen, let alone had a relationship with her.
4. The group liked Seymour's essay "Beginner's Mind;" we had never thought about thinking in that way.
5. Ms. Deutch asked, "Wilhelm, did you just now say, I hate this stuff?" ▆

## MECHANICS

Small matters count in writing. Spelling, grammar, and punctuation can make a difference in your meaning. Then, too, basic errors can reflect poorly on your ethos.

**HANDBOOK Mechanics**

## ACTIVITY 19

Try to correct any errors in mechanics in these sentences (apostrophes, hyphens, italics, capitalization, abbreviations, and numbers). Explain your corrections, if you can. Don't worry about being right or wrong; use your best judgment.

1. Johns older sister was to be married in April.
2. The childrens' toys were scattered everywhere.
3. The president believes its appropriate to support the war.
4. Whooping cough, caused by the bacterium bordetella pertussis was contagious and rampant throughout the early half of the 20th century.
5. My teacher said she enjoyed my well written essay. ▪

## Apostrophe

### Use Apostrophes Correctly to Show Possession

| | |
|---|---|
| Singular nouns, add **'s** | the boy's bike |
| | a writer's notebook |
| | Sue's video collection |
| Singular nouns ending in **s**, add apostrophe and **s** | Mr. Jones's house |
| | James's promotion |
| | the goddess's hair |
| Singular indefinite pronouns, add **'s** | one's options |
| | anyone's problem |
| Plural nouns ending in **s**, add only the apostrophe | the boys' bikes |
| | the girls' school |
| Plural nouns not ending in s, add **'s** | the men's shoes |
| | the women's rights |
| | the children's toys |

Personal pronouns (*I, we, us, you, he, she, it*) do *not* use apostrophes to show possession; instead each has a possessive form: *my, mine, our, ours, your, yours, his, hers, its, their, theirs.* The pronoun *it's* isn't possessive: it's a contraction of *it* and *is* or *has*:

| | |
|---|---|
| Joint possession, add **'s** to the last owner named | Tom and Susan's computer |
| Individual ownership, add **'s** to each owner mentioned | Tom's and Susan's computers |
| Abstract or inanimate nouns and familiar expressions follow the normal rules | a day's work |
| | life's difficulties |
| | five dollars' worth |

**HANDBOOK Mechanics**

## Use Apostrophes to Show Omission of Letters in Contractions

Contractions give an informal tone to your writing: they are generally acceptable except in the most formal writing situations:

we're   she'll   you're   haven't   didn't   it's (it is)   isn't

## Use Apostrophes to Show Plurals

Words referred to as words, abbreviations, and letters and numerals referred to as symbols form their plurals by adding **'s.**

p's and q's   C.P.A.'s   rpm's   if's, and's, or but's
I used to think 3's were partly erased 8's.

*Note*: Apostrophes are not required when dates are treated as collective nouns: 1900s, 1990s.

## Hyphen
## Use a Hyphen to Connect Compound-Word Modifiers before a Noun

deep-fried mushrooms     ill-conceived plan     well-written essay

Compound-word modifiers after the word modified are not hyphenated.

The essay was well written.
The plan is ill conceived.

## Hyphenate Words Formed with Certain Prefixes and Suffixes

Words that use the prefixes *all-, cross-, ex-, half-, ill-, well-,* and *self-* and the suffix *-elect* are usually hyphenated.

all-knowing     ex-president     self-conscious     governor-elect

When *self* is a word's root rather than a prefix, it is not hyphenated.

selfhood     selfish

Use a hyphen when the prefixes *un-, anti-,* and *ex-* are attached to a proper noun:

un-American     anti-Communist     ex-New Yorker

## Use a Hyphen for Two-Word Numbers

twenty-one     forty-five     three-fifths

## Use a Hyphen to Avoid Ambiguity or Confusion

She was excited about the re-creation. [The hyphen is needed to distinguish between *re-creation* (a reenactment) and *recreation* (a diversion).]

HANDBOOK
Mechanics

## Use Hyphens to Divide Words at the End of Lines

Dividing words at the end of lines is not accepted in MLA or APA style. When words are too long to fit on the line, take the entire word to the next line. Don't let your computer add hyphens.

## Italics (Underlining) (see also Interchapter 2)
## Use Underlining or Italics for Titles of Long Works

Underline or italicize titles of most publications: books, booklets, pamphlets, magazines, newspapers, long poems, plays, albums (records, tapes, cassettes, CDs), operas, films, works of art, and the names of television series. Do not underline titles of documents such as the Constitution or the Declaration of Independence.

> Many people love the novel <u>The Catcher in the Rye</u>.
> Have you seen <u>The Sopranos</u> on TV?
> I like to read the "My Turn" column in <u>Newsweek</u>.
> Chris loves Edward Hopper's painting <u>Cape Cod Morning</u>.

## Use Italics or Underlining for Pointing Out Words Used as Words

> What does the term *family values* really mean?
> We explored the word *quality* in class.
> I'm not sure what *liberal* means.

## Italicize or Underline Foreign Words and Phrases

> I walked away, thinking to myself *c'est la vie*.

## Italicize or Underline the Names of Ships, Planes, and Trains

> The *Titanic* was the largest and most luxurious ship ever built at the time.
> Charles Lindbergh flew the *Spirit of St. Louis* nonstop across the Atlantic Ocean.

## Italicize or Underline Scientific Names for Animals and Plants

> The doctor announced that I had *Rhus toxicodendron*, poison ivy.

## Italicize or Underline Special or Technical Terms

> The *hypothalamus*, which regulates body temperature, is in the forebrain.

## Capitalization
## Capitalize the First Word of a Sentence

> The only way to become a writer is to write.

## Capitalize the First Word of a Quotation

> My grandfather told me, "The road is better than the inn."

## Do Not Capitalize the First Word of an Incorporated Quote

The process can also change the "flavor, odor, texture, color and nutritional value" of beef ("Food Irradiation").

## Usually, Do Not Capitalize the First Word after a Colon

Losing balance is good: it helps you learn.

The capitalization rules after a colon differ from one authority to the next. In general, don't.

However, do capitalize the first word after a colon if it begins a question or quote, if it is the first word of a subtitle, or if it introduces a rule or principle.

This is the question: Where will we find our evidence?
I enjoyed Pollan's <u>The Omnivore's Dilemma: A Natural History of Four Meals</u>.
Patrick Henry stated his opinion clearly: "Give me liberty, or give me death."

## Capitalize Names, Descriptive Names, and Nicknames

Susan          Babe Ruth, "the Sultan of Swat"
Thomas Edison, "the Wizard of Menlo Park"

## Capitalize the Names of Nationalities, Ethnic Groups

Khmer        German      Tswana      Irish      Indian

## Capitalize Words Formed from Proper Nouns

Proper nouns refer to specific things; common nouns refer to general things. Common nouns are not capitalized.

| Proper Nouns | Common Nouns |
| --- | --- |
| Dr. Richard Selzer | medical doctor |
| Eureka College | college |
| Ford Ranger | truck |
| Orion | constellation |

## Capitalize the Names of Awards, Brand Names, Historical and Cultural Events

Pulitzer Prize      Nobel Peace Prize      Labor Day      Rosh Hashana

## Do Not Capitalize the Common Names of Most Plants and Animals

oak tree      lily      sparrow      rainbow trout

## Do Not Capitalize Derived Words That Have Acquired Special Meaning

french fry      china closet      panama hat      india ink      brazil nut

## Do Not Capitalize Generic Terms without Names

asteroid        moon        meteor

## Do Not Capitalize a Generic Term When It Comes Before a Name

the comet Kohoutek        the asteroid Ceres

## Capitalize Religious Terms

Easter        Passover        Eucharist        Ramadan

## Do Not Capitalize Religious Objects

rosary        menorah        crucifix

## Capitalize Languages, Names with a Degree, Degree Abbreviations, Specific Courses

English    Spanish    French
Catherine Chen, PhD (or Ph.D.)    Dr. Chen
BA    MA    (or B.A.    M.A.)    English 101

## Do Not Capitalize Subjects Other than Languages

history        social studies        economics

## Do Not Capitalize a Degree without a Name

associate        bachelor's        master of arts        doctorate

## Do Not Capitalize School Years or Rank

freshman        sophomore        junior        senior

## Capitalize Geographic Features, Places

Ohio        Grand Canyon        Mt. Rushmore        Center Street
Great Bear Lake        Big Two-Hearted River

## Do Not Capitalize the Names of Seasons

winter        spring        summer        fall

## Capitalize Geographical Areas, Not Directions

Capitalize *north, south, east, west* and their derivatives only when they refer to specific geographical areas, not when they refer to directions.

Bob lived in the South for ten years before he moved to the East Coast.
From Canada we drove south to Bismark.
To find the drugstore, go north two blocks and then west one block.

## Capitalize Institutions, Organizations

| | | |
|---|---|---|
| the Red Cross | Department of Labor | Federal Bureau of Investigation |
| the Republican Party | United States Congress | General Motors |

## Capitalize Military Groups, Battles, Wars

Vietnam War     U.S. Army     U.S. Navy

## Do Not Capitalize Informal References to the Military

army     navy     the armed services
Hank is joining the army, and I'm joining the marines.

## Capitalize Heavenly Bodies

Mars     Jupiter     comet Halley     asteroid Juno

## Capitalize the Names of Ships, Planes, Trains

*Titanic*     space shuttle *Columbia*     the *California Zephyr*

## Capitalize Titles of Address, Position, Rank

the Queen     Mrs. or Ms. Clinton     Dr. Philip Truman

## Do Not Capitalize Titles of Office Without Names Nor When the Name Comes First

| | | |
|---|---|---|
| the governor | Chris Brown, governor | Governor Chris Brown |
| the president | President Bush | |
| the senator | Senator Kennedy | |

## Do Not Capitalize Family Members Except in Place of/or with Names

my mother     my dad     Aunt Jan     Uncle Fred
We believe Mother will be elected to the task force.

## Capitalize Important Words in Titles of Publications, Documents

Capitalize the first word, the last word, and all significant words between, except articles (*a, an, the*), most prepositions (*in, to, of, from, by . . .*), and conjunctions (*and, but, or*).

We read the story "A Temple of the Holy Ghost" by Flannery O'Connor.
The essay "The Uses and Ethics of Stem Cell Research" surprised me.

## Do Not Use "The" as Part of a Newspaper Title in Your Works Cited (MLA Style)

Staples, Brent. "What Adolescents Miss When We Let Them Grow Up in Cyberspace." <u>New York Times</u> 29 May 2004, late ed.: A14.

**HANDBOOK**
**Mechanics**

But use the full title in your text (MLA style).

I enjoyed Staples's article in <u>The New York Times</u>.

## Abbreviations and Numbers

### Abbreviate Titles before and after Names

| | | |
|---|---|---|
| Dr. Smith | Cathy Smith, PhD (or Ph.D.) | Ms. Jones |
| Rev. David Hooper | Martin Luther King Jr. | John Stone, MD |

### Abbreviate Institutions, Companies, Agencies, Organizations

EPA     FDA     CIA     FBI

### Abbreviate Time, Dates, and Measures with Specific Numbers

12:00 a.m. (or A.M. small caps)     3:00 pm or p.m. (or P.M. small caps)
500 BC (or B.C.)   AD 55 or A.D. 55   (note the order of BC and AD dates)
12 qts.          No. 6          9 mm.

### Abbreviate Latin Words

Latin abbreviations such as ibid. for *ibidem* (another reference to the immediately preceding source) are seldom used with parenthetic references. For subsequent references, you can give the author's name and page: Lewis 38. Here are three common Latin abbreviations:

e.g. (for example)   i.e. (that is)   etc. (and so forth)
Al Pacino has starred in some great films (e.g., <u>Godfather</u>, <u>Dog Day Afternoon</u>, and <u>Scent of a Woman</u>).

Many readers are unfamiliar with these abbreviations and for them the English equivalents are generally preferable. Check with your instructor before you use Latin abbreviations.

### Spell Out Numbers Expressed as One or Two Words

twelve      sixty-eight      forty million

### Spell Out Numbers That Start Sentences

Two hundred and fifty-two students graduated.

### Use Numerals for Numbers Expressed as More than Two Words

1,568      7,120,000      3½

Scientific writing generally prefers numerals:

The vial held 2 drops of solution.
The experiment required 12 mice as subjects

## ACTIVITY 20

Try to correct any errors in capitalization in these sentences. Explain your corrections, if you can.

1. Children enjoy the sounds of nursery rhymes like little miss muffett sat on a tuffet long before they are able to comprehend them.
2. Halley's comet is named for the british astronomer Edmund Halley.
3. I love visiting yellowstone national park.
4. After the speeches the audience was left somewhat puzzled: what, after all, was the point?
5. A likely first-year schedule would contain some math, english, history, and biology, and possibly a second language like french or german.

## GLOSSARY OF USAGE

*Usage* refers to customs and traditions of language use (or disuse) of certain words or word forms accepted by educated readers and writers. There may not be 100% agreement about some usage items; language use changes over time. For example, the word *ain't* was once considered polite usage, but today it is seldom found in educated language except when used deliberately to indicate an uneducated speaker.

## ACTIVITY 21

Some of these sentences may contain errors in usage. Underline the correct answers. Try to explain any error if you can.

1. Golden rod and other fall flowers and weeds can have a serious (affect/effect) on allergies.
2. Renu hoped she might be (accepted/excepted) by God for having tried to live as the church required.
3. We were (already/all ready) to go when we discovered the car had a flat.
4. Elizabeth is an (alumnus/alumna) of Eureka College.
5. We were fascinated by the magician's (allusion/illusion) of causing his assistant to rise up and float in the air.
6. Clorinda was devastated by the (amount/number) of errors she had made on her final exam.
7. The jury concluded it would be (alright/all right) to sentence the boy to time served.

8. "Hurry up," Donny yelled. "(Your/You're) going to make us late."
9. "Talk to anyone (who/whom) will listen to you," the sales manager said.
10. The professor made the class happy when she said (their/there) papers were excellent.
11. The film <u>Little Miss Sunshine</u> (infers/implies) that winning is not everything.
12. Everyone seemed to be (affected/effected) by the emotional movie.
13. The old neighborhood is beginning to look rundown and in need of (a lot/alot) of rehabilitation.
14. Mother said it was (alright/all right) with her if we went to the cinema.
15. Historian Barbara Tuchman's advice to young writers is to interpret the events of history, (since/because) otherwise readers get only a grocery list of names and dates.
16. The Secretary of State believed it was necessary to live among the people of the third world (a while/awhile) in order to understand them.
17. Harry's note ended, "Please keep this between you and (I/me)."
18. Researchers must (cite/site) the sources of their information.
19. It seemed clear that with just a little more money we could (of/have) bought enough tickets to win the lottery.
20. The media today (seem/seems) too fascinated with the private lives of celebrities.
21. The government claimed (its/it's) financial planning was responsible for massive surpluses in the budget.
22. Granny said she felt tired and needed to (lay/lie) down for a short nap.
23. Many critics have asserted that the United States is a (prejudice/prejudiced) country.
24. Several of the older representatives favored voting (themselves/themself) a large raise.
25. The great Dane, of course, is a much larger dog (than/then) the golden Labrador. ▮

**a, an**   Use *a* before words beginning with a consonant sound: *a* man, *a* woman, *a* child. Use *an* before words beginning with a vowel sound or a silent *h*: *an* apple, *an* index, *an* exhibit, *an* hour, *an* honor, *an* honest answer. Use *a* before a word beginning with *h* that is pronounced: *a* historical novel, *a* hospital, *a* Hebrew text.

**accept, except**   *Accept*, a verb, means "to receive or to take": I *accept* your apology. *Except*, a preposition, means "but": Everyone was invited *except* Irving.

**advice, advise**   *Advice* is a noun and means "a recommendation or suggestion": Our *advice* is to buy the cheaper model. *Advise* is a verb and means "to give a recommendation or suggestion": They *advise* us to buy the cheaper model.

**affect, effect**   *Affect* means "to influence": The weather *affects* my mood. Living in a dorm *affected* my grades. *Effect* usually means "result or outcome": An *effect* of too much sun can be skin cancer. What are the *effects* of sleep deprivation? But *effect* can have another meaning: "to bring about or make happen." The first-year students can *effect* that policy if they want.

**all of**   The *of* is usually not necessary: We have bought *all* [not all of] the newspapers we need.

**allude, refer**   *Refer* means "to mention or point out specifically"; *allude* means "to make an indirect reference." The report *alluded* to Iraq as "a disruptive influence in the Middle East" but did not *refer* to Iraq by name.

**a lot**   This is two words. It is commonly misspelled as one word: *alot*. Compare with *a little*.

**already, all ready**   *Already* means "before, previously": We had *already* mailed the check when the bill arrived. *All ready* means "everything is ready": The students are *all ready* for the trip.

**all right**   This is two words. It is commonly misspelled as one word: *alright*. Compare with *all wrong*.

**altogether, all together**   *Altogether* means "completely, entirely." *All together* means "everyone is here; everything is assembled." The scientists worked *all together* on the project until the work was *altogether* finished.

**alumna, alumnus**   Latin terms for female (*alumna*) and male (*alumnus*) graduates. Their plurals are *alumnae* (female) and *alumni* (male). Use the word *graduates* to avoid the Latin if you wish.

**among, between**   *Between* suggests two; *among* suggests more than two: The argument was *between* the dean and the provost. The money was divided *among* members of the team.

**amount, number**   Use *amount* for measurement by volume: *amount* of wheat, *amount* of snow. Use *number* for things that can be counted: *number* of people, *number* of essays. In general, use *amount* of money and *number* of dollars. The *amount* of sugar for the cookies varies. A large *number* of students attended the speech.

**and etc.**   Redundant.

**ante-, anti-**   *Ante-* means "before," as in a pronoun's antecedent. *Anti-* means "against" as in *anti-Semitic*. *Anti-* requires a hyphen when the next letter is either a capital or the letter *i*: *anti*-intellectual.

**as, for, since**   None of these is a good substitute when you mean "because." We ordered new rheostats *because* [not as, for, since] the old ones were burned out.

**as if, as though**   Formal writing requires *were* as the verb with either of these, but *was* is accepted in less formal writing. The substance behaved *as if* it *were* [not was] alive. Elly felt *as though* she *were* flying with Peter Pan.

**at, to**   Avoid adding a redundant *at* or *to* to questions and statements about place. Where are my keys [not *keys at*]? I don't know where my cookbook is [not *is at*]. Where are you going [not *going to*]?

**a while, awhile**   *A while* is a phrase that follows a preposition: We talked for *a while*. We promised to leave in *a while*. *Awhile* is an adverb to describe actions: We talked *awhile*. We sat *awhile* and looked at the stars.

**bad, badly**   Use *bad* to describe emotions, state of health, or negative conditions and actions. She felt *bad* all day. "Hey, how are you?" "Not *bad*, thanks." Use *badly* as an adverb to describe actions. They spoke English *badly*. My brother drives *badly*.

**beside, besides**   *Beside* means "next to"; *besides* means "in addition to." The police were lined up *beside* the limousine. Many research labs can do this kind of work *besides* ours.

**better, best**   Use *better* to express comparison between only two items. He is the *better* [not best] of the two players. Avoid double comparisons like *more better, more slower, more taller*. *Best* is the superlative, indicating superior to all: highest, greatest, finest.

**between you and me**   This is correct. *Between you and I* is incorrect—a pronoun error. The word *me* should follow the preposition *between. Between you and me*, this course is actually fun.

**can, may**   Many writers ignore distinctions between these words. But careful writers prefer precision in thought: *can* means "ability" while *may* means "permission." *Can* you lift all those books? *Can* you hit that tree with a snowball? *May* I ask you a question? *May* I kiss you?

**cite, site**   *Cite* means "to refer to": The footnote *cited* Shakespeare. *Site* means "place": The corner of Superior and Center is the *site* of the new performing arts center.

**compare, contrast**   *Compare* means "to show similarities and differences." Saying "compare and contrast" is not necessary because *contrast* is already implied in compare. Contrast means "to show differences." After we had *compared* the two models, we understood their advantages and disadvantages. The comparison revealed that their *contrasts* were only minor.

**compliment, complement**   *Compliment* means "to praise." Heather's ballet performance drew many *compliments*. *Complement* means "to complete or to balance": The soothing music *complemented* the candlelight in the room.

**conscience, conscious**   *Conscience* means "moral sense": If you lie, should you have a guilty *conscience*? *Conscious* means "being aware": After the accident I was not *conscious* of anything.

**continuous, continual**   *Continuous* means "without interruption": The earth's rotation is *continuous. Continual* means "happening frequently but not always": Ken grew tired of the *continual* e-mails from advertisers.

**could of**   Nonstandard for *could have*.

**data, media, criteria**   In formal writing these plural words are treated as plural: These *data* are [not this data is] insufficient. The *media* have been [not has been] notified. The judges selected three *criteria*. The singular form of *media* is *medium:* Television is a powerful *medium*. The singular form of *criteria* is *criterion:* One *criterion* of good writing is clarity. However, many writers use *data* as both singular [The *data* is too old] and plural [The *data* are unreliable]. The singular for *data* is *datum*, but it is seldom used.

**different from**   Formal writing requires *different from*—not different than. Essays are *different from* short stories. Lake Michigan beaches *differ from* North Carolina beaches.

**eminent, imminent** *Eminent* means "well known, outstanding": She is an *eminent* chemist. *Imminent* means "approaching": They are in *imminent* danger.

**farther, further** *Farther* suggests physical distance: We had walked *farther* than anyone else. *Further* suggests degree or progress in time: The *further* I read, the angrier I got. *Further* also means "additional": *Further* surprises awaited us.

**few, less** *Few* suggests countable items: *few* trees, *few* students. *Less* suggests items measured by volume or degree: *less* water, *less* heat.

**good, well** Use *good* to mean "pleasing": This café looks *good* to me. I see *good* critical thinking here. Use *well* to describe actions: You write *well*. The computer works *well*.

**hanged, hung** *Hanged* means "executed by hanging": The prisoner *hanged* himself in his cell. *Hung* means "suspended": She *hung* her coat on the hook.

**incident, incidence** An *incident* is an event: The *incident* at the fraternity will never happen again. *Incidence* means "rate of occurrence": Doctors have reported a high *incidence* of lung cancer in smokers.

**infer, imply** *Infer* means "to draw a conclusion": I *inferred* what the poem meant. From listening to the lecture, I *infer* the teacher is philosophical. *Imply* means "to suggest": The poet *implied* meanings she did not state directly. My boss *implied* I was not getting enough sleep.

**it's, its** *It's* means "it is" or "it has": *It's* now twelve o'clock. *It's* fun to read a book you love. *It's* fallen 10 degrees. *Its* is the possessive form of *it*: The table has lost *its* shine. The dog found *its* bone.

**lie, lay** (See earlier discussion in this Handbook.)

**like, as** Formal writing avoids using *like* in place of *as*. *Like* is a preposition or a verb: Your son looks *like* you. They *like* ice cream. *As* is a conjunction or joining word: We persuaded Mom to sing again *as* [not like] she had in the old days.

**loose, lose** *Loose* means "free, unrestrained": The horse broke *loose* from the barn. My pants are too *loose*. *Lose* means "misplace": We can't afford to *lose* the horse. If I gamble, I may *lose* a lot of money.

**ourself, themself** Nonstandard. We did the work *ourselves* [not ourself]. The children did all the research *themselves* [not themself].

**prejudice** Nonstandard for *prejudiced*: The scientists were *prejudiced* [not "prejudice"] against the student's new idea.

**principal, principle** *Principal* means "the chief or main thing": as the school *principal*, the *principal* battle in the war, the *principal* sum of money (on which interest is earned). *Principle* refers to "a truth or law": The *principle* of nonviolence is difficult for many Americans to understand. Academic freedom is a highly regarded *principle* by teachers.

**sit, set** *Sit* means "to take a seat": *Sit* down. *Sit* over there please. *Set* means "to put or place": *Set* the books on the desk. *Set* the table for dinner, please.

**than, then** *Than* is used in comparisons: Tracy is shorter *than* Dabney. This new yogurt has fewer calories *than* my old yogurt. *Then* suggests time: I read a chapter, and *then* I wrote a rough draft of my essay.

**there, their, they're**     *There* refers to a place: I went *there* for some peace. Put the chair *there*, please. *There* also is an expletive—a false start on a sentence: *There* are many students who use the Internet on campus. [Better: Many students use the Internet on campus.] *Their* is a possessive pronoun: *Their* term papers were excellent. The children wore *their* coats on the playground. *They're* is a contraction for *they are:* *They're* going to graduate from school next fall. *They're* student volunteers who work at the Red Cross.

**to, too, two**     *To* is a preposition: I'm going *to* the library. *Too* refers to "very" or "also": There is *too* much here to eat. I'm going to the library, *too.* *Two* is a number: I'll take *two* pens to class.

**who, which, that**     Use *who* to refer to people and to animals with names: Clyde is a young man *who* knows what he wants. Our dog Buddy—*who* has been with us for 10 years—is lovable. Use *which* only for animals, objects, and ideas—not people: The opossum, *which* is the only American marsupial, has a prehensile tail. The books, *which* seemed lost, finally arrived. We studied nihilism, *which* is the theory that life has no meaning or purpose. Use *that* to refer to animals, things, and collective people: The FBI computer *that* [or which] failed did not affect national security. The dog *that* [or which] barked all night disappeared. Senior citizens *that* [or who] exercise daily feel better emotionally.

**who, whom**     (See earlier discussion in this Handbook.)

**your, you're**     *Your* is a possessive pronoun: *Your* grades arrived today. *You're* is a contraction meaning "you are": *You're* going to be surprised.

## ACTIVITY 22

Handbook review: underline the correct answers.

1. The one who always has the answer is (her/she).
2. Our team's racing shell (sank/sunk) in six feet of water.
3. Vaughn is one of those industrious students who (is/are) forever studying.
4. No one can (lay/lie) in bed forever, Manny.
5. I knew he was guilty when I (saw/seen) him look away.
6. (A) Mr. Oppenheimer asked his wife, "Can you lend me a 20 until payday, dear"?
   (B) Mr. Oppenheimer asked his wife, "Can you lend me a 20 until payday, dear?"
7. Pete finally was able to ask Vilma to sit and stay (a while/awhile) with him.
8. I felt so (bad/badly) about missing the algebra test that I went back to sleep.
9. (A) Thelma's only line in the play is "Yes, sir," and, then she leaves the stage forever.
   (B) Thelma's only line in the play is "Yes, sir," and then she leaves the stage forever.
10. The lecture board had arranged for an (eminent/imminent) physicist to speak about genetics.

11. I had been reading for an hour when suddenly I (find/found) this marvelous quote.
12. It's easy to guess (who/whom) you mean.
13. (Is/was) it Hamlet or Macbeth who says "To be or not to be, that is the question"?
14. The party was quite a surprise for (her and me/she and I).
15. Bernice hoped she would be (accepted/excepted) into the sorority.
16. The (affect/effect) of dropping water in the acid was a minor explosion of steam.
17. It is conceivable that (a lot/alot) of the chatter comes from loose bearings.
18. Most people assume the bridge is (alright/all right).
19. (A) We saw the redwood trees of California, some were big enough to drive through.
    (B) We saw the redwood trees of California; some were big enough to drive through.
20. The (amount/number) of tools required to fix an electric clock (are/is) staggering.
21. What if a terrorist group actually (was/were) to set off an atomic bomb?
22. It was clear that they were (bias/biased) against people of her race.
23. (A) Riding my bike through the forest, a grizzly bear suddenly appeared on the road.
    (B) Riding my bike through the forest, I saw a grizzly bear suddenly appear on the road.
24. Wyoming has been chosen as the (cite/site) for the new missile silos.
25. We painted a darker border at the base to (complement/compliment) the pale green walls.
26. With more time we could (of/have) done our project much better.
27. The old dog was so tired it could do nothing but (lay/lie) on the porch all day.
28. We thought we heard (a/an) elk outside, near our cabin late last night.
29. Our dog has been acting strangely ever since we had (its/it's) tail cropped.
30. There can never be any secrets between you and (I/me), Seymour whispered.

# Credits

## Chapter 1

Page 4, Reprinted by permission of Renée Bancroft.

Page 6, "My Turn: Stop the Clock" by Amy Wu, <u>Newsweek</u>, 1/22/96, p. 14. Copyright ©1996 by Newsweek, Inc. All rights reserved. Used by permission and protected under the Copyright Laws of the United States. The printing, copying, redistribution, or retransmission of the Material without express written permission is prohibited.

Page 9, "My Turn: Freedom from Choice" by Brian A. Courtney, <u>Newsweek</u>, 2/13/95, p. 16. Copyright ©1995 by Newsweek, Inc. All rights reserved. Used by permission and protected under the Copyright Laws of the United States. The printing, copying, redistribution, or retransmission of the Material without express written permission is prohibited.

Page 21, "Gore's Tear-Jerking Speech Belies Background" by Joan Beck, <u>Detroit Free Press</u>, September 4, 1996, p. A9. Copyright ©1996. Reprinted by permission of The Permissions Group, Inc., on behalf of TMS/MCT Reprints.

Page 24, "My Turn: If I Told You, Would You Want to Hear?" by Julia Kraus, <u>Newsweek</u>, 8/29/05, p. 16. Copyright ©2005 by Newsweek, Inc. All rights reserved. Used by permission and protected under the Copyright Laws of the United States. The printing, copying, redistribution, or retransmission of the Material without express written permission is prohibited.

Page 26, "Making Up for Lost Time" by Rick Reilly, <u>Sports Illustrated</u>, August 21, 2006, p. 134. Copyright ©2006 by Time Inc. Reprinted by permission of Time Inc. Sports Illustrated is a trademark of Time Inc.

Page 28, From DAVE BARRY TALKS BACK by Dave Barry. Copyright ©1991 by Dave Barry. Illustrations copyright ©1991 by Jeff MacNelly. Used by permission of Crown Publishers, a division of Random House, Inc.

Page 32, "Making of a Candidate" by John Edwards, <u>The New York Times</u>, Op-Ed Section, March 1, 2004, p. A21. Copyright ©2004 by The New York Times. Reprinted by permission of The New York Times New Services Division/Syndication Sales Corporation.

Page 35, "A Moment of Grace" from <u>The New York Times</u>, Editorial Section, August 17, 2005, p. 18. Copyright ©2005 by The New York Times. All rights reserved. Used by permission and protected by the Copyright Laws of the United States. The printing, copying, redistribution, or retransmission of the Material without express written permission is prohibited.

## Interchapter 1

## Chapter 2

## Chapter 3

## Interchapter 3

Page 233, "Baby, Baby, Baby, 3 Has Its Charms" by Susan Ager, <u>Detroit Free Press</u>, November 15, 1994, p. D1. Copyright ©1994. Reprinted by permission of the Detroit Free Press.

## Chapter 4

Page 251, "The Tense Middle" by Roald Hoffmann, This I Believe, July 3, 2006. Copyright ©2006 by Roald Hoffmann. Reprinted by arrangement with This I Believe, Inc. <www.thisibelieve.org>.

Page 256, "The Lessons I Didn't Learn in College" by Caitlin Petre, <u>Newsweek</u>, 11/13/06, p. 20. Copyright ©2006 by Newsweek, Inc. All rights reserved. Used by permission and protected under the Copyright Laws of the United States. The printing, copying, redistribution, or retransmission of the Material without express written permission is prohibited.

Page 258, "Eating for Credit" by Alice Waters, <u>The New York Times</u>, Editorial Section, February 24, 2006, p. 23. Copyright ©2006 by The New York Times. All rights reserved. Used by permission and protected by the Copyright Laws of the United States. The printing, copying, redistribution, or retransmission of the Material without express written permission is prohibited.

Page 259, "Serve or Fail" by Dave Eggers, <u>The New York Times</u>, Editorial Section, June 13, 2004, p.13. Copyright ©2004 by The New York Times. All rights reserved. Used by permission and protected by the Copyright Laws of the United States. The printing, copying, redistribution, or retransmission of the Material without express written permission is prohibited.

Page 274, Excerpted from pp. 85–87 in MEN, WOMEN AND RELATIONSHIPS by John Gray. Copyright ©1993 by John Gray. Reprinted by permission of Beyond Words Publishing, Inc., Hillsboro, OR.

## Chapter 5

Page 314, "Keepers of Bush Image Lift Stagecraft to New Heights" by Elizabeth Bumillar, Staff Writer, <u>The New York Times</u>, Editorial Section, May 16, 2003, p. A1. Copyright ©2003 by The New York Times. All rights reserved. Used by permission and protected by the Copyright Laws of the United States. The printing, copying, redistribution, or retransmission of the Material without express written permission is prohibited.

Page 318, Reprinted by permission of Duncan Ferguson.

Page 320, Reprinted by permission of Elizabeth Nichols.

Page 329, Reprinted by permission of Kristen Westdorp.

Page 330, Reprinted by permission of Mary Kate Lesko.

Page 337, "Happy Father's Day Jerk" by Kathleen Parker, <u>Townhall.com</u>, June 15, 2007. Copyright ©2007 by The Washington Post Writers Group. Reprinted by permission of The Washington Post Writers Group.

Page 343, Reprinted by permission of Brett Sanborn.

Page 345, Reprinted by permission of Elizabeth Nichols.

Page 347, "Avast, Me Critics! Ye Kill the Fun: Critics and the Masses Disagree about Film Choices" by Anthony Scott, <u>The New York Times</u>, Foreign Section, July 18, 2006, p. 1.

Page 356, Reprinted by permission of Alex Montoye.

Page 358, Reprinted by permission of Sol Cortez.

## Interchapter 5

Page 365, "Letter from Birmingham Jail" April 16th, 1963 Martin Luther King, Jr. Reprinted by arrangement with the Estate of Martin Luther King Jr., c/o Writers House as agent for the proprietor, New York, NY. Copyright ©1963 by Dr. Martin Luther King, Jr. Copyright renewed 1991 by Coretta Scott King.

Page 366, Reprinted by permission of Megan Crawford.

Page 368, "The Swooshification of the World" by Rick Reilly, <u>Sports Illustrated</u>, February 24, 1997, p. 78. Copyright ©1997 by Time Inc. Reprinted by permission of Time Inc. Sports Illustrated is a trademark of Time Inc.

Page 370, Reprinted by permission of Gavin McMacken.

Page 373, "The Abiding Legacy of My Mother—the Listener" by Ellen Goodman, <u>The Boston Globe</u>, December 8, 2006. Copyright ©2006 by The Washington Post Writers Group. Reprinted by permission of The Washington Post Writers Group.

Page 375, From DAVE BARRY IS FROM MARS AND VENUS by Dave Barry. Copyright ©1997 by Dave Barry. Used by permission of Crown Publishers, a division of Random House, Inc.

Page 377, "I Have a Dream" by Martin Luther King, Jr. Reprinted by arrangement with the Estate of Martin Luther King Jr., c/o Writers House as agent for the proprietor, New York, NY. Copyright ©1963 by Dr. Martin Luther King, Jr. Copyright renewed 1991 by Coretta Scott King.

## Chapter 6

Page 381, "My Papa's Waltz" from COLLECTED POEMS OF THEODORE ROETHKE by Theodore Roethke. Copyright ©1942 by Hearst Magazines, Inc. Used by permission of Doubleday, a division of Random House, Inc.

Page 383, "A narrow fellow in the grass" from THE POEMS OF EMILY DICKINSON edited by Thomas H. Johnson, Cambridge, Mass.: The Belknap Press of Harvard University Press. Copyright ©1951, 1955, 1979, 1983 by the President and Fellows of Harvard College. Reprinted by permission of the publishers and the Trustees of Amherst College.

Page 386, "Metaphors" from CROSSING THE WATER by Sylvia Plath. Copyright ©1960 by Ted Hughes. Reprinted by permission of HarperCollins Publishers and Faber & Faber Ltd.

Page 386, "Root Cellar" from COLLECTED POEMS OF THEODORE ROETHKE by Theodore Roethke. Copyright ©1943 by Modern Poetry Association, Inc. Used by permission of Doubleday, a division of Random House, Inc.

## Chapter 7

## Chapter 8

## Chapter 9

Page 491, "Chris Cecil, Plagairism Gets You Fired" by Leonard Pitts Jr., <u>The Miami Herald</u>, June 3, 2005, p. B1. Copyright ©2005. Reprinted by permission of Copyright Clearance Center on behalf of the publisher.

## Chapter 10

Page 527, Reprinted by permission of Mary Wendt.

Page 554, Figure 1, "Proportional Contribution to Premature Death" from "We Can Do Better—Improving the Health of the American People" by Steven A. Schroeder, <u>New England Journal of Medicine</u> 357 (2007):1222. Copyright ©2007 by Massachusetts Medical Society. All rights reserved. Reprinted by permission of The Publishing Division of the Massachusetts Medical Society.

# Index